SECOND EDITION INSTRUCTOR'S ANNOTATED EDITION

¡ADELANTE! DOS

An Invitation to Spanish

D1442002

José A. Blanco

VISTA
HIGHER LEARNING

Boston, Massachusetts

Publisher: José A. Blanco
President: Janet Dracksdorf
Editorial Development: Deborah Coffey, Jo Hanna Kurth
Project Management: Maria Rosa Alcaraz, Natalia González Peña, Hillary Gospodarek, Sharon Inglis
Technology Production: Jamie Kostecki, Paola Ríos Schaaf
Design: Robin Herr, Michelle Ingari, Jhoany Jiménez, Nick Ventullo
Production: Oscar Díez, Jennifer López, Lina Lozano, Fabian Montoya, Andrés Vanegas

© 2015 by Vista Higher Learning, Inc. All rights reserved.

No part of this work may be reproduced or distributed in any form or by any means, electronic or mechanical, including photocopying and recording, or by any information storage or retrieval system without prior written permission from Vista Higher Learning, 500 Boylston Street, Suite 620, Boston, MA 02116-3736.

Student Text ISBN: 978-1-61857-896-9

Instructor's Annotated Edition ISBN: 978-1-61857-899-0

Library of Congress Control Number: 2013950422

1 2 3 4 5 6 7 8 9 TC 18 17 16 15 14 13

Printed in Canada.

Instructor's Annotated Edition
Table of Contents

THE VISTA HIGHER LEARNING STORY
Your Specialized Foreign Language Publisher

Independent, specialized, and privately owned, Vista Higher Learning was founded in 2000 with one mission: to raise the teaching and learning of world languages to a higher level. This mission is based on the following beliefs:

- It is essential to prepare students for a world in which learning another language is a necessity, not a luxury.
- Language learning should be fun and rewarding, and all students should have the tools necessary for achieving success.
- Students who experience success learning a language will be more likely to continue their language studies both inside and outside the classroom.

With this in mind, we decided to take a fresh look at all aspects of language instructional materials. Because we are specialized, we dedicate 100 percent of our resources to this goal and base every decision on how well it supports language learning.

That is where you come in. Since our founding in 2000, we have relied on the continuous and invaluable feedback from language instructors and students nationwide. This partnership has proved to be the cornerstone of our success by allowing us to constantly improve our programs to meet your instructional needs.

The result? Programs that make language learning exciting, relevant, and effective through:

- an unprecedented access to resources
- a wide variety of contemporary, authentic materials
- the integration of text, technology, and media, and
- a bold and engaging textbook design

By focusing on our singular passion, we let you focus on yours.

The Vista Higher Learning Team

VISTA®
HIGHER LEARNING

500 Boylston Street, Suite 620, Boston, MA 02116-3736 TOLL-FREE: 800-618-7375
TELEPHONE: 617-426-4910 FAX: 617-426-5209 www.vistahigherlearning.com

Getting to Know ¡ADELANTE!

¡ADELANTE!, Second Edition, offers a student-friendly approach to introductory Spanish. Its goal is to make learning Spanish easier and more rewarding so that students will be successful language learners. To this end, **¡ADELANTE!** emphasizes an interactive, communicative approach. It develops speaking, listening, reading, and writing skills so students are capable of communicating with confidence in real-life situations.

NEW to the Second Edition

- A dynamic new **Fotonovela,** filmed in the Yucatan Peninsula and Mexico City, that presents language and culture in an engaging context
- Enhanced Supersite—a simplified, user-friendly interface that highlights current assignments and makes all resources easy to find
- iPad®-friendly* access—get Supersite on the go!
- Online chat activities for synchronous communication and oral practice—2 per lesson
- New **A primera vista** questions that use previously learned vocabulary and grammar to ask about lesson opener photos
- 3 new **Lectura** readings, plus Supersite audio-sync technology for all **Lectura** readings
- Expanded **Adelante** skill-building section, with new **Escritura, Escuchar, En pantalla,** and **Flash cultura** pages for each lesson
- New audio for activities on **Escuchar** pages
- New **En pantalla** TV clips and short films showcasing Spanish from diverse locations in the Spanish-speaking world
- In-text integration of the enormously successful **Flash cultura**
- A new Activity Pack—an online instructor resource that provides additional vocabulary, grammar, communication, and review activities for each lesson
- An expanded Testing Program with new tests, plus vocabulary and grammar quizzes

Plus, the original hallmark features of ¡ADELANTE!

- Easy-to-carry, spiral-bound worktext with perforated pages and folders
- Inclusion of Workbook, Video Manual, and Lab Manual pages at the end of each worktext lesson
- Review lessons at the beginning of **¡ADELANTE! DOS** and **¡ADELANTE! TRES**
- Additional Vocabulary and Notes pages at the end of each lesson for students to write on
- Tabs and color coding for ease of navigation
- Clear and concise grammar and vocabulary sections
- Two compelling cultural videos: **Flash cultura** and **Panorama cultural**

* Students must use a computer for audio recording and select presentations and tools that require Flash or Shockwave.

table of contents

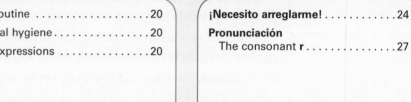

cultura

estructura

cultura

estructura

adelante

Ancillaries

	contextos	fotonovela

Ancillaries

cultura	estructura	adelante

Consulta

The ¡ADELANTE! Supersite

The **¡ADELANTE!** Supersite is your online source for integrating text and technology resources. The Supersite enhances language learning and facilitates simple course management. With powerful functionality, a focus on language learning, and a simplified user experience, the Supersite offers features based directly on feedback from thousands of users.

- **An End to Student Frustration:** Make it a cinch for students to track due dates, save work, and access all assignments and resources.
- **Set-Up Ease:** Customize your course and section settings, create your own grading categories, plus copy previous settings to save time.
- **All-in-One Gradebook:** Add your own activities or use the new grade adjustment tool for a true, cumulative grade.
- **Grading Options:** Choose to grade student-by-student, question-by-question, or spot check. Plus, give targeted feedback via in-line editing and voice comments.
- **Accessible Student Data:** Conveniently share information one-on-one, or issue class reports in the formats that best fit you and your department.

For Instructors

- A gradebook to manage rosters, assignments, and grades
- Time-saving auto-graded activities, plus question-by-question and automated spot-checking
- A communication center for announcements, notifications, and help requests
- Downloadable digital image bank (PDF), pre-made syllabi and lesson plans (RTF), and Testing Program (RTF)
- Instructor Resources (answer keys, audio-video scripts, translations, grammar slides)
- Online administration of quizzes and exams, now with time limits and password protection
- Tools to add your own content to the Supersite
  - Create and assign Partner Chat and open-ended activities
  - Upload and assign videos and outside resources
- Single sign-on feature for integration with your LMS
- Activity Pack (PDF) with additional activities for every lesson
- MP3 files of the complete Worktext, Lab, and Testing Audio Programs
- Live Chat for video chat, audio chat, and instant messaging
- Voiceboards for oral assignments, group discussions, and projects

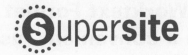
Supersite

Each section of your worktext comes with activities on the ¡ADELANTE! Supersite, many of which are auto-graded for immediate feedback. Plus, the Supersite is iPad®-friendly*, so it can be accessed on the go! Visit **vhlcentral.com** to explore this wealth of exciting resources.

CONTEXTOS
- Vocabulary tutorials
- Image-based vocabulary activity with audio
- Audio activities
- Worktext activities
- Additional activities for extra practice
- Chat activities for conversational skill-building and oral practice

FOTONOVELA
- Streaming video of **Fotonovela**, with instructor-managed options for subtitles and transcripts in Spanish and English
- Worktext activities
- Additional activities for extra practice
- Audio files for **Pronunciación**
- Record-compare practice

CULTURA
- Reading available online
- Keywords and support for **Conexión Internet**
- Worktext activities
- Additional activities for extra practice
- Additional reading

ESTRUCTURA
- Animated grammar tutorials
- Grammar presentations available online
- Worktext activities
- Additional activities for extra practice
- Chat activities for conversational skill-building and oral practice
- Diagnostics in **Recapitulación** section

ADELANTE
- Audio-synced reading in **Lectura**
- Additional reading
- Writing activity in **Escritura** with composition engine
- Audio files for listening activity in **Escuchar**
- Worktext activities and additional activities for extra practice
- Streaming **En pantalla** TV clips or short films, with instructor-managed options for subtitles and transcripts in Spanish and English
- Streaming video of **Flash cultura** series, with instructor-managed options for subtitles and transcripts in Spanish and English

VOCABULARIO
- Vocabulary list with audio
- Flashcards with audio

PANORAMA
- Interactive map
- Worktext activities
- Additional activities for extra practice
- Streaming video of **Panorama cultural** series, with instructor-managed options for subtitles and transcripts in Spanish and English

Plus! Also found on the Supersite:

- All worktext and lab audio MP3 files
- Communication center for instructor notifications and feedback
- Live Chat tool for video chat, audio chat, and instant messaging without leaving your browser
- A single gradebook for all Supersite activities
- WebSAM online Workbook/Video Manual and Lab Manual

Supersite features vary by access level. Visit **vistahigherlearning.com** to explore which Supersite level is right for you.

* Students must use a computer for audio recording and select presentations and tools that require Flash or Shockwave.

Worktext Format
delivers materials in a convenient, user-friendly package.

Spiral binding A unique binding allows easier handling of materials in class, at home, or wherever you may be.

Perforation Perforated pages allow you to easily hand in assignments or travel with just what you need.

Folders and notes For your convenience, folders and note papers are included.

Tab navigation Clearly marked tabs ensure that you always know exactly where you are in the worktext.

Built-in ancillaries The Workbook, Video Manual, and Lab Manual activities are included after each worktext lesson, eliminating the need to carry these components to and from class.

Lesson Openers
outline the content and features of each lesson.

Communicative Goals

You will learn how to:
• Talk about your classes and school life
• Discuss everyday activities
• Ask questions in Spanish
• Describe the location of people and things

En la universidad 2

contextos
pages 62–65
• The classroom and academic life
• Days of the week
• Fields of study and academic subjects
• Class schedules

fotonovela
pages 66–69
Felipe takes Marissa around Mexico City. Along the way, they meet some friends and discuss the upcoming semester.

cultura
pages 70–71
• Universities and majors in the Spanish-speaking world
• The University of Salamanca

estructura
pages 72–89
• Present tense of -ar verbs
• Forming questions in Spanish
• Present tense of estar
• Numbers 31 and higher
• Recapitulación

adelante
pages 90–97
Lectura: A brochure for a summer course in Madrid
Escritura: A description of yourself
Escuchar: A conversation about courses
En pantalla
Flash cultura
Panorama: España

A PRIMERA VISTA
• ¿Hay dos chicos en la foto?
• ¿Hay tres cuadernos o siete?
• ¿Son turistas o estudiantes?
• ¿Qué hora es, la una de la mañana o de la tarde?

Más práctica
Workbook pages 99–110
Video Manual pages 111–116
Lab Manual pages 117–122

A primera vista activities jump-start the lessons, allowing you to use the Spanish you know to talk about the photos.

Communicative goals highlight the real-life tasks you will be able to carry out in Spanish by the end of each lesson.

Supersite

Supersite resources are available for every section of the lesson at **vhlcentral.com**. Icons show you which textbook activities are also available online, and where additional practice activities are available. The description next to the (S) icon indicates what additional resources are available for each section: videos, recordings, tutorials, presentations, and more!

Contextos
presents vocabulary in meaningful contexts.

Más vocabulario boxes call out other important theme-related vocabulary in easy-to-reference Spanish-English lists.

Variación léxica presents alternate words and expressions used throughout the Spanish-speaking world.

Illustrations High-frequency vocabulary is introduced through expansive, full-color illustrations.

Recursos The icons in the **Recursos** boxes let you know exactly which print and technology ancillaries you can use to reinforce and expand on every section of every lesson.

Práctica This section always begins with two listening exercises and continues with activities that practice the new vocabulary in meaningful contexts.

Comunicación activities allow you to use the vocabulary creatively in interactions with a partner, a small group, or the entire class.

Supersite

- Vocabulary tutorials
- Audio support for vocabulary presentation
- Worktext activities
- Additional online-only practice activities
- Chat activities for conversational skill-building and oral practice
- Vocabulary activities in Activity Pack

Fotonovela
follows the adventures of a group of students living and traveling in Mexico.

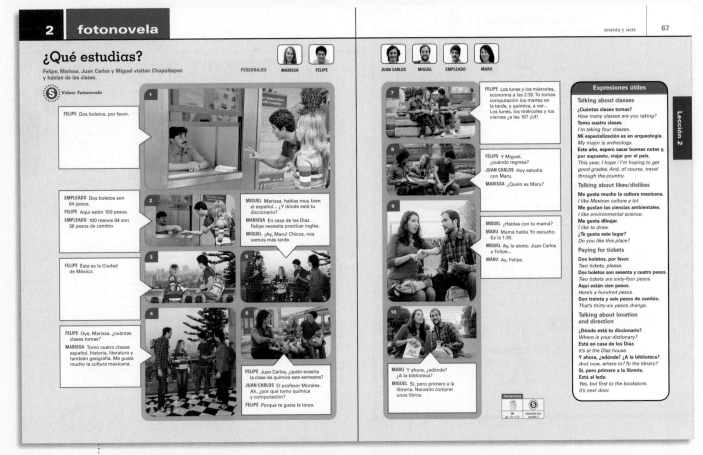

Personajes The photo-based conversations take place among a cast of recurring characters—a Mexican family with two college-age children, and their group of friends.

Icons signal activities by type (pair, group, audio, info gap) and let you know which activities can be completed online.

Fotonovela Video Updated for the Second Edition, the NEW! video episodes that correspond to this section are available for viewing online.

Expresiones útiles These expressions organize new, active structures by language function so you can focus on using them for real-life, practical purposes.

Conversations Taken from the NEW! **Fotonovela** Video, the conversations reinforce vocabulary from **Contextos**. They also preview structures from the upcoming **Estructura** section in context and in a comprehensible way.

Supersite

- Streaming video of the **Fotonovela** episode
- Worktext activities
- Additional online-only practice activities

Pronunciación & Ortografía
present the rules of Spanish pronunciation and spelling.

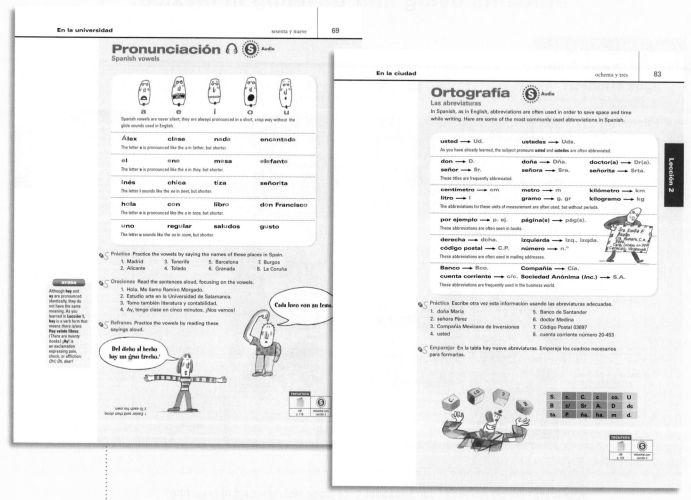

Pronunciación explains the sounds and pronunciation of Spanish in ¡ADELANTE! UNO and Lessons 1–3 of ¡ADELANTE! DOS.

Ortografía focuses on topics related to Spanish spelling in Lessons 4–6 of ¡ADELANTE! DOS and in all of ¡ADELANTE! TRES.

Supersite

- Audio for pronunciation explanation
- Record-compare worktext activities

Cultura
exposes you to different aspects of Hispanic culture tied to the lesson theme.

En detalle & Perfil(es) Two articles on the lesson theme focus on a specific place, custom, person, group, or tradition in the Spanish-speaking world. In Spanish starting in **¡ADELANTE! DOS** Lesson 1, these features also provide reading practice.

Coverage While the **Panorama** section takes a regional approach to cultural coverage, **Cultura** is theme-driven, covering several Spanish-speaking regions in every lesson.

Así se dice & El mundo hispano Lexical and comparative features expand cultural coverage to people, traditions, customs, trends, and vocabulary throughout the Spanish-speaking world.

Supersite

- **Cultura** article
- Worktext activities
- Additional online-only practice activities

- **Conexión Internet** activity with questions and keywords related to lesson theme
- Additional cultural reading

Estructura
presents Spanish grammar in a graphic-intensive format.

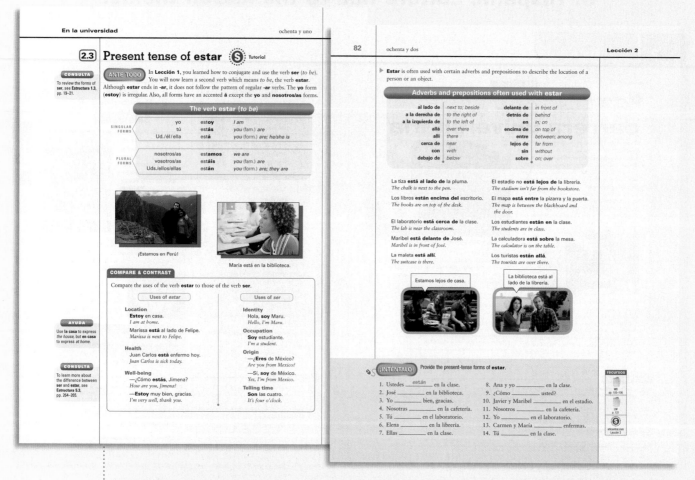

Ante todo Ease into grammar with definitions of grammatical terms, reminders about what you already know of English grammar, and Spanish grammar you have learned in earlier lessons.

Charts To help you learn, colorful, easy-to-use charts call out key grammatical structures and forms, as well as important related vocabulary.

Compare & Contrast This feature focuses on aspects of grammar that native speakers of English may find difficult, clarifying similarities and differences between Spanish and English.

Student sidebars provide you with on-the-spot linguistic, cultural, or language-learning information directly related to the materials in front of you.

Diagrams Clear and easy-to-grasp grammar explanations are reinforced by colorful diagrams that present sample words, phrases, and sentences.

¡Inténtalo! offers an easy first step into each grammar point.

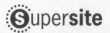upersite

- Animated grammar tutorials
- Worktext activities

Estructura
provides directed and communicative practice.

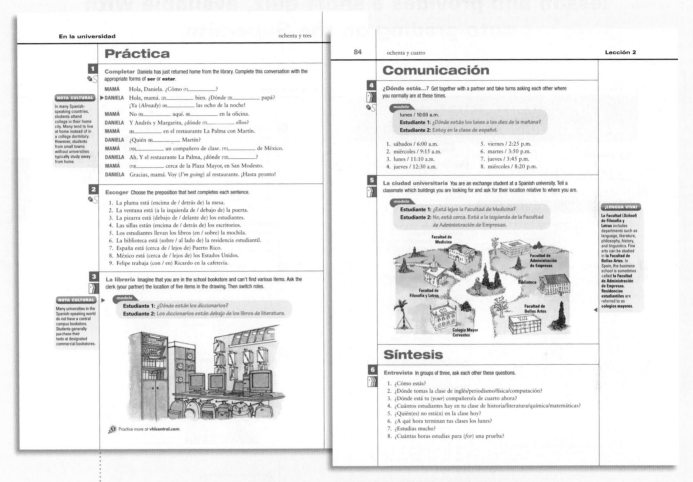

Práctica Guided, yet meaningful exercises weave current and previously learned vocabulary together with the current grammar point.

Information Gap activities You and your partner each have only half of the information you need, so you must work together to accomplish the task at hand.

Comunicación Opportunities for creative expression use the lesson's grammar and vocabulary.

Sidebars The **Notas culturales** expand coverage of the cultures of Spanish-speaking peoples and countries, while **Ayuda** sidebars provide on-the-spot language support.

Síntesis activities integrate the current grammar point with previously learned points, providing built-in, consistent review.

Ⓢupersite

- Worktext activities
- Additional online-only practice activities
- Chat activities for conversational skill-building and oral practice

- Grammar and communication activities in Activity Pack

Estructura
Recapitulación reviews the grammar of each lesson and provides a short quiz, available with auto-grading on the Supersite.

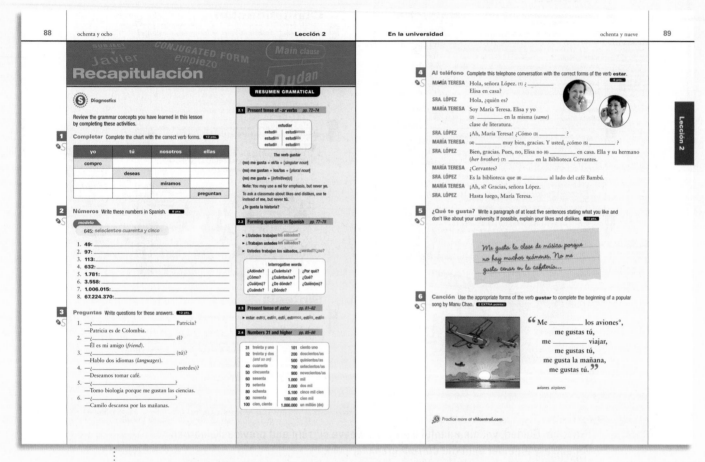

Resumen gramatical This review panel provides you with an easy-to-study summary of the basic concepts of the lesson's grammar, with page references to the full explanations.

Points Each activity is assigned a point value to help you track your progress. All **Recapitulación** sections add up to fifty points, plus two additional points for successfully completing the bonus activity.

Activities A series of activities, moving from directed to open-ended, systematically test your mastery of the lesson's grammar. The section ends with a riddle or puzzle using the grammar from the lesson.

Supersite

- Worktext activities with follow-up support and practice
- Additional online-only review activities
- Review activities in Activity Pack
- Practice quiz

Adelante
Lectura develops reading skills in the context of the lesson theme.

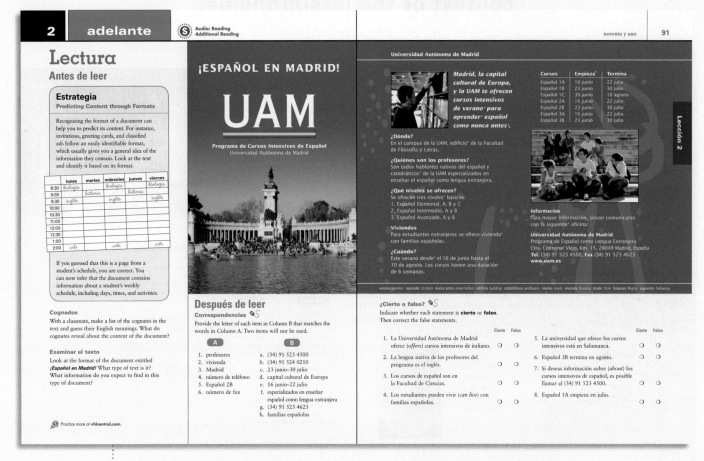

Below the textbook page spread:

Antes de leer Valuable reading strategies and pre-reading activities strengthen your reading abilities in Spanish.

Readings Selections related to the lesson theme recycle vocabulary and grammar you have learned. The selections in **¡ADELANTE! UNO** and **¡ADELANTE! DOS** are cultural texts, while those in **¡ADELANTE! TRES** are literary pieces.

Después de leer Activities include post-reading exercises that review and check your comprehension of the reading as well as expansion activities.

ⓢupersite

- Audio-sync reading that highlights text as it is being read
- Worktext activities
- Additional reading

Adelante NEW!

Escritura develops writing skills while *Escuchar* practices listening skills in the context of the lesson theme.

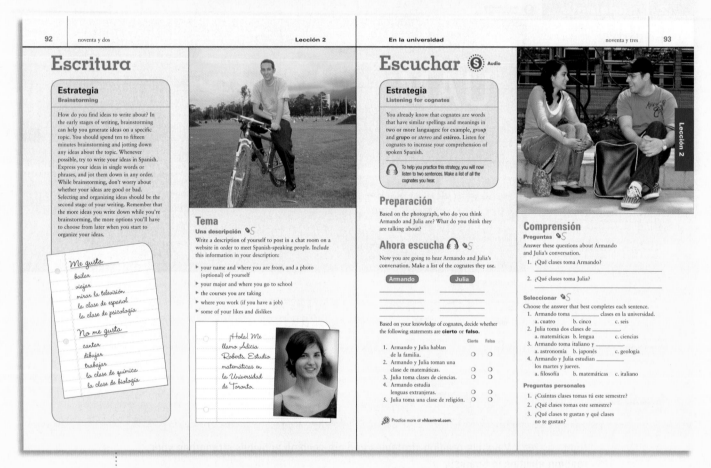

Estrategia Strategies help you prepare for the writing and listening tasks to come.

Escritura The **Tema** describes the writing topic and includes suggestions for approaching it.

Escuchar A recorded conversation or narration develops your listening skills in Spanish. **Preparación** prepares you for listening to the recorded passage.

Ahora escucha walks you through the passage, and **Comprensión** checks your listening comprehension.

Supersite

- Composition engine for writing activity in **Escritura**
- Audio for listening activity in **Escuchar**
- Worktext activities
- Additional online-only practice activities

Adelante NEW!
En pantalla and Flash cultura present additional video tied to the lesson theme.

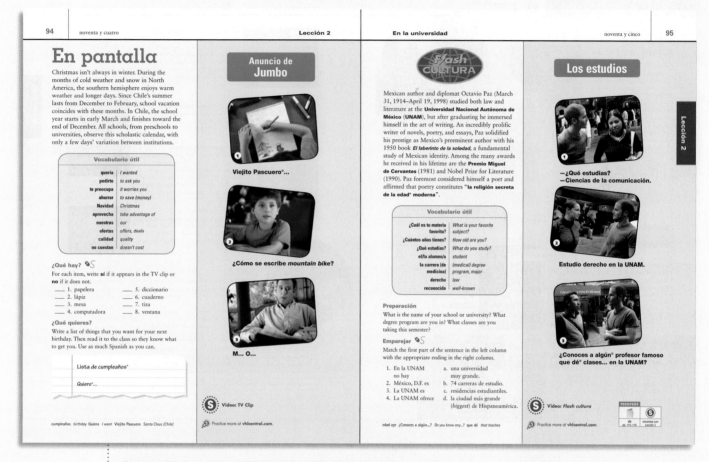

En pantalla TV clips, **NEW!** to this edition, give you additional exposure to authentic language. The clips include commercials, newscasts, short films, and TV shows that feature the language, vocabulary, and theme of the lesson.

Presentation Cultural notes, video stills with captions, and vocabulary support all prepare you to view the clips. Activities check your comprehension and expand on the ideas presented.

Flash cultura An icon lets you know that the enormously successful **Flash cultura** Video offers specially shot content tied to the lesson theme.

NEW! Activities Due to the overwhelming popularity of the **Flash cultura** Video, previewing support and comprehension activities are now integrated into the student text.

Supersite

- Streaming video of **En pantalla** and **Flash cultura**
- Worktext activities
- Additional online-only practice activities

Panorama
presents the nations of the Spanish-speaking world.

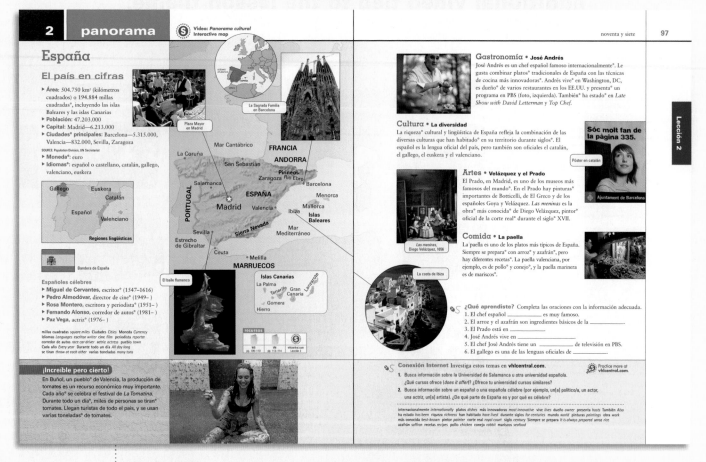

El país en cifras presents interesting key facts about the featured country.

¡Increíble pero cierto! highlights an intriguing fact about the country or its people.

Maps point out major cities, rivers, and geographical features and situate the country in the context of its immediate surroundings and the world.

Readings A series of brief paragraphs explores facets of the country's culture such as history, places, fine arts, literature, and aspects of everyday life.

***Panorama cultural* Video** This video's authentic footage takes you to the featured Spanish-speaking country, letting you experience the sights and sounds of an aspect of its culture.

ⓢupersite

- Interactive map
- Streaming video of the **Panorama cultural** program
- Worktext activities
- Additional online-only practice activities
- **Conexión Internet** activity with questions and keywords related to lesson theme

Vocabulario
summarizes all the active vocabulary of the lesson.

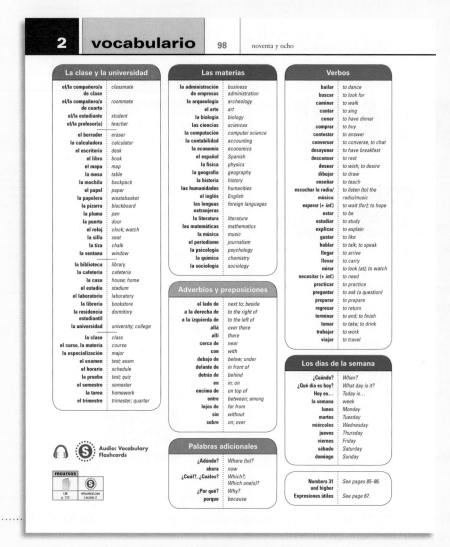

| 2 | vocabulario | 98 | noventa y ocho |

La clase y la universidad

el/la compañero/a de clase	classmate
el/la compañero/a de cuarto	roommate
el/la estudiante	student
el/la profesor(a)	teacher
el borrador	eraser
la calculadora	calculator
el escritorio	desk
el libro	book
el mapa	map
la mesa	table
la mochila	backpack
el papel	paper
la papelera	wastebasket
la pizarra	blackboard
la pluma	pen
la puerta	door
el reloj	clock; watch
la silla	seat
la tiza	chalk
la ventana	window
la biblioteca	library
la cafetería	cafeteria
la casa	house; home
el estadio	stadium
el laboratorio	laboratory
la librería	bookstore
la residencia estudiantil	dormitory
la universidad	university; college
la clase	class
el curso, la materia	course
la especialización	major
el examen	test; exam
el horario	schedule
la prueba	test; quiz
el semestre	semester
la tarea	homework
el trimestre	trimester; quarter

Las materias

la administración de empresas	business administration
la arqueología	archeology
el arte	art
la biología	biology
las ciencias	sciences
la computación	computer science
la contabilidad	accounting
la economía	economics
el español	Spanish
la física	physics
la geografía	geography
la historia	history
las humanidades	humanities
el inglés	English
las lenguas extranjeras	foreign languages
la literatura	literature
las matemáticas	mathematics
la música	music
el periodismo	journalism
la psicología	psychology
la química	chemistry
la sociología	sociology

Adverbios y preposiciones

al lado de	next to; beside
a la derecha de	to the right of
a la izquierda de	to the left of
allá	over there
allí	there
cerca de	near
con	with
debajo de	below; under
delante de	in front of
detrás de	behind
en	in; on
encima de	on top of
entre	between; among
lejos de	far from
sin	without
sobre	on; over

Palabras adicionales

¿Adónde?	Where (to)?
ahora	now
¿Cuál?, ¿Cuáles?	Which?; Which one(s)?
¿Por qué?	Why?
porque	because

Verbos

bailar	to dance
buscar	to look for
caminar	to walk
cantar	to sing
cenar	to have dinner
comprar	to buy
contestar	to answer
conversar	to converse, to chat
desayunar	to have breakfast
descansar	to rest
desear	to wish; to desire
dibujar	to draw
enseñar	to teach
escuchar la radio/ música	to listen (to) the radio/music
esperar (+ inf.)	to wait (for); to hope
estar	to be
estudiar	to study
explicar	to explain
gustar	to like
hablar	to talk; to speak
llegar	to arrive
llevar	to carry
mirar	to look (at); to watch
necesitar (+ inf.)	to need
practicar	to practice
preguntar	to ask (a question)
preparar	to prepare
regresar	to return
terminar	to end; to finish
tomar	to take; to drink
trabajar	to work
viajar	to travel

Los días de la semana

¿Cuándo?	When?
¿Qué día es hoy?	What day is it?
Hoy es…	Today is…
la semana	week
lunes	Monday
martes	Tuesday
miércoles	Wednesday
jueves	Thursday
viernes	Friday
sábado	Saturday
domingo	Sunday
Numbers 31 and higher	See pages 85–86.
Expresiones útiles	See page 67.

Audio: Vocabulary Flashcards

recursos

LM p. 122 | vhlcentral.com Lección 2

Vocabulario The end-of-lesson page lists the active vocabulary from each lesson. This is the vocabulary that may appear on quizzes or tests.

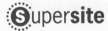

Super**site**

- Audio for all vocabulary items
- Vocabulary flashcards with audio

Workbook and Video Manual

Workbook

Nombre _____
Fecha _____ **105**

2.3 Present tense of **estar**

1 **Están en...** Answer the questions based on the pictures. Write complete sentences.

1. ¿Dónde están Cristina y Bruno? _____
2. ¿Dónde están la profesora y el estudiante? _____
3. ¿Dónde está la puerta? _____

4. ¿Dónde está la mochila? _____
5. ¿Dónde está el pasajero? _____
6. ¿Dónde está José Miguel? _____

2 **¿Dónde están?** Use these cues and the correct form of **estar** to write complete sentences. Add any missing words.

1. libros / cerca / escritorio
2. ustedes / al lado / puerta
3. calculadora / entre / computadoras
4. lápices / sobre / cuaderno
5. estadio / lejos / residencias
6. mochilas / debajo / mesa
7. tú / en / clase de psicología
8. reloj / a la derecha / ventana
9. Rita / a la izquierda / Julio

Video Manual

Nombre _____
Fecha _____ **113**

Panorama: España

Lección 2
Panorama cultural

Antes de ver el video

1 **Más vocabulario** Look over these useful words before you watch the video.

Vocabulario útil		
antiguo *ancient*	empezar *to start*	niños *children*
blanco *white*	encierro *running of bulls*	pañuelo *neckerchief, bandana*
cabeza *head*	esta *this*	peligroso *dangerous*
calle *street*	feria *fair, festival*	periódico *newspaper*
cohete *rocket (firework)*	fiesta *party, festival*	rojo *red*
comparsa *parade*	gente *people*	ropa *clothing*
correr *to run*	gigante *giant*	toro *bull*
defenderse *to defend oneself*	mitad *half*	ver *to see*

2 **Festivales** In this video, you are going to learn about a Spanish festival. List the things you would probably do and see at a festival.

Mientras ves el video

3 **Ordenar** Number the items in the order in which they appear in the video.

____ a. cohete
____ b. cuatro mujeres en un balcón
____ c. gigante
____ d. toros
____ e. mitad hombre, mitad animal

Después de ver el video

4 **Fotos** Describe the video stills.

Video Manual

Workbook The Workbook section provides additional practice for the **Contextos**, **Estructura**, and **Panorama** sections.

Video Manual The three Video Manual sections correspond to the **Fotonovela, Panorama cultural**, and **Flash cultura** video programs. These activities provide pre-, while-, and post-viewing practice.

Recursos Within each lesson, **recursos** boxes let you know which Workbook, Lab Manual, and Video Manual materials can be used.

Supersite

• Streaming video of **Fotonovela, Panorama cultural**, and **Flash cultura**

Lab Manual and Notes

Nombre _____

Fecha _____

117

contextos

Lección 2

1 Identificar Look at each drawing and listen to the statement. Indicate whether the statement is **cierto** or **falso**.

Cierto Falso   Cierto Falso   Cierto Falso

1. ○ ○   2. ○ ○   3. ○ ○

4. ○ ○   5. ○ ○   6. ○ ○

2 ¿Qué día es? Your friend Diego is never sure what day of the week it is. Respond to his questions saying that it is the day before the one he mentions. Then repeat the correct answer after the speaker. (6 *items*)

modelo
Hoy es domingo, ¿no?
No, hoy es sábado.

3 Preguntas You will hear a series of questions. Look at Susana's schedule for today and answer each question. Then repeat the correct response after the speaker.

martes 18	
9:00 economía — Sr. Rivera	1:30 prueba de contabilidad — Sr. Ramos
11:00 química — Sra. Hernández	3:00 matemáticas — Srta. Torres
12:15 cafetería — Carmen	4:30 laboratorio de computación — Héctor

Lab Manual

Notes

Lab Manual The Lab Manual section further practices listening and speaking skills related to the **Contextos**, **Pronunciación**, and **Estructura** materials.

Notes pages The Notes pages at the end of each lesson provide a place to write new vocabulary words and notes.

Supersite

• Audio for Lab Manual activities

A full three-volume series includes
¡ADELANTE! UNO

¡ADELANTE! UNO starts the program with the present tense and ends with an introduction to the preterite. These concepts will be reviewed and recycled throughout the next two volumes.

ⓢupersite

- Animated grammar tutorials
- Worktext activities
- Additional online-only practice activities
- Vocabulary flashcards with audio

A full three-volume series includes
¡ADELANTE! TRES

SECOND EDITION

¡ADELANTE! *TRES*

An Invitation to Spanish

BLANCO

Contextos
- Nature and the environment
- City life, daily chores
- Health and well-being, exercise and physical activity, nutrition
- Professions and occupations, the workplace, job interviews
- The arts, movies and television
- Current events and politics, the media

Estructura
- The subjunctive with verbs of emotion and with conjunctions
- The subjunctive with doubt, disbelief, and denial
- The subjunctive in adjective clauses
- **Nosotros/as** commands
- Past participles used as adjectives
- The present perfect and the past perfect
- The present perfect subjunctive and the past perfect subjunctive
- The future and the future perfect
- The past subjunctive and the present perfect subjunctive
- The conditional and the conditional perfect

¡ADELANTE! TRES begins with a lesson that reviews what was covered in **¡ADELANTE! DOS**. You also continue to expand your knowledge of the Spanish language by covering the subjunctive mood, the future tense, and the conditional tense.

Ⓢupersite

Visit vistahigherlearning.com/highered/adelante for a full Table of Contents covering **¡ADELANTE! UNO**, **¡ADELANTE! DOS**, and **¡ADELANTE! TRES**.

Icons and *Recursos* boxes

Icons

Familiarize yourself with these icons that appear throughout **¡ADELANTE!, Second Edition**.

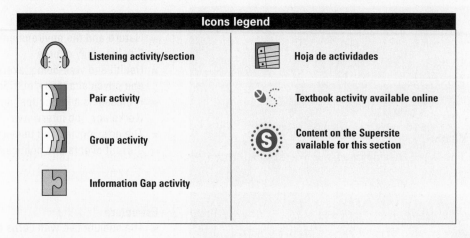

- The Information Gap activities and those involving **Hojas de actividades** (*activity sheets*) require handouts from the Activity Pack on the Supersite.

- You will see the listening icon in each lesson's **Contextos, Pronunciación, Escuchar,** and **Vocabulario** sections.

- A note next to the Supersite icon will let you know what type of content is available online.

- Additional practice on the Supersite, not included in the worktext, is indicated with this icon:

 Practice more at **vhlcentral.com.**

Recursos

Recursos boxes let you know exactly what print and technology ancillaries you can use to reinforce and expand on every section of the lessons in your worktext. They even include page numbers when applicable.

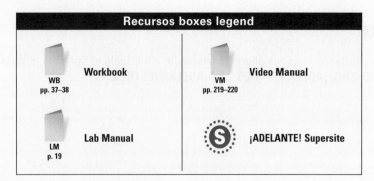

Student Ancillaries

- **Workbook/Video Manual/Lab Manual**
  All of these materials are available right inside your worktext, at the end of each lesson.

- **Lab Audio Program**
  The audio files to accompany the Lab Manual are available on the Supersite.

- **Worktext Audio Program MP3s**
  The Worktext Audio Program MP3s, available on the Supersite, are the audio recordings for the listening-based activities and recordings of the active vocabulary in each lesson of the **¡ADELANTE!** program.

- **WebSAM**
  The WebSAM delivers the Workbook, Video Manual, and Lab Manual online.

Instructor Ancillaries

- **Instructor's Annotated Edition (IAE)**
  The IAE contains a wealth of teaching information. Answers for discrete-item activities are overprinted on the student pages for both the lesson itself and the Workbook, Lab Manual, and Video Manual tabs. Additionally, the principal lessons contain teaching suggestions, ideas for expansion, and more.

- **DVD set**
  One DVD for each level of **¡ADELANTE!** provides the **Fotonovela, Flash cultura,** and **Panorama cultural** segments that correspond to each level.

- **Supersite**
  In addition to access to the student site, the password-protected instructor site offers a robust course management system that allows instructors to assign and track student progress. The Supersite contains Instructor Resources such as answers to directed activities in the worktext, audioscripts and videoscripts, English translations of the videos, a sample lesson plan, and a syllabus. It also has the following:

  - **Digital Image Bank and Grammar Presentation Slides**
    The Digital Image Bank includes maps of all Spanish-speaking countries, the **Contextos** vocabulary drawings, and other selected drawings from the student text. Also included on PowerPoint are presentations of each grammar point in **Estructura**.

  - **Workbook/ Video Manual/ Lab Manual Answer Key**
    Answers to the Workbook, Video Manual, and Lab Manual portions of each lesson are provided, should instructors wish to distribute them for self-correction.

  - **Testing Program**
    The Testing Program contains vocabulary and grammar quizzes, six versions of tests for each worktext lesson, exams for each level of **¡ADELANTE!**, listening scripts, answer keys, and optional cultural, video, and reading test items. The Testing Program is provided in customizable RTF files or PDFs.

Fotonovela Video Program

The cast NEW!

Here are the main characters you will meet in the **Fotonovela** Video:

From Mexico,
Jimena Díaz Velázquez

From Argentina,
Juan Carlos Rossi

From Mexico,
Felipe Díaz Velázquez

From the U.S.,
Marissa Wagner

From Mexico,
María Eugenia (Maru) Castaño Ricaurte

From Spain,
Miguel Ángel Lagasca Martínez

Brand-new and fully integrated with your text, the **¡ADELANTE! 2/e Fotonovela** Video is a dynamic and contemporary window into the Spanish language. The new video centers around the Díaz family, whose household includes two college-aged children and a visiting student from the U.S. Over the course of an academic year, Jimena, Felipe, Marissa, and their friends explore **el D.F.** and other parts of Mexico as they make plans for their futures. Their adventures take them through some of the greatest natural and cultural treasures of the Spanish-speaking world, as well as the highs and lows of everyday life.

The **Fotonovela** section in each worktext lesson is actually an abbreviated version of the dramatic episode featured in the video. Therefore, each **Fotonovela** section can be done before you see the corresponding video episode, after it, or as a section that stands alone.

In each dramatic segment, the characters interact using the vocabulary and grammar you are studying. As the storyline unfolds, the episodes combine new vocabulary and grammar with previously taught language, exposing you to a variety of authentic accents along the way. At the end of each episode, the **Resumen** section highlights the grammar and vocabulary you are studying.

We hope you find the new **Fotonovela** Video to be an engaging and useful tool for learning Spanish!

En pantalla Video Program

The **¡ADELANTE!** Supersite features an authentic video clip for each lesson. Clip formats include commercials, news stories, and even short films. These clips, **NEW!** to the Second Edition, have been carefully chosen to be comprehensible for students learning Spanish, and are accompanied by activities and vocabulary lists to facilitate understanding. More importantly, though, these clips are a fun and motivating way to improve your Spanish!

Here are the countries represented in each lesson in **En pantalla:**

¡ADELANTE! UNO	*¡ADELANTE!* DOS	*¡ADELANTE!* TRES
Lesson 1 U.S.	Lesson 1 Argentina	Lesson 1 Argentina
Lesson 2 Chile	Lesson 2 Peru	Lesson 2 Argentina
Lesson 3 U.S.	Lesson 3 Chile	Lesson 3 Mexico
Lesson 4 Peru	Lesson 4 Spain	Lesson 4 Spain
Lesson 5 Mexico	Lesson 5 Colombia	Lesson 5 Mexico
Lesson 6 Mexico	Lesson 6 Spain	Lesson 6 Mexico

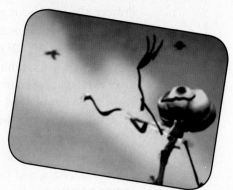

Flash cultura Video Program

In the dynamic **Flash cultura** Video, young people from all over the Spanish-speaking world share aspects of life in their countries with you. The similarities and differences among Spanish-speaking countries that come up through their adventures will challenge you to think about your own cultural practices and values. The segments provide valuable cultural insights as well as linguistic input; the episodes will introduce you to a variety of accents and vocabulary as they gradually move into Spanish.

Panorama cultural Video Program

The **Panorama cultural** Video is integrated with the **Panorama** section in each lesson. Each segment is 2–3 minutes long and consists of documentary footage from each of the countries featured. The images were specially chosen for interest level and visual appeal, while the all-Spanish narrations were carefully written to reflect the vocabulary and grammar covered in the worktexts.

¡ADELANTE! and the *Standards for Foreign Language Learning*

Since 1982, when the *ACTFL Proficiency Guidelines* were first published, that seminal document and its subsequent revisions have influenced the teaching of modern languages in the United States. **¡ADELANTE!** was created with the concerns and philosophy of the *ACTFL Proficiency Guidelines* in mind, incorporating a proficiency-oriented approach from its planning stages.

The pedagogy of **¡ADELANTE!** was also informed from its inception by the *Standards for Foreign Language Learning in the 21st Century*. First published in 1996 under the auspices of the National Standards in Foreign Language Education Project, the Standards are organized into five goal areas, often called the Five Cs: Communication, Cultures, Connections, Comparisons, and Communities.

Since **¡ADELANTE!** takes a communicative approach to the teaching and learning of Spanish, the Communication goal is central to the student text. For example, the diverse formats used in **Comunicación** and **Síntesis** activities—pair work, small group work, class circulation, information gap, task-based, and so forth—engage students in communicative exchanges, providing and obtaining information, and expressing feelings and emotions.

The Cultures goal is most evident in the lessons' **Cultura** sections, **Nota cultural** student sidebars, and **En pantalla, Flash cultura,** and **Panorama** sections, but **¡ADELANTE!** also weaves culture into virtually every page, exposing students to the multiple facets of practices, products, and perspectives of the Spanish-speaking world. In keeping with the Connections goal, students can connect with other disciplines such as geography, history, fine arts, and science in the **Panorama** section; they can acquire information and recognize distinctive cultural viewpoints in the non-literary and literary texts of the **Lectura** sections. The **Estructura** sections, with their clear explanations and special *Compare & Contrast* features, reflect the Comparisons goal. Students can work toward the Connections and Communities goal when they do the **Cultura** and **Panorama** sections' **Conexión Internet** activities, as well as the activities and information on the **¡ADELANTE!** Supersite. In addition, special Standards icons appear on the student text pages of your IAE to call out sections that have a particularly strong relationship with the Standards. These are a few examples of how **¡ADELANTE!** was created with the Standards firmly in mind, but you will find many more as you use the worktext.

Communication Understand and be understood: read and listen to understand the Spanish-speaking world, converse with others, and share your thoughts clearly through speaking and writing.

Cultures Experience Spanish-speaking cultures through their own viewpoints, in the places, objects, behaviors, and beliefs important to the people who live them.

Connections Apply what you learn in your Spanish course to your other studies; apply what you know from other courses to your Spanish studies.

Comparisons Discover in which ways the Spanish language and Spanish-speaking cultures are like your own—and how they differ.

Communities Engage with Spanish-speaking communities locally, nationally, and internationally both in your courses and beyond—for life.

Your Instructor's Annotated Edition

The **¡ADELANTE!, Second Edition,** Instructor's Annotated Edition features student text pages, overprinted with answers, and a wealth of teaching resources. The annotations complement and support varied teaching styles, extending the already rich content of the student worktext and saving you time in class preparation and course management.

This section is designed as a quick orientation to the principal types of instructor annotations you will find in the **¡ADELANTE! 2/e** IAE. As you familiarize yourself with them, it is important to keep in mind that the annotations are merely suggestions. Any Spanish questions, or simulated instructor-student exchanges are not meant to be prescriptive. You are encouraged to view these suggested "scripts" as flexible points of departure that will help you achieve your instructional goals.

- A correlation to instructor ancillaries

- **Teaching Tips** Suggestions for recycling language, leading into the corresponding section, working with materials, and carrying out specific activities

- Expansions and variations for the activities in the student worktext

- **Possible Conversation** Answers based on known vocabulary, grammar, and language functions that students might produce

- **Video Recap** Questions to help students recall the events of the previous lesson's **Fotonovela** episode

- **Video Synopsis** A summary of each lesson's **Fotonovela** episode

- **Expresiones útiles** Suggestions for introducing upcoming **Estructura** grammar points incorporated into the **Fotonovela** episode

- Suggestions for working with the reading, writing, and listening strategies presented in the **Lectura, Escritura,** and **Escuchar** sections, respectively

- Ideas for presenting and expanding the writing assignment topic in **Escritura**

- **Successful Language Learning** Strategies to enhance students' language-learning experience

- **Extra Practice, Pairs, Small Groups, and Large Groups** Additional activities intended to supplement those in the student worktext

- **Game** Games that practice the language of the section and/or recycle previously learned language

- **TPR** Total Physical Response activities that engage students physically in learning Spanish

- **Variación léxica** Extra information related to the **Variación léxica** boxes in **Contextos,** terms that come up in **Lectura,** and terms from the Spanish-speaking countries featured in **Panorama**

- **Heritage Speakers** Suggestions and activities tailored to heritage speakers, who in many colleges and universities are enrolled in the same introductory courses as non-heritage speakers

- **Video** Techniques and activities for using the **¡ADELANTE!** video program with Fotonovela and other lesson sections

General Teaching Considerations

Orienting Students to the Student Worktext

Because **¡ADELANTE! 2/e** treats graphic design as an integral part of students' language-learning experience, you may want to take a few minutes to orient students to the student worktext. Have them flip through one lesson, and point out that all lessons are organized exactly the same way. Also point out how the major sections of each lesson are color-coded for easy navigation: red for **Contextos**, purple for **Fotonovela**, orange for **Cultura**, blue for **Estructura**, green for **Adelante**, and gold for **Vocabulario**. Let them know that, because of these design elements, they can be confident that they will always know "where they are" in their worktext.

Emphasize that sections are self-contained, occupying either a full page or a spread of two facing pages, thereby eliminating "bad breaks" and the need to flip back and forth to do activities or to work with explanatory material. Call students' attention to the use of color to highlight key information in elements such as charts, diagrams, word lists, and activity **modelos**, titles, and sidebars.

Point out that following the major sections of each lesson are the Workbook, Video Manual, and Lab Manual pages for that lesson. Each recto page has a side tab identifying its ancillary. Also call attention to the Additional Vocabulary and Notes pages at the end of each lesson.

Flexible Lesson Organization

¡ADELANTE! 2/e uses a flexible lesson organization designed to accommodate diverse teaching styles, institutions, and instructional goals. For example, you can begin with the lesson opener page and progress sequentially through a lesson. If you do not want to devote class time to grammar, you can assign the **Estructura** explanations for outside study, freeing up class time for other purposes like developing oral communication skills; building listening, reading, or writing skills; learning more about the Spanish-speaking world; or working with the video program. You might decide to work extensively with the **Cultura** and **Adelante** sections in order to focus on students' reading, writing, and listening skills and their knowledge of the Spanish-speaking world. Or, you might prefer to use these sections periodically in response to your students' interests as the opportunity arises. If you plan on using the **¡ADELANTE!** Testing Program, however, be aware that the quizzes, tests, and exams check language presented in **Contextos**, **Estructura**, and the **Expresiones útiles** boxes of **Fotonovela**.

Identifying Active Vocabulary

All words and expressions taught in the illustrations and **Más vocabulario** lists in **Contextos** are considered active, testable vocabulary. Any items in the **Variación léxica** or **Así se dice** boxes, however, are intended for receptive learning and are presented for enrichment only. The words and expressions in the **Expresiones útiles** boxes in **Fotonovela**, as well as words in charts, word lists, **¡Atención!** sidebars, and sample sentences in **Estructura** are also part of the active vocabulary load. At the end of each lesson, **Vocabulario** provides a convenient one-page summary of the items students should know and that may appear on tests and exams. Point this out to students and tell them that an easy way to study from **Vocabulario** is to cover up the Spanish half of each section, leaving only the English equivalents exposed. They can then quiz themselves on the Spanish items. To focus on the English equivalents of the Spanish entries, they simply reverse this process.

Taking into Account the Affective Dimension

While many factors contribute to the quality and success rate of learning experiences, two factors are particularly germane to language learning. One is students' beliefs about how language is learned; the other is language-learning anxiety.

As studies show and experienced instructors know, students often come to modern language courses either with a lack of knowledge about how to approach language learning or with mistaken notions about how to do so. For example, many students believe that making mistakes when speaking the target language must be avoided because doing so will lead to permanent errors. Others are convinced that learning another language is like learning any other academic subject. In other words, they believe that success is guaranteed, provided they attend class regularly, learn the assigned vocabulary words and grammar rules, and study for exams. In fact, in a study of college-level beginning language learners in the United States, over one-third of the participants thought that they could become fluent if they studied the language for only one hour a day for two years or less. Mistaken and unrealistic beliefs such as these can cause frustration and ultimately demotivation, thereby significantly undermining students' ability to achieve a successful language-learning experience.

Another factor that can negatively impact students' language-learning experience is language-learning anxiety. As Professor Elaine K. Horwitz of The University of Texas at Austin wrote, "Surveys indicate that up to one-third of American foreign language students feel moderately to highly anxious about studying another language. Physical symptoms of foreign language anxiety can include heart-pounding or palpitations, sweating, trembling, fast breathing, and general feelings of unease." The late Dr. Philip Redwine Donley, author of articles on language-learning anxiety, spoke with many students who reported feeling nervous or apprehensive in their classes. They mentioned freezing when called on by their instructors or going inexplicably blank when taking tests. Some so dreaded their classes that they skipped them or dropped the course.

¡ADELANTE! contains several features aimed at reducing students' language anxiety and supporting successful language-learning. Its highly structured, visually dramatic design was conceived as a learning tool to make students feel comfortable with the content and confident about navigating the lessons. The Instructor's Annotated Edition includes *Successful Language Learning* annotations with learning strategies for enhancing students' learning experiences. In addition, the student text provides a wealth of helpful sidebars that assist students by making relevant connections with new information or reminding them of previously learned concepts.

Student Sidebars

¡Atención! Provides active, testable information about the vocabulary or grammar point

Ayuda Offers specific grammar and vocabulary reminders related to a particular activity or suggests pertinent language-learning strategies

Consulta References related material introduced in previous or upcoming lessons

¡Lengua viva! Presents relevant information on everyday language use

Nota cultural Provides a wide range of cultural information relevant to the topic of an activity or section

General Suggestions for Using the
NEW! ¡ADELANTE! *Fotonovela* Video

¡ADELANTE!, Second Edition, features a brand-new, specially shot dramatic storyline video. Although the **Fotonovela** is new, the instructional design surrounding it remains true to the original program. The **Fotonovela** section in each lesson of the student worktext and the **¡ADELANTE!** Fotonovela Video were created as interlocking pieces. All photos in this section are images from the corresponding video module, while the printed conversations are abbreviated versions of the video module's dramatic segment. Both the **Fotonovela** conversations and their expanded video versions represent comprehensible input at the discourse level; they were purposely written to use language from the corresponding lesson's **Contextos** and **Estructura** sections. Thus, as of **¡ADELANTE! UNO** Lección 2, they recycle known language, preview grammar points students will study later in the lesson, and, in keeping with the concept of "i + 1," contain a small amount of unknown language.

You can use the **Fotonovela** Video and corresponding worktext section in many ways. For instance, you can use the **Fotonovela** spread as an advance organizer, presenting it before showing the video module. You can also show the video module first. You can even use Fotonovela as a stand-alone, video-independent

section. You might decide to show all video modules in class or to assign them solely for viewing outside of the classroom. You could begin by showing the first one or two episodes in class to gain familiarity with the characters, storyline, style, and **Resumen** sections. After that, you could work in class only with **Fotonovela** pages and have students view the remaining episodes outside of class. For each episode, there are **¿Qué pasó?** activities in the **Fotonovela** section of the corresponding worktext lesson and video activities in the Video Manual section of the worktext and on the Supersite.

You might also want to use the **Fotonovela** Video in class when working with Estructura. You could play parts of the dramatic episode that demonstrate the grammar point you are teaching or show selected scenes that review old grammar points and ask students to identify them. In class, you could play the parts of the **Resumen** section that exemplify individual grammar points as you progress through each **Estructura** section. You could also wait until you complete an **Estructura** section and review it by showing the corresponding **Resumen** section in its entirety.

No matter which approach you choose, students have ample materials to support viewing the video independently and processing it in a meaningful way. We hope you and your students will continue to find the **Fotonovela** Video and corresponding materials to be an engaging and effective tool for language-learning.

General Suggestions for Using the ¡ADELANTE!
Panorama cultural and *Flash cultura* Videos

The **Panorama cultural** Video contains documentary and travelogue footage of each country featured in the lesson's **Panorama** section. The **Flash cultura** Video expands on an aspect of the lesson theme in the format of a news broadcast. Like the conversations in the **Fotonovela** Video, these video segments deliver comprehensible input. Each was written to make the most of the vocabulary and grammar students learned in the corresponding and previous lessons, while still providing a controlled amount of unknown language.

Activities for the **Flash cultura** and **Panorama cultural** Videos are located in the Video Manual section of the ¡ADELANTE! worktext and on the Supersite. They follow a process approach of pre-viewing, while-viewing, and post-viewing and use a variety of formats to prepare students for watching the video segments, to focus them while watching, and to check comprehension after they have watched the footage.

When showing the **videos** in class, you might also want to implement a process approach. You could start with an activity that prepares students for the video segment by taking advantage of what they learned in previous lessons. This could be followed by an activity that students do while you play certain parts or all of the video segment. The final activity, done in the same class period or in the next one as warm-up, could recap what students saw and heard and expand on the video segment's topic. The following suggestions for working with the **Flash cultura** Video in class can be carried out as described or expanded upon in any number of ways.

Before viewing

- After students have practiced the lesson's vocabulary and grammar and worked through the **Cultura** section of the student worktext, mention the video segment's title and ask them to guess what the segment might be about.

- Have pairs make a list of the lesson vocabulary they expect to hear in the video segment.

- Read the class a list of true/false or multiple-choice questions about the video. Students must use what they learned in the **Cultura** section to guess the answers. Confirm their guesses after watching the segment.

While viewing

- Show the video segment with the audio turned off and ask students to use lesson vocabulary and structures to describe what is happening. Have them confirm their guesses by showing the segment again with the audio on.

- Have students refer to the list of words they brainstormed before viewing the video and put a check mark in front of any words they actually see in the segment.

- First, have students simply watch the video. Then, show it again and ask students to take notes on what they see and hear. Finally, have them compare their notes in pairs or groups for confirmation.

- Photocopy the segment's Videoscript from the Supersite and white out words and expressions related to the lesson theme, in order to create cloze paragraphs. Distribute the scripts for pairs or groups to complete the sentences.

After viewing

- Have students say what aspects of the cultural information presented in their worktext appear in the video segment.

- Ask groups to write a brief summary of the content of the video segment. Have them exchange papers with another group for peer editing.

- Ask students to discuss any aspects of the featured country and topic of which they were unaware before watching. Encourage them to explain why they did not expect those aspects to be true of the country in question.

- Have students pick one characteristic about the country and topic that they learned from watching the video segment. Have them research additional information about that topic and write a brief composition that expands on it.

Acknowledgments

Vista Higher Learning expresses its sincere appreciation to the many instructors and college professors across the U.S. and Canada who contributed their ideas and suggestions.

¡ADELANTE!, Second Edition, is the direct result of extensive reviews and ongoing input from instructors using the First Edition. Accordingly, we gratefully acknowledge those who shared their suggestions, recommendations, and ideas as we prepared this Second Edition.

We express our sincere appreciation to the instructors who completed our online review.

Reviewers

Amy Altamirano South Milwaukee High School South Milwaukee, WI

Barbara Bessette Cayuga Community College

Deborah Bock University of Alaska Anchorage

Teresa Borden Columbia College

Dennis Bricault North Park University

Patrice Burns University of Wisconsin—Milwaukee: School of Continuing Education

Katherine Cash Crown College, MN

Carole A. Champagne, Ph.D. University of Maryland Eastern Shore, Salisbury University

Darren Crasto Houston Community College

Kathie Filby Greenville College

José M. Garcia-Paine, Ph.D. Metropolitan State University of Denver

Nancy Hake Park University

Dominique Hitchcock Norco College

Lola Jerez-Moya Monterey Peninsula College

Aggie Johnson Flagler College

Kevin Kaber University of Wisconsin—Milwaukee: School of Continuing Education

Victoria Kildal Prince William Sound Community College

Isabel Killough Norfolk State University

Teresa Lane Hawai'i Pacific University

Michael Langer Wake Technical Community College

Marilyn Manley Rowan University

Estela Sánchez Márquez East Los Angeles College

Lisa Mathelier Morton College

Lizette S. Moon Houston Community College Northwest

M. Margarita Nodarse, Ph.D. Barry University

Chaiya Mohanty Ortiz Northern Virginia Community College

William Paulino Delaware Technical Community College

Emley Poloche Andrews University

Jeff Ruth East Stroudsburg University

Lisbet Sanchez Mt. San Antonio College

Norma Sánchez California State University Los Angeles

Lowell E. "Buddy" Sandefur Eastern Oklahoma State College

Sarah Shanebrook University of Wisconsin—Milwaukee: School of Continuing Education

Cristina Sparks-Early Northern Virginia Community College

David Thomson Luther College, IA

Jeff Tuttle Northeast Mississippi Community College

Adriana Vecino Bilingual Education Institute

Hugo M. Viera Westfield State University

Sandra Watts University of North Carolina at Charlotte

Charlotte Whittle York School Monterey, CA

Karen L. Woelfle-Potter University of Wisconsin—Milwaukee: School of Continuing Education

Wendy Woodrich Lewis & Clark College

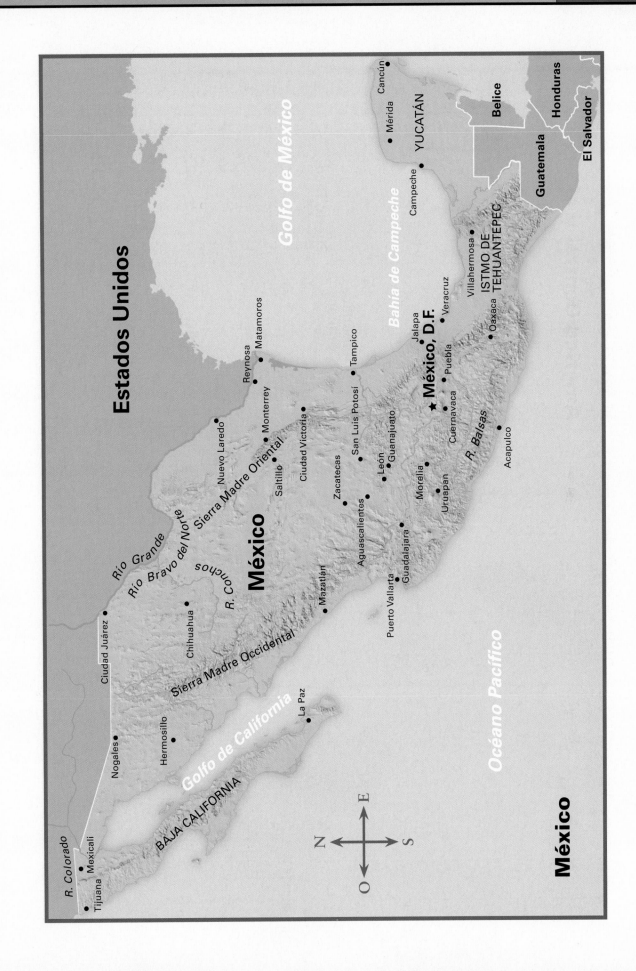

México

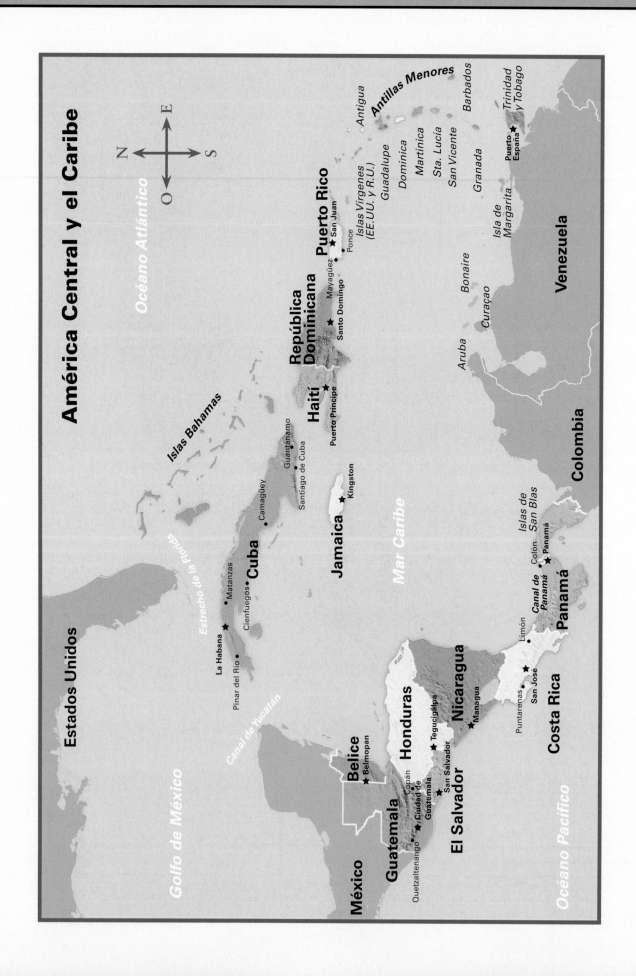

América Central y el Caribe

Estados Unidos

Golfo de México

México

Guatemala

Quetzaltenango

Ciudad de Guatemala

Copán

Belice

Belmopan

El Salvador

San Salvador

Honduras

Tegucigalpa

Nicaragua

Managua

Costa Rica

San José

Puntarenas

Océano Pacífico

Limón

Colón

Panamá

Panamá

Canal de Panamá

Islas de San Blas

Colombia

Venezuela

Mar Caribe

Jamaica

Kingston

Cuba

La Habana

Pinar del Río

Matanzas

Cienfuegos

Camagüey

Santiago de Cuba

Guantánamo

Canal de Yucatán

Estrecho de la Florida

Islas Bahamas

Océano Atlántico

Haití

Puerto Príncipe

República Dominicana

Santo Domingo

Puerto Rico

Mayagüez

San Juan

Ponce

Islas Vírgenes (EE.UU. y R.U.)

Antillas Menores

Antigua

Guadalupe

Dominica

Martinica

Sta. Lucía

San Vicente

Granada

Barbados

Trinidad y Tobago

Puerto España

Isla de Margarita

Bonaire

Curaçao

Aruba

N E S O

América del Sur

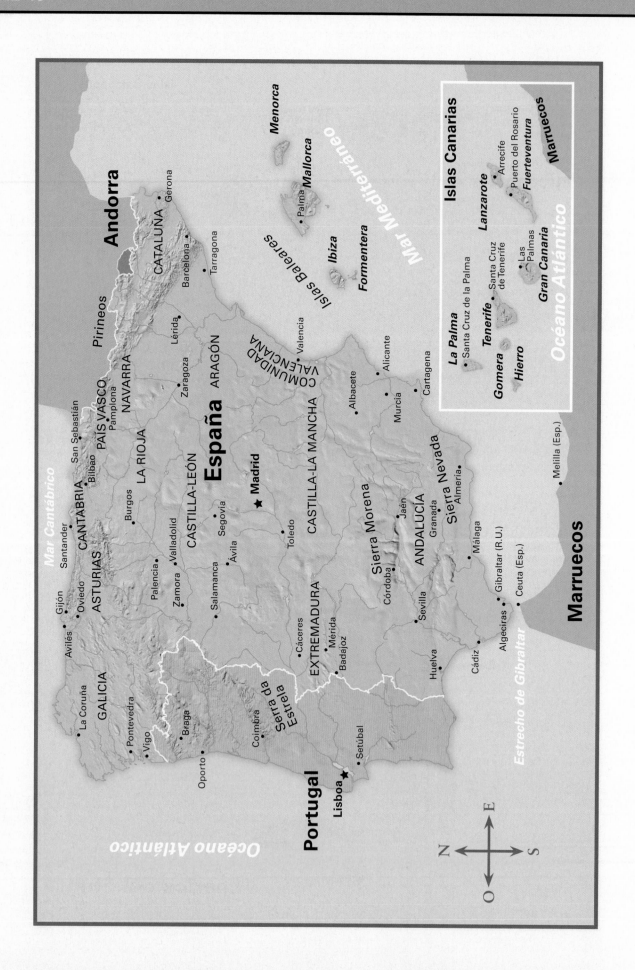

Lección de repaso

Communicative Goals

You will review how to:

- Describe people and things
- Discuss pastimes and sports
- Talk about the seasons and the weather
- Tell what happened in the past

Práctica

1 Identificar Indica la palabra que no pertenece al grupo. `8 pts.`

1. lluvia • (tomar el sol) • botas • impermeable
2. traje de baño • bucear • playa • (abrigo)
3. (nadar) • nieve • esquiar • invierno
4. matemáticas • (mochila) • historia • computación
5. estudiar • tomar un examen • (viajar) • hacer la tarea
6. sandalias • camiseta • (guantes) • pantalones cortos
7. (semana) • ayer • mañana • hoy
8. tío • prima • abuelo • (dependienta)

2 Listas Completa cada lista con las palabras que faltan. `10 pts.`

DÍAS: lunes, (1) ___martes___, miércoles, jueves, (2) ___viernes___, sábado, (3) ___domingo___

MESES: (4) ___enero___, febrero, marzo, abril, (5) ___mayo___, junio, julio, (6) ___agosto___, septiembre, (7) ___octubre___, noviembre, (8) ___diciembre___

ESTACIONES: (9) ___primavera___, verano, otoño, (10) ___invierno___

3 Oraciones Completa cada oración con una palabra de la lista. `6 pts.`

biblioteca	periodismo
historia	pruebas
lápiz	psicología
lenguas extranjeras	reloj
matemáticas	ventana
mochila	vestido

1. Para ser reportero en la televisión, tienes que estudiar ___periodismo___.

2. Si te gustan los números y las ecuaciones, puedes estudiar ___matemáticas___.

3. Para comunicarte con personas de otros países y culturas, debes estudiar ___lenguas extranjeras___.

4. El profesor les hace ___pruebas___ a los estudiantes para comprobar (*check*) lo que aprendieron.

5. Cuando los estudiantes están aburridos, miran el ___reloj___ esperando el final de la clase.

6. Para estudiar en un lugar tranquilo y tener acceso a muchos libros, puedes ir a la ___biblioteca___.

For additional vocabulary, see p. 18.

This overview presents key vocabulary from *¡ADELANTE! UNO*. For further review, follow the cross-references.

El invierno

diciembre *December*
enero *January*
febrero *February*   **Nieva. (nevar)**

¿Qué tiempo hace? *What's the weather like?*
Hace frío. *It's cold.*

estudiar *to study*
patinar *to skate*
tomar el examen *to take an exam*
trabajar *to work*

el esquí *skiing*
el hockey *hockey*

el abrigo *coat*
la bota *boot*
los guantes *gloves*

esquiar

el año *year*
el día *day*
la semana *week*

lunes *Monday*
martes *Tuesday*
miércoles *Wednesday*
jueves *Thursday*
viernes *Friday*
sábado *Saturday*
domingo *Sunday*

el mes

La primavera

marzo *March*
abril *April*
mayo *May*

Extra Practice In small groups, have students list as many related vocabulary words as they can remember. Call on several volunteers to share their lists with the class.

Hace mal tiempo. *The weather is bad.*

ir de excursión *to go on a hike*
pasear *to take a walk; to stroll*
pasear en bicicleta *to ride a bicycle*
practicar deportes *to play sports*

la contabilidad *accounting*
el periodismo *journalism*
la prueba *test; quiz*

Llueve. (llover)

la blusa *blouse*
la camisa *shirt*
el impermeable *raincoat*
el traje *suit*
el vestido *dress*

el reloj

Lección de repaso

El verano

junio *June*
julio *July*
agosto *August*

Hace buen tiempo. *The weather is good.*
Hace sol. *It's sunny.*

bucear *to scuba dive*
nadar *to swim*
tomar el sol *to sunbathe*
viajar *to travel*

el campo *countryside*
el mar *sea*

Hace (mucho) calor.

TPR To review additional vocabulary, play a word association game. Have students stand in a large circle; then throw a foam or paper ball to a student and call out a word. The student must quickly respond with a related word, then throw the ball to another student, who must come up with a new association for that word. (Ex: **jugar: deportes: el tenis: los zapatos de tenis: la ropa**) When a student is "stumped," he or she takes a seat. Call out another word and begin again. The last player standing is the winner.

la playa
el vóleibol *volleyball*

la camiseta *t-shirt*
las gafas de sol *sunglasses*
los pantalones cortos *shorts*
las sandalias *sandals*
el traje de baño *bathing suit*

El otoño

septiembre *September*
octubre *October*
noviembre *November*

Hace fresco. *It's cool.*

comenzar las clases *to start classes*
escalar montañas *to climb mountains*
jugar (u:ue) al fútbol americano *to play football*

Hace viento.

la biblioteca *library*
la cafetería *cafeteria*
la computación *computer science*
las lenguas extranjeras *foreign languages*
las matemáticas *math*
la mochila *backpack*

montar a caballo

la chaqueta *jacket*
los bluejeans *jeans*
el suéter *sweater*

For a complete list of related vocabulary go to *¡ADELANTE!* **UNO**, pp. 38, 98, 160, 220, 282, and 340.

---

4 **Describir** Describe el tiempo que hace en cada escena y el tipo de actividad que hacen las personas. **12 pts.**

Some answers will vary. Sample answers:

> **modelo**
> Hace buen tiempo. Él está paseando en bicicleta.

1. Hace viento. Ella está paseando por la ciudad.

2. Hace fresco. Ellos están acampando.

3. Hace buen tiempo. Él está corriendo.

4. Está nublado. Él está montando a caballo.

5. Está lloviendo. Ella está paseando por el parque.

6. Hace calor. Ellos están jugando al vóleibol.

5 **Preparando un viaje** Escribe una conversación entre dos amigos que están haciendo las maletas para irse de viaje una semana. Uno va a esquiar en Argentina, donde es invierno, y el otro va a Florida, donde es verano. **14 pts.** Answers will vary.

- ¿Qué actividades pueden hacer?
- ¿Qué tiempo va a hacer?
- ¿Qué ropa tienen que llevar?
- ¿Qué medios de transporte van a usar?
- ¿Dónde se van a quedar?

 Practice more at **vhlcentral.com**.

Práctica  Tutorials

1 **Género y número** Completa las tablas cambiando las palabras femeninas a masculinas, las singulares a plurales y viceversa. `14 pts.`

Masculino	Femenino
el pintor	la pintora
el cuñado	**la cuñada**
el huésped	**la huésped**
el turista	la turista
el dependiente	**la dependienta**
el pasajero	la pasajera
el inspector	**la inspectora**

Singular	Plural
una clase	unas clases
un autobús	unos autobuses
una excursión	**unas excursiones**
una comunidad	unas comunidades
un lápiz	**unos lápices**
una revista	**unas revistas**
un calcetín	unos calcetines

2 **Completar** Completa cada oración con el verbo **ser**. `6 pts.`

1. Maite ____es____ de España, ¿verdad?
2. ¿Quiénes ____son____ los huéspedes de la habitación 347?
3. Juan y yo ____somos____ vendedores en aquel centro comercial.
4. ¿De dónde ____eres____ tú?
5. ____Son____ las nueve de la mañana.
6. Yo ____soy____ puertorriqueño pero vivo en Costa Rica.

3 **El primer día de clases** Completa la conversación con las formas correctas del verbo **estar**. `5 pts.`

JULIO Hola, Martín. ¿Cómo (1) ____estás____ (tú)?

MARTÍN Bien. Oye, ¿sabes dónde (2) ____está____ el gimnasio?
Mis compañeros del equipo de béisbol (3) ____están____ allí.

JULIO Pero, hombre, ¡yo también (4) ____estoy____ en el equipo!
Vamos juntos al gimnasio, (nosotros) (5) ____estamos____
muy cerca.

MARTÍN ¡Pero qué tonto soy! No recordaba que tú también estás en
el equipo. OK, vamos.

Resumen gramatical

This overview presents key grammatical concepts from *¡ADELANTE!* UNO. For further review, follow the cross-references.

R.1 | **Nouns and articles** | *¡ADELANTE!* UNO
L1 pp. 12-14

Gender of nouns

Nouns that refer to living things

	Masculine		Feminine
-o	el chico	-a	la chica
-or	el profesor	-ora	la profesora
-ista	el turista	-ista	la turista

Nouns that refer to non-living things

	Masculine		Feminine
-o	el libro	-a	la cosa
-ma	el programa	-ción	la lección
-s	el autobús	-dad	la nacionalidad

Plural of nouns

► ending in vowels + *-s*   la chica → las chicas
► ending in consonant + *-es*   el señor → los señores
   (-z → -ces **un lápiz** → **unos lápices**)

Definite articles: el, la, los, las

Indefinite articles: un, una, unos, unas

R.2 | **Present of ser and estar** | *¡ADELANTE!* UNO
L1 pp. 19-21, L2 pp. 81–82

> ¿Y ustedes de dónde son?

> Yo soy de Buenos Aires, Argentina. Miguel es de España.

ser			
yo	soy	nosotros/as	somos
tú	eres	vosotros/as	sois
Ud./él/ella	es	Uds./ellos/ellas	son

► **Uses of ser:** nationality, origin, profession or occupation, characteristics, generalizations, possession, what something is made of, time and date, time and place of events

estar			
yo	estoy	nosotros/as	estamos
tú	estás	vosotros/as	estáis
Ud./él/ella	está	Uds./ellos/ellas	están

▶ Uses of **estar**: location, health, physical states and conditions, emotional states, weather expressions, ongoing actions

▶ **Ser** and **estar** can both be used with many of the same adjectives, but the meaning will change.

Juan **es** listo.   Juan **está** listo.
Juan is smart.   *Juan is ready.*

R.3 Adjectives   ↻ *¡ADELANTE!* **UNO**
L3 pp. 134–136, 139

Eres gordo, antipático y muy feo.

▶ Adjectives are words that describe nouns. In Spanish, adjectives agree with the nouns they modify in both gender and number.

Descriptive adjectives

Masculine		Feminine	
Singular	Plural	Singular	Plural
alto	altos	alta	altas
inteligente	inteligentes	inteligente	inteligentes
trabajador	trabajadores	trabajadora	trabajadoras

▶ To refer to a mixed group, use the masculine plural form.

Juan y Ana son trabajador**es**.

▶ Descriptive adjectives and adjectives of nationality follow the noun: **el chico rubio, la mujer española**

▶ Adjectives of quantity precede the noun: **muchos libros**

▶ Before a masculine noun, these adjectives are shortened.

bueno → buen   **malo → mal**   **grande → gran**

Possessive adjectives

Singular		Plural	
mi	nuestro/a	mis	nuestros/as
tu	vuestro/a	tus	vuestros/as
su	su	sus	sus

▶ Possesive adjectives are always placed before the nouns they modify: **nuestros amigos, mi madre**

---

4 **¿Ser o estar?** Completa el texto con **ser** o **estar**. **9 pts.**

Me llamo Julio. Mis padres (1) ___son___ de México, pero mi familia ahora (2) ___está___ en Arizona. Mi padre (3) ___es___ médico en el hospital; el hospital (4) ___está___ cerca de nuestra casa. Nosotros tres (5) ___somos___ altos y morenos. Yo (6) ___soy___ estudiante de periodismo. Mis clases (7) ___son___ buenas, pero a veces (yo) (8) ___estoy___ demasiado ocupado con las tareas. Todos mis compañeros (9) ___están___ nerviosos porque hoy empiezan los exámenes finales.

5 **Posesivos** Completa con el adjetivo posesivo correcto. **8 pts.**

1. Él es ___mi___ (*my*) hermano.
2. ___Tu___ (*Your,* fam.) familia es muy simpática.
3. ___Nuestro___ (*Our*) sobrino es italiano.
4. ¿Ella es ___su___ (*his*) profesora?
5. ___Su___ (*Your,* form.) maleta es de color verde.
6. ___Sus___ (*Her*) amigos son de Colombia.
7. Son ___nuestras___ (*our*) compañeras de clase.
8. ___Mis___ (*My*) padres están en el trabajo.

6 **Opuestos** Escribe oraciones completas con los elementos dados y los adjetivos opuestos a los que están subrayados. **¡Ojo!** Recuerda conjugar los verbos. **8 pts.**

> **modelo**
> casa / de Silvia / ser / grande / pero / mi casa / ser / ¿?
> *La casa de Silvia es grande, pero mi casa es pequeña.*

1. habitación / de mi hermana / siempre / estar / sucia / pero / mi habitación / estar / ¿?
   La habitación de mi hermana siempre está sucia, pero mi habitación está limpia/ordenada.

2. (yo) estar / contento / porque / (nosotros) estar / de vacaciones / pero / mis padres / estar / ¿? / porque / (ellos) tener / que trabajar
   Estoy contento/a porque estamos de vacaciones, pero mis padres están tristes/enojados porque tienen que trabajar.

3. tu primo / ser / alto y moreno / pero / tú / ser / ¿? y ¿?
   Tu primo es alto y moreno, pero tú eres bajo/a y rubio/a.

4. mi amigo Fernando / decir / que las matemáticas / ser / difíciles / pero / yo / creer / que / ser / ¿?
   Mi amigo Fernando dice que las matemáticas son difíciles, pero yo creo que son fáciles.

Extra Practice Add a visual aspect to this grammar review. Bring in magazine pictures. Ask students to describe the people, places, and objects using **ser** and **estar**. Focus on verb forms, articles, and adjective agreement.

 Practice more at **vhlcentral.com**.

Práctica y Comunicación

1 Correo
Completa el mensaje de correo electrónico con la forma correcta de **ser** o **estar**.

¡Hola Carlos!

¿Cómo estás? Yo (1) __estoy__ muy preocupada porque tenemos un examen mañana en la clase de español y el profesor (2) __es__ muy estricto. Mi amiga Ana (3) __está__ estudiando en la biblioteca y quiero ir a verla para que me ayude. Ella (4) __es__ una estudiante muy buena y sus notas (*grades*) (5) __son__ excelentes.

Este fin de semana hay una excursión a las montañas. Mis amigos y yo (6) __estamos__ muy contentos porque el lugar que vamos a visitar (7) __es__ muy hermoso. Ana también quiere ir a la excursión, pero (ella) (8) __está__ enojada porque tiene que trabajar.

Bueno, antes de ir a la biblioteca voy a dormir la siesta porque (9) __estoy__ muy cansada.

¡Hasta pronto!
Susana

2 La vida de Marina
Completa cada oración con la forma correcta de los cuatro adjetivos.

1. Marina busca una compañera de cuarto <u>ordenada, honesta, alegre, amable</u>. (ordenado, honesto, alegre, amable)

2. Se lleva bien con las personas <u>alegres, trabajadoras, interesantes, sensibles</u> (alegre, trabajador, interesante, sensible)

3. Los padres de Marina son <u>simpáticos, inteligentes, altos, felices</u> (simpático, inteligente, alto, feliz)

4. A Marina le gusta la ropa <u>elegante, buena, bonita, barata</u>. (elegante, bueno, bonito, barato)

5. Marina tiene un novio <u>trabajador, simpático, pelirrojo, listo</u>. (trabajador, simpático, pelirrojo, listo)

Marina

3 ¿Es o no es?
Responde a cada pregunta usando el adjetivo opuesto.

> **modelo**
> ¿Es alto tu tío? No, es bajo.

1. ¿Es viejo el agente de viajes? <u>No, es joven.</u>
2. ¿Son malas las amigas de Glenda? <u>No, son buenas.</u>
3. ¿Es antipática la vendedora? <u>No, es simpática.</u>
4. ¿Son guapos los primos de Omar? <u>No, son feos.</u>
5. ¿Son morenas las excursionistas? <u>No, son rubias.</u>
6. ¿Es feo el yerno de doña Ana? <u>No, es guapo.</u>

1 To practice adjective agreement, have students circle all the adjectives in the e-mail, then replace them with different adjectives. Call on several volunteers to read their revised e-mails and have the class check for accuracy.

1 For expansion, have students write a similar e-mail to a friend, using at least six forms of **ser** and **estar**. Have them exchange their messages with a partner for peer editing.

2 For additional practice, have students add two more adjectives to each sentence.

3 Give students these additional items: **7. ¿Es grande la biblioteca? (No, es pequeña.) 8. ¿Son difíciles tus clases? (No, son fáciles.) 9. ¿Son caros estos pantalones? (No, son baratos.) 10. ¿Es largo el vestido? (No, es corto.)**

Extra Practice Briefly review adjectives that change in meaning when used with **ser** and **estar**. Ex: **listo, malo, aburrido, verde, vivo, seguro**

4 For expansion, bring in photos or magazine pictures that show several people performing a variety of activities. Have students use **ser** and **estar** to describe the scenes.

4 Ask these additional questions about the drawing:
6. ¿Qué estación es?
7. ¿Qué tiempo hace?
8. ¿Quiénes están de vacaciones?

5 Encourage students to think about these categories: personality, physical characteristics, strengths and weaknesses, health, current feelings, and emotions.

5 Ask follow-up questions to practice gender and number agreement. Ex: **John es alto. ¿Y Paula? ¿Cómo es? (Paula es baja.) Carmen y Melissa son rubias. ¿Y Frank? (Él es rubio también. / Los tres son rubios.)**

¡AL RESCATE!

To review vocabulary related to family and friends, go to *¡ADELANTE!* **UNO**, **Lesson 3**, **Contextos**, pp. 124-125.

7 Circulate around the classroom, providing assistance as needed. If necessary, help students brainstorm useful verbs and briefly review present-tense conjugations.

4

En el parque Mira la imagen y contesta las preguntas usando **ser** y **estar**. Puedes inventar las respuestas para algunas preguntas. Answers will vary.

1. ¿Quién es cada una de estas personas?

2. ¿Qué están haciendo?

3. ¿Cómo están?

4. ¿Cómo son?

5. ¿Dónde están?

5

Entrevista Escribe tantos (*as many*) adjetivos descriptivos como puedas (*as you can*) sobre ti mismo/a (*yourself*) en tres minutos. Luego, en parejas, usa **ser** o **estar** para preguntarle a tu compañero/a si él/ella tiene las mismas características. Finalmente, comparte con la clase lo que tienen en común. Answers will vary.

> **modelo**
>
> **(Yo):** delgada, baja, morena, trabajadora, contenta, simpática
> **(Preguntas):** ¿Tú eres trabajadora? ¿Estás contenta?
> **(Oración):** Somos morenas, estamos contentas y somos trabajadoras.

6

Mi familia y mis amigos Escribe una breve descripción de tu familia, tus parientes y tus amigos. Usa tantos adjetivos posesivos como puedas para identificar a la(s) persona(s) que estás describiendo. Answers will vary.

7

Una cita (*date*) Mañana vas a tener una cita con un(a) muchacho/a maravilloso/a. Quieres contarle a tu mejor amigo/a y pedirle consejos. Tu amigo/a es muy curioso/a y te va a hacer muchas preguntas. En parejas, representen la conversación. Éstos son algunos aspectos que pueden incluir.
Answers will vary.

Tu amigo/a quiere saber:
- cómo te sientes (*you feel*) antes de la cita
- qué crees que va a pasar
- cómo es el lugar adonde van a ir
- cómo es la persona con quien vas a tener la cita

Tú quieres consejos sobre:
- qué ropa usar
- temas de los que pueden hablar
- adónde ir
- quién debe pagar la cuenta (*bill*)

EN DETALLE

Unas vacaciones de
voluntario

¿Qué hiciste durante las vacaciones de verano? Muchos estudiantes contestarían° esta pregunta con historias de cómo disfrutaron° de su tiempo libre. Pero hay otra actividad que ha recibido° atención recientemente: el trabajo voluntario durante las vacaciones.

En Latinoamérica, se le llama **aprendizaje-servicio**°, una combinación de educación formal y voluntariado°. En países como México, Argentina y Chile, los estudiantes reciben crédito académico mientras° usan su creatividad y su talento en beneficio de los demás°. Así se promueve° la participación activa de los estudiantes en la sociedad. Los

voluntarios también viven experiencias que no podrían° obtener en el salón de clases: en Buenos Aires, un grupo de alumnos° de los colegios más exclusivos ayuda con las tareas en centros comunitarios; en una escuela de Resistencia, en Argentina, los chicos de barrios marginales° les enseñan computación a los adultos desocupados° de su propia comunidad.

En 2001, la Secretaría de Educación de Argentina creó el Programa Nacional de Escuela y Comunidad para los proyectos de aprendizaje-servicio por todo el país. Y tú, ¿alguna vez has participado en servicio comunitario?

Otras vacaciones de voluntarios

En León, Nicaragua, 16 estudiantes costarricenses construyeron casas para familias nicaragüenses como parte del programa Hábitat para la Humanidad. Adrián, un voluntario, dijo: "Fue una experiencia increíble. Pude° divertirme y al mismo tiempo hacer algo útil° y beneficiar a otras personas durante mis vacaciones".

Los estudiantes de la escuela técnica de Junín de los Andes, Argentina, adaptaron molinos de viento° a las necesidades de las poblaciones mapuches°. Por este proyecto ganaron un premio° en la Feria Mundial de Ciencias.

---

contestarían *would answer* disfrutaron *they enjoyed* ha recibido *has received* aprendizaje-servicio *service learning* voluntariado *volunteerism* mientras *while* los demás *others* Así se promueve *Thus it promotes* no podrían *they could not* alumnos *students* barrios marginales *disadvantaged neighborhoods* desocupados *unemployed* Pude *I was able to* útil *useful* molinos de viento *windmills* mapuches *indigenous people of Central and Southern Chile and Southern Argentina* premio *prize*

ACTIVIDADES

1 **¿Cierto o falso?** Indica si lo que dice cada oración es cierto o falso. Corrige la información falsa.

1. El aprendizaje-servicio es ir a cursos de verano. Falso. Es una combinación de educación formal y voluntariado.
2. En este programa, los jóvenes voluntarios aprenden cosas que no se aprenden en el salón de clases. Cierto.
3. Los estudiantes de Resistencia, Argentina, les enseñan computación a los chicos de los colegios más exclusivos. Falso. Les enseñan computación a los adultos desocupados de su propia comunidad.

4. En 2001, la Secretaría de Educación de Argentina creó un programa nacional de aprendizaje-servicio. Cierto.
5. De su experiencia como voluntario en Nicaragua, el joven Adrián dijo: "Fue una experiencia horrible". Falso. Adrián dijo: "Fue una experiencia increíble".
6. Los estudiantes de una escuela técnica adaptaron molinos de viento a las necesidades de las poblaciones indígenas de su país. Cierto.

ASÍ SE DICE

el buceo	*diving*
la carrera de autos	*car race*
el/la ciclista	*cyclist*
la lucha libre	*freestyle wrestling*
la ola	*[ocean] wave*
los países hispanohablantes	**los países donde se habla español**
surfear, hacer surf	*to surf*
el/la surfista, el/la surfero/a, el/la surfo/a, el/la tablista	*surfer*

EL MUNDO HISPANO

Deportes importantes

No cabe duda° que el fútbol es el deporte más popular en Latinoamérica. Sin embargo°, también se practican otros deportes en el mundo hispano.

Deporte	Lugar(es)
el béisbol	Puerto Rico, República Dominicana, Cuba, México, Venezuela
el ciclismo	Colombia, España y otras regiones montañosas
el rugby	Argentina, Chile
el baloncesto (básquetbol)	España, Puerto Rico, Colombia, Centroamérica
el jai-alai	Originado en el País Vasco (España), también es popular en México y los EE.UU.
la equitación (montar a caballo)	México, Argentina, España
el surf	las Islas Canarias (España), México, Chile, Perú, Colombia

No cabe duda *there is no doubt* Sin embargo *nevertheless*

PERFIL

Surfistas hispanos

Se dice que para hacer surf hay que "sentir" la ola°, pararse° en la tabla° y "agarrarla°". La frase "agarrar la ola" tiene un significado que sólo entienden realmente los que practican el surf. Originado en Hawai, es popular en muchas partes del mundo. Sólo necesitas una tabla y una costa marina. Dos de los surfistas hispanos más reconocidos son **Gabriel Villarán** y **Ornella Pellizzari**.

Ornella Pellizzari

Gabriel Villarán es probablemente el surfista hispanoamericano más famoso del mundo. Nació en 1984 en Lima, Perú, donde su madre, su padre y su hermano eran° surfistas. Villarán fue campeón° latinoamericano dos veces y en enero de 2006 ganó el primer lugar en los Juegos Panamericanos de Surf.

A los once años, la argentina Ornella Pellizzari se compró una tabla con el dinero que había ahorrado°. A los dieciocho años, ganó el Campeonato Latinoamericano de Surf Profesional femenino. Dice Pellizzari: "Una vez que empecé a surfear, no salí más del agua".

ola *wave* pararse *to stand* la tabla *surfboard* agarrarla *to grab it* eran *were* campeón *champion* había ahorrado *she had saved*

Conexión Internet

¿Quiénes son otros atletas hispanos famosos?	Go to **vhlcentral.com** to find more cultural information related to this **Cultura** section.

ACTIVIDADES

2 **Comprensión** Completa las oraciones.

1. El deporte del surf se originó en ___Hawai___.
2. Gabriel Villarán nació en ___Lima, Perú___.
3. Los países donde se habla español son conocidos como países ___hispanohablantes___
4. A los dieciocho años, Pellizzari ganó el Campeonato Latinoamericano de Surf Profesional para ___mujeres___.
5. El deporte del ___jai-alai___ tiene su origen en el País Vasco.

3 **¿Qué vamos a hacer?** Your class has the opportunity to go on a week's vacation. Working in a small group, decide whether **el aprendizaje-servicio** or **los deportes** best suits the group's talents and interests. Plan activities you can agree on, including where you might go. Present your vacation plans to the class. Answers will vary.

 Practice more at **vhlcentral.com**.

Práctica  Tutorials

1 **Verbos** Completa la tabla con las formas de los verbos. `10 pts.`

Infinitive	yo	nosotros/as	ellos/as
comprar	compro	compramos	**compran**
poder	**puedo**	podemos	pueden
comenzar	comienzo	**comenzamos**	comienzan
hacer	hago	**hacemos**	**hacen**
oír	oigo	oímos	oyen
jugar	**juego**	jugamos	juegan
repetir	repito	repetimos	**repiten**
estudiar	estudio	**estudiamos**	estudian

2 **Ir** Completa el párrafo con las formas de **ir**. `8 pts.`

El sábado yo (1) ___voy___ al Museo de Bellas Artes porque mi artista favorito (2) ___va___ a presentar una exposición. Mis amigos no (3) ___van___ al museo conmigo porque todos (4) ___van___ a jugar al fútbol, pero yo voy a (5) ___ir___ porque yo (6) ___voy___ a ser artista. ¿(7) ___Vas___ (tú) al museo también? ¿Por qué no (8) ___vamos___ juntos?

3 **Conversación** Completa la conversación con las formas de los verbos. Puedes usar algunos verbos más de una vez. `7 pts.`

> empezar   poder
> jugar   querer
> pensar   recordar
> perder   volver

PABLO Óscar, voy al centro ahora. Necesito hacer varias diligencias (*errands*).

ÓSCAR ¿A qué hora (1) ___vuelves___? El partido de fútbol (2) ___empieza___ a las dos.

PABLO Regreso a la una. (3) ___Quiero/Pienso___ ver el partido. ¡Va a estar muy reñido (*hard-fought*)!

ÓSCAR ¿(4) ___Recuerdas___ (tú) que nuestro equipo ganó los tres partidos anteriores (*previous*)? Es muy bueno. ¡Estoy seguro de que vamos a ganar!

PABLO No, yo (5) ___pienso___ que vamos a (6) ___perder___. Los jugadores de Guadalajara son salvajes (*wild*) cuando (7) ___juegan___.

Resumen gramatical

This overview presents key grammatical concepts from *¡ADELANTE!* **UNO**. For further review, follow the cross-references.

R.4 **Present of regular verbs**
¡ADELANTE! **UNO**
L2 pp. 72–74, L3 pp. 142–143

▶ To create the present-tense forms of most regular verbs, drop the infinitive endings (**-ar, -er, -ir**) and add the endings that correspond to the different subject pronouns.

	hablar	comer	escribir
yo	hablo	como	escribo
tú	hablas	comes	escribes
él	habla	come	escribe
nos.	hablamos	comemos	escribimos
vos.	habláis	coméis	escribís
ellas	hablan	comen	escriben

R.5 **Present of tener and venir**
¡ADELANTE! **UNO**
L3 pp. 146–147

> Tía Nayeli, ¿cuántos años tienen tus hijas?

> Marta tiene ocho años y Valentina doce.

tener		venir	
tengo	tenemos	vengo	venimos
tienes	tenéis	vienes	venís
tiene	tienen	viene	vienen

▶ **Tener** is used in many common phrases.

> **tener... años** *to be... (years old)*
> **tener calor** *to be hot*
> **tener frío** *to be cold* a
> **tener ganas de** [+ *inf.*] *to feel like doing something*
> **tener hambre** *to be hungry*
> **tener prisa** *to be in a hurry*
> **tener que** [+ *inf.*] *to have to do something*
> **tener razón** *to be right*
> **tener sed** *to be thirsty*

Lección de repaso

R.6 Present of **ir** ↻ *¡ADELANTE!* UNO
L4 p.196

pedir			
yo	voy	nosotros/as	vamos
tú	vas	vosotros/as	vais
el	va	ellas	van

▶ **Ir** has many everyday uses, including expressing future plans: **ir a** + [infinitivo] = *to be going to* + [*infinitive*]
vamos a + [infinitivo] = *let's* [*do something*]

R.7 Present of irregular verbs ↻ *¡ADELANTE!* UNO
L4 pp. 199–200, 203, 206–207

No encuentro su nombre.
Ah, no, ahora sí lo veo.

e:ie, o:ue, u:ue stem-changing verbs

	empezar	volver	jugar
yo	empiezo	vuelvo	juego
tú	empiezas	vuelves	juegas
él	empieza	vuelve	juega
nos.	empezamos	volvemos	jugamos
vos.	empezáis	volvéis	jugáis
ellas	empiezan	vuelven	juegan

▶ Other e:ie verbs: **comenzar, entender, pensar, querer**

▶ Other o:ue verbs: **almorzar, dormir, encontrar, mostrar**

e:i stem-changing verbs

pedir			
yo	pido	nosotros/as	pedimos
tú	pides	vosotros/as	pedís
el	pide	ellas	piden

▶ Other e:i verbs: **conseguir, decir, repetir, seguir**

Verbs with irregular yo forms

hacer	poner	salir	suponer	traer
hago	pongo	salgo	supongo	traigo

▶ **ver: veo, ves, ve, vemos, veis, ven**

▶ **oír: oigo, oyes, oye, oímos, oís, oyen**

↻ For a complete list of verb conjugations, go to Apéndice D, pp. A-9 to A-18, at the end of your worktext.

---

4 **Oraciones** Escribe oraciones completas con estos elementos.
¡Ojo! Recuerda conjugar los verbos. **10 pts.**

1. tú / tener / unos amigos / muy interesante
   Tú tienes unos amigos muy interesantes.

2. yo / venir / en autobús / de / el centro comercial
   Yo vengo en autobús del centro comercial.

3. ellos / no / tener / mucho / dinero / hoy
   Ellos no tienen mucho dinero hoy.

4. yo / ir / a / el cine / todos / el sábado
   Yo voy al cine todos los sábados.

5. los estudiantes / de español / ir / a / leer / una revista
   Los estudiantes de español van a leer una revista.

5 **Tener** Describe qué hacen las personas. Usa expresiones con **tener** y sigue el modelo. **15 pts.**

Él tiene (mucha) prisa.

1. Ella tiene (mucho) calor.

2. Ella tiene veintiún años.

3. Ellos tienen (mucha) hambre.

4. Ellos tienen (mucho) frío.

5. Él tiene (mucha) sed.

TPR Make sets of cards with infinitives of verbs that are easy to act out (include regular and stem-changing verbs, as well as **tener** expressions). Divide the class into groups of five. Have students take turns drawing a card and acting out the verb for the group. Once someone has guessed the verb, the group members must take turns providing the conjugated forms.

 Practice more at **vhlcentral.com**.

Práctica y Comunicación

1

Completar Completa las oraciones con las formas apropiadas de los verbos de la lista.
Some answers may vary.

aprender	correr	jugar	pedir	salir	vivir
bailar	hablar	oír	recibir	ver	volver

1. Rosa ___baila___ un tango en el teatro.
2. Mis amigos ___hablan___ francés muy bien.
3. Yo no ___salgo___ de casa cuando hace demasiado calor.
4. Mi hermano y yo ___aprendemos___ a nadar en la piscina.
5. Nosotros ___vivimos___ en la residencia estudiantil.
6. ¿Tú ___recibes___ regalos en el día de tu cumpleaños?
7. Los estudiantes ___corren___ a casa por la tarde.
8. Yo ___veo___ una película.
9. Usted nunca ___pide___ ayuda, ¿verdad?
10. Mis hermanos ___juegan___ al fútbol después de las clases.
11. Ustedes siempre ___oyen___ ese programa de radio.
12. ¿Mañana ___vuelven___ tus padres de Roma?

1 For additional practice, call out different subject pronouns for each item and have volunteers restate the sentence.

2 For expansion, ask pairs to write one question for each of the interrogative words listed in ¡Al rescate! Then have them exchange their questions with another pair and take turns asking and answering the questions.

2

Contestar Trabaja con un(a) compañero/a para formar preguntas completas. Luego, túrnense para hacerse las preguntas que crearon.   Answers will vary.

> **modelo**
>
> pedir / en la cafetería
> **Estudiante 1:** ¿Qué pides en la cafetería?
> **Estudiante 2:** En la cafetería, yo pido pizza.

1. horas / dormir cada noche
2. preferir / hacer la tarea de matemáticas
3. ir / cuando salir con amigos/as
4. empezar / tus clases los miércoles
5. tipo de música / preferir
6. pensar / ir a / ser / esta clase

¡AL RESCATE!

Here are some interrogative words.
¿A qué hora?
At what time?
¿Adónde? *Where to?*
¿Cómo? *How?*
¿Cuál(es)? *Which?;
Which one(s)?*
¿Cuándo? *When?*
¿Cuántos/as?
How many?
¿Dónde? *Where?*
¿Qué? *What?*
To review more about forming questions in Spanish, go to
¡ADELANTE! UNO,
Estructura 2.2,
pp. 77–78.

3

Combinar En parejas, túrnense para combinar elementos de las dos columnas y crear oraciones completas.   Answers will vary.

A

yo
mis compañeros/as de clase
mi mejor amigo/a
tú
mi familia
mis amigos/as y yo

B

hacer la tarea todas las tardes
levantarse a las doce del día
ir al cine todos los viernes
conseguir gangas en Internet
pedir favores
almorzar en casa los domingos

4

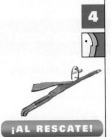

¡AL RESCATE!

The present progressive indicates what someone is doing *right now*. It consists of the present tense of **estar** and the present participle of another verb.

Estamos hablando.

To review the present progressive, go to **¡ADELANTE! UNO**, **Estructura 5.2**, pp. 260–261.

Frecuencia Indica qué actividades haces **todos los días**, cuáles haces **una vez al mes**, cuáles haces **una vez al año** y cuáles estás haciendo **ahora mismo** (*right now*). Escribe por lo menos (*at least*) dos oraciones para cada categoría. Intercambia tus oraciones con las de un(a) compañero/a. Answers will vary.

> **modelo**
>
> **Estudiante 1:** Yo juego al baloncesto todos los días.
> **Estudiante 2:** Yo pierdo mis llaves una vez al año.

decir	jugar
dormir	leer
encontrar	pedir
hablar	perder
hacer	trabajar
¿?	¿?

4 Before beginning this activity, briefly review the present progressive, including **-ir** stem-changing verbs. Ex: **diciendo, durmiendo, sintiendo.**

5

¡AL RESCATE!

Use direct object pronouns to keep your writing concise and clear by avoiding repeating nouns already mentioned.

El domingo voy a visitar a mi abuela. **La voy a ver a las nueve para desayunar.**

To read more about direct object nouns and pronouns, go to **¡ADELANTE! UNO**, **Estructura 5.4**, pp. 268–269.

Encuesta Circula por la clase preguntándoles a tus compañeros si hacen estas actividades con frecuencia (*frequently*). Trata de encontrar personas que respondan **sí** o **no** a cada pregunta y escribe sus nombres en la columna correcta. Prepárate para compartir tus conclusiones con la clase. Answers will vary.

> **modelo**
>
> **Tú:** ¿Escribes cartas con frecuencia?
> **Ana:** Sí, las escribo con frecuencia.
> **Luis:** No, no las escribo con frecuencia.

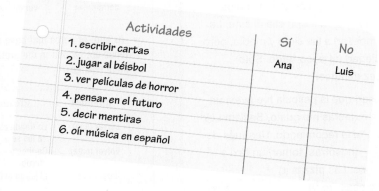

Actividades	Sí	No
1. escribir cartas		
2. jugar al béisbol	Ana	Luis
3. ver películas de horror		
4. pensar en el futuro		
5. decir mentiras		
6. oír música en español		

5 Call on several students to share their results and ask follow-up questions. Ex: ¿_____, cuándo escribes cartas? ¿_____, qué otros deportes juegas con frecuencia?

5 To practice **ir a** + [*infinitive*], have students repeat the activity, this time asking classmates which activities they plan to do today. Ex: **¿Vas a leer correo electrónico hoy?**

6

Escribir Escribe lo que haces en un día típico y tus planes para el fin de semana. Answers will vary.

Un día típico

Hola, me llamo Julia y vivo en Vancouver, Canadá. Por la mañana, yo...

6 Remind students that direct object pronouns can be placed before an infinitive construction (Ex: **te voy a llamar**) or attached to the infinitive. (Ex: **voy a llamarte**).

Práctica  Tutorials

1 **Verbos** Completa la tabla con las formas correctas de los verbos. `10 pts.`

Infinitive	yo	él/ella/usted	ellos/as
buscar	busqué	buscó	**buscaron**
cerrar	**cerré**	cerró	cerraron
comer	comí	comió	**fueron**
jugar	jugué	**jugó**	jugaron
leer	**leí**	leyó	leyeron
pagar	pagué	pagó	**pagaron**
salir	salí	**salió**	salieron
volver	volví	volvió	**volvieron**

2 **El sábado** Completa el mensaje con el pretérito de los verbos. `8 pts.`

De:	cecilia@webmail.es
Para:	julián@todomail.com
Asunto:	El sábado
Fecha:	24 de noviembre

¡Hola, Julián!

¿Cómo estás? Yo estoy muy bien. El sábado mi amiga Matilde me (1) _____invitó_____ (invitar) a ir con ella al cine. La película (2) _____empezó_____ (empezar) a las siete y media, pero nosotras (3) _____llegamos_____ (llegar) un poco tarde. Sólo perdimos los primeros diez minutos.

Yo (4) _____pensé_____ (pensar) que la película fue (*was*) un poco larga, pero de todas maneras me gustó. Se llama *Un día en el centro comercial*, te la recomiendo. Después de salir del cine, (5) _____tomamos_____ (nosotras, tomar) un taxi a Mama Pizza con más amigos. Las pizzas (6) _____resultaron_____ (resultar) (*turned out*) deliciosas. Yo (7) _____pedí_____ (pedir) la de salami, ¡qué ricura!

Y tú, ¿cómo (8) _____pasaste_____ (pasar) la noche del sábado? María Luisa me dijo que te vio (*saw you*) en la fiesta de Antonio y que estabas (*you were*) muy bien acompañado. ¿Nos vemos el miércoles por la tarde y me cuentas los detalles?

Un abrazo,

Cecilia

Resumen gramatical

This overview presents key grammatical concepts from *¡ADELANTE!* **UNO** . For further review, follow the cross-references.

R.8 **Preterite of regular verbs** *¡ADELANTE!* **UNO** L6 p. 322

Y ustedes, ¿qué compraron?

▶ To form the preterite of most regular verbs, attach the appropriate ending to the infinitive stem.

comprar	vender	escribir
compré	vendí	escribí
compraste	vendiste	escribiste
compró	vendió	escribió
compramos	vendimos	escribimos
comprasteis	vendisteis	escribisteis
compraron	vendieron	escribieron

▶ **-Ar** and **-er** verbs that have a stem change in the present tense are regular in the preterite. They do *not* have a stem change.

Infinitive	Present	Preterite
cerrar (e:ie)	La tienda **cierra** a las seis.	La tienda **cerró** a las seis.
volver (o:ue)	Carlitos **vuelve** tarde.	Carlitos **volvió** tarde.
jugar (u:ue)	Él **juega** al fútbol.	Él **jugó** al fútbol.

▶ **¡Atención!** **-Ir** verbs that have a stem change in the present tense also have a stem change in the preterite.

	dormirse	conseguir
yo	me dormí	conseguí
tú	te dormiste	conseguiste
él/ella/Ud.	se durmió	consiguió
nosotros/as	nos dormimos	conseguimos
vosotros/as	os dormisteis	conseguisteis
ellos/ellas	se durmieron	consiguieron

Lección de repaso

R.9 Some irregular preterites  L6 p. 323

► There are many verbs with irregularities in the preterite. Here are some of them. You will learn more in **Lecciones 1, 2,** and **3.**

► Verbs that end in **-car, -gar,** and **-zar** have a spelling change in the first person singular (**yo** form).

buscar	busc-	qu-	yo busqué
llegar	lleg-	gu-	yo llegué
empezar	empez-	c-	yo empecé

► Except for the **yo** form, all other forms of **-car, -gar,** and **-zar** verbs are regular in the preterite.

► Three other verbs—**creer, leer,** and **oír**—have spelling changes in the preterite.

creer	cre-	creí, creíste, creyó, creímos, creísteis, creyeron
leer	le-	leí, leíste, leyó, leímos, leísteis, leyeron
oír	o-	oí, oíste, oyó, oímos, oísteis, oyeron

Jimena leyó un libro en Xochimilco.

► **Ver** is regular in the preterite, but none of its forms has an accent.

ver → vi, viste, vio, vimos, visteis, vieron

—¿A quiénes **vieron** en su viaje a Costa Rica?

—**Vimos** a nuestra prima Mariana y a nuestros amigos Leonardo y Teresa.

Marissa vio una blusa rosada en el mercado.

3 **Preguntas** Completa la conversación con el pretérito de los verbos de la lista. **7 pts.**

atacar	olvidar (*to forget*)
correr	robar
leer	sufrir (*to suffer,*
ocurrir	*to undergo*)

SANDRA ¿Cuándo (1) __corriste__ en el parque por última vez?

MARCOS Corrí en el parque el domingo por la mañana. ¿Por qué?

SANDRA ¿(2) __Leíste__ las noticias (*news*) de ayer?

MARCOS No, (3) __olvidé__ comprar el periódico. ¿Qué (4) __ocurrió__?

SANDRA Unos ladrones (*thieves*) (5) __atacaron__ a un corredor.

MARCOS ¿En serio?

SANDRA Sí, y le (6) __robaron__ el reproductor de MP3.

MARCOS ¿Y resultó herido (*harmed*)?

SANDRA No, sólo (7) __sufrió__ rasguños (*scratches*).

MARCOS ¡Qué fuerte! Mejor vamos a correr juntos. Es más seguro.

4 **Oraciones** Escribe oraciones completas con estos elementos, conjugando los verbos en el pretérito. **10 pts.**

1. tú / esperar / quince minutos / en / la puerta de / el cine
   Tú esperaste quince minutos en la puerta del cine.

2. nosotros / tomar / café / ayer / por la noche
   Nosotros tomamos café ayer por la noche.

3. los jugadores / no / perder / la esperanza / de ganar / el partido
   Los jugadores no perdieron la esperanza de ganar el partido.

4. yo / llegar / tarde / a / la cita / de anoche
   Yo llegué tarde a la cita de anoche.

5. ustedes / leer / el anuncio (*ad*) / con / mucha atención
   Ustedes leyeron el anuncio con mucha atención.

5 **La semana pasada** Escribe un mensaje electrónico de al menos cinco oraciones donde les cuentas a tus padres lo que hiciste durante la semana. Usa al menos cinco verbos diferentes en el pretérito. **15 pts.**
Answers will vary.

modelo

¡Hola, papá y mamá! ¿Cómo están? Esta semana por fin compré el libro de Esmeralda Santiago que me recomendaron...

Extra Practice Briefly review the use of **acabar de** + [*infinitive*] to say that something has just occurred. Ex: **Acabo de llegar.**

 Practice more at **vhlcentral.com.**

Práctica y Comunicación

1

Completar y contestar Completa las preguntas con las formas apropiadas de los verbos de la lista y luego hazle las preguntas a un(a) compañero/a. Some answers may vary.

acompañar	estudiar	llamar	oír	perder	ver
aprender	leer	llegar	pasar	recibir	volver

¿Cuándo fue (*was*) la última vez que...

1. (tú) ___viste___ una película?
2. tus padres te ___llamaron___ por teléfono?
3. (tú) ___perdiste___ las llaves de tu casa?
4. tu mejor amigo/a te ___acompañó___ a ir de compras?
5. nosotros ___estudiamos___ juntos para un examen?
6. (tú) ___recibiste___ una mala nota?
7. tus amigos ___volvieron___ a casa más temprano que tú?
8. (tú) ___leíste___ una novela?
9. tu familia y tú ___pasaron___ el fin de semana juntos?
10. el/la profesor(a) ___llegó___ tarde a clase?

2

Contestar Trabaja con un(a) compañero/a para formar preguntas completas. Luego, túrnense para hacerse las preguntas que crearon. Answers will vary.

> **modelo**
>
> desayunar / esta mañana
> **Estudiante 1:** ¿Qué desayunaste esta mañana?
> **Estudiante 2:** Esta mañana desayuné cereales.

1. comprar / la ropa que llevas hoy
2. llegar / a clase hoy
3. salir / el fin de semana pasado
4. jugar / tu último partido
5. escuchar la radio / por última vez
6. ir / en tus últimas vacaciones

3

Completar y combinar En parejas, túrnense para completar las frases con el pretérito de los verbos. Luego inventen un complemento para crear oraciones lógicas. Answers will vary.

> **modelo**
>
> cuando el/la profesor(a) / entrar / en la clase
> Cuando la profesora entró en la clase, todos
> los estudiantes aplaudieron (clapped).

1. cuando yo / almorzar / en la cafetería
2. el/la estudiante / abrir / el libro
3. yo / buscar / la cartera
4. cuando / mis padres / visitarme / por última vez
5. cuando nosotros / salir / de casa
6. mis hermanos/as / comprarme / un perrito

1 Write these verbs on the board and ask students to come up with additional questions using the preterite: **bailar, hablar, jugar, pedir, salir.**

Pairs For additional practice with the preterite of **-ir** stem-changing verbs, list these verbs on the board: **dormir, conseguir, pedir, preferir, repetir, seguir.** Have students work in pairs to write sentences with the **Ud./él/ella** and **Uds./ellos/ellas** preterite forms.

2 To practice additional preterite forms, divide the class into groups of three. Have each student take turns asking questions to the other two students, using the **ustedes** form. Call on group members to compare each other's responses. Encourage a variety of **yo, nosotros, él/ella,** and **ellos/as** forms. Ex: **Sara y yo llegamos a clase a las nueve. / Anita y Will compraron en Gap la ropa que llevan.**

3 To simplify, have students write down all the conjugated phrases before creating complete sentences.

Lección de repaso

4

En el parque En parejas, túrnense para describir lo que hicieron (*did*) estas personas en el parque el sábado pasado.

1. Ella tomó el sol. _____

2. Ellos leyeron (el periódico). _____

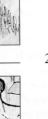

3. Él nadó en la piscina. _____

4. Ellos pasearon. _____

5. Ellos jugaron a la pelota/al fútbol. _____

6. Ella patinó (en línea). _____

4 To help students get started, help them brainstorm a list of infinitive verbs that could be used to describe the activities in each drawing. Review previously learned vocabulary as needed.

5 Have students add two more items to the list before they begin the activity.

Game Divide the class into two teams. Call on a team member. Give an infinitive and a subject, and have the team member supply the correct preterite form. Award one point for each correct answer. Award a bonus point for correctly writing the verb on the board. The team with the most points wins.

6 Have students exchange their paragraphs with a partner for peer editing.

5

Encuesta Circula por la clase preguntando a tus compañeros si hicieron estas actividades la semana pasada. Trata de encontrar personas que respondan **sí** o **no** a cada pregunta y escribe sus nombres en la columna correcta. Prepárate para compartir tus conclusiones con la clase.

Answers will vary.

modelo

Tú: ¿Hablaste por teléfono con tus padres la semana pasada?
Pepe: Sí, hablé por teléfono con mis padres el sábado.
Victoria: No, no hablé por teléfono con mis padres la semana pasada.

Actividades	Sí	No
1. hablar por teléfono con sus padres	Pepe	Victoria
2. leer las noticias por Internet		
3. comer en un restaurante elegante		
4. ver deportes en la televisión		
5. practicar español		
6. pasear con los amigos en el parque		

6

Escribir Escribe una entrada en tu diario contando lo que hiciste (*you did*) durante el verano pasado. Usa por lo menos (*at least*) seis verbos de las páginas 14 y 15. Answers will vary.

La clase y la universidad

el/la compañero/a de clase	classmate
el/la compañero/a de cuarto	roommate
el/la estudiante	student
el/la profesor(a)	teacher
el borrador	eraser
la calculadora	calculator
el escritorio	desk
el libro	book
el mapa	map
la mesa	table
la mochila	backpack
el papel	paper
la papelera	wastebasket
la pizarra	blackboard
la pluma	pen
la puerta	door
el reloj	clock; watch
la silla	seat, chair
la tiza	chalk
la ventana	window
la biblioteca	library
la cafetería	cafeteria
la casa	house; home
el estadio	stadium
el laboratorio	laboratory
la librería	bookstore
la residencia estudiantil	dormitory
la universidad	university; college
la clase	class
el curso, la materia	course
la especialización	major
el examen	test; exam
el horario	schedule
la prueba	test; quiz
el semestre	semester
la tarea	homework
el trimestre	trimester; quarter

Lugares

el café	café
el centro	downtown
el cine	movie theater
el gimnasio	gymnasium
la iglesia	church
el lugar	place
el museo	museum
el parque	park
la piscina	swimming pool
la plaza	city or town square
el restaurante	restaurant

Las materias

la administración de empresas	business administration
la arqueología	archaeology
el arte	art
la biología	biology
las ciencias	sciences
la computación	computer science
la contabilidad	accounting
la economía	economics
el español	Spanish
la física	physics
la geografía	geography
la historia	history
las humanidades	humanities
el inglés	English
las lenguas extranjeras	foreign languages
la literatura	literature
las matemáticas	mathematics
la música	music
el periodismo	journalism
la psicología	psychology
la química	chemistry
la sociología	sociology

Preposiciones

al lado de	next to; beside
a la derecha de	to the right of
a la izquierda de	to the left of
cerca de	near
con	with
debajo de	below; under
delante de	in front of
detrás de	behind
en	in; on
encima de	on top of
entre	between; among
lejos de	far from
sin	without
sobre	on; over

Pasatiempos

andar en patineta	to skateboard
bucear	to scuba dive
escalar montañas (f. pl.)	to climb mountains
escribir una carta	to write a letter
escribir un mensaje electrónico	to write an e-mail message
esquiar	to ski
ganar	to win
hacer (wind)surf	to (wind)surf
ir de excursión	to go on a hike
leer correo electrónico	to read e-mail
leer un periódico	to read a newspaper
leer una revista	to read a magazine
nadar	to swim
pasear	to take a walk
pasear en bicicleta	to ride a bicycle
patinar (en línea)	to (in-line) skate
practicar deportes (m. pl.)	to play sports
tomar el sol	to sunbathe
ver películas (f. pl.)	to see movies
visitar monumentos (m. pl.)	to visit monuments
la diversión	fun activity; entertainment; recreation
el fin de semana	weekend
el pasatiempo	pastime; hobby
los ratos libres	spare (free) time
el videojuego	video game

Deportes

el baloncesto	basketball
el béisbol	baseball
el ciclismo	cycling
el equipo	team
el esquí (acuático)	(water) skiing
el fútbol	soccer
el fútbol americano	football
el golf	golf
el hockey	hockey
el/la jugador(a)	player
la natación	swimming
el partido	game; match
la pelota	ball
el tenis	tennis
el vóleibol	volleyball

For a complete list of related vocabulary go to *¡ADELANTE!* UNO, pp. 38, 98, 160, 220, 282, and 340.

S Flashcards

La rutina diaria

Communicative Goals

You will learn how to:

- Describe your daily routine
- Talk about personal hygiene
- Reassure someone

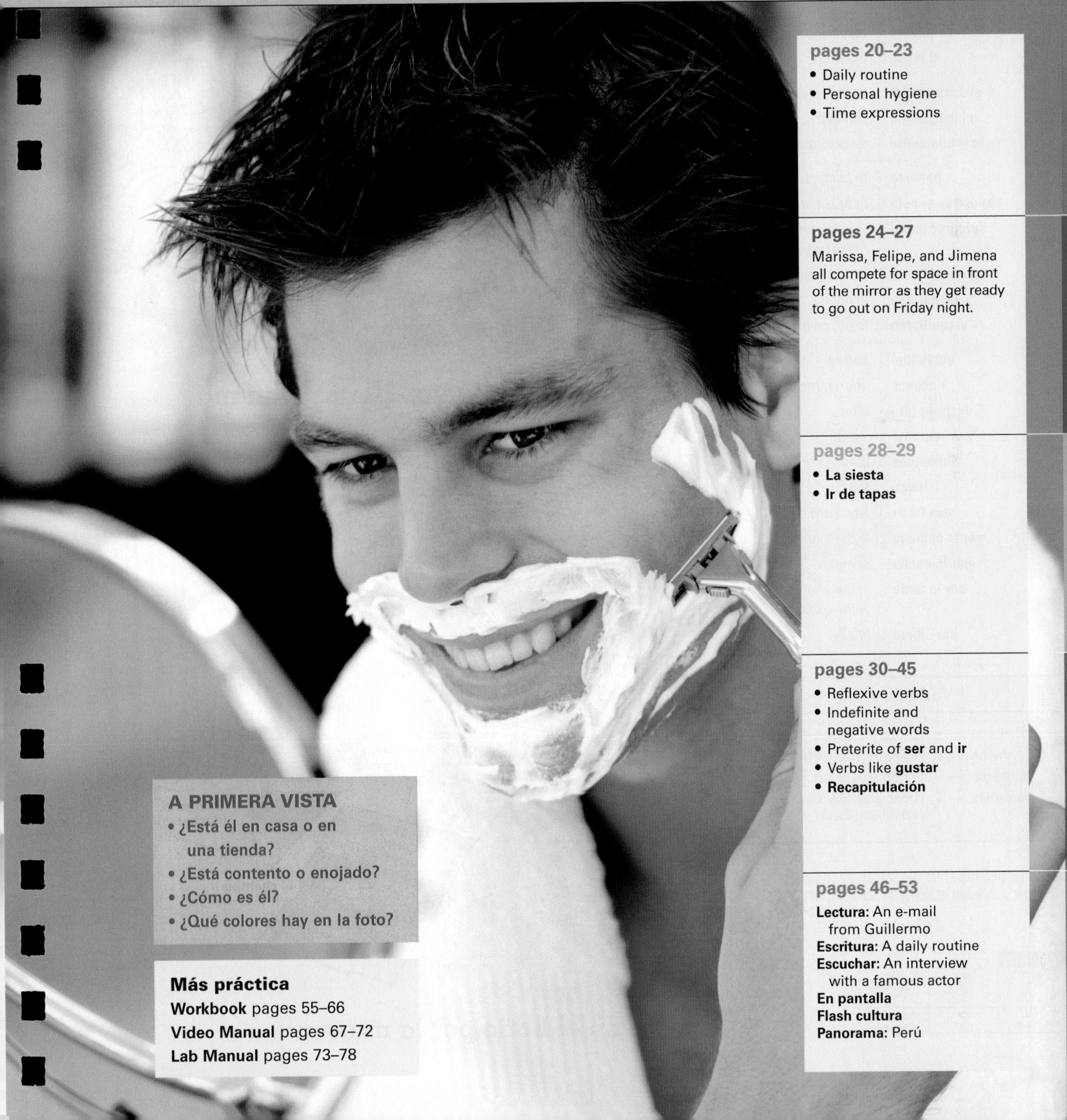

A PRIMERA VISTA

- ¿Está él en casa o en una tienda?
- ¿Está contento o enojado?
- ¿Cómo es él?
- ¿Qué colores hay en la foto?

La rutina diaria

Más vocabulario

el baño, el cuarto de baño	bathroom
el inodoro	toilet
el jabón	soap
el despertador	alarm clock
el maquillaje	makeup
la rutina diaria	daily routine
bañarse	to bathe; to take a bath
cepillarse el pelo	to brush one's hair
dormirse (o:ue)	to go to sleep; to fall asleep
lavarse la cara	to wash one's face
levantarse	to get up
maquillarse	to put on makeup
antes (de)	before
después	afterwards; then
después (de)	after
durante	during
entonces	then
luego	then
más tarde	later (on)
por la mañana	in the morning
por la noche	at night
por la tarde	in the afternoon; in the evening
por último	finally

Variación léxica

afeitarse	⟷	rasurarse (Méx., Amér. C.)
ducha	⟷	regadera (Col., Méx., Venez.)
ducharse	⟷	bañarse (Amér. L.)
pantuflas	⟷	chancletas (Méx., Col.); zapatillas (Esp.)

Supersite: MP3 Audio Files and Scripts, Digital Image Bank, Activity Pack, Testing Program (Quizzes), *Vocabulario adicional*

recursos

WB pp. 55–56	LM p. 73	vhlcentral.com Lección 1

En la habitación por la mañana

En el baño por la mañana

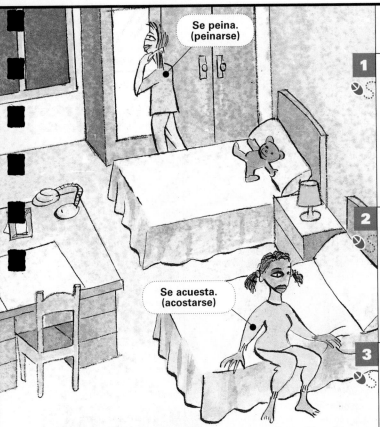

Se peina. (peinarse)

Se acuesta. (acostarse)

En la habitación por la noche

Se lava las manos. (lavarse las manos)

Se cepilla los dientes. (cepillarse los dientes)

la toalla

la pasta de dientes

las pantuflas

En el baño por la noche

Práctica ① ② Supersite: MP3 Audio Files, Scripts

1 **Escuchar** 🎧 Escucha las oraciones e indica si cada oración es **cierta** o **falsa**, según el dibujo.

① ② To prepare students for the listening activities, have volunteers provide the third-person forms of each verb in **Contextos**. Additional reflexive verb forms will be presented in **Estructura 1.1**.

1. _falsa_
2. _cierta_
3. _falsa_
4. _cierta_
5. _falsa_
6. _falsa_
7. _falsa_
8. _cierta_
9. _falsa_
10. _cierta_

2 **Ordenar** 🎧 Escucha la rutina diaria de Marta. Después ordena los verbos según lo que escuchaste.

_5_ a. almorzar
_2_ b. ducharse
_4_ c. peinarse
_7_ d. ver la televisión
_3_ e. desayunar
_8_ f. dormirse
_1_ g. despertarse
_6_ h. estudiar en la biblioteca

3 **Seleccionar** Selecciona la palabra que no está relacionada con cada grupo.

1. lavabo • toalla • despertador • jabón _despertador_
2. manos • antes de • después de • por último _manos_
3. acostarse • jabón • despertarse • dormirse _jabón_
4. espejo • lavabo • despertador • entonces _entonces_
5. dormirse • toalla • vestirse • levantarse _toalla_
6. pelo • cara • manos • inodoro _inodoro_
7. espejo • champú • jabón • pasta de dientes _espejo_
8. maquillarse • vestirse • peinarse • dientes _dientes_
9. baño • dormirse • despertador • acostarse _baño_
10. ducharse • luego • bañarse • lavarse _luego_

4 **Identificar** Con un(a) compañero/a, identifica las cosas que cada persona necesita. Sigue el modelo. Some answers will vary.

modelo

Jorge / lavarse la cara

Estudiante 1: ¿Qué necesita Jorge para lavarse la cara?
Estudiante 2: Necesita jabón y una toalla.

1. Mariana / maquillarse   maquillaje y un espejo
2. Gerardo / despertarse   un despertador
3. Celia / bañarse   jabón y una toalla
4. Gabriel / ducharse   una ducha, una toalla y jabón
5. Roberto / afeitarse   un espejo y crema de afeitar
6. Sonia / lavarse el pelo   champú y una toalla
7. Vanesa / lavarse las manos   un lavabo, jabón y una toalla
8. Manuel / vestirse   su ropa/una camiseta/unos pantalones/etc.
9. Simón / acostarse   una cama
10. Daniela / cepillarse los dientes   pasta de dientes y cepillo de dientes

Heritage Speakers Ask heritage speakers to look at the illustration and provide additional lexical variations. Ex: **cepillarse los dientes/lavarse la boca; la toalla/el paño; la habitación/la alcoba**.

5 **La rutina de Andrés** Ordena esta rutina de una manera lógica.

a. Se afeita después de cepillarse los dientes. __4__

b. Se acuesta a las once y media de la noche. __9__

c. Por último, se duerme. __10__

d. Después de afeitarse, sale para las clases. __5__

e. Asiste a todas sus clases y vuelve a su casa. __6__

f. Andrés se despierta a las seis y media de la mañana. __1__

g. Después de volver a casa, come un poco. Luego estudia en su habitación. __7__

h. Se viste y entonces se cepilla los dientes. __3__

i. Se cepilla los dientes antes de acostarse. __8__

j. Se ducha antes de vestirse. __2__

6 **La rutina diaria** Con un(a) compañero/a, mira los dibujos y describe lo que hacen Ángel y Lupe.

Some answers may vary. Suggested answers:

1.

Ángel se afeita y mira la televisión.

2.

Lupe se maquilla y escucha la radio.

3.

Ángel se ducha y canta.

4.

Lupe se baña y lee.

5.

Ángel se lava la cara con jabón.

6.

Lupe se lava el pelo con champú en la ducha.

7.

Ángel se cepilla el pelo.

8.
Lupe se cepilla los dientes.

Practice more at **vhlcentral.com**.

5 To simplify, have students read all items and identify the expressions of time before putting the sentences in order.

5 Ask students if **Andrés's** schedule represents that of a "typical" student. Ask: **Un estudiante típico, ¿se despierta normalmente a las seis y media de la mañana? ¿A qué hora se despiertan ustedes?**

6 Ask brief comprehension questions about the actions in the drawings. Ex: **¿Quién se maquilla? (Lupe) ¿Quién se cepilla el pelo? (Ángel)**

6 If students ask, point out that in drawing number 7, **Ángel se mira en el espejo**. Reflexive pronouns and verbs will be formally presented in **Estructura 1.1**. For now it is enough just to explain that *he is looking at himself*, hence the use of the pronoun **se**.

6 For item 7, point out that **el pelo** is used only with the verb **cepillarse**, never with **peinarse**.

Small Groups In groups of three or four, have students think of a famous person or character and describe his or her daily routine. In their descriptions, students may use names of friends or family of the famous person or character. Have groups read their descriptions aloud for the rest of the class to guess.

Extra Practice Name daily routine activities and have students list all the words that they associate with each activity, such as things, places, and parts of the body. Ex: **lavarse las manos: el jabón, el cuarto de baño, el agua, la toalla.** How many associations can the class make for each activity?

Comunicación

7 Ask small groups to write a competing ad for another pharmacy. Have each group present its ad to the class, who will vote for the most persuasive one.

Small Groups Have students prepare and perform a brief skit in which three or four roommates are trying to get ready for their morning classes at the same time. The problem: they have only one bathroom. Have the class vote for the funniest skit.

Heritage Speakers Ask heritage speakers to write paragraphs describing their daily routine when living with their families. Remind them to use the present tense and several expressions of time from **Contextos** (**por la mañana, antes, durante,** etc.) Have students read their paragraphs to the class, then verify comprehension by calling on volunteers to describe their classmates' routines.

8 Ask volunteers to read their descriptions aloud. Ask other pairs who chose the same people if their descriptions are similar and how they differ.

7

La farmacia Lee el anuncio y responde a las preguntas con un(a) compañero/a.

Answers will vary.

LA FARMACIA NUEVO SOL tiene todo
lo que necesitas para la vida diaria.

Esta semana tenemos grandes rebajas.

Con poco dinero puedes comprar lo que necesitas para el cuarto de baño ideal.

Para los hombres ofrecemos…
Excelentes cremas de afeitar de Guapo y Máximo

Para las mujeres ofrecemos…
Nuevo maquillaje de Marisol y jabones de baño Ilusiones y Belleza

Y para todos tenemos los mejores jabones, pastas de dientes y cepillos de dientes.

¡Visita **LA FARMACIA NUEVO SOL**!
Tenemos los mejores precios. Visita nuestra tienda muy cerca de tu casa.

1. ¿Qué tipo de tienda es? Es una farmacia.
2. ¿Qué productos ofrecen para las mujeres? maquillaje, jabones de baño
3. ¿Qué productos ofrecen para los hombres? cremas de afeitar
4. Haz (*Make*) una lista de los verbos que asocias con los productos del anuncio.
5. ¿Dónde compras tus productos de higiene? Answers will vary.
6. ¿Tienes una tienda favorita? ¿Cuál es? Answers will vary.

Suggested answers: afeitarse, maquillarse, cepillarse los dientes, ducharse/bañarse

8

Rutinas diarias Trabajen en parejas para describir la rutina diaria de dos o tres de estas personas. Pueden usar palabras de la lista. Answers will vary.

antes (de)	entonces	primero
después (de)	luego	tarde
durante el día	por último	temprano

- un(a) profesor(a) de la universidad
- un(a) turista
- un hombre o una mujer de negocios (*businessman/woman*)
- un vigilante nocturno (*night watchman*)
- un(a) jubilado/a (*retired person*)
- el presidente/primer ministro de tu país
- un niño de cuatro años
▶ • Daniel Espinosa

NOTA CULTURAL

Daniel Espinosa (México, 1961) es un famoso diseñador de joyería (*jewelry*). Su trabajo es vanguardista (*avant-garde*), arriesgado (*risky*) e innovador. Su material favorito es la plata (*silver*). Entre sus clientes están Nelly Furtado, Eva Longoria, Salma Hayek, Lindsay Lohan y Daisy Fuentes.

Lección 1

Video Synopsis **Marissa**, **Felipe**, and **Jimena** all have plans to go out on a Friday night but must compete for space in front of the mirror as they get ready. **Felipe** wins and manages to shave. **Marissa** convinces **Jimena** to skip the library and go with her to the movies.

¡Necesito arreglarme!

Es viernes por la tarde y Marissa, Jimena y Felipe se preparan para salir.

PERSONAJES

 MARISSA

 JIMENA

S Video: Fotonovela

1

MARISSA ¿Hola? ¿Está ocupado?

JIMENA Sí. Me estoy lavando la cara.

MARISSA Necesito usar el baño.

MARISSA Tengo que terminar de arreglarme. Voy al cine esta noche.

JIMENA Yo también tengo que salir. ¿Te importa si me maquillo primero? Me voy a encontrar con mi amiga Elena en una hora.

2

JIMENA No te preocupes, Marissa. Llegaste primero. Entonces, te arreglas el pelo y después me maquillo.

FELIPE ¿Y yo? Tengo crema de afeitar en la cara. No me voy a ir. Estoy aquí y aquí me quedo.

3

JIMENA ¡Felipe! ¿Qué estás haciendo?

FELIPE Me estoy afeitando. ¿Hay algún problema?

JIMENA ¡Siempre haces lo mismo!

FELIPE Pues, yo no vi a nadie aquí.

5

6

JIMENA ¿Por qué no te afeitaste por la mañana?

FELIPE Porque cada vez que quiero usar el baño, una de ustedes está aquí. O bañándose o maquillándose.

4

MARISSA Tú ganas. ¿Adónde vas a ir esta noche, Felipe?

FELIPE Juan Carlos y yo vamos a ir a un café en el centro. Siempre hay música en vivo. (*Se despide.*) Me siento guapísimo. Todavía me falta cambiarme la camisa.

Lección 1

FELIPE

Expresiones útiles Draw attention to the verb forms **fue** and **fuimos** in the caption of video still 9. Tell students that these are preterite forms of the verbs **ser** and **ir**, respectively. Explain that the context clarifies which verb is used. Point out the phrases **Me estoy lavando**, **me maquillo**, **te arreglas**, and **No te preocupes**. Tell the class that these are forms of the reflexive verbs **lavarse**, **maquillarse**, **arreglarse**, and **preocuparse**. Then point out the phrases **Me fascinan**, **Me encanta**, and **Me molesta**. Explain that these are examples of verbs that have constructions similar to that of **gustar**. Finally, draw attention to the caption for video still 3 and point out the words **algún**, **Siempre**, and **nadie**. Explain that **algún** and **Siempre** are indefinite words and **nadie** is a negative word. Tell students that they will learn more about these concepts in **Estructura**.

MARISSA ¿Adónde vas esta noche?

JIMENA A la biblioteca.

MARISSA ¡Es viernes! ¡Nadie debe estudiar los viernes! Voy a ver una película de Pedro Almodóvar con unas amigas.

MARISSA ¿Por qué no vienen tú y Elena al cine con nosotras? Después, podemos ir a ese café y molestar a Felipe.

JIMENA No sé.

MARISSA ¿Cuándo fue la última vez que viste a Juan Carlos?

JIMENA Cuando fuimos a Mérida.

MARISSA A ti te gusta ese chico.

JIMENA No tengo idea de qué estás hablando. Si no te importa, nos vemos en el cine.

Expresiones útiles

Talking about getting ready

Necesito arreglarme.
I need to get ready.

Me estoy lavando la cara.
I'm washing my face.

¿Te importa si me maquillo primero?
Is it OK with you if I put on my makeup first?

Tú te arreglas el pelo y después yo me maquillo.
You fix your hair and then I'll put on my makeup.

Todavía me falta cambiarme la camisa.
I still have to change my shirt.

Reassuring someone

Tranquilo/a.
Relax.

No te preocupes.
Don't worry.

Talking about past actions

¿Cuándo fue la última vez que viste a Juan Carlos?
When was the last time you saw Juan Carlos?

Cuando fuimos a Mérida.
When we went to Mérida.

Talking about likes and dislikes

Me fascinan las películas de Almodóvar.
I love Almodóvar's movies.

Me encanta la música en vivo.
I love live music.

Me molesta compartir el baño.
It bothers me to share the bathroom.

Additional vocabulary

encontrarse con *to meet up with*
molestar *to bother*
nadie *no one*

Teaching Tips
- Play the video segment and have students jot down notes on what they see and hear. Then have them work in groups of three to prepare a brief plot summary. Play the segment again and then ask groups to refine their summaries. Discuss the plot as a class.
- For expansion, ask students to write a short description of what they think the daily routine of one of the characters is like. Then have students who picked the same character get together to find similarities and differences in their descriptions.

recursos

VM
pp. 67–68

vhlcentral.com
Lección 1

TPR Ask students to write **Marissa**, **Jimena**, and **Felipe** on separate pieces of paper. Read several statements aloud and have students hold up the corresponding name. Ex: **Me quiero arreglar el pelo.** (Marissa) **Mi hermano se está afeitando.** (Jimena) **Me siento muy guapo.** (Felipe)

¿Qué pasó?

1 **¿Cierto o falso?** Indica si lo que dicen estas oraciones es **cierto** o **falso**. Corrige las oraciones falsas

1. Marissa va a ver una película de Pedro Almodóvar con unas amigas.
   Cierto.
2. Jimena se va a encontrar con Elena en dos horas.
   Falso. Jimena se va a encontrar con Elena en una hora.
3. Felipe se siente muy feo después de afeitarse.
   Falso. Felipe se siente guapísimo después de afeitarse.
4. Jimena quiere maquillarse.
   Cierto.
5. Marissa quiere ir al café para molestar a Juan Carlos.
   Falso. Marissa quiere ir al café para molestar a Felipe.

2 **Identificar** Identifica quién puede decir estas oraciones. Puedes usar cada nombre más de una vez.

1. No puedo usar el baño porque siempre están aquí, o bañándose o maquillándose. _____Felipe_____
2. Quiero arreglarme el pelo porque voy al cine esta noche. _____Marissa_____
3. Hoy voy a ir a la biblioteca. _____Jimena_____
4. ¡Necesito arreglarme! Marissa/Jimena/Felipe
5. Te gusta Juan Carlos. _____Marissa_____
6. ¿Por qué quieres afeitarte cuando estamos en el baño? _____Jimena/Marissa_____

MARISSA

FELIPE

JIMENA

3 **Ordenar** Ordena correctamente los planes que tiene Marissa.

__5__ a. Voy al café.
__2__ b. Me arreglo el pelo.
__6__ c. Molesto a Felipe.
__3__ d. Me encuentro con unas amigas.
__1__ e. Entro al baño.
__4__ f. Voy al cine.

4 **En el baño** Trabajen en parejas para representar los papeles de dos compañeros/as de cuarto que deben usar el baño al mismo tiempo para hacer su rutina diaria. Usen las instrucciones como guía.

Answers will vary.

Estudiante 1

Di (*Say*) que quieres arreglarte porque vas a ir al cine.

Pregunta si puedes secarte (*dry*) el pelo.

Di que puede lavarse la cara, pero que después necesitas secarte el pelo.

Estudiante 2

Di (*Say*) que necesitas arreglarte porque te vas a encontrar con tus amigos/as.

Responde que no porque necesitas lavarte la cara.

Di que puede secarse el pelo, pero que después necesitas peinarte.

NATIONAL communication STANDARDS

1 Give students these additional items: **6. Felipe y Juan Carlos van a una discoteca.** (Falso. Ellos van a un café.) **7. La última vez que Jimena vio a Juan Carlos fue ayer.** (Falso. Fue en Mérida.)

2 Give students these additional items: **7. Quiero ponerme otra camisa.** (Felipe) **8. Debes venir al cine.** (Marissa)

3 Ask pairs to imagine another character's plans and list them using the **yo** form of the verbs, as in the activity. Then have pairs share their lists with the class.

4 Possible conversation: **E1: Quiero arreglarme porque voy a ir al cine. E2: Pues, necesito arreglarme porque voy a encontrarme con mis amigos. E1: ¿Puedo secarme el pelo? E2: No, porque necesito lavarme la cara. E1: Está bien. Puedes lavarte la cara, pero después necesito secarme el pelo. E2: De acuerdo. Puedes secarte el pelo, pero después necesito peinarme.**

NATIONAL comparisons STANDARDS

Teaching Tips

- Before students repeat the sample words, ask the class to imitate the sound of a motorcycle. To avoid frustration, remind students that most native English speakers have difficulty with the trilled **r** sound and that their ability to pronounce it will improve with practice.
- To help students discriminate between **r** and **rr**, write on the board the pairs **caro/carro** and **pero/perro**. Then pronounce each pair several times in random order, pausing after each for students to repeat. Ex: **caro, carro, caro, carro, carro, caro**.
- Call on volunteers to write down other words they have learned with **r** and **rr**. Model pronunciation and have the class repeat.

Perro que ladra no muerde.[1]

Video Play the video segment again and pause to have students repeat and write down words with **r** and **rr**. Go over as a class to check spelling.

Pronunciación   Audio
The consonant r

Supersite: MP3 Audio Files, Listening Scripts

ropa	rutina	rico	Ramón

In Spanish, **r** has a strong trilled sound at the beginning of a word. No English words have a trill, but English speakers often produce a trill when they imitate the sound of a motor.

gustar	durante	primero	crema

In any other position, **r** has a weak sound similar to the English *tt* in *better* or the English *dd* in *ladder*. In contrast to English, the tongue touches the roof of the mouth behind the teeth.

pizarra	corro	marrón	aburrido

The letter combination **rr**, which only appears between vowels, always has a strong trilled sound.

caro	carro	pero	perro

Between vowels, the difference between the strong trilled **rr** and the weak **r** is very important, as a mispronunciation could lead to confusion between two different words.

Práctica Lee las palabras en voz alta, prestando (*paying*) atención a la pronunciación de la **r** y la **rr**.

1. Perú
2. Rosa
3. borrador
4. madre
5. comprar
6. favor
7. rubio
8. reloj
9. Arequipa
10. tarde
11. cerra
12. despertador

Oraciones Lee las oraciones en voz alta, prestando atención a la pronunciación de la **r** y la **rr**.

1. Ramón Robles Ruiz es programador. Su esposa Rosaura es artista.
2. A Rosaura Robles le encanta regatear en el mercado.
3. Ramón nunca regatea... le aburre regatear.
4. Rosaura siempre compra cosas baratas.
5. Ramón no es rico, pero prefiere comprar cosas muy caras.
6. ¡El martes Ramón compró un carro nuevo!

Refranes Lee en voz alta los refranes, prestando atención a la **r** y a la **rr**.

No se ganó Zamora en una hora.[2]

Extra Practice Write the names of a few Peruvian cities on the board and ask for a volunteer to pronounce each name. Ex: **Huaraz, Cajamarca, Trujillo, Puerto Maldonado, Cerro de Pasco, Piura.** Then write the names of a few Peruvian literary figures on the board and repeat the process. Ex: **Ricardo Palma, Ciro Alegría, Mario Vargas Llosa, César Vallejo.**

Heritage Speakers Call on heritage speakers to model pronunciation for the class. Ask them to list several additional words on the board for practice. You may wish to point out regional variations in strength and use of the trilled **r** sound.

recursos
LM p. 74
vhlcentral.com Lección 1

Lección 1

EN DETALLE

Additional Reading

La siesta

¿Sientes cansancio° después de comer?
¿Te cuesta° volver al trabajo° o a clase después
del almuerzo? Estas sensaciones son normales.
A muchas personas les gusta relajarse° después de
almorzar. Este momento de descanso es **la siesta**. La
siesta es popular en los países hispanos y viene de
una antigua costumbre° del área del Mediterráneo.
La palabra *siesta* viene del latín, es una forma
corta de decir "sexta hora". La sexta hora del día
es después del mediodía, el momento de más calor.
Debido al° calor y al cansancio, los habitantes
de España, Italia, Grecia y Portugal tienen la
costumbre de dormir la siesta desde hace° más
de° dos mil años. Los españoles y los portugueses
llevaron la costumbre a los países americanos.

Aunque° hoy día esta costumbre está
desapareciendo° en las grandes ciudades, la siesta
todavía es importante en la cultura hispana. En
pueblos pequeños, por ejemplo, muchas oficinas°
y tiendas tienen la costumbre de cerrar por dos o
tres horas después del mediodía. Los empleados

van a su casa, almuerzan con sus familias,
duermen la siesta o hacen actividades, como ir
al gimnasio, y luego regresan al trabajo entre las
2:30 y las 4:30 de la tarde.

Los estudios científicos explican que una
siesta corta después de almorzar ayuda° a trabajar
más y mejor° durante la tarde. Pero ¡cuidado! Esta
siesta debe durar° sólo entre veinte y cuarenta
minutos. Si dormimos más, entramos en la fase de
sueño profundo y es difícil despertarse.

Hoy, algunas empresas° de los EE.UU., Canadá,
Japón, Inglaterra y Alemania tienen salas° especiales
donde los empleados pueden dormir la siesta.

¿Dónde duermen la siesta?

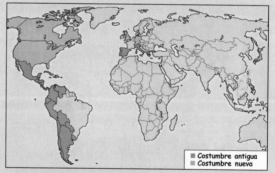

◼ Costumbre antigua
◼ Costumbre nueva

**En los lugares donde la siesta es una costumbre antigua, las
personas la duermen en su casa. En los países donde la siesta
es una costumbre nueva, la gente duerme en sus lugares de
trabajo o en centros de siesta.**

Sientes cansancio *Do you feel tired* Te cuesta *Is it hard for you* trabajo *work*
relajarse *to relax* antigua costumbre *old custom* Debido al *Because (of)*
desde hace *for* más de *more than* Aunque *Although* está desapareciendo *is
disappearing* oficinas *offices* ayuda *helps* mejor *better* durar *last* algunas
empresas *some businesses* salas *rooms*

ACTIVIDADES

1 **¿Cierto o falso?** Indica si lo que dicen las oraciones es
cierto o falso. Corrige la información falsa.

1. La costumbre de la siesta empezó en Asia. **Falso.**
   La costumbre de la siesta empezó en el área del Mediterráneo.
2. La palabra *siesta* está relacionada con la sexta hora del día.
   Cierto.
3. Los españoles y los portugueses llevaron la costumbre de la
   siesta a Latinoamérica. **Cierto.**

4. La siesta ayuda a trabajar más y mejor durante la tarde. **Cierto.**

5. Los horarios de trabajo de las grandes ciudades hispanas son los
   mismos que los pueblos pequeños. **Falso.** En las grandes ciudades
   hispanas la costumbre de la siesta está desapareciendo.
6. Una siesta larga siempre es mejor que una siesta corta.
   Falso. La siesta debe durar entre veinte y cuarenta minutos.
7. En los Estados Unidos, los empleados de algunas empresas
   pueden dormir la siesta en el trabajo. **Cierto.**

8. Es fácil despertar de un sueño profundo.
   Falso. Es difícil despertar de un sueño profundo.

ASÍ SE DICE

El cuidado personal

el aseo; el excusado; el servicio; el váter (Esp.)	el baño
el cortaúñas	*nail clippers*
el desodorante	*deodorant*
el enjuague bucal	*mouthwash*
el hilo dental/ la seda dental	*dental floss*
la máquina de afeitar/ de rasurar (Méx.)	*electric razor*

EL MUNDO HISPANO

Costumbres especiales

- **México y El Salvador** Los vendedores pasan por las calles anunciando a gritos° su mercancía°: tanques de gas y flores° en México; pan y tortillas en El Salvador.

- **Costa Rica** Para encontrar las direcciones°, los costarricenses usan referencias a anécdotas, lugares o características geográficas. Por ejemplo: *200 metros norte de la iglesia Católica, frente al° supermercado Mi Mega.*

- **Argentina** En Tigre, una ciudad junto al Río° de la Plata, la gente usa barcos particulares°, barcos colectivos° y barcos-taxi para ir de una isla a otra. Todas las mañanas, un barco colectivo recoge° a los niños y los lleva a la escuela.

gritos *shouts* mercancía *merchandise* flores *flowers* direcciones *addresses* frente al *opposite* Río *River* particulares *private* colectivos *collective* recoge *picks up*

PERFIL

El mate

El mate es una parte muy importante de la rutina diaria en muchos países. Es una bebida° muy similar al té que se consume en Argentina, Uruguay y Paraguay. Tradicionalmente se bebe caliente° con una *bombilla°* y en un recipiente° que también se llama *mate.* Por ser amarga°, algunos le agregan° azúcar para suavizar su sabor°. El mate se puede tomar a cualquier° hora y en cualquier lugar, aunque en Argentina las personas prefieren sentarse en círculo e ir pasando el mate de mano en mano mientras° conversan. Los uruguayos, por otra parte, acostumbran llevar el agua° caliente para el mate en un termo°

bajo el brazo° y lo beben mientras caminan. Si ves a una persona con un termo bajo el brazo y un mate en la mano, ¡es casi seguro que es de Uruguay!

bebida *drink* caliente *hot* bombilla *straw (in Argentina)* recipiente *container* amarga *bitter* agregan *add* suavizar su sabor *soften its flavor* cualquier *any* mientras *while* agua *water* termo *thermos* bajo el brazo *under their arm*

Conexión Internet

¿Qué costumbres son populares en los países hispanos?

Go to **vhlcentral.com** to find more cultural information related to this **Cultura** section.

ACTIVIDADES

2 **Comprensión** Completa las oraciones.

1. Uso <u>el hilo dental/la seda dental</u> para limpiar (*to clean*) entre los dientes.

2. En <u>El Salvador</u> las personas compran pan y tortillas a los vendedores que pasan por la calle.

3. El <u>mate</u> es una bebida similar al té.

4. Los uruguayos beben mate mientras <u>caminan</u>.

3 **¿Qué costumbres tienes?** Escribe cuatro oraciones sobre una costumbre que compartes con tus amigos o con tu familia (por ejemplo: ir al cine, ir a eventos deportivos, leer, comer juntos, etc.). Explica qué haces, cuándo lo haces y con quién. Answers will vary.

3 To simplify, write time expressions on the board that students can use in their descriptions (Ex: **siempre, todos los años, cada mes**).

Practice more at **vhlcentral.com**.

1.1 Reflexive verbs  Tutorial

ANTE TODO A reflexive verb is used to indicate that the subject does something to or for himself or herself. In other words, it "reflects" the action of the verb back to the subject. Reflexive verbs always use reflexive pronouns.

SUBJECT	REFLEXIVE VERB
Joaquín	**se ducha** por la mañana.

The verb **lavarse** (*to wash oneself*)

SINGULAR FORMS	yo	**me lavo**	*I wash (myself)*
	tú	**te lavas**	*you wash (yourself)*
	Ud.	**se lava**	*you wash (yourself)*
	él/ella	**se lava**	*he/she washes (himself/herself)*
PLURAL FORMS	nosotros/as	**nos lavamos**	*we wash (ourselves)*
	vosotros/as	**os laváis**	*you wash (yourselves)*
	Uds.	**se lavan**	*you wash (yourselves)*
	ellos/ellas	**se lavan**	*they wash (themselves)*

▶ The pronoun **se** attached to an infinitive identifies the verb as reflexive: **lavarse.**

▶ When a reflexive verb is conjugated, the reflexive pronoun agrees with the subject.

Me afeito.   **Te despiertas** a las siete.

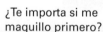

¿Te importa si me maquillo primero?

A las chicas les encanta maquillarse durante horas y horas.

▶ Like object pronouns, reflexive pronouns generally appear before a conjugated verb. With infinitives and present participles, they may be placed before the conjugated verb or attached to the infinitive or present participle.

Ellos **se** van a vestir.   **Nos** estamos lavando las manos.
Ellos van a vestir**se.**   Estamos lavándo**nos** las manos.
They are going to get dressed.   *We are washing our hands.*

▶ **¡Atención!** When a reflexive pronoun is attached to a present participle, an accent mark is added to maintain the original stress.

bañando ⟶ bañándo**se**   durmiendo ⟶ durmiéndo**se**

NATIONAL comparisons STANDARDS

Teaching Tips
• Model the first-person reflexive by talking about yourself. Ex: **Me levanto a las cinco de la mañana.** Then model the second person by asking questions. Ex: **Y tú, _____, ¿a qué hora te levantas?** Use follow-up questions to introduce the third person. Ex: **¿A qué hora se levanta _____?**

AYUDA

Except for **se,** reflexive pronouns have the same forms as direct and indirect object pronouns.

• • •

Se is used for both singular and plural subjects—there is no individual plural form:
Pablo **se** lava.
Ellos **se** lavan.

• For visual learners, use drawings or magazine pictures to clarify forms for third-person singular and plural. Ex: **se lava las manos** and **se lavan las manos.**
• On the board, summarize the three positions for reflexive pronouns: **X verbo conjugado, infinitivoX, gerundioX.** Remind students they have already learned these positions for object pronouns.

Extra Practice To provide oral practice with reflexive verbs, create sentences that follow the pattern of the sentences in the examples. Say the sentence, have students repeat it, then say a different subject, varying the gender and number. Have students then say the sentence with the new subject, changing pronouns and verbs as necessary.

Lección 1

Common reflexive verbs

acordarse (de) (o:ue)	to remember	**llamarse**	to be called; to be named
acostarse (o:ue)	to go to bed		
afeitarse	to shave	**maquillarse**	to put on makeup
bañarse	to bathe; to take a bath	**peinarse**	to comb one's hair
cepillarse	to brush	**ponerse**	to put on
despedirse (de) (e:i)	to say goodbye (to)	**ponerse (+ adj.)**	to become (+ adj.)
despertarse (e:ie)	to wake up	**preocuparse (por)**	to worry (about)
dormirse (o:ue)	to go to sleep; to fall asleep	**probarse** (o:ue)	to try on
		quedarse	to stay; to remain
ducharse	to shower; to take a shower	**quitarse**	to take off
		secarse	to dry (oneself)
enojarse (con)	to get angry (with)	**sentarse** (e:ie)	to sit down
irse	to go away; to leave	**sentirse** (e:ie)	to feel
lavarse	to wash (oneself)	**vestirse** (e:i)	to get dressed
levantarse	to get up		

AYUDA

You have already learned several adjectives that can be used with **ponerse** when it means *to become*: **alegre, cómodo/a, contento/a, elegante, guapo/a, nervioso/a, rojo/a,** and **triste**.

Teaching Tips
- Contrast the difference between reflexive and non-reflexive verbs with personal examples. Ex: **Los lunes, me despierto a las seis. A las siete, despierto a mi hijo.** You may wish to use a doll or other visual aspect for this presentation.
- To practice reflexive verbs in the preterite and periphrastic future (**ir a +** [*infinitive*]), talk about what you did yesterday and plan to do tomorrow. Ex: **Ayer me levanté a las seis. Pero el sábado me voy a levantar a las nueve.** Then ask volunteers to talk about what they did and plan to do.
- Explain that the definite article is used rather than a possessive because reflexive pronouns make it clear whose part of the body or clothing it is.

COMPARE & CONTRAST

Unlike English, a number of verbs in Spanish can be reflexive or non-reflexive. If the verb acts upon the subject, the reflexive form is used. If the verb acts upon something other than the subject, the non-reflexive form is used. Compare these sentences.

Lola **lava** los platos.

Lola **se lava** la cara.

As the preceding sentences show, reflexive verbs sometimes have different meanings than their non-reflexive counterparts. For example, **lavar** means *to wash*, while **lavarse** means *to wash oneself, to wash up*.

▶ **¡Atención!** Parts of the body or clothing are generally not referred to with possessives, but with articles.

La niña se quitó **un** zapato.   Necesito cepillarme **los** dientes.

recursos

WB
pp. 57–58

LM
p. 75

(S)
vhlcentral.com
Lección 1

¡INTÉNTALO!

Indica el presente de estos verbos reflexivos.

despertarse

1. Mis hermanos <u>se despiertan</u> tarde.
2. Tú <u>te despiertas</u> tarde.
3. Nosotros <u>nos despertamos</u> tarde.
4. Benito <u>se despierta</u> tarde.
5. Yo <u>me despierto</u> tarde.

ponerse

1. Él <u>se pone</u> una chaqueta.
2. Yo <u>me pongo</u> una chaqueta.
3. Usted <u>se pone</u> una chaqueta.
4. Nosotras <u>nos ponemos</u> una chaqueta.
5. Las niñas <u>se ponen</u> una chaqueta.

TPR Model gestures for a few of the reflexive verbs. Ex: **acordarse** (tap side of head), **acostarse** (lay head on folded hands). Have students stand. Begin by practicing as a class using only the **nosotros** form, saying expressions at random (Ex: **Nos lavamos la cara.**). Then vary the verb forms and point to the student who should perform the appropriate gesture. Keep a brisk pace. Vary by pointing to more than one student (Ex: **Ustedes se peinan.**).

Práctica

1

Nuestra rutina La familia de Blanca sigue la misma rutina todos los días. Según Blanca, ¿qué hacen ellos?

> **1** To practice the formal register, describe situations and have students tell you what you are going to do. Ex: **Hace frío y nieva, pero necesito salir. (Usted va a ponerse el abrigo.)**

modelo

mamá / despertarse a las 5:00
Mamá *se despierta* a las *cinco*.

1. Roberto y yo / levantarse a las 7:00   Roberto y yo nos levantamos a las siete.
2. papá / ducharse primero y / luego afeitarse   Papá se ducha primero y luego se afeita.
3. yo / lavarse la cara y / vestirse antes de tomar café   Yo me lavo la cara y me visto antes de tomar café.
4. mamá / peinarse y / luego maquillarse   Mamá se peina y luego se maquilla.
5. todos (nosotros) / sentarse a la mesa para comer   Todos nos sentamos a la mesa para comer.
6. Roberto / cepillarse los dientes después de comer   Roberto se cepilla los dientes después de comer.
7. yo / ponerse el abrigo antes de salir   Yo me pongo el abrigo antes de salir.
8. nosotros / despedirse de mamá   Nosotros nos despedimos de mamá.

NOTA CULTURAL

Como en los EE.UU., **tomar café** en el desayuno es muy común en los países hispanos.

En muchas familias, incluso los niños toman café con leche (*milk*) en el desayuno antes de ir a la escuela.

El café en los países hispanos generalmente es más fuerte que en los EE.UU., y el descafeinado no es muy popular.

2

La fiesta elegante Selecciona el verbo apropiado y completa las oraciones con la forma correcta.

1. Tú ____lavas____ (lavar / lavarse) el auto antes de ir a la fiesta.
2. Nosotros no __nos acordamos__ (acordar / acordarse) de comprar los regalos.
3. Para llegar a tiempo, Raúl y Marta ____acuestan____ (acostar / acostarse) a los niños antes de salir.
4. Yo ____me siento____ (sentir / sentirse) cómoda en mi vestido nuevo.
5. Mis amigos siempre ____se visten____ (vestir / vestirse) con ropa muy elegante.
6. Los cocineros ____prueban____ (probar / probarse) la comida antes de servirla.
7. Usted ____se preocupa____ (preocupar / preocuparse) mucho por llegar antes que (*before*) los demás invitados, ¿no?
8. En general, ____me afeito____ (afeitar / afeitarse) yo mismo, pero hoy es un día especial y el barbero (*barber*) me ____afeita____ (afeitar / afeitarse). ¡Será una fiesta inolvidable!

¡LENGUA VIVA!

In Spain a car is called **un coche**, while in many parts of Latin America it is known as **un carro**. Although you'll be understood using either of these terms, using **auto (automóvil)** will surely get you where you want to go.

3

Describir Mira los dibujos y describe lo que estas personas hacen.   Some answers may vary.

1. el joven   El joven se quita/se pone los zapatos.

2. Carmen   Carmen se duerme/se acuesta/ se despierta.

3. Juan   Juan se pone/se quita la camiseta.

4. ellos   Ellos se despiden/se saludan.

5. Estrella   Estrella se maquilla.

6. Toni   Toni se enoja con el perro.

2 For expansion, ask students to write five sentence pairs contrasting reflexive and non-reflexive forms. Ex: **Me despierto a las siete. Despierto a mi compañero de cuarto a las ocho.**

3 Repeat the activity as a pattern drill, supplying different subjects for each drawing. Ex: **Número uno, yo. (Me quito los zapatos.) Número cinco, nosotras. (Nosotras nos maquillamos.)**

Extra Practice Repeat the activity using the present progressive. Ask students to provide both possible sentences. Ex: **1. El joven se está quitando los zapatos./ El joven está quitándose los zapatos.**

Comunicación

4

4 Ask volunteers to call out some of their answers. The class should add information by speculating on the reason behind each answer. Ex: **Hablas por teléfono con tus amigos cuando te sientes triste porque ellos te comprenden muy bien.** Have the volunteer confirm or refute the speculation.

5 Ask each group to present their best **charada** to the class.

6 Before assigning groups, go over some of the things men and women do to get ready to go out. Ex: **Las mujeres se maquillan. Los hombres se afeitan.** Then ask students to indicate their opinion on the question; divide the class into groups accordingly.

7 Ask groups of four to imagine they all live in the same house, and have them put together a message board to reflect their different schedules.

Extra Practice Add an auditory aspect to this grammar practice. Prepare descriptions of five celebrities or fictional characters, using reflexives. Write their names randomly on the board. Then read the descriptions aloud and have students match each one to a name. Ex: **Se preocupa por todo. Siempre se viste de pantalones cortos negros y una camiseta amarilla. Tiene un amigo que se llama Linus. (Charlie Brown)**

Preguntas personales En parejas, túrnense para hacerse estas preguntas. Answers will vary.

1. ¿A qué hora te levantas durante la semana?
2. ¿A qué hora te levantas los fines de semana?
3. ¿Prefieres levantarte tarde o temprano? ¿Por qué?
4. ¿Te enojas frecuentemente con tus amigos?
5. ¿Te preocupas fácilmente? ¿Qué te preocupa?
6. ¿Qué te pone contento/a?
7. ¿Qué haces cuando te sientes triste?
8. ¿Y cuando te sientes alegre?
9. ¿Te acuestas tarde o temprano durante la semana?
10. ¿A qué hora te acuestas los fines de semana?

5

Charadas En grupos, jueguen a las charadas. Cada persona debe pensar en dos oraciones con verbos reflexivos. La primera persona que adivina la charada dramatiza la siguiente. Answers will vary.

6

Debate En grupos, discutan este tema: ¿Quiénes necesitan más tiempo para arreglarse (*to get ready*) antes de salir, los hombres o las mujeres? Hagan una lista de las razones (*reasons*) que tienen para defender sus ideas e informen a la clase. Answers will vary.

7

La coartada Hoy se cometió un crimen entre las 7 y las 11 de la mañana. En parejas, imaginen que uno de ustedes es un sospechoso y el otro un policía investigador. El policía le pregunta al sospechoso qué hace habitualmente a esas horas y el sospechoso responde. Luego, el policía presenta las respuestas del sospechoso ante el jurado (la clase) y entre todos deciden si es culpable o no.
Answers will vary.

Síntesis   Supersite: Activity Pack

8

La familia ocupada Tú y tu compañero/a asisten a un programa de verano en Lima, Perú. Viven con la familia Ramos. Tu profesor(a) te va a dar la rutina incompleta que la familia sigue en las mañanas. Trabaja con tu compañero/a para completarla. Answers will vary.

> **modelo**
> **Estudiante 1:** ¿Qué hace el señor Ramos a las seis y cuarto?
> **Estudiante 2:** El señor Ramos se levanta.

Practice more at **vhlcentral.com**.

Lección 1

1.2 | Indefinite and negative words  Tutorial

ANTE TODO   Indefinite words refer to people and things that are not specific, for example, *someone* or *something*. Negative words deny the existence of people and things or contradict statements, for instance, *no one* or *nothing*. Spanish indefinite words have corresponding negative words, which are opposite in meaning.

Indefinite and negative words

Indefinite words		Negative words	
algo	*something; anything*	**nada**	*nothing; not anything*
alguien	*someone; somebody; anyone*	**nadie**	*no one; nobody; not anyone*
alguno/a(s), algún	*some; any*	**ninguno/a, ningún**	*no; none; not any*
o... o	*either... or*	**ni... ni**	*neither... nor*
siempre	*always*	**nunca, jamás**	*never, not ever*
también	*also; too*	**tampoco**	*neither; not either*

▶ There are two ways to form negative sentences in Spanish. You can place the negative word before the verb, or you can place **no** before the verb and the negative word after.

Nadie se levanta temprano.
No one gets up early.

No se levanta nadie temprano.
No one gets up early.

Ellos **nunca gritan**.
They never shout.

Ellos **no gritan nunca**.
They never shout.

¿Hay algún problema?

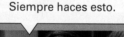

Siempre haces esto.

▶ Because they refer to people, **alguien** and **nadie** are often used with the personal **a**. The personal **a** is also used before **alguno/a, algunos/as,** and **ninguno/a** when these words refer to people and they are the direct object of the verb.

—Perdón, señor, ¿busca usted **a alguien**?
—No, gracias, señorita, no busco **a nadie**.

—Tomás, ¿buscas **a alguno** de tus hermanos?
—No, mamá, no busco **a ninguno**.

▶ **¡Atención!** Before a masculine singular noun, **alguno** and **ninguno** are shortened to **algún** and **ningún**.

—¿Tienen ustedes **algún** amigo peruano?

—No, no tenemos **ningún** amigo peruano.

Teaching Tips
• Present negative words by complaining dramatically in a whining tone. Ex: **Nadie me llama por teléfono. Jamás recibo un correo electrónico de ningún estudiante. Ni mi esposo ni mis hijos se acuerdan de mi cumpleaños.** Then smile radiantly and state the opposite. Ex: **Alguien me llama por teléfono.**
• Add a visual aspect to this grammar presentation. Use magazine pictures to compare and contrast indefinite and negative words. Ex: **La señora tiene algo en las manos. ¿El señor tiene algo también? No, el señor no tiene nada.**

Pairs Have students take turns giving one-word indefinite and negative word prompts and having the other respond in complete sentences. Ex: **E1: siempre E2: Siempre le mando un mensaje electrónico a mi madre por la mañana. E1: tampoco E2: Yo no me levanto temprano tampoco.**

AYUDA

Alguno/a, algunos/as are not always used in the same way English uses *some* or *any.* Often, **algún** is used where *a* would be used in English.

¿Tienes algún libro que hable de los incas? *Do you have a book that talks about the Incas?*

Note that **ninguno/a** is rarely used in the plural.

—**¿Visitaste algunos museos?**
—**No, no visité ninguno.**

Lección 1

Teaching Tips
• Emphasize that there is no limit to the number of negative words that can be strung together in a sentence in Spanish. Ex: **No hablo con nadie nunca de ningún problema, ni con mi familia ni con mis amigos.**
• Elicit negative responses by asking questions whose answers will clearly be negative. Ex: **¿Alguien lleva zapatos de lunares? (No, nadie lleva zapatos de lunares.) ¿Piensas comprar un barco mañana? (No, no pienso comprar ninguno/ningún barco.) ¿Tienes nietos? (No, no tengo ninguno/ningún nieto.)**

Pairs Have pairs create sentences about your community using indefinite and negative words. Ex: **En nuestra ciudad no hay ningún mercado al aire libre. Hay algunos restaurantes de tapas. El equipo de béisbol juega bien, pero no gana muchos partidos.**

Small Groups Give small groups five minutes to write a description of **un señor muy, pero muy antipático.** Tell them to use as many indefinite and negative words as possible to describe what makes this person so unpleasant. Encourage exaggeration and creativity.

Video Show the **Fotonovela** again to give students more input containing indefinite and negative words. Stop the video where appropriate to discuss how these words are used.

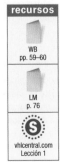

recursos

WB
pp. 59–60

LM
p. 76

vhlcentral.com
Lección 1

COMPARE & CONTRAST

In English, it is incorrect to use more than one negative word in a sentence. In Spanish, however, sentences frequently contain two or more negative words. Compare these Spanish and English sentences.

Nunca le escribo a **nadie**.	**No** me preocupo por **nada nunca**.
I never write to anyone.	*I do not ever worry about anything.*

As the preceding sentences show, once an English sentence contains one negative word (for example, *not* or *never*), no other negative word may be used. Instead, indefinite (or affirmative) words are used. In Spanish, however, once a sentence is negative, no other affirmative (that is, indefinite) word may be used. Instead, all indefinite ideas must be expressed in the negative.

▶ **Pero** is used to mean *but*. The meaning of **sino** is *but rather* or *on the contrary*. It is used when the first part of the sentence is negative and the second part contradicts it.

Los estudiantes no se acuestan temprano **sino** tarde.	Esas gafas son caras, **pero** bonitas.
The students don't go to bed early, but rather late.	*Those glasses are expensive, but pretty.*
María no habla francés **sino** español.	José es inteligente, **pero** no saca buenas notas.
María doesn't speak French, but rather Spanish.	*José is intelligent but doesn't get good grades.*

¡INTÉNTALO!   Cambia las oraciones para que sean negativas.

1. Siempre se viste bien.
   ___Nunca___ se viste bien.
   ___No___ se viste bien ___nunca___.

2. Alguien se ducha.
   ___Nadie___ se ducha.
   ___No___ se ducha ___nadie___.

3. Ellas van también.
   Ellas ___tampoco___ van.
   Ellas ___no___ van ___tampoco___.

4. Alguien se pone nervioso.
   ___Nadie___ se pone nervioso.
   ___No___ se pone nervioso ___nadie___.

5. Tú siempre te lavas las manos.
   Tú ___nunca / jamás___ te lavas las manos.
   Tú ___no___ te lavas las manos ___nunca / jamás___.

6. Voy a traer algo.
   ___No___ voy a traer ___nada___.

7. Juan se afeita también.
   Juan ___tampoco___ se afeita.
   Juan ___no___ se afeita ___tampoco___.

8. Mis amigos viven en una residencia o en casa.
   Mis amigos ___no___ viven ___ni___ en una residencia ___ni___ en casa.

9. La profesora hace algo en su escritorio.
   La profesora ___no___ hace ___nada___ en su escritorio.

10. Tú y yo vamos al mercado.
    ___Ni___ tú ___ni___ yo vamos al mercado.

11. Tienen un espejo en su casa.
    ___No___ tienen ___ningún___ espejo en su casa.

12. Algunos niños se ponen sus abrigos.
    ___Ningún___ niño se pone su abrigo.

Práctica

1 **¿Pero o sino?** Forma oraciones sobre estas personas usando **pero** o **sino**.

> **modelo**
>
> muchos estudiantes viven en residencias estudiantiles / muchos de ellos quieren vivir fuera del (*off*) campus
> *Muchos estudiantes viven en residencias estudiantiles, pero muchos de ellos quieren vivir fuera del campus.*

1. Marcos nunca se despierta temprano / siempre llega puntual a clase
   Marcos nunca se despierta temprano, pero siempre llega puntual a clase.
2. Lisa y Katarina no se acuestan temprano / muy tarde
   Lisa y Katarina no se acuestan temprano sino muy tarde.
3. Alfonso es inteligente / algunas veces es antipático
   Alfonso es inteligente, pero algunas veces es antipático.
4. los directores de la residencia no son ecuatorianos / peruanos
   Los directores de la residencia no son ecuatorianos sino peruanos.
5. no nos acordamos de comprar champú / compramos jabón
   No nos acordamos de comprar champú, pero compramos jabón.
6. Emilia no es estudiante / profesora
   Emilia no es estudiante sino profesora.
7. no quiero levantarme / tengo que ir a clase
   No quiero levantarme, pero tengo que ir a clase.
8. Miguel no se afeita por la mañana / por la noche
   Miguel no se afeita por la mañana sino por la noche.

2 **Completar** Completa esta conversación. Usa expresiones negativas en tus respuestas. Luego, dramatiza la conversación con un(a) compañero/a. Answers will vary.

AURELIO   Ana María, ¿encontraste algún regalo para Eliana?
ANA MARÍA (1)___No, no encontré ningún regalo/nada para Eliana.___

AURELIO   ¿Viste a alguna amiga en el centro comercial?
ANA MARÍA (2)___No, no vi a ninguna amiga/ninguna/nadie en el centro comercial.___

AURELIO   ¿Me llamó alguien?
ANA MARÍA (3)___No, nadie te llamó./No, no te llamó nadie.___

AURELIO   ¿Quieres ir al teatro o al cine esta noche?
ANA MARÍA (4)___No, no quiero ir ni al teatro ni al cine.___

AURELIO   ¿No quieres salir a comer?
ANA MARÍA (5)___No, no quiero salir a comer (tampoco).___

AURELIO   ¿Hay algo interesante en la televisión esta noche?
ANA MARÍA (6)___No, no hay nada interesante en la televisión.___

AURELIO   ¿Tienes algún problema?
ANA MARÍA (7)___No, no tengo ningún problema/ninguno.___

🕹️ Practice more at **vhlcentral.com**.

1 Have pairs create four sentences, two with **sino** and two with **pero**. Have them "dehydrate" their sentences as in the **modelo** and exchange papers with another pair, who will write the complete sentences.

1 To challenge students, ask them to change each sentence so that the opposite choice (**pero** or **sino**) would be correct. Ex: **Muchos estudiantes no viven en la residencia estudiantil, sino en apartamentos.**

2 Review indefinite and negative words by using them in short sentences and asking volunteers to contradict your statements. Ex: **Veo a alguien en la puerta. (No, usted no ve a nadie en la puerta.) Nunca vengo a clase con el libro. (No, usted siempre viene a clase con el libro.)**

Extra Practice To provide oral practice with indefinite and negative words, create prompts that follow the pattern of the sentences in **Actividad 1** and **Actividad 2**. Say the first part of the sentence, then have students repeat it and finish the sentence. Ex: **1. _____ no se viste de azul hoy, sino _____. (de verde) 2. _____ no llegó temprano a clase hoy, sino _____. (tarde)**

2 For follow-up, ask students to summarize the conversation. Ex: **Ana María no encontró ningún regalo para Eliana. Tampoco vio a ninguna amiga en el centro comercial.**

Lección 1

Comunicación

3 Give students these additional items: **5. Mis padres no son ____ sino ____. 6. Mi compañero/a de cuarto es ____ pero ____.**

3 Use personal examples to preview the activity. Ex: **Mi hijo es inteligente, pero no le gusta estudiar. Mi amiga no es norteamericana, sino española.**

4 Have pairs of students create two additional sentences about your school.

5 Divide the class into all-male and all-female groups. Then have each group make two different lists: **Quejas que tienen los hombres de las mujeres** and **Quejas que tienen las mujeres de los hombres.** After five minutes, compare and contrast the answers and perceptions.

7 Have students write five sentences using information obtained through the survey. Ex: **Nadie va a la biblioteca durante el fin de semana, pero muchos vamos durante la semana.**

Extra Practice Have students complete this cloze activity using **pero, sino,** and **tampoco:** Yo me levanto temprano y hago mi tarea, ____ mi compañera de apartamento prefiere hacerla por la noche y acostarse muy tarde. (pero) Ella no tiene exámenes este semestre ____ proyectos. (sino) Yo no tengo exámenes ____. (tampoco) Sólo tengo mucha, mucha tarea.

3 **Opiniones** Completa estas oraciones de una manera lógica. Luego, compara tus respuestas con las de un(a) compañero/a. Answers will vary.

1. Mi habitación es _____, pero _____.
2. Por la noche me gusta _____, pero _____.
3. Un(a) profesor(a) ideal no es _____, sino _____.
4. Mis amigos son _____, pero _____.

4 **En el campus** En parejas, háganse preguntas sobre qué hay en su universidad: residencias bonitas, departamento de ingeniería, cines, librerías baratas, estudiantes guapos/as, equipo de fútbol, playa, clases fáciles, museo, profesores/as estrictos/as. Sigan el modelo. Answers will vary.

modelo
Estudiante 1: ¿Hay algunas residencias bonitas?
Estudiante 2: Sí, hay una/algunas. Está(n) detrás del estadio.
Estudiante 1: ¿Hay algún museo?
Estudiante 2: No, no hay ninguno.

5 **Quejas** En parejas, hagan una lista de cinco quejas (*complaints*) comunes que tienen los estudiantes. Usen expresiones negativas. Answers will vary.

modelo
Nadie me entiende.

Ahora hagan una lista de cinco quejas que los padres tienen de sus hijos.

modelo
Nunca limpian sus habitaciones.

6 **Anuncios** En parejas, lean el anuncio y contesten las preguntas. Some answers will vary.

1. ¿Es el anuncio positivo o negativo? ¿Por qué? Answers will vary.
2. ¿Qué palabras indefinidas hay? algún, siempre, algo
3. Escriban el texto del anuncio cambiando todo por expresiones negativas. ¿No buscas ningún producto especial? ¡Nunca hay nada para nadie en las tiendas García!

Ahora preparen su propio (*own*) anuncio usando expresiones afirmativas y negativas.

¿Buscas algún producto especial?
¡Siempre hay algo para todos en las tiendas García!

Síntesis
Supersite: Activity Pack

7 **Encuesta** Tu profesor(a) te va a dar una hoja de actividades para hacer una encuesta. Circula por la clase y pídeles a tus compañeros que comparen las actividades que hacen durante la semana con las que hacen durante los fines de semana. Escribe las respuestas. Answers will vary.

1.3 Preterite of **ser** and **ir** Tutorial

ANTE TODO   In *¡ADELANTE! UNO*, **Lección 6**, you learned how to form the preterite tense of regular **-ar**, **-er**, and **-ir** verbs. The following chart contains the preterite forms of **ser** (*to be*) and **ir** (*to go*). Since these forms are irregular, you will need to memorize them.

Preterite of **ser** and **ir**

		ser *(to be)*	**ir** *(to go)*
SINGULAR FORMS	yo	fui	fui
	tú	fuiste	fuiste
	Ud./él/ella	fue	fue
PLURAL FORMS	nosotros/as	fuimos	fuimos
	vosotros/as	fuisteis	fuisteis
	Uds./ellos/ellas	fueron	fueron

▶ Since the preterite forms of **ser** and **ir** are identical, context clarifies which of the two verbs is being used.

Él **fue** a comprar champú y jabón.
He went to buy shampoo and soap.

¿Cómo **fue** la película anoche?
How was the movie last night?

¿Cuándo fue la última vez que viste a Juan Carlos?

Cuando fuimos a Mérida.

¡INTÉNTALO!   Completa las oraciones usando el pretérito de **ser** e **ir**.

ir

1. Los viajeros ___fueron___ a Perú.
2. Patricia ___fue___ a Cuzco.
3. Tú ___fuiste___ a Iquitos.
4. Gregorio y yo ___fuimos___ a Lima.
5. Yo ___fui___ a Trujillo.
6. Ustedes ___fueron___ a Arequipa.
7. Mi padre ___fue___ a Lima.
8. Nosotras ___fuimos___ a Cuzco.
9. Él ___fue___ a Machu Picchu.
10. Usted ___fue___ a Nazca.

ser

1. Usted ___fue___ muy amable.
2. Yo ___fui___ muy cordial.
3. Ellos ___fueron___ simpáticos.
4. Nosotros ___fuimos___ muy tontos.
5. Ella ___fue___ antipática.
6. Tú ___fuiste___ muy generoso.
7. Ustedes ___fueron___ cordiales.
8. La gente ___fue___ amable.
9. Tomás y yo ___fuimos___ muy felices.
10. Los profesores ___fueron___ buenos.

NATIONAL STANDARDS / comparisons

Teaching Tips
• Use pairs of sentences to contrast the preterite of ser and ir. Ex: **Ayer fue domingo. No fui al supermercado ayer.**

AYUDA

Note that, whereas regular **-er** and **-ir** verbs have accent marks in the **yo** and **Ud./él/ella** forms of the preterite, **ser** and **ir** do not.

• Ask questions to further clarify how context determines meaning. Ex: **¿Quiénes fueron al partido de fútbol el sábado? ¿Fue divertido el partido?**

Video Replay the **Fotonovela** segment and have students listen for preterite forms of **ser** and **ir**. Stop the video with each example to illustrate how context makes the meaning of the verb clear.

Extra Practice To reverse the activity, have students close their books. Read several completed sentences at random and have students state whether the verb is **ser** or **ir**.

recursos

WB
p. 61

LM
p. 77

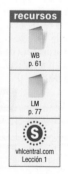
vhlcentral.com
Lección 1

Práctica y Comunicación

1

Completar Completa estas conversaciones con la forma correcta del pretérito de **ser** o **ir**. Indica el infinitivo de cada forma verbal.

Conversación 1

			ser	ir
RAÚL	¿Adónde (1)_____ fueron _____ ustedes de vacaciones?		○	⊘
PILAR	(2)_____ Fuimos _____ a Perú.		○	⊘
RAÚL	¿Cómo (3)_____ fue _____ el viaje?		⊘	○
▶ **PILAR**	¡(4)_____ Fue _____ estupendo! Machu Picchu y El Callao son increíbles.		⊘	○
RAÚL	¿(5)_____ Fue _____ caro el viaje?		⊘	○
PILAR	No, el precio (6)_____ fue _____ muy bajo. Sólo costó tres mil dólares.		⊘	○

Conversación 2

		ser	ir
ISABEL	Tina y Vicente (7)_____ fueron _____ novios, ¿no?	⊘	○
LUCÍA	Sí, pero ahora no. Anoche Tina (8)_____ fue _____ a comer con Gregorio	○	⊘
	y la semana pasada ellos (9)_____ fueron _____ al partido de fútbol.	○	⊘
ISABEL	¿Ah sí? Javier y yo (10)_____ fuimos _____ al partido y no los vimos.	○	⊘

NOTA CULTURAL

La ciudad peruana de **El Callao**, fundada en 1537, fue por muchos años el puerto (*port*) más activo de la costa del Pacífico en Suramérica. En el siglo XVIII, se construyó (*was built*) una fortaleza allí para proteger (*protect*) la ciudad de los ataques de piratas y bucaneros.

---

2 Ask a volunteer to say one of his or her sentences aloud. Point to another student, and call out an interrogative word in order to cue a question. Ex: **E1: No fui a un restaurante anoche.** Say: **¿Adónde? E2: ¿Adónde fuiste? E1: Fui al cine.**

3 Have students form new pairs and describe the movie that their first partner saw, based on the information they learned from items 3–6. The other student should guess what movie it was, asking for more information as needed.

TPR Read aloud a series of sentences using **ser** and **ir** in the preterite. Have students raise their right hand if the verb is **ser**, and their left hand for **ir**. Ex: **Yo fui camarero a los dieciocho años.** (right hand)

Small Groups Have small groups of students prepare and perform a TV interview with astronauts who have just returned from a long stay on Mars. Review previous vocabulary as needed. Students should include three uses each of **ser** and **ir** in the preterite.

2 **Descripciones** Forma oraciones con estos elementos. Usa el pretérito. Answers will vary.

A	B	C	D
yo	(no) ir	a un restaurante	ayer
tú	(no) ser	en autobús	anoche
mi compañero/a		estudiante	anteayer
nosotros		muy simpático/a	la semana pasada
mis amigos		a la playa	año pasado
ustedes		dependiente/a en una tienda	

3 **Preguntas** En parejas, túrnense para hacerse estas preguntas. Answers will vary.

1. ¿Cuándo fuiste al cine por última vez? ¿Con quién fuiste?
2. ¿Fuiste en auto, en autobús o en metro? ¿Cómo fue el viaje?
3. ¿Cómo fue la película?
4. ¿Fue una película de terror, de acción o un drama?
5. ¿Fue una de las mejores películas que viste? ¿Por qué?
6. ¿Fueron buenos los actores o no? ¿Cuál fue el mejor?
7. ¿Adónde fuiste/fueron después?
8. ¿Fue una buena idea ir al cine?
9. ¿Fuiste feliz ese día?

4 **El viaje** En parejas, escriban un diálogo de un(a) viajero/a hablando con el/la agente de viajes sobre un viaje que hizo recientemente. Usen el pretérito de **ser** e **ir**. Answers will vary.

> **modelo**
>
> **Agente:** ¿Cómo fue el viaje?
> **Viajero:** El viaje fue maravilloso/horrible…

 Practice more at **vhlcentral.com**.

Lección 1

1.4 Verbs like **gustar** Tutorial

ANTE TODO In *¡ADELANTE! UNO*, **Lección 2**, you learned how to express preferences with **gustar**. You will now learn more about the verb **gustar** and other similar verbs. Observe these examples.

Me gusta ese champú.

> ENGLISH EQUIVALENT
> *I like that shampoo.*
> LITERAL MEANING
> *That shampoo is pleasing to me.*

¿Te gustaron las clases?

> ENGLISH EQUIVALENT
> *Did you like the classes?*
> LITERAL MEANING
> *Were the classes pleasing to you?*

▶ As the examples show, constructions with **gustar** do not have a direct equivalent in English. The literal meaning of this construction is *to be pleasing to* (*someone*), and it requires the use of an indirect object pronoun.

INDIRECT OBJECT PRONOUN	VERB	SUBJECT		SUBJECT	VERB	DIRECT OBJECT
Me	**gusta**	ese champú.		*I*	*like*	*that shampoo.*

▶ In the diagram above, observe how in the Spanish sentence the object being liked **(ese champú)** is really the subject of the sentence. The person who likes the object, in turn, is an indirect object because it answers the question: *To whom is the shampoo pleasing?*

¿Te gusta Juan Carlos?

Me gustan los cafés que tienen música en vivo.

▶ Other verbs in Spanish are used in the same way as **gustar**. Here is a list of the most common ones.

Verbs like **gustar**

aburrir	to bore	**importar**	to be important to; to matter
encantar	to like very much; to love (inanimate objects)	**interesar**	to be interesting to; to interest
faltar	to lack; to need	**molestar**	to bother; to annoy
fascinar	to fascinate; to like very much	**quedar**	to be left over; to fit (clothing)

Teaching Tip Ask questions to briefly review the verb **gustar**. Ex: _____, ¿te gustan las canciones de Shakira? ¿Qué tipo de música les gusta a tus padres?

Game Divide the class into small teams. Give a prompt including subject and object (Ex: **ella/películas de horror**). Allow teams one minute to construct a sentence using one of the verbs that follow the pattern of **gustar**. Then one member from each team will write the sentence on the board. Award one point to each team for each correct response.

Heritage Speakers Ask heritage speakers to add to the list of verbs like **gustar**. Ex: **doler, preocupar, sorprender**. Have them use each verb in a sentence about themselves; then ask volunteers to report on their statements.

¡ATENCIÓN!

Faltar expresses what is lacking or missing. **Me falta una página.** *I'm missing one page.*

Quedar expresses how much of something is left. **Nos quedan tres pesos.** *We have three pesos left.*

•••

Quedar also means *to fit.* It can be used to tell how something looks (on someone). **Estos zapatos me quedan bien.** *These shoes fit me well.*

Esa camisa te queda muy bien. *That shirt looks good on you.*

Large Group Have the class sit in a circle. Student A begins by saying **Me encanta** and an activity he or she enjoys. Ex: **Me encanta correr.** Student B reports what student A said and adds his or her own favorite activity. **A Frank le encanta correr. A mí me fascina bailar.** Student C reports the preferences of the first two students and adds his or her own, and so forth. This activity may be used with any verb that follows the pattern of **gustar**.

▶ The most commonly used verb forms of **gustar** and similar verbs are the third person (singular and plural). When the object or person being liked is singular, the singular form (**gusta**) is used. When two or more objects or persons are being liked, the plural form (**gustan**) is used. Observe the following diagram:

me, te, le, nos, os, les	SINGULAR	encanta / interesó	→	la película / el concierto
	PLURAL	importan / fascinaron	→	las vacaciones / los museos de Lima

▶ To express what someone likes or does not like to do, use an appropriate verb followed by an infinitive. The singular form is used even if there is more than one infinitive.

Nos molesta comer a las nueve.
It bothers us to eat at nine o'clock.

Les encanta bailar y **cantar** en las fiestas.
They love to dance and sing at parties.

▶ As you learned in *¡ADELANTE!* **UNO**, **Lección 2**, the construction **a** + [*pronoun*] (**a mí, a ti, a usted, a él,** etc.) is used to clarify or to emphasize who is pleased, bored, etc. The construction **a** + [*noun*] can also be used before the indirect object pronoun to clarify or to emphasize who is pleased.

A los turistas les gustó mucho Machu Picchu.
The tourists liked Machu Picchu a lot.

A ti te gusta cenar en casa, pero **a mí** me aburre.
You like eating dinner at home, but I get bored.

▶ **¡Atención! Mí** (*me*) has an accent mark to distinguish it from the possessive adjective **mi** (*my*).

AYUDA

Note that the **a** must be repeated if there is more than one person. **A Armando** y a **Carmen** les molesta levantarse temprano.

Extra Practice Add an auditory aspect to this grammar presentation. Read a series of sentences aloud, pausing to allow students to write. Ex: **1. A todos en mi familia nos encanta viajar. 2. Nos gusta viajar en avión, pero nos molestan los aviones pequeños. 3. A mi hijo le interesan las culturas latinoamericanas, a mi esposo le encantan los países de Asia y a mí me fascina Europa. 4. Todavía nos quedan muchos lugares por visitar y nos falta el tiempo necesario.**

recursos

WB pp. 62–63

LM p. 78

Ⓢ vhlcentral.com Lección 1

¡INTÉNTALO! Indica el pronombre de objeto indirecto y la forma del tiempo presente adecuados en cada oración.

fascinar

1. A él _le fascina_ viajar.
2. A mí _me fascina_ bailar.
3. A nosotras _nos fascina_ cantar.
4. A ustedes _les fascina_ leer.
5. A ti _te fascina_ correr y patinar.
6. A ellos _les fascinan_ los aviones.
7. A mis padres _les fascina_ caminar.
8. A usted _le fascina_ jugar al tenis.
9. A mi esposo y a mí _nos fascina_ dormir.
10. A Alberto _le fascina_ dibujar y pintar.
11. A todos _nos/les fascina_ opinar.
12. A Pili _le fascinan_ los sombreros.

aburrir

1. A ellos _les aburren_ los deportes.
2. A ti _te aburren_ las películas.
3. A usted _le aburren_ los viajes.
4. A mí _me aburren_ las revistas.
5. A Jorge y a Luis _les aburren_ los perros.
6. A nosotros _nos aburren_ las vacaciones.
7. A ustedes _les aburre_ el béisbol.
8. A Marcela _le aburren_ los libros.
9. A mis amigos _les aburren_ los museos.
10. A ella _le aburre_ el ciclismo.
11. A Omar _le aburre_ ir de compras.
12. A ti y a mí _nos aburre_ el baile.

Pairs Ask students to write five questions using verbs like **gustar**, then exchange with a partner. Remind them to use complete sentences in their responses.

Práctica

1

Completar Completa las oraciones con todos los elementos necesarios.

1. ___A___ Adela __le encanta__ (encantar) la música de Tito "El Bambino". ◄
2. A ___mí___ me __interesa__ (interesar) la música de otros países.
3. A mis amigos __les encantan__ (encantar) las canciones (*songs*) de Calle 13.
4. A Juan y ___a___ Rafael no les __molesta__ (molestar) la música alta (*loud*).
5. ___A___ nosotros __nos fascinan__ (fascinar) los grupos de pop latino.
6. ___Al___ señor Ruiz __le interesa__ (interesar) más la música clásica.
7. A ___mí___ me __aburre__ (aburrir) la música clásica.
8. ¿A ___ti___ te __falta__ (faltar) dinero para el concierto de Carlos Santana?
9. No. Ya compré el boleto y __me quedan__ (quedar) cinco dólares.
10. ¿Cuánto dinero te __queda__ (quedar) a ___ti___?

NOTA CULTURAL

Hoy día, la música latina es popular en los EE.UU. gracias a artistas como **Shakira**, de nacionalidad colombiana, y **Tito "El Bambino"**, puertorriqueño. Otros artistas, como **Carlos Santana** y **Gloria Estefan**, difundieron (*spread*) la música latina en los años 60, 70, 80 y 90.

2

Describir Mira los dibujos y describe lo que está pasando. Usa los verbos de la lista. Answers will vary. Suggested answers:

aburrir	faltar	molestar
encantar	interesar	quedar

1. a Ramón   A Ramón le molesta despertarse temprano.

2. a nosotros   A nosotros nos encanta esquiar.

3. a ti   A ti no te queda bien este vestido. A ti te queda mal/grande este vestido.

LIBROS DE ARTE MODERNO

4. a Sara   A Sara le interesan los libros de arte moderno.

3

Gustos Forma oraciones con los elementos de las columnas. Answers will vary.

> *modelo*
>
> A ti te interesan las ruinas de Machu Picchu.

A	B	C
yo	aburrir	despertarse temprano
tú	encantar	mirarse en el espejo
mi mejor amigo/a	faltar	la música rock
mis amigos y yo	fascinar	las pantuflas rosadas
Bart y Homero Simpson	interesar	la pasta de dientes con menta (*mint*)
Shakira	molestar	las ruinas de Machu Picchu
Antonio Banderas		los zapatos caros

 Practice more at **vhlcentral.com**.

1 Have students use the verbs in the activity to write a paragraph describing their own musical tastes.

1 To simplify, have students underline the subject in each sentence before filling in the blanks.

2 Repeat the activity using the preterite. Invite students to provide additional details. Ex: **1. A Ramón le molestó el despertador ayer. 2. A nosotros nos encantó esquiar en Vail.**

TPR Have students stand and form a circle. Begin by tossing a foam or paper ball to a student, who should state a complaint using a verb like **gustar** (Ex: **Me falta dinero para comprar los libros**) and then toss the ball to another student. The next student should offer advice (Ex: **Debes pedirle dinero a tus padres**) and throw the ball to another person, who will air another complaint. Repeat the activity with positive statements (**Me fascinan las películas cómicas**) and advice (**Debes ver las películas de Will Ferrell**).

3 Ask students to create two additional sentences using verbs from column B. Have students read their sentences aloud. After everyone has had a turn, ask the class how many similar or identical sentences they heard and what they were.

NATIONAL communication STANDARDS

Lección 1

Comunicación

4 Take a class survey of the answers and write the results on the board. Ask volunteers to use verbs like **gustar** to summarize them.

5 For items that start with **A mi(s)…** , have pairs compare their answers and then report to the class: first answers in common, then answers that differed. Ex: **A mis padres les importan los estudios, pero a los padres de _____ les importa más el dinero.**

6 Divide the class into pairs and distribute the handouts from the Activity Pack on the Supersite that correspond to this information gap activity.

Pairs Have pairs prepare short TV commercials in which they use the target verbs presented in **Estructura 1.4** to sell a particular product.

Extra Practice Add a visual aspect to this grammar practice. Bring in magazine pictures of people enjoying or not enjoying what they are doing. Have them create sentences with verbs like **gustar**. Ex: **A los chicos no les interesa estudiar biología.**

7 To simplify, have students prepare for their roles by brainstorming a list of words and phrases. Remind students to use the formal register in this conversation.

4

Preguntas En parejas, túrnense para hacer y contestar estas preguntas. Answers will vary.

1. ¿Te gusta levantarte temprano o tarde? ¿Por qué? ¿Y a tu compañero/a de cuarto?
2. ¿Te gusta acostarte temprano o tarde? ¿Y a tu compañero/a de cuarto?
3. ¿Te gusta dormir la siesta?
4. ¿Te encanta acampar o prefieres quedarte en un hotel cuando estás de vacaciones?
5. ¿Qué te gusta hacer en el verano?
6. ¿Qué te fascina de esta universidad? ¿Qué te molesta?
7. ¿Te interesan más las ciencias o las humanidades? ¿Por qué?
8. ¿Qué cosas te aburren?

5

Completar Trabajen en parejas. Túrnense para completar estas frases de una manera lógica. Answers will vary.

1. A mi novio/a le fascina(n)…
2. A mi mejor (*best*) amigo/a no le interesa(n)…
3. A mis padres les importa(n)…
4. A nosotros nos molesta(n)…
5. A mis hermanos les aburre(n)…
6. A mi compañero/a de cuarto le aburre(n)…
7. A los turistas les interesa(n)…
8. A los jugadores profesionales les encanta(n)…
9. A nuestro/a profesor(a) le molesta(n)…
10. A mí me importa(n)…

6

La residencia Tú y tu compañero/a de clase son los directores de una residencia estudiantil en Perú. Su profesor(a) les va a dar a cada uno de ustedes las descripciones de cinco estudiantes. Con la información tienen que escoger quiénes van a ser compañeros de cuarto. Después, completen la lista. Answers will vary.

Síntesis

7

Situación Trabajen en parejas para representar los papeles de un(a) cliente/a y un(a) dependiente/a en una tienda de ropa. Usen las instrucciones como guía. Answers will vary.

Dependiente/a

Saluda al/a la cliente/a y pregúntale en qué le puedes servir.

Pregúntale si le interesan los estilos modernos y empieza a mostrarle la ropa.

Habla de los gustos del/de la cliente/a.

Da opiniones favorables al/a la cliente/a (las botas te quedan fantásticas…).

Cliente/a

Saluda al/a la dependiente/a y dile (*tell him/her*) qué quieres comprar y qué colores prefieres.

Explícale que los estilos modernos te interesan. Escoge las cosas que te interesan.

Habla de la ropa (me queda(n) bien/mal, me encanta(n)…).

Decide cuáles son las cosas que te gustan y qué vas a comprar.

NATIONAL communication STANDARDS

Recapitulación

 **Diagnostics**

Completa estas actividades para repasar los conceptos de gramática que aprendiste en esta lección.

1 Completar Completa la tabla con la forma correcta de los verbos. **6 pts.**

yo	tú	nosotros	ellas
me levanto	te levantas	nos levantamos	se levantan
me afeito	**te afeitas**	nos afeitamos	se afeitan
me visto	te vistes	**nos vestimos**	se visten
me seco	te secas	nos secamos	**se secan**

2 Hoy y ayer Cambia los verbos del presente al pretérito. **5 pts.**

1. Vamos de compras hoy. _Fuimos_ de compras hoy.
2. Por último, voy a poner el despertador. Por último, _fui_ a poner el despertador.
3. Lalo es el primero en levantarse. Lalo _fue_ el primero en levantarse.
4. ¿Vas a tu habitación? ¿_Fuiste_ a tu habitación?
5. ¿Ustedes son profesores. Ustedes _fueron_ profesores.

3 Reflexivos Completa cada conversación con la forma correcta de los verbos reflexivos. **11 pts.**

TOMÁS Yo siempre (1) __me baño__ (bañarse) antes de (2) __acostarme__ (acostarse). Esto me relaja porque no (3) __me duermo__ (dormirse) fácilmente. Y así puedo (4) __levantarme__ (levantarse) más tarde. Y tú, ¿cuándo (5) __te duchas__ (ducharse)?

LETI Pues por la mañana, para poder (6) __despertarme__ (despertarse).

DAVID ¿Cómo (7) __se siente__ (sentirse) Pepa hoy?

MARÍA Todavía está enojada.

DAVID ¿De verdad? Ella nunca (8) __se enoja__ (enojarse) con nadie.

BETO ¿(Nosotros) (9) __Nos vamos__ (Irse) de esta tienda? Estoy cansado.

SARA Pero antes vamos a (10) __probarnos__ (probarse) estos sombreros. Si quieres, después (nosotros) (11) __nos sentamos__ (sentarse) un rato.

3 Remind students of the different positions for reflexive pronouns and the need for an infinitive after a phrase like **antes de** or a conjugated verb, such as **puedo**.

RESUMEN GRAMATICAL

1.1 Reflexive verbs *pp. 30–31*

lavarse	
me lavo	nos lavamos
te lavas	os laváis
se lava	se lavan

1.2 Indefinite and negative words *pp. 34–35*

Indefinite words	Negative words
algo	nada
alguien	nadie
alguno/a(s), algún	ninguno/a, ningún
o... o	ni... ni
siempre	nunca, jamás
también	tampoco

1.3 Preterite of ser and ir *p. 38*

▶ The preterite of **ser** and **ir** are identical. Context will determine the meaning.

ser and ir	
fui	fuimos
fuiste	fuisteis
fue	fueron

1.4 Verbs like gustar *pp. 40–41*

aburrir	importar
encantar	interesar
faltar	molestar
fascinar	quedar

me, te, le, nos, os, les

SINGULAR
encanta → la película
interesó → el concierto

PLURAL
importan → las vacaciones
fascinaron → los museos

▶ Use the construction a + [*noun/pronoun*] to clarify the person in question.

A mí me encanta ver películas, ¿y a ti?

Lección 1

4

4 Have students create four additional sentences using the remaining indefinite and negative words from the word bank.

Game Play a game of **Diez Preguntas**. Ask a volunteer to think of a person in the class. Other students get one chance each to ask a question using indefinite and negative words. Ex: **¿Es alguien que siempre llega temprano a clase?**

5 Give students these sentences as items 5–8:
5. yo / faltar / dinero (A mí me falta dinero.)
6. Pedro y yo / fascinar / cantar y bailar (A Pedro y a mí nos fascina cantar y bailar.) 7. usted / quedar / muy bien / esas gafas de sol (A usted le quedan muy bien esas gafas de sol.) 8. ¿ / ustedes / interesar / conocer / otros países / ? (¿A ustedes les interesa conocer otros países?)

7 To challenge students, have them work in small groups to create a riddle using grammar and/or vocabulary from this lesson. Have groups share their riddles with the class.

Conversaciones Completa cada conversación de manera lógica con palabras de la lista. No tienes que usar todas las palabras. **8 pts.**

algo	nada	ningún	siempre
alguien	nadie	nunca	también
algún	ni... ni	o... o	tampoco

1. —¿Tienes __algún__ plan para esta noche?

   —No, prefiero quedarme en casa. Hoy no quiero ver a __nadie__.

   —Yo __también__ me quedo. Estoy muy cansado.

2. —¿Puedo entrar? ¿Hay __alguien__ en el cuarto de baño?

   —Sí. ¡Un momento! Ahora mismo salgo.

3. —¿Puedes prestarme __algo__ para peinarme? No encuentro __ni__ mi cepillo __ni__ mi peine.

   —Lo siento, yo __tampoco__ encuentro los míos (*mine*).

4. —¿Me prestas tu maquillaje?

   —Lo siento, no tengo. __Nunca__ me maquillo.

Oraciones Forma oraciones completas con los elementos dados (*given*). Usa el presente de los verbos. **8 pts.**

1. David y Juan / molestar / levantarse temprano   A David y a Juan les molesta levantarse temprano.
2. Lucía / encantar / las películas de terror   A Lucía le encantan las películas de terror.
3. todos (nosotros) / importar / la educación   A todos nos importa la educación.
4. tú / aburrir / ver / la televisión.   A ti te aburre ver la televisión.

Rutinas Escribe seis oraciones que describan las rutinas de dos personas que conoces. **12 pts.**

Answers will vary.

> **modelo**
>
> Mi tía se despierta temprano, pero mi primo...

Adivinanza Completa la adivinanza con las palabras que faltan y adivina la respuesta. **¡2 puntos EXTRA!**

" Cuanto más° __te seca__ (*it dries you*), más se moja°. "
¿Qué es?__La toalla__

Cuanto más *The more* se moja *it gets wet*

 Practice more at **vhlcentral.com**.

Lectura

Antes de leer

Estrategia

Predicting content from the title

Prediction is an invaluable strategy in reading for comprehension. For example, we can usually predict the content of a newspaper article from its headline. We often decide whether to read the article based on its headline. Predicting content from the title will help you increase your reading comprehension in Spanish.

Examinar el texto

Lee el título de la lectura y haz tres predicciones sobre el contenido. Escribe tus predicciones en una hoja de papel. Answers will vary.

Compartir

Comparte tus ideas con un(a) compañero/a de clase.

Cognados

Haz una lista de seis cognados que encuentres en la lectura. Answers will vary.

1. _____
2. _____
3. _____
4. _____
5. _____
6. _____

¿Qué te dicen los cognados sobre el tema de la lectura?

Teaching Tip Display or make up several cognate-rich headlines from Spanish newspapers and ask students to predict the content of each article. Ex: **Científicos anuncian que Plutón ya no es planeta. Decenas de miles recuerdan la explosión atómica en Hiroshima.**

Extra Practice Ask students to skim the selection for verbs like **gustar**, then use **le** and **les** to rewrite the sentences in third person. Ex: **A Guillermo le aburre la biología.**

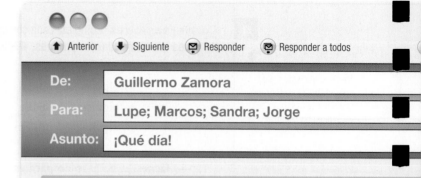

Anterior   Siguiente   Responder   Responder a todos

De: Guillermo Zamora

Para: Lupe; Marcos; Sandra; Jorge

Asunto: ¡Qué día!

Hola, chicos:

La semana pasada me di cuenta° de que necesito organizar mejor° mi rutina… pero especialmente debo prepararme mejor para los exámenes. Me falta disciplina, me molesta no tener control de mi tiempo y nunca deseo repetir los eventos de la semana pasada.

El miércoles pasé todo el día y toda la noche estudiando para el examen de biología del jueves por la mañana. Me aburre la biología y no empecé a estudiar hasta el día antes del examen. El jueves a las 8, después de no dormir en toda la noche, fui exhausto al examen. Fue difícil, pero afortunadamente° me acordé de todo el material. Esa noche me acosté temprano y dormí mucho.

Me desperté a las 7, y fue extraño° ver a mi compañero de cuarto, Andrés, preparándose para ir a dormir. Como° siempre se enferma°, tiene problemas para dormir y no hablamos mucho, no le comenté nada. Fui al baño a cepillarme los dientes

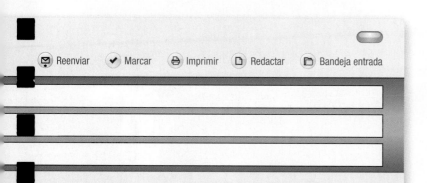

Reenviar ✔ Marcar 🖨 Imprimir 📄 Redactar 📥 Bandeja entrada

para ir a clase. ¿Y Andrés? Él se acostó. "Debe estar enfermo°, ¡otra vez!", pensé.

Mi clase es a las 8, y fue necesario hacer las cosas rápido. Todo empezó a ir mal... eso pasa siempre cuando uno tiene prisa. Cuando busqué mis cosas para el baño, no las encontré. Entonces me duché sin jabón, me cepillé los dientes sin cepillo de dientes y me peiné con las manos. Tampoco encontré ropa limpia y usé la sucia. Rápido, tomé mis libros. ¿Y Andrés? Roncando°... ¡a las 7:50!

Cuando salí corriendo para la clase, la prisa no me permitió ver el campus desierto. Cuando llegué a la clase, no vi a nadie. No vi al profesor ni a los estudiantes. Por último miré mi reloj, y vi la hora. Las 8 en punto... ¡de la noche!

¡Dormí 24 horas!

Guillermo

me di cuenta *I realized* **mejor** *better* **afortunadamente** *fortunately*
extraño *strange* **Como** *Since* **se enferma** *he gets sick* **enfermo** *sick*
Roncando *Snoring*

Después de leer

Seleccionar 🔊

Selecciona la respuesta correcta.

1. ¿Quién es el/la narrador(a)? c
   a. Andrés
   b. una profesora
   c. Guillermo
2. ¿Qué le molesta al narrador? b
   a. Le molestan los exámenes de biología.
   b. Le molesta no tener control de su tiempo.
   c. Le molesta mucho organizar su rutina.
3. ¿Por qué está exhausto? c
   a. Porque fue a una fiesta la noche anterior.
   b. Porque no le gusta la biología.
   c. Porque pasó la noche anterior estudiando.
4. ¿Por qué no hay nadie en clase? a
   a. Porque es de noche.
   b. Porque todos están de vacaciones.
   c. Porque el profesor canceló la clase.
5. ¿Cómo es la relación de Guillermo y Andrés? b
   a. Son buenos amigos.
   b. No hablan mucho.
   c. Tienen una buena relación.

Pairs For expansion, have pairs create three additional items, then exchange with another pair to complete the activity.

Ordenar 🔊

Ordena los sucesos de la narración. Utiliza los números del 1 al 9.

a. Toma el examen de biología. __2__
b. No encuentra sus cosas para el baño. __5__
c. Andrés se duerme. __7__
d. Pasa todo el día y toda la noche estudiando para un examen. __1__
e. Se ducha sin jabón. __6__
f. Se acuesta temprano. __3__
g. Vuelve a su cuarto después de las 8 de la noche. __9__
h. Se despierta a las 7 y su compañero de cuarto se prepara para dormir. __4__
i. Va a clase y no hay nadie. __8__

Contestar 🔊

Contesta estas preguntas. Answers will vary.

1. ¿Cómo es tu rutina diaria? ¿Muy organizada?
2. ¿Cuándo empiezas a estudiar para los exámenes?
3. ¿Tienes compañero/a de cuarto? ¿Es tu amigo/a?
4. Para comunicarte con tus amigos/as, ¿prefieres el teléfono o el correo electrónico? ¿Por qué?

Small Groups In groups of four, have students list all the verbs in the preterite, then use those verbs to summarize Guillermo's day.

Escritura

Estrategia

Sequencing events

Paying strict attention to sequencing in a narrative will ensure that your writing flows logically from one part to the next.

Every composition should have an introduction, a body, and a conclusion. The introduction presents the subject, the setting, the situation, and the people involved. The main part, or the body, describes the events and people's reactions to these events. The conclusion brings the narrative to a close.

Adverbs and adverbial phrases are sometimes used as transitions between the introduction, the body, and the conclusion. Here is a list of commonly used adverbs in Spanish:

Adverbios

además; también	*in addition; also*
al principio; en un principio	*at first*
antes (de)	*before*
después	*then*
después (de)	*after*
entonces; luego	*then*
más tarde	*later (on)*
primero	*first*
pronto	*soon*
por fin; finalmente	*finally*
al final	*finally*

Teaching Tip Tell students to consult the **Plan de escritura** on page A-2 for step-by-step writing instructions.

Tema

Escribe tu rutina

Imagina tu rutina diaria en uno de estos lugares:

▶ una isla desierta

▶ el Polo Norte

▶ un crucero° transatlántico

▶ un desierto

Escribe una composición en la que describes tu rutina diaria en uno de estos lugares o en algún otro lugar interesante que imagines°. Mientras planeas tu composición, considera cómo cambian algunos de los elementos más básicos de tu rutina diaria en el lugar que escogiste°. Por ejemplo, ¿dónde te acuestas en el Polo Norte? ¿Cómo te duchas en el desierto?

Usa el presente de los verbos reflexivos que conoces e incluye algunos de los adverbios de esta página para organizar la secuencia de tus actividades. Piensa también en la información que debes incluir en cada sección de la narración. Por ejemplo, en la introducción puedes hacer una descripción del lugar y de las personas que están allí, y en la conclusión puedes dar tus opiniones acerca del° lugar y de tu vida diaria allí.

---

crucero *cruise ship* que imagines *that you dream up* escogiste *you chose* acerca del *about the*

Escuchar Audio

Supersite: MP3 Audio Files and Listening Scripts

Estrategia
Using background information

Once you discern the topic of a conversation, take a minute to think about what you already know about the subject. Using this background information will help you guess the meaning of unknown words or linguistic structures.

 To help you practice this strategy, you will now listen to a short paragraph. Jot down the subject of the paragraph, and then use your knowledge of the subject to listen for and write down the paragraph's main points.

Preparación
Teaching Tip Read the directions with students, then have them identify the situation depicted in the photo.

Según la foto, ¿dónde están Carolina y Julián? Piensa en lo que sabes de este tipo de situación. ¿De qué van a hablar? Answers will vary.

Ahora escucha

Ahora escucha la entrevista entre Carolina y Julián, teniendo en cuenta (*taking into account*) lo que sabes sobre este tipo de situación. Elige la información que completa correctamente cada oración.

1. Julián es __c__.
   a. político
   b. deportista profesional
   c. artista de cine
2. El público de Julián quiere saber de __b__.
   a. sus películas
   b. su vida
   c. su novia
3. Julián habla de __a__.
   a. sus viajes y sus rutinas
   b. sus parientes y amigos
   c. sus comidas favoritas
4. Julián __b__.
   a. se levanta y se acuesta a diferentes horas todos los días
   b. tiene una rutina diaria
   c. no quiere hablar de su vida

Comprensión

¿Cierto o falso?

Indica si las oraciones son **ciertas** o **falsas** según la información que Julián da en la entrevista.

1. Es difícil despertarme; generalmente duermo hasta las diez. Falsa
2. Pienso que mi vida no es más interesante que las vidas de ustedes. Cierta
3. Me gusta tener tiempo para pensar y meditar. Cierta
4. Nunca hago mucho ejercicio; no soy una persona activa. Falsa
5. Me fascinan las actividades tranquilas, como escribir y escuchar música clásica. Cierta
6. Los viajes me parecen aburridos. Falsa

Preguntas?   Answers will vary.

1. ¿Qué tiene Julián en común con otras personas de su misma profesión?
2. ¿Te parece que Julián siempre fue rico? ¿Por qué?
3. ¿Qué piensas de Julián como persona?

 Practice more at **vhlcentral.com**.

En pantalla

(NATIONAL STANDARDS — communication cultures)

En la mayor parte de Argentina, Uruguay y Paraguay, y en algunas partes de Chile, Colombia y Centroamérica, las personas tienen la costumbre° de usar **vos** en lugar de **tú** al hablar o escribir. Este uso es conocido como **el voseo** y se refleja también en la manera de conjugar los verbos. El uso de **vos** como tratamiento de respeto pasó a ser° de uso coloquial a partir del° siglo° XVI.

Vocabulario útil	
rehacé	*redo (en el voseo)*
volvete	*become (en el voseo)*

Opciones

Escoge la opción correcta para cada oración

1. El plomero (*plumber*) va a romper el __c__ del chico.
   a. cepillo   b. lavabo   c. espejo

2. El chico y la chica __b__ la primera vez que se ven (*they see each other*).
   a. bailan   b. gritan   c. se peinan

3. Al chico __a__ conocer a la chica.
   a. le interesa   b. le molesta   c. le aburre

4. Al final __b__ rompe el espejo.
   a. la chica   b. el chico   c. el plomero

La cita

En parejas, imaginen que los chicos del anuncio tienen una primera cita (*date*). Escriban una conversación entre ellos donde hablen sobre lo que les encanta y lo que les molesta. Después dramatícenla para la clase y decidan entre todos si los chicos son compatibles o no.

Answers will vary.

Small Groups Have groups of three work together to create and perform their own **Sedal** shampoo commercial. Encourage them to use reflexive verbs, verbs like **gustar**, and indefinite and negative words to sell the product.

costumbre *custom* pasó a ser *became* a partir del *starting in the* siglo *century* Acá hay... *We need to break it here.* ¿Salís? ¿Sales? (en el voseo) ¿por? *why?*

Anuncio de champú Sedal

1

Acá hay que romper°.

2

—Soledad.
—Mariano.

3

—¿Salís°?
—Sí, ¿por°?

 Video: TV Clip

 Practice more at **vhlcentral.com**.

Lección 1

En este episodio de *Flash cultura* vas a conocer unos entremeses° españoles llamados **tapas**. Hay varias teorías sobre el origen de su nombre. Una dice que viene de la costumbre antigua° de **tapar**° los vasos de vino para evitar° que insectos o polvo entren en° ellos. Otra teoría cuenta que el rey Alfonso X debía° beber un poco de vino por indicación médica y decidió acompañarlo° con algunos bocados° para tapar los efectos del alcohol. Cuando estuvo° mejor, ordenó que siempre en Castilla se sirviera° algo de comer con las bebidas° alcohólicas.

Vocabulario útil	
económicas	*inexpensive*
montaditos	*bread slices with assorted toppings*
pagar propinas	*to tip*
tapar el hambre	*to take the edge off (lit. putting the lid on one's hunger)*

Preparación

En el área donde vives, ¿qué hacen las personas normalmente después del trabajo (*work*)? ¿Van a sus casas? ¿Salen con amigos? ¿Comen? Answers will vary.

  Ordenar To simplify, have students read through the items before watching the video.

Ordena estos sucesos de manera lógica

___5___ a. El empleado cuenta los palillos (*counts the toothpicks*) de los montaditos que Mari Carmen comió.

___2___ b. Mari Carmen va al barrio de la Ribera.

___1___ c. Un hombre en un bar explica cuándo sale a tomar tapas.

___3___ d. Un hombre explica la tradición de los montaditos o pinchos.

___4___ e. Carmen le pregunta a la chica si los montaditos son buenos para la salud.

Tapas para todos los días

①

Estamos en la Plaza Cataluña, el puro centro de Barcelona.

②

—¿Cuándo sueles° venir a tomar tapas?
—Generalmente después del trabajo.

③

Éstos son los montaditos, o también llamados pinchos. ¿Te gustan?

 Video: *Flash cultura*

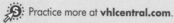 Practice more at **vhlcentral.com**.

recursos

VM pp. 71–72 | vhlcentral.com Lección 1

---

entremeses *hors d'oeuvres* antigua *ancient* tapar *cover* evitar *avoid*
entren en *would get in* debía *should* acompañarlo *accompany it* bocados *snacks*
estuvo *he was* se sirviera *they should serve* bebidas *drinks* sueles *do you tend*

Perú

NATIONAL
connections
cultures
STANDARDS

El país en cifras

▸ **Área:** 1.285.220 km² (496.224 millas²),
un poco menos que el área de Alaska

▸ **Población:** 31.197.000

▸ **Capital:** Lima —9.659.000

▸ **Ciudades principales:** Arequipa —848.000,
Trujillo, Chiclayo, Callao, Iquitos

SOURCE: Population Division, UN Secretariat

*Iquitos es un puerto muy importante en el río
Amazonas. Desde Iquitos se envían° muchos
productos a otros lugares, incluyendo goma°,
nueces°, madera°, arroz°, café y tabaco. Iquitos
es también un destino popular para
los ecoturistas que visitan la selva°.*

▸ **Moneda:** nuevo sol

▸ **Idiomas:** español (oficial);
quechua, aimara y otras
lenguas indígenas (oficiales
en los territorios donde se usan)

Bandera de Perú

Peruanos célebres

▸ **Clorinda Matto de Turner,** escritora (1854–1909)

▸ **César Vallejo,** poeta (1892–1938)

▸ **Javier Pérez de Cuéllar,** diplomático (1920–)

▸ **Mario Vargas Llosa,** escritor (1936–)

Mario Vargas Llosa, Premio
Nobel de Literatura 2010

se envían *are shipped* goma *rubber* nueces *nuts* madera *timber*
arroz *rice* selva *jungle* Hace más de *More than... ago*
grabó *engraved* tamaño *size*

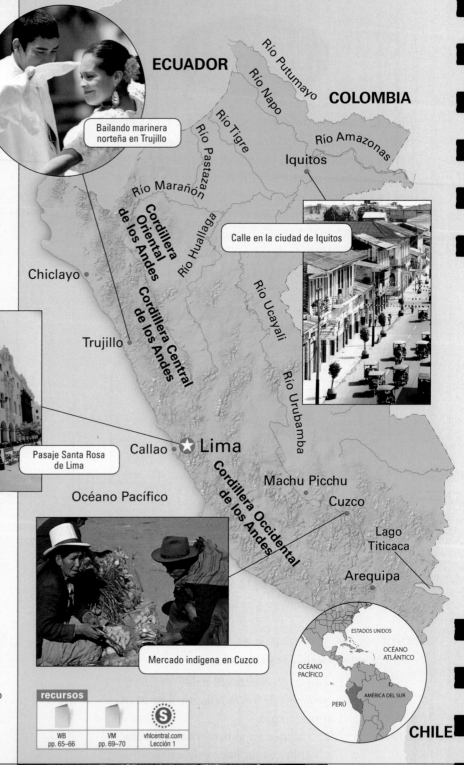

ECUADOR

COLOMBIA

Río Putumayo

Río Napo

Río Tigre

Río Pastaza

Río Amazonas

Iquitos

Río Marañón

Río Huallaga

Cordillera
Oriental
de los Andes

Cordillera Central
de los Andes

Bailando marinera
norteña en Trujillo

Calle en la ciudad de Iquitos

Río Ucayali

Río Urubamba

Chiclayo

Trujillo

Pasaje Santa Rosa
de Lima

Callao ★ Lima

Océano Pacífico

Cordillera Occidental
de los Andes

Machu Picchu

Cuzco

Lago
Titicaca

Arequipa

Mercado indígena en Cuzco

ESTADOS UNIDOS

OCÉANO
ATLÁNTICO

OCÉANO
PACÍFICO

AMÉRICA DEL SUR

PERÚ

CHILE

recursos

WB
pp. 65–66

VM
pp. 69–70

vhlcentral.com
Lección 1

¡Increíble pero cierto!

Hace más de° dos mil años la civilización nazca
de Perú grabó° más de dos mil kilómetros
de líneas en el desierto. Los dibujos sólo son
descifrables desde el aire. Uno de ellos es un
cóndor del tamaño° de un estadio. Las Líneas
de Nazca son uno de los grandes misterios de
la humanidad.

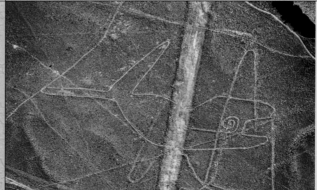

Lección 1

Lugares • **Lima**

Lima es una ciudad moderna y antigua° a la vez°. La Iglesia de San Francisco es notable por su arquitectura barroca colonial. También son fascinantes las exhibiciones sobre los incas en el Museo Oro del Perú y en el Museo Nacional de Antropología y Arqueología. Barranco, el barrio° bohemio de la ciudad, es famoso por su ambiente cultural y sus bares y restaurantes.

BRASIL

Historia • **Machu Picchu**

A 80 kilómetros al noroeste de Cuzco está Machu Picchu, una ciudad antigua del Imperio inca. Está a una altitud de 2.350 metros (7.710 pies), entre dos cimas° de los Andes. Cuando los españoles llegaron a Perú y recorrieron la región, nunca encontraron Machu Picchu. En 1911, el arqueólogo estadounidense Hiram Bingham la descubrió. Todavía no se sabe ni cómo se construyó° una ciudad a esa altura, ni por qué los incas la abandonaron. Sin embargo°, esta ciudad situada en desniveles° naturales es el ejemplo más conocido de la arquitectura inca.

Artes • **La música andina**

Machu Picchu aún no existía° cuando se originó la música cautivadora° de las culturas indígenas de los Andes. Los ritmos actuales de la música andina tienen influencias españolas y africanas. Varios tipos de flauta°, entre ellos la quena y la zampoña, caracterizan esta música. En las décadas de los sesenta y los setenta se popularizó un movimiento para preservar la música andina, y hasta° Simon y Garfunkel incorporaron a su repertorio la canción *El cóndor pasa.*

Economía • **Llamas y alpacas**

Perú se conoce por sus llamas, alpacas, guanacos y vicuñas, todos ellos animales mamíferos° parientes del camello. Estos animales todavía tienen una enorme importancia en la economía del país. Dan lana para exportar a otros países y para hacer ropa, mantas°, bolsas y otros artículos artesanales. La llama se usa también para la carga y el transporte.

BOLIVIA

 ¿Qué aprendiste? Responde a las preguntas con una oración completa.

1. ¿Qué productos envía Iquitos a otros lugares? *Iquitos envía goma, nueces, madera, arroz, café y tabaco a otros lugares.*
2. ¿Cuáles son las lenguas oficiales de Perú? *Las lenguas oficiales de Perú son el español, el quechua, el aimara y otras lenguas indígenas.*
3. ¿Por qué es notable la Iglesia de San Francisco en Lima? *Es notable por su arquitectura barroca colonial.*
4. ¿Qué información sobre Machu Picchu no se sabe todavía? *No se sabe ni cómo se construyó ni por qué la abandonaron.*
5. ¿Qué son la quena y la zampoña? *Son tipos de flauta.*
6. ¿Qué hacen los peruanos con la lana de sus llamas y alpacas? *La exportan a otros países y hacen ropa, mantas, bolsas y otros artículos artesanales.*

 Conexión Internet Investiga estos temas en **vhlcentral.com**.

1. Investiga la cultura incaica. ¿Cuáles son algunos de los aspectos interesantes de su cultura?
2. Busca información sobre dos artistas, escritores o músicos peruanos y presenta un breve informe a tu clase.

 Practice more at **vhlcentral.com**.

Variación léxica Point out familiar words that have entered both Spanish and English from the Quechua language. Ex: **el cóndor, la llama, el puma, la vicuña**

antigua *old* a la vez *at the same time* barrio *neighborhood* cimas *summits* se construyó *was built* Sin embargo *However* desniveles *uneven pieces of land* aún no existía *didn't exist yet* cautivadora *captivating* flauta *flute* hasta *even* mamíferos *mammalian* mantas *blankets*

Supersite/DVD: You may want to wrap up this section by playing the **Panorama cultural** video footage for this lesson.

Los verbos reflexivos

acordarse (de) (o:ue)	to remember
acostarse (o:ue)	to go to bed
afeitarse	to shave
bañarse	to bathe; to take a bath
cepillarse el pelo	to brush one's hair
cepillarse los dientes	to brush one's teeth
despedirse (de) (e:i)	to say goodbye (to)
despertarse (e:ie)	to wake up
dormirse (o:ue)	to go to sleep; to fall asleep
ducharse	to shower; to take a shower
enojarse (con)	to get angry (with)
irse	to go away; to leave
lavarse la cara	to wash one's face
lavarse las manos	to wash one's hands
levantarse	to get up
llamarse	to be called; to be named
maquillarse	to put on makeup
peinarse	to comb one's hair
ponerse	to put on
ponerse (+ *adj.*)	to become (+ *adj.*)
preocuparse (por)	to worry (about)
probarse (o:ue)	to try on
quedarse	to stay; to remain
quitarse	to take off
secarse	to dry oneself
sentarse (e:ie)	to sit down
sentirse (e:ie)	to feel
vestirse (e:i)	to get dressed

Supersite: MP3 Audio Files, Testing Program

Palabras de secuencia

antes (de)	before
después	afterwards; then
después (de)	after
durante	during
entonces	then
luego	then
más tarde	later (on)
por último	finally

Palabras afirmativas y negativas

algo	something; anything
alguien	someone; somebody; anyone
alguno/a(s), algún	some; any
jamás	never; not ever
nada	nothing; not anything
nadie	no one; nobody; not anyone
ni... ni	neither... nor
ninguno/a, ningún	no; none; not any
nunca	never; not ever
o... o	either... or
siempre	always
también	also; too
tampoco	neither; not either

En el baño

el baño, el cuarto de baño	bathroom
el champú	shampoo
la crema de afeitar	shaving cream
la ducha	shower
el espejo	mirror
el inodoro	toilet
el jabón	soap
el lavabo	sink
el maquillaje	makeup
la pasta de dientes	toothpaste
la toalla	towel

Verbos similares a gustar

aburrir	to bore
encantar	to like very much; to love (inanimate objects)
faltar	to lack; to need
fascinar	to fascinate; to like very much
importar	to be important to; to matter
interesar	to be interesting to; to interest
molestar	to bother; to annoy
quedar	to be left over; to fit (clothing)

Palabras adicionales

el despertador	alarm clock
las pantuflas	slippers
la rutina diaria	daily routine
por la mañana	in the morning
por la noche	at night
por la tarde	in the afternoon; in the evening

Expresiones útiles	See page 25.

recursos

LM p. 78 | vhlcentral.com Lección 1

Audio: Vocabulary Flashcards

contextos

Lección 1

1 **Las rutinas** Complete each sentence with a word from **Contextos**.

1. Susana se lava el pelo con _____champú_____.

2. La ducha y el lavabo están en el _baño/cuarto de baño_.

3. Manuel se lava las manos con _____jabón_____.

4. Después de lavarse las manos, usa la _____toalla_____.

5. Luis tiene un _____despertador_____ para levantarse temprano.

6. Elena usa el _____espejo/maquillaje_____ para maquillarse.

2 **¿En el baño o en la habitación?** Write **en el baño** or **en la habitación** to indicate where each activity takes place.

1. bañarse _____en el baño_____

2. levantarse _____en la habitación_____

3. ducharse _____en el baño_____

4. lavarse la cara _____en el baño_____

5. acostarse _____en la habitación_____

6. afeitarse _____en el baño_____

7. cepillarse los dientes _____en el baño_____

8. dormirse _____en la habitación_____

3 **Ángel y Lupe** Look at the drawings, and choose the appropriate phrase to describe what Ángel or Lupe are doing. Use complete sentences.

| afeitarse por la mañana | cepillarse los dientes después de comer |
| bañarse por la tarde | ducharse antes de salir |

1. Lupe se cepilla los dientes después de comer.

2. Ángel se afeita por la mañana.

3. Lupe se baña por la tarde. _____

4. Ángel se ducha antes de salir. _____

---

4. La palabra diferente Fill in each blank with the word that doesn't belong in each group.

1. luego, después, más tarde, entonces, antes _____antes_____

2. maquillarse, cepillarse el pelo, despertarse, peinarse, afeitarse _____despertarse_____

3. bailar, despertarse, acostarse, levantarse, dormirse _____bailar_____

4. champú, despertador, jabón, maquillaje, crema de afeitar _____despertador_____

5. entonces, bañarse, lavarse las manos, cepillarse los dientes, ducharse _____entonces_____

6. pelo, vestirse, dientes, manos, cara _____vestirse_____

---

6. La rutina de Silvia Rewrite this paragraph, selecting the correct sequencing words from the parentheses.

(Por la mañana, Durante el día) Silvia se prepara para salir. (Primero, Antes de) se levanta y se ducha. (Después, Antes) de ducharse, se viste. (Entonces, Durante) se maquilla. (Primero, Antes) de salir, come algo y bebe un café. (Durante, Por último) se peina y se pone una chaqueta. (Durante el día, Antes de) Silvia no tiene tiempo (*time*) de volver a su casa. (Más tarde, Antes de) come algo en la cafetería de la universidad y estudia en la biblioteca. (Por la tarde, Por último), Silvia trabaja en el centro comercial. (Por la noche, Primero) llega a su casa y está cansada. (Más tarde, Después de) prepara algo de comer y mira la televisión un rato. (Antes de, Después de) acostarse a dormir siempre estudia un rato.

Por la mañana Silvia se prepara para salir. Primero se levanta y se ducha. Después de ducharse, se viste. Entonces se maquilla. Antes de salir come algo y bebe un café. Por último se peina y se pone una chaqueta. Durante el día Silvia no tiene tiempo de volver a su casa. Más tarde come algo en la cafetería de la universidad y estudia en la biblioteca. Por la tarde, Silvia trabaja en el centro comercial. Por la noche llega a su casa y está cansada. Más tarde prepara algo de comer y mira la televisión un rato. Antes de acostarse a dormir siempre estudia un rato.

Workbook

estructura

1.1 Reflexive verbs

1 **Completar** Complete each sentence with the correct present tense forms of the verb in parentheses.

1. Marcos y Gustavo _____se enojan_____ (enojarse) con Javier.

2. Mariela _____se despide_____ (despedirse) de su amiga en la estación de tren.

3. (yo) _____Me acuesto_____ (acostarse) temprano porque tengo clase por la mañana.

4. Los jugadores _____se secan_____ (secarse) con toallas nuevas.

5. (tú) _____Te preocupas_____ (preocuparse) por tu novio porque siempre pierde las cosas.

6. Usted _____se lava_____ (lavarse) la cara con un jabón especial.

7. Mi mamá _____se pone_____ (ponerse) muy contenta cuando llego temprano a casa.

2 **Lo hiciste** Answer the questions positively, using complete sentences.

1. ¿Te cepillaste los dientes después de comer?
   Sí, me cepillé los dientes después de comer.

2. ¿Se maquilla Julia antes de salir a bailar?
   Sí, Julia se maquilla antes de salir a bailar.

3. ¿Se duchan ustedes antes de nadar en la piscina?
   Sí, nos duchamos antes de nadar en la piscina.

4. ¿Se ponen sombreros los turistas cuando van a la playa?
   Sí, los turistas se ponen sombreros cuando van a la playa.

5. ¿Nos ponemos las pantuflas cuando llegamos a casa?
   Sí, se ponen/nos ponemos las pantuflas cuando llegan/llegamos a casa.

3 **Terminar** Complete each sentence with the correct reflexive verbs. You may use some verbs more than once.

| acordarse | cepillarse | enojarse | maquillarse |
| acostarse | dormirse | levantarse | quedarse |

1. Mi mamá _____se enoja_____ porque no queremos _____levantarnos/acostarnos_____ temprano.

2. La profesora _____se enoja_____ con nosotros cuando no _____nos acordamos_____ de los verbos.

3. Mi hermano _____se cepilla_____ los dientes cuando _____se levanta_____.

4. Mis amigas y yo _____nos quedamos_____ estudiando en la biblioteca por la noche y por la mañana _____me levanto_____ muy cansada.

5. Muchas noches _____me duermo/me quedo_____ delante del televisor, porque no quiero _____acostarme_____.

4 **Escoger** Choose the correct verb from the parentheses, then fill in the blank with its correct form.

1. (lavar/lavarse)

   Josefina _____se lava_____ las manos en el lavabo.

   Josefina _____lava_____ la ropa en casa de su madre.

2. (peinar/peinarse)

   (yo) _____Peino_____ a mi hermana todas las mañanas.

   (yo) _____Me peino_____ en el baño, delante del espejo.

3. (poner/ponerse)

   (nosotros) _____Nos ponemos_____ nerviosos antes de un examen.

   (nosotros) _____Ponemos_____ la toalla al lado de la ducha.

4. (levantar/levantarse)

   Los estudiantes _____se levantan_____ muy temprano.

   Los estudiantes _____levantan_____ la mano y hacen preguntas.

5 **El incidente** Complete the paragraph with reflexive verbs from the word bank. Use each verb only once.

acordarse	irse	maquillarse	quedarse
acostarse	lavarse	ponerse	secarse
despertarse	levantarse	preocuparse	sentarse
enojarse	llamarse	probarse	vestirse

Luis (1) _se levanta/se despierta_ todos los días a las seis de la mañana. Luego entra en la

ducha y (2) _____se lava_____ el pelo con champú. Cuando sale de la ducha, usa la crema de

afeitar para (3) _____afeitarse_____ delante del espejo. Come algo con su familia y él y sus

hermanos (4) _____se quedan_____ hablando un rato.

Cuando sale tarde, Luis (5) _____se preocupa_____ porque no quiere llegar tarde a la clase de

español. Los estudiantes (6) _____se ponen_____ nerviosos porque a veces (*sometimes*) tienen

pruebas sorpresa en la clase.

Ayer por la mañana, Luis (7) _____se enojó_____ con su hermana Marina porque ella

(8) _se levantó/se despertó_ tarde y pasó mucho tiempo en el cuarto de baño con la puerta cerrada.

—¿Cuándo sales, Marina?— le preguntó Luis.

—¡Tengo que (9) _____maquillarme_____ porque voy a salir con mi novio y quiero estar bonita!—,

dijo Marina.

—¡Tengo que (10) _____irme_____ ya, Marina! ¿Cuándo terminas?

—Ahora salgo, Luis. Tengo que (11) _____vestirme_____. Me voy a poner mi vestido favorito.

—Tienes que (12) _____acordarte_____ de que viven muchas personas en esta casa, Marina.

1.2 Indefinite and negative words

1 **Alguno o ninguno** Complete the sentences with indefinite and negative words from the word bank.

alguien	algunas	ninguna
alguna	ningún	tampoco

1. No tengo ganas de ir a _____ningún_____ lugar hoy.

2. ¿Tienes _____algunas_____ ideas para mejorar (*to improve*) la economía?

3. ¿Viene _____alguien_____ a la fiesta de mañana?

4. No voy a _____ningún_____ estadio nunca.

5. ¿Te gusta _____alguna_____ de estas corbatas?

6. Jorge, tú no eres el único. Yo _____tampoco_____ puedo ir de vacaciones.

2 **Estoy de mal humor** Your classmate Jaime is in a terrible mood. Complete his complaints with negative words.

1. No me gustan estas gafas. _____No_____ quiero comprar _____ninguna_____ de ellas.

2. Estoy muy cansado. _____No_____ quiero ir a _____ningún_____ restaurante.

3. No tengo hambre. _____No_____ quiero comer _____nada_____.

4. A mí no me gusta la playa. _____No_____ quiero ir a la playa _____nunca_____.

5. Soy muy tímido. _____No_____ hablo con _____nadie_____ _____nunca_____.

6. No me gusta el color rojo, _____ni_____ el color rosado _____tampoco_____.

3 **¡Amalia!** Your friend Amalia is chronically mistaken. Change her statements as necessary to correct her; each statement should be negative.

> **modelo**
> Buscaste algunos vestidos en la tienda.
> **No busqué ningún vestido en la tienda.**

1. Las dependientas venden algunas blusas.
   Las dependientas no venden ninguna blusa/ninguna.

2. Alguien va de compras al centro comercial.
   Nadie va de compras al centro comercial.

3. Siempre me cepillo los dientes antes de salir.
   Nunca te cepillas los dientes antes de salir.

4. Te voy a traer algún programa de computadora.
   No me vas a traer ningún programa de la computadora/ninguno.

5. Mi hermano prepara algo de comer.
   Tu hermano no prepara nada de comer.

6. Quiero tomar algo en el café de la librería.
   No quieres tomar nada en el café de la librería.

4 **No, no es cierto** Now your friend Amalia realizes that she's usually wrong and is asking you for the correct information. Answer her questions negatively.

> **modelo**
>
> ¿Comes siempre en casa?
> No, nunca como en casa./No, no como en casa nunca.

1. ¿Tienes alguna falda?

   No, no tengo ninguna falda/no tengo ninguna.

2. ¿Sales siempre los fines de semana?

   No, nunca salgo los fines de semana/no salgo nunca los fines de semana.

3. ¿Quieres comer algo ahora?

   No, no quiero comer nada (ahora).

4. ¿Le prestaste algunos discos de jazz a César?

   No, no le presté ningún disco de jazz (a César)/no le presté ninguno (a César).

5. ¿Podemos ir a la playa o nadar en la piscina?

   No, no podemos ni ir a la playa ni nadar en la piscina.

6. ¿Encontraste algún cinturón barato en la tienda?

   No, no encontré ningún cinturón barato en la tienda/no encontré ninguno.

7. ¿Buscaron ustedes a alguien en la playa?

   No, no buscamos a nadie (en la playa).

8. ¿Te gusta alguno de estos trajes?

   No, no me gusta ninguno de estos trajes/no me gusta ninguno.

5 **Lo opuesto** Rodrigo's good reading habits have changed since this description was written. Rewrite the paragraph, changing the positive words to negative ones.

Rodrigo siempre está leyendo algún libro. También lee el periódico. Siempre lee algo. Leyó algunos libros de Vargas Llosa el año pasado. También leyó algunas novelas de Gabriel García Márquez. Siempre quiere leer o libros de misterio o novelas fantásticas.

Rodrigo nunca está leyendo ningún libro. Tampoco lee el periódico. Nunca lee nada.

No leyó ningún libro de Vargas Llosa el año pasado. Tampoco leyó ninguna novela de

Gabriel García Márquez. Nunca quiere leer ni libros de misterio ni novelas fantásticas.

_____

_____

_____

_____

_____

1.3 Preterite of **ser** and **ir**

1 **¿Ser o ir?** Complete the sentences with the preterite of **ser** or **ir**. Then write the infinitive form of the verb you used.

1. Ayer María y Javier _____fueron_____ a la playa con sus amigos. _____ir_____.

2. La película del sábado por la tarde _____fue_____ muy bonita. _____ser_____.

3. El fin de semana pasado (nosotros) _____fuimos_____ al centro comercial. _____ir_____.

4. La abuela y la tía de Maricarmen _____fueron_____ doctoras. _____ser_____.

5. (nosotros) _____Fuimos_____ muy simpáticos con la familia de Claribel. _____ser_____.

6. Manuel _____fue_____ a la universidad en septiembre. _____ir_____.

7. Los vendedores _____fueron_____ al almacén muy temprano. _____ir_____.

8. Lima _____fue_____ la primera parada (*stop*) de nuestro viaje. _____ser_____.

9. (yo) _____Fui_____ a buscarte a la cafetería, pero no te encontré. _____ir_____.

10. Mi compañera de cuarto _____Fue_____ a la tienda a comprar champú. _____ir_____.

2 **Viaje a Perú** Complete the paragraph with the preterite of **ser** and **ir**. Then fill in the chart with the infinitive form of the verbs you used.

El mes pasado mi amiga Clara y yo (1) _____fuimos_____ de vacaciones a Perú. El vuelo (*flight*) (2) _____fue_____ un miércoles por la mañana y (3) _____fue_____ cómodo. Primero Clara y yo (4) _____fuimos_____ a Lima y (5) _____fuimos_____ a comer a un restaurante de comida peruana. La comida (6) _____fue_____ muy buena. Luego (7) _____fuimos_____ al hotel y nos (8) _____fuimos_____ a dormir. El jueves (9) _____fue_____ un día nublado. Nos (10) _____fuimos_____ a Cuzco, y el viaje en autobús (11) _____fue_____ largo. Yo (12) _____fui_____ la primera en despertarse y ver la ciudad de Cuzco. Aquella mañana, el paisaje (13) _____fue_____ impresionante. Luego Clara y yo (14) _____fuimos_____ de excursión a Machu Picchu. El cuarto día nos levantamos muy temprano y (15) _____fuimos_____ a la ciudad inca. El amanecer sobre Machu Picchu (16) _____fue_____ hermoso. La excursión (17) _____fue_____ una experiencia inolvidable (*unforgettable*). ¿(18) _____Fuiste_____ tú a Perú el año pasado?

1. _____ir_____	7. _____ir_____	13. _____ser_____
2. _____ser_____	8. _____ir_____	14. _____ir_____
3. _____ser_____	9. _____ser_____	15. _____ir_____
4. _____ir_____	10. _____ir_____	16. _____ser_____
5. _____ir_____	11. _____ser_____	17. _____ser_____
6. _____ser_____	12. _____ser_____	18. _____ir_____

1.4 Verbs like **gustar**

1 **La fotonovela** Rewrite each sentence, choosing the correct form of the verb in parentheses.

1. Maru, te (quedan, queda) bien las faldas y los vestidos.

   Maru, te quedan bien las faldas y los vestidos.

2. A Jimena y a Juan Carlos no les (molesta, molestan) la lluvia.

   A Jimena y a Juan Carlos no les molesta la lluvia.

3. A los chicos no les (importa, importan) ir de compras.

   A los chicos no les importa ir de compras.

4. A don Diego y a Felipe les (aburre, aburren) probarse ropa en las tiendas.

   A don Diego y a Felipe les aburre probarse ropa en las tiendas.

5. A Jimena le (fascina, fascinan) las tiendas y los almacenes.

   A Jimena le fascinan las tiendas y los almacenes.

6. A Felipe le (falta, faltan) dos años para terminar la carrera (*degree*).

   A Felipe le faltan dos años para terminar la carrera.

7. A los chicos les (encanta, encantan) pescar y nadar en el mar.

   A los chicos les encanta pescar y nadar en el mar.

8. A Miguel le (interesan, interesa) el arte.

   A Miguel le interesa el arte.

2 **Nos gusta el fútbol** Complete the paragraph with the correct forms of the verbs in parentheses.

A mi familia le (1) _____ fascina _____ (fascinar) el fútbol. A mis hermanas les

(2) _____ encantan _____ (encantar) los jugadores porque son muy guapos. También les

(3) _____ gusta _____ (gustar) la emoción (*excitement*) de los partidos. A mi papá le

(4) _____ interesan _____ (interesar) mucho los partidos y, cuando puede, los ve por Internet.

A mi mamá le (5) _____ molesta _____ (molestar) nuestra afición porque no hacemos las

tareas de la casa cuando hay partidos. A ella generalmente le (6) _____ aburren _____ (aburrir)

los partidos. Pero cuando al equipo argentino le (7) _____ falta _____ (faltar) un gol para

ganar, le (8) _____ encantan _____ (encantar) los minutos finales del partido.

3 **El viaje** You and your friend are packing and planning your upcoming vacation to the Caribbean. Rewrite her sentences, substituting the subject with the one in parentheses. Make all the necessary changes.

> **modelo**
>
> A mis amigos les fascinan los partidos de béisbol. (la comida peruana)
> A mis amigos les fascina la comida peruana.

1. Te quedan bien los vestidos largos. (la blusa cara)
   Te queda bien la blusa cara.

2. Les molesta la música estadounidense. (las canciones populares)
   Les molestan las canciones populares.

3. ¿No te interesa aprender a bailar salsa? (nadar)
   ¿No te interesa nadar/aprender a nadar?

4. Les encantan las tiendas. (el centro comercial)
   Les encanta el centro comercial.

5. Nos falta practicar el español. (unas semanas de clase)
   Nos faltan unas semanas de clase.

6. No les importa esperar un rato. (buscar unos libros nuestros)
   No les importa buscar unos libros nuestros.

4 **¿Qué piensan?** Complete the sentences with the correct pronouns and forms of the verbs in parentheses.

1. A mí ___me encantan___ (encantar) las películas de misterio.

2. A Gregorio ___le molestan___ (molestar) mucho la nieve y el frío.

3. A ustedes ___les falta___ (faltar) un libro de esa colección.

4. ¿ ___Te quedan___ (quedar) bien los sombreros a ti?

5. A ella no ___le importan___ (importar) las apariencias (*appearances*).

6. A mí los deportes por televisión ___me aburren___ (aburrir) mucho.

5 **Mi rutina diaria** Answer these questions using verbs like **gustar** in complete sentences. Answers will vary.

1. ¿Te molesta levantarte temprano durante la semana?

   _____

2. ¿Qué te interesa hacer por las mañanas?

   _____

3. ¿Te importa despertarte temprano los fines de semana?

   _____

4. ¿Qué te encanta hacer los domingos?

   _____

Síntesis

Interview a friend or relative about an interesting vacation he or she took. Then gather the answers into a report. Answer the following questions:

• What did he or she like or love about the vacation? What interested him or her?
• Where did he or she stay, what were the accommodations like, and what was his or her daily routine like during the trip?
• Where did he or she go, what were the tours like, what were the tour guides like, and what were his or her travelling companions like?
• What bothered or angered him or her? What bored him or her during the vacation?

Be sure to address both the negative and positive aspects of the vacation. Answers will vary.

_____

_____

_____

_____

_____

_____

_____

_____

_____

_____

_____

_____

_____

_____

_____

_____

_____

_____

_____

_____

_____

_____

panorama

Perú

1   **Datos de Perú** Complete the sentences with the correct words.

1. _____Lima_____ es la capital de Perú y _____Arequipa_____ es la segunda ciudad más poblada.

2. _____Iquitos_____ es un puerto muy importante en el río Amazonas.

3. El barrio bohemio de la ciudad de Lima se llama _____Barranco_____.

4. Hiram Bingham descubrió las ruinas de _____Machu Picchu_____ en los Andes.

5. Las llamas, alpacas, guanacos y vicuñas son parientes del _____camello_____.

6. Las Líneas de _____Nazca_____ son uno de los grandes misterios de la humanidad.

2   **Perú** Fill in the blanks with the names and places described. Then use the word in the vertical box to answer the final question.

1. barrio bohemio de Lima
2. animales que se usan para carga y transporte
3. en Perú se habla este idioma
4. capital de Perú
5. montañas de Perú
6. dirección de Machu Picchu desde Cuzco

7. puerto en el río Amazonas
8. animales que dan lana
9. esta civilización peruana dibujó líneas
10. profesión de César Vallejo

¿Por dónde se llega caminando a Machu Picchu?
Se llega por el _____Camino Inca_____.

1	B	a	r	r	a	n	c	o

2	l	l	a	m	a	s

3	a	i	m	a	r	a

4	L	i	m	a

5	A	n	d	e	s

6	n	o	r	o	e	s	t	e

7	I	q	u	i	t	o	s

8	g	u	a	n	a	c	o	s

9	n	a	z	c	a

10	p	o	e	t	a

3   **Ciudades peruanas** Fill in the blanks with the names of the appropriate cities in Peru.

1. ciudad al sureste de Cuzco _____Arequipa_____

2. se envían productos por el Amazonas _____Iquitos_____

3. Museo Oro del Perú _____Lima_____

4. está a 80 km de Machu Picchu _____Cuzco_____

5. ciudad antigua del Imperio inca _____Machu Picchu_____

4 **¿Cierto o falso?** Indicate whether each statement is **cierto** or **falso**. Correct the false statements.

1. Trujillo es un destino popular para los ecoturistas que visitan la selva.
   Falso. Iquitos es un destino popular para los ecoturistas que visitan la selva.

2. Mario Vargas Llosa es un novelista peruano famoso.
   Cierto.

3. La Iglesia de San Francisco es notable por la influencia de la arquitectura árabe.
   Falso. La Iglesia de San Francisco es notable por la influencia de la arquitectura barroca colonial.

4. Las ruinas de Machu Picchu están en la cordillera de los Andes.
   Cierto.

5. Las llamas se usan para la carga y el transporte en Perú.
   Cierto.

6. La civilización inca hizo dibujos que sólo son descifrables desde el aire.
   Falso. La civilización nazca hizo dibujos que sólo son descifrables desde el aire.

5 **El mapa de Perú** Label the map of Peru.

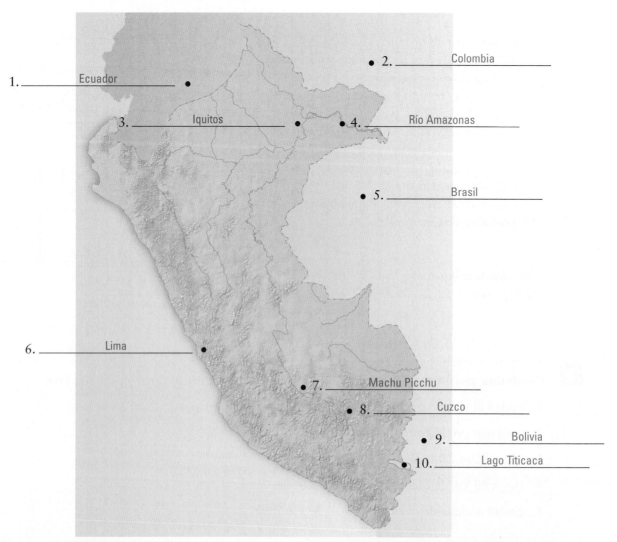

1. ____ Ecuador ____

2. ____ Colombia

3. ____ Iquitos ____

4. ____ Río Amazonas

5. ____ Brasil

6. ____ Lima ____

7. ____ Machu Picchu

8. ____ Cuzco

9. ____ Bolivia

10. ____ Lago Titicaca

¡Necesito arreglarme!

Antes de ver el video

1   **En el baño** In this episode, Marissa, Felipe, and Jimena want to get ready at the same time. What do you think they might say?   Answers will vary.

_____

_____

_____

_____

_____

_____

_____

Mientras ves el video

2   **¿Marissa o Felipe?** Watch **¡Necesito arreglarme!** and put a check mark in a column to show whether the plans are Marissa's or Felipe's.

Actividad	Marissa	Felipe
1. ir al cine	✗	
2. afeitarse		✗
3. ir al café a molestar a su amigo	✗	
4. arreglarse el pelo	✗	
5. ir al café con Juan Carlos		✗

3   **Ordenar** Number the following events from one to six, in the order they occurred.

  6   a. Jimena termina de maquillarse.

  3   b. Todos quieren usar el espejo al mismo tiempo.

  1   c. Marissa quiere entrar al baño y la puerta está cerrada.

  5   d. Las chicas comparten el espejo.

  4   e. Marissa busca una toalla.

  2   f. Felipe entra al baño.

4   **Completar** Fill in the blanks.

1. **FELIPE**   Cada vez que quiero usar el _____ baño _____, una de ustedes está aquí.

2. **JIMENA**   Me estoy _____ lavando _____ la cara.

3. **MARISSA**   ¡_____ Nadie _____ debe estudiar los viernes!

4. **JIMENA**   ¿Por qué no te _____ afeitaste _____ por la mañana?

5. **FELIPE**   Siempre hay _____ música _____ en vivo.

Después de ver el video

5 **Preguntas** Answer these questions in Spanish.

1. ¿Qué está haciendo Jimena cuando Marissa quiere entrar al baño?
   Jimena se está lavando la cara.

2. ¿Por qué Jimena quiere maquillarse primero?
   Jimena quiere maquillarse primero porque va a encontrarse con su amiga Elena en una hora.

3. ¿Por qué se quiere afeitar Felipe?
   Felipe se quiere afeitar porque va a ir con Juan Carlos a un café.

4. ¿Cómo es el café adonde van a ir Felipe y Juan Carlos?
   Es muy divertido. Siempre hay música en vivo y muchas chicas.

5. ¿Por qué Marissa quiere arreglarse?
   Marissa quiere arreglarse porque va a ir al cine con unas amigas.

6. ¿Cuándo fue la última vez que Jimena vio a Juan Carlos?
   La última vez que Jimena vio a Juan Carlos fue cuando fueron a Mérida.

6 **Preguntas personales** Answer these questions in Spanish. Answers will vary.

1. ¿A qué hora te levantas durante la semana? ¿Y los fines de semana?

2. ¿Te gusta más bañarte o ducharte? ¿Por qué?

3. ¿Cuántas veces por día (*How many times a day*) te cepillas los dientes?

4. ¿Te lavas el pelo todos los días (*every day*)? ¿Por qué?

5. ¿Cómo cambia tu rutina los días que vas a la universidad y los días que sales con tus amigos?

7 **Escribir** Describe in Spanish what happened, from the point of view of Jimena, Marissa, or Felipe.
Answers will vary.

Panorama: Perú

Antes de ver el video

1 **Más vocabulario** Look over these useful words and expressions before you watch the video.

Vocabulario útil		
canoa *canoe*	**exuberante naturaleza**	**ruta** *route, path*
dunas *sand dunes*	*lush countryside*	**tabla** *board*

2 **Preferencias** In this video you are going to learn about unusual sports. In preparation for watching the video, answer these questions about your interest in sports. Answers will vary.

1. ¿Qué deportes practicas?

_____

2. ¿Dónde los practicas?

_____

3. ¿Qué deportes te gusta ver en televisión?

_____

Mientras ves el video

3 **Fotos** Describe the video stills. Write at least three sentences in Spanish for each still. Answers will vary.

_____
_____
_____
_____
_____
_____

_____
_____
_____
_____
_____

Después de ver el video

4 **¿Cierto o falso?** Indicate whether each statement is **cierto** or **falso**. Correct the false statements.

1. Pachacamac es el destino favorito para los que pasean en bicicletas de montaña.

   Cierto.

2. El *sandboard* es un deporte antiguo en Perú.

   Falso. El *sandboard* es un deporte nuevo en Perú.

3. El *sandboard* se practica en Ocucaje porque en este lugar hay muchos parques.

   Falso. El *sandboard* se practica en Ocucaje porque allí hay grandes dunas.

4. El Camino Inca termina en Machu Picchu.

   Cierto.

5. El Camino Inca se puede completar en dos horas.

   Falso. El Camino Inca se puede completar en tres o cuatro días.

6. La pesca en pequeñas canoas es un deporte tradicional.

   Cierto.

5 **Completar** Complete the following sentences with words from the box.

aventura	kilómetros	pesca
excursión	llamas	restaurante
exuberante	parque	tradicional

1. En Perú se practican muchos deportes de _____aventura_____.

2. Pachacamac está a 31 _____kilómetros_____ de Lima.

3. La naturaleza en Santa Cruz es muy _____exuberante_____.

4. En Perú, uno de los deportes más antiguos es la _____pesca_____ en pequeñas canoas.

5. Caminar con _____llamas_____ es uno de los deportes tradicionales en Perú.

6. Santa Cruz es un sitio ideal para ir de _____excursión_____ por las bolsas.

6 **Escribir** Imagine that you just completed the **Camino Inca** in the company of a nice llama. In Spanish, write a short letter to a friend telling him or her about the things you did and saw.

Answers will vary.

Tapas para todos los días

Antes de ver el video

1 **Más vocabulario** Look over these useful words and expressions before you watch the video.

Vocabulario útil		
los caracoles *snails*	informal *casual, informal*	preparaban unos platillos
Cataluña *Catalonia (an*	País Vasco *Basque Country*	*used to prepare little dishes*
autonomous community	*(autonomous community*	las tortillas de patata *Spanish*
in Spain)	*in Spain)*	*potato omelets*
contar los palillos *counting*	el pan *bread*	el trabajo *job; work*
the toothpicks	las porciones de comida	único/a *unique*
la escalivada *grilled vegetables*	*food portions*	

2 **Completar** Complete this paragraph about **tapas**.

Las tapas son pequeñas (1) ___porciones de comida___ que se sirven en bares y restaurantes de España.

Hay diferentes tipos de tapas: los (2) ___caracoles___ y las (3) ___tortillas/escalivadas___ son algunos

ejemplos. En algunos bares, los camareros (*waiters*) traen la comida, pero en lugares más (*more*)

(4) ___informales___ el cliente toma las tapas en la barra (*bar*). Es muy común salir solo o con

amigos a tomar tapas después del trabajo. Sin duda, ¡salir de tapas en España es una experiencia

fantástica y (5) ___única___!

3 **¡En español!** Look at the video still. Imagine what Mari Carmen will say about **tapas** in
Barcelona, and write a two- or three-sentence introduction to this episode. Answers will vary.

Mari Carmen, España

¡Hola! Hoy estamos en Barcelona. Esta bonita ciudad... _____

_____

_____

_____

_____

Mientras ves el video

4 **Montaditos** Indicate whether these statements about **montaditos** are **cierto** or **falso**.

1. Los clientes cuentan los palillos para saber cuánto pagar. ___cierto___
2. Los montaditos son informales. ___cierto___
3. Los montaditos son caros. ___falso___
4. Los montaditos se preparan siempre con pan. ___cierto___
5. Hay montaditos en bares al aire libre solamente. ___falso___

Video Manual

5 **Completar** (03:13–03:29) Watch these people talk about **tapas** and complete this conversation.

MARI CARMEN ¿Cuándo sueles venir a (1) _____tomar_____ tapas?

HOMBRE Generalmente (2) _____después_____ del trabajo. Cuando al salir de trabajar (3) _____tengo_____ hambre, vengo (4) _____aquí_____.

MARI CARMEN ¿Y vienes solo, vienes con amigos o da igual (*doesn't it matter*)?

HOMBRE Da igual. Si alguien (5) _____viene_____ conmigo, mejor; y si no, vengo solo.

Después de ver el video

6 **¿Cierto o falso?** Indicate whether these statements are **cierto** or **falso**.

1. Mari Carmen pasea en motocicleta por el centro de Barcelona. _____cierto_____

2. Mari Carmen entrevista a personas sobre sus hábitos después de ir al trabajo. _____cierto_____

3. Una versión sobre el origen de las tapas dice que un rey (*king*) necesitaba (*needed*) comer pocas veces al día. _____falso_____

4. Los restaurantes elegantes y caros sirven montaditos. _____falso_____

5. La tradición del montadito proviene (*comes from*) del País Vasco. _____cierto_____

6. Los pinchos son sólo platos fríos. _____falso_____

7 **Un día en la vida de...** Select one of these people and imagine a typical workday. Consider his or her daily routine as well as the time he or she gets up, goes to work, spends with friends, goes back home and goes to sleep. Use the words provided. Answers will vary.

| más tarde | se acuesta | se levanta |
| por la noche | se cepilla los dientes | va al trabajo |

_____

_____

_____

_____

_____

_____

contextos

Lección 1

1 **Describir** For each drawing, you will hear two statements. Choose the one that corresponds to the drawing.

1. a. (b.)   2. a. (b.)

11:05 p.m.

3. (a.)   b.   4. (a.)   b.

2 **Preguntas** Clara is going to baby-sit your nephew. Answer her questions about your nephew's daily routine using the cues in your lab manual. Repeat the correct response after the speaker.

> **modelo**
> *You hear:* ¿A qué hora va a la escuela?
> *You see:* 8:30 a.m.
> *You say:* Va a la escuela a las ocho y media de la mañana.

1. 7:00 a. m.
2. se lava la cara
3. por la noche

4. champú para niños
5. 9:00 p. m.
6. después de comer

3 **Entrevista** Listen to this interview. Then read the statements in your lab manual and decide whether they are **cierto** or **falso**.

	Cierto	Falso
1. Sergio Santos es jugador de fútbol.	○	☑
2. Sergio se levanta a las 5:00 a. m.	○	☑
3. Sergio se ducha por la mañana y por la noche.	☑	○
4. Sergio se acuesta a las 11:00 p. m.	☑	○

Lab Manual

pronunciación

The consonant **r**

In Spanish, **r** has a strong trilled sound at the beginning of a word. No English words have a trill, but English speakers often produce a trill when they imitate the sound of a motor.

| ropa | rutina | rico | **R**amón |

In any other position, **r** has a weak sound similar to the English *tt* in *better* or the English *dd* in *ladder*. In contrast to English, the tongue touches the roof of the mouth behind the teeth.

| gustar | durante | primero | crema |

The letter combination **rr**, which only appears between vowels, always has a strong trilled sound.

| pizarra | corro | marrón | aburrido |

Between vowels, the difference between the strong trilled **rr** and the weak **r** is very important, as a mispronunciation could lead to confusion between two different words.

| caro | carro | pero | perro |

1 **Práctica** Repeat each word after the speaker, to practice the **r** and the **rr**.

1. Perú	5. comprar	9. Arequipa
2. Rosa	6. favor	10. tarde
3. borrador	7. rubio	11. cerrar
4. madre	8. reloj	12. despertador

2 **Oraciones** When you hear the number, read the corresponding sentence aloud, focusing on the **r** and **rr** sounds. Then listen to the speaker and repeat the sentence.

1. Ramón Robles Ruiz es programador. Su esposa Rosaura es artista.
2. A Rosaura Robles le encanta regatear en el mercado.
3. Ramón nunca regatea… le aburre regatear.
4. Rosaura siempre compra cosas baratas.
5. Ramón no es rico, pero prefiere comprar cosas muy caras.
6. ¡El martes Ramón compró un carro nuevo!

3 **Refranes** Repeat each saying after the speaker to practice the **r** and the **rr**.

1. Perro que ladra no muerde.
2. No se ganó Zamora en una hora.

4 **Dictado** You will hear seven sentences. Each will be said twice. Listen carefully and write what you hear.

1. Ramiro y Roberta Torres son peruanos.
2. Ramiro es pelirrojo, gordo y muy trabajador.
3. Hoy él quiere jugar al golf y descansar, pero Roberta prefiere ir de compras.
4. Hay grandes rebajas y ella necesita un regalo para Ramiro.
5. ¿Debe comprarle una cartera marrón o un suéter rojo?
6. Por la tarde, Ramiro abre su regalo.
7. Es ropa interior.

estructura

1.1 Reflexive verbs

1 **Describir** For each drawing, you will hear two statements. Choose the one that corresponds to the drawing.

1. (a.)　　　　b.　　　　　　2. a.　　　　(b.)

¡A+!

3. (a.)　　　　b.　　　　　　4. a.　　　　(b.)

2 **Preguntas** Answer each question you hear in the affirmative. Repeat the correct response after the speaker. (*7 items*)

> **modelo**
> ¿Se levantó temprano Rosa?
> Sí, Rosa se levantó temprano.

3 **¡Esto fue el colmo! (*The last straw!*)** Listen as Julia describes what happened in her dorm yesterday. Then choose the correct ending for each statement in your lab manual.

1. Julia se ducha en cinco minutos porque...

   a. siempre se levanta tarde. 　　　　(b.) las chicas de su piso comparten un cuarto de baño.

2. Ayer la chica nueva...

   (a.) se quedó dos horas en el baño. 　　　　b. se preocupó por Julia.

3. Cuando salió, la chica nueva...

   a. se enojó mucho. 　　　　(b.) se sintió (*felt*) avergonzada.

1.2 Indefinite and negative words

1 **¿Lógico o ilógico?** You will hear some questions and the responses. Decide if they are **lógico** or **ilógico**.

	Lógico	Ilógico		Lógico	Ilógico
1.	O	⊘	5.	⊘	O
2.	⊘	O	6.	O	⊘
3.	⊘	O	7.	⊘	O
4.	O	⊘	8.	⊘	O

2 **¿Pero o sino?** You will hear some sentences with a beep in place of a word. Decide if **pero** or **sino** should complete each sentence and circle it.

> **modelo**
>
> *You hear:* Ellos no viven en Lima (*beep*) en Arequipa.
> *You circle:* **sino** *because the sentence is* **Ellos no viven en Lima sino en Arequipa.**

1.	pero	(sino)	5.	(pero)	sino
2.	(pero)	sino	6.	pero	(sino)
3.	pero	(sino)	7.	(pero)	sino
4.	pero	(sino)	8.	(pero)	sino

3 **Transformar** Change each sentence you hear to say the opposite is true. Repeat the correct answer after the speaker. (*6 items*)

> **modelo**
>
> Nadie se ducha ahora.
> Alguien se ducha ahora.

4 **Preguntas** Answer each question you hear in the negative. Repeat the correct response after the speaker. (*6 items*)

> **modelo**
>
> ¿Qué estás haciendo?
> No estoy haciendo nada.

5 **Entre amigos** Listen to this conversation between Felipe and Mercedes. Then decide whether the statements in your lab manual are **cierto** or **falso**.

	Cierto	Falso
1. No hay nadie en la residencia.	⊘	O
2. Mercedes quiere ir al Centro Estudiantil.	⊘	O
3. Felipe tiene un amigo peruano.	O	⊘
4. Mercedes no visitó ni Machu Picchu ni Cuzco.	⊘	O
5. Felipe nunca visitó Perú.	⊘	O

1.3 Preterite of **ser** and **ir**

1 **Escoger** Listen to each sentence and indicate whether the verb is a form of **ser** or **ir**.

1. ser (ir)
2. (ser) ir
3. ser (ir)
4. ser (ir)
5. ser (ir)
6. (ser) ir
7. (ser) ir
8. ser (ir)

2 **Cambiar** Change each sentence from the present to the preterite. Repeat the correct answer after the speaker. (8 items)

> **modelo**
> Ustedes van en avión.
> *Ustedes fueron en avión.*

3 **Preguntas** Answer each question you hear using the cue in your lab manual. Repeat the correct response after the speaker.

> **modelo**
> *You hear:* ¿Quién fue tu profesor de química?
> *You see:* el señor Ortega
> *You say:* El señor Ortega fue mi profesor de química.

1. al mercado al aire libre
2. muy buenas
3. no
4. fabulosa
5. al parque
6. difícil

4 **¿Qué hicieron (*did they do*) anoche?** Listen to this telephone conversation and answer the questions in your lab manual.

1. ¿Adónde fue Carlos anoche?
   Carlos fue al estadio.

2. ¿Cómo fue el partido? ¿Por qué?
   El partido fue estupendo porque su equipo favorito ganó.

3. ¿Adónde fueron Katarina y Esteban anoche?
   Katarina y Esteban fueron al cine.

4. Y Esteban, ¿qué hizo (*did he do*) allí?
   Esteban se durmió durante la película.

1.4 Verbs like **gustar**

1 **Escoger** Listen to each question and choose the most logical response.

1. (a.) Sí, me gusta. b. Sí, te gusta.
2. (a.) No, no le interesa. b. No, no le interesan.
3. (a.) Sí, les molestan mucho. b. No, no les molesta mucho.
4. (a.) No, no nos importa. b. No, no les importa.
5. a. Sí, le falta. (b.) Sí, me falta.
6. a. Sí, les fascina. (b.) No, no les fascinan.

2 **Cambiar** Form a new sentence using the cue you hear. Repeat the correct answer after the speaker. (*6 items*)

> *modelo*
> A ellos les interesan las ciencias. (a Ricardo)
> A Ricardo le interesan las ciencias.

3 **Preguntas** Answer each question you hear using the cue in your lab manual. Repeat the correct response after the speaker.

> *modelo*
> *You hear:* ¿Qué te encanta hacer?
> *You see:* patinar en línea
> *You say:* Me encanta patinar en línea.

1. la familia y los amigos 4. $2,00 7. no / nada
2. sí 5. el baloncesto y el béisbol 8. sí
3. las computadoras 6. no

4 **Preferencias** Listen to this conversation. Then fill in the chart with Eduardo's preferences and answer the question in your lab manual.

Le gusta	No le gusta
nadar (la natación)	el tenis
ir de excursión al campo	el sol
el cine	ir de compras

¿Qué van a hacer los chicos esta tarde? Los chicos van a quedarse/se van a quedar en casa esta tarde.

vocabulario

You will now hear the vocabulary found in your textbook on the last page of this lesson. Listen and repeat each Spanish word or phrase after the speaker.

Additional Vocabulary

Additional Vocabulary

Notes

Notes

La comida

2

A PRIMERA VISTA
• ¿Dónde está ella?
• ¿Qué hace?
• ¿Es parte de su rutina diaria?
• ¿Qué colores hay en la foto?

Más práctica
Workbook pages 117–128
Video Manual pages 129–134
Lab Manual pages 135–140

La comida

Más vocabulario

el/la camarero/a	waiter/waitress
la comida	food; meal
la cuenta	bill
el/la dueño/a	owner; landlord
los entremeses	hors d'oeuvres; appetizers
el menú	menu
el plato (principal)	(main) dish
la propina	tip
la sección de (no) fumar	(non) smoking section
el agua (mineral)	(mineral) water
la bebida	drink
la cerveza	beer
la leche	milk
el refresco	soft drink; soda
el ajo	garlic
las arvejas	peas
los cereales	cereal; grains
los frijoles	beans
el melocotón	peach
el pollo (asado)	(roast) chicken
el queso	cheese
el sándwich	sandwich
el yogur	yogurt
el aceite	oil
la margarina	margarine
la mayonesa	mayonnaise
el vinagre	vinegar
delicioso/a	delicious
sabroso/a	tasty; delicious
saber	to taste; to know
saber a	to taste like

Variación léxica

camarones ←→ gambas (*Esp.*)

camarero ←→ mesero (*Amér. L.*), mesonero (*Ven.*), mozo (*Arg., Chile, Urug., Perú*)

refresco ←→ gaseosa (*Amér. C., Amér. S.*)

Las frutas

la pera
la banana
las uvas
la naranja
el limón

Las verduras

el maíz
la cebolla
la lechuga
el champiñón
la zanahoria
el tomate

recursos

WB pp. 117–118

LM p. 135

vhlcentral.com Lección 2

Supersite: MP3 Audio Files and Scripts, Digital Image Bank, Activity Pack, Testing Program (Quizzes), **Vocabulario adicional**

Heritage Speakers Ask heritage speakers to share regional variations in food-related vocabulary. Ex: **el guisante, el banano, el cambur, el hongo, la habichuela, la patata.**

Práctica

1 2 Supersite: MP3 Audio Files, Scripts

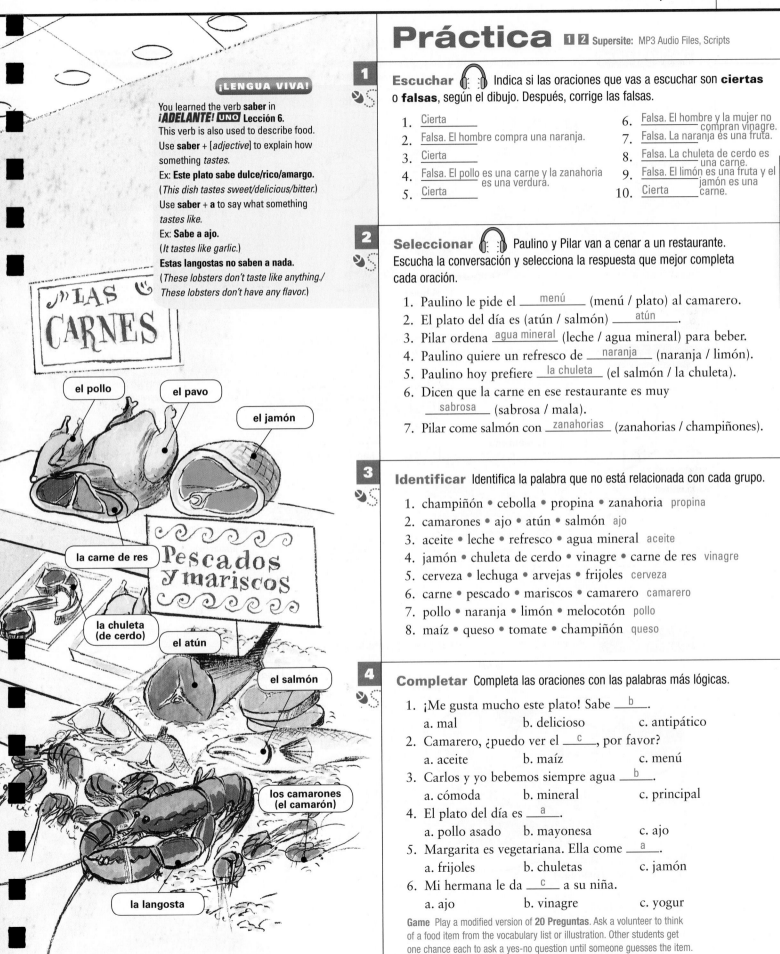

1 Escuchar 🎧 Indica si las oraciones que vas a escuchar son **ciertas** o **falsas**, según el dibujo. Después, corrige las falsas.

1. Cierta
2. Falsa. El hombre compra una naranja.
3. Cierta
4. Falsa. El pollo es una carne y la zanahoria es una verdura.
5. Cierta
6. Falsa. El hombre y la mujer no compran vinagre.
7. Falsa. La naranja es una fruta.
8. Falsa. La chuleta de cerdo es una carne.
9. Falsa. El limón es una fruta y el jamón es una carne.
10. Cierta

2 Seleccionar 🎧 Paulino y Pilar van a cenar a un restaurante. Escucha la conversación y selecciona la respuesta que mejor completa cada oración.

1. Paulino le pide el ___menú___ (menú / plato) al camarero.
2. El plato del día es (atún / salmón) ___atún___.
3. Pilar ordena ___agua mineral___ (leche / agua mineral) para beber.
4. Paulino quiere un refresco de ___naranja___ (naranja / limón).
5. Paulino hoy prefiere ___la chuleta___ (el salmón / la chuleta).
6. Dicen que la carne en ese restaurante es muy ___sabrosa___ (sabrosa / mala).
7. Pilar come salmón con ___zanahorias___ (zanahorias / champiñones).

3 Identificar Identifica la palabra que no está relacionada con cada grupo.

1. champiñón • cebolla • propina • zanahoria propina
2. camarones • ajo • atún • salmón ajo
3. aceite • leche • refresco • agua mineral aceite
4. jamón • chuleta de cerdo • vinagre • carne de res vinagre
5. cerveza • lechuga • arvejas • frijoles cerveza
6. carne • pescado • mariscos • camarero camarero
7. pollo • naranja • limón • melocotón pollo
8. maíz • queso • tomate • champiñón queso

4 Completar Completa las oraciones con las palabras más lógicas.

1. ¡Me gusta mucho este plato! Sabe ___b___.
   a. mal   b. delicioso   c. antipático
2. Camarero, ¿puedo ver el ___c___, por favor?
   a. aceite   b. maíz   c. menú
3. Carlos y yo bebemos siempre agua ___b___.
   a. cómoda   b. mineral   c. principal
4. El plato del día es ___a___.
   a. pollo asado   b. mayonesa   c. ajo
5. Margarita es vegetariana. Ella come ___a___.
   a. frijoles   b. chuletas   c. jamón
6. Mi hermana le da ___c___ a su niña.
   a. ajo   b. vinagre   c. yogur

Game Play a modified version of **20 Preguntas**. Ask a volunteer to think of a food item from the vocabulary list or illustration. Other students get one chance each to ask a yes-no question until someone guesses the item.

¡LENGUA VIVA!

You learned the verb **saber** in *¡ADELANTE!* **UNO** Lección 6. This verb is also used to describe food. Use **saber** + [*adjective*] to explain how something *tastes*.

Ex: **Este plato sabe dulce/rico/amargo.** (*This dish tastes sweet/delicious/bitter.*)

Use **saber** + **a** to say what something *tastes like*.

Ex: **Sabe a ajo.** (*It tastes like garlic.*)

Estas langostas no saben a nada. (*These lobsters don't taste like anything./ These lobsters don't have any flavor.*)

LAS CARNES

el pollo
el pavo
el jamón
la carne de res
la chuleta (de cerdo)
el atún
el salmón
los camarones (el camarón)
la langosta

Pescados y mariscos

el desayuno

Teaching Tips
• Ask students to name their favorite foods for each of the three meals. Introduce additional items as necessary (ex: **la pizza, los espaguetis**).

el jugo (de fruta)
el café
el pan (tostado)
el azúcar
la mantequilla
la salchicha
el huevo

NOTA CULTURAL

En Guatemala, un desayuno típico incluye huevos, frijoles, fruta, tortillas, jugo y café.

Otros desayunos populares son:

madalenas (*muffins*) España

pan dulce (*assorted breads/pastries*) México

champurradas (*sugar cookies*) Guatemala

gallo pinto (*fried rice and beans*) Costa Rica

perico (*scrambled eggs with peppers and onions*) Venezuela

el almuerzo

• Point out that in Spanish-speaking countries, lunch (also called **la comida**) is usually the main meal of the day. **La cena** is typically much lighter than **el almuerzo**.

el pan
la manzana
el té helado
la hamburguesa
las papas/patatas fritas

• At this point you may want to present **Vocabulario adicional: Más vocabulario relacionado con la comida** (Supersite).

Más vocabulario

escoger	*to choose*
merendar (e:ie)	*to snack*
probar (o:ue)	*to taste; to try*
recomendar (e:ie)	*to recommend*
servir (e:i)	*to serve*
el té	*tea*
el vino blanco	*white wine*

la cena

• For expansion, discuss favorite desserts (**postres**) and snacks (**meriendas**). Introduce new terms as needed (ex: **el helado, el pastel, las galletas**).

la sal
el vino tinto
la pimienta
la sopa
el arroz
la ensalada
los espárragos
el bistec

Extra Practice Add an auditory aspect to this vocabulary presentation. Prepare descriptions of five to seven different meals, with a mix of breakfasts, lunches, and dinners. As you read each description aloud, have students write down what you say as a dictation and then guess the meal it describes.

Lección 2

5 Get students to talk about what they eat. Ex: **¿Comen ustedes carne sólo una vez a la semana o menos? ¿Qué comidas comen ustedes dos o más veces al día?**

5 Ask follow-up questions about the food pyramid. Ex: **¿Qué se debe comer todos los días? ¿Cuáles son los productos que aparecen en el grupo cuatro? ¿Y en el grupo siete?**

Extra Practice Have students draw food pyramids based not on what they should eat, but on what they actually do eat as part of their diet. Encourage them to include drawings or magazine cutouts to enhance the visual presentation. Then have students present their pyramids to the class.

5

Completar Trabaja con un(a) compañero/a de clase para relacionar cada producto con el grupo alimenticio (*food group*) correcto.

modelo

> ___La carne___ es del grupo uno.

el aceite	las bananas	los cereales	la leche
el arroz	el café	los espárragos	el pescado
el azúcar	la carne	los frijoles	el vino

1. ___La leche___ y el queso son del grupo cuatro.
2. ___Los frijoles___ son del grupo ocho.
3. ___El pescado___ y el pollo son del grupo tres.
4. ___El aceite___ es del grupo cinco.
5. ___El azúcar___ es del grupo dos.
6. Las manzanas y ___las bananas___ son del grupo siete.
7. ___El café___ es del grupo seis.
8. ___Los cereales___ son del grupo diez.
9. ___Los espárragos___ y los tomates son del grupo nueve.
10. El pan y ___el arroz___ son del grupo diez.

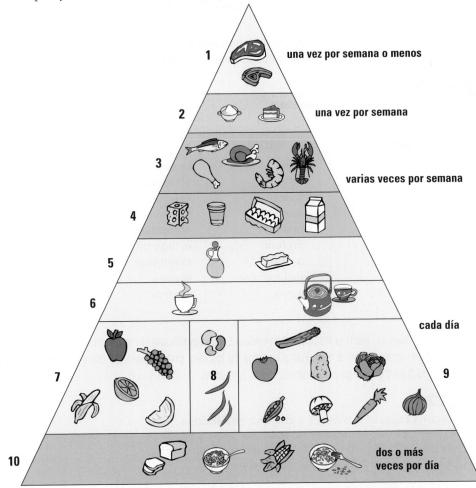

La Pirámide Alimenticia Latinoamericana

6

¿Cierto o falso? Consulta la Pirámide Alimenticia Latinoamericana de la página 83 e indica si lo que dice cada oración es **cierto** o **falso**. Si la oración es falsa, escribe las comidas que sí están en el grupo indicado.

> **modelo**
>
> El queso está en el grupo diez.
> Falso. En ese grupo están el maíz, el pan, los cereales y el arroz.

1. La manzana, la banana, el limón y las arvejas están en el grupo siete.
   Falso. En ese grupo están la manzana, las uvas, la banana, la naranja y el limón.
2. En el grupo cuatro están los huevos, la leche y el aceite.
   Falso. En ese grupo están los huevos, la leche, el queso y el yogur.
3. El azúcar está en el grupo dos.
   Cierto.
4. En el grupo diez están el pan, el arroz y el maíz.
   Cierto.
5. El pollo está en el grupo uno.
   Falso. En ese grupo están la carne de res/el bistec/el jamón y la chuleta de cerdo.
6. En el grupo nueve están la lechuga, el tomate, las arvejas, la naranja, la papa, los espárragos y la cebolla.   Falso. En ese grupo están la lechuga, el tomate, las arvejas, la zanahoria, la papa, los espárragos, la cebolla y el champiñón.
7. El café y el té están en el mismo grupo.
   Cierto.
8. En el grupo cinco está el arroz.
   Falso. En ese grupo están el aceite y la mantequilla.
9. El pescado, el yogur y el bistec están en el grupo tres.
   Falso. En ese grupo están el pescado, el pollo, el pavo, los camarones y la langosta.

7

Combinar Combina palabras de cada columna, en cualquier (*any*) orden, para formar diez oraciones lógicas sobre las comidas. Añade otras palabras si es necesario.   Answers will vary.

> **modelo**
>
> La camarera nos sirve la ensalada.

A	B	C
el/la camarero/a	almorzar	la sección de no fumar
el/la dueño/a	escoger	el desayuno
mi familia	gustar	la ensalada
mi novio/a	merendar	las uvas
mis amigos y yo	pedir	el restaurante
mis padres	preferir	el jugo de naranja
mi hermano/a	probar	el refresco
el/la médico/a	recomendar	el plato
yo	servir	el arroz

8

Un menú En parejas, usen la Pirámide Alimenticia Latinoamericana de la página 83 para crear un menú para una cena especial. Incluyan alimentos de los diez grupos para los entremeses, los platos principales y las bebidas. Luego presenten el menú a la clase.   Answers will vary.

> **modelo**
>
> La cena especial que vamos a preparar es deliciosa.
> Primero, hay dos entremeses: ensalada César y sopa
> de langosta. El plato principal es salmón con salsa de
> ajo y espárragos. También vamos a servir arroz...

Extra Practice To review and practice the preterite along with food vocabulary, have students write a paragraph in which they describe what they ate yesterday. Students should also indicate whether this collection of meals represents a typical day for them. If not, they should explain why.

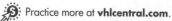 Practice more at **vhlcentral.com**.

6 In pairs, have students create three additional true/false statements for their partners to answer.

7 To simplify, ask individual students what people in the activity logically do. Point out that there are many possible answers to your questions. Ex: **¿Qué hace la camarera en el restaurante? ¿Qué hace el dueño?**

8 Emphasize that students must include at least one item from each group in the **pirámide alimenticia**.

NOTA CULTURAL

El arroz es un alimento básico en el Caribe, Centroamérica y México, entre otros países. Aparece frecuentemente como acompañamiento del plato principal y muchas veces se sirve con frijoles. Un plato muy popular en varios países es **el arroz con pollo** (*chicken and rice casserole*).

Small Groups In groups of three, students role-play a situation in a restaurant. Two students play the customers and the other plays the **camarero/a**. Write these sentences on the board as suggested phrases: **¿Están listos/as para pedir?, ¿Qué nos recomienda usted?, ¿Me trae ____, por favor?, ¿Y para empezar?, A sus órdenes. La especialidad de la casa.**

Comunicación

9

9 Ask the same questions of individual students. Ask other students to restate what their classmates answered.

Small Groups In groups of two to four, ask students to prepare brief skits related to food. The skits may involve being in a market, in a restaurant, in a café, inviting people over for dinner, and so forth. Allow groups time to rehearse before performing their skits for the class, who will vote for the most creative one.

10

10 For expansion, repeat the activity with additional photos of people in eating situations.

Conversación En parejas, túrnense para hacerse estas preguntas. Answers will vary.

1. ¿Meriendas mucho durante el día? ¿Qué comes? ¿A qué hora?
2. ¿Qué te gusta cenar?
3. ¿A qué hora, dónde y con quién almuerzas?
4. ¿Cuáles son las comidas más (*most*) típicas de tu almuerzo?
5. ¿Desayunas? ¿Qué comes y bebes por la mañana?
6. ¿Qué comida te gusta más? ¿Qué comida no conoces y quieres probar?
7. ¿Comes cada día alimentos de los diferentes grupos de la pirámide alimenticia? ¿Cuáles son las comidas y bebidas más frecuentes en tu dieta?
8. ¿Qué comida recomiendas a tus amigos? ¿Por qué?
9. ¿Eres vegetariano/a? ¿Crees que ser vegetariano/a es una buena idea? ¿Por qué?
10. ¿Te gusta cocinar (*to cook*)? ¿Qué comidas preparas para tus amigos? ¿Para tu familia?

Describir Con dos compañeros/as de clase, describe las dos fotos, contestando estas preguntas.
Answers will vary.

▶ ¿Quiénes están en las fotos?

▶ ¿Dónde están?

▶ ¿Qué hora es?

▶ ¿Qué comen y qué beben?

Supersite:
Activity Pack

11

11 Have groups create another type of word puzzle, such as a wordsearch, to share with the class. It should contain additional food- and meal-related vocabulary.

Crucigrama Tu profesor(a) les va a dar a ti y a tu compañero/a un crucigrama (*crossword puzzle*) incompleto. Tú tienes las palabras que necesita tu compañero/a y él/ella tiene las palabras que tú necesitas. Tienen que darse pistas (*clues*) para completarlo. No pueden decir la palabra; deben utilizar definiciones, ejemplos y frases. Answers will vary.

> **modelo**
> **6 vertical:** Es un *condimento que normalmente viene con* la sal.
> **12 horizontal:** Es una *fruta amarilla.*

Game Play a game of continuous narration. One student begins with **Voy a preparar** (*name of dish*) **y voy al mercado. Necesito comprar...** and names one food item. Each student repeats the entire narration, adding an additional food item. Repeat the prompt with a new dish as necessary.

Video Synopsis **Miguel** and **Maru** are at one of Mexico City's best restaurants enjoying a romantic dinner to celebrate their second anniversary. **Felipe** and **Juan Carlos** show up and, while **Juan Carlos** distracts the waiter, **Felipe** serves the couple their food, making a mess of the table.

Una cena... romántica

Maru y Miguel quieren tener una cena romántica,
pero les espera una sorpresa.

PERSONAJES   MARU   MIGUEL

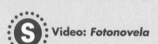 Video: *Fotonovela*

MARU No sé qué pedir. ¿Qué me recomiendas?

MIGUEL No estoy seguro. Las chuletas de cerdo se ven muy buenas.

MARU ¿Vas a pedirlas?

MIGUEL No sé.

MIGUEL ¡Qué bonitos! ¿Quién te los dio?

MARU Me los compró un chico muy guapo e inteligente.

MIGUEL ¿Es tan guapo como yo?

MARU Sí, como tú, guapísimo.

MIGUEL Por nosotros.

MARU Dos años.

(El camarero llega a la mesa.)

CAMARERO ¿Les gustaría saber nuestras especialidades del día?

MARU Sí, por favor.

CAMARERO Para el entremés, tenemos ceviche de camarón. De plato principal ofrecemos bistec con verduras a la plancha.

MARU Voy a probar el jamón.

CAMARERO Perfecto. ¿Y para usted, caballero?

MIGUEL Pollo asado con champiñones y papas, por favor.

CAMARERO Excelente.

(en otra parte del restaurante)

JUAN CARLOS Disculpe. ¿Qué me puede contar del pollo? ¿Dónde lo consiguió el chef?

CAMARERO ¡Oiga! ¿Qué está haciendo?

Video Recap: **Lección 1** Before doing this **Fotonovela** section, review the previous episode with these questions: 1. ¿Adónde va a ir Marissa?
(Va al cine.) 2. ¿Qué necesita hacer antes de salir? (Necesita arreglarse el pelo.) 3. ¿Qué está haciendo Felipe en el baño? (Está afeitándose.)
4. ¿Qué planes tiene Jimena? ¿Adónde decide ir al final? (Tiene que estudiar en la biblioteca. Decide ir al cine con Marissa.)   ochenta y siete   **87**

CAMARERO

JUAN CARLOS

FELIPE

GERENTE

Lección 2

FELIPE Los espárragos están sabrosísimos esta noche. Usted pidió el pollo, señor. Estos champiñones saben a mantequilla.

GERENTE ¿Qué pasa aquí, Esteban?

CAMARERO Lo siento, señor. Me quitaron la comida.

GERENTE (*a Felipe*) Señor, ¿quién es usted? ¿Qué cree que está haciendo?

JUAN CARLOS Felipe y yo les servimos la comida a nuestros amigos. Pero desafortunadamente, salió todo mal.

FELIPE Soy el peor camarero del mundo. ¡Lo siento! Nosotros vamos a pagar la comida.

JUAN CARLOS ¿Nosotros?

FELIPE Todo esto fue idea tuya, Juan Carlos.

JUAN CARLOS ¿Mi idea? ¡Felipe! (*al gerente*) Señor, él es más responsable que yo.

GERENTE Tú y tú, vamos.

Expresiones útiles

Ordering food

¿Qué me recomiendas?
What do you recommend?
Las chuletas de cerdo se ven muy buenas.
The pork chops look good.
¿Les gustaría saber nuestras especialidades del día?
Would you like to hear our specials?
Para el entremés, tenemos ceviche de camarón.
For an appetizer, we have shrimp ceviche.
De plato principal ofrecemos bistec con verduras a la plancha.
For a main course, we have beef with grilled vegetables.
Voy a probar el jamón.
I am going to try the ham.

Describing people and things

¡Qué bonitos! ¿Quién te los dio?
How pretty! Who gave them to you?
Me los compró un chico muy guapo e inteligente.
A really handsome, intelligent guy bought them for me.
¿Es tan guapo como yo?
Is he as handsome as I am?
Sí, como tú, guapísimo.
Yes, like you, gorgeous.
Soy el peor camarero del mundo.
I am the worst waiter in the world.
Él es más responsable que yo.
He is more responsible than I am.

Additional vocabulary

el/la gerente *manager*
caballero *gentleman, sir*

Expresiones útiles Have the class read the caption for video still 2, and draw attention to the double object pronouns **te los** and **Me los**. Explain that these are examples of indirect object pronouns and direct object pronouns used together. Then point out that **tan guapo como** is an example of a comparison of two things that are equal. Have the class read the caption for video still 10, and tell them that **más responsible que** is an example of a comparison of two unequal things. Then, for video still 9, point out that **el peor camarero del mundo** is an example of a superlative. Tell students that they will learn more about these concepts in **Estructura**.

recursos

VM
pp. 129–130

vhlcentral.com
Lección 2

¿Qué pasó?

1 **Escoger** Escoge la respuesta que completa mejor cada oración.

1. Miguel lleva a Maru a un restaurante para __c__.
   a. almorzar   b. desayunar   c. cenar
2. El camarero les ofrece __b__ como plato principal.
   a. ceviche de camarón   b. bistec con verduras a la plancha
   c. pescado, arroz y ensalada
3. Miguel va a pedir __a__.
   a. pollo asado con champiñones y papas
   b. langosta al horno   c. pescado con verduras a la mantequilla
4. Felipe les lleva la comida a sus amigos y prueba __c__.
   a. el jamón y los vinos   b. el atún y la lechuga
   c. los espárragos y los champiñones

2 **Identificar** Indica quién puede decir estas oraciones.

1. Qué desastre. Soy un camarero muy malo. Felipe
2. Les recomiendo el bistec con verduras a la plancha. camarero
3. Tal vez escoja las chuletas de cerdo, creo que son muy sabrosas. Miguel
4. ¿Qué pasa aquí? gerente
5. Dígame las especialidades del día, por favor. Maru/Miguel
6. No fue mi idea. Felipe es más responsable que yo. Juan Carlos

FELIPE   MARU   JUAN CARLOS

CAMARERO   MIGUEL   GERENTE

2 For expansion, give students additional items.
Ex: **Me quitaron la comida.** (camarero)

3 **Preguntas** Contesta estas preguntas sobre la **Fotonovela.** Some answers may vary. Sample answers:

1. ¿Por qué fueron Maru y Miguel a un restaurante?
   Maru y Miguel fueron a un restaurante para tener una cena romántica.
2. ¿Qué entremés es una de las especialidades del día?
   El ceviche de camarón es el entremés del día.
3. ¿Qué pidió Maru?
   Maru pidió vino, sopa de frijoles y jamón con espárragos.
4. ¿Quiénes van a pagar la cuenta?
   Juan Carlos y Felipe van a pagar la cuenta.

4 **En el restaurante** Answers will vary.

1. Prepara con un(a) compañero/a una conversación en la que le preguntas si conoce algún buen restaurante en tu comunidad. Tu compañero/a responde que él/ella sí conoce un restaurante que sirve una comida deliciosa. Lo/La invitas a cenar y tu compañero/a acepta. Determinan la hora para verse en el restaurante y se despiden.

2. Trabaja con un(a) compañero/a para representar los papeles de un(a) cliente/a y un(a) camarero/a en un restaurante. El/La camarero/a te pregunta qué te puede servir y tú preguntas cuál es la especialidad de la casa. El/La camarero/a te dice cuál es la especialidad y te recomienda algunos platos del menú. Tú pides entremeses, un plato principal y escoges una bebida. El/La camarero/a te sirve la comida y tú le das las gracias.

Large Groups Have students work in groups of five or six to prepare a skit in which a family goes to a restaurant, is seated by a server, examines the menu, and orders dinner. Each family member should ask a question about the menu and then order an entree and a drink. Have one or two groups perform the skit in front of the class.

 Practice more at **vhlcentral.com.**

NOTA CULTURAL

El **ceviche** es un plato típico de varios países hispanos como México, Perú y Costa Rica. En México, se prepara con pescado o mariscos frescos, jugo de limón, jitomate, cebolla, chile y cilantro. Se puede comer como plato fuerte, pero también como entremés o botana (*snack*). Casi siempre se sirve con tostadas (*fried tortillas*) o galletas saladas (*crackers*).

4 Possible conversation (1):
E1: Oye, María, ¿conoces un buen restaurante en esta ciudad?
E2: Sí… el restaurante El Pescador sirve comida riquísima.
E1: ¿Por qué no vamos a El Pescador esta noche?
E2: ¿A qué hora?
E1: ¿A las ocho?
E2: Perfecto.
E1: Está bien. Nos vemos a las ocho.
E2: Adiós.
Possible conversation (2):
E1: ¿Qué le puedo traer?
E2: Bueno, ¿cuáles son las especialidades del día?
E1: Hay ceviche de atún. También le recomiendo la langosta con arroz y verduras.
E2: Mmm… voy a pedir el ceviche y el bistec con verduras. De tomar, voy a pedir el té helado.
E1: Gracias, señor.

CONSULTA

To review indefinite words like **algún**, see **Estructura 1.2**, p. 34.

communication
NATIONAL STANDARDS

Pronunciación   Audio
ll, ñ, c, and z

Supersite: MP3 Audio Files, Listening Scripts

Teaching Tips
• As you model the pronunciation of these sounds with the class, write additional words on the board and have students repeat.
• You may wish to bring in additional audio samples to compare and contrast the pronunciation of **c** and **z** in Spain and Latin America.

Pairs Have the class work in pairs to practice the pronunciation of the sentences in **Fotonovela** captions. Encourage students to help their partner if he or she has trouble pronouncing a particular word.

Game Divide students into teams of four. With books closed, give them two minutes to write down as many words as they can with **ll**. Then have students in each group take turns reading the words aloud. Groups earn a point for each word that is spelled and pronounced correctly. Repeat with **ñ**, **c**, and **z**.

| **pollo** | **llave** | **ella** | **cebolla** |

Most Spanish speakers pronounce the letter **ll** like the *y* in *yes*.

| **mañana** | **señor** | **baño** | **niña** |

The letter **ñ** is pronounced much like the *ny* in *canyon*.

| **café** | **colombiano** | **cuando** | **rico** |

Before **a**, **o**, or **u**, the Spanish **c** is pronounced like the *c* in *car*.

| **cereales** | **delicioso** | **conducir** | **conocer** |

Before **e** or **i**, the Spanish **c** is pronounced like the *s* in *sit*. (In parts of Spain, **c** before **e** or **i** is pronounced like the *th* in *think*.)

| **zeta** | **zanahoria** | **almuerzo** | **cerveza** |

The Spanish **z** is pronounced like the *s* in *sit*. (In parts of Spain, **z** is pronounced like the *th* in *think*.)

Práctica Lee las palabras en voz alta.

1. mantequilla	5. español	9. quince	
2. cuñada	6. cepillo	10. compañera	
3. aceite	7. zapato	11. almorzar	
4. manzana	8. azúcar	12. calle	

Heritage Speakers Call on heritage speakers to model pronunciation for the class. Ask them to list several additional words on the board for practice. You may wish to point out regional variations in the pronunciation of **ll**.

Oraciones Lee las oraciones en voz alta.

1. Mi compañero de cuarto se llama Toño Núñez. Su familia es de la ciudad de Guatemala y de Quetzaltenango.
2. Dice que la comida de su mamá es deliciosa, especialmente su pollo al champiñón y sus tortillas de maíz.
3. Creo que Toño tiene razón porque hoy cené en su casa y quiero volver mañana para cenar allí otra vez.

Refranes Lee los refranes en voz alta.

Panza llena, corazón contento.[2]

Las apariencias engañan.[1]

1 Looks can be deceiving.
2 A full belly makes a happy heart.

recursos

LM p. 136 | vhlcentral.com Lección 2

Lección 2

EN DETALLE

Additional Reading

Frutas y verduras de América

Imagínate una pizza sin salsa° de tomate o una hamburguesa sin papas fritas. Ahora piensa que quieres ver una película, pero las palomitas de maíz° y el chocolate no existen. ¡Qué mundo° tan insípido°! Muchas de las comidas más populares del mundo tienen ingredientes esenciales que son originarios del continente llamado Nuevo Mundo. Estas frutas y verduras no fueron introducidas en Europa sino hasta° el siglo° XVI.

El tomate, por ejemplo, era° usado como planta ornamental cuando llegó por primera vez a Europa porque pensaron que era venenoso°. El maíz, por su parte, era ya la base de la comida de muchos países latinoamericanos muchos siglos antes de la llegada de los españoles.

La papa fue un alimento° básico para los incas. Incluso consiguieron deshidratarla para almacenarla° por largos períodos de tiempo. El cacao (planta con la que se hace el chocolate) fue muy importante para los aztecas y los mayas. Ellos usaban sus semillas° como moneda° y como ingrediente de diversas salsas. También las molían° para preparar una bebida, mezclándolas° con agua ¡y con chile!

El aguacate°, la guayaba°, la papaya, la piña y el maracuyá (o fruta de la pasión) son otros ejemplos de frutas originarias de América que son hoy día conocidas en todo el mundo.

Mole

¿En qué alimentos encontramos estas frutas y verduras?

Tomate: pizza, ketchup, salsa de tomate, sopa de tomate

Maíz: palomitas de maíz, tamales, tortillas, arepas (Colombia y Venezuela), pan

Papa: papas fritas, frituras de papa°, puré de papas°, sopa de papas, tortilla de patatas (España)

Cacao: mole (México), chocolatinas°, cereales, helados°, tartas°

Aguacate: guacamole (México), coctel de camarones, sopa de aguacate, nachos, enchiladas hondureñas

salsa *sauce* palomitas de maíz *popcorn* mundo *world* insípido *flavorless* hasta *until* siglo *century* era *was* venenoso *poisonous* alimento *food* almacenarla *to store it* semillas *seeds* moneda *currency* las molían *they used to grind them* mezclándolas *mixing them* aguacate *avocado* guayaba *guava* frituras de papa *chips* puré de papas *mashed potatoes* chocolatinas *chocolate bars* helados *ice cream* tartas *cakes*

ACTIVIDADES

1 **¿Cierto o falso?** Indica si lo que dicen las oraciones es cierto o falso. Corrige la información falsa.

1. El tomate se introdujo a Europa como planta ornamental. **Cierto.**
2. Los incas sólo consiguieron almacenar las papas por poco tiempo. **Falso.** Los incas pudieron almacenar las papas por largo tiempo.
3. Los aztecas y los mayas usaron las papas como moneda. **Falso.** Los aztecas y los mayas usaron las semillas de cacao como moneda.
4. El maíz era una comida poco popular en Latinoamérica. **Falso.** El maíz era muy popular en Latinoamérica.
5. El aguacate era el alimento básico de los incas. **Falso.** La papa era el alimento básico de los incas.
6. En México se hace una salsa con chocolate. **Cierto.**
7. El aguacate, la guayaba, la papaya, la piña y el maracuyá son originarios de América. **Cierto.**
8. Las arepas se hacen con cacao. **Falso.** Las arepas se hacen con maíz.
9. El aguacate es un ingrediente del cóctel de camarones. **Cierto.**
10. En España hacen una tortilla con papas. **Cierto.**

Lección 2

ASÍ SE DICE

La comida

el banano (Col.), el cambur (Ven.), el guineo (Nic.), el plátano (Amér. L., Esp.)	la banana
el choclo (Amér. S.), el elote (Méx.), el jojoto (Ven.), la mazorca (Esp.)	*corncob*
las caraotas (Ven.), los porotos (Amér. S.), las habichuelas (P. R.)	los frijoles
el durazno (Méx.)	el melocotón
el jitomate (Méx.)	el tomate

EL MUNDO HISPANO

Algunos platos típicos

- **Ceviche peruano:** Es un plato de pescado crudo° que se marina° en jugo de limón, con sal, pimienta, cebolla y ají°. Se sirve con lechuga, maíz, camote° y papa amarilla.

- **Gazpacho andaluz:** Es una sopa fría típica del sur de España. Se hace con verduras crudas y molidas°: tomate, ají, pepino° y ajo. También lleva pan, sal, aceite y vinagre.

- **Sancocho colombiano:** Es una sopa de pollo, pescado o carne con plátano, maíz, zanahoria, yuca, papas, cebolla, cilantro y ajo. Se sirve con arroz blanco.

crudo *raw* se marina *gets marinated* ají *pepper* camote *sweet potato* molidas *mashed* pepino *cucumber*

PERFIL

Ferran Adrià: arte en la cocina°

¿Qué haces si un amigo te invita a comer croquetas líquidas o paella de *Kellogg's*? ¿Piensas que es una broma°? ¡Cuidado! Puedes estar perdiendo la oportunidad de probar los platos de uno de los chefs más innovadores del mundo°: **Ferran Adrià.**

Este artista de la cocina basa su éxito° en la creatividad y en la química. Adrià modifica combinaciones de ingredientes y juega con contrastes de gustos y sensaciones: frío-caliente, crudo-cocido°, dulce°-salado°...

Aire de zanahorias

A partir de nuevas técnicas, altera la textura de los alimentos sin alterar su sabor°. Sus platos sorprendentes° y divertidos atraen a muchos nuevos chefs a su academia de cocina experimental. Quizás un día compraremos° en el supermercado té esférico°, carne líquida y espuma° de tomate.

cocina *kitchen* broma *joke* mundo *world* éxito *success* cocido *cooked* dulce *sweet* salado *savory* sabor *taste* sorprendentes *surprising* compraremos *we will buy* esférico *spheric* espuma *foam*

Conexión Internet

¿Qué platos comen los hispanos en los Estados Unidos?	Go to **vhlcentral.com** to find more cultural information related to this **Cultura** section.

ACTIVIDADES

2 **Comprensión** Empareja cada palabra con su definición.

1. fruta amarilla d
2. sopa típica de Colombia c
3. ingrediente del ceviche e
4. chef español b

a. gazpacho
b. Ferran Adrià
c. sancocho
d. guineo
e. pescado

3 **¿Qué plato especial hay en tu región?** Escribe cuatro oraciones sobre un plato típico de tu región. Explica los ingredientes que contiene y cómo se sirve. Answers will vary.

3 For expansion, ask students to create a **menú del día** in which they suggest complementary dishes (appetizers, drinks, or dessert).

 Practice more at **vhlcentral.com**.

2.1 Preterite of stem-changing verbs ⓢ Tutorial

ANTE TODO As you learned in *¡ADELANTE!* **UNO** Lección 6, -ar and -er stem-changing verbs have no stem change in the preterite. -Ir stem-changing verbs, however, do have a stem change. Study the following chart and observe where the stem changes occur.

CONSULTA

There are a few high-frequency irregular verbs in the preterite. You will learn more about them in **Estructura 3.1**, p. 152.

Preterite of **-ir** stem-changing verbs		
	servir *(to serve)*	**dormir** *(to sleep)*
SINGULAR FORMS		
yo	serví	dormí
tú	serviste	dormiste
Ud./él/ella	s**i**rvió	d**u**rmió
PLURAL FORMS		
nosotros/as	servimos	dormimos
vosotros/as	servisteis	dormisteis
Uds./ellos/ellas	s**i**rvieron	d**u**rmieron

▶ Stem-changing **-ir** verbs, in the preterite only, have a stem change in the third-person singular and plural forms. The stem change consists of either **e** to **i** or **o** to **u**.

(e → i) pedir: p**i**dió, p**i**dieron   (o → u) morir *(to die)*: m**u**rió, m**u**rieron

¿Quién pidió el jamón?

Yo lo pedí.

Teaching Tips
• Review present-tense forms of **-ir** stem-changing verbs like **pedir** and **dormir**. Also review formation of the preterite of regular **-ir** verbs using **escribir** and **recibir**.
• Ask students questions using stem-changing **-ir** verbs in the preterite. Ex: **¿Cuántas horas dormiste anoche?** Then have other students summarize the answers. Ex: _____ durmió seis horas, pero _____ durmió ocho. _____ y _____ durmieron cinco horas.
• Point out that **morir** means *to die* and provide sample sentences using third-person preterite forms of the verb. Ex: **No tengo bisabuelos. Ya murieron.**
• Other **-ir** verbs that change their stem vowel in the preterite are **conseguir, despedirse, divertirse, pedir, preferir, repetir, seguir, sentir, sugerir,** and **vestirse.**

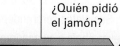
¡INTÉNTALO!   Cambia cada infinitivo al pretérito.

Extra Practice Have students write five original sentences using stem-changing preterite forms. Encourage them to include lesson vocabulary.

1. Yo __serví, dormí, pedí...__ . (servir, dormir, pedir, preferir, repetir, seguir)
   preferí, repetí, seguí

2. Usted _____. (morir, conseguir, pedir, sentirse, despedirse, vestirse)
   murió, consiguió, pidió, se sintió, se despidió, se vistió

3. Tú _____. (conseguir, servir, morir, pedir, dormir, repetir)
   conseguiste, serviste, moriste, pediste, dormiste, repetiste

4. Ellas _____. (repetir, dormir, seguir, preferir, morir, servir)
   repitieron, durmieron, siguieron, prefirieron, murieron, sirvieron

5. Nosotros _____. (seguir, preferir, servir, vestirse, despedirse, dormirse)
   seguimos, preferimos, servimos, nos vestimos, nos despedimos, nos dormimos

6. Ustedes _____. (sentirse, vestirse, conseguir, pedir, despedirse, dormirse)
   se sintieron, se vistieron, consiguieron, pidieron, se despidieron, se durmieron

7. Él _____. (dormir, morir, preferir, repetir, seguir, pedir)
   durmió, murió, prefirió, repitió, siguió, pidió

recursos

WB pp. 119–120

LM p. 137

ⓢ vhlcentral.com Lección 2

Práctica

1

Completar Completa estas oraciones para describir lo que pasó anoche en el restaurante El Famoso.

NOTA CULTURAL

El horario de las comidas en España es distinto al de los EE.UU. El desayuno es ligero (*light*). La hora del almuerzo es entre las 2 y las 3 de la tarde. Es la comida más importante del día. Mucha gente merienda o come unas tapas por la tarde. La cena, normalmente ligera, suele (*tends*) ser entre las 9 y las 11 de la noche.

▶ 1. Paula y Humberto Suárez llegaron al restaurante El Famoso a las ocho y ____siguieron____ (seguir) al camarero a una mesa en la sección de no fumar.

2. El señor Suárez ____pidió____ (pedir) una chuleta de cerdo.

3. La señora Suárez ____prefirió____ (preferir) probar los camarones.

4. De tomar, los dos ____pidieron____ (pedir) vino tinto.

5. El camarero ____repitió____ (repetir) el pedido (*the order*) para confirmarlo.

6. La comida tardó mucho (*took a long time*) en llegar y los señores Suárez ____se durmieron____ (dormirse) esperando la comida.

7. A las nueve y media el camarero les ____sirvió____ (servir) la comida.

8. Después de comer la chuleta, el señor Suárez ____se sintió____ (sentirse) muy mal.

9. Pobre señor Suárez... ¿por qué no ____pidió____ (pedir) los camarones?

2

El camarero loco En el restaurante La Hermosa trabaja un camarero muy distraído que siempre comete muchos errores. Indica lo que los clientes pidieron y lo que el camarero les sirvió.

2 In pairs, have students repeat the activity, this time role-playing the customer and the server. Model the first interaction: **E1: Perdón, pero pedí papas fritas y usted me sirvió maíz. E2: ¡Ay, perdón! Le traigo papas fritas enseguida.** Have students switch roles for each item number.

Video Show the **Fotonovela** again to give students more input with stem-changing -**ir** verbs in the preterite. Have them write down the stem-changing forms they hear. Stop the video where appropriate to discuss how certain verbs were used and to ask comprehension questions. Ex: **¿Qué pidió Maru? ¿Quién les sirvió la comida a Maru y a Miguel?**

modelo

Armando / papas fritas

Armando pidió papas fritas, pero el camarero le sirvió maíz.

1. nosotros / jugo de naranja Nosotros pedimos jugo de naranja, pero el camarero nos sirvió papas.

2. Beatriz / queso Beatriz pidió queso, pero el camarero le sirvió uvas.

3. tú / arroz Tú pediste arroz, pero el camarero te sirvió arvejas/sopa.

4. Elena y Alejandro / atún Elena y Alejandro pidieron atún, pero el camarero les sirvió camarones/mariscos.

5. usted / agua mineral Usted pidió agua mineral, pero el camarero le sirvió vino tinto.

6. yo / hamburguesa Yo pedí una hamburguesa, pero el camarero me sirvió zanahorias.

 Practice more at **vhlcentral.com**.

Comunicación

3

El almuerzo Trabajen en parejas. Túrnense para completar las oraciones de César de una manera lógica. Answers will vary.

> **modelo**
>
> Mi compañero de cuarto se despertó temprano, pero yo...
> Mi compañero de cuarto se despertó temprano, pero yo me desperté tarde.

1. Yo llegué al restaurante a tiempo, pero mis amigos...
2. Beatriz pidió la ensalada de frutas, pero yo...
3. Yolanda les recomendó el bistec, pero Eva y Paco...
4. Nosotros preferimos las papas fritas, pero Yolanda...
5. El camarero sirvió la carne, pero yo...
6. Beatriz y yo pedimos café, pero Yolanda y Paco...
7. Eva se sintió enferma, pero Paco y yo...
8. Nosotros repetimos postre (*dessert*), pero Eva...
9. Ellos salieron tarde, pero yo...
10. Yo me dormí temprano, pero mi compañero de cuarto...

3 To check preterite verb forms, ask volunteers to write their sentences on the board. Have the class correct errors as needed.

¡LENGUA VIVA!

In Spanish, the verb **repetir** is used to express *to have a second helping (of something).*
Cuando mi mamá prepara sopa de champiñones, yo siempre repito.
When my mom makes mushroom soup, I always have a second helping.

4

Entrevista Trabajen en parejas y túrnense para entrevistar a su compañero/a. Answers will vary.

1. ¿Te acostaste tarde o temprano anoche? ¿A qué hora te dormiste? ¿Dormiste bien?
2. ¿A qué hora te despertaste esta mañana? Y, ¿a qué hora te levantaste?
3. ¿A qué hora vas a acostarte esta noche?
4. ¿Qué almorzaste ayer? ¿Quién te sirvió el almuerzo?
5. ¿Qué cenaste ayer?
6. ¿Cenaste en un restaurante recientemente? ¿Con quién(es)?
7. ¿Qué pediste en el restaurante? ¿Qué pidieron los demás?
8. ¿Se durmió alguien en alguna de tus clases la semana pasada? ¿En qué clase?

4 To practice the formal register, have students ask you the same questions.

Síntesis

5

Describir En grupos, estudien la foto y las preguntas. Luego, describan la primera (¿y la última?) cita de César y Libertad. Answers will vary.

▶ ¿Adónde salieron a cenar?

▶ ¿Qué pidieron?

▶ ¿Les gustó la comida?

▶ ¿Quién prefirió una cena vegetariana? ¿Por qué?

▶ ¿Cómo se vistieron?

▶ ¿De qué hablaron? ¿Les gustó la conversación?

▶ ¿Van a volver a verse? ¿Por qué?

Pairs For expansion, have students describe a memorable experience in a restaurant (ex: a first date, a celebration, a wonderful or terrible meal).

CONSULTA

To review words commonly associated with the preterite, such as **anoche**, see **¡ADELANTE! UNO Estructura 6.3**, p. 323.

5 Have groups present their description to the class in the form of a narration. Remind them to use transition words, such as **primero**, **después**, **luego**, and **también**.

Lección 2

2.2 Double object pronouns Tutorial

Teaching Tips
- Briefly review direct and indirect object pronouns. Give sentences and have students convert objects into object pronouns. Ex: **Sara escribió la carta. (Sara la escribió.) Mis padres escribieron una carta. (yo) (Mis padres me escribieron una carta.**

- Model additional examples for students, asking them to make the conversion with **se.** Ex: **Le pedí papas fritas. (Se las pedí.) Les servimos café. (Se lo servimos.)**

Pairs In pairs, ask students to write five sentences that contain both direct and indirect objects (not pronouns). Have them exchange papers with another pair, who will restate the sentences using double object pronouns.

ANTE TODO In *¡ADELANTE! UNO* **Lecciones 5** and **6,** you learned that direct and indirect object pronouns replace nouns and that they often refer to nouns that have already been referenced. You will now learn how to use direct and indirect object pronouns together. Observe the following diagram.

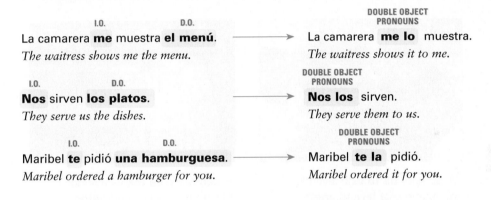

Indirect Object Pronouns		Direct Object Pronouns	
me	nos	lo	los
te	os	la	las
le (se)	les (se)		

+

▶ When direct and indirect object pronouns are used together, the indirect object pronoun always precedes the direct object pronoun.

I.O.   D.O.
La camarera **me** muestra **el menú**.
The waitress shows me the menu.

DOUBLE OBJECT PRONOUNS
La camarera **me lo** muestra.
The waitress shows it to me.

I.O.   D.O.
Nos sirven **los platos**.
They serve us the dishes.

DOUBLE OBJECT PRONOUNS
Nos los sirven.
They serve them to us.

I.O.   D.O.
Maribel **te** pidió **una hamburguesa**.
Maribel ordered a hamburger for you.

DOUBLE OBJECT PRONOUNS
Maribel **te la** pidió.
Maribel ordered it for you.

Video Show the **Fotonovela** again to give students more input containing double object pronouns. Stop the video where appropriate to discuss how double object pronouns were used and to ask comprehension questions.

Extra Practice Write six sentences on the board for students to restate using double object pronouns. Ex: **Rita les sirvió la cena a los clientes. (Rita se la sirvió.)**

¿Quién te los dio?

Me los compró un chico muy guapo.

▶ In Spanish, two pronouns that begin with the letter **l** cannot be used together. Therefore, the indirect object pronouns **le** and **les** always change to **se** when they are used with **lo, los, la,** and **las**.

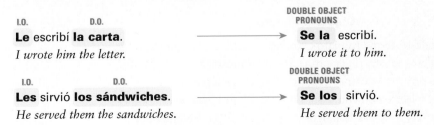

I.O.   D.O.
Le escribí **la carta**.
I wrote him the letter.

DOUBLE OBJECT PRONOUNS
Se la escribí.
I wrote it to him.

I.O.   D.O.
Les sirvió **los sándwiches**.
He served them the sandwiches.

DOUBLE OBJECT PRONOUNS
Se los sirvió.
He served them to them.

▶ Because **se** has multiple meanings, Spanish speakers often clarify to whom the pronoun refers by adding **a usted, a él, a ella, a ustedes, a ellos,** or **a ellas.**

¿El sombrero? Carlos **se** lo
vendió **a ella.**
The hat? Carlos sold it to her.

¿Las verduras? Ellos **se** las
compran **a usted.**
The vegetables? They are buying them for you.

▶ Double object pronouns are placed before a conjugated verb. With infinitives and present participles, they may be placed before the conjugated verb or attached to the end of the infinitive or present participle.

DOUBLE OBJECT
PRONOUNS
Te   lo   voy a mostrar.

DOUBLE OBJECT
PRONOUNS
Voy a mostrár**telo.**

DOUBLE OBJECT
PRONOUNS
Nos las están comprando.

DOUBLE OBJECT
PRONOUNS
Están comprándo**noslas.**

Mi abuelo **me lo** está leyendo.
Mi abuelo está leyéndo**melo.**

El camarero **se los** va a servir.
El camarero va a servír**selos.**

▶ As you can see above, when double object pronouns are attached to an infinitive or a present participle, an accent mark is added to maintain the original stress.

¡INTÉNTALO!   Escribe el pronombre de objeto directo o indirecto que falta en cada oración.

Objeto directo

1. ¿La ensalada? El camarero nos ___la___ sirvió.
2. ¿El salmón? La dueña me ___lo___ recomienda.
3. ¿La comida? Voy a preparárte___la___.
4. ¿Las bebidas? Estamos pidiéndose___las___.
5. ¿Los refrescos? Te ___los___ puedo traer ahora.
6. ¿Los platos de arroz? Van a servírnos___los___ después.

Objeto indirecto

1. ¿Puedes traerme tu plato? No, no ___te___ lo puedo traer.
2. ¿Quieres mostrarle la carta? Sí, voy a mostrár___se___la ahora.
3. ¿Les serviste la carne? No, no ___se___ la serví.
4. ¿Vas a leerle el menú? No, no ___se___ lo voy a leer.
5. ¿Me recomiendas la langosta? Sí, ___te___ la recomiendo.
6. ¿Cuándo vas a prepararnos la cena? ___Se___ la voy a preparar en una hora.

Teaching Tips
• Ask questions to elicit third-person double object pronouns. Ex: **¿Le recomiendas el restaurante Acapulco a _____?** (Sí, se lo recomiendo.) **¿Le traes sándwiches a tus compañeros?** (No, no se los traigo.)

• Practice pronoun placement with infinitives and present participles by giving sentences that show one method of pronoun placement and asking students to restate them another way. Ex: **Se lo voy a mandar.** (Voy a mandárselo.)

Game Play **Concentración.** Write sentences that use double object pronouns on each of eight cards. Ex: **Óscar se las muestra.** On another eight cards, draw or paste a picture that matches each sentence. Ex: A photo of a boy showing photos to his grandparents. Place the cards face-down in four rows of four. In pairs, students select two cards. If the two cards match, the pair keeps them. If they do not match, students replace them in their original position. The pair with the most cards at the end wins.

Pairs Have students create five dehydrated sentences for their partner to complete. They should include the following elements: subject / action / direct object / indirect object (name or pronoun). Ex: **Carlos / escribe / carta / Marta** Their partners should "hydrate" the sentences using double object pronouns. Ex: **Carlos se la escribe (a Marta).**

recursos

WB
pp. 121–122

LM
p. 138

Ⓢ
vhlcentral.com
Lección 2

Práctica

1

Responder Imagínate que trabajas de camarero/a en un restaurante. Responde a los pedidos (*requests*) de estos clientes usando pronombres.

> **modelo**
>
> Sra. Gómez: Una ensalada, por favor.
> Sí, señora. Enseguida (*Right away*) se la traigo.

1 Do the activity with the class, selecting two students for each exchange. Encourage them to vary their responses with the phrases in the sidebar.

AYUDA

Here are some other useful expressions:

ahora mismo
right now

inmediatamente
immediately

¡A la orden!
At your service!

¡Ya voy!
I'm on my way!

1. Sres. López: La mantequilla, por favor.   Sí, señores. Enseguida se la traigo.
2. Srta. Rivas: Los camarones, por favor.   Sí, señorita. Enseguida se los traigo.
3. Sra. Lugones: El pollo asado, por favor.   Sí, señora. Enseguida se lo traigo.
4. Tus compañeros/as de cuarto: Café, por favor.   Sí, chicos/as. Enseguida se lo traigo.
5. Tu profesor(a) de español: Papas fritas, por favor.   Sí, profesor(a). Enseguida se las traigo.
6. Dra. González: La chuleta de cerdo, por favor.   Sí, doctora. Enseguida se la traigo.
7. Tu padre: Los champiñones, por favor.   Sí, papá. Enseguida te los traigo.
8. Dr. Torres: La cuenta, por favor.   Sí, doctor. Enseguida se la traigo.

2

¿Quién? La señora Cevallos está planeando una cena. Se pregunta cómo va a resolver ciertas situaciones. En parejas, túrnense para decir lo que ella está pensando. Cambien los sustantivos subrayados por pronombres de objeto directo y hagan los otros cambios necesarios.

2 For each item, change the subject in parentheses so that students practice different forms of the verbs.

> **modelo**
>
> ¡No tengo carne! ¿Quién va a traerme la carne del supermercado? (mi esposo)
> Mi *esposo* va a traérmela./Mi *esposo* me la va a traer.

2 Add a visual aspect to this activity. Hold up magazine pictures and ask students who is doing what to or for whom. Ex: **La señora les muestra la casa a los jóvenes. Se la muestra a los jóvenes.**

1. ¡Las invitaciones! ¿Quién les manda <u>las invitaciones</u> a los invitados (*guests*)? (mi hija)   Mi hija se las manda.
2. No tengo tiempo de ir a la bodega. ¿Quién me puede comprar <u>el vino</u>? (mi hijo)   Mi hijo puede comprármelo./Mi hijo me lo puede comprar.
3. ¡Ay! No tengo suficientes platos (*plates*). ¿Quién puede prestarme <u>los platos</u> que necesito? (mi mamá)   Mi mamá puede prestármelos./Mi mamá me los puede prestar.
4. Nos falta mantequilla. ¿Quién nos trae <u>la mantequilla</u>? (mi cuñada)   Mi cuñada nos la trae.
5. ¡Los entremeses! ¿Quién está preparándonos <u>los entremeses</u>? (Silvia y Renata)   Silvia y Renata están preparándonoslos./Silvia y Renata nos los están preparando.
6. No hay suficientes sillas. ¿Quién nos trae <u>las sillas</u> que faltan? (Héctor y Lorena)   Héctor y Lorena nos las traen.
7. No tengo tiempo de pedirle el aceite a Mónica. ¿Quién puede pedirle <u>el aceite</u>? (mi hijo)   Mi hijo puede pedírselo./Mi hijo se lo puede pedir.
8. ¿Quién va a servirles <u>la cena</u> a los invitados? (mis hijos)   Mis hijos van a servírsela./Mis hijos se la van a servir.
9. Quiero poner buena música de fondo (*background*). ¿Quién me va a recomendar <u>la música</u>? (mi esposo)   Mi esposo va a recomendármela./Mi esposo me la va a recomendar.
10. ¡Los postres! ¿Quién va a preparar <u>los postres</u> para los invitados? (Sra. Villalba)   La señora Villalba va a preparárselos./La señora Villalba se los va a preparar.

NOTA CULTURAL

Los vinos de Chile son conocidos internacionalmente. **Concha y Toro** es el productor y exportador más grande de vinos de Chile. Las zonas más productivas de vino están al norte de Santiago, en el Valle Central.

Large Groups Split the class into two groups. Give cards that contain verbs that can take a direct object to one group. The other group gets cards containing nouns. Then select one member from each group to stand up and show his or her card. Another student converts the two elements into a sentence using double object pronouns. Ex: **mostrar / el libro** ➔ [*Name of student*] **Se lo va a mostrar**.

 Practice more at **vhlcentral.com**.

Comunicación

3

Contestar Trabajen en parejas. Túrnense para hacer preguntas, usando las palabras interrogativas **¿Quién?** o **¿Cuándo?**, y para responderlas. Sigan el modelo.   Answers will vary.

> **modelo**
>
> nos enseña español
> **Estudiante 1:** ¿Quién nos enseña español?
> **Estudiante 2:** La profesora Camacho nos lo enseña.

3 To simplify, begin by having students read through each item. Guide them in choosing **¿Quién?** or **¿Cuándo?** for each one.

3 Continue the **modelo** exchange by asking: **¿Cuándo nos lo enseña?** (**Nos lo enseña los lunes, miércoles, jueves y viernes.**)

1. te puede explicar la tarea cuando no la entiendes
2. les vende el almuerzo a los estudiantes
3. vas a comprarme boletos (*tickets*) para un concierto
4. te escribe mensajes de texto
5. nos prepara los entremeses
6. me vas a prestar tu computadora
7. te compró esa bebida
8. nos va a recomendar el menú de la cafetería
9. le enseñó español al/a la profesor(a)
10. me vas a mostrar tu casa o apartamento

4

Preguntas En parejas, túrnense para hacerse estas preguntas.   Answers will vary.

> **modelo**
>
> **Estudiante 1:** ¿Les prestas tu casa a tus amigos? ¿Por qué?
> **Estudiante 2:** No, no se la presto a mis amigos porque no son muy responsables.

1. ¿Me prestas tu auto? ¿Ya le prestaste tu auto a otro/a amigo/a?
2. ¿Quién te presta dinero cuando lo necesitas?
3. ¿Les prestas dinero a tus amigos? ¿Por qué?
4. ¿Nos compras el almuerzo a mí y a los otros compañeros de clase?
5. ¿Les mandas correo electrónico a tus amigos? ¿Y a tu familia?
6. ¿Les das regalos a tus amigos? ¿Cuándo?
7. ¿Quién te va a preparar la cena esta noche?
8. ¿Quién te va a preparar el desayuno mañana?

Síntesis

5

Regalos de Navidad Tu profesor(a) te va a dar a ti y a un(a) compañero/a una parte de la lista de los regalos de Navidad (*Christmas gifts*) que Berta pidió y los regalos que sus parientes le compraron. Conversen para completar sus listas.   Answers will vary.

> **modelo**
>
> **Estudiante 1:** ¿Qué le pidió Berta a su mamá?
> **Estudiante 2:** Le pidió una computadora. ¿Se la compró?
> **Estudiante 1:** Sí, se la compró.

Supersite: Activity Pack

Game Divide the class into two groups. Give each member of the first group a strip of paper with a question on it. Ex: **¿Te compró ese suéter tu novia?** Give each member of the second group the answer to one of the questions. Ex: **Sí, ella me lo compró.** Students must find their partners. Take care not to create sentences that can have more than one match.

5 Have different pairs make a list of the gifts they each received for their last birthday or other occasion. Then have them point to each item on their list and, using double object pronouns, tell their partner who bought it for them. Ex: **zapatos nuevos** (**Me los compró mi prima.**)

Heritage Speakers Ask heritage speakers if they or their families celebrate **el Día de los Reyes Magos** (The Feast of the Epiphany, January 6). Ask them to expand on the information given in the **Nota cultural** box and to tell whether **el Día de los Reyes** is more important for them than **la Navidad**.

NOTA CULTURAL

Las fiestas navideñas (*Christmas season*) en los países hispanos duran hasta enero. En muchos lugares celebran **la Navidad** (*Christmas*), pero no se dan los regalos hasta el seis de enero, **el Día de los Reyes Magos** (*Three Kings' Day/The Feast of the Epiphany*).

2.3 # Comparisons Tutorial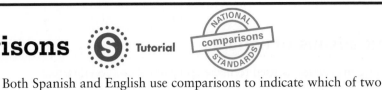

NATIONAL STANDARDS comparisons

ANTE TODO Both Spanish and English use comparisons to indicate which of two people or things has a lesser, equal, or greater degree of a quality.

> **Comparisons**

menos interesante	**más grande**	**tan sabroso como**
less interesting	*bigger*	*as delicious as*

Comparisons of inequality

▶ Comparisons of inequality are formed by placing **más** (*more*) or **menos** (*less*) before adjectives, adverbs, and nouns and **que** (*than*) after them.

$$\textbf{más/menos} + \begin{bmatrix} \textit{adjective} \\ \textit{adverb} \\ \textit{noun} \end{bmatrix} + \textbf{que}$$

▶ **¡Atención!** Note that while English has a comparative form for short adjectives (*tall**er***), such forms do not exist in Spanish (**más** alto).

> **adjectives**

Los bistecs son **más caros que** el pollo.	Estas uvas son **menos ricas que** esa pera.
Steaks are more expensive than chicken.	*These grapes are less tasty than that pear.*

> **adverbs**

Me acuesto **más tarde que** tú.	Luis se despierta **menos temprano que** yo.
I go to bed later than you (do).	*Luis wakes up less early than I (do).*

> **nouns**

Juan prepara **más platos que** José.	Susana come **menos carne que** Enrique.
Juan prepares more dishes than José (does).	*Susana eats less meat than Enrique (does).*

La ensalada es menos cara que la sopa.

¿El pollo es más rico que el jamón?

▶ When the comparison involves a numerical expression, **de** is used before the number instead of **que**.

Hay más **de** cincuenta naranjas.	Llego en menos **de** diez minutos.
There are more than fifty oranges.	*I'll be there in less than ten minutes.*

▶ With verbs, this construction is used to make comparisons of inequality.

$$\begin{bmatrix} \textit{verb} \end{bmatrix} + \textbf{más/menos que}$$

Mis hermanos **comen más que** yo.	Arturo **duerme menos que** su padre.
My brothers eat more than I (do).	*Arturo sleeps less than his father (does).*

Teaching Tips
• Write **más** + [*adjective*] + **que** and **menos** + [*adjective*] + **que** on the board, explaining their meaning. Illustrate with examples. Ex: **Esta clase es más grande que la clase de la tarde. La clase de la tarde es menos trabajadora que ésta**. Repeat with adverbs and nouns.

• Point out that **que** and what follows it are optional if the items being compared are evident. Ex: **Los bistecs son más caros (que el pollo).**

Extra Practice Ask students questions that make comparisons of inequality using adjectives, adverbs, and nouns. Ex: **¿Qué es más sabroso que una ensalada de frutas? ¿Quién se despierta más tarde que tú? ¿Quién tiene más libros que yo?** Then ask questions that use verbs in their construction. Ex: **¿Quién habla más que yo en la clase?**

Heritage Speakers Ask heritage speakers to give four to five sentences in which they compare themselves to members of their families. Make sure that the comparisons are ones of inequality. Ask other students in the class to report what the heritage speakers said to verify comprehension.

Comparisons of equality

▶ This construction is used to make comparisons of equality.

$$\textbf{tan} + \begin{bmatrix} \textit{adjective} \\ \textit{adverb} \end{bmatrix} + \textbf{como} \qquad \textbf{tanto/a(s)} + \begin{bmatrix} \textit{singular noun} \\ \textit{plural noun} \end{bmatrix} + \textbf{como}$$

¿Es tan guapo como yo?

¿Aquí vienen tantos mexicanos como extranjeros?

▶ **¡Atención!** Note that unlike **tan**, **tanto** acts as an adjective and therefore agrees in number and gender with the noun it modifies.

Estas uvas son **tan ricas como** aquéllas.
These grapes are as tasty as those ones (are).

Yo probé **tantos platos como** él.
I tried as many dishes as he did.

▶ **Tan** and **tanto** can also be used for emphasis, rather than to compare, with these meanings: **tan** *so*, **tanto** *so much*, **tantos/as** *so many*.

¡Tu almuerzo es **tan** grande!
Your lunch is so big!

¡Comes **tantas** manzanas!
You eat so many apples!

¡Comes **tanto**!
You eat so much!

¡Preparan **tantos** platos!
They prepare so many dishes!

▶ Comparisons of equality with verbs are formed by placing **tanto como** after the verb. Note that in this construction **tanto** does not change in number or gender.

$$\begin{bmatrix} \textit{verb} \end{bmatrix} + \textbf{tanto como}$$

Tú viajas **tanto como** mi tía.
You travel as much as my aunt (does).

Ellos hablan **tanto como** mis hermanas.
They talk as much as my sisters.

Sabemos **tanto como** ustedes.
We know as much as you (do).

No estudio **tanto como** Felipe.
I don't study as much as Felipe (does).

Teaching Tips
- Ask the class questions to elicit comparisons of equality. Ex: **¿Quién es tan bonita como Jennifer Lawrence? ¿Quién tiene tanto dinero como J.K. Rowling?**
- Ask questions that involve comparisons with yourself. Ex: **¿Quién es tan alto/a como yo? ¿Quién se acostó tan tarde como yo?**
- Involve the class in a conversation about themselves and classroom objects. Ex: _____, **¿por qué tienes tantas plumas? _____, ¡tu mochila es tan grande! Puedes llevar muchos libros, ¿no? ¿Quién más tiene una mochila tan grande?**

Game Divide the class into two teams, A and B. Place the names of twenty famous people into a hat. Select a member from each team to draw a name. The student from team A then has ten seconds to compare those two famous people. If the student has made a logical comparison, team A gets a point. Then it is team B's turn to make a different comparison. The team with the most points at the end wins.

Extra Practice Have students write three original comparative sentences that describe themselves. Ex: **Soy tan bajo como Ellen Page**. Then collect the papers, shuffle them, and read the sentences aloud. See if the rest of the class can guess who wrote each description.

Teaching Tip Ask questions and give examples to practice irregular comparative forms. Ex: (Pointing to two students) **Lisa tiene diecinueve años y Shawn tiene veintiún años. ¿Lisa es mayor que Shawn? (No, Lisa es menor que Shawn.)** Then ask questions about celebrities. Ex: **¿Quién canta mejor, Adele o Avril Lavigne?**

Irregular comparisons

▶ Some adjectives have irregular comparative forms.

Irregular comparative forms			
Adjective		**Comparative form**	
bueno/a	good	**mejor**	better
malo/a	bad	**peor**	worse
grande	grown, adult	**mayor**	older
pequeño/a	young	**menor**	younger
joven	young	**menor**	younger
viejo/a	old	**mayor**	older

CONSULTA

To review how descriptive adjectives like **bueno**, **malo**, and **grande** are shortened before nouns, see *¡ADELANTE!* **UNO** **Estructura** 3.1, p. 136.

▶ When **grande** and **pequeño/a** refer to age, the irregular comparative forms, **mayor** and **menor**, are used. However, when these adjectives refer to size, the regular forms, **más grande** and **más pequeño/a**, are used.

Yo soy **menor** que tú.
I'm younger than you.

Pedí un plato **más pequeño**.
I ordered a smaller dish.

Pairs Write on the board the heading **Nuestra universidad vs.** [*another nearby university*]. Underneath, write a list of categories. Ex: **la ciudad universitaria, los estudiantes, las residencias estudiantiles, el equipo de fútbol americano.** Have pairs take turns making comparisons about the universities. Encourage them to be creative and to use a variety of comparative forms. Ex: **Los estudiantes de nuestra universidad estudian tanto como los estudiantes de** [*other university*].

Nuestro hijo es **mayor** que el hijo de los Andrade.
Our son is older than the Andrades' son.

La ensalada de Isabel es **más grande** que ésa.
Isabel's salad is bigger than that one.

▶ The adverbs **bien** and **mal** have the same irregular comparative forms as the adjectives **bueno/a** and **malo/a**.

Julio nada **mejor** que los otros chicos.
Julio swims better than the other boys.

Ellas cantan **peor** que las otras chicas.
They sing worse than the other girls.

recursos

WB
pp. 123–124

LM
p. 139

S
vhlcentral.com
Lección 2

¡INTÉNTALO! Escribe el equivalente de las palabras en inglés.

1. Ernesto mira más televisión ___que___ (*than*) Alberto.
2. Tú eres ___menos___ (*less*) simpático que Federico.
3. La camarera sirve ___tanta___ (*as much*) carne como pescado.
4. Recibo ___más___ (*more*) propinas que tú.
5. No estudio ___tanto como___ (*as much as*) tú.
6. ¿Sabes jugar al tenis tan bien ___como___ (*as*) tu hermana?
7. ¿Puedes beber ___tantos___ (*as many*) refrescos como yo?
8. Mis amigos parecen ___tan___ (*as*) simpáticos como ustedes.

Large Groups Divide the class into groups of six. Give cards with adjectives listed on this page to one group. Give cards with the corresponding irregular comparative form to another group. Students must find their partners. To avoid confusion, make duplicate cards of **mayor** and **menor**.

Práctica

1 Escoger Escoge la palabra correcta para comparar a dos hermanas muy diferentes. Haz los cambios necesarios.

1. Lucila es más alta y más bonita ____que____ Tita. (de, más, menos, que)
2. Tita es más delgada porque come ____más____ verduras que su hermana. (de, más, menos, que)
3. Lucila es más ____simpática____ que Tita porque es alegre. (listo, simpático, bajo)
4. A Tita le gusta comer en casa. Va a ____menos____ restaurantes que su hermana. (más, menos, que) Es tímida, pero activa. Hace ____más____ ejercicio (*exercise*) que su hermana. (más, tanto, menos) Todos los días toma más ____de____ cinco vasos (*glasses*) de agua mineral. (que, tan, de)
5. Lucila come muchas papas fritas y se preocupa ____menos____ que Tita por comer frutas. (de, más, menos) ¡Son ____tan____ diferentes! Pero se llevan (*they get along*) muy bien. (como, tan, tanto)

2 Emparejar Compara a Mario y a Luis, los novios de Lucila y Tita, completando las oraciones de la columna A con las palabras o frases de la columna B.

A

1. Mario es ____tan interesante____ como Luis.
2. Mario viaja tanto ____como____ Luis.
3. Luis toma ____tantas____ clases de cocina (*cooking*) como Mario.
4. Luis habla ____francés____ tan bien como Mario.
5. Mario tiene tantos ____amigos extranjeros____ como Luis.
6. ¡Qué casualidad (*coincidence*)! Mario y Luis también son hermanos, pero no hay tanta ____diferencia____ entre ellos como entre Lucila y Tita.

B

tantas
diferencia
tan interesante
amigos extranjeros
como
francés

3 Oraciones Combina elementos de las columnas A, B y C para hacer comparaciones. Escribe oraciones completas. Answers will vary.

> **modelo**
> Arnold Schwarzenegger tiene tantos autos como Jennifer Aniston.
> Jennifer Aniston es menos musculosa que Arnold Schwarzenegger.

A

la comida japonesa
el fútbol
Arnold Schwarzenegger
el pollo
la gente de Vancouver
la primera dama (*lady*) de los EE.UU.
las universidades privadas
las espinacas
la música rap

B

costar
saber
ser
tener
¿?

C

la gente de Montreal
la música *country*
el brócoli
el presidente de los EE.UU.
la comida italiana
el hockey
Jennifer Aniston
las universidades públicas
la carne de res

 Practice more at **vhlcentral.com**.

1 Quickly review the use of **de** before numerals in comparisons.

1 Ask two students a question, then have another student compare them. Ex: **¿Cuántas horas de televisión miras cada día? ¿Y tú, ____? ____, haz una comparación.**

1 Ask several pairs of students different types of questions for later comparison. Ex: **¿Cuáles prefieres, las películas de aventuras o los dramas? ¿Estudias más para la clase de español o para la clase de matemáticas?**

2 Turn the activity statements into questions and ask them of students. Have them make up answers that involve comparisons. Ex: **¿Cómo es Mario?**

TPR Give the same types of objects to different students but in different numbers. For example, hand out three books to one student, one book to another, and four to another. Then call on individuals to make comparisons between the students based on the number of objects they have. Have students continue the activity in groups, using pens, sheets of paper, and other classroom objects.

3 To simplify, guide students in pairing up elements from columns A and C and brainstorming possible infinitives for each pair of elements.

Large Groups Divide the class into two groups. Survey each group to get information about various topics. Ex: **¿Quiénes hacen ejercicio todos los días? ¿Quiénes van al cine cada fin de semana? ¿Quiénes comen comida rápida tres veces a la semana?** Ask for a show of hands and tally the number of hands. Then have students make comparisons between the two groups based on the information given.

Comunicación

NATIONAL communication STANDARDS

4

AYUDA

You can use these adjectives in your comparisons:
bonito/a
caro/a
elegante
interesante
inteligente

4 Ask pairs of volunteers to present one of their conversations to the class. Then survey the class to see with which of the students the class agrees more.

Intercambiar En parejas, hagan comparaciones sobre diferentes cosas. Pueden usar las sugerencias de la lista u otras ideas. Answers will vary.

▶ **modelo**

Estudiante 1: Los pollos de *Pollitos del Corral* son muy ricos.
Estudiante 2: Pues yo creo que los pollos de *Rostipollos* son tan buenos como los pollos de *Pollitos del Corral.*
Estudiante 1: Ummm... no tienen tanta mantequilla como los pollos de *Pollitos del Corral.* Tienes razón. Son muy sabrosos.

restaurantes en tu ciudad/pueblo
cafés en tu comunidad
tiendas en tu ciudad/pueblo

periódicos en tu ciudad/pueblo
revistas favoritas
libros favoritos

comidas favoritas
los profesores
los cursos que toman

5

5 Model the activity by making a few comparisons between yourself and a celebrity.

Conversar En grupos, túrnense para hacer comparaciones entre ustedes mismos (*yourselves*) y una persona de cada categoría de la lista. Answers will vary.

▶ una persona de tu familia

▶ un(a) amigo/a especial

▶ una persona famosa

Síntesis

NATIONAL communication STANDARDS

6

6 Have students create a drawing of a family similar to the one on this page. Tell them not to let anyone see their drawings. Then pair students up and have them describe their drawings to one another. Each student must draw the family described by his or her partner.

La familia López En grupos, túrnense para hablar de Sara, Sabrina, Cristina, Ricardo y David y hacer comparaciones entre ellos. Answers will vary.

modelo

Estudiante 1: Sara es tan alta como Sabrina.
Estudiante 2: Sí, pero David es más alto que ellas.
Estudiante 3: En mi opinión, él es guapo también.

Lección 2

2.4 Superlatives Tutorial

 Both English and Spanish use superlatives to express the highest or lowest degree of a quality.

el/la mejor	**el/la peor**	**el/la más alto/a**
the best	*the worst*	*the tallest*

▶ This construction is used to form superlatives. Note that the noun is always preceded by a definite article and that **de** is equivalent to the English *in* or *of*.

$$\text{el/la/los/las} + \boxed{noun} + \text{más/menos} + \boxed{adjective} + \text{de}$$

▶ The noun can be omitted if the person, place, or thing referred to is clear.

¿El restaurante Las Delicias?
  Es **el más elegante** de la ciudad.
  The restaurant Las Delicias?
  It's the most elegant (one) in the city.

Recomiendo el pollo asado.
  Es **el más sabroso** del menú.
  I recommend the roast chicken.
  It's the most delicious on the menu.

▶ Here are some irregular superlative forms.

Irregular superlatives

Adjective		Superlative form	
bueno/a	*good*	**el/la mejor**	*(the) best*
malo/a	*bad*	**el/la peor**	*(the) worst*
grande	*grown, adult*	**el/la mayor**	*(the) oldest*
pequeño/a	*young*	**el/la menor**	*(the) youngest*
joven	*young*	**el/la menor**	*(the) youngest*
viejo/a	*old*	**el/la mayor**	*(the) oldest*

▶ The absolute superlative is equivalent to *extremely*, *super*, or *very*. To form the absolute superlative of most adjectives and adverbs, drop the final vowel, if there is one, and add **-ísimo/a(s)**.

malo → mal- → **malísimo**   mucho → much- → **muchísimo**

¡El bistec está **malísimo**!   Comes **muchísimo**.

▶ Note these spelling changes.

rico → **riquísimo**   largo → **larguísimo**   feliz → **felicísimo**

fácil → **facilísimo**   joven → **jovencísimo**   trabajador → **trabajadorcísimo**

 Escribe el equivalente de las palabras en inglés.

1. Marisa es ___la más inteligente___ (*the most intelligent*) de todas.
2. Ricardo y Tomás son ___los menos aburridos___ (*the least boring*) de la fiesta.
3. Miguel y Antonio son ___los peores___ (*the worst*) estudiantes de la clase.
4. Mi profesor de biología es ___el mayor___ (*the oldest*) de la universidad.

Teaching Tips
Practice superlative questions by asking for students' opinions. Ex: **¿Cuál es la clase más difícil de esta universidad? ¿Y la más fácil?** Include a mix of regular and irregular forms.

¡ATENCIÓN!

While **más** alone means *more*, after **el**, **la**, **los** or **las**, it means *most*. Likewise, **menos** can mean *less* or *least*.
Es **el café más rico del** país.
It's the most delicious coffee in the country.
Es **el menú menos caro de** todos éstos.
It is the least expensive menu of all of these.

CONSULTA

The rule you learned in **Estructura 2.3** (p. 101) regarding the use of **mayor/menor** with age, but not with size, is also true with superlative forms.

Heritage Speakers Ask heritage speakers to discuss whether absolute superlatives are common in their culture (some regions use them less frequently than others).

recursos

WB
pp. 125–126

LM
p. 140

vhlcentral.com
Lección 2

Práctica y Comunicación

1

1 Give these sentences to students as items 5–7: **5. Esas películas son malísimas, ¿no? (Hollywood) (Sí, son las peores de Hollywood.) 6. El centro comercial Galerías es grandísimo, ¿no? (ciudad) (Sí, es el más grande de la ciudad.) 7. Tus bisabuelos son viejísimos, ¿no? (familia) (Sí, son los mayores de mi familia.)**

Supersite: Activity Pack

Extra Practice Add an auditory aspect to this grammar practice. Prepare ten superlative sentences and read them aloud slowly, pausing after each sentence to allow students to write the direct opposite. Ex: **Ernesto es el menor de la familia. (Ernesto es el mayor de la familia.)**

El más... Responde a las preguntas afirmativamente. Usa las palabras entre paréntesis.

modelo
El cuarto está sucísimo, ¿no? (residencia)
Sí, es el más sucio de la residencia.

1. El almacén Velasco es buenísimo, ¿no? (centro comercial) Sí, es el mejor del centro comercial.
2. La silla de tu madre es comodísima, ¿no? (casa) Sí, es la más cómoda de la casa.
3. Ángela y Julia están nerviosísimas por el examen, ¿no? (clase) Sí, son las más nerviosas de la clase.
4. Jorge es jovencísimo, ¿no? (mis amigos) Sí, es el menor de mis amigos.

2

Completar Tu profesor(a) te va a dar una hoja de actividades con descripciones de José Valenzuela Carranza y Ana Orozco Hoffman. Completa las oraciones con las palabras de la lista. Some answers may vary. Suggested answers:

altísima	del	mayor	peor
atlética	guapísimo	mejor	periodista
bajo	la	menor	trabajadorcísimo
de	más	Orozco	Valenzuela

1. José tiene 22 años; es el ___menor___ y el más ___bajo___ de su familia. Es ___guapísimo___ y ___trabajadorcísimo___. Es el mejor ___periodista___ de la ciudad y el ___peor___ jugador de baloncesto.
2. Ana es la más ___atlética___ y ___la___ mejor jugadora de baloncesto del estado. Es la ___mayor___ de sus hermanos (tiene 28 años) y es ___altísima___. Estudió la profesión ___más___ difícil ___de___ todas: medicina.
3. Jorge es el ___mejor___ jugador de videojuegos de su familia.
4. Mauricio es el menor de la familia ___Orozco___.
5. El abuelo es el ___mayor___ de todos los miembros de la familia Valenzuela.
6. Fifí es la perra más antipática ___del___ mundo.

3

3 Encourage students to create as many superlatives as they can for each item. Have volunteers share their most creative statements with the class.

3 For item 6, briefly describe these novels for students who are not familiar with them.

Superlativos Trabajen en parejas para hacer comparaciones. Usen los superlativos.
Answers will vary.

modelo
Angelina Jolie, Bill Gates, Jimmy Carter
Estudiante 1: Bill Gates es el más rico de los tres.
Estudiante 2: Sí, ¡es riquísimo! Y Jimmy Carter es el mayor de los tres.

1. Guatemala, Argentina, España
2. Jaguar, Prius, Smart
3. la comida mexicana, la comida francesa, la comida árabe
4. Rachel McAdams, Meryl Streep, Jennifer Lawrence
5. Ciudad de México, Buenos Aires, Nueva York
6. *Don Quijote de la Mancha*, *Cien años de soledad*, *Como agua para chocolate*
7. el fútbol americano, el golf, el béisbol
8. las películas románticas, las películas de acción, las películas cómicas

 Practice more at **vhlcentral.com**.

Recapitulación

S Diagnostics

Completa estas actividades para repasar los conceptos de gramática que aprendiste en esta lección.

1 Completar
Completa la tabla con la forma correcta del pretérito. **9 pts.**

Infinitive	yo	usted	ellos
dormir	dormí	durmió	durmieron
servir	serví	sirvió	sirvieron
vestirse	me vestí	se vistió	se vistieron

2 La cena
Completa la conversación con el pretérito de los verbos. **7 pts.**

PAULA ¡Hola, Daniel! ¿Qué tal el fin de semana?

DANIEL Muy bien. Marta y yo (1) <u>conseguimos</u> (conseguir) hacer muchas cosas, pero lo mejor fue la cena del sábado.

PAULA Ah, ¿sí? ¿Adónde fueron?

DANIEL Al restaurante Vistahermosa. Es elegante, así que (nosotros) (2) <u>nos vestimos</u> (vestirse) bien.

PAULA Y, ¿qué platos (3) <u>pidieron</u> (pedir, ustedes)?

DANIEL Yo (4) <u>pedí</u> (pedir) camarones y Marta (5) <u>prefirió</u> (preferir) el pollo. Y al final, el camarero nos (6) <u>sirvió</u> (servir) flan.

PAULA ¡Qué rico!

DANIEL Sí. Pero después de la cena Marta no (7) <u>se sintió</u> (sentirse) bien.

3 Camareros
Genaro y Úrsula son camareros en un restaurante. Completa la conversación que tienen con su jefe usando pronombres. **8 pts.**

JEFE Úrsula, ¿le ofreciste agua fría al cliente de la mesa 22?

ÚRSULA Sí, (1) <u>se la ofrecí</u> de inmediato.

JEFE Genaro, ¿los clientes de la mesa 5 te pidieron ensaladas?

GENARO Sí, (2) <u>me las pidieron</u>.

ÚRSULA Genaro, ¿recuerdas si ya me mostraste los vinos nuevos?

GENARO Sí, ya (3) <u>te los mostré</u>.

JEFE Genaro, ¿van a pagarte la cuenta los clientes de la mesa 5?

GENARO Sí, (4) <u>me la van a pagar/van a</u> ahora mismo.

                <u>pagármela</u>

3 Remind students that indirect object pronouns always precede direct object pronouns.

RESUMEN GRAMATICAL

2.1 Preterite of stem-changing verbs   *p. 92*

servir	dormir
serví	dormí
serviste	dormiste
sirvió	durmió
servimos	dormimos
servisteis	dormisteis
sirvieron	durmieron

2.2 Double object pronouns   *pp. 95–96*

Indirect Object Pronouns: **me, te, le (se), nos, os, les (se)**

Direct Object Pronouns: **lo, la, los, las**

Le escribí la carta. → Se la escribí.
Nos van a servir los platos. → Nos los van a servir./
                         Van a servírnoslos.

2.3 Comparisons   *pp. 99–101*

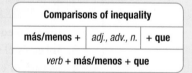

Comparisons of inequality

más/menos +	*adj., adv., n.*	+ que
verb + **más/menos** + **que**		

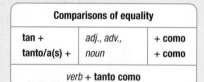

Comparisons of equality

tan +	*adj., adv.,*	+ como
tanto/a(s) +	*noun*	+ como
verb + **tanto como**		

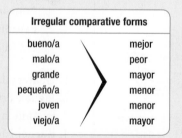

Irregular comparative forms

bueno/a	mejor
malo/a	peor
grande	mayor
pequeño/a	menor
joven	menor
viejo/a	mayor

Lección 2

4 Remind students that the comparative **tanto/a** must agree in gender and number with the noun it modifies.

TPR Have students write a celebrity's name, a place, and a thing on separate slips of paper. Collect the papers in three envelopes, separated by category. Then divide the class into two teams, **comparativos** and **superlativos**, and have them line up. Draw out two or three slips of paper (alternate randomly) and read the terms aloud. The corresponding team member has five seconds to create a logical comparison or superlative statement.

Pairs Have pairs imagine they went to a restaurant where the server mixed up all the orders. Call on pairs to share their experiences, using **pedir** and **servir** as well as double object pronouns. Ex: **Fui a un restaurante italiano. Pedí la pasta primavera. ¡El camarero me sirvió la sopa de mariscos! ¡Y me la sirvió fría!**

5 To help students organize their ideas, have them divide their paper into two columns: **mejor** and **peor**. Under each category, have students list the different reasons why their chosen restaurants are the best or worst.

6 Have students work in small groups to create an original riddle related to food. Have groups read their riddles for the class to guess.

2.4 **Superlatives**   *p. 104*

el/la/ los/las +	noun	+ más/ menos +	adjective	+ de

▶ Irregular superlatives follow the same pattern as irregular comparatives.

---

4 **El menú** Observa el menú y sus características. Completa las oraciones basándote en los elementos dados. Usa comparativos y superlativos. **14 pts.**

Ensaladas	*Precio*	*Calorías*
Ensalada de tomates	$9.00	170
Ensalada de mariscos	$12.99	325
Ensalada de zanahorias	$9.00	200

Platos principales		
Pollo con champiñones	$13.00	495
Cerdo con papas	$10.50	725
Atún con espárragos	$18.95	495

1. ensalada de mariscos / otras ensaladas / costar
   La ensalada de mariscos _____cuesta más que_____ las otras ensaladas.
2. pollo con champiñones / cerdo con papas / calorías
   El pollo con champiñones tiene _____menos calorías que_____ el cerdo con papas.
3. atún con espárragos / pollo con champiñones / calorías
   El atún con espárragos tiene _____tantas calorías como_____ el pollo con champiñones.
4. ensalada de tomates / ensalada de zanahorias / caro
   La ensalada de tomates es _____tan cara como_____ la ensalada de zanahorias.
5. cerdo con papas / platos principales / caro
   El cerdo con papas es _____el menos caro de_____ los platos principales.
6. ensalada de zanahorias / ensalada de tomates / costar
   La ensalada de zanahorias _____cuesta tanto como_____ la ensalada de tomates.
7. ensalada de mariscos / ensaladas / caro
   La ensalada de mariscos es _____la más cara de_____ las ensaladas.

5 **Dos restaurantes** ¿Cuál es el mejor restaurante que conoces? ¿Y el peor? Escribe un párrafo de por lo menos (*at least*) seis oraciones donde expliques por qué piensas así. Puedes hablar de la calidad de la comida, el ambiente, los precios, el servicio, etc. **12 pts.** Answers will vary.

6 **Adivinanza** Completa la adivinanza y adivina la respuesta. **¡2 puntos EXTRA!**

"En el campo yo nací°,
mis hermanos son
los ___ajos___ (*garlic, pl.*),
y aquél que llora° por mí
me está partiendo°
en pedazos°.**"**
¿Quién soy? ___La cebolla___

nací *was born* llora *cries* partiendo *cutting* pedazos *pieces*

 Practice more at **vhlcentral.com**.

Lectura

Antes de leer

Estrategia

Reading for the main idea

As you know, you can learn a great deal about a reading selection by looking at the format and looking for cognates, titles, and subtitles. You can skim to get the gist of the reading selection and scan it for specific information. Reading for the main idea is another useful strategy; it involves locating the topic sentences of each paragraph to determine the author's purpose for writing a particular piece. Topic sentences can provide clues about the content of each paragraph, as well as the general organization of the reading. Your choice of which reading strategies to use will depend on the style and format of each reading selection.

Examinar el texto

En esta sección tenemos dos textos diferentes. ¿Qué estrategias puedes usar para leer la crítica culinaria°? ¿Cuáles son las apropiadas para familiarizarte con el menú? Utiliza las estrategias más eficaces° para cada texto. ¿Qué tienen en común? ¿Qué tipo de comida sirven en el restaurante?

Identificar la idea principal

Lee la primera oración de cada párrafo de la crítica culinaria del restaurante **La feria del maíz.** Apunta° el tema principal de cada párrafo. Luego lee todo el primer párrafo. ¿Crees que el restaurante le gustó al autor de la crítica culinaria? ¿Por qué? Ahora lee la crítica entera. En tu opinión, ¿cuál es la idea principal de la crítica? ¿Por qué la escribió el autor? Compara tus opiniones con las de un(a) compañero/a.

Teaching Tips
• Review previous reading strategies: have students scan the text for cognates; ask how the title and format give clues to the content; and have students skim the article.
• Ask groups to create a dinner menu featuring their favorite dishes, including lists of ingredients similar to those in the menu above. Have groups present their menus to the class.

crítica culinaria *restaurant review* eficaces *efficient*
Apunta *Jot down*

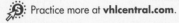 Practice more at **vhlcentral.com**.

MENÚ

Entremeses

Tortilla servida con
• Ajiaceite (chile, aceite) • Ajicomino (chile, comino)

Pan tostado servido con
• Queso frito a la pimienta • Salsa de ajo y mayonesa

Sopas

• Tomate • Cebolla • Verduras • Pollo y huevo
• Carne de res • Mariscos

Entradas

Tomaticán
(tomate, papas, maíz, chile, arvejas y zanahorias)

Tamales
(maíz, azúcar, ajo, cebolla)

Frijoles enchilados
(frijoles negros, carne de cerdo o de res, arroz, chile)

Chilaquil
(tortilla de maíz, queso, hierbas y chile)

Tacos
(tortillas, pollo, verduras y salsa)

Cóctel de mariscos
(camarones, langosta, vinagre, sal, pimienta, aceite)

Postres°

• Plátanos caribeños • Cóctel de frutas al ron°
• Uvate (uvas, azúcar de caña y ron) • Flan napolitano
• Helado° de piña y naranja • Pastel° de yogur

Después de leer

Preguntas

En parejas, contesten estas preguntas sobre la crítica culinaria de **La feria del maíz.**

1. ¿Quién es el dueño y chef de **La feria del maíz**?
   Ernesto Sandoval
2. ¿Qué tipo de comida se sirve en el restaurante?
   tradicional
3. ¿Cuál es el problema con el servicio?
   Se necesitan más camareros.
4. ¿Cómo es el ambiente del restaurante?
   agradable
5. ¿Qué comidas probó el autor? las tortillas, el ajiaceite, la sopa de mariscos, los tamales, los tacos de pollo y los plátanos caribeños
6. ¿Quieren ir ustedes al restaurante **La feria del maíz**?
   ¿Por qué? Answers will vary.

Teaching Tip Ask additional comprehension questions. Ex: ¿Cómo fue el camarero que atendió al crítico? ¿Cuál fue la opinión del crítico con respecto a la comida? ¿Cómo son los precios de La feria del maíz?

23F

Gastronomía
Por Eduardo Fernández

Lección 2

La feria del maíz

Sobresaliente°. En el nuevo restaurante **La feria del maíz** va a encontrar la perfecta combinación entre la comida tradicional y el encanto° de la vieja ciudad de Antigua. Ernesto Sandoval, antiguo jefe de cocina° del famoso restaurante **El fogón**, está teniendo mucho éxito° en su nueva aventura culinaria.

El gerente°, el experimentado José Sierra, controla a la perfección la calidad del servicio. El camarero que me atendió esa noche fue muy amable en todo momento. Sólo hay que comentar que,

La feria del maíz
13 calle 4-41 Zona 1
La Antigua, Guatemala
2329912

lunes a sábado
10:30am-11:30pm
domingo 10:00am-10:00pm

Comida ♈♈♈♈♈

Servicio ♈♈♈

Ambiente ♈♈♈♈

Precio ♈♈♈

debido al éxito inmediato de **La feria del maíz**, se necesitan más camareros para atender a los clientes de una forma más eficaz. En esta ocasión, el mesero se

tomó unos veinte minutos en traerme la bebida.

Afortunadamente, no me importó mucho la espera entre plato y plato, pues el ambiente es tan agradable que me sentí como en casa. El restaurante mantiene el estilo colonial de Antigua. Por dentro°, es elegante y rústico a la vez. Cuando el tiempo lo permite, se puede comer también en el patio, donde hay muchas flores.

El servicio de camareros y el ambiente agradable del local pasan a un segundo plano cuando llega la comida, de una calidad extraordinaria. Las tortillas de casa se sirven con un ajiaceite delicioso. La sopa

de mariscos es excelente y los tamales, pues, tengo que confesar que son mejores que los de mi abuelita. También recomiendo los tacos de pollo, servidos con un mole buenísimo. De postre, don Ernesto me preparó su especialidad, unos plátanos caribeños sabrosísimos.

Los precios pueden parecer altos° para una comida tradicional, pero la calidad de los productos con que se cocinan los platos y el exquisito ambiente de **La feria del maíz** garantizan° una experiencia inolvidable°.

Bebidas

- Cerveza negra • Chilate (bebida de maíz, chile y cacao)
- Jugos de fruta • Agua mineral • Té helado
- Vino tinto/blanco • Ron

Postres *Desserts* ron *rum* Helado *Ice cream* Pastel *Cake* Sobresaliente *Outstanding* encanto *charm* jefe de cocina *head chef* éxito *success* gerente *manager* Por dentro *Inside* altos *high* garantizan *guarantee* inolvidable *unforgettable*

Large Groups In groups of eight, have students role-play the situation depicted in the activity. Assign these roles: **camarero/a, guía turístico/a, la señora Johnson, los señores Petit, el señor Smith, la hija del señor Smith**, and **la señorita Jackson**. Have groups perform their skits for the class.

Un(a) guía turístico/a 🌰

Tú eres un(a) guía turístico/a en Guatemala. Estás en el restaurante **La feria del maíz** con un grupo de turistas norteamericanos. Ellos no hablan español y quieren pedir de comer, pero necesitan tu ayuda. Lee nuevamente el menú e indica qué error comete cada turista.

1. La señora Johnson es diabética y no puede comer azúcar. Pide sopa de verduras y tamales. No pide nada de postre.
   No debe pedir los tamales porque tienen azúcar.

2. Los señores Petit son vegetarianos y piden sopa de tomate, frijoles enchilados y plátanos caribeños.
   No deben pedir los frijoles enchilados porque tienen carne.

3. El señor Smith, que es alérgico al chocolate, pide tortilla servida con ajiaceite, chilaquil y chilate para beber.
   No debe pedir chilate porque tiene cacao.

4. La adorable hija del señor Smith tiene sólo cuatro años y le gustan mucho las verduras y las frutas naturales. Su papá le pide tomaticán y un cóctel de frutas.
   No debe pedir el cóctel de frutas porque tiene ron.

5. La señorita Jackson está a dieta y pide uvate, flan napolitano y helado.
   No debe pedir postres porque está a dieta.

Heritage Speakers Ask a heritage speaker of Guatemalan origin or a student who has visited Guatemala and dined in restaurants or cafés to prepare a short presentation about his or her experiences there. Of particular interest would be a comparison and contrast of city vs. small-town restaurants. If possible, the presentation should be illustrated with menus from the restaurants, advertisements, or photos of and articles about the country.

Escritura

Estrategia

Expressing and supporting opinions

Written reviews are just one of the many kinds of writing which require you to state your opinions. In order to convince your reader to take your opinions seriously, it is important to support them as thoroughly as possible. Details, facts, examples, and other forms of evidence are necessary. In a restaurant review, for example, it is not enough just to rate the food, service, and atmosphere. Readers will want details about the dishes you ordered, the kind of service you received, and the type of atmosphere you encountered. If you were writing a concert or album review, what kinds of details might your readers expect to find?

It is easier to include details that support your opinions if you plan ahead. Before going to a place or event that you are planning to review, write a list of questions that your readers might ask. Decide which aspects of the experience you are going to rate and list the details that will help you decide upon a rating. You can then organize these lists into a questionnaire and a rating sheet. Bring these forms with you to help you make your opinions and to remind you of the kinds of information you need to gather in order to support those opinions. Later, these forms will help you organize your review into logical categories. They can also provide the details and other evidence you need to convince your readers of your opinions.

Tema

Escribir una crítica

Escribe una crítica culinaria° sobre un restaurante local para el periódico de la universidad. Clasifica el restaurante dándole de una a cinco estrellas° y anota tus recomendaciones para futuros clientes del restaurante. Incluye tus opiniones acerca de°:

▶ La comida
  ¿Qué tipo de comida es? ¿Qué tipo de ingredientes usan?
  ¿Es de buena calidad? ¿Cuál es el mejor plato? ¿Y el peor?
  ¿Quién es el/la chef?

▶ El servicio
  ¿Es necesario esperar mucho para conseguir una mesa?
  ¿Tienen los camareros un buen conocimiento del menú?
  ¿Atienden a los clientes con rapidez° y cortesía?

▶ El ambiente
  ¿Cómo es la decoración del restaurante?
  ¿Es el ambiente informal o elegante?
  ¿Hay música o algún tipo de entretenimiento°?
  ¿Hay un bar? ¿Un patio?

▶ Información práctica
  ¿Cómo son los precios?
  ¿Se aceptan tarjetas de crédito?
  ¿Cuál es la dirección° y el número de teléfono?
  ¿Quién es el/la dueño/a? ¿El/La gerente?

Teaching Tip Go over the directions with the class, explaining that each student will rate (**puntuar**) a local restaurant and write a review of a meal there, including a recommendation for future patrons.

crítica culinaria *restaurant review* estrellas *stars* acerca de *about* rapidez *speed* entretenimiento *entertainment* dirección *address*

Escuchar Audio

Estrategia

Jotting down notes as you listen

Jotting down notes while you listen to a conversation in Spanish can help you keep track of the important points or details. It will help you to focus actively on comprehension rather than on remembering what you have heard.

> To practice this strategy, you will now listen to a paragraph. Jot down the main points you hear.

Preparación

Mira la foto. ¿Dónde están estas personas y qué hacen? ¿Sobre qué crees que están hablando?

Ahora escucha

Rosa y Roberto están en un restaurante. Escucha la conversación entre ellos y la camarera y toma nota de cuáles son los especiales del día, qué pidieron y qué bebidas se mencionan.

Especiales del día

Entremeses
salmón y langosta

Plato principal
arroz con pollo

cerdo con salsa de champiñones y papas

bistec a la criolla

¿Qué pidieron?

Roberto
cerdo con salsa de champiñones y papas

Rosa
especial de arroz con pollo

Bebidas

Inca Kola

jugo de naranja

Comprensión

Seleccionar

Usa tus notas para seleccionar la opción correcta para completar cada oración.

1. Dos de los mejores platos del restaurante son ___c___.
   a. los entremeses del día y el cerdo
   b. el salmón y el arroz con pollo
   c. la carne y el arroz con pollo

2. La camarera ___b___.
   a. los lleva a su mesa, les muestra el menú y les sirve el postre
   b. les habla de los especiales del día, les recomienda unos platos y ellos deciden qué van a comer
   c. les lleva unas bebidas, les recomienda unos platos y les sirve pan

3. Roberto va a comer ___a___ Rosa.
   a. tantos platos como
   b. más platos que
   c. menos platos que

Teaching Tip Invite students to look at the photo and predict where **Roberto** and **Rosa** are and what they are doing.

Preguntas

En grupos de tres o cuatro, respondan a las preguntas: ¿Conocen los platos que Rosa y Roberto pidieron? ¿Conocen platos con los mismos ingredientes? ¿En qué son diferentes o similares? ¿Cuál les gusta más? ¿Por qué?   Answers will vary.

Practice more at **vhlcentral.com**.

En pantalla

NATIONAL · communication cultures · STANDARDS

Los niños en los países hispanos suelen° comer algunos platos que no son muy comunes en los hogares° estadounidenses. Por ejemplo, muchos de los dulces° tradicionales de Colombia se hacen con frutas naturales. En algunas familias mexicanas se sirven pepinos° y jícamas° con limón y chile en polvo° como merienda a media tarde. Y para la comida, en muchos países, les sirven hígado o morcilla° a los niños porque son muy nutritivos. En este anuncio, vas a conocer a un niño peruano al que no le gusta el hígado.

Vocabulario útil

el cuco	bogeyman
fascículos	parts
el hígado	liver
nutritivo	nutritious
recetas	recipes
se los lleva...	are taken away by...
te dijo	told you

Ordenar

Pon en orden lo que ves en el anuncio de televisión. No vas a usar dos elementos.

- 6 a. pescado
- 4 b. periódicos
- 0 c. sal y pimienta
- 3 d. mamá
- 2 e. cuco
- 0 f. langosta
- 1 g. niño
- 5 h. recetas

Los platos

Responde a las preguntas. Después comparte tus respuestas con dos o tres compañeros/as para saber quién es el/la más osado/a (*daring*). Answers will vary.

1. ¿Cuál es tu plato favorito?
2. ¿Cuál es el plato más exótico que has probado (*that you have tried*)? ¿Te gustó o no?
3. ¿Qué plato exótico te gustaría (*would you like*) probar?
4. ¿Qué plato no quieres probar nunca? ¿Por qué?

Teaching Tip Before you show the video, have students read the title and the video captions and predict what type of product is being advertised.

suelen *are in the habit of* **hogares** *homes* **dulces** *candy* **pepinos** *cucumbers* **jícamas** *yam beans* **polvo** *powder* **morcilla** *blood sausage*

Anuncio de El Comercio

¡Grrrrrrr!

Y tú, ¿quién eres?

El cuco...

Teaching Tip Ask additional questions to facilitate a class discussion: **¿Es importante probar nuevas comidas? ¿Qué importancia tiene la comida en la cultura de un país? ¿Qué opinan de la comida en los EE.UU. y Canadá?**

S Video: TV Clip

 Practice more at **vhlcentral.com**.

España y la mayoría de los países de Latinoamérica tienen una producción muy abundante de frutas y verduras. Es por esto que en los hogares° hispanos se acostumbra° cocinar° con productos frescos° más que con alimentos° que vienen en latas° o frascos°. Las salsas mexicanas, el gazpacho español y el sancocho colombiano, por ejemplo, deben prepararse con ingredientes frescos para que mantengan° su sabor° auténtico. Actualmente, en los Estados Unidos está creciendo el interés en cocinar con productos frescos y orgánicos. Cada vez hay más mercados donde los agricultores° pueden vender sus frutas y verduras directamente° al público. Además, las personas prefieren consumir productos locales de temporada°. En este episodio de *Flash cultura* vas a ver algunas de las frutas y verduras típicas de la comida hispana.

Vocabulario útil

blanda	*soft*
cocinar	*to cook*
dura	*hard*
¿Está lista para ordenar?	*Are you ready to order?*
el plato	*dish (in a meal)*
pruébala	*try it, taste it*
las ventas	*sales*

Preparación

¿Probaste alguna vez comida latina? ¿La compraste en un supermercado o fuiste a un restaurante? ¿Qué plato(s) probaste? ¿Te gustó? Answers will vary.

¿Cierto o falso?

Indica si cada oración es **cierta** o **falsa**.

1. En Los Ángeles hay comida de países latinoamericanos y de España. Cierto.
2. Leticia explica que la tortilla del taco americano es blanda y la del taco mexicano es dura. Falso.
3. Las ventas de salsa son bajas en los Estados Unidos. Falso.
4. Leticia fue a un restaurante ecuatoriano. Falso.
5. Leticia probó Inca Kola en un supermercado. Cierto.

hogares *homes* se acostumbra *they are used* cocinar *to cook* frescos *fresh* alimentos *foods* latas *cans* frascos *jars* para que mantengan *so that they keep* sabor *flavor* agricultores *farmers* directamente *directly* de temporada *seasonal* mostrará *will show*

La comida latina

La mejor comida latina no sólo se encuentra en los grandes restaurantes.

Marta nos mostrará° algunos de los platos de la comida mexicana.

... hay más lugares donde podemos comprar productos hispanos.

Teaching Tip Have students work in pairs and correct the false statements in the ¿Cierto o falso? activity.

 **Video:** *Flash cultura*

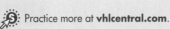 Practice more at **vhlcentral.com**.

recursos

VM pp. 133–134 | vhlcentral.com Lección 2

Guatemala

NATIONAL
connections
cultures
STANDARDS

El país en cifras

▸ **Área:** 108.890 km² (42.042 millas²),
un poco más pequeño que Tennessee

▸ **Población:** 16.227.000

▸ **Capital:** Ciudad de Guatemala—1.281.000

▸ **Ciudades principales:** Quetzaltenango,
Escuintla, Mazatenango, Puerto Barrios

SOURCE: Population Division, UN Secretariat

▸ **Moneda:** quetzal

▸ **Idiomas:** español (oficial),
lenguas mayas, xinca, garífuna
*El español es la lengua de un
60 por ciento° de la población;
el otro 40 por ciento tiene como
lengua materna el xinca, el
garífuna o, en su mayoría°, una
de las lenguas mayas (cakchiquel,
quiché y kekchícomo, entre
otras). Una palabra que las
lenguas mayas tienen en común
es ixim, que significa 'maíz', un
cultivo° de mucha importancia
en estas culturas.*

Bandera de Guatemala

Guatemaltecos célebres

▸ **Carlos Mérida,** pintor (1891–1984)

▸ **Miguel Ángel Asturias,** escritor (1899–1974)

▸ **Margarita Carrera,** poeta y ensayista (1929–)

▸ **Rigoberta Menchú Tum,** activista (1959–),
Premio Nobel de la Paz° en 1992

por ciento *percent* en su mayoría *most of them* cultivo *crop*
Paz *Peace* telas *fabrics* tinte *dye* aplastados *crushed*
hace... destiñan *keeps the colors from running*

ESTADOS UNIDOS
OCÉANO ATLÁNTICO
GUATEMALA
OCÉANO PACÍFICO
AMÉRICA DEL SUR

Palacio Nacional de la Cultura
en la Ciudad de Guatemala

MÉXICO

Sierra de Lacandón
Río Usumacinta
Lago Petén Itzá
Río de la Pasión
BELICE

Mujeres indígenas limpiando cebollas

Sierra Madre
Quetzaltenango
Lago de Atitlán

Lago de Izabal
Sierra de las Minas
Río Motagua

★ Guatemala
Antigua Guatemala
Mazatenango

Escuintla

Iglesia de la Merced en
Antigua Guatemala

EL SALVADOR

Océano Pacífico

recursos

WB
pp. 127–128

VM
pp. 131–132

vhlcentral.com
Lección 2

¡Increíble pero cierto!

¿Qué "ingrediente" secreto se encuentra en las
telas° tradicionales de Guatemala? ¡El mosquito! El
excepcional tinte° de estas telas es producto de una
combinación de flores y de mosquitos aplastados°.
El insecto hace que los colores no se destiñan°.
Quizás es por esto que los artesanos representan
la figura del mosquito en muchas de sus telas.

Lección 2

Mar Caribe

Golfo de
Honduras

Puerto
Barrios

HONDURAS

Ciudades • Antigua Guatemala

Antigua Guatemala fue fundada en 1543. Fue una capital de gran importancia hasta 1773, cuando un terremoto° la destruyó. Sin embargo, conserva el carácter original de su arquitectura y hoy es uno de los centros turísticos del país. Su celebración de la Semana Santa° es, para muchas personas, la más importante del hemisferio.

Naturaleza • El quetzal

El quetzal simbolizó la libertad para los antiguos° mayas porque creían° que este pájaro° no podía° vivir en cautiverio°. Hoy el quetzal es el símbolo nacional. El pájaro da su nombre a la moneda nacional y aparece también en los billetes° del país. Desafortunadamente, está en peligro° de extinción. Para su protección, el gobierno mantiene una reserva ecológica especial.

Historia • Los mayas

Desde 1500 a.C. hasta 900 d.C., los mayas habitaron gran parte de lo que ahora es Guatemala. Su civilización fue muy avanzada. Los mayas fueron arquitectos y constructores de pirámides, templos y observatorios. También descubrieron° y usaron el cero antes que los europeos, e inventaron un calendario complejo° y preciso.

Artesanía • La ropa tradicional

La ropa tradicional de los guatemaltecos se llama *huipil* y muestra el amor° de la cultura maya por la naturaleza. Ellos se inspiran en las flores°, plantas y animales para crear sus diseños° de colores vivos° y formas geométricas. El diseño y los colores de cada *huipil* indican el pueblo de origen y a veces también el sexo y la edad° de la persona que lo lleva.

¿Qué aprendiste? Responde a cada pregunta con una oración completa.

1. ¿Qué significa la palabra *ixim*?
   La palabra *ixim* significa "maíz".
2. ¿Quién es Rigoberta Menchú?
   Rigoberta Menchú es una activista de Guatemala.
3. ¿Qué pájaro representa a Guatemala?
   El quetzal representa a Guatemala.
4. ¿Qué simbolizó el quetzal para los mayas?
   El quetzal simbolizó la libertad para los mayas.
5. ¿Cuál es la moneda nacional de Guatemala?
   La moneda nacional de Guatemala es el quetzal.
6. ¿De qué fueron arquitectos los mayas?
   Los mayas fueron arquitectos de pirámides, templos y observatorios.

7. ¿Qué celebración de la Antigua Guatemala es la más importante del hemisferio para muchas personas? La celebración de la Semana Santa de la Antigua Guatemala es la más importante del hemisferio.
8. ¿Qué descubrieron los mayas antes que los europeos? Los mayas descubrieron el cero antes que los europeos.
9. ¿Qué muestra la ropa tradicional de los guatemaltecos? La ropa muestra el amor a la naturaleza.
10. ¿Qué indica un *huipil* con su diseño y sus colores? Con su diseño y colores, un *huipil* indica el pueblo de origen, el sexo y la edad de la persona.

Conexión Internet Investiga estos temas en **vhlcentral.com**.

1. Busca información sobre Rigoberta Menchú. ¿De dónde es? ¿Qué libros publicó? ¿Por qué es famosa?
2. Estudia un sitio arqueológico de Guatemala para aprender más sobre los mayas y prepara un breve informe para tu clase.

Practice more at **vhlcentral.com**.

terremoto *earthquake* Semana Santa *Holy Week* antiguos *ancient* creían *they believed* pájaro *bird* no podía *couldn't* cautiverio *captivity* los billetes *bills* peligro *danger* descubrieron *they discovered* complejo *complex* amor *love* flores *flowers* diseños *designs* vivos *bright* edad *age*
Supersite/DVD: You may want to wrap up this section by playing the **Panorama cultural** video footage for this lesson.

Las comidas

el/la camarero/a	waiter/waitress
la comida	food; meal
la cuenta	bill
el/la dueño/a	owner; landlord
el menú	menu
la propina	tip
la sección de (no) fumar	(non) smoking section
el almuerzo	lunch
la cena	dinner
el desayuno	breakfast
los entremeses	hors d'oeuvres; appetizers
el plato (principal)	(main) dish
delicioso/a	delicious
rico/a	tasty; delicious
sabroso/a	tasty; delicious

Las frutas

la banana	banana
las frutas	fruits
el limón	lemon
la manzana	apple
el melocotón	peach
la naranja	orange
la pera	pear
la uva	grape

Las verduras

las arvejas	peas
la cebolla	onion
el champiñón	mushroom
la ensalada	salad
los espárragos	asparagus
los frijoles	beans
la lechuga	lettuce
el maíz	corn
las papas/patatas (fritas)	(fried) potatoes; French fries
el tomate	tomato
las verduras	vegetables
la zanahoria	carrot

La carne y el pescado

el atún	tuna
el bistec	steak
los camarones	shrimp
la carne	meat
la carne de res	beef
la chuleta (de cerdo)	(pork) chop
la hamburguesa	hamburger
el jamón	ham
la langosta	lobster
los mariscos	shellfish
el pavo	turkey
el pescado	fish
el pollo (asado)	(roast) chicken
la salchicha	sausage
el salmón	salmon

Otras comidas

el aceite	oil
el ajo	garlic
el arroz	rice
el azúcar	sugar
los cereales	cereal; grains
el huevo	egg
la mantequilla	butter
la margarina	margarine
la mayonesa	mayonnaise
el pan (tostado)	(toasted) bread
la pimienta	black pepper
el queso	cheese
la sal	salt
el sándwich	sandwich
la sopa	soup
el vinagre	vinegar
el yogur	yogurt

Las bebidas

el agua (mineral)	(mineral) water
la bebida	drink
el café	coffee
la cerveza	beer
el jugo (de fruta)	(fruit) juice
la leche	milk
el refresco	soft drink; soda
el té (helado)	(iced) tea
el vino (blanco/ tinto)	(white/red) wine

Verbos

escoger	to choose
merendar (e:ie)	to snack
morir (o:ue)	to die
pedir (e:i)	to order (food)
probar (o:ue)	to taste; to try
recomendar (e:ie)	to recommend
saber	to taste; to know
saber a	to taste like
servir (e:i)	to serve

Las comparaciones

como	like; as
más de (+ number)	more than
más... que	more... than
menos de (+ number)	fewer than
menos... que	less... than
tan... como	as... as
tantos/as... como	as many... as
tanto... como	as much... as
el/la mayor	the oldest
el/la mejor	the best
el/la menor	the youngest
el/la peor	the worst
mejor	better
peor	worse

Expresiones útiles	See page 87.

recursos

LM p. 140
vhlcentral.com Lección 2

Audio: Vocabulary Flashcards

Supersite: MP3 Audio Files, Testing Program

contextos

Lección 2

1 **¿Qué comida es?** Read the descriptions and write the names of the food in the blanks.

1. Son rojos y se sirven (*they are served*) en las ensaladas. <u>los tomates</u>

2. Se come (*It is eaten*) antes del plato principal; es líquida y caliente (*hot*). <u>la sopa</u>

3. Son unas verduras anaranjadas, largas y delgadas. <u>las zanahorias</u>

4. Hay de naranja y de manzana; se bebe en el desayuno. <u>el jugo</u>

5. Son dos rebanadas (*slices*) de pan con queso y jamón. <u>el sándwich</u>

6. Es comida rápida; se sirven con hamburguesas y se les pone sal. <u>las papas/patatas fritas</u>

7. Son pequeños y rosados; viven en el mar. <u>los camarones</u>

8. Son frutas amarillas; con ellas, agua y azúcar se hace una bebida de verano. <u>los limones</u>

2 **Categorías** Categorize the foods listed in the word bank.

aceite	cebollas	jamón	mantequilla	peras	salmón
arvejas	champiñones	langosta	manzanas	pimienta	tomates
atún	chuletas de	leche	mayonesa	pollo	uvas
azúcar	cerdo	lechuga	melocotones	queso	vinagre
bananas	espárragos	limones	naranjas	sal	yogur
bistec	hamburguesas	maíz	papas	salchichas	zanahorias
camarones					

Verduras	Productos lácteos (*dairy*)	Condimentos	Carnes y aves (*poultry*)	Pescados y mariscos	Frutas
arvejas	leche	aceite	bistec	atún	bananas
cebollas	mantequilla	azúcar	chuletas de cerdo	camarones	limones
champiñones	queso	mayonesa	hamburguesas	langosta	manzanas
espárragos	yogur	pimienta	jamón	salmón	melocotones
lechuga		sal	pollo		naranjas
maíz		vinagre	salchichas		peras
papas					tomates
tomates					uvas
zanahorias					

3 **¿Qué es?** Label the food item shown in each drawing. Suggested answers:

1. _el vino tinto_

2. _las zanahorias_

3. _los camarones_

4. _las uvas_

4 **¿Cuándo lo comes?** Read the lists of meals, then categorize when the meals would be eaten.

1. un sándwich de jamón y queso, unas chuletas de cerdo con arroz y frijoles, un yogur y un café con leche

Desayuno _un yogur y un café con leche_
Almuerzo _un sándwich de jamón y queso_
Cena _unas chuletas de cerdo con arroz y frijoles_

2. una langosta con papas y espárragos, huevos fritos y jugo de naranja, una hamburguesa y un refresco

Desayuno _huevos fritos y jugo de naranja_
Almuerzo _una hamburguesa y un refresco_
Cena _una langosta con papas y espárragos_

3. pan tostado con mantequilla, un sándwich de atún y un té helado, un bistec con cebolla y arroz

Desayuno _pan tostado con mantequilla_
Almuerzo _un sándwich de atún y un té helado_
Cena _un bistec con cebolla y arroz_

4. una sopa y una ensalada, cereales con leche, pollo asado con ajo y champiñones

Desayuno _cereales con leche_
Almuerzo _una sopa y una ensalada_
Cena _pollo asado con ajo y champiñones_

estructura

2.1 Preterite of stem-changing verbs

1 **En el pasado** Rewrite each sentence, conjugating the verbs into the preterite tense.

1. Ana y Enrique piden unos refrescos fríos.

   Ana y Enrique pidieron unos refrescos fríos.

2. Mi mamá nos sirve arroz con frijoles y carne.

   Mi mamá nos sirvió arroz con frijoles y carne.

3. Tina y Linda duermen en un hotel de Lima.

   Tina y Linda durmieron en un hotel de Lima.

4. Las flores (*flowers*) de mi tía mueren durante el otoño.

   Las flores de mi tía murieron durante el otoño.

5. Ustedes se sienten bien porque ayudan a las personas.

   Ustedes se sintieron bien porque ayudaron a las personas.

2 **¿Qué hicieron?** For each sentence, choose the correct verb from those in parentheses. Then complete the sentence by writing the preterite form of the verb.

1. Rosana y Héctor _____repitieron_____ las palabras del profesor. (repetir, dormir, morir)

2. El abuelo de Luis _____murió_____ el año pasado. (despedirse, morir, servir)

3. (yo) _____Serví_____ camarones y salmón de cena en mi casa. (morir, conseguir, servir)

4. Lisa y tú _____pidieron_____ pan tostado con queso y huevos. (sentirse, seguir, pedir)

5. Elena _____durmió_____ en casa de su prima el sábado. (dormir, pedir, repetir)

6. Gilberto y su familia _____prefirieron_____ ir al restaurante francés. (servir, preferir, vestirse)

3 **No pasó así** Your brother is very confused today. Correct his mistakes by rewriting each sentence, replacing the subject with the one given in parentheses.

1. Anoche nos despedimos de nuestros abuelos en el aeropuerto. (mis primos)

   Anoche mis primos se despidieron de nuestros abuelos en el aeropuerto.

2. Melinda y Juan siguieron a Camelia por la ciudad en el auto. (yo)

   (Yo) Seguí a Camelia por la ciudad en el auto.

3. Alejandro prefirió quedarse en casa. (ustedes)

   Ustedes prefirieron quedarse en casa.

4. Pedí un plato de langosta con salsa de mantequilla. (ellas)

   Ellas pidieron un plato de langosta con salsa de mantequilla.

5. Los camareros les sirvieron una ensalada con atún y espárragos. (tu esposo)

   Tu esposo les sirvió una ensalada con atún y espárragos.

4 **En el restaurante** Create sentences from the elements provided. Use the preterite form of the verbs.

1. (nosotros) / preferir / este restaurante al restaurante italiano

   Preferimos este restaurante al restaurante italiano.

2. mis amigos / seguir / a Gustavo para encontrar el restaurante

   Mis amigos siguieron a Gustavo para encontrar el restaurante.

3. la camarera / servirte / huevos fritos y café con leche

   La camarera te sirvió huevos fritos y café con leche.

4. ustedes / pedir / ensalada de mariscos y vino blanco

   Ustedes pidieron ensalada de mariscos y vino blanco.

5. Carlos / preferir / las papas fritas

   Carlos prefirió las papas fritas.

6. (yo) / conseguir / el menú del restaurante

   Conseguí el menú del restaurante.

5 **La planta de la abuela** Complete this message with the preterite form of the verbs from the word bank. Use each verb only once.

conseguir	dormir	pedir	repetir	servir
despedirse	morir	preferir	seguir	vestirse

Querida mamá:

El fin de semana pasado fui a visitar a mi abuela Lilia en el campo. (Yo) Le

(1) _____ conseguí _____ unos libros en la librería de la universidad porque ella me los

(2) _____ pidió _____ . Cuando llegué, mi abuela me (3) _____ sirvió _____

un plato sabroso de arroz con frijoles. La encontré triste porque la semana pasada

su planta de tomates (4) _____ murió _____ y ahora tiene que comprar los tomates en

el mercado. Me invitó a quedarme, y yo (5) _____ dormí _____ en su casa. Por la

mañana, abuela Lilia se despertó temprano, (6) _____ se vistió _____ y salió a

comprar huevos para el desayuno. Me levanté inmediatamente y la

(7) _____ seguí _____ porque quería ir con ella al mercado. En el mercado, ella me

(8) _____ repitió _____ que estaba triste por la planta de tomates. Le pregunté:

¿Debemos comprar otra planta de tomates?, pero ella (9) _____ prefirió _____

esperar hasta el verano. Después del desayuno (10) _____ me despedí _____ de ella

y volví a la universidad. Quiero mucho a la abuela. ¿Cuándo la vas a visitar?

Chau,

Mónica

2.2 Double object pronouns

1　**Buena gente** Rewrite each sentence, replacing the direct objects with direct object pronouns.

1. La camarera te sirvió el plato de pasta con mariscos.

   La camarera te lo sirvió.

2. Isabel nos trajo la sal y la pimienta a la mesa.

   Isabel nos las trajo (a la mesa).

3. Javier me pidió el aceite y el vinagre anoche.

   Javier me los pidió (anoche).

4. El dueño nos busca una mesa para seis personas.

   El dueño nos la busca (para seis personas).

5. Tu madre me consigue unos melocotones deliciosos.

   Tu madre me los consigue.

6. ¿Te recomendaron este restaurante Lola y Paco?

   ¿Te lo recomendaron Lola y Paco?

2　**En el restaurante** Last night, you and some friends ate in a popular new restaurant. Rewrite what happened there, using double object pronouns in each sentence.

1. La dueña nos abrió la sección de no fumar.

   La dueña nos la abrió.

2. Le pidieron los menús al camarero.

   Se los pidieron.

3. Nos buscaron un lugar cómodo y nos sentamos.

   Nos lo buscaron y nos sentamos.

4. Les sirvieron papas fritas con el pescado a los clientes.

   Se las sirvieron (con el pescado).

5. Le llevaron unos entremeses a la mesa a Marcos.

   Se los llevaron (a la mesa).

6. Me trajeron una ensalada de lechuga y tomate.

   Me la trajeron.

7. El dueño le compró la carne al señor Gutiérrez.

   El dueño se la compró.

8. Ellos te mostraron los vinos antes de servirlos.

   Ellos te los mostraron (antes de servirlos).

3 **¿Quiénes son?** Answer the questions, using double object pronouns.

1. ¿A quiénes les escribiste las postales? (a ellos) _Se las escribí a ellos._

2. ¿Quién le recomendó ese plato? (su tío) _Se lo recomendó su tío./Su tío se lo recomendó._

3. ¿Quién nos va a abrir la puerta a esta hora? (Sonia) _Sonia nos la va a abrir./Sonia va a abrírnosla._

4. ¿Quién les sirvió el pescado asado? (Miguel) _Se lo sirvió Miguel./Miguel se lo sirvió._

5. ¿Quién te llevó los entremeses? (mis amigas) _Me los llevaron mis amigas./Mis amigas me los llevaron._

6. ¿A quién le ofrece frutas Roberto? (a su familia) _(Roberto) Se las ofrece a su familia._

4 **La cena** Read the two conversations. Then answer the questions, using double object pronouns.

CELIA	(*A Tito*) Rosalía me recomendó este restaurante.
DUEÑO	Buenas noches, señores. Les traigo unos entremeses, cortesía del restaurante.
CAMARERO	Buenas noches. ¿Quieren ver el menú?
TITO	Sí, por favor. ¿Está buena la langosta?
CAMARERO	Sí, es la especialidad del restaurante.
CELIA	¿Cuánto vale la langosta?
CAMARERO	Vale treinta dólares.
TITO	Entonces queremos pedir dos.
CELIA	Y yo quiero una copa (*glass*) de vino tinto, por favor.
CAMARERO	Tenemos flan y fruta de postre (*for dessert*).
CELIA	Perdón, ¿me lo puede repetir?
CAMARERO	Tenemos flan y fruta.
CELIA	Yo no quiero nada de postre, gracias.
DUEÑO	¿Les gustó la cena?
TITO	Sí, nos encantó. Muchas gracias. Fue una cena deliciosa.

1. ¿Quién le recomendó el restaurante a Celia? _Se lo recomendó Rosalía./Rosalía se lo recomendó._

2. ¿Quién les sirvió los entremeses a Celia y a Tito? _Se los sirvió el dueño./El dueño se los sirvió._

3. ¿Quién les trajo los menús a Celia y a Tito? _Se los trajo el camarero./El camarero se los trajo._

4. ¿A quién le preguntó Celia el precio de la langosta? _Se lo preguntó al camarero._

5. ¿Quién le pidió las langostas al camarero? _Se las pidió Tito./Tito se las pidió._

6. ¿Quién le pidió un vino tinto al camarero? _Se lo pidió Celia./Celia se lo pidió._

7. ¿Quién le repitió a Celia la lista de postres? _Se la repitió el camarero./El camarero se la repitió._

8. ¿A quién le dio las gracias Tito cuando se fueron? _Se las dio al dueño._

2.3 Comparisons

1 **¿Cómo se comparan?** Complete the sentences with the Spanish of the comparison in parentheses.

1. Puerto Rico es _____ más pequeño que _____ (*smaller than*) Guatemala.

2. Felipe corre _____ más rápido que _____ (*faster than*) su amigo Juan Carlos.

3. Los champiñones son _____ tan ricos/deliciosos/sabrosos como _____ (*as tasty as*) los espárragos.

4. Los jugadores de baloncesto son _____ más altos que _____ (*taller than*) los otros estudiantes.

5. Laura es _____ más trabajadora que _____ (*more hard-working than*) su novio Pablo.

6. Marisol es _____ menos inteligente que _____ (*less intelligent than*) su hermana mayor.

7. La nueva novela de ese escritor es _____ tan mala como _____ (*as bad as*) su primera novela.

8. Agustín y Mario están _____ menos gordos que _____ (*less fat than*) antes.

2 **Lo obvio** Your friend Francisco is always sharing his opinions with you, even though his comparisons are always painfully obvious. Write sentences that express his opinions, using the adjectives in parentheses.

> **modelo**
>
> (inteligente) Albert Einstein / Homer Simpson
> **Albert Einstein es más inteligente que Homer Simpson.**

1. (famoso) Nelly Furtado / mi hermana
   Nelly Furtado es más famosa que mi hermana.

2. (difícil) estudiar química orgánica / leer una novela
   Estudiar química orgánica es más difícil que leer una novela.

3. (malo) el tiempo en Boston / el tiempo en Florida
   El tiempo en Boston es peor que el tiempo en Florida.

4. (barato) los restaurantes elegantes / los restaurantes de comida rápida
   Los restaurantes elegantes son menos baratos que los restaurantes de comida rápida.

5. (viejo) mi abuelo / mi sobrino
   Mi abuelo es mayor que mi sobrino.

3 **¿Por qué?** Complete the sentences with the correct comparisons.

> **modelo**
>
> Darío juega mejor al fútbol que tú.
> **Es porque Darío practica más que tú.**

1. Mi hermano es más gordo que mi padre. Es porque mi hermano come más que mi padre/más que él .

2. Natalia conoce más países que tú. Es porque Natalia viaja más que tú .

3. Estoy más cansado que David. Es porque duermo menos que David/menos que él .

4. Rolando tiene más hambre que yo. Va a comer más que yo .

5. Mi vestido favorito es más barato que el tuyo. Voy a pagar menos que tú .

6. Julia gana más dinero que Lorna. Es porque Julia trabaja más que Lorna/más que ella .

4 **Comparaciones** Form complete sentences using one word from each column. Answers will vary.

la carne	bueno	el aceite
la comida rápida	caro	el almuerzo
el desayuno	malo	las chuletas de cerdo
la fruta	pequeño	la ensalada
la mantequilla	rico	los entremeses
el pollo	sabroso	el pescado

> **modelo**
>
> La carne es más cara que el pescado.

1. _____
2. _____
3. _____

4. _____
5. _____
6. _____

5 **Tan... como** Compare Jorge and Marcos using comparisons of equality and the following words. Be creative in your answers. Answers will vary.

alto	delgado	inteligente
bueno	guapo	joven

Marcos

Jorge

> **modelo**
>
> Marcos no es tan inteligente como Jorge.

1. _____
2. _____
3. _____

4. _____
5. _____
6. _____

6 **¿Más o menos?** Read the pairs of sentences. Then write a new sentence comparing the first item to the second one.

> **modelo**
>
> Ese hotel tiene cien habitaciones. El otro hotel tiene cuarenta habitaciones.
> Ese hotel tiene más habitaciones que el otro.

1. La biblioteca tiene ciento cincuenta sillas. El laboratorio de lenguas tiene treinta sillas.
   La biblioteca tiene más sillas que el laboratorio de lenguas.

2. Ramón compró tres corbatas. Roberto compró tres corbatas.
   Ramón compró tantas corbatas como Roberto.

3. Yo comí un plato de pasta. Mi hermano comió dos platos de pasta.
   Yo comí menos que mi hermano./Yo comí menos pasta que mi hermano.

4. Anabel durmió ocho horas. Amelia durmió ocho horas.
   Anabel durmió tanto como Amelia./Anabel durmió tantas horas como Amelia.

5. Mi primo toma seis clases. Mi amiga Tere toma ocho clases.
   Mi primo toma menos clases que mi amiga Tere.

2.4 Superlatives

1 **El mejor...** Complete with the appropriate information in each case. Form complete sentences using the superlatives. Answers will vary. Sample answers:

> **modelo**
>
> el restaurante _____ / bueno / ciudad
>
> *El restaurante Dalí es el mejor restaurante de la ciudad.*

1. la película _____ / mala / la historia del cine
   La película *Cobardes* es la peor de la historia del cine.

2. la comida _____ / sabrosa / todas
   La comida mexicana es la más sabrosa de todas.

3. mi _____ / joven / mi familia
   Mi sobrino es el menor de mi familia.

4. el libro _____ / interesante / biblioteca
   El libro *El Quijote* es el más interesante de la biblioteca.

5. las vacaciones de _____ / buenas / año
   Las vacaciones de verano son las mejores del año.

2 **Facilísimo** Rewrite each sentence, using absolute superlatives.

1. Miguel y Maru están muy cansados. Miguel y Maru están cansadísimos.

2. Felipe es muy joven. Felipe es jovencísimo.

3. Jimena es muy inteligente. Jimena es inteligentísima.

4. La madre de Marissa está muy contenta. La madre de Marissa está contentísima.

5. Estoy muy aburrido. Estoy aburridísimo.

3 **Compárate** Compare yourself with the members of your family and the students in your class. Write at least two complete sentences using comparisons of equality and inequality, superlatives, and absolute superlatives. Answers will vary.

> **modelo**
>
> En mi familia, yo soy más bajo que mi hermano.

_____

_____

_____

> **modelo**
>
> En mi clase, mi amigo Evan es tan inteligente como yo.

_____

_____

_____

Workbook

Síntesis

Interview a friend or a relative and ask him or her to describe two restaurants where he or she recently ate.

- How was the quality of the food at each restaurant?
- How was the quality of the service at each restaurant?
- How did the prices of the two restaurants compare?
- What did his or her dining companions think about the restaurants?
- How was the ambience different at each restaurant?
- How convenient are the restaurants? Are they centrally located? Are they accessible by public transportation? Do they have parking?

When you are finished with the interview, write up a comparison of the two restaurants based on the information you collected. Use as many different types of comparisons and superlative phrases as possible in your report. Answers will vary.

panorama

Guatemala

1   **Guatemala** Complete the sentences with the correct words.

1. La _____moneda_____ de Guatemala recibe su nombre de un pájaro que simboliza la libertad.

2. Un _____cuarenta_____ por ciento de la población guatemalteca tiene una lengua materna diferente del español.

3. El _____diseño_____ y los colores de cada *huipil* indican el pueblo de origen de la persona que lo lleva.

4. El _____quetzal_____ es un pájaro en peligro de extinción.

5. La civilización maya inventó un _____calendario_____ complejo y preciso.

6. La ropa tradicional refleja el amor de la cultura maya por la _____naturaleza_____.

2   **Preguntas** Answer the questions with complete sentences. Answers will vary. Sample answers:

1. ¿Cuál es un cultivo de mucha importancia en la cultura maya? _____

El maíz es un cultivo de mucha importancia en la cultura maya.

2. ¿Quién es Miguel Ángel Asturias? _____

Miguel Ángel Asturias es un escritor guatemalteco célebre.

3. ¿Qué países limitan con (*border*) Guatemala? _____

México, Belice, El Salvador y Honduras limitan con Guatemala.

4. ¿Hasta cuándo fue la Antigua Guatemala una capital importante? ¿Qué pasó? _____

La Antigua Guatemala fue una capital importante hasta 1773, cuando un terremoto la destruyó.

5. ¿Por qué simbolizó el quetzal la libertad para los mayas? _____

El quetzal simbolizó la libertad para los mayas porque creían que este pájaro no podía vivir en cautiverio.

6. ¿Qué hace el gobierno para proteger al quetzal? _____

El gobierno mantiene una reserva ecológica especial para proteger al quetzal.

3   **Fotos de Guatemala** Label each photo.

1. _____el quetzal_____

2. _____el huipil/los huipiles_____

4 **Comparar** Read the sentences about Guatemala. Then rewrite them, using comparisons and superlatives. Do not change the meaning.

> **modelo**
>
> La Ciudad de Guatemala no es una ciudad pequeña.
> La Ciudad de Guatemala es la más grande del país.

1. El área de Guatemala no es más grande que la de Tennessee.

   El área de Guatemala es más pequeña que la de Tennessee.

2. Un componente muy interesante de las telas (*fabrics*) de Guatemala es el mosquito.

   Un componente interesantísimo de las telas de Guatemala es el mosquito.

3. Las lenguas mayas no se hablan tanto como el español.

   Las lenguas mayas se hablan menos que el español.

4. Rigoberta Menchú no es mayor que Margarita Carrera.

   Rigoberta Menchú es menor que Margarita Carrera.

5. La celebración de la Semana Santa en la Antigua Guatemala es importantísima para muchas personas.

   La celebración de la Semana Santa en la Antigua Guatemala es la más importante del hemisferio para muchas personas.

5 **¿Cierto o falso?** Indicate whether the statements about Guatemala are **cierto** or **falso**. Correct the false statements.

1. Rigoberta Menchú ganó el Premio Nobel de la Paz en 1992.

   Cierto.

2. La lengua materna de muchos guatemaltecos es una lengua inca.

   Falso. La lengua materna de muchos guatemaltecos es una lengua maya.

3. La civilización de los mayas no era avanzada.

   Falso. La civilización de los mayas era muy avanzada.

4. Guatemala es un país que tiene costas en dos océanos.

   Cierto.

5. Hay muchísimos quetzales en los bosques de Guatemala.

   Falso. Los quetzales están en peligro de extinción.

6. La civilización maya descubrió y usó el cero antes que los europeos.

   Cierto.

Una cena... romántica

Antes de ver el video

1   **En un restaurante** What do you do and say when you have dinner at a restaurant? Answers will vary.

_____

_____

_____

_____

_____

_____

_____

Mientras ves el video

2   **¿Quién?** Watch **Una cena... romántica** and write the name of the person who says each sentence.

Oración	Nombre
1. La ensalada viene con aceite y vinagre.	camarero
2. Vino blanco para mí.	Maru
3. Mejor pido la ensalada de pera con queso.	Miguel
4. Los espárragos están sabrosísimos esta noche.	Felipe
5. Señor, él es más responsable que yo.	Juan Carlos

3   **Ordenar** Show the order in which the following took place.

_3_ a. Felipe les pone pimienta a los platillos.

_1_ b. Miguel pide una cerveza.

_2_ c. El camarero recomienda la sopa de frijoles.

_4_ d. El gerente llega a la mesa de Maru y Miguel.

4   **Completar** Fill in the missing words.

1. **MARU**   No sé qué pedir. ¿Qué me ___recomiendas___ ?

2. **CAMARERO**   ¿Ya decidieron qué ___entremés___ quieren?

3. **MARU**   Tienes razón, Felipe. Los espárragos están ___deliciosos___.

4. **FELIPE**   ¿Quién ___pidió___ jamón?

5. **JUAN CARLOS**   ¿Aquí vienen ___tantos___ mexicanos ___como___ extranjeros?

Después de ver el video

5   **Opiniones** Say who expressed the following opinions, either verbally or through body language.

     <u>   Maru   </u>   1. Los mariscos parecen tan ricos como el jamón.

     <u>   camarero   </u>   2. Este joven me está molestando con sus preguntas.

     <u>   Felipe   </u>   3. Los champiñones están deliciosos.

     <u>   Juan Carlos   </u>   4. Felipe tiene la culpa (*is guilty*) de lo que pasó.

     <u>   gerente   </u>   5. Vamos a la cocina para que paguen lo que hicieron.

6   **Corregir** Correct these statements.

1. Miguel le dice a Maru que la langosta se ve muy buena.

     Miguel le dice a Maru que las chuletas de cerdo se ven muy buenas.

2. De beber, Maru y Miguel piden té.

     De beber, Maru pide vino blanco y Miguel pide cerveza.

3. El plato principal es ceviche de camarones con cilantro y limón.

     El entremés es ceviche de camarones con limón y cilantro./El plato principal es bistec con verduras a la plancha.

4. Maru pide el jamón con arvejas.

     Maru pide el jamón con espárragos.

5. Felipe dice que los champiñones saben a vinagre.

     Felipe dice que los champiñones saben a mantequilla.

6. Felipe dice que es el mejor camarero del mundo.

     Felipe dice que es el peor camarero del mundo.

7   **Preguntas personales** Answer these questions in Spanish.   Answers will vary.

1. ¿Almuerzas en la cafetería de tu universidad? ¿Por qué? _____

     _____

2. ¿Cuál es tu plato favorito? ¿Por qué? _____

     _____

3. ¿Cuál es el mejor restaurante de tu comunidad? Explica (*Explain*) tu opinión. _____

     _____

4. ¿Cuál es tu restaurante favorito? ¿Cuál es la especialidad de ese restaurante? _____

     _____

5. ¿Sales mucho a cenar con tus amigos/as? ¿Adónde van a cenar? _____

     _____

Panorama: Guatemala

Lección 2
Panorama cultural

Antes de ver el video

1 **Más vocabulario** Look over these useful words and expressions before you watch the video.

Vocabulario útil		
alfombra *carpet*	destruir *to destroy*	ruinas *ruins*
artículos *items*	época colonial *colonial times*	sobrevivir *to survive*
calle *street*	indígenas *indigenous people*	terremoto *earthquake*

2 **Describir** In this video you are going to learn about an open-air market that takes place in Guatemala. In Spanish, describe one open-air market that you have been to or that you know about.
Answers will vary.
mercado: ______________________________

____

____

____

____

3 **Categorías** Categorize the words listed in the word bank.

bonitas	espectaculares	indígenas	quieres
calles	grandes	mercado	región
colonial	habitantes	monasterios	sentir
conocer	iglesias	mujeres	vieja

Lugares	Personas	Verbos	Adjetivos
calles	habitantes	conocer	bonitas
iglesia	indígenas	quieres	colonial
mercado	mujeres	sentir	espectaculares
monasterios			grandes
región			vieja

Mientras ves el video

4 | **Marcar** Check off what you see while watching the video.

✔ 1. fuente (*fountain*)
✔ 2. hombres con vestidos morados
___ 3. mujer bailando
✔ 4. mujer llevando bebé en el mercado
✔ 5. mujeres haciendo alfombras de flores

✔ 6. niñas sonriendo
___ 7. niño dibujando
✔ 8. personas hablando
✔ 9. ruinas
___ 10. turista mirando el paisaje

Después de ver el video

5 | **Completar** Complete the sentences with words from the word bank.

| aire libre | alfombras | atmósfera | fijo | indígenas | regatear |

1. En Semana Santa las mujeres hacen ___alfombras___ con miles de flores.
2. En Chichicastenango hay un mercado al ___aire libre___ los jueves y domingos.
3. En el mercado los artículos no tienen un precio ___fijo___.
4. Los clientes tienen que ___regatear___ cuando hacen sus compras.
5. En las calles de Antigua, los turistas pueden sentir la ___atmósfera___ del pasado.
6. Muchos ___indígenas___ de toda la región van al mercado a vender sus productos.

6 | **¿Cierto o falso?** Indicate whether each statement is **cierto** or **falso**. Correct the false statements.

1. Antigua fue la capital de Guatemala hasta 1773.
Cierto.

2. Una de las celebraciones más importantes de Antigua es la de la Semana Santa.
Cierto.

3. En esta celebración, muchas personas se visten con ropa de color verde.
Falso. En esta celebración muchas personas se visten con ropa de color morado.

4. Antigua es una ciudad completamente moderna. Falso. En Antigua (todavía) hay ruinas de la vieja capital/
hay muchas iglesias y monasterios de arquitectura colonial/se puede sentir la atmósfera del pasado.

5. Chichicastenango es una ciudad mucho más grande que Antigua.
Falso. Chichicastenango es más pequeña que Antigua.

6. El terremoto de 1773 destruyó todas las iglesias y monasterios en Antigua.
Falso. Muchas iglesias y monasterios sobrevivieron al terremoto.

7 | **Comparar** Write four sentences comparing the cities Antigua and Chichicastenango. Answers will vary.

La comida latina

Antes de ver el video

1 **Más vocabulario** Look over these useful words before you watch the video.

Vocabulario útil		
el arroz congrí *mixed rice and beans from Cuba*	**el frijol** *bean*	**la rebanada** *slice*
el azafrán *saffron*	**el perejil** *parsley*	**el taco al pastor** *Shepherd-style taco*
la carne molida *ground beef*	**el picadillo a la habanera** *Cuban-style ground beef*	**la torta al pastor** *traditional sandwich from Tijuana*
la carne picada *diced beef*	**el plátano** *banana*	
el cerdo *pork*	**el pollo** *chicken*	**la ropa vieja** *Cuban shredded beef*

2 **¡En español!** Look at the video still. Imagine what Leticia will say about **la comida latina** in Los Angeles, and write a two- or three-sentence introduction to this episode. Answers will vary.

Leticia, Estados Unidos

¡Hola! Soy Leticia Arroyo desde Los Ángeles. Hoy vamos a hablar sobre… _____

_____

_____

_____

_____

_____

_____

_____

Mientras ves el video

3 **Completar** (04:15–04:48) Watch Leticia ask other customers in the restaurant for recommendations and complete this conversation.

LETICIA Señoritas, ¿qué estamos (1) ___comiendo___ de rico?

CLIENTE 1 Mojito.

LETICIA ¿Y de qué se trata el (2) ___plato___?

CLIENTE 1 Es pollo con cebolla, arroz blanco, (3) ___frijoles___ negros y plátanos fritos. Es delicioso.

LETICIA Rico. ¿Y el tuyo?

CLIENTE 2 Yo estoy comiendo (4) ___arroz___ con pollo, que es arroz amarillo, pollo y plátanos fritos.

LETICIA ¿Y otras cosas en el (5) ___menú___ que están ricas también?

CLIENTE 2 A mí me (6) ___encanta___ la ropa vieja.

4   **Ordenar** Put these events in the correct order.

   _3_ a. Toma un café en el restaurante cubano.

   _4_ b. Leticia habla con el gerente (*manager*) de un supermercado.

   _2_ c. Leticia come picadillo, un plato típico cubano.

   _1_ d. La dueña de una taquería mexicana le muestra a Leticia diferentes platos mexicanos.

   _5_ e. Leticia compra frutas y verduras en un supermercado hispano.

Después de ver el video

5   **Emparejar** Match these expressions to the appropriate situations.

   _b_ 1. ¿Qué me recomienda?   _c_ 4. ¿Está listo/a para ordenar?

   _e_ 2. ¡Se me hace agua la boca!   _a_ 5. A la orden.

   _d_ 3. ¡Que se repita!

    a. Eres un(a) empleado/a de una tienda. Ayudaste a un(a) cliente/a a hacer una compra. Él/Ella se despide y te dice gracias. ¿Qué le respondes?

    b. Estás en un restaurante. Miraste el menú, pero todavía no sabes qué quieres comer. ¿Qué le dices al/a la camarero/a?

    c. El/La camarero/a te dio el menú hace cinco minutos y ahora se acerca para preguntarte si sabes lo que quieres pedir. ¿Qué pregunta te hace?

    d. Terminas de comer y pagas, estás muy contento/a por la comida y el servicio que recibiste. ¿Qué le dices al/a la camarero/a?

    e. Acabas de entrar en un supermercado. Tienes mucha hambre y ves unos postres que te parecen (*seem*) deliciosos. ¿Qué dices?

6   **Un plato típico** Research one of these typical dishes or drinks from the Hispanic world. Find out about its ingredients, where it is typical, and any other information that you find interesting. Answers will vary.

ropa vieja	picadillo a la habanera	horchata
Inca Kola	malta Hatuey	mate

_____

_____

_____

_____

_____

_____

_____

contextos

Lección 2

1 **Identificar** Listen to each question and mark an **X** in the appropriate category.

> **modelo**
> You hear: ¿Qué es la piña?
> You mark: an **X** under **fruta**.

	carne	pescado	verdura	fruta	bebida
Modelo				X	
1.		✗			
2.					✗
3.			✗		
4.		✗			
5.	✗				
6.				✗	
7.	✗				
8.					✗

2 **Describir** Listen to each sentence and write the number of the sentence below the drawing of the food or drink mentioned.

a. _____4_____   b. _____6_____   c. _____9_____   d. _____1_____

  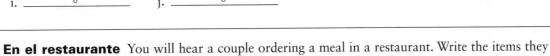

e. _____7_____   f. _____3_____   g. _____10_____   h. _____2_____

i. _____8_____   j. _____5_____

3 **En el restaurante** You will hear a couple ordering a meal in a restaurant. Write the items they order in the appropriate categories.

	SEÑORA	SEÑOR
Primer plato	ensalada de lechuga y tomate	sopa de verduras
Plato principal	hamburguesa con queso y papas fritas	pollo asado con arvejas y zanahorias
Bebida	agua mineral	agua mineral

pronunciación

ll, ñ, c, and z

Most Spanish speakers pronounce the letter **ll** like the *y* in *yes*.

po**ll**o	**ll**ave	e**ll**a	cebo**ll**a

The letter **ñ** is pronounced much like the *ny* in *canyon*.

ma**ñ**ana	se**ñ**or	ba**ñ**o	ni**ñ**a

Before **a**, **o**, or **u**, the Spanish **c** is pronounced like the *c* in *car*.

café	**c**olombiano	**c**uando	ri**c**o

Before **e** or **i**, the Spanish **c** is pronounced like the *s* in *sit*. In parts of Spain, **c** before **e** or **i** is pronounced like the *th* in *think*.

cereales	deli**c**ioso	condu**c**ir	cono**c**er

The Spanish **z** is pronounced like the *s* in *sit*. In parts of Spain, **z** before a vowel is pronounced like the *th* in *think*.

zeta	**z**anahoria	almuer**z**o	cerve**z**a

1 **Práctica** Repeat each word after the speaker to practice pronouncing **ll**, **ñ**, **c**, and **z**.

1. mantequilla
2. cuñado
3. aceite
4. manzana
5. español
6. cepillo
7. zapato
8. azúcar
9. quince
10. compañera
11. almorzar
12. calle

2 **Oraciones** When the speaker pauses, repeat the corresponding sentence or phrase, focusing on **ll**, **ñ**, **c**, and **z**.

1. Mi compañero de cuarto se llama Toño Núñez. Su familia es de la ciudad de Guatemala y de Quetzaltenango.
2. Dice que la comida de su mamá es deliciosa, especialmente su pollo al champiñón y sus tortillas de maíz.
3. Creo que Toño tiene razón porque hoy cené en su casa y quiero volver mañana para cenar allí otra vez.

3 **Refranes** Repeat each saying after the speaker to practice pronouncing **ll**, **ñ**, **c**, and **z**.

1. Las aparencias engañan.
2. Panza llena, corazón contento.

4 **Dictado** You will hear five sentences. Each will be said twice. Listen carefully and write what you hear.

1. Catalina compró mantequilla, chuletas de cerdo, refrescos y melocotones en el mercado.
2. Ese señor español quiere almorzar en un restaurante francés.
3. El mozo le recomendó los camarones con arroz.
4. En mi casa empezamos la comida con una sopa.
5. Guillermo llevó a Alicia al Café Azul anoche.

estructura

2.1 Preterite of stem-changing verbs

1 **Identificar** Listen to each sentence and decide whether the verb is in the present or the preterite tense. Mark an **X** in the appropriate column.

> **modelo**
>
> *You hear:* Pido bistec con papas fritas.
> *You mark:* an **X** under **Present**.

	Present	Preterite
Modelo	X	
1.	X	
2.	X	
3.		X
4.	X	
5.	X	
6.		X
7.		X
8.		X

2 **Cambiar** Change each sentence you hear substituting the new subject given. Repeat the correct response after the speaker. (*6 items*)

> **modelo**
>
> Tú no dormiste bien anoche. (Los niños)
> *Los niños no durmieron bien anoche.*

3 **Preguntas** Answer each question you hear using the cue in your lab manual. Repeat the correct response after the speaker.

> **modelo**
>
> *You hear:* ¿Qué pediste?
> *You see:* pavo asado con papas y arvejas
> *You say:* Pedí pavo asado con papas y arvejas.

1. Sí   3. leche   5. No
2. No   4. Sí   6. la semana pasada

4 **Un día largo** Listen as Ernesto describes what he did yesterday. Then read the statements in your lab manual and decide whether they are **cierto** or **falso**.

	Cierto	Falso
1. Ernesto se levantó a las seis y media de la mañana.	○	●
2. Se bañó y se vistió en poco tiempo.	●	○
3. Los clientes empezaron a llegar a la una.	○	●
4. Almorzó temprano.	○	●
5. Pidió pollo asado con papas.	●	○
6. Después de almorzar, Ernesto y su primo siguieron trabajando.	●	○

2.2 Double object pronouns

1 **Escoger** The manager of El Gran Pavo Restaurant wants to know what items the chef is going to serve to the customers today. Listen to each question and choose the correct response.

> **modelo**
>
> *You hear:* ¿Les vas a servir sopa a los clientes?
> *You read:* a. Sí, se la voy a servir.   b. No, no se lo voy a servir.
> *You mark:* **a because it refers to la sopa**.

1. a. Sí, se las voy a servir.　　　　(b.) No, no se los voy a servir.
2. (a.) Sí, se la voy a servir.　　　　b. No, no se lo voy a servir.
3. (a.) Sí, se los voy a servir.　　　　b. No, no se las voy a servir.
4. a. Sí, se los voy a servir.　　　　(b.) No, no se las voy a servir.
5. a. Sí, se la voy a servir.　　　　(b.) No, no se lo voy a servir.
6. (a.) Sí, se lo voy a servir.　　　　b. No, no se la voy a servir.

2 **Cambiar** Repeat each statement, replacing the direct object noun with a pronoun. (*6 items*)

> **modelo**
>
> María te hace ensalada.
> María **te la hace**.

3 **Preguntas** Answer each question using the cue you hear and object pronouns. Repeat the correct response after the speaker. (*5 items*)

> **modelo**
>
> ¿Me recomienda usted los mariscos? (sí)
> Sí, **se los recomiendo**.

4 **Una fiesta** Listen to this conversation between Eva and Marcela. Then read the statements in your lab manual and decide whether they are **cierto** or **falso**.

	Cierto	Falso
1. Le van a hacer una fiesta a Sebastián.	⊘	○
2. Le van a preparar langosta.	○	⊘
3. Le van a preparar una ensalada de mariscos.	⊘	○
4. Van a tener vino tinto, cerveza, agua mineral y té helado.	○	⊘
5. Clara va a comprar cerveza.	○	⊘
6. Le compraron un cinturón.	○	⊘

2.3 Comparisons

1 **Escoger** You will hear a series of descriptions. Choose the statement in your lab manual that expresses the correct comparison.

1. a. Yo tengo más dinero que Rafael.
   (b.) Yo tengo menos dinero que Rafael.
2. (a.) Elena es mayor que Juan.
   b. Elena es menor que Juan.
3. a. Enrique come más hamburguesas que José.
   (b.) Enrique come tantas hamburguesas como José.
4. (a.) La comida de la Fonda es mejor que la comida del Café Condesa.
   b. La comida de la Fonda es peor que la comida del Café Condesa.
5. a. Las langostas cuestan tanto como los camarones.
   (b.) Los camarones cuestan menos que las langostas.

2 **Comparar** Look at each drawing and answer the question you hear with a comparative statement. Repeat the correct response after the speaker.

1. **Ricardo   Sara**

2. **Héctor   Alejandro**

3. **Leonor   Melissa**

3 **Al contrario** You are babysitting Anita, a small child, who starts boasting about herself and her family. Respond to each statement using a comparative of equality. Then repeat the correct answer after the speaker. (*6 items*)

> **modelo**
> Mi mamá es más bonita que tu mamá.
> Al contrario, mi mamá es tan bonita como tu mamá.

2.4 Superlatives

1

Superlativos You will hear a series of descriptions. Choose the statement in your lab manual that expresses the correct superlative.

1. a. Tus pantalones no son los más grandes de la tienda.
   (b.) Tus pantalones son los más grandes de la tienda.
2. (a.) La camisa blanca es la más bonita del centro comercial.
   b. La camisa blanca no es tan bonita como otras camisas de la tienda.
3. a. Las rebajas del centro comercial son peores que las rebajas de la tienda.
   (b.) En el centro comercial puedes encontrar las mejores rebajas.
4. (a.) El vestido azul es el más caro de la tienda.
   b. El vestido azul es el más barato de la tienda.
5. (a.) Sebastián es el mejor vendedor de la tienda.
   b. Sebastián es el peor vendedor de la tienda.

2

Preguntas Answer each question you hear using the absolute superlative. Repeat the correct response after the speaker. (*6 items*)

> modelo
>
> La comida de la cafetería es mala, ¿no?
> Sí, es malísima.

3

Anuncio Listen to this advertisement. Then read the statements and decide whether they are **cierto** or **falso**.

	Cierto	Falso
1. Ningún almacén de la ciudad es tan grande como El Corte Inglés.	⊘	○
2. La mejor ropa es siempre carísima.	○	⊘
3. Los zapatos de El Corte Inglés son muy elegantes.	⊘	○
4. En El Corte Inglés gastas menos dinero y siempre tienes muy buena calidad.	⊘	○
5. El horario de El Corte Inglés es tan flexible como el horario de otras tiendas del centro.	○	⊘

vocabulario

You will now hear the vocabulary found in your textbook on the last page of this lesson. Listen and repeat each Spanish word or phrase after the speaker.

Additional Vocabulary

Additional Vocabulary

Notes

Notes

Las fiestas

3

A PRIMERA VISTA

- ¿Se conocen ellos?
- ¿Cómo se sienten, alegres o tristes?
- ¿Está el hombre más contento que la mujer?
- ¿De qué color es su ropa?

Más práctica

Las fiestas

Más vocabulario

la alegría	happiness
la amistad	friendship
el amor	love
el beso	kiss
la sorpresa	surprise
el aniversario (de bodas)	(wedding) anniversary
la boda	wedding
el cumpleaños	birthday
el día de fiesta	holiday
el divorcio	divorce
el matrimonio	marriage
la Navidad	Christmas
la quinceañera	young woman celebrating her fifteenth birthday
el/la recién casado/a	newlywed
cambiar (de)	to change
celebrar	to celebrate
divertirse (e:ie)	to have fun
graduarse (de/en)	to graduate (from/in)
invitar	to invite
jubilarse	to retire (from work)
nacer	to be born
odiar	to hate
pasarlo bien/mal	to have a good/bad time
reírse (e:i)	to laugh
relajarse	to relax
sonreír (e:i)	to smile
sorprender	to surprise
juntos/as	together
¡Felicidades!/ ¡Felicitaciones!	Congratulations!

Variación léxica

pastel	⟷	torta (*Arg., Col., Venez.*)
comprometerse	⟷	prometerse (*Esp.*)

Supersite: MP3 Audio Files and Scripts, Digital Image Bank, Activity Pack, Testing Program (Quizzes), **Vocabulario adicional**

recursos

WB
pp. 173–174

LM
p. 189

vhlcentral.com
Lección 3

el pastel (de chocolate)

la botella de vino

el flan de caramelo

las galletas

los postres

el champán

los dulces

Práctica 1 2 Supersite: MP3 Audio Files, Scripts

1

Escuchar  Escucha la conversación e indica si las oraciones son **ciertas** o **falsas**.

1. A Silvia no le gusta mucho el chocolate. Falsa.
2. Silvia sabe que sus amigos le van a hacer una fiesta. Falsa.
3. Los amigos de Silvia le compraron un pastel de chocolate. Cierta.
4. Los amigos brindan por Silvia con refrescos. Falsa.
5. Silvia y sus amigos van a comer helado. Cierta.
6. Los amigos de Silvia le van a servir flan y galletas. Falsa.

2

Ordenar Escucha la narración y ordena las oraciones de acuerdo con los eventos de la vida de Beatriz.

___5___ a. Beatriz se compromete con Roberto.

___4___ b. Beatriz se gradúa.

___3___ c. Beatriz sale con Emilio.

___2___ d. Sus padres le hacen una gran fiesta.

___6___ e. La pareja se casa.

___1___ f. Beatriz nace en Montevideo.

3

Emparejar Indica la letra de la frase que mejor completa cada oración.

a. cambió de	d. nos divertimos	g. se llevan bien
b. lo pasaron mal	e. se casaron	h. sonrió
c. nació	f. se jubiló	i. tenemos una cita

1. María y sus compañeras de cuarto ___g___. Son buenas amigas.
2. Pablo y yo ___d___ en la fiesta. Bailamos y comimos mucho.
3. Manuel y Felipe ___b___ en el cine. La película fue muy mala.
4. ¡Tengo una nueva sobrina! Ella ___c___ ayer por la mañana.
5. Mi madre ___a___ profesión. Ahora es artista.
6. Mi padre ___f___ el año pasado. Ahora no trabaja.
7. Jorge y yo ___i___ esta noche. Vamos a ir a un restaurante muy elegante.
8. Jaime y Laura ___e___ el septiembre pasado. La boda fue maravillosa.

4

Definiciones En parejas, definan las palabras y escriban una oración para cada ejemplo. Answers will vary. Suggested answers below.

> **modelo**
>
> **romper (con)** una pareja termina la relación
> Marta rompió con su novio.

1. regalar dar un regalo
2. helado una comida fría y dulce
3. pareja dos personas enamoradas
4. invitado una persona que va a una fiesta
5. casarse ellos deciden estar juntos para siempre
6. pasarlo bien divertirse
7. sorpresa la persona no sabe lo que va a pasar
8. amistad la relación entre dos personas que se llevan bien

Heritage Speakers Ask heritage speakers to describe Hispanic holidays or other celebrations that their families celebrate. Ex: **el Cinco de Mayo, la fiesta de quince años**

FELIZ CUMPLEAÑOS

brindar

el invitado

regalar

el helado

Relaciones personales

casarse (con)	to get married (to)
comprometerse (con)	to get engaged (to)
divorciarse (de)	to get divorced (from)
enamorarse (de)	to fall in love (with)
llevarse bien/mal (con)	to get along well/badly (with)
romper (con)	to break up (with)
salir (con)	to go out (with); to date
separarse (de)	to separate (from)
tener una cita	to have a date; to have an appointment

Las etapas de la vida de Sergio

el nacimiento

la niñez

la adolescencia

la juventud

la madurez

la vejez

Más vocabulario

la edad	age
el estado civil	marital status
las etapas de la vida	the stages of life
la muerte	death
casado/a	married
divorciado/a	divorced
separado/a	separated
soltero/a	single
viudo/a	widower/widow

5 Ask students to create five sentences using words from the **Más vocabulario** box on this page.

NOTA CULTURAL

Viña del Mar es una ciudad en la costa de Chile, situada al oeste de Santiago. Tiene playas hermosas, excelentes hoteles, casinos y buenos restaurantes. El poeta Pablo Neruda pasó muchos años allí.

¡LENGUA VIVA!

The term **quinceañera** refers to a girl who is celebrating her 15th birthday. The party is called **la fiesta de quince años**.

AYUDA

Other ways to contradict someone:

No es verdad.
It's not true.

Creo que no.
I don't think so.

¡Claro que no!
Of course not!

¡Qué va!
No way!

---

5 **Las etapas de la vida** Identifica las etapas de la vida que se describen en estas oraciones.

1. Mi abuela se jubiló y se mudó (*moved*) a Viña del Mar. la vejez
2. Mi padre trabaja para una compañía grande en Santiago. la madurez
3. ¿Viste a mi nuevo sobrino en el hospital? Es precioso y ¡tan pequeño! el nacimiento
4. Mi abuelo murió este año. la vejez/la muerte
5. Mi hermana celebró su fiesta de quince años. la adolescencia
6. Mi hermana pequeña juega con muñecas (*dolls*). la niñez

6 **Cambiar** En parejas, imaginen que son dos hermanos/as de diferentes edades. Cada vez que el/la hermano/a menor dice algo, se equivoca. El/La hermano/a mayor lo/la corrige (*corrects him/her*), cambiando las expresiones subrayadas (*underlined*). Túrnense para ser mayor y menor, decir algo equivocado y corregir.

> **modelo**
>
> **Estudiante 1:** La niñez es cuando trabajamos mucho.
> **Estudiante 2:** No, te equivocas (*you're wrong*). La madurez es cuando trabajamos mucho.

1. El nacimiento es el fin de la vida. La muerte
2. La juventud es la etapa cuando nos jubilamos. La vejez
3. A los sesenta y cinco años, muchas personas comienzan a trabajar. se jubilan
4. Julián y nuestra prima se divorcian mañana. se casan
5. Mamá odia a su hermana. quiere/se lleva bien con
6. El abuelo murió, por eso la abuela es separada. viuda
7. Cuando te gradúas de la universidad, estás en la etapa de la adolescencia. la juventud
8. Mi tío nunca se casó; es viudo. soltero

6 Explain that students are to give the opposite of the underlined words in their answers.

Practice more at **vhlcentral.com**.

Comunicación

Lección 3

7

Una fiesta Trabaja con dos compañeros/as para planear una fiesta. Recuerda incluir la siguiente información. Answers will vary.

1. ¿Qué tipo de fiesta es? ¿Dónde va a ser? ¿Cuándo va a ser?
2. ¿A quiénes van a invitar?
3. ¿Qué van a comer? ¿Quiénes van a llevar o a preparar la comida?
4. ¿Qué van a beber? ¿Quiénes van a traer las bebidas?
5. ¿Cómo planean entretener a los invitados? ¿Van a bailar o a jugar algún juego?
6. Después de la fiesta, ¿quiénes van a limpiar (*to clean*)?

7 To simplify, create a six-column chart on the board, with the headings **Lugar, Fecha y hora, Invitados, Comida, Bebidas,** and **Actividades.** Have groups brainstorm a few items for each category.

7 Have students make invitations for their party. Ask the class to judge which invitation is the cleverest, funniest, most elegant, and so forth.

8

Encuesta Tu profesor(a) va a darte una hoja de actividades. Haz las preguntas de la hoja a dos o tres compañeros/as de clase para saber qué actitudes tienen en sus relaciones personales. Luego comparte los resultados de la encuesta con la clase y comenta tus conclusiones. Answers will vary.

Supersite: Activity Pack

Preguntas	Nombres	Actitudes
1. ¿Te importa la amistad? ¿Por qué?		
2. ¿Es mejor tener un(a) buen(a) amigo/a o muchos/as amigos/as?		
3. ¿Cuáles son las características que buscas en tus amigos/as?		
4. ¿Tienes novio/a? ¿A qué edad es posible enamorarse?		
5. ¿Deben las parejas hacer todo juntos? ¿Deben tener las mismas opiniones? ¿Por qué?		

¡LENGUA VIVA!

While a **buen(a) amigo/a** is a *good friend*, the term **amigo/a íntimo/a** refers to a *close friend*, or a very good friend, without any romantic overtones.

Extra Practice Add a visual aspect to this vocabulary practice. Using magazine pictures, display images that pertain to parties or celebrations, stages of life, or interpersonal relations. Have students describe the pictures and make guesses about who the people are, how they are feeling, etc.

9

9 To simplify, read through the word list as a class and have students name the stage(s) of life that correspond to each word.

Minidrama En parejas, consulten la ilustración de la página 144 y luego, usando las palabras de la lista, preparen un minidrama para representar las etapas de la vida de Sergio. Pueden inventar más información sobre su vida. Answers will vary.

amor	celebrar	enamorarse	romper
boda	comprometerse	graduarse	salir
cambiar	cumpleaños	jubilarse	separarse
casarse	divorciarse	nacer	tener una cita

Video Synopsis The **Díaz** family gets ready for **Día de Muertos**. The whole family participates in the preparations, and **Ana María** shows **Marissa** and **Jimena** how to make **mole**. **Juan Carlos** is invited to accompany the family to the cemetery.

El Día de Muertos

communication
cultures

NATIONAL
STANDARDS

La familia Díaz conmemora el Día de Muertos.

PERSONAJES

 MARISSA   **JIMENA**   **FELIPE**   **JUAN CARLOS**

S Video: *Fotonovela*

MAITE FUENTES El Día de Muertos se celebra en México el primero y el segundo de noviembre. Como pueden ver, hay calaveras de azúcar, flores, música y comida por todas partes. Ésta es una fiesta única que todos deben ver por lo menos una vez en la vida.

MARISSA *Holy moley!* ¡Está delicioso!

TÍA ANA MARÍA Mi mamá me enseñó a prepararlo. El mole siempre fue el plato favorito de mi papá. Mi hijo Eduardo nació el día de su cumpleaños. Por eso le pusimos su nombre.

MARISSA ¿Cómo se conocieron?

TÍA ANA MARÍA En la fiesta de un amigo. Fue amor a primera vista.

MARISSA (*Señala la foto.*) La voy a llevar al altar.

TÍO RAMÓN ¿Dónde están mis hermanos?

JIMENA Mi papá y Felipe están en el otro cuarto. Esos dos antipáticos no quieren decirnos qué están haciendo. Y la tía Ana María...

TÍO RAMÓN ... está en la cocina.

TÍA ANA MARÍA Marissa, ¿le puedes llevar esa foto que está ahí a Carolina? La necesita para el altar.

MARISSA Sí. ¿Son sus padres?

TÍA ANA MARÍA Sí, el día de su boda.

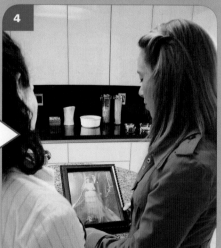

TÍA ANA MARÍA Ramón, ¿cómo estás?

TÍO RAMÓN Bien, gracias. ¿Y Mateo? ¿No vino contigo?

TÍA ANA MARÍA No. Ya sabes que me casé con un doctor y, pues, trabaja muchísimo.

Video Recap: Lección 2 Before doing this **Fotonovela** section, review the previous episode with these questions.
1. ¿Qué pidió de plato principal Maru? ¿Y Miguel? (Maru pidió el jamón y Miguel pidió el pollo asado con champiñones y papas. 2.¿Quiénes pagaron la comida de Maru y Miguel? (Felipe y Juan Carlos la pagaron.)

ciento cuarenta y siete   **147**

 SRA. DÍAZ
 SR. DÍAZ
 TÍA ANA MARÍA
 TÍO RAMÓN
 TÍA NAYELI
 DON DIEGO
 MARTA
 VALENTINA
MAITE FUENTES

Lección 3

7

SR. DÍAZ Familia Díaz, deben prepararse...

FELIPE ... ¡para la sorpresa de sus vidas!

8

JUAN CARLOS Gracias por invitarme.

SR. DÍAZ Juan Carlos, como eres nuestro amigo, ya eres parte de la familia.

(En el cementerio)

JIMENA Yo hice las galletas y el pastel. ¿Dónde los puse?

MARTA Postres... ¿Cuál prefiero? ¿Galletas? ¿Pastel? ¡Dulces!

VALENTINA Me gustan las galletas.

9

10

SR. DÍAZ Brindamos por ustedes, mamá y papá.

TÍO RAMÓN Todas las otras noches estamos separados. Pero esta noche estamos juntos.

TÍA ANA MARÍA Con gratitud y amor.

Expresiones útiles Draw attention to **pusimos** (video still 2) and explain that it is an irregular preterite form of the verb **poner**. Then point out the forms **vino** (video still 6) and **hice** and **puse** (video still 9). Tell students that these are irregular preterite forms of the verbs **venir, hacer,** and **poner**. Finally, draw attention to the phrase **Cómo se conocieron** and explain that **conocer** in the preterite means *to meet*. Tell students that they will learn more about these concepts in **Estructura**.

Teaching Tips
• Have students read the first line of dialogue in each caption and guess what happens in this episode.
• Go through the **Fotonovela**, asking volunteers to read the various parts.

recursos

VM
pp. 183–184

vhlcentral.com
Lección 3

Expresiones útiles

Discussing family history

El mole siempre fue el plato favorito de mi papá.
Mole *was always my dad's favorite dish.*
Mi hijo Eduardo nació el día de su cumpleaños.
My son Eduardo was born on his birthday.
Por eso le pusimos su nombre.
That's why we named him after him (after my father).
¿Cómo se conocieron sus padres?
How did your parents meet?
En la fiesta de un amigo. Fue amor a primera vista.
At a friend's party. It was love at first sight.

Talking about a party/celebration

Ésta es una fiesta única que todos deben ver por lo menos una vez.
This is a unique celebration that everyone should see at least once.
Gracias por invitarme.
Thanks for inviting me.
Brindamos por ustedes.
A toast to you.

Additional vocabulary

alma *soul*
altar *altar*
ángel *angel*
calavera de azúcar *skull made out of sugar*
cementerio *cemetery*
cocina *kitchen*
disfraz *costume*

Game Divide the class into two teams, A and B. Give a member from team A a card with the name of an item from the **Fotonovela** or **Expresiones útiles** (Ex: **flores, cocina, foto**). He or she has thirty seconds to draw the item, while team A has to guess what it is. Award one point per correct answer. If team A cannot guess the item within the time limit, team B may try to "steal" the point.

¿Qué pasó?

1 Completar Completa las oraciones con la información correcta, según la **Fotonovela**.

1. El Día de Muertos es una ___fiesta___ única que todos deben ver.
2. La tía Ana María preparó ___mole___ para celebrar.
3. Marissa lleva la ___foto___ al altar.
4. Jimena hizo las ___galletas___ y el ___pastel___.
5. Marta no sabe qué ___postre___ prefiere.

2 Identificar Identifica quién puede decir estas oraciones. Vas a usar un nombre dos veces.

SR. DÍAZ   **MAITE FUENTES**

1. Mis padres se conocieron en la fiesta de un amigo.
   tía Ana María
2. El Día de Muertos se celebra con flores, calaveras de azúcar, música y comida. Maite Fuentes
3. Gracias por invitarme a celebrar este Día de Muertos.
   Juan Carlos
4. Los de la foto son mis padres el día de su boda.
   tía Ana María
5. A mí me gustan mucho las galletas. Valentina
6. ¡Qué bueno que estás aquí, Juan Carlos! Eres uno más de la familia. Sr. Díaz

JUAN CARLOS   **VALENTINA**

TÍA ANA MARÍA

3 Seleccionar Selecciona algunas de las opciones de la lista para completar las oraciones.

amor	días de fiesta	pasarlo bien	salieron
el champán	divorciarse	postres	se enamoraron
cumpleaños	flan	la quinceañera	una sorpresa

1. El Sr. Díaz y Felipe prepararon ___una sorpresa___ para la familia.
2. Los ___días de fiesta___, como el Día de Muertos, se celebran con la familia.
3. Eduardo, el hijo de Ana María, nació el día del ___cumpleaños___ de su abuelo.
4. La tía Ana María siente gratitud y ___amor___ hacia (*toward*) sus padres.
5. Los días de fiesta también son para ___pasarlo bien___ con los amigos.
6. El Día de Muertos se hacen muchos ___postres___.
7. Los padres de la tía Ana María ___se enamoraron___ a primera vista.

4 Una cena Trabajen en grupos para representar una conversación en una cena de Año Nuevo.

Answers will vary.

- Una persona brinda por el año que está por comenzar y por estar con su familia y amigos.
- Cada persona del grupo habla de cuál es su comida favorita en año nuevo.
- Después de la cena, una persona del grupo dice que es hora de (*it's time to*) comer las uvas.
- Cada persona del grupo dice qué desea para el año que empieza.
- Después, cada persona del grupo debe desear Feliz Año Nuevo a las demás.

 Practice more at **vhlcentral.com**.

1 Have students work in pairs or small groups and write questions that would have elicited these statements.

3 Have pairs create additional sentences with the leftover items from the word bank.

Pairs Have students tell each other about celebrations they have with their own families. Remind them to use new vocabulary from the **Fotonovela** and **Contextos**.

NOTA CULTURAL

Comer doce uvas a las doce de la noche del 31 de diciembre de cada año es una costumbre que nació en España y que también se observa en varios países de Latinoamérica. Se debe comer una uva por cada una de las 12 campanadas (*strokes*) del reloj y se cree que (*it's believed that*) quien lo hace va a tener un año próspero.

Lección 3

Pronunciación (S) Audio
The letters h, j, and g

Supersite: MP3 Audio Files, Listening Scripts

helado	**h**ombre	**h**ola	**h**ermosa

The Spanish **h** is always silent.

José	**j**ubilarse	de**j**ar	pare**j**a

The letter **j** is pronounced much like the English *h* in *his*.

a**g**encia	**g**eneral	**G**il	**G**isela

The letter **g** can be pronounced three different ways. Before **e** or **i**, the letter **g** is pronounced much like the English *h*.

Gustavo, **g**racias por llamar el domin**g**o.

At the beginning of a phrase or after the letter **n**, the Spanish **g** is pronounced like the English *g* in *girl*.

Me **g**radué en a**g**osto.

In any other position, the Spanish **g** has a somewhat softer sound.

Guerra	conse**gui**r	**gua**ntes	a**gua**

In the combinations **gue** and **gui**, the **g** has a hard sound and the **u** is silent. In the combination **gua**, the **g** has a hard sound and the **u** is pronounced like the English *w*.

Práctica Lee las palabras en voz alta, prestando atención a la **h**, la **j** y la **g**.

1. hamburguesa	5. geografía	9. seguir	13. Jorge
2. jugar	6. magnífico	10. gracias	14. tengo
3. oreja	7. espejo	11. hijo	15. ahora
4. guapa	8. hago	12. galleta	16. guantes

Oraciones Lee las oraciones en voz alta, prestando atención a la **h**, la **j** y la **g**.

1. Hola. Me llamo Gustavo Hinojosa Lugones y vivo en Santiago de Chile.
2. Tengo una familia grande; somos tres hermanos y tres hermanas.
3. Voy a graduarme en mayo.
4. Para celebrar mi graduación, mis padres van a regalarme un viaje a Egipto.
5. ¡Qué generosos son!

Refranes Lee los refranes en voz alta, prestando atención a la **h**, la **j** y la **g**.

A la larga, lo más dulce amarga.[1]

El hábito no hace al monje.[2]

1 *Too much of a good thing.*
2 *The clothes don't make the man.*

Teaching Tips
- As you model the pronunciation of these sounds with the class, write additional words on the board and have students repeat.
- Contrast the pronunciations of the English *hotel* and the Spanish **hotel**. Repeat with *Julia* and **Julia**, *Gilbert* and **Gilberto**.
- Have students use the English words *guess* and *Guinness* to help them remember the silent **u** in the Spanish combinations **gue** and **gui**.
- For additional auditory practice, say several words with **h**, **j**, and **g** aloud. Have the class repeat and then write down the words. Go over as a class to check spelling.

Video Photocopy the **Fotonovela** script (Supersite) and white out words with **h**, **j**, and **g** to create a cloze activity. Play the video again and have students fill in the words as they watch the episode. Have volunteers write answers on the board to check spelling and repeat as a class.

Heritage Speakers Provide heritage speakers with several words and phrases containing the letter **g** and ask them to read them aloud. Have the class underline the words with a hard **g** sound, circle the words with a softer **g** sound, and put an X on words with the English *h* sound.

recursos

LM
p. 190

vhlcentral.com
Lección 3

EN DETALLE

Ⓢ Additional Reading

connections cultures
NATIONAL STANDARDS

Semana Santa: vacaciones y tradición

¿Te imaginas pasar veinticuatro horas tocando un tambor° entre miles de personas? Así es como mucha gente celebra el Viernes Santo° en el pequeño pueblo de **Calanda**, España.

De todas las celebraciones hispanas, la Semana Santa° es una de las más espectaculares y únicas.

Procesión en Sevilla, España

Semana Santa es la semana antes de Pascua°, una celebración religiosa que conmemora la Pasión de Jesucristo. Generalmente, la gente tiene unos días de vacaciones en esta semana. Algunas personas aprovechan° estos días para viajar, pero otras prefieren participar en las tradicionales celebraciones religiosas en las calles. En **Antigua**, Guatemala, hacen alfombras° de flores° y altares; también organizan Vía Crucis° y danzas. En las famosas procesiones y desfiles° religiosos de **Sevilla**, España, los fieles°

sacan a las calles imágenes religiosas. Las imágenes van encima de plataformas ricamente decoradas con abundantes flores y velas°. En la procesión, los penitentes llevan túnicas y unos sombreros cónicos que les cubren° la cara°. En sus manos llevan faroles° o velas encendidas.

Si visitas algún país hispano durante la Semana Santa, debes asistir a un desfile. Las playas y las discotecas pueden esperar hasta la semana siguiente.

Alfombra de flores en Antigua, Guatemala

Otras celebraciones famosas

Ayacucho, Perú: Además de alfombras de flores y procesiones, aquí hay una antigua tradición llamada "quema de la chamiza"°.

Iztapalapa, Ciudad de México: Es famoso el Vía Crucis del cerro° de la Estrella. Es una representación del recorrido° de Jesucristo con la cruz°.

Popayán, Colombia: En las procesiones "chiquitas" los niños llevan imágenes que son copias pequeñas de las que llevan los mayores.

tocando un tambor *playing a drum* Viernes Santo *Good Friday* Semana Santa *Holy Week* Pascua *Easter Sunday* aprovechan *take advantage of* alfombras *carpets* flores *flowers* Vía Crucis *Stations of the Cross* desfiles *parades* fieles *faithful* velas *candles* cubren *cover* cara *face* faroles *lamps* quema de la chamiza *burning of brushwood* cerro *hill* recorrido *route* cruz *cross*

ACTIVIDADES

1 ¿Cierto o falso? Indica si lo que dicen las oraciones sobre Semana Santa en países hispanos es **cierto** o **falso**. Corrige las falsas.

1. La Semana Santa se celebra después de Pascua.
   Falso. La Semana Santa es la semana antes de Pascua.
2. Las personas tienen días libres durante la Semana Santa.
   Cierto.
3. Todas las personas asisten a las celebraciones religiosas.
   Falso. Algunas personas aprovechan estos días para viajar.
4. En los países hispanos, las celebraciones se hacen en las calles.
   Cierto.

5. En Antigua y en Ayacucho es típico hacer alfombras de flores.
   Cierto.
6. En Sevilla, sacan imágenes religiosas a las calles.
   Cierto.
7. En Sevilla, las túnicas cubren la cara.
   Falso. Los sombreros cónicos cubren la cara.
8. En la procesión en Sevilla algunas personas llevan flores en sus manos.
   Falso. En sus manos llevan faroles o velas encendidas.
9. El Vía Crucis de Iztapalapa es en el interior de una iglesia.
   Falso. Es en el cerro de la Estrella.
10. Las procesiones "chiquitas" son famosas en Sevilla, España.
    Falso. Son famosas en Popayán, Colombia.

Lección 3

ASÍ SE DICE

Fiestas y celebraciones

la despedida de soltero/a	*bachelor(ette) party*
el día feriado/festivo	**el día de fiesta**
disfrutar	*to enjoy*
festejar	**celebrar**
los fuegos artificiales	*fireworks*
pasarlo en grande	**divertirse mucho**
la vela	*candle*

EL MUNDO HISPANO

Celebraciones latinoamericanas

• **Oruro, Bolivia** Durante el carnaval de Oruro se realiza la famosa Diablada, una antigua danza° que muestra la lucha° entre el Bien y el Mal: ángeles contra° demonios.

• **Panchimalco, El Salvador** La primera semana de mayo, Panchimalco se cubre de flores y de color. También hacen el Desfile de las palmas° y bailan danzas antiguas.

• **Quito, Ecuador** El mes de agosto es el Mes de las Artes. Danza, teatro, música, cine, artesanías° y otros eventos culturales inundan la ciudad.

• **San Pedro Sula, Honduras** En junio se celebra la Feria Juniana. Hay comida típica, bailes, desfiles, conciertos, rodeos, exposiciones ganaderas° y eventos deportivos y culturales.

danza *dance* lucha *fight* contra *versus* palmas *palm leaves* artesanías *handcrafts* exposiciones ganaderas *cattle shows*

PERFIL

Festival de Viña del Mar

En 1959 unos estudiantes de **Viña del Mar**, Chile, celebraron una fiesta en una casa de campo conocida como la Quinta Vergara donde hubo° un espectáculo° musical. En 1960 repitieron el evento. Asistió tanta gente que muchos vieron el espectáculo parados° o sentados en el suelo°. Algunos se subieron a los árboles°.

Años después, se convirtió en el **Festival Internacional de la Canción**. Este evento se celebra en febrero, en el mismo lugar donde empezó. ¡Pero ahora nadie necesita subirse a un árbol para verlo! Hay un anfiteatro con capacidad para quince mil personas.

En el festival hay concursos° musicales y conciertos de artistas famosos como Calle 13 y Nelly Furtado.

Nelly Furtado

hubo *there was* espectáculo *show* parados *standing* suelo *floor* se subieron a los árboles *climbed trees* concursos *competitions*

 Conexión Internet

¿Qué celebraciones hispanas hay en los Estados Unidos y Canadá?

Go to **vhlcentral.com** to find more cultural information related to this **Cultura** section.

ACTIVIDADES

2 **Comprensión** Responde a las preguntas.

1. ¿Cuántas personas por día pueden asistir al Festival de Viña del Mar? quince mil

2. ¿Qué es la Diablada? Es una antigua danza que muestra la lucha entre el bien y el mal.

3. ¿Qué celebran en Quito en agosto? Celebran el Mes de las Artes.

4. Nombra dos atracciones en la Feria Juniana de San Pedro Sula. Answers will vary.

5. ¿Qué es la Quinta Vergara? una casa de campo donde empezó el Festival de Viña del Mar.

3 **¿Cuál es tu celebración favorita?** Escribe un pequeño párrafo sobre la celebración que más te gusta de tu comunidad. Explica cómo se llama, cuándo ocurre y cómo es. Answers will vary.

3 Have students exchange papers with a classmate for peer editing.

Practice more at **vhlcentral.com**.

3.1 Irregular preterites  Tutorial

ANTE TODO You already know that the verbs **ir** and **ser** are irregular in the preterite. You will now learn other verbs whose preterite forms are also irregular.

Preterite of tener, venir, and decir

		tener (**u**-stem)	**venir** (**i**-stem)	**decir** (**j**-stem)
SINGULAR FORMS	yo	tuv**e**	vin**e**	dij**e**
	tú	tuv**iste**	vin**iste**	dij**iste**
	Ud./él/ella	tuv**o**	vin**o**	dij**o**
PLURAL FORMS	nosotros/as	tuv**imos**	vin**imos**	dij**imos**
	vosotros/as	tuv**isteis**	vin**isteis**	dij**isteis**
	Uds./ellos/ellas	tuv**ieron**	vin**ieron**	dij**eron**

▶ **¡Atención!** The endings of these verbs are the regular preterite endings of **-er/-ir** verbs, except for the **yo** and **usted/él/ella** forms. Note that these two endings are unaccented.

▶ These verbs observe similar stem changes to **tener, venir,** and **decir.**

INFINITIVE	U-STEM	PRETERITE FORMS
poder	pud-	pude, pudiste, pudo, pudimos, pudisteis, pudieron
poner	pus-	puse, pusiste, puso, pusimos, pusisteis, pusieron
saber	sup-	supe, supiste, supo, supimos, supisteis, supieron
estar	estuv-	estuve, estuviste, estuvo, estuvimos, estuvisteis, estuvieron

INFINITIVE	I-STEM	PRETERITE FORMS
querer	quis-	quise, quisiste, quiso, quisimos, quisisteis, quisieron
hacer	hic-	hice, hiciste, hizo, hicimos, hicisteis, hicieron

INFINITIVE	J-STEM	PRETERITE FORMS
traer	traj-	traje, trajiste, trajo, trajimos, trajisteis, trajeron
conducir	conduj-	conduje, condujiste, condujo, condujimos, condujisteis, condujeron
traducir	traduj-	traduje, tradujiste, tradujo, tradujimos, tradujisteis, tradujeron

▶ **¡Atención!** Most verbs that end in **-cir** are **j**-stem verbs in the preterite. For example, **producir → produje, produjiste.**

> **Produjimos** un documental sobre los accidentes en la casa.
> *We produced a documentary about accidents in the home.*

▶ Notice that the preterites with **j**-stems omit the letter **i** in the **ustedes/ellos/ellas** form.

> Mis amigos **trajeron** comida a la fiesta.
> *My friends brought food to the party.*

> Ellos **dijeron** la verdad.
> *They told the truth.*

NATIONAL comparisons STANDARDS

Teaching Tips
- Quickly review the present tense of a stem-changing verb such as **pedir**. Write the paradigm on the board and ask volunteers to point out the stem-changing forms.
- Work through the preterite paradigms of **tener, venir,** and **decir,** modeling the pronunciation.
- Add a visual aspect to this grammar presentation. Use magazine pictures to ask about social events in the past. Ex: ¿**Con quién vino este chico a la fiesta? (Vino con esa chica rubia.) ¿Qué se puso esta señora para ir a la boda? (Se puso un sombrero.)**
- Write the preterite paradigm for **estar** on the board. Then erase the initial **es-** for each form and point out that the preterite of **estar** and **tener** are identical except for the initial **es-**.

Extra Practice Do a pattern practice drill. Name an infinitive and ask individuals to provide conjugations for the different subject pronouns and/or names you provide. Reverse the activity by saying a conjugated form and asking students to give an appropriate subject pronoun.

Game Divide the class into two teams. Indicate one team member at a time, alternating between teams. Give a verb in its infinitive form and a subject pronoun (Ex: **querer/tú**). The team member should give the correct preterite form (Ex: **quisiste**). Give one point per correct answer. Deduct one point for each wrong answer. The team with the most points at the end wins.

The preterite of dar

yo	d**i**	nosotros/as	d**imos**
tú	d**iste**	vosotros/as	d**isteis**
Ud./él/ella	d**io**	Uds./ellos/ellas	d**ieron**

SINGULAR FORMS   PLURAL FORMS

▶ The endings for **dar** are the same as the regular preterite endings for **-er** and **-ir** verbs, except that there are no accent marks.

La camarera me **dio** el menú.
The waitress gave me the menu.

Le **di** a Juan algunos consejos.
I gave Juan some advice.

Los invitados le **dieron** un regalo.
The guests gave him/her a gift.

Nosotros **dimos** una gran fiesta.
We gave a great party.

▶ The preterite of **hay** (*inf.* **haber**) is **hubo** (*there was; there were*).

Marissa le dio la foto a la Sra. Díaz.

Hubo una celebración en casa de los Díaz.

Teaching Tips
• Point out that **dar** has the same preterite endings as **ver**.
• Drill the preterite of **dar** by asking students about what they gave their family members for their last birthdays or other special occasion. Ex: **¿Qué le diste a tu hermano para su cumpleaños?** Then ask what other family members gave them. Ex: **¿Qué te dio tu padre? ¿Y tu madre?**

CONSULTA

Note that there are other ways to say *there was* or *there were* in Spanish. See **Estructura 4.1**, p. 206.

Video Show the **Fotonovela** again to give students more input containing irregular preterite forms. Stop the video where appropriate to discuss how certain verbs were used and to ask comprehension questions.

Extra Practice Ask personalized questions to elicit irregular preterite forms. Ex: ____, ¿qué hiciste el sábado? Ah, hubo una fiesta para tu hermano. ¿Le dieron muchos regalos?

¡INTÉNTALO!   Escribe la forma correcta del pretérito de cada verbo que está entre paréntesis.

1. (querer) tú ___quisiste___
2. (decir) usted ___dijo___
3. (hacer) nosotras ___hicimos___
4. (traer) yo ___traje___
5. (conducir) ellas ___condujeron___
6. (estar) ella ___estuvo___
7. (tener) tú ___tuviste___
8. (dar) ella y yo ___dimos___
9. (traducir) yo ___traduje___
10. (haber) ayer ___hubo___
11. (saber) usted ___supo___
12. (poner) ellos ___pusieron___

13. (venir) yo ___vine___
14. (poder) tú ___pudiste___
15. (querer) ustedes ___quisieron___
16. (estar) nosotros ___estuvimos___
17. (decir) tú ___dijiste___
18. (saber) ellos ___supieron___
19. (hacer) él ___hizo___
20. (poner) yo ___puse___
21. (traer) nosotras ___trajimos___
22. (tener) yo ___tuve___
23. (dar) tú ___diste___
24. (poder) ustedes ___pudieron___

recursos

WB
pp. 175–176

LM
p. 191

S
vhlcentral.com
Lección 3

Práctica

1

Completar Completa estas oraciones con el pretérito de los verbos entre paréntesis.

1. El sábado ___hubo___ (haber) una fiesta sorpresa para Elsa en mi casa.
2. Sofía ___hizo___ (hacer) un pastel para la fiesta y Miguel ___trajo___ (traer) un flan.
3. Los amigos y parientes de Elsa ___vinieron___ (venir) y ___trajeron___ (traer) regalos.
4. El hermano de Elsa no ___vino___ (venir) porque ___tuvo___ (tener) que trabajar.
5. Su tía María Dolores tampoco ___pudo___ (poder) venir.
6. Cuando Elsa abrió la puerta, todos gritaron: "¡Feliz cumpleaños!" y su esposo le ___dio___ (dar) un beso.
7. Elsa no ___supo___ (saber) cómo reaccionar (*react*). ___Estuvo___ (Estar) un poco nerviosa al principio, pero pronto sus amigos ___pusieron___ (poner) música y ella ___pudo___ (poder) relajarse bailando con su esposo.
8. Al final de la noche, todos ___dijeron___ (decir) que se divirtieron mucho.

2

Describir En parejas, usen verbos de la lista para describir lo que estas personas hicieron. Deben dar por lo menos dos oraciones por cada dibujo. Some answers may vary. Suggested answers:

dar	hacer	tener	traer
estar	poner	traducir	venir

1. el señor López
El señor López le dio/trajo dinero a su hijo.

2. Norma
Norma puso el pavo en la mesa./Norma trajo el pavo a la mesa.

3. anoche nosotros
Anoche nosotros tuvimos/hicimos/dimos una fiesta de Navidad./Anoche nosotros estuvimos en una fiesta de Navidad.

4. Roberto y Elena
Roberto y Elena le trajeron/dieron un regalo a su amigo.

Practice more at **vhlcentral.com**.

NOTA CULTURAL

El **flan** es un postre muy popular en los países de habla hispana. Se prepara con huevos, leche y azúcar y se sirve con salsa de caramelo. Existen variedades deliciosas como el flan de chocolate o el flan de coco.

1 Ask individual students about the last time they threw a party. Ex: **La última vez que diste una fiesta, ¿quiénes estuvieron allí? ¿Fue alguien que no invitaste? ¿Qué llevaron los invitados?**

1 Assign students to groups of three. Tell them they are going to write a narrative about a wedding. You will begin the story, then each student will add a sentence using an irregular verb in the preterite. Each group member should have at least two turns. Ex: **El domingo se casaron Carlos y Susana. (E1: Tuvieron una boda muy grande. E2: Vinieron muchos invitados. E3: Hubo un pastel enorme y elegante.)**

2 To challenge students, have them see how many sentences they can come up with to describe each drawing using the target verbs.

Small Groups In groups of three or four, have each student write three sentences using irregular preterites. Two of the sentences should be true and the third should be false. As students read their sentences aloud, the other members of the group have to guess which of the sentences is the false one. This can also be done with the whole class.

Lección 3

Comunicación

3 To practice the formal register, call on different students to ask you the questions in the activity.

4 Distribute the **Hoja de actividades** for this activity from the Activity Pack on the Supersite. Point out that to get information, students must form questions using the **tú** forms of the infinitives.

3 **Preguntas** En parejas, túrnense para hacerse y responder a estas preguntas. Answers will vary.

1. ¿Fuiste a una fiesta de cumpleaños el año pasado? ¿De quién?
2. ¿Quiénes fueron a la fiesta?
3. ¿Quién condujo el auto?
4. ¿Cómo estuvo el ambiente de la fiesta?
5. ¿Quién llevó regalos, bebidas o comida? ¿Llevaste algo especial?
6. ¿Hubo comida? ¿Quién la hizo? ¿Hubo champán?
7. ¿Qué regalo hiciste tú? ¿Qué otros regalos trajeron los invitados?
8. ¿Cuántos invitados hubo en la fiesta?
9. ¿Qué tipo de música hubo?
10. ¿Qué te dijeron algunos invitados de la fiesta?

4 **Encuesta** Tu profesor(a) va a darte una hoja de actividades. Para cada una de las actividades de la lista, encuentra a alguien que hizo esa actividad en el tiempo indicado. Answers will vary.

Supersite: Activtity Pack

Large Groups Divide the class into two groups. Give each member of the first group a strip of paper with a question. Ex: **¿Quién me trajo el pastel de cumpleaños?** Give each member of the second group a strip of paper with an answer. Ex: **Marta te lo trajo.** Students must find their partners.

5 Have pairs work in groups of four to write a paragraph combining the most interesting or unusual aspects of each pair's conversation. Ask a group representative to read the paragraph to the class, who will vote for the most creative or funniest paragraph.

modelo

traer dulces a clase
Estudiante 1: ¿Trajiste dulces a clase?
Estudiante 2: Sí, traje galletas y helado a la fiesta del fin del semestre.

Actividades | Nombres

1. ponerse un disfraz (*costume*) de Halloween
2. traer dulces a clase
3. conducir su auto a clase
4. estar en la biblioteca ayer
5. dar un regalo a alguien ayer
6. poder levantarse temprano esta mañana
7. hacer un viaje a un país hispano en el verano
8. tener una cita anoche
9. ir a una fiesta el fin de semana pasado
10. tener que trabajar el sábado pasado

Síntesis

5 **Conversación** En parejas, preparen una conversación en la que uno/a de ustedes va a visitar a su hermano/a para explicarle por qué no fue a su fiesta de graduación y para saber cómo estuvo la fiesta. Incluyan esta información en la conversación: Answers will vary.

- cuál fue el menú
- quiénes vinieron a la fiesta y quiénes no pudieron venir
- quiénes prepararon la comida o trajeron algo
- si él/ella tuvo que preparar algo
- lo que la gente hizo antes y después de comer
- cómo lo pasaron, bien o mal

3.2 Verbs that change meaning in the preterite

 **Tutorial**

ANTE TODO The verbs **conocer, saber, poder,** and **querer** change meanings when used in the preterite. Because of this, each of them corresponds to more than one verb in English, depending on its tense.

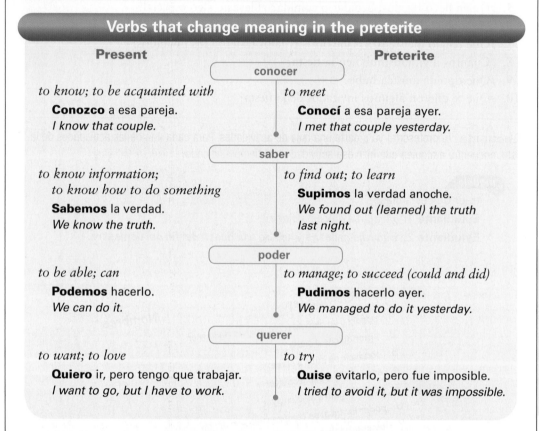

Verbs that change meaning in the preterite

Present	Preterite
conocer	
to know; to be acquainted with	*to meet*
Conozco a esa pareja.	**Conocí** a esa pareja ayer.
I know that couple.	*I met that couple yesterday.*
saber	
to know information;	*to find out; to learn*
to know how to do something	**Supimos** la verdad anoche.
Sabemos la verdad.	*We found out (learned) the truth*
We know the truth.	*last night.*
poder	
to be able; can	*to manage; to succeed (could and did)*
Podemos hacerlo.	**Pudimos** hacerlo ayer.
We can do it.	*We managed to do it yesterday.*
querer	
to want; to love	*to try*
Quiero ir, pero tengo que trabajar.	**Quise** evitarlo, pero fue imposible.
I want to go, but I have to work.	*I tried to avoid it, but it was impossible.*

¡INTÉNTALO! Elige la respuesta más lógica.

1. Yo no hice lo que me pidieron mis padres. ¡Tengo mis principios! a
   a. No quise hacerlo.
   b. No supe hacerlo.

2. Hablamos por primera vez con Nuria y Ana en la boda. a
   a. Las conocimos en la boda.
   b. Les dijimos en la boda.

3. Por fin hablé con mi hermano después de llamarlo siete veces. b
   a. No quise hablar con él.
   b. Pude hablar con él.

4. Josefina se acostó para relajarse. Se durmió inmediatamente. a
   a. Pudo relajarse.
   b. No pudo relajarse.

5. Después de mucho buscar, encontraste la definición en el diccionario. b
   a. No supiste la respuesta.
   b. Supiste la respuesta.

6. Las chicas fueron a la fiesta. Cantaron y bailaron mucho. a
   a. Ellas pudieron divertirse.
   b. Ellas no supieron divertirse.

Teaching Tips
- Prepare sentences using **conocer, saber, poder,** and **querer** in the present tense that will be logical when converted into the preterite. Have students convert them and explain how the meanings of the sentences change. Ex: **Sé la fecha de la fiesta. (Supe la fecha de la fiesta.)**
- Give both affirmative and negative examples with **poder** and **querer**. Ex: **Pude leer todas sus composiciones anoche, pero no pude leer las composiciones de la otra clase.**

¡ATENCIÓN!

In the preterite, the verbs **poder** and **querer** have different meanings, depending on whether they are used in affirmative or negative sentences.
pude *I succeeded*
no pude *I failed (to)*
quise *I tried (to)*
no quise *I refused (to)*

Video Show the **Fotonovela** again to give students more input containing verbs that change meaning in the preterite. Stop the video where appropriate to discuss how certain verbs were used and to ask comprehension questions.

recursos

WB
p. 177

LM
p. 192

vhlcentral.com
Lección 3

Práctica y Comunicación

Lección 3

1

Carlos y Eva Forma oraciones con los siguientes elementos. Usa el pretérito y haz todos los cambios necesarios. Al final, inventa la razón del divorcio de Carlos y Eva.

NOTA CULTURAL

La isla de Pascua es un remoto territorio chileno situado en el océano Pacífico Sur. Sus inmensas estatuas son uno de los mayores misterios del mundo: nadie sabe cómo o por qué se crearon. Para más información, véase **Panorama**, p. 171.

1. anoche / mi esposa y yo / saber / que / Carlos y Eva / divorciarse
   Anoche mi esposa y yo supimos que Carlos y Eva se divorciaron.

▶ 2. los / conocer / viaje / isla de Pascua
   Los conocimos en un viaje a la isla de Pascua.

3. no / poder / hablar / mucho / con / ellos / ese día
   No pudimos hablar mucho con ellos ese día.

4. pero / ellos / ser / simpático / y / nosotros / hacer planes / vernos / con más / frecuencia
   Pero ellos fueron simpáticos y nosotros hicimos planes para vernos con más frecuencia.

5. yo / poder / encontrar / su / número / teléfono / páginas / amarillo
   Yo pude encontrar su número de teléfono en las páginas amarillas.

6. (yo) querer / llamar / los / ese día / pero / no / tener / tiempo
   Quise llamarlos ese día, pero no tuve tiempo.

7. cuando / los / llamar / nosotros / poder / hablar / Eva
   Cuando los llamé, nosotros pudimos hablar con Eva.

8. nosotros / saber / razón / divorcio / después / hablar / ella
   Nosotros supimos la razón del divorcio después de hablar con ella.

9. _____
   Answers will vary.

2 Preview the activity by describing some recent things you found out, tried to do, failed to do, etc.

2

Completar Completa estas frases de una manera lógica.   Answers will vary.

1. Ayer mi compañero/a de cuarto supo…
2. Esta mañana no pude…
3. Conocí a mi mejor amigo/a en…
4. Mis padres no quisieron…
5. Mi mejor amigo/a no pudo…
6. Mi novio/a y yo nos conocimos en…
7. La semana pasada supe…
8. Ayer mis amigos quisieron…

3

Pairs In pairs, have students write three sentences using verbs that change meaning in the preterite. Two of the sentences should be true and the third should be false. Partners have to guess which of the sentences is the false one.

3 Point out that unlike their U.S. counterparts, Hispanic soap operas run for a limited period of time, like a miniseries.

Telenovela En parejas, escriban el diálogo para una escena de una telenovela (*soap opera*). La escena trata de una situación amorosa entre tres personas: Mirta, Daniel y Raúl. Usen el pretérito de **conocer, poder, querer** y **saber** en su diálogo.   Answers will vary.

PASIÓN   AVENTURA
SUSPENSO   VENGANZA

LA MUJER DOBLE

Síntesis

4 Have pairs repeat the activity, this time describing another person. Ask students to share their descriptions with the class, who will guess the person being described.

4

Conversación En una hoja de papel, escribe dos listas: las cosas que hiciste durante el fin de semana y las cosas que quisiste hacer, pero no pudiste. Luego, compara tu lista con la de un(a) compañero/a, y expliquen ambos por qué no pudieron hacer esas cosas.   Answers will vary.

 Practice more at **vhlcentral.com**.

3.3 **¿Qué? and ¿cuál?** **S** Tutorial

ANTE TODO You've already learned how to use interrogative words and phrases. As you know, **¿qué?** and **¿cuál?** or **¿cuáles?** mean *what?* or *which?* However, they are not interchangeable.

▶ **¿Qué?** is used to ask for a definition or an explanation.

¿Qué es el flan?	**¿Qué** estudias?
What is flan?	*What do you study?*

▶ **¿Cuál(es)?** is used when there is more than one possibility to choose from.

¿Cuál de los dos prefieres, el vino o el champán?	**¿Cuáles** son tus medias, las negras o las blancas?
Which of these (two) do you prefer, wine or champagne?	*Which ones are your socks, the black ones or the white ones?*

▶ **¿Cuál?** cannot be used before a noun; in this case, **¿qué?** is used.

¿Qué sorpresa te dieron tus amigos?	**¿Qué** colores te gustan?
What surprise did your friends give you?	*What colors do you like?*

▶ **¿Qué?** used before a noun has the same meaning as **¿cuál?**

¿Qué regalo te gusta?	**¿Qué dulces** quieren ustedes?
What (Which) gift do you like?	*What (Which) sweets do you want?*

Review of interrogative words and phrases

¿a qué hora?	at what time?	**¿cuántos/as?**	how many?
¿adónde?	(to) where?	**¿de dónde?**	from where?
¿cómo?	how?	**¿dónde?**	where?
¿cuál(es)?	what?; which?	**¿por qué?**	why?
¿cuándo?	when?	**¿qué?**	what?; which?
¿cuánto/a?	how much?	**¿quién(es)?**	who?

 **¡INTÉNTALO!** Completa las preguntas con **¿qué?** o **¿cuál(es)?**, según el contexto.

1. ¿ __Cuál__ de los dos te gusta más?
2. ¿ __Cuál__ es tu teléfono?
3. ¿ __Qué__ tipo de pastel pediste?
4. ¿ __Qué__ es una galleta?
5. ¿ __Qué__ haces ahora?
6. ¿ __Cuáles__ son tus platos favoritos?
7. ¿ __Qué__ bebidas te gustan más?
8. ¿ __Qué__ es esto?
9. ¿ __Cuál__ es el mejor?
10. ¿ __Cuál__ es tu opinión?
11. ¿ __Qué__ fiestas celebras tú?
12. ¿ __Qué__ botella de vino prefieres?
13. ¿ __Cuál__ es tu helado favorito??
14. ¿ __Qué__ pones en la mesa?
15. ¿ __Qué__ restaurante prefieres?
16. ¿ __Qué__ estudiantes estudian más?
17. ¿ __Qué__ quieres comer esta noche?
18. ¿ __Cuál__ es la sorpresa mañana?
19. ¿ __Qué__ postre prefieres?
20. ¿ __Qué__ opinas?

Teaching Tips
• Write incomplete questions on the board and ask students which interrogative word best completes each sentence. Ex: 1. ¿____ es tu número de teléfono? (Cuál) 2. ¿____ es esto? (Qué)
• Give students pairs of questions and have them explain the difference in meaning. Ex: **¿Qué es tu número de teléfono? ¿Cuál es tu número de teléfono?** Emphasize that the first question would be asked by someone who has no idea what a phone number is (asking for a definition) and, in the second question, someone wants to know *which* number (out of all the phone numbers in the world) is yours.
• Review the chart of interrogative words and phrases. Ask personalized questions (Ex: **¿Cuál es tu película favorita? ¿Adónde vas después de la clase?**) and call on volunteers to ask you questions.

Extra Practice Ask students to write one question using each of the interrogative words or phrases in the chart on this page. Then have them ask those questions of a partner, who must answer in complete sentences.

recursos

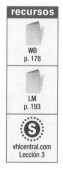

WB
p. 178

LM
p. 193

S
vhlcentral.com
Lección 3

Lección 3

Práctica y Comunicación

NATIONAL
communication
STANDARDS

1 Conduct a conversation with the whole class to find consensus on some of the questions.

1 **Completar** Tu clase de español va a crear un sitio web. Completa estas preguntas con alguna(s) palabra(s) interrogativa(s). Luego, con un(a) compañero/a, hagan y contesten las preguntas para obtener la información para el sitio web.

1. ¿_____Cuál_____ es la fecha de tu cumpleaños?
2. ¿_Dónde/Cuándo/A qué hora_ naciste?
3. ¿_____Cuál_____ es tu estado civil?
4. ¿_Cómo/Cuándo/Dónde_ te relajas?
5. ¿__Quién/Cómo__ es tu mejor amigo/a?
6. ¿_____Qué_____ cosas te hacen reír?
7. ¿_____Qué_____ postres te gustan? ¿_____Cuál_____ te gusta más?
8. ¿_____Qué_____ problemas tuviste en la primera cita con alguien?

2 For expansion, have students ask additional questions using the interrogative words and phrases on p. 158. Ex: **¿A qué hora es la ceremonia?**

2 **Una invitación** En parejas, lean esta invitación. Luego, túrnense para hacer y contestar preguntas con **qué** y **cuál** basadas en la información de la invitación. Answers will vary.

modelo

Estudiante 1: ¿Cuál es el nombre del padre de la novia?
Estudiante 2: Su nombre es Fernando Sandoval Valera.

¡LENGUA VIVA!

The word **invitar** is not always used exactly like *invite*. Sometimes, if you say **Te invito un café**, it means that you are offering to buy that person a coffee.

> Fernando Sandoval Valera   Lorenzo Vásquez Amaral
> Isabel Arzipe de Sandoval   Elena Soto de Vásquez
>
> tienen el agrado de invitarlos
> a la boda de sus hijos
>
> María Luisa y José Antonio
>
> La ceremonia religiosa tendrá lugar
> el sábado 10 de junio a las dos de la tarde
> en el Templo de Santo Domingo
> (Calle Santo Domingo, 961).
>
> Después de la ceremonia, sírvanse pasar a la recepción en el salón
> de baile del Hotel Metrópoli (Sotero del Río, 465).

Supersite: Activity Pack

3 Divide the class into pairs and distribute the handouts from the Activity Pack on the Supersite that correspond to this information gap activity.

3 **Quinceañera** Trabaja con un(a) compañero/a. Uno/a de ustedes es el/la director(a) del salón de fiestas "Renacimiento". La otra persona es el padre/la madre de Sandra, quien quiere hacer la fiesta de quince años de su hija gastando menos de $25 por invitado. Su profesor(a) va a darles la información necesaria para confirmar la reservación. Answers will vary.

modelo

Estudiante 1: ¿Cuánto cuestan los entremeses?
Estudiante 2: Depende. Puede escoger champiñones por 50 centavos o camarones por dos dólares.
Estudiante 1: ¡Uf! A mi hija le gustan los camarones, pero son muy caros.
Estudiante 2: Bueno, también puede escoger quesos por un dólar por invitado.

 Practice more at **vhlcentral.com**.

3.4 **Pronouns after prepositions**  Tutorial

ANTE TODO In Spanish, as in English, the object of a preposition is the noun or pronoun that follows a preposition. Observe the following diagram.

PREPOSITION	NOUN	PREPOSITION	PRONOUN
La sopa es para	Alicia	y para	él.

Prepositional pronouns

	Singular			Plural	
	mí	me		**nosotros/as**	us
	ti	you (fam.)		**vosotros/as**	you (fam.)
preposition +	**Ud.**	you (form.)		**Uds.**	you (form.)
	él	him		**ellos**	them (m.)
	ella	her		**ellas**	them (f.)

▶ Note that, except for **mí** and **ti,** these pronouns are the same as the subject pronouns. **¡Atención!** **Mí** (*me*) has an accent mark to distinguish it from the possessive adjective **mi** (*my*).

▶ The preposition **con** combines with **mí** and **ti** to form **conmigo** and **contigo**, respectively.

—¿Quieres venir **conmigo** a Concepción?
Do you want to come with me to Concepción?

—Sí, gracias, me gustaría ir **contigo**.
Yes, thanks, I would like to go with you.

▶ The preposition **entre** is followed by **tú** and **yo** instead of **ti** and **mí**.

Papá va a sentarse **entre tú y yo**.
Dad is going to sit between you and me.

 **¡INTÉNTALO!** Completa estas oraciones con las preposiciones y los pronombres apropiados.

1. (*with him*) No quiero ir ___con él___.
2. (*for her*) Las galletas son ___para ella___.
3. (*for me*) Los mariscos son ___para mí___.
4. (*with you*, pl. form.) Preferimos estar ___con ustedes___.
5. (*with you*, sing. fam.) Me gusta salir ___contigo___.
6. (*with me*) ¿Por qué no quieres tener una cita ___conmigo___?
7. (*for her*) La cuenta es ___para ella___.
8. (*for them*, m.) La habitación es muy pequeña ___para ellos___.
9. (*with them*, f.) Anoche celebré la Navidad ___con ellas___.
10. (*for you*, sing. fam.) Este beso es ___para ti___.
11. (*with you*, sing. fam.) Nunca me aburro ___contigo___.
12. (*with you*, pl. form.) ¡Qué bien que vamos ___con ustedes___!
13. (*for you*, sing. fam.) ___Para ti___ la vida es muy fácil.
14. (*for them*, f.) ___Para ellas___ no hay sorpresas.

Teaching Tips
• Review previously learned prepositions before beginning this grammar presentation.
• Ask personalized questions to elicit prepositional pronouns. Ex: _____, ¿quién está detrás de ti? ¿Quién está delante de ella? ¿Ese libro es para mí?
• Point out that students have already been using prepositional pronouns after **a** with verbs like **gustar** and to clarify indirect object pronouns.

Game Divide the class into two teams. One student from the first team chooses an item in the classroom and writes it down. Call on five students from the other team to ask questions about the item's location. Ex: ¿Está cerca de mí? The first student can respond with **sí, no, caliente,** or **frío.** If a team guesses the item within five tries, give them a point. If not, give the other team a point. The team with the most points wins.

CONSULTA

For more prepositions, refer to *¡ADELANTE!* **UNO** **Estructura 2.3,** p. 82.

Video Show the **Fotonovela** again to give students more input containing prepositional pronouns. Stop the video where appropriate to discuss how certain pronouns were used and to ask comprehension questions.

recursos

WB
pp. 179–180

LM
p. 194

vhlcentral.com
Lección 3

Lección 3

Práctica y Comunicación

1 Remind students that they are to fill in the blanks with prepositional pronouns, not names of the characters in the conversation.

1

Completar David sale con sus amigos a comer. Para saber quién come qué, lee el mensaje electrónico que David le envió (*sent*) a Cecilia dos días después y completa el diálogo en el restaurante con los pronombres apropiados.

> **modelo**
>
> **Camarero:** Los camarones en salsa verde, ¿para quién son?
> **David:** Son para ___ella___.

Para: Cecilia	Asunto: El menú

Hola, Cecilia:

¿Recuerdas la comida del viernes? Quiero repetir el menú en mi casa el miércoles. Ahora voy a escribir lo que comimos, luego me dices si falta algún plato. Yo pedí el filete de pescado y Maribel camarones en salsa verde. Tatiana pidió un plato grandísimo de machas a la parmesana. Diana y Silvia pidieron langostas, ¿te acuerdas? Y tú, ¿qué pediste? Ah, sí, un bistec grande con papas. Héctor también pidió un bistec, pero más pequeño. Miguel pidió pollo y vino tinto para todos. Y la profesora comió ensalada verde porque está a dieta. ¿Falta algo? Espero tu mensaje. Hasta pronto. David.

CAMARERO	El filete de pescado, ¿para quién es?
DAVID	Es para (1)___mí___.
CAMARERO	Aquí está. ¿Y las machas a la parmesana y las langostas?
DAVID	Las machas son para (2)___ella___.
SILVIA Y DIANA	Las langostas son para (3)___nosotras___.
CAMARERO	Tengo un bistec grande...
DAVID	Cecilia, es para (4)___ti___, ¿no es cierto? Y el bistec más pequeño es para (5)___él___.
CAMARERO	¿Y la botella de vino?
MIGUEL	Es para todos (6)___nosotros___, y el pollo es para (7)___mí___.
CAMARERO	(*a la profesora*) Entonces la ensalada verde es para (8)___usted___.

NOTA CULTURAL

Las **machas a la parmesana** son un plato muy típico de Chile. Se prepara con machas, un tipo de almeja (*clam*) que se encuentra en Suramérica. Las machas a la parmesana se hacen con queso parmesano, limón, sal, pimienta y mantequilla, y luego se ponen en el horno (*oven*).

Supersite: Activity Pack

2 Using both versions of the drawing as a guide, ask questions of the class to find out where the people are. Ex: **¿Quién sabe dónde está la señora Blanco?**

2 Verify that all students labeled the characters correctly by suggesting changes to the drawing and using prepositions to ask about their new locations. Ex: **Yolanda y Carlos cambian de lugar. ¿Quién está al lado de Yolanda ahora? (Rubén)**

2

Compartir Tu profesor(a) va a darte una hoja de actividades en la que hay un dibujo. En parejas, hagan preguntas para saber dónde está cada una de las personas en el dibujo. Ustedes tienen dos versiones diferentes de la ilustración. Al final deben saber dónde está cada persona. Answers will vary.

> **modelo**
>
> **Estudiante 1:** ¿Quién está al lado de Óscar?
> **Estudiante 2:** Alfredo está al lado de él.

Alfredo	Dolores	Graciela	Raúl
Sra. Blanco	Enrique	Leonor	Rubén
Carlos	Sra. Gómez	Óscar	Yolanda

AYUDA

Here are some other useful prepositions: **al lado de, debajo de, a la derecha de, a la izquierda de, cerca de, lejos de, delante de, detrás de, entre.**

Recapitulación

S **Diagnostics**

Completa estas actividades para repasar los conceptos de gramática que aprendiste en esta lección.

1 **Completar** Completa la tabla con el pretérito de los verbos. **9 pts.**

Infinitive	yo	ella	nosotros
conducir	conduje	condujo	condujimos
hacer	hice	hizo	hicimos
saber	supe	supo	supimos

2 **Mi fiesta** Completa este mensaje electrónico con el pretérito de los verbos de la lista. Vas a usar cada verbo sólo una vez. **10 pts.**

> dar   haber   tener
> decir   hacer   traer
> estar   poder   venir
>   poner

2 Have students work in pairs to write a response e-mail from **Omar**. Tell them to use the preterite tense to ask for more details about the party.

Hola, Omar:

Como tú no (1) __pudiste__ venir a mi fiesta de cumpleaños, quiero contarte cómo fue. El día de mi cumpleaños, muy temprano por la mañana, mis hermanos me (2) __dieron__ una gran sorpresa: ellos (3) __pusieron__ un regalo delante de la puerta de mi habitación: ¡una bicicleta roja preciosa! Mi madre nos preparó un desayuno riquísimo. Después de desayunar, mis hermanos y yo (4) __tuvimos__ que limpiar toda la casa, así que (*therefore*) no (5) __hubo__ más celebración hasta la tarde. A las seis y media (nosotros) (6) __hicimos__ una barbacoa en el patio de la casa. Todos los invitados (7) __trajeron__ bebidas y regalos. (8) __Vinieron__ todos mis amigos, excepto tú, ¡qué pena! :-(La fiesta (9) __estuvo__ muy animada hasta las diez de la noche, cuando mis padres (10) __dijeron__ que los vecinos (*neighbors*) iban a (*were going to*) protestar y entonces todos se fueron a sus casas.

TPR Have students stand and form a circle. Call out an infinitive from **Resumen gramatical** and a subject pronoun (Ex: **poder/nosotros**) and toss a foam or paper ball to a student, who will give the correct preterite form (Ex: **pudimos**). He or she then tosses the ball to another student, who must use the verb correctly in a sentence before throwing the ball back to you. Ex: **No pudimos comprar los regalos.**

RESUMEN GRAMATICAL

3.1 **Irregular preterites** *pp. 152–153*

u-stem	estar	estuv-	
	poder	pud-	
	poner	pus-	
	saber	sup-	
	tener	tuv-	
i-stem	hacer	hic-	-e, -iste,
	querer	quis-	-o, -imos,
	venir	vin-	-isteis, -(i)eron
j-stem	conducir	conduj-	
	decir	dij-	
	traducir	traduj-	
	traer	traj-	

▶ Preterite of **dar: di, diste, dio, dimos, disteis, dieron**

▶ Preterite of **hay** (*inf.* **haber**): **hubo**

3.2 **Verbs that change meaning in the preterite** *p. 156*

Present	Preterite
conocer	
to know; to be acquainted with	to meet
saber	
to know info.; to know how to do something	to find out; to learn
poder	
to be able; can	to manage; to succeed
querer	
to want; to love	to try

3.3 **¿Qué? and ¿cuál?** *p. 158*

▶ Use **¿qué?** to ask for a definition or an explanation.

▶ Use **¿cuál(es)?** when there is more than one possibility to choose from.

▶ **¿Cuál?** cannot be used before a noun; use **¿qué?** instead.

▶ **¿Qué?** used before a noun has the same meaning as **¿cuál?**

Lección 3

3 To challenge students, ask them to explain why they chose the preterite or present tense in each case.

3

¿Presente o pretérito? Escoge la forma correcta de los verbos en paréntesis. **6 pts.**

1. Después de muchos intentos (*tries*), (podemos/pudimos) hacer una piñata.
2. —¿Conoces a Pepe?
   —Sí, lo (conozco/conocí) en tu fiesta.
3. Como no es de aquí, Cristina no (sabe/supo) mucho de las celebraciones locales.
4. Yo no (quiero/quise) ir a un restaurante grande, pero tú decides.
5. Ellos (quieren/quisieron) darme una sorpresa, pero Nina me lo dijo todo.
6. Mañana se terminan las vacaciones; por fin (podemos/pudimos) volver a la escuela.

3.4 | **Pronouns after prepositions**   *p. 160*

Prepositional pronouns

	Singular	Plural
Preposition +	**mí**	**nosotros/as**
	ti	**vosotros/as**
	Ud.	**Uds.**
	él	**ellos**
	ella	**ellas**

► Exceptions: **conmigo, contigo, entre tú y yo**

4 Give students these additional items:
5. —¿? / libro / comprar —Voy a comprar el libro de viajes. (¿Qué libro vas a comprar?)
6. —¿? / ser / última película / ver —Vi la película *Volver*. (¿Cuál fue la última película que viste?)
7. —¿? / ser / número de la suerte —Mi número de la suerte es el ocho. (¿Cuál es tu número de la suerte?) 8. —¿? / ser / nacimiento —El nacimiento es la primera etapa de la vida. (¿Qué es el nacimiento?)

4

Preguntas Escribe una pregunta para cada respuesta con los elementos dados. Empieza con **qué, cuál** o **cuáles** de acuerdo con el contexto y haz los cambios necesarios. **8 pts.**

1. —¿? / pastel / querer —Quiero el pastel de chocolate. 1. ¿Qué pastel quieres?
2. —¿? / ser / sangría —La sangría es una bebida típica española. 2. ¿Qué es la sangría?
3. —¿? / ser / restaurante favorito —Mis restaurantes favoritos son Dalí y Jaleo. 3. ¿Cuáles son tus restaurantes favoritos?
4. —¿? / ser / dirección electrónica —Mi dirección electrónica es paco@email.com. 4. ¿Cuál es tu dirección electrónica?

5

¿Dónde me siento? Completa la conversación con los pronombres apropiados. **7 pts.**

JUAN A ver, te voy a decir dónde te vas a sentar. Manuel, ¿ves esa silla? Es para __ti__. Y esa otra silla es para tu novia, que todavía no está aquí.

MANUEL Muy bien, yo la reservo para __ella__.

HUGO ¿Y esta silla es para __mí__ (*me*)?

JUAN No, Hugo. No es para __ti__. Es para Carmina, que viene con Julio.

HUGO No, Carmina y Julio no pueden venir. Hablé con __ellos__ y me avisaron.

JUAN Pues ellos se lo pierden (*it's their loss*). ¡Más comida para __nosotros__ (*us*)!

CAMARERO Aquí tienen el menú. Les doy un minuto y enseguida estoy con __ustedes__.

6 To simplify, have students make an idea map to help them organize their ideas. In the center circle, have them write **Mi último cumpleaños**. Help them brainstorm labels for the surrounding circles, such as **lugar, invitados, regalos**. You may also want to provide a list of infinitives that students may use in their descriptions.

6

Cumpleaños feliz Escribe cinco oraciones que describan cómo celebraste tu último cumpleaños. Usa el pretérito y los pronombres que aprendiste en esta lección. **10 pts.**

7 You may want to point out the example of **leísmo** in line 4 (**le miraste**). Explain that some Spanish speakers tend to use **le** or **les** as direct object pronouns. In this case, **le** replaces the direct object pronoun **lo**, which refers to **mi corazón**.

7

Poema Completa este fragmento del poema *Elegía nocturna* de Carlos Pellicer con el pretérito de los verbos entre paréntesis. **¡2 puntos EXTRA!**

“ Ay de mi corazón° que nadie __quiso__ (querer)
tomar de entre mis manos desoladas.
Tú __viniste__ (venir) a mirar sus llamaradas°
y le miraste arder° claro° y sereno. ”

corazón *heart* llamaradas *flames* arder *to burn* claro *clear*

 Practice more at **vhlcentral.com**.

Lectura

 communication cultures NATIONAL STANDARDS

Antes de leer

Estrategia

Recognizing word families

Recognizing root words can help you guess the meaning of words in context, ensuring better comprehension of a reading selection. Using this strategy will enrich your Spanish vocabulary as you will see below.

Examinar el texto

Familiarízate con el texto usando las estrategias de lectura más efectivas para ti. ¿Qué tipo de documento es? ¿De qué tratan° las cuatro secciones del documento? Explica tus respuestas.

Raíces°

Completa el siguiente cuadro° para ampliar tu vocabulario. Usa palabras de la lectura de esta lección y vocabulario de las lecciones anteriores. ¿Qué significan las palabras que escribiste en el cuadro? Some answers may vary. Suggested answers:

Verbos	Sustantivos	Otras formas
1. agradecer *to thank, to be grateful for*	agradecimiento/ gracias *gratitude/thanks*	agradecido *grateful, thankful*
2. estudiar	estudiante *student*	estudiado *studied*
3. celebrar *to celebrate*	celebración *celebration*	celebrado
4. bailar *to dance*	baile	bailable *danceable*
5. bautizar	bautismo *baptism*	bautizado *baptized*

Teaching Tips
- Have students fill in the chart after they have read **Vida social.**
- Write **conocer** (*to know*) on the board. Next to it, write **conocimiento** and **conocido** and guide students to recognize their meanings (*knowledge* and *known*). Explain that recognizing word families will help students infer the meaning of new words.

Extra Practice Write additional related words on the board and ask students to guess their meanings. Ex: **hablar, hablador, hablante, hablado; ideal, idealizar, idealista**

¿De qué tratan...? *What are... about?* **Raíces** *Roots* **cuadro** *chart*

 Practice more at **vhlcentral.com.**

Teaching Tip Divide the class into groups of three and assign each one a section of the article (Ex: **Matrimonio**). Group members should take turns reading aloud, then write three comprehension questions about their section for the class to answer.

Vida social

Matrimonio
Espinoza Álvarez- Reyes Salazar

El día sábado 17 de junio a las 19 horas, se celebró el matrimonio de Silvia Reyes y Carlos Espinoza en la catedral de Santiago. La ceremonia fue oficiada por el pastor Federico Salas y participaron los padres de los novios, el señor Jorge Espinoza y señora y el señor José Alfredo Reyes y señora. Después de la ceremonia, los padres de los recién casados ofrecieron una fiesta bailable en el restaurante La Misión.

Bautismo
José María recibió el bautismo el 26 de junio.

Sus padres, don Roberto Lagos Moreno y doña María Angélica Sánchez, compartieron la alegría de la fiesta con todos sus parientes y amigos. La ceremonia religiosa tuvo lugar° en la catedral de Aguas Blancas. Después de la ceremonia, padres, parientes y amigos celebraron una fiesta en la residencia de la familia Lagos.

32B

Fiesta de quince años

El doctor don Amador Larenas Fernández y la señora Felisa Vera de Larenas celebraron los quince años de su hija Ana Ester junto a sus parientes y amigos. La quinceañera reside en la ciudad de Valparaíso y es estudiante del Colegio Francés. La fiesta de presentación en sociedad de la señorita Ana Ester fue el día viernes 2 de mayo a las 19 horas en el Club Español. Entre los invitados especiales asistieron el alcalde° de la ciudad, don Pedro Castedo, y su esposa. La música estuvo a cargo de la Orquesta Americana. ¡Feliz cumpleaños, le deseamos a la señorita Ana Ester en su fiesta bailable!

Expresión de gracias
Carmen Godoy Tapia

Agradecemos° sinceramente a todas las personas que nos acompañaron en el último adiós a nuestra apreciada esposa, madre, abuela y tía, la señora Carmen Godoy Tapia. El funeral tuvo lugar el día 28 de junio en la ciudad de Viña del Mar. La vida de Carmen Godoy fue un ejemplo de trabajo, amistad, alegría y amor para todos nosotros. Su esposo, hijos y familia agradecen de todo corazón° su asistencia° al funeral a todos los parientes y amigos.

tuvo lugar *took place* alcalde *mayor* Agradecemos *We thank*
de todo corazón *sincerely* asistencia *attendance*

Después de leer

Corregir
Escribe estos comentarios otra vez para corregir la información errónea.

1. El alcalde y su esposa asistieron a la boda de Silvia y Carlos. El alcalde y su esposa asistieron a la fiesta de quince años de Ana Ester.
2. Todos los anuncios (*announcements*) describen eventos felices. Tres de los anuncios tratan de eventos felices. Uno trata de una muerte.
3. Felisa Vera de Larenas cumple quince años. Ana Ester Larenas cumple quince años.
4. Roberto Lagos y María Angélica Sánchez son hermanos. Roberto Lagos y María Angélica Sánchez están casados/son esposos.
5. Carmen Godoy Tapia les dio las gracias a las personas que asistieron al funeral. La familia de Carmen Godoy Tapia les dio las gracias a las personas que asistieron al funeral.

Identificar
Escribe el nombre de la(s) persona(s) descrita(s) (*described*).

1. Dejó viudo a su esposo el 28 de junio. Carmen Godoy Tapia
2. Sus padres y todos los invitados brindaron por él, pero él no entendió por qué. José María
3. El Club Español les presentó una cuenta considerable. don Amador Larenas Fernández y doña Felisa Vera de Larenas
4. Unió a los novios en santo matrimonio. el pastor Federico Salas
5. Su fiesta de cumpleaños se celebró en Valparaíso. Ana Ester

Un anuncio
Trabajen en grupos pequeños para inventar un anuncio breve sobre una celebración importante. Puede ser una graduación, un matrimonio o una gran fiesta en la que ustedes participan. Incluyan la siguiente información. Answers will vary.

1. nombres de los participantes
2. la fecha, la hora y el lugar
3. qué se celebra
4. otros detalles de interés

Extra Practice Have pairs visit the website of a Spanish-language newspaper, such as *El Heraldo* (Colombia) or *El Norte* (Mexico). Tell them to print photos and/or articles from the society section (**Gente, Sociedad,** or **Sociales**) and present the events to the class.

Teaching Tips
• Provide examples from Spanish-language newspapers.
• After presenting their announcements to the class, have students combine the articles to create their own **Vida social** page for a class newspaper.

Escritura

Estrategia

Planning and writing a comparative analysis

Writing any kind of comparative analysis requires careful planning. Venn diagrams are useful for organizing your ideas visually before comparing and contrasting people, places, objects, events, or issues. To create a Venn diagram, draw two circles that overlap one another and label the top of each circle. List the differences between the two elements in the outer rings of the two circles, then list their similarities where the two circles overlap. Review the following example.

Diferencias y similitudes

Boda de Silvia Reyes y Carlos Espinoza

Diferencias:
1. Primero hay una celebración religiosa.
2. Se celebra en un restaurante.

Similitudes:
1. Las dos fiestas se celebran por la noche.
2. Las dos fiestas son bailables.

Fiesta de quince años de Ana Ester Larenas Vera

Diferencias:
1. Se celebra en un club.
2. Vienen invitados especiales.

La lista de palabras y expresiones a la derecha puede ayudarte a escribir este tipo de ensayo (*essay*).

Tema

Escribir una composición

Compara una celebración familiar (como una boda, una fiesta de cumpleaños o una graduación) a la que tú asististe recientemente con otro tipo de celebración. Utiliza palabras y expresiones de esta lista.

Para expresar similitudes

además; también	*in addition; also*
al igual que	*the same as*
como	*as; like*
de la misma manera	*in the same manner (way)*
del mismo modo	*in the same manner (way)*
tan + [*adjetivo*] + como	*as + [adjective] + as*
tanto/a(s) + [*sustantivo*] + como	*as many/much + [noun] + as*

Para expresar diferencias

a diferencia de	*unlike*
a pesar de	*in spite of*
aunque	*although*
en cambio	*on the other hand*
más/menos... que	*more/less ... than*
no obstante	*nevertheless; however*
por el contrario	*on the contrary*
por otro lado	*on the other hand*
sin embargo	*nevertheless; however*

Teaching Tip Explain to students that to write a comparative analysis, they will need to use words that signal similarities (**similitudes**) and differences (**diferencias**). Model the pronunciation of the words and expressions under **Escribir una composición**. Then have volunteers use them in sentences to express the similarities and differences listed in the Venn diagram.

Escuchar Audio

Estrategia

Guessing the meaning of words through context

When you hear an unfamiliar word, you can often guess its meaning by listening to the words and phrases around it.

 To practice this strategy, you will now listen to a paragraph. Jot down the unfamiliar words that you hear. Then listen to the paragraph again and jot down the word or words that give the most useful clues to the meaning of each unfamiliar word.

Preparación

Lee la invitación. ¿De qué crees que van a hablar Rosa y Josefina?

Ahora escucha

Ahora escucha la conversación entre Josefina y Rosa. Cuando oigas una de las palabras de la columna A, usa el contexto para identificar el sinónimo o la definición en la columna B.

A	B
_d_ 1. festejar	a. conmemoración religiosa de una muerte
_c_ 2. dicha	b. tolera
_h_ 3. bien parecido	c. suerte
_g_ 4. finge (fingir)	d. celebrar
_b_ 5. soporta (soportar)	e. me divertí
_e_ 6. yo lo disfruté (disfrutar)	f. horror
	g. crea una ficción
	h. guapo

Margarita Robles de García
y Roberto García Olmos

Piden su presencia en la celebración
del décimo aniversario de bodas
el día 13 de marzo
con una misa en la Iglesia Virgen del Coromoto
a las 6:30

seguida por cena y baile
en el restaurante El Campanero,
Calle Principal, Las Mercedes
a las 8:30

Comprensión

¿Cierto o falso?

Lee cada oración e indica si lo que dice es **cierto** o **falso**. Corrige las oraciones falsas.

1. No invitaron a mucha gente a la fiesta de Margarita y Roberto porque ellos no conocen a muchas personas
   Falso. Fueron muchos invitados.

2. Algunos fueron a la fiesta con pareja y otros fueron sin compañero/a. Cierto.

3. Margarita y Roberto decidieron celebrar el décimo aniversario porque no hicieron una fiesta el día de su boda. Falso. Celebraron el décimo aniversario porque les gustan las fiestas.

4. Rafael les parece interesante a Rosa y a Josefina.
   Cierto.

5. Josefina se divirtió mucho en la fiesta porque bailó toda la noche con Rafael. Falso. Josefina se divirtió mucho, pero bailó con otros, no con Rafael.

Preguntas

Responde a estas preguntas con oraciones completas.
Answers will vary.

1. ¿Son solteras Rosa y Josefina? ¿Cómo lo sabes?

2. ¿Tienen las chicas una amistad de mucho tiempo con la pareja que celebra su aniversario? ¿Cómo lo sabes?

En pantalla

NATIONAL STANDARDS *communication cultures*

Desfiles°, música, asados°, fuegos artificiales° y baile son los elementos de una buena fiesta. ¿Celebrar durante toda una semana? ¡Eso sí que es una fiesta espectacular! El 18 de septiembre Chile conmemora su independencia de España y los chilenos demuestran su orgullo° nacional durante una semana llena de celebraciones. Durante las Fiestas Patrias° casi todas las oficinas° y escuelas se cierran para que la gente se reúna° a festejar. Desfiles y rodeos representan la tradición de los vaqueros° del país, y la gente baila cueca, el baile nacional. Las familias y los amigos se reúnen para preparar y disfrutar platos tradicionales como las empanadas y asados. Otra de las tradiciones de estas fiestas es hacer volar cometas°, llamadas volantines. Mira el video para descubrir cómo se celebran otras fiestas en Chile.

Vocabulario útil

conejo	*bunny*
disfraces	*costumes*
mariscal	*traditional Chilean soup with raw seafood*
sustos	*frights*
vieja (Chi.)	*mother*

Seleccionar 🖱️

Selecciona la palabra que no está relacionada con cada grupo.

1. disfraces • noviembre • arbolito • sustos arbolito
2. volantines • arbolito • regalos • diciembre volantines
3. conejo • enero • huevitos • chocolates enero
4. septiembre • volantines • disfraces • asado disfraces

Fiesta

Trabajen en grupos de tres. Imaginen que van a organizar una fiesta para celebrar el 4 de julio. Escriban una invitación electrónica para invitar a sus parientes y amigos a la fiesta. Describan los planes que tienen para la fiesta y díganles a sus amigos qué tiene que traer cada uno. Answers will vary.

Desfiles/Paradas *Parades* asados *barbecues* fuegos artificiales *fireworks* orgullo *pride* Fiestas Patrias *Independence Day celebrations* oficinas *offices* se reúna *would get together* vaqueros *cowboys* cometas/volantines *kites*

Fiestas patrias: Chilevisión

Noviembre: disfraces, dulces...

Mayo: besito, tarjeta, tecito con la mamá...

Septiembre... Septiembre: familia, parada militar...

Teaching Tip For the first three items of Seleccionar, have students name a holiday that they associate with the three related words. Have students write a sentence using each of the words that doesn't belong.

Ⓢ **Video: TV Clip**

Practice more at **vhlcentral.com**.

El Día de los Reyes Magos* es una celebración muy popular en muchos países hispanos. No sólo es el día en que los reyes les traen regalos a los niños, también es una fiesta llena° de tradiciones. La tarde del 5 de enero, en muchas ciudades como Barcelona, España, se hace un desfile° en que los reyes regalan dulces a los niños y reciben sus cartas con peticiones. Esa noche, antes de irse a dormir, los niños deben dejar un zapato junto a la ventana y un bocado° para los reyes. En Puerto Rico, por ejemplo, los niños ponen una caja con hierba° bajo su cama para alimentar a los camellos° de los reyes.

Vocabulario útil

los cabezudos	*carnival figures with large heads*
los carteles	*posters*
fiesta de pueblo	*popular celebration*
santos de palo	*wooden saints*

Preparación

¿Se celebra la Navidad en tu país? ¿Qué otras fiestas importantes se celebran? En cada caso, ¿cuántos días dura la fiesta? ¿Cuáles son las tradiciones y actividades típicas? ¿Hay alguna comida típica en esa celebración?

Answers will vary.

Elegir 🔵S

Indica cuál de las dos opciones resume mejor este episodio

(a.) Las Navidades puertorriqueñas son las más largas y terminan después de las fiestas de la calle San Sebastián. Esta fiesta de pueblo se celebra con baile, música y distintas expresiones artísticas típicas.

b. En la celebración de las Navidades puertorriqueñas, los cabezudos son una tradición de España y son el elemento más importante de la fiesta. A la gente le gusta bailar y hacer procesiones por la noche.

---

* *According to the Christian tradition, the Three Wise Men were the three kings that traveled to Bethlehem after the birth of Baby Jesus, carrying with them gifts of gold, frankincense, and myrrh to pay him homage.*

llena *full* desfile *parade* bocado *snack*
hierba *grass* alimentar los camellos *feed the camels*

Las fiestas

Los cabezudos son una tradición [...] de España.

Hay mucha gente y mucho arte.

Es una fiesta de pueblo... una tradición. Vengo todos los años.

Teaching Tip To challenge students, have them write a brief summary, in their own words, that is no more than a paragraph in length.

 **Video:** *Flash cultura*

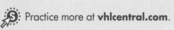 Practice more at **vhlcentral.com**.

recursos

| VM pp. 187–188 | vhlcentral.com Lección 3 |

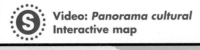

Chile

NATIONAL
connections
cultures
STANDARDS

El país en cifras

▶ **Área:** 756.950 km² (292.259 millas²), *dos veces el área de Montana*

▶ **Población:** 17.926.000
Aproximadamente el 80 por ciento de la población del país es urbana.

▶ **Capital:** Santiago de Chile—6.237.000

▶ **Ciudades principales:** Valparaíso—911.000, Concepción, Viña del Mar, Temuco

SOURCE: Population Division, UN Secretariat

▶ **Moneda:** peso chileno

▶ **Idiomas:** español (oficial), mapuche

Bandera de Chile

Chilenos célebres

▶ **Bernardo O'Higgins,** militar° y héroe nacional (1778–1842)

▶ **Gabriela Mistral,** Premio Nobel de Literatura, 1945; poeta y diplomática (1889–1957)

▶ **Pablo Neruda,** Premio Nobel de Literatura, 1971; poeta (1904–1973)

▶ **Isabel Allende,** novelista (1942–)

Pablo Neruda

militar *soldier* desierto *desert* el más seco *the driest* mundo *world* han tenido *have had* ha sido usado *has been used* Marte *Mars*

PERÚ

Pampa del Tamarugal

Cordillera de los Andes

BOLIVIA

La costa de Viña del Mar

El puerto de Valparaíso

Edificio antiguo en Santiago

Océano Pacífico

Viña del Mar
Valparaíso

Santiago de Chile

ARGENTINA

Concepción

Temuco

Torres del Paine

Una celebración en Temuco

Lago Buenos Aires

Océano Atlántico

Punta Arenas

Estrecho de Magallanes

recursos

| WB pp. 181–182 | VM pp. 185–186 | vhlcentral.com Lección 3 |

Isla Grande de Tierra del Fuego

¡Increíble pero cierto!

El desierto° de Atacama, en el norte de Chile, es el más seco° del mundo°. Con más de cien mil km² de superficie, algunas zonas de este desierto nunca han tenido° lluvia. Atacama ha sido usado° como escenario para representar a Marte° en películas y series de televisión.

Lección 3

Lugares • **La isla de Pascua**

La isla de Pascua° recibió ese nombre porque los exploradores holandeses° llegaron a la isla por primera vez el día de Pascua de 1722. Ahora es parte del territorio de Chile. La isla de Pascua es famosa por los *moái*, estatuas enormes que representan personas con rasgos° muy exagerados. Estas estatuas las construyeron los *rapa nui*, los antiguos habitantes de la zona. Todavía no se sabe mucho sobre los *rapa nui*, ni tampoco se sabe por qué decidieron abandonar la isla.

Deportes • **Los deportes de invierno**

Hay muchos lugares para practicar deportes de invierno en Chile porque las montañas nevadas de los Andes ocupan gran parte del país. El Parque Nacional Villarrica, por ejemplo, situado al pie de un volcán y junto a° un lago, es un sitio popular para el esquí y el *snowboard*. Para los que prefieren deportes más extremos, el centro de esquí Valle Nevado organiza excursiones para practicar heliesquí.

Ciencias • **Astronomía**

Los observatorios chilenos, situados en los Andes, son lugares excelentes para las observaciones astronómicas. Científicos° de todo el mundo van a Chile para estudiar las estrellas° y otros cuerpos celestes. Hoy día Chile está construyendo nuevos observatorios y telescopios para mejorar las imágenes del universo.

Economía • **El vino**

La producción de vino comenzó en Chile en el siglo° XVI. Ahora la industria del vino constituye una parte importante de la actividad agrícola del país y la exportación de sus productos está aumentando° cada vez más. Los vinos chilenos son muy apreciados internacionalmente por su gran variedad, sus ricos y complejos sabores° y su precio moderado. Los más conocidos son los vinos de Aconcagua y del valle del Maipo.

 ¿Qué aprendiste? Responde a cada pregunta con una oración completa.

1. ¿Qué porcentaje (*percentage*) de la población chilena es urbana?
   El 80 por ciento de la población chilena es urbana.

2. ¿Qué son los *moái*? ¿Dónde están? Los *moái* son estatuas enormes. Están en la isla de Pascua.

3. ¿Qué deporte extremo ofrece el centro de esquí Valle Nevado?
   Ofrece la práctica de heliesquí.

4. ¿Por qué van a Chile científicos de todo el mundo? Porque los observatorios chilenos son excelentes para las observaciones astronómicas.

5. ¿Cuándo comenzó la producción de vino en Chile?
   Comenzó en el siglo XVI.

6. ¿Por qué son apreciados internacionalmente los vinos chilenos? Son apreciados por su variedad, sus ricos y complejos sabores y su precio moderado.

 Conexión Internet Investiga estos temas en **vhlcentral.com**.

1. Busca información sobre Pablo Neruda e Isabel Allende. ¿Dónde y cuándo nacieron? ¿Cuáles son algunas de sus obras (*works*)? ¿Cuáles son algunos de los temas de sus obras?

2. Busca información sobre sitios donde los chilenos y los turistas practican deportes de invierno en Chile. Selecciona un sitio y descríbeselo a tu clase.

 Practice more at **vhlcentral.com**.

....

La isla de Pascua *Easter Island* holandeses *Dutch* rasgos *features* junto a *beside* Científicos *Scientists* estrellas *stars* siglo *century* aumentando *increasing* complejos sabores *complex flavors*

Supersite/DVD: You may want to wrap up this section by playing the **Panorama cultural** video footage for this lesson.

Las celebraciones

el aniversario (de bodas)	(wedding) anniversary
la boda	wedding
el cumpleaños	birthday
el día de fiesta	holiday
la fiesta	party
el/la invitado/a	guest
la Navidad	Christmas
la quinceañera	young woman celebrating her fifteenth birthday
la sorpresa	surprise
brindar	to toast (drink)
celebrar	to celebrate
divertirse (e:ie)	to have fun
invitar	to invite
pasarlo bien/mal	to have a good/bad time
regalar	to give (a gift)
reírse (e:i)	to laugh
relajarse	to relax
sonreír (e:i)	to smile
sorprender	to surprise

Los postres y otras comidas

la botella (de vino)	bottle (of wine)
el champán	champagne
los dulces	sweets; candy
el flan (de caramelo)	baked (caramel) custard
la galleta	cookie
el helado	ice cream
el pastel (de chocolate)	(chocolate) cake; pie
el postre	dessert

Las relaciones personales

la amistad	friendship
el amor	love
el divorcio	divorce
el estado civil	marital status
el matrimonio	marriage
la pareja	(married) couple; partner
el/la recién casado/a	newlywed
casarse (con)	to get married (to)
comprometerse (con)	to get engaged (to)
divorciarse (de)	to get divorced (from)
enamorarse (de)	to fall in love (with)
llevarse bien/mal (con)	to get along well/ badly (with)
odiar	to hate
romper (con)	to break up (with)
salir (con)	to go out (with); to date
separarse (de)	to separate (from)
tener una cita	to have a date; to have an appointment
casado/a	married
divorciado/a	divorced
juntos/as	together
separado/a	separated
soltero/a	single
viudo/a	widower/widow

Las etapas de la vida

la adolescencia	adolescence
la edad	age
el estado civil	marital status
las etapas de la vida	the stages of life
la juventud	youth
la madurez	maturity; middle age
la muerte	death
el nacimiento	birth
la niñez	childhood
la vejez	old age
cambiar (de)	to change
graduarse (de/en)	to graduate (from/in)
jubilarse	to retire (from work)
nacer	to be born

Palabras adicionales

la alegría	happiness
el beso	kiss
conmigo	with me
contigo	with you
¡Felicidades!/ ¡Felicitaciones!	Congratulations!
¡Feliz cumpleaños!	Happy birthday!

Expresiones útiles	See page 147.

Supersite: MP3 Audio Files, Testing Program

recursos

LM p. 194   vhlcentral.com Lección 3

Audio: Vocabulary Flashcards

contextos

Lección 3

1   **Identificar** Label the following terms as **estado civil**, **fiesta**, or **etapa de la vida**.

1. casada ___estado civil___

2. adolescencia ___etapa de la vida___

3. viudo ___estado civil___

4. juventud ___etapa de la vida___

5. Navidad ___fiesta___

6. niñez ___etapa de la vida___

7. vejez ___etapa de la vida___

8. aniversario de bodas ___fiesta___

9. divorciado ___estado civil___

10. madurez ___etapa de la vida___

11. cumpleaños ___fiesta___

12. soltera ___estado civil___

2   **Las etapas de la vida** Label the stages of life on the timeline.

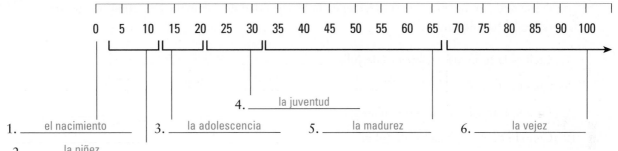

0 5 10 15 20 25 30 35 40 45 50 55 60 65 70 75 80 85 90 100

1. ___el nacimiento___

2. ___la niñez___

3. ___la adolescencia___

4. ___la juventud___

5. ___la madurez___

6. ___la vejez___

3   **Escribir** Fill in the blanks with the stage of life in which these events would normally occur.

1. jubilarse ___la vejez/la madurez___

2. graduarse en la universidad ___la juventud___

3. cumplir nueve años ___la niñez___

4. conseguir el primer trabajo ___la juventud___

5. graduarse de la escuela secundaria ___la adolescencia___

6. morir o quedar viudo ___la vejez___

7. casarse (por primera vez) ___la juventud___

8. tener un hijo ___la juventud___

9. celebrar el aniversario de bodas número cincuenta ___la vejez___

10. tener la primera cita ___la adolescencia___

4 **Información personal** Read the descriptions and answer these questions.

"Me llamo Jorge Rosas. Nací el 26 de enero de 1952. Mi esposa murió el año pasado. Tengo dos hijos: Marina y Daniel. Terminé mis estudios de sociología en la Universidad Interamericana en 1974. Me voy a jubilar este año. Voy a celebrar este evento con una botella de champán."

1. ¿Cuál es la fecha de nacimiento de Jorge? _____ el 26 de enero de 1952 _____

2. ¿Cuál es el estado civil de Jorge? _____ viudo _____

3. ¿En qué etapa de la vida está Jorge? _____ en la madurez _____

4. ¿Cuándo es el cumpleaños de Jorge? _____ el 26 de enero _____

5. ¿Cuándo se graduó Jorge? _____ en 1974 _____

6. ¿Cómo va a celebrar la jubilación (*retirement*) Jorge? _____ con una botella de champán _____

"Soy Julia Jiménez. Nací el 11 de marzo de 1982. Me comprometí a los veinte años, pero rompí con mi novio antes de casarme. Ahora estoy saliendo con un músico cubano. Soy historiadora del arte desde que terminé mi carrera (*degree*) en la Universidad de Salamanca en 2004. Mi postre favorito es el flan de caramelo."

7. ¿Cuál es la fecha de nacimiento de Julia? _____ el 11 de marzo de 1982 _____

8. ¿Cuál es el estado civil de Julia? _____ soltera _____

9. ¿En qué etapa de la vida está Julia? _____ en la juventud _____

10. ¿Cuándo es el cumpleaños de Julia? _____ el 11 de marzo _____

11. ¿Cuándo se graduó Julia? _____ en 2004 _____

12. ¿Qué postre le gusta a Julia? _____ el flan de caramelo _____

"Me llamo Manuel Blanco y vivo en Caracas. Mi esposa y yo nos comprometimos a los veintiséis años, y la boda fue dos años después. Pasaron quince años y tuvimos tres hijos. Me gustan mucho los dulces."

13. ¿Dónde vive Manuel? _____ en Caracas _____

14. ¿En qué etapa de la vida se comprometió Manuel? _____ en la juventud _____

15. ¿A qué edad se casó Manuel? _____ a los veintiocho años _____

16. ¿Cuál es el estado civil de Manuel? _____ casado _____

17. ¿Cuántos hijos tiene Manuel? _____ tres _____

18. ¿Qué postre le gusta a Manuel? _____ los dulces _____

estructura

3.1 Irregular preterites

1 **¿Hay o hubo?** Complete these sentences with the correct tense of **haber**.

1. Ahora _____ hay _____ una fiesta de graduación en el patio de la universidad.

2. _____ Hubo _____ muchos invitados en la fiesta de aniversario anoche.

3. Ya _____ hubo _____ una muerte en su familia el año pasado.

4. Siempre _____ hay _____ galletas y dulces en esas conferencias.

5. _____ Hubo _____ varios entremeses en la cena de ayer.

6. Por las mañanas _____ hay _____ unos postres deliciosos en esa tienda.

2 **¿Cómo fue?** Complete these sentences with the preterite of the verb in parentheses.

1. Cristina y Lara _____ estuvieron _____ (estar) en la fiesta anoche.

2. (yo) _____ Tuve _____ (Tener) un problema con mi pasaporte y lo pasé mal en la aduana.

3. Rafaela _____ vino _____ (venir) temprano a la fiesta y conoció a Humberto.

4. El padre de la novia _____ hizo _____ (hacer) un brindis por los novios.

5. Román _____ puso _____ (poner) las maletas en el auto antes de salir.

3 **¿Qué hicieron?** Complete these sentences, using the preterite of **decir**, **conducir**, **traducir**, and **traer**.

1. Felipe y Silvia _____ dijeron _____ que no les gusta ir a la playa.

2. Claudia le _____ tradujo _____ unos papeles al inglés a su hermano.

3. David _____ condujo _____ su motocicleta nueva durante el fin de semana.

4. Rosario y Pepe me _____ trajeron _____ un pastel de chocolate de regalo.

5. Cristina y yo les _____ dijimos _____ a nuestras amigas que vamos a bailar.

4 **Es mejor dar...** Rewrite these sentences in the preterite tense.

1. Antonio le da un beso a su madre.

   Antonio le dio un beso a su madre.

2. Los invitados le dan las gracias a la familia.

   Los invitados le dieron las gracias a la familia.

3. Tú les traes una sorpresa a tus padres.

   Tú les trajiste una sorpresa a tus padres.

4. Rosa y yo le damos un regalo al profesor.

   Rosa y yo le dimos un regalo al profesor.

5. Carla nos trae mucha comida para el viaje.

   Carla nos trajo mucha comida para el viaje.

5 **Combinar** Create logical sentences in the preterite using one element from each column. Notice that, using each word once, there is only one correct match between second and third columns. Answers will vary. Suggested answers:

Rita y Sara	decir	una cámara
ellos	estar	a este lugar
tú	hacer	un examen
mi tía	poner	galletas
ustedes	producir	una película
Rosa	tener	en Perú
nosotras	traer	la televisión
yo	venir	la verdad

1. Rosa hizo galletas.

2. Mi tía estuvo en el Perú.

3. Yo vine a este lugar.

4. Rita y Sara dijeron la verdad.

5. Ustedes pusieron la televisión.

6. Ellos produjeron una película.

7. Nosotras trajimos una cámara.

8. Tú tuviste un examen.

6 **Ya lo hizo** Your friend Miguel is very forgetful. Answer his questions negatively, indicating that the action has already occurred. Use the phrases or words in parentheses.

> **modelo**
>
> ¿Quiere Pepe cenar en el restaurante japonés? (restaurante chino)
> **No, Pepe ya cenó en el restaurante chino.**

1. ¿Vas a estar en la biblioteca hoy? (ayer)

   No, ya estuve en la biblioteca ayer.

2. ¿Quieren dar una fiesta Elena y Miguel este fin de semana? (el sábado pasado)

   No, Elena y Miguel ya dieron una fiesta el sábado pasado.

3. ¿Debe la profesora traducir esa novela este semestre? (el año pasado)

   No, la profesora ya tradujo esa novela el año pasado.

4. ¿Va a haber pastel de limón en la cena de hoy? (anoche)

   No, ya hubo un pastel de limón (en la cena de) anoche.

5. ¿Deseas poner los abrigos en la silla? (sobre la cama)

   No, ya puse los abrigos sobre la cama.

6. ¿Van ustedes a tener un hijo? (tres hijos)

   No, ya tuvimos/tenemos tres hijos.

3.2 Verbs that change meaning in the preterite

1

Completar Complete these sentences with the preterite tense of the verbs in parentheses.

1. Liliana no _____pudo_____ (poder) llegar a la fiesta de cumpleaños de Esteban.

2. Las chicas _____conocieron_____ (conocer) a muchos estudiantes en la biblioteca.

3. Raúl y Marta no _____quisieron_____ (querer) invitar al padre de Raúl a la boda.

4. Lina _____supo_____ (saber) ayer que sus tíos se van a divorciar.

5. (nosotros) _____Pudimos_____ (poder) regalarle una bicicleta a Marina.

6. María _____quiso_____ (querer) romper con su novio antes del verano.

2

Traducir Use these verbs to translate the sentences into Spanish.

> conocer   querer
> poder   saber

1. I failed to finish the book on Wednesday.

   No pude terminar el libro el miércoles.

2. Inés found out last week that Vicente is divorced.

   Inés supo la semana pasada que Vicente es/está divorciado.

3. Her girlfriends tried to call her, but they failed to.

   Sus amigas quisieron llamarla (por teléfono), pero no pudieron.

4. Susana met Alberto's parents last night.

   Susana conoció a los padres de Alberto anoche.

5. The waiters managed to serve dinner at eight.

   Los camareros pudieron servir la cena a las ocho.

6. Your mother refused to go to your brother's house.

   Tu madre no quiso ir a la casa de tu hermano.

3

Raquel y Ronaldo Complete the paragraph with the preterite of the verbs in the word bank.

> conocer   querer
> poder   saber

El año pasado Raquel (1) _____conoció_____ al muchacho que ahora es su esposo, Ronaldo.

Primero, Raquel no (2) _____quiso_____ salir con él porque él vivía (*was living*) en una ciudad

muy lejos de ella. Ronaldo (3) _____quiso_____ convencerla durante muchos meses, pero no

(4) _____pudo_____ hacerlo. Finalmente, Raquel decidió darle una oportunidad a Ronaldo.

Cuando empezaron a salir, Raquel y Ronaldo (5) _____supieron_____ inmediatamente que eran el

uno para el otro (*they were made for each other*). Raquel y Ronaldo (6) _____pudieron_____

comprar una casa en la misma ciudad y se casaron ese verano.

3.3 ¿Qué? and ¿cuál?

1

¿Qué o cuál? Complete these sentences with **qué**, **cuál**, or **cuáles**.

1. ¿_____Qué_____ estás haciendo ahora?

2. ¿_____Qué_____ gafas te gustan más?

3. ¿_____Cuál_____ prefieres, el vestido largo o el corto?

4. ¿Sabes _____cuál_____ de éstos es mi disco favorito?

5. ¿_____Qué_____ es un departamento de hacienda?

6. ¿_____Cuáles_____ trajiste, las de chocolate o las de limón?

7. ¿_____Qué_____ auto compraste este año?

8. ¿_____Cuál_____ es la tienda más elegante del centro?

2

¿Cuál es la pregunta? Write questions that correspond to these responses. Use each word or phrase from the word bank only once.

¿a qué hora?	¿cuál?	¿cuándo?	¿de dónde?	¿qué?
¿adónde?	¿cuáles?	¿cuántos?	¿dónde?	¿quién?

1. ¿Cuál es la camisa que más te gusta?

   La camisa que más me gusta es ésa.

2. ¿Qué quieres hacer hoy?

   Hoy quiero descansar durante el día.

3. ¿Quién es tu profesora de matemáticas?

   Mi profesora de matemáticas es la señora Aponte.

4. ¿De dónde eres?/¿De dónde es usted?

   Soy de Buenos Aires, Argentina.

5. ¿Cuáles son tus gafas favoritas?

   Mis gafas favoritas son las azules.

6. ¿Dónde está el pastel de cumpleaños?

   El pastel de cumpleaños está en el refrigerador.

7. ¿A qué hora empieza la fiesta sorpresa?

   La fiesta sorpresa empieza a las ocho en punto de la noche.

8. ¿Cuándo cierra el restaurante?

   El restaurante cierra los lunes.

9. ¿Cuántos invitados hay en la lista?

   Hay ciento cincuenta invitados en la lista.

10. ¿Adónde van ustedes?

    Vamos a la fiesta de cumpleaños de Inés.

3.4 Pronouns after prepositions

1 **Antes de la fiesta** Choose and write the correct pronouns to complete the paragraph.

Hoy voy al mercado al aire libre cerca de mi casa con mi tía Carmen. Me gusta ir con

(1) _____ella_____ (usted, ella) porque sabe escoger las mejores frutas y verduras del mercado.

Y a ella le gusta ir (2) _____conmigo_____ (contigo, conmigo) porque sé regatear mejor que nadie.

—Entre (3) _____tú_____ (tú, ellas) y yo, debes saber que a (4) _____mí_____

(ella, mí) no me gusta gastar mucho dinero. Me gusta venir (5) _____contigo_____ (con usted,

contigo) porque me ayudas a ahorrar (*save*) dinero —me confesó un día en el mercado. Hoy la

vienen a visitar sus hijos porque es su cumpleaños, y ella quiere hacer una ensalada de frutas para

(6) _____ellos_____ (ellos, nosotros).

—Estas peras son para (7) _____ti_____ (mí, ti), por venir conmigo al mercado.

También me llevo unos hermosos melocotones para el novio de Verónica, que viene con

(8) _____ella_____ (ella, nosotras). Siempre compro frutas para (9) _____él_____

(mí, él) porque le encantan y no consigue muchas frutas en el lugar donde vive —dice (*says*) mi tía.

—¿Voy a conocer al novio de Verónica?

—Sí, ¡queremos invitarte a (10) _____ti_____ (ti, él) a la fiesta de cumpleaños!

2 **El pastel de Carlota** Some friends are having Carlota's birthday cake. Complete the conversation with the correct pronouns.

SR. MARTÍNEZ Chicos, voy a buscar a mi esposa, en un momento estoy con
(1) _____ustedes_____.

TOMÁS Sí, señor Martínez, no se preocupe por (2) _____nosotros_____.

YOLANDA ¡Qué rico está el pastel! A (3) _____mí_____ me encantan los pasteles.
Tomás, ¿quieres compartir un pedazo (*slice*) (4) _____conmigo_____?

TOMÁS ¡Claro! Para (5) _____mí_____ el chocolate es lo más delicioso.

CARLOTA Pero no se lo terminen... Víctor, quiero compartir el último (*last*) pedazo
(6) _____contigo_____.

VÍCTOR Mmmh, está bien; sólo por (7) _____ti_____ hago este sacrificio.

CARLOTA Toma, Víctor, este pedazo es especial para (8) _____ti_____.

TOMÁS ¡Oh, no! Mira, Yolanda, ¡hay más miel (*honey*) en (9) _____ellos/él_____
que en cien pasteles!

Síntesis

Research the life of a famous person who has had a stormy personal life, such as Elizabeth Taylor or Henry VIII. Write a brief biography of the person, including the following information:

- When was the person born?
- What was that person's childhood like?
- With whom did the person fall in love?
- Whom did the person marry?
- Did he or she have children?

- Did the person get divorced?
- Did the person go to school, and did he or she graduate?
- How did his or her career or lifestyle vary as the person went through different stages in life?

Answers will vary.

panorama

Chile

1   **Datos chilenos** Complete the chart with the correct information about Chile.

Ciudades más grandes	Deportes de invierno	Países fronterizos (*bordering*)	Escritores
Santiago de Chile	el esquí	Perú	Gabriela Mistral
Concepción	el *snowboard*	Bolivia	Pablo Neruda
Viña del Mar	el heliesquí	Argentina	Isabel Allende

2   **¿Cierto o falso?** Indicate whether the sentences are **cierto** or **falso**. Correct the false sentences.

1. Una quinta parte de los chilenos vive en Santiago de Chile.
   Falso. Una tercera parte de los chilenos vive en Santiago de Chile.

2. En Chile se hablan el idioma español y el mapuche.
   Cierto.

3. La mayoría (*most*) de las playas de Chile están en la costa del océano Atlántico.
   Falso. La mayoría de las playas de Chile están en la costa del océano Pacífico.

4. El desierto de Atacama es el más seco del mundo.
   Cierto.

5. La isla de Pascua es famosa por sus observatorios astronómicos.
   Falso. La isla de Pascua es famosa por los *moái*, unas estatuas enormes.

6. El Parque Nacional Villarrica está situado al pie de un volcán y junto a un lago.
   Cierto.

7. Se practican deportes de invierno en los Andes chilenos.
   Cierto.

8. La exportación de vinos chilenos se redujo (*decreased*) en los últimos años.
   Falso. La exportación de vinos está subiendo cada vez más.

3   **Información de Chile** Complete the sentences with the correct words.

1. La moneda de Chile es el _____ peso chileno _____.

2. Bernardo O'Higgins fue un militar y _____ héroe _____ nacional de Chile.

3. Los exploradores _____ holandeses _____ descubrieron la isla de Pascua.

4. Desde los _____ observatorios _____ chilenos de los Andes, los científicos estudian las estrellas.

5. La producción de _____ vino _____ es una parte importante de la actividad agrícola de Chile.

6. El país al este de Chile es _____ Argentina _____.

4   **Fotos de Chile** Label the photos.

1.   edificio antiguo en Santiago

2.   los *moái* de la isla de Pascua

5   **El pasado de Chile** Complete the sentences with the preterite of the correct verbs from the word bank.

> comenzar   escribir
> decidir   recibir

1. Pablo Neruda _____ escribió _____ muchos poemas románticos durante su vida.

2. La isla de Pascua _____ recibió _____ su nombre porque la descubrieron el Día de Pascua.

3. No se sabe por qué los *rapa nui* _____ decidieron _____ abandonar la isla de Pascua.

4. La producción de vino en Chile _____ comenzó _____ en el siglo XVI.

6   **Preguntas chilenas** Write questions that correspond to the answers below. Vary the interrogative words you use.

1. ¿Cuántos habitantes hay en/tiene Chile? _____

Hay más de diecisiete millones de habitantes en Chile.

2. ¿Cuál es la capital chilena/de Chile? _____

Santiago de Chile es la capital chilena.

3. ¿Qué idiomas se hablan en Chile?/¿Cuáles son los idiomas que se hablan en Chile? _____

Los idiomas que se hablan en Chile son el español y el mapuche.

4. ¿Quiénes descubrieron la isla de Pascua?/¿Qué descubrieron los exploradores holandeses? _____

Los exploradores holandeses descubrieron la isla de Pascua.

5. ¿Qué tipo de excursiones organiza el centro de esquí Valle Nevado? _____

El centro de esquí Valle Nevado organiza excursiones de heliesquí.

6. ¿Cuándo/En qué siglo comenzó la producción de vino en Chile? _____

La producción de vino en Chile comenzó en el siglo XVI.

El Día de Muertos

Antes de ver el video

Lección 3
Fotonovela

1 **La celebración** In this episode, the Díaz family celebrates the Day of the Dead. What kinds of things do you expect to see? Answers will vary.

_____

_____

_____

_____

_____

_____

_____

_____

Mientras ves el video

2 **Ordenar** Put the following events in order.

__3__ a. La tía Ana María le dice a Marissa cómo se enamoraron sus papás.

__5__ b. El señor Díaz brinda por los abuelos de la familia.

__2__ c. Marissa prueba el mole que prepara la tía Ana María.

__1__ d. Maite Fuentes habla del Día de Muertos en la televisión.

__4__ e. Jimena pregunta dónde puso las galletas y el pastel.

3 **¿Qué ves?** Place a check mark beside each thing you see.

____ 1. una botella   ✔ 5. calaveras de azúcar   ____ 9. un regalo de Navidad

✔ 2. una foto de boda   ____ 6. una quinceañera   ____ 10. helados

____ 3. una graduación   ✔ 7. galletas   ✔ 11. un altar

✔ 4. flores   ✔ 8. bolsas   ____ 12. un flan

4 **¿Quién lo dijo?** Write a name next to each sentence to indicate who says it.

_____Marissa_____ 1. Su familia es muy interesante.

_____Maite Fuentes_____ 2. El Día de Muertos se celebra en México el primero y el dos de noviembre.

_____don Diego_____ 3. ¡Estoy seguro que se lo van a pasar bien!

_____tía Ana María_____ 4. Al principio, mi abuela no quiso aceptar el matrimonio.

Después de ver el video

5　**Corregir** Rewrite these sentences to reflect what took place.

1. El Día de Muertos se celebra con flores, calaveras de azúcar, música y champán.

   El Día de Muertos se celebra con flores, calaveras de azúcar, música y comida.

2. El mole siempre fue el plato favorito de la mamá de la tía Ana María.

   El mole siempre fue el plato favorito del papá de la tía Ana María.

3. Jimena intentó preparar mole para la fiesta de aniversario de sus tíos.

   Jimena intentó preparar mole para la fiesta de aniversario de sus papás.

4. La tía Ana María se casó con un ingeniero que trabaja muchísimo.

   La tía Ana María se casó con un doctor que trabaja muchísimo.

5. Felipe y su papá prepararon pastel de chocolate para la familia.

   Felipe y su papá prepararon una sorpresa para la familia.

6. A Valentina le gusta el helado.

   A Valentina le gustan las galletas.

6　**Eventos importantes** Describe in Spanish the three most important events in this episode, and explain your choices.　Answers will vary.

_____

_____

_____

_____

_____

_____

_____

7　**Preguntas personales** Answer these questions in Spanish.　Answers will vary.

1. ¿Qué días de fiesta celebras con tu familia? _____

   _____

2. De los días de fiesta, ¿cuál es tu favorito? ¿Por qué? _____

   _____

3. ¿Qué haces el Día de Acción de Gracias? _____

   _____

4. ¿Cómo celebras tu cumpleaños? ¿Te gusta recibir regalos? _____

   _____

Panorama: Chile

Antes de ver el video

Lección 3
Panorama cultural

1 **Más vocabulario** Look over these useful words and expressions before you watch the video.

Vocabulario útil
disfrutar (de) *to take advantage (of)*   **isla** *island*
grados *degrees*   **recursos naturales** *natural resources*
hace miles de años *thousands of years ago*   **repartidas** *spread throughout, distributed*
indígena *indigenous*   **vista** *view*

2 **Escribir** This video talks about Chile's Easter Island. In preparation for watching the video, answer the following questions. Answers will vary.

1. ¿Has estado (*Have you been*) en una isla o conoces alguna? ¿Cómo se llama?

_____

2. ¿Dónde está? ¿Cómo es?

_____

Mientras ves el video

3 **Fotos** Describe the video stills. Write at least three sentences in Spanish for each still. Answers will vary.

Después de ver el video

4

Completar Complete the sentences with words from the word bank.

atracción	indígena
característico	llega
diferente	recursos
difícil	remoto
escalan	repartidas

1. *Rapa Nui* es el nombre de la isla de Pascua en la lengua _____indígena_____ de la región.

2. Esta isla está en un lugar _____remoto_____.

3. Los habitantes de esta isla no tenían muchos _____recursos_____ naturales.

4. En un día de verano la temperatura _____llega_____ a los noventa grados.

5. Las esculturas *moái* son el elemento más _____característico_____ de esta isla.

6. Hay más de novecientas esculturas _____repartidas_____ por toda la isla.

7. Otra gran _____atracción_____ de la isla es el gran cráter Rano Kau.

8. Los visitantes _____escalan_____ el cráter para disfrutar de la espectacular vista.

5

Preferencias In Spanish, list at least two things you like about this video and explain your choices. Answers will vary.

_____

_____

_____

_____

_____

_____

_____

_____

_____

_____

_____

_____

Las fiestas

Lección 3
Flash cultura

Antes de ver el video

1 **Más vocabulario** Look over these useful words before you watch the video.

Vocabulario útil		
alegrar *to make happy*	**el cartel** *poster*	**la parranda** *party*
las artesanías *crafts*	**la clausura** *closing ceremony*	**la pintura** *painting*
el/la artesano/a *craftsperson; artisan*	**destacarse** *to stand out*	**el santo de palo** *wooden saint*
los cabezudos *carnival figures with large heads*	**el Día de Reyes** *Three Kings' Day*	**tocar el tambor** *playing drums*
la canción de Navidad *Christmas carol*	**las frituras** *fried foods; fritters*	**los Tres Santos Reyes/Reyes Magos** *Three Kings*
	la madera *wood*	
	la misa *mass*	

2 **Completar** Complete this paragraph about **la Navidad** in Puerto Rico.

En Puerto Rico, las Navidades no terminan después del (1) _____Día de Reyes_____, como en el resto de los países hispanos, sino después de las Fiestas de la Calle San Sebastián. Hay muchas expresiones artísticas de (2) _____artesanos_____ locales; entre ellas se destacan los (3) _____santo de palo_____, que son pequeñas estatuas (*statues*) de madera de vírgenes y santos. La (4) _____parranda_____ empieza por la noche cuando las personas salen a disfrutar del baile y la música con amigos y familiares.

3 **¡En español!** Look at the video still. What do you think this episode will be about? Imagine what Diego will say and write a two- or three-sentence introduction to this episode. Answers will vary.

Diego Palacios, Puerto Rico

¡Bienvenidos! Soy Diego Palacios, de Puerto Rico. Hoy les quiero mostrar… _____

_____

_____

_____

_____

Mientras ves el video

4 **Ordenar** Ordena cronológicamente lo que Diego hizo (*did*).

___5___ a. Les preguntó a personas qué disfrutaban más de las fiestas.

___1___ b. Bailó con los cabezudos en la calle.

___2___ c. Habló con artesanos sobre los santos de palo.

___4___ d. Tomó un helado de coco.

___3___ e. Comió unas frituras.

5   **Emparejar** Match the captions to the appropriate elements.

1. __b__

2. __d__

3. __c__

4. __a__

a. el güiro   b. los cabezudos   c. los santos de palo   d. el pandero   e. los carteles

Después de ver el video

6   **¿Cierto o falso?** Indicate whether each statement is **cierto** or **falso**.

1. Las Navidades en Puerto Rico terminan con del Día de Reyes. _____falso_____

2. Los artistas hacen cuadros y carteles sobre la Navidad. _____cierto_____

3. En Puerto Rico, todas las celebraciones navideñas son religiosas. _____falso_____

4. Los santos de palo representan a personajes puertorriqueños. _____falso_____

5. Según un artesano, la pieza de artesanía más popular es la de los Tres Santos Reyes.
   _____cierto_____

6. El güiro y el pandero son algunos de los instrumentos típicos de la música de estas fiestas.
   _____cierto_____

7   **¡De parranda!** Imagine that you are an exchange student in Puerto Rico and that you are attending this celebration. You are dancing on the street when suddenly Diego spots you and decides to interview you. Tell him how you feel and what cultural aspects catch your attention. Make sure to include these words.

| artistas | bailar | cabezudos | de parranda | en la calle | tocar el tambor |

Answers will vary.

_____

_____

_____

_____

contextos

Lección 3

1 **¿Lógico o ilógico?** You will hear some statements. Decide if they are **lógico** or **ilógico**.

1. Lógico (Ilógico)   5. Lógico (Ilógico)
2. (Lógico) Ilógico   6. (Lógico) Ilógico
3. (Lógico) Ilógico   7. (Lógico) Ilógico
4. Lógico (Ilógico)   8. Lógico (Ilógico)

2 **Escoger** For each drawing, you will hear three statements. Choose the one that corresponds to the drawing.

1. a.   b.   (c.)   2. a.   (b.)   c.

3. (a.)   b.   c.   4. a.   b.   (c.)

3 **Una celebración** Listen as señora Jiménez talks about a party she has planned. Then answer the questions in your lab manual.

1. ¿Para quién es la fiesta?

   La fiesta es para Martín, su hijo.

2. ¿Cuándo es la fiesta?

   La fiesta es el viernes a las ocho y media.

3. ¿Por qué hacen la fiesta?

   Porque él/Martín/su hijo se gradúa.

4. ¿Quiénes van a la fiesta?

   La familia y los amigos (de la universidad) de Martín van a la fiesta.

5. ¿Qué van a hacer los invitados en la fiesta?

   Los invitados van a cenar, a bailar y a comer pastel.

pronunciación

The letters **h**, **j**, and **g**

The Spanish **h** is always silent.

helado   **h**ombre   **h**ola   **h**ermosa

The letter **j** is pronounced much like the English *h* in *his*.

José   **j**ubilarse   de**j**ar   pare**j**a

The letter **g** can be pronounced three different ways. Before **e** or **i**, the letter **g** is pronounced much like the English *h*.

a**g**encia   **g**eneral   **G**il   **G**isela

At the beginning of a phrase or after the letter **n**, the Spanish **g** is pronounced like the English *g* in *girl*.

Gustavo, **g**racias por llamar el domin**g**o.

In any other position, the Spanish **g** has a somewhat softer sound.

Me **g**radué en a**g**osto.

In the combinations **gue** and **gui**, the **g** has a hard sound and the **u** is silent. In the combination **gua**, the **g** has a hard sound and the **u** is pronounced like the English *w*.

Guerra   conse**gui**r   **gua**ntes   a**gua**

1 **Práctica** Repeat each word after the speaker to practice pronouncing **h**, **j**, and **g**.

1. hamburguesa	4. guapa	7. espejo	10. gracias	13. Jorge
2. jugar	5. geografía	8. hago	11. hijo	14. tengo
3. oreja	6. magnífico	9. seguir	12. galleta	15. ahora

2 **Oraciones** When you hear the number, read the corresponding sentence aloud. Then listen to the speaker and repeat the sentence.

1. Hola. Me llamo Gustavo Hinojosa Lugones y vivo en Santiago de Chile.
2. Tengo una familia grande; somos tres hermanos y tres hermanas.
3. Voy a graduarme en mayo.
4. Para celebrar mi graduación, mis padres van a regalarme un viaje a Egipto.
5. ¡Qué generosos son!

3 **Refranes** Repeat each saying after the speaker to practice pronouncing **h**, **j**, and **g**.

1. A la larga, lo más dulce amarga.   2. El hábito no hace al monje.

4 **Dictado** Victoria is talking to her friend Mirta on the phone. Listen carefully and during the pauses write what she says. The entire passage will then be repeated so that you can check your work.

Mirta, sabes que el domingo es el aniversario de bodas de Héctor y Ángela, ¿no? Sus hijos quieren hacerles una fiesta

grande e invitar a todos sus amigos. Pero a Ángela y a Héctor no les gusta la idea. Ellos quieren salir juntos a algún

restaurante y después relajarse en casa.

estructura

3.1 Irregular preterites

1 **Escoger** Listen to each question and choose the most logical response.

1. (a.) No, no conduje hoy.   b. No, no condujo hoy.
2. a. Te dije que tengo una cita con   (b.) Me dijo que tiene una cita con
   Gabriela esta noche.   Gabriela esta noche.
3. (a.) Estuvimos en la casa de Marta.   b. Estuvieron en la casa de Marta.
4. (a.) Porque tuvo que estudiar.   b. Porque tiene que estudiar.
5. a. Lo supieron la semana pasada.   (b.) Lo supimos la semana pasada.
6. (a.) Los pusimos en la mesa.   b. Los pusiste en la mesa.
7. a. No, sólo tradujimos un poco.   (b.) No, sólo traduje un poco.
8. (a.) Sí, le di $20.   b. Sí, le dio $20.

2 **Cambiar** Change each sentence from the present to the preterite. Repeat the correct answer after the speaker. (*8 items*)

> **modelo**
> Él pone el flan sobre la mesa.
> Él *puso el flan sobre la mesa.*

3 **Preguntas** Answer each question you hear using the cue in your lab manual. Substitute object pronouns for the direct object when possible. Repeat the correct answer after the speaker.

> **modelo**
> *You hear:* ¿Quién condujo el auto?
> *You see:* yo
> *You say:* Yo lo conduje.

1. Gerardo   3. nosotros   5. ¡Felicitaciones!
2. Mateo y Yolanda   4. muy buena   6. mi papá

4 **Completar** Listen to the following description and write the missing words in your lab manual.

(1) _____Supe_____ por un amigo que los Márquez (2) _____vinieron_____ a visitar a su hija.

Me (3) _____dijo_____ que (4) _____condujeron_____ desde Antofagasta y que se

(5) _____quedaron_____ en el Hotel Carrera. Les (6) _____hice_____ una llamada (*call*)

anoche, pero no (7) _____contestaron_____ el teléfono. Sólo (8) _____pude_____ dejarles un

mensaje. Hoy ellos me (9) _____llamaron_____ y me (10) _____preguntaron_____ si mi esposa y yo

teníamos tiempo para almorzar con ellos. Claro que les (11) _____dije_____ que sí.

3.2 Verbs that change meaning in the preterite

1 **Identificar** Listen to each sentence and mark and **X** in the column for the subject of the verb.

> **modelo**
>
> *You hear:* ¿Cuándo lo supiste?
> *You mark:* an **X** under **tú**.

	yo	tú	él/ella	nosotros/as	ellos/ellas
Modelo		X			
1.				X	
2.			X		
3.	X				
4.		X			
5.					X
6.	X				
7.					X
8.			X		

2 **Preguntas** Answer each question you hear using the cue in your lab manual. Substitute object pronouns for the direct object when possible. Repeat the correct response after the speaker.

> **modelo**
>
> *You hear:* ¿Conocieron ellos a Sandra?
> *You see:* sí
> *You say:* Sí, la conocieron.

1. sí   2. en la casa de Ángela   3. el viernes   4. no   5. no   6. anoche

3 **¡Qué lástima! (What a shame!)** Listen as José talks about some news he recently received. Then read the statements and decide whether they are **cierto** or **falso**.

	Cierto	Falso
1. Supieron de la muerte ayer.	○	⊘
2. Se sonrieron cuando oyeron las noticias (*news*).	○	⊘
3. Carolina no se pudo comunicar con la familia.	⊘	○
4. Francisco era (*was*) joven.	⊘	○
5. Mañana piensan llamar a la familia de Francisco.	○	⊘

4 **Relaciones amorosas** Listen as Susana describes what happened between her and Pedro. Then answer the questions in your lab manual.

1. ¿Por qué no pudo salir Susana con Pedro? <u>No pudo salir con Pedro porque pasó toda la noche estudiando.</u>

2. ¿Qué supo por su amiga? <u>Supo que Pedro salió/fue al cine con Mónica esa noche.</u>

3. ¿Cómo se puso Susana cuando Pedro llamó? <u>Se puso muy enojada./Se enojó mucho.</u>

4. ¿Qué le dijo Susana a Pedro? <u>Le dijo que supo que el domingo él salió con Mónica.</u>

3.3 ¿Qué? and ¿cuál?

1 **¿Lógico o ilógico?** You will hear some questions and the responses. Decide if they are **lógico** or **ilógico**.

1. Lógico (Ilógico)
2. (Lógico) Ilógico
3. Lógico (Ilógico)
4. (Lógico) Ilógico
5. Lógico (Ilógico)
6. Lógico (Ilógico)
7. (Lógico) Ilógico
8. (Lógico) Ilógico

2 **Preguntas** You will hear a series of responses to questions. Using **¿qué?** or **¿cuál?**, form the question that prompted each response. Repeat the correct answer after the speaker. (8 items)

> **modelo**
> Santiago de Chile es la capital de Chile.
> ¿Cuál es la capital de Chile?

3 **De compras** Look at Marcela's shopping list for Christmas and answer each question you hear. Repeat the correct response after the speaker. (6 items)

Raúl	2 camisas, talla 17
Cristina	blusa, color azul
Pepe	bluejeans y tres pares de calcetines blancos
Abuelo	cinturón
Abuela	suéter blanco

4 **Escoger** Listen to this radio commercial and choose the most logical response to each question.

1. ¿Qué hace Fiestas Mar?
   (a.) Organiza fiestas.   b. Es una tienda que vende cosas para fiestas.   c. Es un club en el mar.

2. ¿Para qué tipo de fiesta no usaría Fiestas Mar?
   a. Para una boda.   b. Para una fiesta de sorpresa.   (c.) Para una cena con los suegros.

3. ¿Cuál de estos servicios no ofrece Fiestas Mar?
   a. Poner las decoraciones.   b. Proveer (*Provide*) el lugar.   (c.) Proveer los regalos.

4. ¿Qué tiene que hacer el cliente si usa los servicios de Fiestas Mar?
   (a.) Tiene que preocuparse por la lista de invitados.   b. Tiene que preocuparse por la música.
   c. Tiene que preparar la comida.

5. Si uno quiere contactar Fiestas Mar, ¿qué debe hacer?
   a. Debe escribirles un mensaje electrónico.   (b.) Debe llamarlos.   c. Debe ir a Casa Mar.

3.4 Pronouns after prepositions

1 **Cambiar** Listen to each statement and say that the feeling is not mutual. Use a pronoun after the preposition in your response. Then repeat the correct answer after the speaker. (*6 items*)

> **modelo**
>
> Carlos quiere desayunar con nosotros.
> *Pero nosotros no queremos desayunar con él.*

2 **Preguntas** Answer each question you hear using the appropriate pronoun after the preposition and the cue in your lab manual. Repeat the correct response after the speaker.

> **modelo**
>
> *You hear:* ¿Almuerzas con Alberto hoy?
> *You see:* No
> *You say:* No, no almuerzo con él hoy.

1. Sí
2. Luis
3. Sí
4. Sí
5. No
6. Francisco

3 **Preparativos (*Preparations*)** Listen to this conversation between David and Andrés. Then answer the questions in your lab manual.

1. ¿Qué necesitan comprar para la fiesta?

   Necesitan comprar jamón, pan, salchicha y queso.

2. ¿Con quién quiere Alfredo ir a la fiesta?

   Alfredo quiere ir a la fiesta con Sara.

3. ¿Por qué ella no quiere ir con él?

   Ella no quiere ir con él porque está muy enojada.

4. ¿Con quién va Sara a la fiesta?

   Sara va con Andrés.

5. ¿Para quién quieren comprar algo especial?

   Quieren comprar algo especial para Alfredo.

vocabulario

You will now hear the vocabulary found in your textbook on the last page of this lesson. Listen and repeat each Spanish word or phrase after the speaker.

Additional Vocabulary

Additional Vocabulary

Notes

Notes

En el consultorio

4

A PRIMERA VISTA
- ¿Están en una farmacia o en un hospital?
- ¿La mujer es médico o dentista?
- ¿Qué hace ella, una operación o un examen médico?
- ¿Crees que la paciente está nerviosa?

Más práctica
Workbook pages 231–244
Video Manual pages 245–250
Lab Manual pages 251–256

En el consultorio

Más vocabulario

la clínica	clinic
el consultorio	doctor's office
el/la dentista	dentist
el examen médico	physical exam
la farmacia	pharmacy
el hospital	hospital
la operación	operation
la sala de emergencia(s)	emergency room
el cuerpo	body
el oído	(sense of) hearing; inner ear
el accidente	accident
la salud	health
el síntoma	symptom
caerse	to fall (down)
darse con	to bump into; to run into
doler (o:ue)	to hurt
enfermarse	to get sick
estar enfermo/a	to be sick
poner una inyección	to give an injection
recetar	to prescribe
romperse (la pierna)	to break (one's leg)
sacar(se) un diente	to have a tooth removed
sufrir una enfermedad	to suffer an illness
torcerse (o:ue) (el tobillo)	to sprain (one's ankle)
toser	to cough

Variación léxica

gripe	⟷	gripa (Col., Gua., Méx.)
resfriado	⟷	catarro (Cuba, Esp., Gua.)
sala de emergencia(s)	⟷	sala de urgencias (Arg., Col., Esp., Méx.)
romperse	⟷	quebrarse (Arg., Gua.)

Supersite: MP3 Audio Files and Scripts, Digital Image Bank, Activity Pack, Testing Program (Quizzes), **Vocabulario adicional**

recursos

WB pp. 231–232	LM p. 251	vhlcentral.com Lección 4

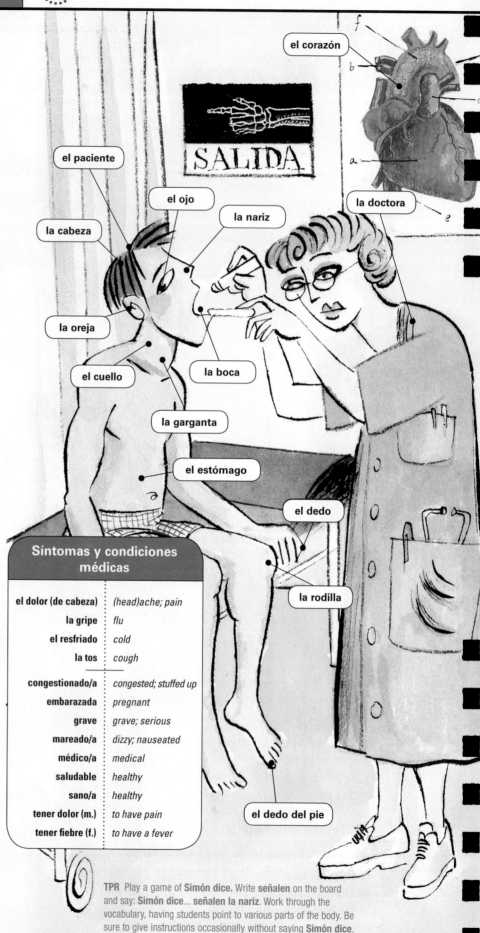

el corazón

SALIDA

el paciente

el ojo

la nariz

la doctora

la cabeza

la oreja

el cuello

la boca

la garganta

el estómago

el dedo

la rodilla

Síntomas y condiciones médicas

el dolor (de cabeza)	(head)ache; pain
la gripe	flu
el resfriado	cold
la tos	cough
congestionado/a	congested; stuffed up
embarazada	pregnant
grave	grave; serious
mareado/a	dizzy; nauseated
médico/a	medical
saludable	healthy
sano/a	healthy
tener dolor (m.)	to have pain
tener fiebre (f.)	to have a fever

el dedo del pie

TPR Play a game of **Simón dice.** Write **señalen** on the board and say: **Simón dice... señalen la nariz.** Work through the vocabulary, having students point to various parts of the body. Be sure to give instructions occasionally without saying **Simón dice.**

la radiografía

el hueso

la enfermera

la paciente

Estornuda.

Toma la temperatura.

el brazo

la pierna

el tobillo

La medicina

el antibiótico	antibiotic
la aspirina	aspirin
la pastilla	pill; tablet
la receta	prescription

Lección 4

Práctica 1 2 **Supersite:** MP3 Audio Files, Scripts

1 Escuchar Escucha las preguntas y selecciona la respuesta más adecuada.

    a. Tengo dolor de cabeza y fiebre.
    b. No fui a la clase porque estaba (*I was*) enfermo.
    c. Me caí la semana pasada jugando al tenis.
    d. Debes ir a la farmacia.
    e. Porque tengo gripe.
    f. Sí, tengo mucha tos por las noches.
    g. Lo llevaron directamente a la sala de emergencia.
    h. No sé. Todavía tienen que tomarme la temperatura.

1. __c__ 3. __g__ 5. __f__ 7. __a__
2. __e__ 4. __d__ 6. __h__ 8. __b__

2 Seleccionar Escucha la conversación entre Daniel y su doctor y selecciona la respuesta que mejor complete cada oración.

1. Daniel cree que tiene __a__.
    a. gripe   b. un resfriado   c. la temperatura alta
2. A Daniel le duele la cabeza, estornuda, tose y __c__.
    a. se cae   b. tiene fiebre   c. está congestionado
3. El doctor le __b__.
    a. pone una inyección   b. toma la temperatura
    c. mira el oído
4. A Daniel no le gustan __a__.
    a. las inyecciones   b. los antibióticos   c. las visitas al doctor
5. El doctor dice que Daniel tiene __b__.
    a. gripe   b. un resfriado   c. fiebre
6. Después de la consulta Daniel va a __c__.
    a. la sala de emergencia   b. la clínica   c. la farmacia

3 Completar Completa las oraciones con una palabra de la misma familia de la palabra subrayada. Usa la forma correcta de cada palabra.

1. Cuando <u>oyes</u> algo, usas el __oído__.
2. Cuando te <u>enfermas</u>, te sientes __enfermo/a__ y necesitas ir al consultorio para ver a la __enfermera__.
3. ¿Alguien __estornudó__? Creo que oí un <u>estornudo</u> (*sneeze*).
4. No puedo <u>arrodillarme</u> (*kneel down*) porque me lastimé la __rodilla__ en un accidente de coche.
5. ¿Vas al __consultorio__ para <u>consultar</u> al médico?
6. Si te rompes un <u>diente</u>, vas al __dentista__.

4 Contestar Mira el dibujo y contesta las preguntas. Answers will vary.

1. ¿Qué hace la doctora?   4. ¿Qué hace el paciente?
2. ¿Qué hay en la pared (*wall*)?   5. ¿A quién le duele la garganta?
3. ¿Qué hace la enfermera?   6. ¿Qué tiene la paciente?

4 Ask additional questions about the doctor's office scene. Ex: **¿Qué hace la chica? (Estornuda.)**

5   **Asociaciones** Trabajen en parejas para identificar las partes del cuerpo que ustedes asocian con estas actividades. Sigan el modelo. Answers will vary.

> **modelo**
>
> nadar
> **Estudiante 1:** Usamos los brazos para nadar.
> **Estudiante 2:** Usamos las piernas también.

1. hablar por teléfono
2. tocar el piano
3. correr en el parque
4. escuchar música
5. ver una película
6. toser
7. llevar zapatos
8. comprar perfume
9. estudiar biología
10. comer pollo asado

AYUDA

Remember that in Spanish, parts of the body are usually referred to with an article and not a possessive adjective: **Me duelen los pies.** The indirect object pronoun **me** is used to express the concept of *my.*

6   **Cuestionario** Contesta el cuestionario seleccionando las respuestas que reflejen mejor tus experiencias. Suma (*Add*) los puntos de cada respuesta y anota el resultado. Después, con el resto de la clase, compara y analiza los resultados del cuestionario y comenta lo que dicen de la salud y de los hábitos de todo el grupo. Answers will vary.

¿Tienes buena salud?

27–30 puntos	Salud y hábitos excelentes
23–26 puntos	Salud y hábitos buenos
22 puntos o menos	Salud y hábitos problemáticos

1. ¿Con qué frecuencia te enfermas? (resfriados, gripe, etc.)
Cuatro veces por año o más. (1 punto)
Dos o tres veces por año. (2 puntos)
Casi nunca. (3 puntos)

2. ¿Con qué frecuencia tienes dolores de estómago o problemas digestivos?
Con mucha frecuencia. (1 punto)
A veces. (2 puntos)
Casi nunca. (3 puntos)

3. ¿Con qué frecuencia sufres de dolores de cabeza?
Frecuentemente. (1 punto)
A veces. (2 puntos)
Casi nunca. (3 puntos)

4. ¿Comes verduras y frutas?
No, casi nunca como verduras ni frutas. (1 punto)
Sí, a veces. (2 puntos)
Sí, todos los días. (3 puntos)

5. ¿Eres alérgico/a a algo?
Sí, a muchas cosas. (1 punto)
Sí, a algunas cosas. (2 puntos)
No. (3 puntos)

6. ¿Haces ejercicios aeróbicos?
No, casi nunca hago ejercicios aeróbicos. (1 punto)
Sí, a veces. (2 puntos)
Sí, con frecuencia. (3 puntos)

7. ¿Con qué frecuencia te haces un examen médico?
Nunca o casi nunca. (1 punto)
Cada dos años. (2 puntos)
Cada año y/o antes de empezar a practicar un deporte. (3 puntos)

8. ¿Con qué frecuencia vas al dentista?
Nunca voy al dentista. (1 punto)
Sólo cuando me duele un diente. (2 puntos)
Por lo menos una vez por año. (3 puntos)

9. ¿Qué comes normalmente por la mañana?
No como nada por la mañana. (1 punto)
Tomo una bebida dietética. (2 puntos)
Como cereal y fruta. (3 puntos)

10. ¿Con qué frecuencia te sientes mareado/a?
Frecuentemente. (1 punto)
A veces. (2 puntos)
Casi nunca. (3 puntos)

5 For each item, encourage students to list as many parts of the body as they can. For variation, say parts of the body and have students associate each one with at least five activities.

6 Write the three categories with their point totals on the board. Ask for a show of hands for those who fall into each group. Analyze the trends of the class—are your students healthy or unhealthy?

6 Ask for volunteers from each of the three groups to explain whether they think the results of the survey are accurate or not. Ask them to give examples based on their own eating, exercise, and other health habits.

Game Play a modified version of **20 Preguntas**. Ask a volunteer to think of a part of the body. Other students get one chance each to ask a yes/no question until someone guesses the item correctly. Limit attempts to ten questions per item. Encourage students to guess by associating activities with various parts of the body.

Supersite: At this point you may want to present *Vocabulario adicional: Más vocabulario para el consultorio.*

6 For expansion, have students brainstorm a few additional health-related questions and responses, and adjust the point totals accordingly. Ex: **¿Con qué frecuencia te lavas las manos? ¿Con qué frecuencia usas seda dental? ¿Tomas el sol sin bloqueador solar? ¿Comes comida rápida (McDonald's, etc.)? ¿Fumas cigarros? ¿Consumes mucha cafeína?**

Lección 4

NATIONAL
communication
STANDARDS

Comunicación

7

¿Qué les pasó? Trabajen en un grupo de dos o tres personas. Hablen de lo que les pasó y de cómo se sienten las personas que aparecen en los dibujos. Answers will vary.

1. Adela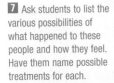

2. Francisco

3. Pilar

4. Pedro

5. Cristina

6. Félix

7 Ask students to list the various possibilities of what happened to these people and how they feel. Have them name possible treatments for each.

7 Bring in magazine pictures related to illness, medicine, and medical appointments. Have students describe what is going on in the images.

8 To practice more verb forms, have students talk about an illness or accident that someone they know had.

Pairs For homework, ask students to draw an alien or other fantastic being. In the next class period, have students describe the alien to a classmate, who will draw it according to the description. Ex: **Tiene una cabeza grande y tres piernas delgadas con pelo en las rodillas. Encima de la cabeza tiene ocho ojos pequeños y uno grande…** Then have students compare the drawings for accuracy.

8 Model this activity by talking about an illness or accident you had.

8

Un accidente Cuéntale a la clase de un accidente o una enfermedad que tuviste. Incluye información que conteste estas preguntas. Answers will vary.

✔ ¿Qué ocurrió?
✔ ¿Dónde ocurrió?
✔ ¿Cuándo ocurrió?
✔ ¿Cómo ocurrió?
✔ ¿Quién te ayudó y cómo?
✔ ¿Tuviste algún problema después del accidente o después de la enfermedad?
✔ ¿Cuánto tiempo tuviste el problema?

9 Have pairs use words from the crossword to role-play a visit to a doctor's office.

Supersite:
Activity Pack

9

Crucigrama Tu profesor(a) les va a dar a ti y a un(a) compañero/a un crucigrama (*crossword*) incompleto. Tú tienes las palabras que necesita tu compañero/a y él/ella tiene las palabras que tú necesitas. Tienen que darse pistas para completarlo. No pueden decir la palabra necesaria; deben utilizar definiciones, ejemplos y frases. Answers will vary.

modelo

10 horizontal: La usamos para hablar.
14 vertical: Es el médico que examina los dientes.

Extra Practice Write **Mido _____ pies y _____ pulgadas** on the board and explain what it means. Have students write physical descriptions of themselves. Students should use as much vocabulary from this lesson as they can. Collect the papers, shuffle them, and read the descriptions aloud. The rest of the class has to guess who is being described.

Video Synopsis While out with her friend **Elena**, **Jimena's** cold symptoms start bothering her. Despite taking **don Diego's** and **Elena's** home remedies, the cold symptoms persist. At her mother's insistence, **Jimena** goes to the doctor, who prescribes some medicine.

¡Qué dolor!

Jimena no se siente bien y tiene que ir al doctor.

PERSONAJES **ELENA** **JIMENA**

S Video: *Fotonovela*

ELENA ¿Cómo te sientes?

JIMENA Me duele un poco la garganta. Pero no tengo fiebre.

ELENA Creo que tienes un resfriado. Te voy a llevar a casa.

JIMENA HOLA, don Diego. Gracias por venir.

DON DIEGO Fui a la farmacia. Aquí están las pastillas para el resfriado. Se debe tomar una cada seis horas con las comidas. Y no se deben tomar más de seis pastillas al día.

ELENA ¿Don Diego ya fue a la farmacia? ¿Cuánto tiempo hace que lo llamaste?

JIMENA Hace media hora. Ay, qué cosas, de niña apenas me enfermaba. No perdí ni un solo día de clases.

ELENA Yo tampoco.

ELENA Nunca tenía resfriados, pero me rompí el brazo dos veces. Mi hermana y yo estábamos paseando en bicicleta y casi me di con un señor que caminaba por la calle. Me caí y me rompí el brazo.

JIMENA ¿Qué es esto?

ELENA Es té de jengibre. Cuando me dolía el estómago, mi mamá siempre me hacía tomarlo. Se dice que es bueno para el dolor de estómago.

JIMENA Pero no me duele el estómago.

(*La Sra. Díaz llama a Jimena.*)

JIMENA Hola, mamá. Don Diego me trajo los medicamentos... ¿Al doctor? ¿Estás segura? Allá nos vemos. (*A Elena*) Mi mamá ya hizo una cita para mí con el Dr. Meléndez.

Video Recap: Lección 3 Before doing this **Fotonovela** section, review the previous episode. Ask:
1. ¿Qué plato hizo la tía Ana María? (Hizo mole.) 2. ¿Quiénes prepararon una sorpresa para llevar al
cementerio? (El Sr. Díaz y Felipe la prepararon.) 3. ¿Qué postres hizo Jimena? (Hizo galletas y pastel.)

doscientos uno **201**

DON DIEGO

SRA. DÍAZ

DR. MELÉNDEZ

Expresiones útiles Point out the phrase **apenas me enfermaba**. Explain that **apenas** is an adverb and that **me enfermaba** is an imperfect tense form, used here to talk about habitual events in the past. Point out **Se dice que** and **Se debe tomar** as examples of impersonal constructions with **se**. Draw attention to **Se me olvidó** and **se le olvidó** and tell students that **se** is also used to describe unplanned or accidental events. Tell students that they will learn more about these concepts in **Estructura**.

Lección 4

SRA. DÍAZ ¿Te pusiste un suéter anoche?

JIMENA No, mamá. Se me olvidó.

SRA. DÍAZ Doctor, esta jovencita salió anoche, se le olvidó ponerse un suéter y parece que le dio un resfriado.

DR. MELÉNDEZ Jimena, ¿cuáles son tus síntomas?

JIMENA Toso con frecuencia y me duele la garganta.

DR. MELÉNDEZ ¿Cuánto tiempo hace que tienes estos síntomas?

JIMENA Hace dos días que me duele la garganta.

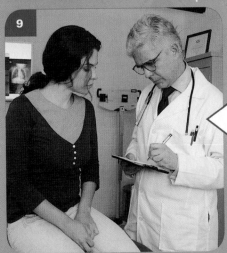

DR. MELÉNDEZ Muy bien. Aquí no tienes infección. No tienes fiebre. Te voy a mandar algo para la garganta. Puedes ir por los medicamentos inmediatamente a la farmacia.

Teaching Tips
• Photocopy the **Fotonovela** Videoscript (Supersite) and white out words related to injuries and illnesses in order to make a master for a cloze activity. Have students fill in the missing words as they watch the episode.
• Ask students to read the **Fotonovela** captions in groups of five. Ask one or two groups to role-play the dialogue for the class.
• On the board, write the paradigms for **hace** + [*time period*] + **que** + [*present*] and **hace** + [*time period*] + **que** + [*preterite*]. Ask a few comprehension questions to contrast their uses. Ex: ¿Cuánto tiempo hace que te graduaste de la escuela secundaria? ¿Cuánto tiempo hace que eres estudiante universitario?

SRA. DÍAZ Doctor, ¿cómo está? ¿Es grave?

DR. MELÉNDEZ No, no es nada grave. Jimena, la próxima vez, escucha a tu mamá. ¡Tienes que usar suéter!

recursos

VM
pp. 245–246

vhlcentral.com
Lección 4

Expresiones útiles

Discussing medical conditions

¿Cómo te sientes?
How do you feel?
Me duele un poco la garganta.
My throat hurts a little.
No me duele el estómago.
My stomach doesn't hurt.
De niño/a apenas me enfermaba.
As a child, I rarely got sick.
¡Soy alérgico/a a chile!
I'm allergic to chili powder!

Discussing remedies

Se dice que el té de jengibre es bueno para el dolor de estómago.
They say ginger tea is good for stomachaches.
Aquí están las pastillas para el resfriado.
Here are the pills for your cold.
Se debe tomar una cada seis horas.
You should take one every six hours.

Expressions with hacer

Hace + [*period of time*] **que** + [*present /preterite*]
¿Cuánto tiempo hace que tienes estos síntomas?
How long have you had these symptoms?
Hace dos días que me duele la garganta.
My throat has been hurting for two days.
¿Cuánto tiempo hace que lo llamaste?
How long has it been since you called him?
Hace media hora.
It's been a half hour (since I called).

Additional vocabulary

canela *cinnamon*
miel *honey*
terco *stubborn*

¿Qué pasó?

1   ¿Cierto o falso? Decide si lo que dicen estas oraciones sobre Jimena es **cierto** o **falso**. Corrige las oraciones falsas.

	Cierto	Falso	
1. Dice que de niña apenas se enfermaba.	●	○	
2. Tiene dolor de garganta y fiebre.	○	●	Tiene dolor de garganta, pero no tiene fiebre
3. Olvidó ponerse un suéter anoche.	●	○	
4. Hace tres días que le duele la garganta.	○	●	Hace dos días que le duele la garganta.
5. El doctor le dice que tiene una infección.	○	●	El doctor le dice que no tiene una infección.

2   Identificar Identifica quién puede decir estas oraciones.

1. Como dice tu mamá, tienes que usar suéter.   Dr. Meléndez
2. Por pasear en bicicleta me rompí el brazo dos veces.   Elena
3. ¿Cuánto tiempo hace que toses y te duele la garganta?   Dr. Meléndez
4. Tengo cita con el Dr. Meléndez.   Jimena
5. Dicen que el té de jengibre es muy bueno para los dolores de estómago.   Elena
6. Nunca perdí un día de clases porque apenas me enfermaba.   Jimena

DR. MELÉNDEZ

ELENA

JIMENA

3   Ordenar Pon estos sucesos en el orden correcto.

a. Jimena va a ver al doctor. ___4___
b. El doctor le dice a la Sra. Díaz que no es nada serio. ___6___
c. Elena le habla a Jimena de cuando se rompió el brazo. ___2___
d. El doctor le receta medicamentos. ___5___
e. Jimena le dice a Elena que le duele la garganta. ___1___
f. Don Diego le trae a Jimena las pastillas para el resfriado. ___3___

4   En el consultorio Trabajen en parejas para representar los papeles de un(a) médico/a y su paciente. Usen las instrucciones como guía.

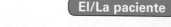

El/La médico/a

Pregúntale al / a la paciente qué le pasó.

Pregúntale cuánto tiempo hace que se cayó.

Mira el dedo. Debes recomendar un tratamiento (*treatment*) al / a la paciente.

El/La paciente

→ Dile que te caíste en casa. Describe tu dolor.

→ Describe la situación. Piensas que te rompiste el dedo.

→ Debes hacer preguntas al / a la médico/a sobre el tratamiento (*treatment*).

Practice more at **vhlcentral.com**.

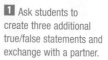

1 Ask students to create three additional true/false statements and exchange with a partner.

2 Give students these additional items: **7. Si quieres, ya puedes ir a la farmacia. (Dr. Meléndez) 8. De pequeña nunca tenía resfriados. (Jimena/Elena)**

4 Possible conversation:
E1: Buenos días. ¿Cómo se lastimó?
E2: Doctor, me caí en casa. Me duele mucho la mano.
E1: ¿Y cuánto tiempo hace que se cayó?
E2: Hace más de dos horas. Creo que me rompí el dedo.
E1: ¿Ah, sí? ¿Le duele mucho?
E2: Me duele muchísimo, doctor. Y estoy mareada.
E1: Bueno, le voy a sacar una radiografía primero.
E2: ¿Está roto el dedo?
E1: No se preocupe. No está roto el dedo. Como le duele mucho, le receto unas pastillas.
E2: Sí, doctor. Gracias.

NATIONAL communication STANDARDS

AYUDA

Here are some useful expressions:
¿Cómo se lastimó...?
¿Qué le pasó?
¿Cuánto tiempo hace que...?
Tengo...
Estoy...
¿Es usted alérgico/a a algún medicamento?
Usted debe...

Heritage Speakers Ask heritage speakers to prepare a poster about the health-care system of their families' countries of origin or other Spanish-speaking countries they have visited. Have them present their posters to the class, who can ask questions about the information.

Ortografía Audio

Supersite: MP3 Audio Files, Listening Scripts

El acento y las sílabas fuertes

The Spanish, written accent marks are used on many words. Here is a review of some of the principles governing word stress and the use of written accents.

Teaching Tips
- You may want to explain that all words in which the spoken stress falls on the antepenultimate syllable or one before will carry a written accent, regardless of the letter they end in.
- As you go through each point in the explanation, write the example words on the board, pronounce them, and have students repeat. Have students provide other words that exemplify each point.
- Point out that **Ortografía** replaces **Pronunciación** in this section from this lesson on, but not in the Lab Manual pages. The **Recursos** box refers to the **Pronunciación** sections found in the Lab Manual for all lessons.

CONSULTA

In Spanish, **a**, **e**, and **o** are considered strong vowels while **i** and **u** are weak vowels. To review this concept, see **¡ADELANTE! UNO Lección 3, Pronunciación**, p. 131.

---

as-pi-ri-na   gri-pe   to-man   an-tes

In Spanish, when a word ends in a vowel, **-n**, or **-s**, the spoken stress usually falls on the next-to-last syllable. Words of this type are very common and do not need a written accent.

a-sí   in-glés   in-fec-ción   hé-ro-e

When a word ends in a vowel, **-n**, or **-s**, and the spoken stress does *not* fall on the next-to-last syllable, then a written accent is needed.

hos-pi-tal   na-riz   re-ce-tar   to-ser

When a word ends in any consonant *other* than **-n** or **-s**, the spoken stress usually falls on the last syllable. Words of this type are very common and do not need a written accent.

lá-piz   fút-bol   hués-ped   sué-ter

When a word ends in any consonant *other* than **-n** or **-s** and the spoken stress does *not* fall on the last syllable, then a written accent is needed.

far-ma-cia   bio-lo-gí-a   su-cio   frí-o

Diphthongs (two weak vowels or a strong and weak vowel together) are normally pronounced as a single syllable. A written accent is needed when a diphthong is broken into two syllables.

sol   pan   mar   tos

Spanish words of only one syllable do not usually carry a written accent (unless it is to distinguish meaning: **se** and **sé**.)

Práctica Busca las palabras que necesitan acento escrito y escribe su forma correcta.

1. sal-mon salmón
2. ins-pec-tor
3. nu-me-ro número
4. fa-cil fácil
5. ju-go
6. a-bri-go
7. ra-pi-do rápido
8. sa-ba-do sábado
9. vez
10. me-nu menú
11. o-pe-ra-cion operación
12. im-per-me-a-ble
13. a-de-mas además
14. re-ga-te-ar
15. an-ti-pa-ti-co antipático
16. far-ma-cia
17. es-qui esquí
18. pen-sion pensión
19. pa-is país
20. per-don perdón

El ahorcado Juega al ahorcado (*hangman*) para adivinar las palabras.

1. _ l _ _ _ _ _ a   Vas allí cuando estás enfermo. clínica
2. _ _ _ _ e _ c _ _ n   Se usa para poner una vacuna (*vaccination*). inyección
3. _ _ _ d _ o _ _ _ _ _ _ a   Permite ver los huesos. radiografía
4. _ _ _ _ i _ o   Trabaja en un hospital. médico
5. a _ _ _ _ b _ _ _ _ _ _ _   Es una medicina. antibiótico

Heritage Speakers Note that heritage speakers may be unfamiliar with the rules that govern written accents. For extra practice, help students come up with additional words to exemplify each point in the chart. Encourage students to think of place names and family names that require accent marks.

recursos

LM p. 252

vhlcentral.com Lección 4

Lección 4

EN DETALLE

Additional Reading

Servicios de salud

¿Sabías que en los países hispanos no necesitas pagar por los servicios de salud? Ésta es una de las diferencias que hay entre países como los Estados Unidos y los países hispanos.

En la mayor parte de estos países, el gobierno ofrece servicios médicos muy baratos o gratuitos° a sus ciudadanos°. Los turistas y extranjeros también pueden tener acceso a los servicios médicos a bajo° costo. La Seguridad Social y organizaciones similares son las responsables de gestionar° estos servicios.

Naturalmente, esto no funciona igual° en todos los países. En Ecuador, México y Perú, la situación varía según las regiones. Los habitantes de las ciudades y pueblos grandes tienen acceso a más servicios médicos, mientras que quienes viven en pueblos remotos sólo cuentan con° pequeñas clínicas.

Por su parte, Costa Rica, Colombia, Cuba y España tienen sistemas de salud muy desarrollados°.

Cruz verde de farmacia en Madrid, España

Las farmacias

Farmacia de guardia: Las farmacias generalmente tienen un horario comercial. Sin embargo°, en cada barrio° hay una farmacia de guardia que abre las veinticuatro horas del día.

Productos farmacéuticos: Todavía hay muchas farmacias tradicionales que están más especializadas en medicinas y productos farmacéuticos. No venden una gran variedad de productos.

Recetas: Muchos medicamentos se venden sin receta médica. Los farmacéuticos aconsejan° a las personas sobre problemas de salud y les dan las medicinas.

Cruz° verde: En muchos países, las farmacias tienen como símbolo una cruz verde. Cuando la cruz verde está encendida°, la farmacia está abierta.

En España, por ejemplo, la mayoría de la gente tiene acceso a ellos y en muchos casos son completamente gratuitos. Según un informe de la Organización Mundial de la Salud, el sistema de salud español ocupa uno de los primeros diez lugares del mundo. Esto se debe no sólo al buen funcionamiento° del sistema, sino también al nivel de salud general de la población. Impresionante, ¿no?

Consulta médica en la República Dominicana

gratuitos *free (of charge)* ciudadanos *citizens* bajo *low*
gestionar *to manage* igual *in the same way* cuentan con *have*
desarrollados *developed* funcionamiento *operation*
Sin embargo *However* barrio *neighborhood* aconsejan *advise*
Cruz *Cross* encendida *lit (up)*

NATIONAL connections cultures STANDARDS

ACTIVIDADES

1 **¿Cierto o falso?** Indica si lo que dicen las oraciones es cierto o falso. Corrige la información falsa.

1. En los países hispanos los gobiernos ofrecen servicios de salud accesibles a sus ciudadanos. **Cierto.**

2. En los países hispanos los extranjeros tienen que pagar mucho dinero por los servicios médicos. **Falso.** Los extranjeros tienen acceso a los servicios médicos a bajo costo.

3. El sistema de salud español es uno de los mejores del mundo. **Cierto.**

4. Las farmacias de guardia abren sólo los sábados y domingos. **Falso.** Las farmacias de guardia abren las 24 horas del día.

5. En los países hispanos las farmacias venden una gran variedad de productos. **Falso.** En los países hispanos las farmacias están más especializadas en medicinas y productos farmacéuticos.

6. Los farmacéuticos de los países hispanos aconsejan a los enfermos y venden algunas medicinas sin necesidad de receta. **Cierto.**

7. En México y otros países, los pueblos remotos cuentan con grandes centros médicos. **Falso.** Cuentan con pequeñas clínicas.

8. Muchas farmacias usan una cruz verde como símbolo. **Cierto.**

ASÍ SE DICE

La salud

el chequeo (Esp., Méx.)	el examen médico
la droguería (Col.)	la farmacia
la herida	*injury; wound*
la píldora	la pastilla
los primeros auxilios	*first aid*
la sangre	*blood*

EL MUNDO HISPANO

Remedios caseros° y plantas medicinales

- **Achiote°** En Suramérica se usa para curar inflamaciones de garganta. Las hojas° de achiote se cuecen° en agua, se cuelan° y se hacen gárgaras° con esa agua.

- **Ají** En Perú se usan cataplasmas° de las semillas° de ají para aliviar los dolores reumáticos y la tortícolis°.

- **Azúcar** En Nicaragua y otros países centroamericanos se usa el azúcar para detener° la sangre en pequeñas heridas.

- **Sábila (aloe vera)** En Latinoamérica, el jugo de las hojas de sábila se usa para reducir cicatrices°. Se recomienda aplicarlo sobre la cicatriz dos veces al día, durante varios meses.

Remedios caseros *Home remedies* Achiote *Annatto* hojas *leaves* se cuecen *are cooked* se cuelan *they are drained* gárgaras *gargles* cataplasmas *pastes* semillas *seeds* tortícolis *stiff neck* detener *to stop* cicatrices *scars*

PERFILES

Curanderos° y chamanes

¿Quieres ser doctor(a), juez(a)°, político/a o psicólogo/a? En algunas sociedades de las Américas **los curanderos** y **los chamanes** no tienen que escoger entre estas profesiones porque ellos son mediadores de conflictos y dan consejos a la comunidad. Su opinión es muy respetada.

Códice Florentino, México, siglo XVI

Desde las culturas antiguas° de las Américas muchas personas piensan que la salud del cuerpo y de la mente sólo puede existir si hay un equilibrio entre el ser humano y la naturaleza. Los curanderos y los chamanes son quienes cuidan este equilibrio.

Los curanderos se especializan más en enfermedades físicas, mientras que los chamanes están más

Cuzco, Perú

relacionados con los males° de la mente y el alma°. Ambos° usan plantas, masajes y rituales y sus conocimientos se basan en la tradición, la experiencia, la observación y la intuición.

Curanderos *Healers* juez(a) *judge* antiguas *ancient* males *illnesses* alma *soul* Ambos *Both*

Conexión Internet

¿Cuáles son algunos hospitales importantes del mundo hispano?

Go to **vhlcentral.com** to find more cultural information related to this **Cultura** section.

ACTIVIDADES

2 **Comprensión** Responde a las preguntas

1. ¿Cómo se les llama a las farmacias en Colombia? droguerías
2. ¿Qué parte del achiote se usa para curar la garganta? las hojas
3. ¿Cómo se aplica la sábila para reducir cicatrices? Se aplica sobre la cicatriz dos veces al día.
4. En algunas partes de las Américas, ¿quiénes mantienen el equilibrio entre el ser humano y la naturaleza? los chamanes y curanderos
5. ¿Qué usan los curanderos y chamanes para curar? Usan plantas, masajes y rituales.

3 **¿Qué haces cuando tienes gripe?** Escribe cuatro oraciones sobre las cosas que haces cuando tienes gripe. Explica si vas al médico, si tomas medicamentos o si sigues alguna dieta especial. Después, comparte tu texto con un(a) compañero/a. Answers will vary.

Heritage Speakers Ask heritage speakers to describe home remedies used in their families.

 Practice more at **vhlcentral.com**.

4.1 The imperfect tense (S) Tutorial

ANTE TODO You have already learned the preterite tense. You will now learn the imperfect, which describes past activities in a different way.

The imperfect of regular verbs

		cantar	beber	escribir
SINGULAR FORMS	yo	cant**aba**	beb**ía**	escrib**ía**
	tú	cant**abas**	beb**ías**	escrib**ías**
	Ud./él/ella	cant**aba**	beb**ía**	escrib**ía**
PLURAL FORMS	nosotros/as	cant**ábamos**	beb**íamos**	escrib**íamos**
	vosotros/as	cant**abais**	beb**íais**	escrib**íais**
	Uds./ellos/ellas	cant**aban**	beb**ían**	escrib**ían**

¡ATENCIÓN!

Note that the imperfect endings of -**er** and -**ir** verbs are the same. Also note that the **nosotros** form of -**ar** verbs always carries an accent mark on the first **a** of the ending. All forms of -**er** and -**ir** verbs in the imperfect carry an accent on the first **i** of the ending.

De niña apenas me enfermaba.

Cuando me dolía el estómago, mi mamá me daba té de jengibre.

▶ There are no stem changes in the imperfect.

entender (e:ie)
servir (e:i)
doler (o:ue)

Entendíamos japonés.
We used to understand Japanese.
El camarero les **servía** el café.
The waiter was serving them coffee.
A Javier le **dolía** el tobillo.
Javier's ankle was hurting.

▶ The imperfect form of **hay** is **había** (*there was; there were; there used to be*).

▶ **¡Atención!** **Ir, ser,** and **ver** are the only verbs that are irregular in the imperfect.

The imperfect of irregular verbs

		ir	ser	ver
SINGULAR FORMS	yo	ib**a**	era	ve**ía**
	tú	ib**as**	eras	ve**ías**
	Ud./él/ella	ib**a**	era	ve**ía**
PLURAL FORMS	nosotros/as	íb**amos**	ér**amos**	ve**íamos**
	vosotros/as	ib**ais**	erais	ve**íais**
	Uds./ellos/ellas	ib**an**	eran	ve**ían**

Teaching Tip Refer to the chart on p. 203 and have students identify which rules govern the use of written accents on -**er** and -**ir** verbs and on the **nosotros** form of -**ar** verbs in the imperfect.

AYUDA

Like **hay**, **había** can be followed by a singular or plural noun.
Había un solo médico en la sala.
Había dos pacientes allí.

TPR Call out a name or subject pronoun and an infinitive (ex: **ellas/ver**). Toss a foam or paper ball to a student, who will say the correct imperfect form (ex: **veían**). He or she should then name another subject and infinitive and throw the ball to another student.

CONSULTA

You will learn more about the contrast between the preterite and the imperfect in **Estructura 4.2**, pp. 210–211.

Teaching Tips
• Ask students to compare and contrast a home video with a snapshot in the family picture album. Then call their attention to the brief description of uses of the imperfect. Which actions would be best captured by a home video? (continuing actions; incomplete actions; what was happening; how things used to be) Which actions are best captured in a snapshot? (a completed action)
• Ask students to answer questions about themselves in the past. Ex: **Y tú, _____, ¿ibas al parque los domingos cuando eras niño/a? ¿Qué hacías mientras tu madre preparaba la comida? ¿Cómo eras de niño/a?**

Extra Practice Ask students to write a description of their first-grade classroom and teacher, using the imperfect. Ex: **En la sala de clases había... La maestra se llamaba... Ella era...** Have students share their descriptions with a classmate.

Extra Practice For additional oral practice, call out a new subject for each activity item and have students restate the sentence.

Uses of the imperfect

▶ As a general rule, the imperfect is used to describe actions which are seen by the speaker as incomplete or "continuing," while the preterite is used to describe actions which have been completed. The imperfect expresses what was happening at a certain time or how things used to be. The preterite, in contrast, expresses a completed action.

—¿Qué te **pasó**?
What happened to you?

—Me **torcí** el tobillo.
I sprained my ankle.

—¿Dónde **vivías** de niño?
Where did you live as a child?

—**Vivía** en San José.
I lived in San José.

▶ These expressions are often used with the imperfect because they express habitual or repeated actions: **de niño/a** (*as a child*), **todos los días** (*every day*), **mientras** (*while*).

Uses of the imperfect

1. **Habitual or repeated actions** . . . .
Íbamos al parque los domingos.
We used to go to the park on Sundays.

2. **Events or actions that were in progress**
Yo **leía** mientras él **estudiaba**.
I was reading while he was studying.

3. **Physical characteristics** . . . .
Era alto y guapo.
He was tall and handsome.

4. **Mental or emotional states** . . . .
Quería mucho a su familia.
He loved his family very much.

5. **Telling time** . . . .
Eran las tres y media.
It was 3:30.

6. **Age** . . . .
Los niños **tenían** seis años.
The children were six years old.

¡INTÉNTALO! Indica la forma correcta de cada verbo en el imperfecto.

1. Mis hermanos _____veían_____ (ver) televisión todas las tardes.
2. Yo _____viajaba_____ (viajar) en el tren de las 3:30.
3. ¿Dónde _____vivía_____ (vivir) Samuel de niño?
4. Tú _____hablabas_____ (hablar) con Javier.
5. Leonardo y yo _____corríamos_____ (correr) por el parque.
6. Ustedes _____iban_____ (ir) a la clínica.
7. Nadia _____bailaba_____ (bailar) merengue.
8. ¿Cuándo _____asistías_____ (asistir) tú a clase de español?
9. Yo _____era_____ (ser) muy feliz.
10. Nosotras _____comprendíamos_____ (comprender) las preguntas.

recursos

WB
pp. 233–234

LM
p. 253

vhlcentral.com
Lección 4

Large Groups Write a list of activities on the board. Ex: **1. tenerle miedo a la oscuridad 2. ir a la escuela en autobús 3. llevar el almuerzo a la escuela 4. creer en Santa Claus.** Have students copy the list and write sentences for each item they used to do when they were in the second grade. Then have them circulate around the room and find other students that used to do the same activities. Ask volunteers to report back to the class. Ex: **Mark y yo creíamos en Santa Claus.**

Lección 4

Práctica

1

Completar Primero, completa las oraciones con el imperfecto de los verbos. Luego, pon las oraciones en orden lógico y compáralas con las de un(a) compañero/a.

a. El doctor dijo que no _____era_____ (ser) nada grave. __7__
b. El doctor _____quería_____ (querer) ver la nariz del niño. __6__
c. Su mamá _____estaba_____ (estar) dibujando cuando Miguelito entró llorando. __3__
d. Miguelito _____tenía_____ (tener) la nariz hinchada (*swollen*). Fueron al hospital. __4__
e. Miguelito no _____iba_____ (ir) a jugar más. Ahora quería ir a casa a descansar. __8__
f. Miguelito y sus amigos _____jugaban_____ (jugar) al béisbol en el patio. __2__
g. _____Eran_____ (Ser) las dos de la tarde. __1__
h. Miguelito le dijo a la enfermera que _____le dolía_____ (dolerle) la nariz. __5__

1 Before assigning the activity, review the forms of the imperfect by calling out an infinitive and a series of subject pronouns. Ask volunteers to give the corresponding forms. Ex: **querer: usted (quería); yo (quería); nosotras (queríamos).** Include irregular verbs.

1 Have students write a conversation between **Miguelito** and his friends in which he relates what happened after the accident.

2

Transformar Forma oraciones completas para describir lo que hacían Julieta y César. Usa las formas correctas del imperfecto y añade todas las palabras necesarias.

1. Julieta y César / ser / paramédicos
   Julieta y César eran paramédicos.
2. trabajar / juntos y / llevarse / muy bien
   Trabajaban juntos y se llevaban muy bien.
3. cuando / haber / accidente, / siempre / analizar / situación / con cuidado
   Cuando había un accidente, siempre analizaban la situación con cuidado.
4. preocuparse / mucho / por / pacientes
   Se preocupaban mucho por los pacientes.
5. si / paciente / tener / mucho / dolor, / ponerle / inyección
   Si el paciente tenía mucho dolor, le ponían una inyección.

2 To challenge students, ask them to identify the reason the imperfect is used in each sentence.

3

En la escuela de medicina Usa los verbos de la lista para completar las oraciones con las formas correctas del imperfecto. Algunos verbos se usan más de una vez. Some answers may vary. Suggested answers:

caerse	enfermarse	ir	querer	tener
comprender	estornudar	pensar	sentirse	tomar
doler	hacer	poder	ser	toser

1. Cuando Javier y Victoria _____eran_____ estudiantes de medicina, siempre _____tenían_____ que ir al médico.
2. Cada vez que él _____tomaba_____ un examen, a Javier le _____dolía_____ mucho la cabeza.
3. Cuando Victoria _____hacía_____ ejercicios aeróbicos, siempre _____se sentía_____ mareada.
4. Todas las primaveras, Javier _____estornudaba/tosía_____ mucho porque es alérgico al polen.
5. Victoria también _____se caía_____ de su bicicleta camino a la escuela.
6. Después de comer en la cafetería, a Victoria siempre le _____dolía_____ el estómago.
7. Javier _____quería/pensaba_____ ser médico para ayudar a los demás.
8. Pero no _____comprendía_____ por qué él _____se enfermaba_____ con tanta frecuencia.
9. Cuando Victoria _____tenía_____ fiebre, no _____podía_____ ni leer el termómetro.
10. A Javier _____le dolían_____ los dientes, pero nunca _____quería_____ ir al dentista.
11. Victoria _____tosía/estornudaba_____ mucho cuando _____se sentía_____ congestionada.
12. Javier y Victoria _____pensaban_____ que nunca _____iban_____ a graduarse.

3 For expansion, write these sentences on the board and have students complete them in pairs.
**1. Fui al doctor porque ____. 2. Tuvo que ir al dentista porque____.
3. El médico le dio unas pastillas porque____.
4. La enfermera le tomó la temperatura porque____.**

Small Groups Ask students to write about a favorite or least favorite doctor or dentist from the past. They should use at least five verbs in the imperfect. Then have them read, compare, and discuss the descriptions in groups of four.

Comunicación

4

Entrevista Trabajen en parejas. Un(a) estudiante usa estas preguntas para entrevistar a su compañero/a. Luego compartan los resultados de la entrevista con la clase. Answers will vary.

1. Cuando eras estudiante de primaria, ¿te gustaban tus profesores/as?
2. ¿Veías mucha televisión cuando eras niño/a?
3. Cuando tenías diez años, ¿cuál era tu programa de televisión favorito?
4. Cuando eras niño/a, ¿qué hacía tu familia durante las vacaciones?
5. ¿Cuántos años tenías en 2005?
6. Cuando estabas en el quinto año escolar, ¿qué hacías con tus amigos/as?
7. Cuando tenías once años, ¿cuál era tu grupo musical favorito?
8. Antes de tomar esta clase, ¿sabías hablar español?

5 After students present their partner's descriptions, call on volunteers to ask one additional question about each student's childhood.

5 You may want to assign this activity as a short written composition.

5

Describir En parejas, túrnense para describir cómo eran sus vidas cuando eran niños. Pueden usar las sugerencias de la lista u otras ideas. Luego informen a la clase sobre la vida de su compañero/a. Answers will vary.

> **modelo**
>
> De niña, mi familia y yo siempre íbamos a Tortuguero. Tomábamos un barco desde Limón, y por las noches mirábamos las tortugas (*turtles*) en la playa. Algunas veces teníamos suerte, porque las tortugas venían a poner (*lay*) huevos. Otras veces, volvíamos al hotel sin ver ninguna tortuga.

- las vacaciones
- ocasiones especiales
- qué hacías durante el verano
- celebraciones con tus amigos/as
- celebraciones con tu familia

- cómo era tu escuela
- cómo eran tus amigos/as
- los viajes que hacías
- a qué jugabas
- qué hacías cuando te sentías enfermo/a

NOTA CULTURAL

El Parque Nacional Tortuguero está en la costa del Caribe, al norte de la ciudad de Limón, en Costa Rica. Varias especies de tortuga (*turtle*) van a las playas del parque para poner (*lay*) sus huevos. Esto ocurre de noche, y hay guías que llevan pequeños grupos de turistas a observar este fenómeno biológico.

Síntesis

6 Have pairs write **Dr. Donoso's** advice for three of the patients. Then have them read the advice to the class and compare it with what other pairs wrote for the same patients.

6

En el consultorio Tu profesor(a) te va a dar una lista incompleta con los pacientes que fueron al consultorio del doctor Donoso ayer. En parejas, conversen para completar sus listas y saber a qué hora llegaron las personas al consultorio y cuáles eran sus problemas. Answers will vary.

Supersite:
Activity Pack

Game Divide the class into teams of three. Each team should choose a historical or fictional villain. When it is their turn, they will use the imperfect to give the class one hint. The other teams are allowed three questions, which must be answered truthfully. At the end of the question/answer session, teams must guess the person's identity. Award one point for each correct guess and two to any team able to stump the class.

Lección 4

4.2 The preterite and the imperfect Tutorial

ANTE TODO   Now that you have learned the forms of the preterite and the imperfect, you will learn more about how they are used. The preterite and the imperfect are not interchangeable. In Spanish, the choice between these two tenses depends on the context and on the point of view of the speaker.

> Me rompí el brazo cuando estaba paseando en bicicleta.

> Tenía dolor de cabeza, pero me tomé una aspirina y se me fue.

COMPARE & CONTRAST

Use the preterite to...	Use the imperfect to...
1. Express actions that are viewed by the speaker as completed	**1.** Describe an ongoing past action with no reference to its beginning or end
Sandra **se rompió** la pierna. *Sandra broke her leg.*	Sandra **esperaba** al doctor. *Sandra was waiting for the doctor.*
Fueron a Buenos Aires ayer. *They went to Buenos Aires yesterday.*	El médico **se preocupaba** por sus pacientes. *The doctor worried about his patients.*
2. Express the beginning or end of a past action	**2.** Express habitual past actions and events
La película **empezó** a las nueve. *The movie began at nine o'clock.*	Cuando **era** joven, **jugaba** al tenis. *When I was young, I used to play tennis.*
Ayer **terminé** el proyecto para la clase de química. *Yesterday I finished the project for chemistry class.*	De niño, Eduardo **se enfermaba** con mucha frecuencia. *As a child, Eduardo used to get sick very frequently.*
3. Narrate a series of past actions or events	**3.** Describe physical and emotional states or characteristics
La doctora me **miró** los oídos, me **hizo** unas preguntas y **escribió** la receta. *The doctor looked in my ears, asked me some questions, and wrote the prescription.*	La chica **quería** descansar. **Se sentía** mal y **tenía** dolor de cabeza. *The girl wanted to rest. She felt ill and had a headache.*
Me di con la mesa, **me caí** y **me lastimé** el pie. *I bumped into the table, I fell, and I injured my foot.*	Ellos **eran** altos y **tenían** ojos verdes. *They were tall and had green eyes.*
	Estábamos felices de ver a la familia. *We were happy to see our family.*

Teaching Tip Give examples as you contrast the preterite and the imperfect. Ex: **La semana pasada fui al dentista porque me dolía mucho el diente.** Then ask personalized questions. Ex: _____, ¿paseabas en bicicleta cuando eras niño/a? Te caíste alguna vez?

AYUDA

These words and expressions, as well as similar ones, commonly occur with the preterite: **ayer, anteayer, una vez, dos veces, tres veces, el año pasado, de repente.** They usually imply that an action has happened at a specific point in time. For a review, see *¡ADELANTE!* UNO Estructura 6.3, p. 323.

AYUDA

These words and expressions, as well as similar ones, commonly occur with the imperfect: **de niño/a, todos los días, mientras, siempre, con frecuencia, todas las semanas.** They usually express habitual or repeated actions in the past.

Teaching Tip Write in English a simple, humorous retelling of a well-known fairy tale. Read it to the class, pausing after each verb in the past to ask the class whether the imperfect or preterite would be used in Spanish. Ex: *Once upon a time there was a girl named Little Red Riding Hood. She wanted to take lunch to her ailing grandmother. She put a loaf of bread, a wedge of cheese, and a bottle of Beaujolais in a basket and set off through the woods. Meanwhile, farther down the path, a big, ugly, snaggletoothed wolf was leaning against a tree, filing his nails...*

Video Photocopy the *Fotonovela* Script (Supersite) and white out all preterite and imperfect verb forms. Provide the infinitive of each verb, then have students predict which verb form will be used. Show the video again so students can confirm their predictions. Go over the uses of each verb form.

Pairs Ask students to narrate the most interesting, embarrassing, exciting, or annoying thing that has happened to them recently. Tell them to describe what happened and how they felt, using the preterite and the imperfect.

Extra Practice After completing ¡Inténtalo!, have students explain why the preterite or imperfect was used in each case. Then call on different students to create other sentences illustrating the same uses.

Lección 4

▶ The preterite and the imperfect often appear in the same sentence. In such cases, the imperfect describes what *was happening*, while the preterite describes the action that "interrupted" the ongoing activity.

Miraba la tele cuando **sonó** el teléfono.
I was watching TV when the phone rang.

Felicia **leía** el periódico cuando **llegó** Ramiro.
Felicia was reading the newspaper when Ramiro arrived.

▶ You will also see the preterite and the imperfect together in narratives such as fiction, news, and the retelling of events. The imperfect provides background information, such as time, weather, and location, while the preterite indicates the specific events that occurred.

Eran las dos de la mañana y el detective ya no **podía** mantenerse despierto. **Se bajó** lentamente del coche, **estiró** las piernas y **levantó** los brazos hacia el cielo oscuro.
It was two in the morning, and the detective could no longer stay awake. He slowly stepped out of the car, stretched his legs, and raised his arms toward the dark sky.

La luna **estaba** llena y no **había** en el cielo ni una sola nube. De repente, el detective **escuchó** un grito espeluznante proveniente del parque.
The moon was full and there wasn't a single cloud in the sky. Suddenly, the detective heard a piercing scream coming from the park.

Un médico colombiano desarrolló una vacuna contra la malaria
En 1986, el doctor colombiano Manuel Elkin Patarroyo creó la primera vacuna sintética para combatir la malaria. Esta enfermedad parecía haberse erradicado hacía décadas en muchas partes del mundo. Sin embargo, justo cuando Patarroyo terminó de elaborar la inmunización, los casos de malaria empezaban a aumentar de nuevo. En mayo de 1993, el doctor colombiano cedió la patente de la vacuna a la Organización Mundial de la Salud en nombre de Colombia. Los grandes laboratorios farmacéuticos presionaron a la OMS porque querían la vacuna. Las presiones no tuvieron éxito y, en 1995, el doctor Patarroyo y la OMS pactaron continuar con el acuerdo inicial: la vacuna seguía siendo propiedad de la OMS.

¡INTÉNTALO! Elige el pretérito o el imperfecto para completar la historia. Explica por qué se usa ese tiempo verbal en cada ocasión. Answers for the second part will vary.

1. _____Eran_____ (Fueron/Eran) las doce.
2. _____Había_____ (Hubo/Había) mucha gente en la calle.
3. A las doce y media, Tomás y yo ___entramos___ (entramos/entrábamos) en el restaurante Tárcoles.
4. Todos los días yo ___almorzaba___ (almorcé/almorzaba) con Tomás al mediodía.
5. El camarero ___llegó___ (llegó/llegaba) inmediatamente con el menú.
6. Nosotros ___empezamos___ (empezamos/empezábamos) a leerlo.
7. Yo ___pedí___ (pedí/pedía) el pescado.
8. De repente, el camarero ___volvió___ (volvió/volvía) a nuestra mesa.
9. Y nos ___dio___ (dio/daba) una mala noticia.
10. Desafortunadamente, no ___tenían___ (tuvieron/tenían) más pescado.
11. Por eso Tomás y yo ___decidimos___ (decidimos/decidíamos) comer en otro lugar.
12. ___Llovía___ (Llovió/Llovía) mucho cuando ___salimos___ (salimos/salíamos) del restaurante.
13. Así que ___regresamos___ (regresamos/regresábamos) al restaurante Tárcoles.
14. Esta vez, ___pedí___ (pedí/pedía) arroz con pollo.

recursos

WB
pp. 235–238

LM
p. 254

S
vhlcentral.com
Lección 4

Práctica

1

En el periódico Completa esta noticia con las formas correctas del pretérito o el imperfecto.

Un accidente trágico

Ayer temprano por la mañana (1)___hubo___ (haber) un trágico accidente en el centro de San José cuando el conductor de un autobús no (2)___vio___ (ver) venir un carro. La mujer que (3)___manejaba___ (manejar) el carro (4)___murió___ (morir) al instante y los paramédicos (5)___tuvieron___ (tener) que llevar al pasajero al hospital porque (6)___sufrió___ (sufrir) varias fracturas. El conductor del autobús (7)___dijo___ (decir) que no (8)___vio___ (ver) el carro hasta el último momento porque (9)___estaba___ (estar) muy nublado y (10)___llovía___ (llover). Él (11)___intentó___ (intentar) (*to attempt*) dar un viraje brusco (*to swerve*), pero (12)___perdió___ (perder) el control del autobús y no (13)___pudo___ (poder) evitar (*to avoid*) el accidente. Según nos informaron, no (14)___se lastimó___ (lastimarse) ningún pasajero del autobús.

2

Seleccionar Utiliza el tiempo verbal adecuado, según el contexto.   Answers will vary. Suggested answers:

1. La semana pasada, Manolo y Aurora ___querían___ (querer) dar una fiesta. ___Decidieron___ (Decidir) invitar a seis amigos y servirles mucha comida.
2. Manolo y Aurora ___estaban___ (estar) preparando la comida cuando Elena ___llamó___ (llamar). Como siempre, ___tenía___ (tener) que estudiar para un examen.
3. A las seis, ___volvió___ (volver) a sonar el teléfono. Su amigo Francisco tampoco ___podía___ (poder) ir a la fiesta, porque ___tenía___ (tener) fiebre. Manolo y Aurora ___se sentían___ (sentirse) muy tristes, pero ___tenían___ (tener) que preparar la comida.
4. Después de otros quince minutos, ___sonó___ (sonar) el teléfono. Sus amigos, los señores Vega, ___estaban___ (estar) en camino (*en route*) al hospital: a su hijo le ___dolía___ (doler) mucho el estómago. Sólo dos de los amigos ___podían___ (poder) ir a la cena.
5. Por supuesto, ___iban___ (ir) a tener demasiada comida. Finalmente, cinco minutos antes de las ocho, ___llamaron___ (llamar) Ramón y Javier. Ellos ___pensaban___ (pensar) que la fiesta ___era___ (ser) la próxima semana.
6. Tristes, Manolo y Aurora ___se sentaron___ (sentarse) a comer solos. Mientras ___comían___ (comer), pronto ___llegaron___ (llegar) a la conclusión de que ___era___ (ser) mejor estar solos: ¡La comida ___estaba___ (estar) malísima!

3

Completar Completa las frases de una manera lógica. Usa el pretérito o el imperfecto. En parejas, comparen sus respuestas.   Answers will vary.

1. De niño/a, yo...
2. Yo conducía el auto mientras...
3. Anoche mi novio/a...
4. Ayer el/la profesor(a)...
5. La semana pasada un(a) amigo/a...
6. Con frecuencia mis padres...
7. Esta mañana en la cafetería...
8. Hablábamos con el doctor cuando...

1 Follow up with comprehension questions. Ex: ¿Qué pasó ayer? (Hubo un accidente.) ¿Qué tiempo hacía? (Estaba muy nublado y llovía.) ¿Qué le pasó a la mujer que manejaba? (Murió al instante.)

AYUDA

Reading Spanish-language newspapers is a good way to practice verb tenses. You will find that both the imperfect and the preterite occur with great regularity. Many newsstands carry international papers, and many Spanish-language newspapers (such as Spain's *El País*, Mexico's *Reforma*, and Argentina's *Clarín*) are on the Web.

2 To simplify, begin by reading through the items as a class. Have students label each blank with an *I* for *imperfect* or *P* for *preterite*.

2 Have volunteers explain why they chose the preterite or imperfect in each case. Ask them to point out any words or expressions that triggered one tense or the other.

3 To challenge students, ask them to expand on one of their sentences, creating a paragraph about an imaginary or actual past experience.

Comunicación

4

Entrevista Usa estas preguntas para entrevistar a un(a) compañero/a acerca de su primer(a) novio/a. Si quieres, puedes añadir otras preguntas. Answers will vary.

1. ¿Quién fue tu primer(a) novio/a?
2. ¿Cuántos años tenías cuando lo/la conociste?
3. ¿Cómo era él/ella?
4. ¿Qué le gustaba hacer? ¿Tenían ustedes los mismos pasatiempos?
5. ¿Por cuánto tiempo salieron ustedes?
6. ¿Adónde iban cuando salían?
7. ¿Pensaban casarse?
8. ¿Cuándo y por qué rompieron?

4 Have students write a summary of their partners' responses, omitting all names. Collect the summaries, then read them to the class. Have students guess who had the relationship described in the summary.

5

La sala de emergencias En parejas, miren la lista e inventen qué les pasó a estas personas que están en la sala de emergencias. Answers will vary.

modelo

Eran las tres de la tarde. Como todos los días, Pablo jugaba al fútbol con sus amigos. Estaba muy contento. De repente, se cayó y se rompió el brazo. Entonces fue a la sala de emergencias.

Paciente	Edad	Hora	Estado
1. Pablo Romero	9 años	15:20	hueso roto (el brazo)
2. Estela Rodríguez	45 años	15:25	tobillo torcido
3. Lupe Quintana	29 años	15:37	embarazada, dolores
4. Manuel López	52 años	15:45	infección de garganta
5. Marta Díaz	3 años	16:00	congestión, fiebre
6. Roberto Salazar	32 años	16:06	dolor de oído
7. Marco Brito	18 años	16:18	daño en el cuello, posible fractura
8. Ana María Ortiz	66 años	16:29	reacción alérgica a un medicamento

5 Remind students that the 24-hour clock is often used for schedules. Go through a few of the times and ask volunteers to provide the equivalent in the 12-hour clock.

5 Have pairs share their answers with the class, without mentioning the patient's name. The class must guess who is being described.

6 Have students decide who in their group would be the most likely thief based on his or her responses. Ask the group to prepare a police report explaining why they believe their suspect is the culprit.

6

Situación Anoche alguien robó (*stole*) el examen de la **Lección 4** de la oficina de tu profesor(a) y tú tienes que averiguar quién lo hizo. Pregúntales a tres compañeros dónde estaban, con quién estaban y qué hicieron entre las ocho y las doce de la noche. Answers will vary.

Síntesis

7

La primera vez En grupos, cuéntense cómo fue la primera vez que les pusieron una inyección, se rompieron un hueso, pasaron la noche en un hospital, estuvieron mareados/as, etc. Incluyan estos datos en su conversación: una descripción del tiempo que hacía, sus edades, qué pasó y cómo se sentían.
Answers will vary.

Lección 4

[4.3] Constructions with se Tutorial

ANTE TODO   In **Lección 1,** you learned how to use **se** as the third person reflexive pronoun (**Él <u>se</u> despierta. Ellos <u>se</u> visten. Ella <u>se</u> baña.**). **Se** can also be used to form constructions in which the person performing the action is not expressed or is de-emphasized.

Impersonal constructions with se

▶ In Spanish, verbs that are not reflexive can be used with **se** to form impersonal constructions. These are statements in which the person performing the action is not defined.

Se habla español en Costa Rica.
Spanish is spoken in Costa Rica.

Se hacen operaciones aquí.
They perform operations here.

Se puede leer en la sala de espera.
You can read in the waiting room.

Se necesitan medicinas enseguida.
They need medicine right away.

▶ **¡Atención!** Note that the third person singular verb form is used with singular nouns and the third person plural form is used with plural nouns.

Se vende ropa.   **Se venden** camisas.

▶ You often see the impersonal **se** in signs, advertisements, and directions.

SE PROHÍBE NADAR

Se necesitan programadores
Grupo Tecno
Tel. 778-34-34

ENTRADA
Se entra por la izquierda

Se for unplanned events

¿Te pusiste un suéter anoche?

No, mamá. Se me olvidó.

▶ **Se** also describes accidental or unplanned events. In this construction, the person who performs the action is de-emphasized, implying that the accident or unplanned event is not his or her direct responsibility. Note this construction.

se	+	[INDIRECT OBJECT PRONOUN]	+	[VERB]	+	[SUBJECT]
Se		me		cayó		la pluma.

NATIONAL comparisons STANDARDS

TPR Use impersonal constructions with **se** to have students draw what you say. Ex: **Se prohíbe entrar** (students draw a door with a diagonal line through it).

AYUDA

In English, the passive voice or indefinite subjects (*you, they, one*) are used where Spanish uses impersonal constructions with **se**.

Teaching Tips
• Ask questions using constructions with **se**. Ex: ¿Se habla español en Inglaterra? (No, se habla inglés.) ¿Dónde se hacen las películas norteamericanas? (Se hacen en Hollywood.)
• Emphasize that using **se** for unplanned events has no exact equivalent in English. Have students examine the model sentences and make up some of their own in order to get a feel for how this construction works.

Heritage Speakers Ask heritage speakers to write a fictional or true account of a day in which everything went wrong. Ask them to include as many constructions with **se** as possible. Have them read their accounts aloud to the class, who will summarize the events.

Teaching Tips
- Test comprehension by asking volunteers to change sentences from plural to singular and vice versa. Ex: **Se me perdieron las llaves. (Se me perdió la llave.)**
- Have students finish sentences using a construction with **se** to express an unplanned event. Ex: **1. Al doctor _____. (se le cayó el termómetro) 2. A la profesora _____. (se le quedaron los papeles en casa)**
- Involve students in a conversation about unplanned events that happened to them recently. Say: **Se me olvidaron las gafas de sol esta mañana. Y a ti, _____, ¿se te olvidó algo esta mañana?**
- Have students use **se** constructions to make excuses in different situations. Ex: You did not bring in a composition to class. **(Se me dañó la computadora.)**

▶ In this type of construction, what would normally be the direct object of the sentence becomes the subject, and it agrees with the verb, not with the indirect object pronoun.

I.O. PRONOUN	VERB		SUBJECT
Se me, te, le, nos, os, les	quedó / cayó / dañó	SINGULAR	la receta. / la taza. / el radio.
	rompieron / olvidaron / perdieron	PLURAL	las botellas. / las pastillas. / las llaves.

▶ These verbs are the ones most frequently used with **se** to describe unplanned events.

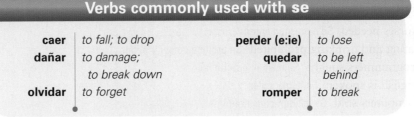

Verbs commonly used with se

caer	to fall; to drop	**perder (e:ie)**	to lose
dañar	to damage; to break down	**quedar**	to be left behind
olvidar	to forget	**romper**	to break

Se me perdió el teléfono de la farmacia.
I lost the pharmacy's phone number.

Se nos olvidaron los pasajes.
We forgot the tickets.

▶ **¡Atención!** While Spanish has a verb for *to fall* (**caer**), there is no direct translation for *to drop*. **Dejar caer** (*To let fall*) or a **se** construction is often used to mean *to drop*.

El médico **dejó caer** la aspirina.
The doctor dropped the aspirin.

A mí **se me cayeron** los cuadernos.
I dropped the notebooks.

▶ To clarify or emphasize who the person involved in the action is, this construction commonly begins with the preposition **a** + [*noun*] or **a** + [*prepositional pronoun*].

Al paciente se le perdió la receta.
The patient lost his prescription.

A ustedes se les quedaron los libros en casa.
You left the books at home.

CONSULTA

For an explanation of prepositional pronouns, refer to **Estructura 3.4**, p. 160.

¡INTÉNTALO!   Completa las oraciones con **se** impersonal y los verbos en presente.

A

1. __Se enseñan__ (enseñar) cinco lenguas en esta universidad.
2. __Se come__ (comer) muy bien en Las Delicias.
3. __Se venden__ (vender) muchas camisetas allí.
4. __Se sirven__ (servir) platos exquisitos cada noche.

Completa las oraciones con **se** y los verbos en pretérito.

B

1. __Se me rompieron__ (*I broke*) las gafas.
2. __Se te cayeron__ (*You* (fam., sing.) *dropped*) las pastillas.
3. __Se les perdió__ (*They lost*) la receta.
4. __Se le quedó__ (*You* (form., sing.) *left*) aquí la radiografía.

recursos

WB pp. 239–240

LM p. 255

vhlcentral.com Lección 4

Extra Practice For homework, have students research the Internet for common icons or international signs. Then pair students to write directions using **se** for each of the icons and signs. Ex: **Se prohíbe pasear en bicicleta. Se prohíbe pasar. Se habla español.**

Lección 4

Práctica

1

¿Cierto o falso? Lee estas oraciones sobre la vida en 1901. Indica si lo que dice cada oración es **cierto** o **falso**. Luego corrige las oraciones falsas.

1. Se veía mucha televisión. Falso. No se veía televisión. Se leía mucho.
2. Se escribían muchos libros. Cierto.
3. Se viajaba mucho en tren. Cierto.
4. Se montaba a caballo. Cierto.
5. Se mandaba correo electrónico. Falso. No se mandaba correo electrónico. Se mandaban cartas y postales.
6. Se preparaban comidas en casa. Cierto.
7. Se llevaban minifaldas. Falso. No se llevaban minifaldas. Se llevaban faldas largas.
8. Se pasaba mucho tiempo con la familia. Cierto.

2

Traducir Traduce estos letreros (*signs*) y anuncios al español.

1. Nurses needed Se necesitan enfermeros/as
2. Eating and drinking prohibited Se prohíbe comer y beber
3. Programmers sought Se buscan programadores
4. English is spoken Se habla inglés
5. Computers sold Se venden computadoras
6. No talking Se prohíbe hablar
7. Teacher needed Se necesita profesor(a)
8. Books sold Se venden libros
9. Do not enter Se prohíbe entrar
10. Spanish is spoken Se habla español

3

¿Qué pasó? Mira los dibujos e indica lo que pasó en cada uno. Some answers will vary. Suggested answers:

1. camarero / pastel
   Al camarero se le cayó el pastel.
2. Sr. Álvarez / espejo
   Al señor Álvarez se le rompió el espejo.

3. Arturo / tarea
   A Arturo se le olvidó la tarea.
4. Sra. Domínguez / llaves
   A la Sra. Domínguez se le perdieron las llaves.

5. Carla y Lupe / botellas de vino
   A Carla y a Lupe se les rompieron las botellas de vino.
6. Juana / platos
   A Juana se le rompieron los platos.

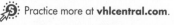
 Practice more at **vhlcentral.com**.

1 Change the date from 1901 to 2014 and go through the exercise again orally.

1 For expansion, have students work in pairs and, using constructions with **se**, write a description of a period in history such as the French or American Revolution, the Sixties, or Prohibition. Then have pairs form groups of six and read their descriptions aloud to their group.

Extra Practice Have students use **se** constructions to show cultural differences between Spanish-speaking countries and their own. Ex: **Aquí se habla inglés, pero en _____ se habla español.**

2 For expansion, ask students to find three signs on campus and translate them using the impersonal **se**.

3 To simplify, have students work in pairs to brainstorm verbs that could be used to complete this activity.

3 Add another visual aspect to this activity. Use magazine pictures to have students continue describing past events using constructions with **se**.

Extra Practice Have students imagine that they have just seen a movie about the future. Have them work in groups to prepare a description of the way of life portrayed in the movie using the imperfect tense and constructions with **se**. Ex: **No se necesitaba trabajar. Se usaban robots para hacer todo. Se viajaba por telepatía. No se comía nada sino en los fines de semana.**

Lección 4

Comunicación

4

4 Have each pair decide on the most unusual answer to the questions. Ask the student who gave it to describe the event to the class.

¿Distraído/a yo? Trabajen en parejas y usen estas preguntas para averiguar cuál de los/las dos es más distraído/a (*absentminded*). Answers will vary.

¿Alguna vez…

1. se te olvidó invitar a alguien a una fiesta o comida? ¿A quién?
2. se te quedó algo importante en la casa? ¿Qué?
3. se te perdió algo importante durante un viaje? ¿Qué?
4. se te rompió algo muy caro? ¿Qué?

¿Sabes…

5. si se permite el ingreso (*admission*) de perros al parque cercano a la universidad?
6. si en el supermercado se aceptan cheques?
7. dónde se arreglan zapatos y botas?
8. qué se sirve en la cafetería de la universidad los lunes?

5 Ask pairs to write similar beginnings to three different statements using **se** constructions. Have pairs exchange papers and finish each other's sentences.

5

Opiniones En parejas, terminen cada oración con ideas originales. Después, comparen los resultados con la clase para ver qué pareja tuvo las mejores ideas. Answers will vary.

1. No se tiene que dejar propina cuando…
2. Antes de viajar, se debe…
3. Si se come bien, …
4. Para tener una vida sana, se debe…
5. Se sirve la mejor comida en…
6. Se hablan muchas lenguas en…

Síntesis

6

Anuncios En grupos, preparen dos anuncios de televisión para presentar a la clase. Usen el imperfecto y por lo menos dos construcciones con **se** en cada uno. Answers will vary.

modelo

Se me cayeron unos libros en el pie y me dolía mucho. Pero ahora no, gracias a SuperAspirina 500. ¡Dos pastillas y se me fue el dolor! Se puede comprar SuperAspirina 500 en todas las farmacias Recetamax.

Extra Practice Write these sentence fragments on the board and ask students to supply several logical endings using a construction with **se**.
1. Una vez, cuando yo comía en un restaurante elegante, ____. (se me rompió un vaso; se me perdió la tarjeta de crédito)
2. Ayer cuando yo venía a clase, ____. (se me dañó la bicicleta; me caí y se me rompió el brazo)
3. Cuando era niño/a, siempre ____. (se me olvidaban las cosas; se me perdían las cosas) 4. El otro día cuando yo lavaba los platos, ____. (se me rompieron tres vasos; se me terminó el detergente)

6 After all the groups have presented their ads, have each group write a letter of complaint. Their letter should be directed to one of the other groups, claiming false advertising.

Adverbs Tutorial

ANTE TODO Adverbs are words that describe how, when, and where actions take place. They can modify verbs, adjectives, and even other adverbs. In previous lessons, you have already learned many Spanish adverbs, such as the ones below.

aquí	hoy	nunca
ayer	mal	siempre
bien	muy	temprano

▶ The most common adverbs end in **-mente**, equivalent to the English ending *-ly*.

verdaderamente *truly, really*   **generalmente** *generally*   **simplemente** *simply*

▶ To form these adverbs, add **-mente** to the feminine form of the adjective. If the adjective does not have a special feminine form, just add **-mente** to the standard form. **¡Atención!** Adjectives do not lose their accents when adding **-mente**.

ADJECTIVE	FEMININE FORM	SUFFIX	ADVERB
seguro	segura	-mente	seguramente
fabuloso	fabulosa	-mente	fabulosamente
enorme		-mente	enormemente
fácil		-mente	fácilmente

▶ Adverbs that end in **-mente** generally follow the verb, while adverbs that modify an adjective or another adverb precede the word they modify.

Maira dibuja **maravillosamente**.   Sergio está **casi siempre** ocupado.
Maira draws wonderfully.   *Sergio is almost always busy.*

Common adverbs and adverbial expressions

a menudo	often	así	like this; so	menos	less
a tiempo	on time	bastante	enough; rather	muchas veces	a lot; many times
a veces	sometimes	casi	almost		
además (de)	furthermore; besides	con frecuencia	frequently	poco	little
				por lo menos	at least
apenas	hardly; scarcely	de vez en cuando	from time to time	pronto	soon
		despacio	slowly	rápido	quickly

 **¡INTÉNTALO!** Transforma los adjetivos en adverbios.

1. alegre *alegremente*
2. constante *constantemente*
3. gradual *gradualmente*
4. perfecto *perfectamente*

5. real *realmente*
6. frecuente *frecuentemente*
7. tranquilo *tranquilamente*
8. regular *regularmente*

9. maravilloso *maravillosamente*
10. normal *normalmente*
11. básico *básicamente*
12. afortunado *afortunadamente*

comparisons
NATIONAL STANDARDS

Teaching Tips
• Use magazine pictures to review known adverbs. Ex: **Hoy esta chica se siente** *bien*, **pero ayer se sentía** *mal*.
• Ask volunteers to use **-mente** to convert known adjectives into adverbs. Ex: **cómodo/cómodamente**.

¡ATENCIÓN!
When a sentence contains two or more adverbs in sequence, the suffix **-mente** is dropped from all but the last adverb.
Ex: **El médico nos habló simple y abiertamente.** *The doctor spoke to us simply and openly.*

Extra Practice Name celebrities and have students create sentences about them, using adverbs. Ex: **Shakira (Shakira baila maravillosamente.)**

¡ATENCIÓN!
Rápido functions as an adjective (**Ella tiene una computadora rápida.**) as well as an adverb (**Ellas corren rápido.**). Note that as an adverb, **rápido** does not need to agree with any other word in the sentence. You can also use the adverb **rápidamente** (**Ella corre rápidamente.**).

recursos

WB
pp. 241–242

LM
p. 256

vhlcentral.com
Lección 4

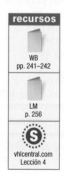

Práctica

1 To simplify, use a three-column chart (*¿Cómo?, ¿Cuándo?,* and *¿Dónde?*) to review adverbs and adverbial expressions.

1

Escoger Completa la historia con los adverbios adecuados.

1. La cita era a las dos, pero llegamos _____tarde_____. (mientras, nunca, tarde)
2. El problema fue que _____ayer_____ se nos dañó el despertador. (aquí, ayer, despacio)
3. La recepcionista no se enojó porque sabe que normalmente llego _____a tiempo_____. (a veces, a tiempo, poco)
4. _____Por lo menos_____ el doctor estaba listo. (Por lo menos, Muchas veces, Casi)
5. _____Apenas_____ tuvimos que esperar cinco minutos. (Así, Además, Apenas)
6. El doctor dijo que nuestra hija Irene necesitaba cambiar su rutina diaria _____inmediatamente_____. (temprano, menos, inmediatamente)
▶ 7. El doctor nos explicó _____bien_____ las recomendaciones del Cirujano General (*Surgeon General*) sobre la salud de los jóvenes. (de vez en cuando, bien, apenas)
8. _____Afortunadamente_____ nos dijo que Irene estaba bien, pero tenía que hacer más ejercicio y comer mejor. (Bastante, Afortunadamente, A menudo)

NOTA CULTURAL

La doctora Antonia Novello, de Puerto Rico, fue la primera mujer y la primera hispana en tomar el cargo de **Cirujana General** de los Estados Unidos (1990–1993).

Comunicación

2 Before assigning the activity, ask some general questions about the ad. Ex: **¿Qué producto se vende?** (aspirina) **¿Dónde se encuentra un anuncio de este tipo?** (en una revista)

2

Aspirina Lee el anuncio y responde a las preguntas con un(a) compañero/a. Answers will vary.

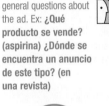

No hay tiempo para el dolor de cabeza.

Si tienes prisa, o simplemente quieres que tu dolor de cabeza se vaya muy pronto, piensa en Capalivia. Se asimila mejor y actúa rápidamente. Ya no se puede perder tiempo por un dolor de cabeza.

ASPIRINA

2 For expansion, have pairs create a similar ad for a different product, using at least four adverbs. Collect the ads and read the descriptions aloud. The class should identify the adverbs and then guess what product is being advertised.

Game Divide the class into teams of three. Each team should have a piece of paper. Say the name of a historical figure and give teams three minutes to write down as many facts as they can about that person, using adverbs and adverbial expressions. At the end of each round, have teams read their answers aloud. Award one point to the team with the most correct answers for each historical figure.

1. ¿Cuáles son los adverbios que aparecen en el anuncio?
2. Según el anuncio, ¿cuáles son las ventajas (*advantages*) de este tipo de aspirina?
3. ¿Tienen ustedes dolores de cabeza? ¿Qué toman para curarlos?
4. ¿Qué medicamentos ven con frecuencia en los anuncios de televisión? Escriban descripciones de varios de estos anuncios. Usen adverbios en sus descripciones.

 Practice more at **vhlcentral.com**.

Lección 4

Recapitulación

SUBJECT → Javier   CONJUGATED FORM   empiezo   Main clause   Dudan

 Diagnostics

Completa estas actividades para repasar los conceptos de gramática que aprendiste en esta lección.

1 Completar Completa el cuadro con la forma correcta del imperfecto. `12 pts.`

yo/Ud./él/ella	tú	nosotros	Uds./ellos/ellas
era	eras	éramos	eran
cantaba	**cantabas**	cantábamos	cantaban
venía	venías	**veníamos**	venían
quería	querías	queríamos	**querían**

2 Adverbios Escoge el adverbio correcto de la lista para completar estas oraciones. Lee con cuidado las oraciones; los adverbios sólo se usan una vez. No vas a usar uno de los adverbios. `8 pts.`

a menudo	apenas	fácilmente
a tiempo	casi	maravillosamente
además	despacio	por lo menos

1. Pablito se cae __a menudo__; un promedio (*average*) de cuatro veces por semana.

2. No me duele nada y no sufro de ninguna enfermedad; me siento __maravillosamente__ bien.

3. —Doctor, ¿cómo supo que tuve una operación de garganta?
   —Muy __fácilmente__, lo leí en su historial (*history*) médico.

4. ¿Le duele mucho la espalda (*back*)? Entonces tiene que levantarse __despacio__.

5. Ya te sientes mucho mejor, ¿verdad? Mañana puedes volver al trabajo; tu temperatura es __casi__ normal.

6. Es importante hacer ejercicio con regularidad, __por lo menos__ tres veces a la semana.

7. El examen médico no comenzó ni tarde ni temprano. Comenzó __a tiempo__, a las tres de la tarde.

8. Parece que ya te estás curando del resfriado. __Apenas__ estás congestionada.

TPR Divide the class into three groups: -**ar** verbs, -**er** verbs, and -**ir** verbs. Read a series of sentences that contain the imperfect tense. Have groups stand up when their verb form is used. Ex: **Mi escuela primaria tenía un patio grande.** (-**er** verb group stands)

RESUMEN GRAMATICAL

4.1 The imperfect tense   *pp. 206–207*

The imperfect of regular verbs		
cantar	**beber**	**escribir**
cantaba	bebía	escribía
cantabas	bebías	escribías
cantaba	bebía	escribía
cantábamos	bebíamos	escribíamos
cantabais	bebíais	escribíais
cantaban	bebían	escribían

► There are no stem changes in the imperfect:
entender (e:ie) → entendía; servir (e:i) → servía;
doler (o:ue) → dolía

► The imperfect of **hay** is **había**.

► Only three verbs are irregular in the imperfect.
ir: iba, ibas, iba, íbamos, ibais, iban
ser: era, eras, era, éramos, erais, eran
ver: veía, veías, veía, veíamos, veíais, veían

4.2 The preterite and the imperfect   *pp. 210–211*

Preterite	Imperfect
1. Completed actions	1. Ongoing past action
Fueron a Buenos Aires ayer.	**Usted miraba el fútbol.**
2. Beginning or end of past action	2. Habitual past actions
La película empezó a las nueve.	**Todos los domingos yo visitaba a mi abuela.**
3. Series of past actions or events	3. Description of states or characteristics
Me caí y me lastimé el pie.	**Ella era alta.** **Quería descansar.**

4.3 Constructions with se   *pp. 214–215*

Impersonal constructions with **se**	
	prohíbe fumar.
Se	habla español.
	hablan varios idiomas.

		Se for unplanned events	
Se	me, te, le, nos, os, les	cayó la taza.	
		dañó el radio.	
		rompieron las botellas.	
		olvidaron las llaves.	

4.4 **Adverbs** *p. 218*

Formation of adverbs
fácil → fá**cilmente**
seguro → segura**mente**
verdadero → verdadera**mente**

3 To challenge students, have them explain why they used the preterite and imperfect in each case and how the meaning might change if the other tense were used.

3 **Un accidente** Escoge el imperfecto o el pretérito según el contexto para completar esta conversación. **10 pts.**

NURIA Hola, Felipe. ¿Estás bien? ¿Qué es eso? ¿(1) (Te lastimaste/Te lastimabas) el pie?

FELIPE Ayer (2) (tuve/tenía) un pequeño accidente.

NURIA Cuéntame. ¿Cómo (3) (pasó/pasaba)?

FELIPE Bueno, (4) (fueron/eran) las cinco de la tarde y (5) (llovió/llovía) mucho cuando (6) (salí/salía) de la casa en mi bicicleta. No (7) (vi/veía) a una chica que (8) (caminó/caminaba) en mi dirección, y los dos (9) (nos caímos/nos caíamos) al suelo (*ground*).

NURIA Y la chica, ¿está bien ella?

FELIPE Sí. Cuando llegamos al hospital, ella sólo (10) (tuvo/tenía) dolor de cabeza.

4 For items 2, 3, and 5, have volunteers rewrite the sentences on the board using other subjects. Ex: **2. (nosotros) ¿Se nos olvidaron las llaves otra vez?**

4 Give students these additional items: **6. (yo) / caer / el vaso de cristal (pretérito) (Se me cayó el vaso de cristal.) 7. (ustedes) / quedar / las maletas en el aeropuerto (pretérito) (A ustedes se les quedaron las maletas en el aeropuerto.) 8. en esta tienda / hablar / español e italiano (presente) (En esta tienda se hablan español e italiano.)**

4 **Oraciones** Escribe oraciones con **se** a partir de los elementos dados (*given*). Usa el tiempo especificado entre paréntesis y añade pronombres cuando sea necesario. **10 pts.**

> **modelo**
>
> Carlos / quedar / la tarea en casa (pretérito)
> *A Carlos se le quedó la tarea en casa.*

1. en la farmacia / vender / medicamentos (presente) En la farmacia se venden medicamentos.

2. ¿(tú) / olvidar / las llaves / otra vez? (pretérito) ¿Se te olvidaron las llaves otra vez?

3. (yo) / dañar / la computadora (pretérito) Se me dañó la computadora.

3. en esta clase / prohibir / hablar inglés (presente) En esta clase se prohíbe hablar inglés.

4. ellos / romper / las gafas / en el accidente (pretérito) A ellos se les rompieron las gafas en el accidente.

5 After writing their paragraphs, have students work in pairs and ask each other follow-up questions about their visits.

5 **En la consulta** Escribe al menos cinco oraciones sobre tu última visita al médico. Incluye cinco verbos en pretérito y cinco en imperfecto. Habla de qué te pasó, cómo te sentías, cómo era el/la doctor(a), qué te dijo, etc. Usa tu imaginación. **10 pts.** Answers will vary.

6 Ask students to give the English equivalent of this phrase.

6 **Refrán** Completa el refrán con las palabras que faltan. **¡2 puntos EXTRA!**

❝ Lo que ___bien___ (*well*) se aprende, nunca ___se___ pierde. ❞

Lectura

Antes de leer

Estrategia

Activating background knowledge

Using what you already know about a particular subject will often help you better understand a reading selection. For example, if you read an article about a recent medical discovery, you might think about what you already know about health in order to understand unfamiliar words or concepts.

Examinar el texto

Utiliza las estrategias de lectura que tú consideras más efectivas para hacer algunas observaciones preliminares acerca del texto. Después trabajen en parejas para comparar sus observaciones acerca del texto. Luego contesten estas preguntas:

- Analicen el formato del texto: ¿Qué tipo de texto es? ¿Dónde creen que se publicó este artículo?
- ¿Quiénes son Carla Baron y Tomás Monterrey?
- Miren la foto del libro. ¿Qué sugiere el título del libro sobre su contenido?

Conocimiento previo

Ahora piensen en su conocimiento previo° sobre el cuidado de la salud en los viajes. Consideren estas preguntas:

- ¿Viajaron alguna vez a otro estado o a otro país?
- ¿Tuvieron problemas durante sus viajes con el agua, la comida o el clima del lugar?
- ¿Olvidaron poner en su maleta algún medicamento que después necesitaron?
- Imaginen que su compañero/a se va de viaje. Díganle por lo menos cinco cosas que debe hacer para prevenir cualquier problema de salud.

conocimiento previo *background knowledge*

Teaching Tips
- Discuss the questions as a class and jot down responses on the board.
- Before reading the selection, ask small groups to write a paragraph summarizing ways to safeguard health while traveling. Encourage them to use the ideas on the board and to draw from previous knowledge and personal experience.

Practice more at **vhlcentral.com**.

Libro de la semana

Cómo hacer un viaje
saludable y feliz

Carla Baron

Después de leer

Correspondencias

Busca las correspondencias entre los problemas y las recomendaciones.

Problemas

1. el agua __b__
2. el sol __d__
3. la comida __a__
4. la identificación __e__
5. el clima __c__

Recomendaciones

a. Hay que adaptarse a los ingredientes desconocidos (*unknown*).
b. Toma sólo productos purificados (*purified*).
c. Es importante llevar ropa adecuada cuando viajas.
d. Lleva loción o crema con alta protección solar.
e. Lleva tu pasaporte.

Pairs Have students work in pairs to read the selection and complete the activities.

Entrevista a Carla Baron
por Tomás Monterrey

Teaching Tip After reading the selection, call on pairs of students to role-play additional interview questions and answers.

Tomás: ¿Por qué escribió su libro *Cómo hacer un viaje saludable y feliz*?

Carla: Me encanta viajar, conocer otras culturas y escribir. Mi primer viaje lo hice cuando era estudiante universitaria. Todavía recuerdo el día en que llegamos a San Juan, Puerto Rico. Era el panorama ideal para unas vacaciones maravillosas, pero al llegar a la habitación del hotel, bebí mucha agua de la llave° y luego pedí un jugo de frutas con mucho hielo°. El clima en San Juan es tropical y yo tenía mucha sed y calor. Los síntomas llegaron en menos de media hora: pasé dos días con dolor de estómago y corriendo al cuarto de baño cada diez minutos. Desde entonces, siempre que viajo sólo bebo agua mineral y llevo un pequeño bolso con medicinas necesarias, como pastillas para el dolor y también bloqueador solar, una crema repelente de mosquitos y un desinfectante.

Tomás: ¿Son reales° las situaciones que se narran en su libro?

Carla: Sí, son reales y son mis propias° historias°. A menudo los autores crean caricaturas divertidas de un turista en dificultades. ¡En mi libro la turista en dificultades soy yo!

Tomás: ¿Qué recomendaciones puede encontrar el lector en su libro?

Carla: Bueno, mi libro es anecdótico y humorístico, pero el tema de la salud se trata° de manera seria. En general, se dan recomendaciones sobre ropa adecuada para cada sitio, consejos para protegerse del sol, y comidas y bebidas adecuadas para el turista que viaja al Caribe o Suramérica.

Tomás: ¿Tiene algún consejo para las personas que se enferman cuando viajan?

Carla: Muchas veces los turistas toman el avión sin saber nada acerca del país que van a visitar. Ponen toda su ropa en la maleta, toman el pasaporte, la cámara fotográfica y ¡a volar°! Es necesario tomar precauciones porque nuestro cuerpo necesita adaptarse al clima, al sol, a la humedad, al agua y a la comida. Se trata de° viajar, admirar las maravillas del mundo y regresar a casa con hermosos recuerdos. En resumen, el secreto es "prevenir en vez de° curar".

llave *faucet* **hielo** *ice* **reales** *true* **propias** *own* **historias** *stories*
se trata *is treated* **¡a volar!** *Off they go!* **Se trata de** *It's a question of*
en vez de *instead of*

Seleccionar

Selecciona la respuesta correcta.

1. El tema principal de este libro es __d__.
   a. Puerto Rico   b. la salud y el agua   c. otras culturas
   d. el cuidado de la salud en los viajes

2. Las situaciones narradas en el libro son __a__.
   a. autobiográficas   b. inventadas   c. ficticias
   d. imaginarias

3. ¿Qué recomendaciones no vas a encontrar en este libro? __d__
   a. cómo vestirse adecuadamente
   b. cómo prevenir las quemaduras solares
   c. consejos sobre la comida y la bebida
   d. cómo dar propina en los países del Caribe o de Suramérica

4. En opinión de la señorita Baron, __b__.
   a. es bueno tomar agua de la llave y beber jugo de frutas con mucho hielo
   b. es mejor tomar solamente agua embotellada (*bottled*)
   c. los minerales son buenos para el dolor abdominal
   d. es importante visitar el cuarto de baño cada diez minutos

5. ¿Cuál de estos productos no lleva la autora cuando viaja a otros países? __c__
   a. desinfectante
   b. crema repelente
   c. detergente
   d. pastillas medicinales

Small Groups Have groups of three select a country they would like to visit, then research specific precautions that should be taken by visitors.
Heritage Speakers Ask heritage speakers to prepare a short presentation on health and travel tips for visitors to their families' countries of origin.

Lección 4

Escritura

Estrategia

Mastering the simple past tenses

In Spanish, when you write about events that occurred in the past you will need to know when to use the preterite and when to use the imperfect tense. A good understanding of the uses of each tense will make it much easier to determine which one to use as you write.

Look at the summary of the uses of the preterite and the imperfect and write your own example sentence for each of the rules described.

Preterite vs. imperfect

Preterite

1. Completed actions

_____

_____

2. Beginning or end of past actions

_____

_____

3. Series of past actions

_____

_____

Imperfect

1. Ongoing past actions

_____

_____

2. Habitual past actions

_____

_____

3. Mental, physical, and emotional states and characteristics in the past

_____

_____

Get together with a few classmates to compare your example sentences. Then use these sentences and the chart as a guide to help you decide which tense to use as you are writing a story or other type of narration about the past.

Tema

Escribir una historia

Escribe una historia acerca de una experiencia tuya° (o de otra persona) con una enfermedad, accidente o problema médico. Tu historia puede ser real o imaginaria y puede tratarse de un incidente divertido, humorístico o desastroso. Incluye todos los detalles relevantes. Consulta la lista de sugerencias° con detalles que puedes incluir.

▶ Descripción del/de la paciente
  nombre y apellidos
  edad
  características físicas
  historial médico°

▶ Descripción de los síntomas
  enfermedades
  accidente
  problemas médicos

▶ Descripción del tratamiento°
  tratamientos
  recetas
  operaciones

Teaching Tips
• Explain that the story should be about something that occurred in the past. Encourage students to brainstorm as many details as possible before they begin writing.
• Remind students to check for the correct use of the preterite and the imperfect whenever they write about the past in Spanish. Refer them to the summary of uses.

tuya *of yours* **sugerencias** *suggestions* **historial médico** *medical history*
tratamiento *treatment*

Escuchar Audio

Estrategia

Listening for specific information

You can listen for specific information effectively once you identify the subject of a conversation and use your background knowledge to predict what kinds of information you might hear.

 To practice this strategy, you will listen to a paragraph from a letter Marta wrote to a friend about her fifteenth birthday celebration. Before you listen to the paragraph, use what you know about this type of party to predict the content of the letter. What kinds of details might Marta include in her description of the celebration? Now listen to the paragraph and jot down the specific information Marta relates. Then compare these details to the predictions you made about the letter.

Preparación

Mira la foto. ¿Con quién crees que está conversando Carlos Peña? ¿De qué están hablando? Answers will vary.

Ahora escucha

Ahora escucha la conversación de la señorita Méndez y Carlos Peña. Marca las oraciones donde se mencionan los síntomas de Carlos.

1. ____ Tiene infección en los ojos.
2. ____ Se lastimó el dedo.
3. ✔ No puede dormir.
4. ✔ Siente dolor en los huesos.
5. ____ Está mareado.
6. ✔ Está congestionado.
7. ____ Le duele el estómago.
8. ✔ Le duele la cabeza.
9. ____ Es alérgico a la aspirina.
10. ✔ Tiene tos.
11. ✔ Le duele la garganta.
12. ____ Se rompió la pierna.
13. ____ Tiene dolor de oído.
14. ✔ Tiene frío.

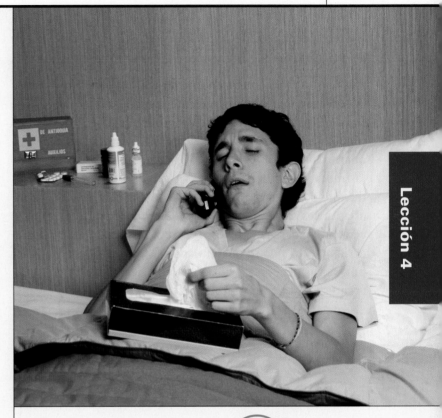

Lección 4

Comprensión

Preguntas

1. ¿Tiene fiebre Carlos? Carlos no sabe si tiene fiebre pero tiene mucho frío y le duelen los huesos.
2. ¿Cuánto tiempo hace que le duele la garganta a Carlos? Hace cinco días que le duele la garganta.
3. ¿Qué tiene que hacer el médico antes de recetarle algo a Carlos? Tiene que ver si tiene una infección.
4. ¿A qué hora es su cita con el médico? Es a las tres de la tarde.
5. Después de darle una cita con el médico, ¿qué otra información le pide a Carlos la señorita del consultorio? Le pide su nombre, su fecha de nacimiento y su número de teléfono.
6. En tu opinión, ¿qué tiene Carlos? ¿Gripe? ¿Un resfriado? ¿Alergias? Explica tu opinión. Answers will vary.

Diálogo

Con un(a) compañero/a, escribe el diálogo entre el Dr. Aguilar y Carlos Peña en el consultorio del médico. Usa la información del diálogo telefónico para pensar en lo que dice el médico mientras examina a Carlos. Imagina cómo responde Carlos y qué preguntas le hace al médico. ¿Cuál es el diagnóstico del médico?

Teaching Tip Have students look at the photo. Guide them to see that **Carlos Peña** is talking to a health care provider about his illness.

 Practice more at **vhlcentral.com**.

En pantalla

Algunas personas piensan que los países hispanos no cuentan con° la más reciente tecnología. La verdad es que sí se tiene acceso a ella, pero muchas personas prefieren conservar cosas como aparatos electrónicos o muebles° sin importar las modas temporales y los constantes avances tecnológicos. Esto es por el aprecio° que les tienen a las cosas más que por limitaciones económicas o tecnológicas. Este fenómeno se ve especialmente en las piezas que se quedan en una familia por varias generaciones, como, por ejemplo, el tocadiscos° que un bisabuelo compró en 1910.

Vocabulario útil	
suaviza	*soothes*
alivio	*relief*

Ordenar

Ordena las palabras o expresiones según aparecen en el anuncio. No vas a usar tres de estas palabras.

  _4_ a. gargantas irritadas   _____ e. pastillas
  _____ b. receta   _5_ f. alivio
  _2_ c. comienzan   _1_ g. a menudo
  _3_ d. calma   _____ h. dolor

Tu música

En el anuncio se escucha un tango muy emotivo como música de fondo (*background*). Escribe el título de una canción que refleje cómo te sientes en cada una de estas situaciones. Después comparte tus ideas con tres compañeros/as.   Answers will vary.

▸ tienes un dolor de cabeza muy fuerte

▸ terminaron las clases

▸ te sacaron un diente

▸ estás enamorado/a

▸ te sientes mareado/a

▸ estás completamente saludable

Anuncio de Strepsils

... los problemas de garganta...

comienzan...

... con un pinchazo°.

Teaching Tip Before you show the TV clip, have students look at the video stills, read the captions, and predict how music might be used to sell throat lozenges.

 Video: TV Clip

 Practice more at **vhlcentral.com**.

---

no cuentan con *don't have*   **muebles** *furniture*   **aprecio** *appreciation*
tocadiscos *record player*   **pinchazo** *sharp pain (lit. puncture)*   **boticarios** *pharmacists*
artesanos *craftsmen*   **ejercían...** *practiced unduidance*

Lección 4

Argentina tiene una gran tradición médica influenciada desde el siglo XIX por la medicina francesa. Tres de los cinco premios Nobel de esta nación están relacionados con investigaciones médicas que han hecho° grandes aportes° al avance de las ciencias de la salud. Además, existen otros adelantos° de médicos argentinos que han hecho historia. Entre ellos se cuentan el *bypass* coronario, desarrollado° por el cirujano° René Favaloro en 1967, y la técnica de cirugía cardiovascular sin circulación extracorpórea° desarrollada en 1978 por Federico Benetti, quien es considerado uno de los padres de la cirugía cardíaca moderna.

La salud

¿Le podría° pedir que me explique qué es la guardia?

Vocabulario útil

la cita previa	previous appointment
la guardia	emergency room
Me di un golpe.	I got hit.
la práctica	rotation (hands-on medical experience)

Preparación

¿Qué haces si tienes un pequeño accidente o quieres hacer una consulta? ¿Visitas a tu médico general o vas al hospital? ¿Debes pedir un turno (*appointment*)?

Answers will vary.

¿Cierto o falso?

Indica si las oraciones son **ciertas** o **falsas**.

1. Silvina tuvo un accidente en su automóvil. Falso.
2. Silvina fue a la guardia del hospital. Cierto.
3. La guardia del hospital está abierta sólo durante el día y es necesario tener cita previa. Falso.
4. Los entrevistados (*interviewees*) tienen enfermedades graves. Falso.
5. En Argentina, los médicos reciben la certificación cuando terminan la práctica. Cierto.

¿Cierto o falso? Have students correct the false statements.

Nuestro hospital público es gratuito para todas las personas.

... la carrera de medicina comienza con el primer año de la universidad.

Teaching Tip You may want to mention that the time of day is probably a factor in determining where one goes for medical care following an accident.

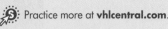 **Video:** *Flash cultura*

han hecho *have done* aportes *contributions* adelantos *advances* desarrollado *developed* cirujano *surgeon* extracorpórea *out-of-body* podría *could*

Practice more at **vhlcentral.com**.

recursos

VM pp. 249–250

vhlcentral.com Lección 4

Ⓢ Video: *Panorama cultural*
Interactive map

Costa Rica

NATIONAL STANDARDS
connections cultures

El país en cifras

▶ **Área:** 51.100 km² (19.730 millas²),
aproximadamente el área de Virginia Occidental°

▶ **Población:** 4.957.000

Costa Rica es el país de Centroamérica con la población más homogénea. El 94% de sus habitantes es blanco y mestizo°. Más del 50% de la población es de ascendencia° española y un alto porcentaje tiene sus orígenes en otros países europeos.

▶ **Capital:** San José —1.655.000

▶ **Ciudades principales:** Alajuela, Cartago, Puntarenas, Heredia

SOURCE: Population Division, UN Secretariat

▶ **Moneda:** colón costarricense

▶ **Idioma:** español (oficial)

Bandera de Costa Rica

Costarricenses célebres

▶ **Carmen Lyra,** escritora (1888–1949)
▶ **Chavela Vargas,** cantante (1919–2012)
▶ **Óscar Arias Sánchez,** ex presidente de Costa Rica (1941–)
▶ **Claudia Poll,** nadadora° olímpica (1972–)

Óscar Arias recibió el Premio Nobel de la Paz en 1987.

Virginia Occidental *West Virginia* mestizo *of indigenous and white parentage* ascendencia *descent* nadadora *swimmer* ejército *army* gastos *expenditures* invertir *to invest* cuartel *barracks*

Mercado Central en San José
NICARAGUA
Vista del volcán Arenal
Río San Juan
Río Tempisque
Cordillera de Guanacaste
Volcán Arenal
Cordillera Central
Cordillera de Tilarán
Alajuela
Puntarenas
Heredia
Río Grande de Tárcoles
Volcán Irazú
San José
Cartago
Cordillera de

Edificio Metálico en San José

Océano Pacífico

Basílica de Nuestra Señora de los Ángeles en Cartago

ESTADOS UNIDOS
OCÉANO ATLÁNTICO
COSTA RICA
OCÉANO PACÍFICO
AMÉRICA DEL SUR

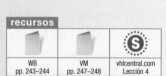
recursos

WB pp. 243–244	VM pp. 247–248	Ⓢ vhlcentral.com Lección 4

¡Increíble pero cierto!

Costa Rica es el único país latinoamericano que no tiene ejército°. Sin gastos° militares, el gobierno puede invertir° más dinero en la educación y las artes. En la foto aparece el Museo Nacional de Costa Rica, antiguo cuartel° del ejército.

MUSEO NACIONAL DE COSTA RICA

Mar Caribe

Limón

Talamanca

PANAMÁ

Parque Morazán
en San José

Lugares • **Los parques nacionales**

El sistema de parques nacionales de Costa Rica ocupa aproximadamente el 12% de su territorio y fue establecido° para la protección de su biodiversidad. En los parques, los ecoturistas pueden admirar montañas, cataratas° y una gran variedad de plantas exóticas. Algunos ofrecen también la oportunidad de ver quetzales°, monos°, jaguares, armadillos y mariposas° en su hábitat natural.

Economía • **Las plantaciones de café**

Costa Rica fue el primer país centroamericano en desarrollar° la industria del café. En el siglo° XIX, los costarricenses empezaron a exportar esta semilla a Inglaterra°, lo que significó una contribución importante a la economía de la nación. Actualmente, más de 50.000 costarricenses trabajan en el cultivo del café. Este producto representa cerca del 15% de sus exportaciones anuales.

Sociedad • **Una nación progresista**

Costa Rica es un país progresista. Tiene un nivel de alfabetización° del 96%, uno de los más altos de Latinoamérica. En 1870, esta nación centroamericana abolió la pena de muerte° y en 1948 eliminó el ejército e hizo obligatoria y gratuita° la educación para todos sus ciudadanos.

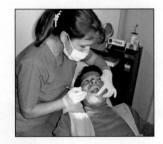

¿Qué aprendiste? Responde a las preguntas con oraciones completas.

1. ¿Cómo se llama la capital de Costa Rica?
   La capital de Costa Rica se llama San José.

2. ¿Quién es Claudia Poll?
   Claudia Poll es una nadadora olímpica.

3. ¿Qué porcentaje del territorio de Costa Rica ocupan los parques nacionales?
   Los parques nacionales ocupan aproximadamente el 12% del territorio de Costa Rica.

4. ¿Para qué se establecieron los parques nacionales? Los parques nacionales
   se establecieron para proteger los ecosistemas de la región y su biodiversidad.

5. ¿Qué pueden ver los turistas en los parques nacionales? En los parques
   nacionales, los turistas pueden ver cataratas, montañas y muchas plantas exóticas.

6. ¿Cuántos costarricenses trabajan en las plantaciones de café hoy día?
   Más de 50.000 costarricenses trabajan en las plantaciones de café hoy día.

7. ¿Cuándo eliminó Costa Rica la pena de muerte?
   Costa Rica eliminó la pena de muerte en 1870.

Conexión Internet Investiga estos temas en **vhlcentral.com**.

Practice more at
vhlcentral.com.

1. Busca información sobre Óscar Arias Sánchez. ¿Quién es? ¿Por qué se le considera (*is he considered*) un costarricense célebre?

2. Busca información sobre los artistas de Costa Rica. ¿Qué artista, escritor o cantante te interesa más? ¿Por qué?

....

establecido *established* **cataratas** *waterfalls* **quetzales** *type of tropical bird* **monos** *monkeys* **mariposas** *butterflies*
en desarrollar *to develop* **siglo** *century* **Inglaterra** *England* **nivel de alfabetización** *literacy rate* **pena de muerte** *death penalty* **gratuita** *free*

Supersite/DVD: You may want to wrap up this section by playing the **Panorama cultural** video footage for this lesson.

El cuerpo

la boca	mouth
el brazo	arm
la cabeza	head
el corazón	heart
el cuello	neck
el cuerpo	body
el dedo	finger
el dedo del pie	toe
el estómago	stomach
la garganta	throat
el hueso	bone
la nariz	nose
el oído	(sense of) hearing; inner ear
el ojo	eye
la oreja	(outer) ear
el pie	foot
la pierna	leg
la rodilla	knee
el tobillo	ankle

La salud

el accidente	accident
el antibiótico	antibiotic
la aspirina	aspirin
la clínica	clinic
el consultorio	doctor's office
el/la dentista	dentist
el/la doctor(a)	doctor
el dolor (de cabeza)	(head)ache; pain
el/la enfermero/a	nurse
el examen médico	physical exam
la farmacia	pharmacy
la gripe	flu
el hospital	hospital
la infección	infection
el medicamento	medication
la medicina	medicine
la operación	operation
el/la paciente	patient
la pastilla	pill; tablet
la radiografía	X-ray
la receta	prescription
el resfriado	cold (illness)
la sala de emergencia(s)	emergency room
la salud	health
el síntoma	symptom
la tos	cough

Verbos

caerse	to fall (down)
dañar	to damage; to break down
darse con	to bump into; to run into
doler (o:ue)	to hurt
enfermarse	to get sick
estar enfermo/a	to be sick
estornudar	to sneeze
lastimarse (el pie)	to injure (one's foot)
olvidar	to forget
poner una inyección	to give an injection
prohibir	to prohibit
recetar	to prescribe
romper	to break
romperse (la pierna)	to break (one's leg)
sacar(se) un diente	to have a tooth removed
ser alérgico/a (a)	to be allergic (to)
sufrir una enfermedad	to suffer an illness
tener dolor (m.)	to have a pain
tener fiebre (f.)	to have a fever
tomar la temperatura	to take someone's temperature
torcerse (o:ue) (el tobillo)	to sprain (one's ankle)
toser	to cough

Adjetivos

congestionado/a	congested; stuffed up
embarazada	pregnant
grave	grave; serious
mareado/a	dizzy; nauseated
médico/a	medical
saludable	healthy
sano/a	healthy

Supersite: MP3 Audio Files, Testing Program

Adverbios

a menudo	often
a tiempo	on time
a veces	sometimes
además (de)	furthermore; besides
apenas	hardly; scarcely
así	like this; so
bastante	enough; rather
casi	almost
con frecuencia	frequently
de niño/a	as a child
de vez en cuando	from time to time
despacio	slowly
menos	less
mientras	while
muchas veces	a lot; many times
poco	little
por lo menos	at least
pronto	soon
rápido	quickly
todos los días	every day

Expresiones útiles	See page 201.

Audio: Vocabulary Flashcards

recursos

LM
p. 256

vhlcentral.com
Lección 4

contextos

Lección 4

1 **El cuerpo humano** Label the parts of the body.

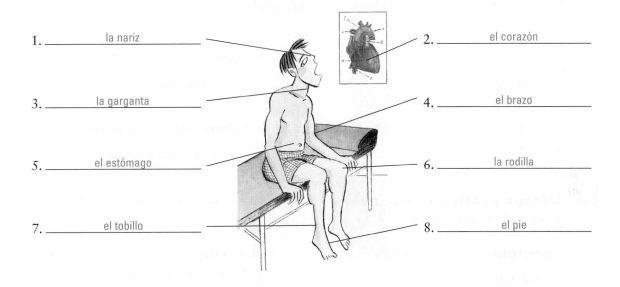

1. _____la nariz_____
2. _____el corazón_____
3. _____la garganta_____
4. _____el brazo_____
5. _____el estómago_____
6. _____la rodilla_____
7. _____el tobillo_____
8. _____el pie_____

2 **¿Adónde vas?** Indicate where you would go in each of the following situations.

la clínica	el dentista	el hospital
el consultorio	la farmacia	la sala de emergencia

1. tienes que comprar aspirinas _la farmacia_
2. te duele un diente _el dentista_
3. te rompes una pierna _la sala de emergencia_
4. te debes hacer un examen médico _la clínica/el consultorio_
5. te van a hacer una operación _el hospital_
6. te van a poner una inyección _la clínica/el consultorio/la farmacia_

3 **Las categorías** List these terms under the appropriate category.

antibiótico	gripe	receta
aspirina	operación	resfriado
estornudos	pastilla	tomar la temperatura
fiebre	radiografía	tos

Síntoma: _fiebre, tos, estornudos_

Enfermedad: _resfriado, gripe_

Diagnóstico: _radiografía, tomar la temperatura_

Tratamiento (*Treatment*): _receta, pastilla, operación, antibiótico, aspirina_

Workbook

4 **En el consultorio** Complete the sentences with the correct words.

1. La señora Gandía va a tener un hijo en septiembre. Está _____embarazada_____.

2. Manuel tiene la temperatura muy alta. Tiene _____fiebre_____.

3. A Rosita le recetaron un antibiótico y le van a poner una _____inyección_____.

4. A Pedro le cayó una mesa en el pie. El pie le _____duele_____ mucho.

5. Durante la primavera, mi tía estornuda mucho y está muy _____congestionada_____.

6. Tienes que llevar la _____receta_____ a la farmacia para que te vendan (*in order for them to sell you*) la medicina.

7. Le tomaron una _____radiografía_____ de la pierna para ver si se le rompió.

8. Los _____síntomas_____ de un resfriado son los estornudos y la tos.

5 **Doctora y paciente** Choose the logical sentences to complete the conversation between Doctora Pérez and José Luis.

DOCTORA ¿Qué síntomas tiene?

JOSÉ LUIS (1) _____
(a.) Tengo tos y me duele la cabeza.
b. Soy muy saludable.
c. Me recetaron un antibiótico.

DOCTORA (2) _____
a. ¿Cuándo fue el accidente?
(b.) ¿Le dio fiebre ayer?
c. ¿Dónde está la sala de emergencia?

JOSÉ LUIS (3) _____
a. Fue a la farmacia.
b. Me torcí el tobillo.
(c.) Sí, mi esposa me tomó la temperatura.

DOCTORA (4) _____
(a.) ¿Está muy congestionado?
b. ¿Está embarazada?
c. ¿Le duele el dedo del pie?

JOSÉ LUIS (5) _____
a. Sí, me hicieron una operación.
b. Sí, estoy mareado.
(c.) Sí, y también me duele la garganta.

DOCTORA (6) _____
a. Tiene que ir al consultorio.
(b.) Es una infección de garganta.
c. La farmacia está muy cerca.

JOSÉ LUIS (7) _____
(a.) ¿Tengo que tomar un antibiótico?
b. ¿Debo ir al dentista?
c. ¿Qué indican las radiografías?

DOCTORA (8) _____
a. Sí, es usted una persona saludable.
b. Sí, se lastimó el pie.
(c.) Sí, ahora se lo voy a recetar.

estructura

4.1 The imperfect tense

1 **¿Cómo eran las cosas?** Complete the sentences with the imperfect forms of the verbs in parentheses.

1. Antes, la familia Álvarez _____cenaba_____ (cenar) a las ocho de la noche.
2. De niña, yo _____cantaba_____ (cantar) en el Coro de Niños de San Juan.
3. Cuando vivían en la costa, ustedes _____nadaban_____ (nadar) por las mañanas.
4. Mis hermanas y yo _____jugábamos_____ (jugar) en un equipo de béisbol.
5. La novia de Raúl _____tenía_____ (tener) el pelo rubio en ese tiempo.
6. Antes de tener la computadora, (tú) _____escribías_____ (escribir) a mano (*by hand*).
7. (nosotros) _____Creíamos_____ (creer) que el concierto era el miércoles.
8. Mientras ellos lo _____buscaban_____ (buscar) en su casa, él se fue a la universidad.

2 **Oraciones imperfectas** Create sentences with the elements provided and the imperfect tense.

1. mi abuela / ser / muy trabajadora y amable

   Mi abuela era muy trabajadora y amable.

2. tú / ir / al teatro / cuando vivías en Nueva York

   Tú ibas al teatro cuando vivías en Nueva York.

3. ayer / haber / muchísimos pacientes en el consultorio

   Ayer había muchísimos pacientes en el consultorio.

4. (nosotros) / ver / tu casa desde allí

   Veíamos tu casa desde allí.

5. ser / las cinco de la tarde / cuando llegamos a San José

   Eran las cinco de la tarde cuando llegamos a San José.

6. ella / estar / muy nerviosa durante la operación

   Ella estaba muy nerviosa durante la operación.

3 **No, pero antes...** Your nosy friend Cristina is asking you many questions. Answer her questions negatively, using the imperfect tense.

> **modelo**
> ¿Juega Daniel al fútbol?
> **No, pero antes jugaba.**

1. ¿Hablas por teléfono? No, pero antes hablaba.
2. ¿Fue a la playa Susana? No, pero antes iba.
3. ¿Come carne Benito? No, pero antes (la) comía.
4. ¿Te trajo muchos regalos tu novio? No, pero antes me traía.
5. ¿Conduce tu mamá? No, pero antes conducía.

4 **¿Qué hacían?** Write sentences that describe what the people in the drawings were doing yesterday at three o'clock in the afternoon. Use the subjects provided and the imperfect tense.

Answers may vary. Suggested answers:

1. Tú

Tú escribías cartas/postales.

2. Rolando

Rolando buceaba en el mar.

3. Pablo y Elena

Pablo y Elena jugaban a las

cartas.

4. Lilia y yo

Lilia y yo tomábamos el sol.

5 **Antes y ahora** Javier is thinking about his childhood—how things were then and how they are now. Write two sentences comparing what Javier used to do and what he does now.

> **modelo**
>
> vivir en casa / vivir en la residencia estudiantil
> **Antes vivía en casa.**
> **Ahora vivo en la residencia estudiantil.**

1. jugar al fútbol con mis primos / jugar en el equipo de la universidad
   Antes jugaba al fútbol con mis primos. Ahora juego en el equipo de la universidad.

2. escribir las cartas a mano / escribir el correo electrónico con la computadora
   Antes escribía las cartas a mano. Ahora escribo el correo electrónico con la computadora.

3. ser gordito (*chubby*) / ser delgado
   Antes era gordito. Ahora soy delgado.

4. tener a mi familia cerca / tener a mi familia lejos
   Antes tenía a mi familia cerca. Ahora tengo a mi familia lejos.

5. estudiar en mi habitación / estudiar en la biblioteca
   Antes estudiaba en mi habitación. Ahora estudio en la biblioteca.

6. conocer a personas de mi ciudad / conocer a personas de todo el (*the whole*) país
   Antes conocía a personas de mi ciudad. Ahora conozco a personas de todo el país.

4.2 The preterite and the imperfect

1   **Los accidentes** Complete the sentences correctly with imperfect or preterite forms of the verbs in parentheses.

1. Claudia _____celebraba_____ (celebrar) su cumpleaños cuando se torció el tobillo.

2. Ramiro tenía fiebre cuando _____llegó_____ (llegar) a la clínica.

3. Mientras el doctor _____miraba_____ (mirar) la radiografía, yo llamé por teléfono a mi novia.

4. (yo) _____Estaba_____ (estar) mirando la televisión cuando mi mamá se lastimó la mano con la puerta.

5. Cuando Sandra llegó a la universidad, _____tenía_____ (tener) un dolor de cabeza terrible.

6. ¿De niño (tú) _____te enfermabas_____ (enfermarse) con frecuencia?

7. El verano pasado, Luis y Olivia _____sufrieron_____ (sufrir) una enfermedad exótica.

8. Anoche, mi primo y yo _____perdimos_____ (perder) la receta de mi tía.

2   **Antes y ayer** Complete each pair of sentences by using the imperfect and preterite forms of the verbs in parentheses.

(bailar)

1. Cuando era pequeña, Sara _____bailaba_____ ballet todos los lunes y miércoles.

2. Ayer Sara _____bailó_____ ballet en el recital de la universidad.

(escribir)

3. La semana pasada, (yo) le _____escribí_____ un mensaje electrónico a mi papá.

4. Antes (yo) _____escribía_____ las cartas a mano o con una máquina de escribir (*typewriter*).

(ser)

5. El novio de María _____era_____ delgado y deportista.

6. El viaje de novios _____fue_____ una experiencia inolvidable (*unforgettable*).

(haber)

7. _____Hubo_____ una fiesta en casa de Maritere el viernes pasado.

8. Cuando llegamos a la fiesta, _____había_____ mucha gente.

(ver)

9. El lunes (yo) _____vi_____ a mi prima Lisa en el centro comercial.

10. De niña, yo _____veía_____ a Lisa todos los días.

3 **¿Qué pasaba?** Look at the drawings, then complete the sentences, using the preterite or imperfect.

1. Cuando llegué a casa anoche, las

niñas _____dormían_____

_____

2. Cuando empezó a llover, Sara

_____cerró la ventana_____

_____

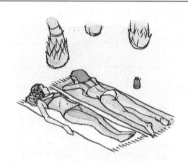

3. Antes de irse de vacaciones, la

señora García ___compró una maleta___

_____

4. Cada verano, las chicas

_____tomaban el sol_____

_____

4 **El pasado** Decide whether the verbs in parentheses should be in the preterite or the imperfect. Then rewrite the sentences.

1. Ayer Clara (ir) a casa de sus primos, (saludar) a su tía y (comer) con ellos.

   Ayer Clara fue a casa de sus primos, saludó a su tía y comió con ellos.

2. Cuando Manuel (vivir) en San José, (conducir) muchos kilómetros todos los días.

   Cuando Manuel vivía en San José, conducía muchos kilómetros todos los días.

3. Mientras Carlos (leer) las traducciones (*translations*), Blanca (traducir) otros textos.

   Mientras Carlos leía las traducciones, Blanca traducía otros textos.

4. El doctor (terminar) el examen médico y me (recetar) un antibiótico.

   El doctor terminó el examen médico y me recetó un antibiótico.

5. La niña (tener) ocho años y (ser) inteligente y alegre.

   La niña tenía ocho años y era inteligente y alegre.

6. Rafael (cerrar) todos los programas, (apagar) la computadora y (irse).

   Rafael cerró todos los programas, apagó la computadora y se fue.

5 **¡Qué diferencia!** Complete this paragraph with the preterite or the imperfect of the verbs in parentheses.

La semana pasada (yo) (1) _____llegué_____ (llegar) a la universidad y me di cuenta (*realized*) de que este año iba a ser muy diferente a los anteriores. Todos los años Laura y yo (2) _____vivíamos_____ (vivir) con Regina, pero la semana pasada (nosotras) (3) _____conocimos_____ (conocer) a nuestra nueva compañera de cuarto, Gisela. Antes Laura, Regina y yo (4) _____teníamos_____ (tener) un apartamento muy pequeño, pero al llegar la semana pasada, (nosotras) (5) _____vimos_____ (ver) el apartamento nuevo: es enorme y tiene mucha luz. Antes de vivir con Gisela, Laura y yo no (6) _____podíamos_____ (poder) leer el correo electrónico desde la casa, pero ayer Gisela (7) _____conectó_____ (conectar) su computadora a Internet y todas (8) _____miramos_____ (mirar) nuestros mensajes. Antes (nosotras) siempre (9) _____caminábamos_____ (caminar) hasta la biblioteca para ver el correo, pero anoche Gisela nos (10) _____dijo_____ (decir) que podemos compartir su computadora. ¡Qué diferencia!

6 **¿Dónde estabas?** Write questions and answers with the words provided. Ask where these people were when something happened.

> **modelo**
> Jimena ⟶ Marissa / salir a bailar // cuarto / dormir la siesta
> ¿Dónde estaba Jimena cuando Marissa salió a bailar?
> Jimena estaba en el cuarto. Dormía la siesta.

1. Miguel ⟶ (yo) / llamar por teléfono // cocina / lavar los platos
   ¿Dónde estaba Miguel cuando llamé por teléfono? Miguel estaba en la cocina. Lavaba los platos.

2. (tú) ⟶ Juan Carlos y yo / ir al cine // casa / leer una revista
   ¿Dónde estabas cuando Juan Carlos y yo fuimos al cine? Estaba en casa. Leía una revista.

3. tu hermano ⟶ empezar a llover // calle / pasear en bicicleta
   ¿Dónde estaba tu hermano cuando empezó a llover? Mi hermano estaba en la calle. Paseaba en bicicleta.

4. ustedes ⟶ Felipe / venir a casa // estadio / jugar al fútbol
   ¿Dónde estaban ustedes cuando Felipe vino a casa? Estábamos en el estadio. Jugábamos al fútbol.

5. Jimena y Felipe ⟶ (tú) / saludarlos // supermercado / hacer la compra
   ¿Dónde estaban Jimena y Felipe cuando los saludaste? Estaban en el supermercado. Hacían la compra.

7 **El diario de Laura** Laura has just found a page from her old diary. Rewrite the page in the past tense, using the preterite and imperfect forms of the verbs as appropriate.

Querido diario:

Estoy pasando el verano en Alajuela, y es un lugar muy divertido. Salgo con mis amigas todas las noches hasta tarde. Bailamos con nuestros amigos y nos divertimos mucho. Durante la semana trabajo: doy clases de inglés. Los estudiantes son alegres y se interesan mucho por aprender. El día de mi cumpleaños conocí a un chico muy simpático que se llama Francisco. Me llamó al día siguiente (*next*) y nos vemos todos los días. Me siento enamorada de él.

Estaba pasando el verano en Alajuela, y era un lugar muy divertido. Salía con mis amigas todas las noches hasta

tarde. Bailaba con nuestros amigos y nos divertíamos mucho. Durante la semana, trabajaba: daba clases de inglés. Los

estudiantes eran alegres y se interesaban mucho por aprender. El día de mi cumpleaños conocí a un chico muy simpático

que se llamaba Francisco. Me llamó al día siguiente y nos veíamos todos los días. Me sentía enamorada de él.

_____

_____

_____

_____

_____

_____

8 **Un día en la playa** Laura is still reading her old diary. Rewrite this paragraph, using the preterite or imperfect forms of the verbs in parentheses as appropriate.

Querido diario:

Ayer mi hermana y yo (ir) a la playa. Cuando llegamos, (ser) un día despejado con mucho sol, y nosotras (estar) muy contentas. A las doce (comer) unos sándwiches de almuerzo. Los sándwiches (ser) de jamón y queso. Luego (descansar) y entonces (nadar) en el mar. Mientras (nadar), (ver) a las personas que (practicar) el esquí acuático. (Parecer) muy divertido, así que (decidir) probarlo. Mi hermana (ir) primero, mientras yo la (mirar). Luego (ser) mi turno. Las dos (divertirse) mucho esa tarde.

Ayer mi hermana y yo fuimos a la playa. Cuando llegamos, era un día despejado con mucho sol, y nosotras estábamos

muy contentas. A las doce comimos unos sándwiches de almuerzo. Los sándwiches eran de jamón y queso. Luego

descansamos y entonces nadamos en el mar. Mientras nadábamos, vimos a las personas que practicaban el esquí

acuático. Parecía muy divertido, así que decidimos probarlo. Mi hermana fue primero, mientras yo la miraba. Luego fue mi

turno. Las dos nos divertimos mucho esa tarde.

_____

_____

_____

4.3 Constructions with **se**

1 **¿Qué se hace?** Complete the sentences with verbs from the word bank. Use impersonal constructions with **se** in the present tense.

caer	hablar	recetar	vender
dañar	poder	servir	vivir

1. En Costa Rica ____se habla____ español.

2. En las librerías ____se venden____ libros y revistas.

3. En los restaurantes ____se sirve____ comida.

4. En los consultorios ____se recetan____ medicinas.

5. En el campo ____se vive____ muy bien.

6. En el mar ____se puede____ nadar y pescar.

2 **Los anuncios** Write advertisements or signs for the situations described. Use impersonal constructions with **se**.

1. "Está prohibido fumar."

> Se prohíbe/No se debe fumar.

2. "Vendemos periódicos."

> Se venden periódicos.

3. "Hablamos español."

> Se habla español.

4. "Necesitamos enfermeras."

> Se necesitan enfermeras.

5. "No debes nadar."

> No se debe nadar./Se prohíbe nadar.

6. "Estamos buscando un auto usado."

> Se busca un auto usado.

3 **¿Qué les pasó?** Complete the sentences with the correct indirect object pronouns.

1. Se ____le____ perdieron las maletas a Roberto.

2. A mis hermanas se ____les____ cayó la mesa.

3. A ti se ____te____ olvidó venir a buscarme ayer.

4. A mí se ____me____ quedó la ropa nueva en mi casa.

5. A las tías de Ana se ____les____ rompieron los vasos.

6. A Isabel y a mí se ____nos____ dañó el auto.

Workbook

4 **Los accidentes** Your classmates are very unlucky. Rewrite what happened to them, using the correct form of the verb in parentheses.

1. A Marina se le (cayó, cayeron) la bolsa.
   A Marina se le cayó la bolsa.

2. A ti se te (olvidó, olvidaron) comprarme la medicina.
   A ti se te olvidó comprarme la medicina.

3. A nosotros se nos (quedó, quedaron) los libros en el auto.
   A nosotros se nos quedaron los libros en el auto.

4. A Ramón y a Pedro se les (dañó, dañaron) el proyecto.
   A Ramón y a Pedro se les dañó el proyecto.

5 **Mala suerte** You and your friends are trying to go on vacation, but everything is going wrong. Use the elements provided, the preterite tense, and constructions with **se** to write sentences.

> **modelo**
> (a Raquel) / olvidar / traer su pasaporte
> *Se le olvidó traer su pasaporte.*

1. (a nosotros) / perder / las llaves del auto
   Se nos perdieron las llaves del auto.

2. (a ustedes) / olvidar / ponerse las inyecciones
   Se les olvidó ponerse las inyecciones.

3. (a ti) / caer / los papeles del médico
   Se te cayeron los papeles del médico.

4. (a Marcos) / romper / la pierna cuando esquiaba
   Se le rompió la pierna cuando esquiaba.

5. (a mí) / dañar / la cámara durante el viaje
   Se me dañó la cámara durante el viaje.

6 **¿Qué pasó?** As the vacation goes on, you and your friends have more bad luck. Answer the questions, using the phrases in parentheses and the preterite tense.

> **modelo**
> ¿Qué le pasó a Roberto? (quedar la cámara nueva en casa)
> *Se le quedó la cámara nueva en casa.*

1. ¿Qué les pasó a Pilar y a Luis? (dañar el coche)
   Se les dañó el coche.

2. ¿Qué les pasó a los padres de Sara? (romper la botella de vino)
   Se les rompió la botella de vino.

3. ¿Qué te pasó a ti? (perder las llaves del hotel)
   Se me perdieron las llaves del hotel.

4. ¿Qué les pasó a ustedes? (quedar las toallas en la playa)
   Se nos quedaron las toallas en la playa.

5. ¿Qué le pasó a Hugo? (olvidar estudiar para el examen en el avión)
   Se le olvidó estudiar para el examen en el avión.

4.4 Adverbs

1

En mi ciudad Complete the sentences by changing the adjectives in the first sentences into adverbs in the second.

1. Los conductores son lentos. Conducen _____lentamente_____.

2. Esa doctora es amable. Siempre nos saluda _____amablemente_____.

3. Los autobuses de mi ciudad son frecuentes. Pasan por la parada _____frecuentemente_____.

4. Rosa y Julia son chicas muy alegres. Les encanta bailar y cantar _____alegremente_____.

5. Mario y tú hablan un español perfecto. Hablan español _____perfectamente_____.

6. Los pacientes visitan al doctor de manera constante. Lo visitan _____constantemente_____.

7. Llegar tarde es normal para David. Llega tarde _____normalmente_____.

8. Me gusta trabajar de manera independiente. Trabajo _____independientemente_____.

2

Completar Complete the sentences with adverbs and adverbial expressions from the word bank. Use each term once.

a menudo	así	por lo menos
a tiempo	bastante	pronto
apenas	casi	

1. Tito no es un niño muy sano. Se enferma _____a menudo_____.

2. El doctor Garrido es muy puntual. Siempre llega al consultorio _____a tiempo_____.

3. Mi madre visita al doctor con frecuencia. Se chequea _____por lo menos_____ una vez cada año.

4. Fui al doctor el año pasado. Tengo que volver _____pronto_____.

5. Llegué tarde al autobús; _____así_____ tengo que ir al centro caminando.

6. El examen fue _____bastante_____ difícil.

3

Traducir Complete the sentences with the adverbs or adverbial phrases that correspond to the words in parentheses.

1. Llegaron temprano al concierto; _____así_____ (*so*), consiguieron asientos muy buenos.

2. El accidente fue _____bastante_____ (*rather*) grave, pero al conductor no se le rompió ningún hueso.

3. Irene y Vicente van a comer _____menos_____ (*less*) porque quieren estar más delgados.

4. Silvia y David _____casi_____ (*almost*) se cayeron de la motocicleta cerca de su casa.

5. Para aprobar (*pass*) el examen, tienes que contestar _____por lo menos_____ (*at least*) el 75 por ciento de las preguntas.

6. Mi mamá _____a veces_____ (*sometimes*) se tuerce el tobillo cuando camina mucho.

4

Háblame de ti Answer the questions using the adverbs and adverbial phrases that you learned in this lesson. Do not repeat the adverb or adverbial phrase of the question. Then, say how long ago you last did each activity.   Answers will vary.

> **modelo**
>
> ¿Vas a la playa siempre?
> No, voy a la playa a veces. Hace cuatro meses que no voy a la playa.

1. ¿Tú y tus amigos van al cine con frecuencia?

2. ¿Comes comida china?

3. ¿Llegas tarde a tu clase de español?

4. ¿Te enfermas con frecuencia?

5. ¿Comes carne?

Síntesis

Think of a summer in which you did a lot of different things on vacation or at home. State exceptional situations or activities that you did just once. Then state the activities that you used to do during that summer; mention which of those things you still do in the present. How often did you do those activities then? How often do you do them now? How long ago did you do some of those things? Create a "photo album" of that summer, using actual photographs if you have them, or drawings that you make. Use your writing about the summer as captions for the photo album.

Answers will vary.

panorama

Costa Rica

1 **El mapa de Costa Rica** Label the map of Costa Rica.

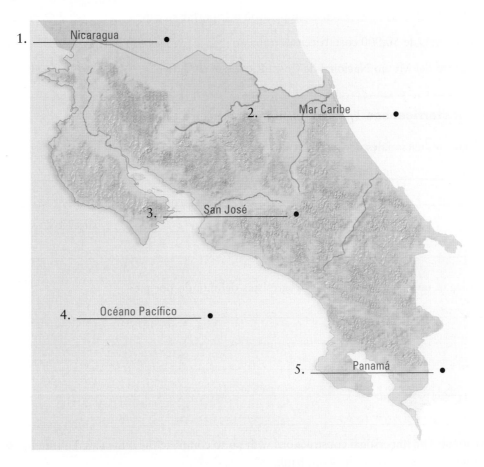

1. _____ Nicaragua _____

2. _____ Mar Caribe _____

3. _____ San José _____

4. _____ Océano Pacífico _____

5. _____ Panamá _____

2 **¿Cierto o falso?** Indicate whether the statements are **cierto** or **falso**. Correct the false statements.

1. Los parques nacionales costarricenses se establecieron para el turismo.

   Falso. Los parques nacionales costarricenses se establecieron para la protección de la biodiversidad.

2. Costa Rica fue el primer país centroamericano en desarrollar la industria del café.

   Cierto.

3. El café representa más del 50% de las exportaciones anuales de Costa Rica.

   Falso. El café representa cerca del 15% de las exportaciones anuales de Costa Rica.

4. Costa Rica tiene un nivel de alfabetización del 96%.

   Cierto.

5. El ejército de Costa Rica es uno de los más grandes y preparados de Latinoamérica.

   Falso. Costa Rica eliminó el ejército en 1948.

6. En Costa Rica se eliminó la educación gratuita para los costarricenses.

   Falso. En 1948 Costa Rica hizo obligatoria y gratuita la educación para todos los costarricenses.

3 **Costa Rica** Complete the sentences with the correct words.

1. Costa Rica es el país de Centroamérica con la población más _____ homogénea _____.

2. La moneda que se usa en Costa Rica es _____ el colón costarricense _____.

3. Costa Rica es el único país latinoamericano que no tiene _____ ejército _____.

4. En el siglo XIX los costarricenses empezaron a exportar su café a _____ Inglaterra _____.

5. Hoy día más de 50.000 costarricenses trabajan _____ cultivando el/en el cultivo del _____ café.

6. El edificio del Museo Nacional de Costa Rica es el antiguo _____ cuartel del ejército _____.

4 **Datos costarricenses** Fill in the blanks with the correct information.

En los parques nacionales de Costa Rica los ecoturistas pueden ver: Order of answers will vary.

1. _____ cataratas _____

2. _____ montañas _____

3. _____ plantas exóticas _____

4. _____ quetzales _____

5. _____ monos _____

6. _____ jaguares _____

7. _____ armadillos _____

8. _____ mariposas _____

Costa Rica es uno de los países más progresistas del mundo porque:

9. Tiene un nivel de alfabetización del 96%.

10. En 1870 eliminó la pena de muerte.

11. En 1948 eliminó el ejército.

12. En 1948 hizo obligatoria y gratuita la educación para todos los costarricenses.

5 **Completar** Use impersonal constructions with **se** to complete the sentences. Be sure to use the correct tense of the verbs in the word bank.

> **modelo**
>
> En Costa Rica ahora *se pone* más dinero en la educación y las artes.

comprar	establecer	eliminar	poder
empezar	invertir	ofrecer	proveer

1. En Costa Rica _____ se compra _____ y se vende en colones.

2. El sistema de parques nacionales _____ se estableció _____ para la protección de los ecosistemas.

3. En los parques, los animales _____ se pueden _____ ver en su hábitat natural.

4. En el siglo XIX _____ se empezó _____ a exportar el café costarricense.

5. En Costa Rica _____ se ofrece _____ educación gratuita a todos los ciudadanos.

6. En 1870 _____ se eliminó _____ la pena de muerte en Costa Rica.

¡Qué dolor!

Lección 4
Fotonovela

Antes de ver el video

1 Una cita Look at the image. Where do you think Jimena is? What is happening? Answers will vary.

_____

_____

_____

_____

_____

_____

_____

_____

Mientras ves el video

2 ¿Quién? Watch **¡Qué dolor!** and use check marks to show who said what.

Expresión	Jimena	Elena	Dr. Meléndez
1. ¿Cuáles son tus síntomas?			✔
2. Tengo un dolor de cabeza terrible.		✔	
3. Empecé a toser esta mañana.	✔		
4. Te voy a mandar algo para la garganta.			✔
5. ¡Es tan sólo un resfriado!	✔		

3 ¿Qué ves? Place a check mark beside the things you see in the video.

✔ 1. un letrero (*sign*) que dice: "Se prohíbe fumar"   ___ 6. una sala de emergencias

✔ 2. un termómetro   ✔ 7. una receta

✔ 3. pastillas para el resfriado   ___ 8. un antibiótico

✔ 4. una radiografía   ✔ 9. un doctor

✔ 5. un consultorio   ✔ 10. una bolsa de la farmacia

4 Completar Write the name of the person who said each sentence and fill in the missing words.

don Diego   1. A mi hermanito le dolía la ___garganta___ con frecuencia.

Dr. Meléndez   2. ¿Cuánto tiempo hace que tienes estos ___síntomas___?

Jimena   3. Tengo ___tos___ y estoy congestionada.

Elena   4. Nunca tenía resfriados, pero me ___rompí___ el brazo dos veces.

Sra. Díaz   5. No tienes ___fiebre___. ¿Te pusiste un suéter anoche?

Después de ver el video

5 **Seleccionar** Write the letter of the word or words that match each sentence.

1. ___ hizo cita con el Dr. Meléndez para llevar a Jimena.

   a. Don Diego   (b.) La señora Díaz   c. Elena   d. Miguel

2. Jimena puede ir inmediatamente a la ___ por los medicamentos.

   a. sala de emergencias   b. clínica   c. dentista   (d.) farmacia

3. Elena toma ___ para ___.

   (a.) aspirina; el dolor de cabeza   b. antibióticos; la gripe

   c. pastillas; el resfriado   d. medicamentos; el dolor de estómago

4. Elena dice que el té de jengibre es bueno para el dolor de ___.

   (a.) estómago   b. garganta   c. cabeza   d. brazos

5. La señora Díaz dice que a Jimena le dio ___ porque olvidó ponerse un suéter.

   a. fiebre   (b.) un resfriado   c. dolor de estómago   d. gripe

6. Cuando era niña, Jimena casi no ___.

   a. tomaba antibióticos   b. tomaba aspirinas   c. se rompía huesos   (d.) se enfermaba

6 **Preguntas** Answer the following questions in Spanish.

1. ¿Tiene fiebre Jimena? ¿Está mareada?

   No, Jimena no tiene fiebre y no está mareada.

2. ¿Cuánto tiempo hace que a Jimena le duele la garganta? ¿Cuándo empezó a toser?

   Hace dos días que a Jimena le duele la garganta y empezó a toser esta mañana.

3. Según (*According to*) don Diego, ¿qué es lo mejor para los dolores de cabeza?

   Según don Diego, lo mejor para los dolores de cabeza es un vaso con/de agua y una aspirina.

4. ¿Cuantas veces se rompió el brazo Elena?

   Elena se rompió el brazo dos veces.

5. ¿Qué le daban al hermanito de don Diego cuando le dolía la garganta?

   Le daban miel con canela cuando le dolía la garganta.

7 **Preguntas personales** Answer these questions in Spanish. Answers will vary.

1. ¿Te gusta ir al/a la médico/a? ¿Por qué? _____

   _____

2. ¿Tienes muchas alergias? ¿Eres alérgico/a a algún medicamento? _____

   _____

3. ¿Cuándo es importante ir a la sala de emergencias? _____

   _____

4. ¿Qué haces cuando tienes fiebre y te duele la garganta? _____

   _____

Panorama: Costa Rica

Lección 4
Panorama cultural

Antes de ver el video

1 **Más vocabulario** Look over these useful words and expressions before you watch the video.

Vocabulario útil		
bosque *forest*	guía certificado *certified guide*	riqueza *wealth*
conservar *to preserve*	nuboso *cloudy*	tiendas de campaña *camping tents*
cubierto *covered*	permitir *to allow*	tocar *to touch*
entrar *to enter*	regla *rule*	tortugas marinas *sea turtles*

2 **Foto** Describe the video still. Write at least three sentences in Spanish. Answers will vary.

_____

_____

_____

_____

_____

_____

_____

3 **Categorías** Categorize the words listed in the word bank.

bosque	guía	pedir	sacar
diferentes	hermosos	permite	Tortuguero
entrar	Monteverde	playa	turistas
exóticas	nuboso	pueblos	visitantes
frágil			

Lugares	Personas	Verbos	Adjetivos
bosque	guía	entrar	diferentes
Monteverde	turistas	pedir	exóticas
playa	visitantes	permite	frágil
pueblos		sacar	hermosos
Tortuguero			nuboso

Mientras ves el video

4 **Marcar** While watching the video, check off the rules that have been put in place to protect nature.

✔ 1. En el parque Monteverde no pueden entrar más de 150 personas al mismo tiempo.

_____ 2. Los turistas tienen que dormir en tiendas de campaña.

_____ 3. Los turistas no pueden visitar Tortuguero en febrero.

✔ 4. Después de las 6 p.m. no se permite ir a la playa sin un guía certificado.

✔ 5. Los turistas no pueden tocar las tortugas.

✔ 6. En Tortuguero está prohibido tomar fotografías.

Después de ver el video

5 **Completar** Complete the sentences with words from the word bank.

| acampan | entrar | pasan | prohíbe |
| conservan | estudiar | prefieren | transportan |

1. En Monteverde se _____conservan_____ más de dos mil especies diferentes de animales.

2. En este parque no pueden _____entrar_____ más de 150 personas al mismo tiempo.

3. Algunos turistas _____acampan_____ en Monteverde.

4. Otros _____prefieren_____ ir a los hoteles de los pueblos que están cerca de Monteverde.

5. Se _____prohíbe_____ sacar fotografías.

6 **Preferencias** Write a brief paragraph in Spanish where you describe which place(s) you would like to visit in Costa Rica and why. Answers will vary.

_____
_____
_____
_____
_____
_____
_____
_____
_____

La salud

Antes de ver el video

1 **Más vocabulario** Look over these useful words before you watch the video.

Vocabulario útil		
atender *to treat; to see (in a hospital)*	cumplir (una función) *to fulfill (a function/role)*	gratuito *free (of charge)*
atendido/a *treated*	esperar *to wait*	herido/a *injured*
brindar *to offer*	estar de guardia *to be on call*	el reportaje *story*
chocar *to crash*	golpeado/a *bruised*	se atienden pacientes *patients are treated*

2 **¡En español!** Look at the video still. Imagine what Silvina will say about hospitals in Argentina, and write a two- or three-sentence introduction to this episode. Answers will vary.

Silvina Márquez, Argentina

¡Hola a todos! Hoy estamos en... _____

_____

_____

_____

_____

_____

Mientras ves el video

3 **Problemas de salud** Match these statements to their corresponding video stills.

1. _b_

2. _e_

3. _d_

a. Tengo dolor de cabeza y me golpeé la cabeza.

b. Mi abuela estaba con un poco de tos.

c. Estoy congestionada.

d. Me chocó una bici.

e. Me salió una alergia.

4 **Completar** Watch Silvina interview a patient, and complete this conversation.

SILVINA ¿Y a vos qué te pasa? ¿Por qué estás aquí en la (1) _____guardia_____ ?

PACIENTE Porque me salió una (2) _____alergia_____ en la (3) _____espalda_____ hace dos días y quería saber qué tenía. ¿Y a vos qué te pasó?

SILVINA Yo tuve un accidente. Me (4) _____chocó_____ una bici en el centro y mirá cómo quedé…

PACIENTE … toda lastimada (*hurt*)…

SILVINA Sí, y aquí también, aquí también… Estoy toda (5) _____golpeada_____ .

Después de ver el video

5 **Ordenar** Put Silvina's actions in the correct order.

___3___ a. Le dio sus datos personales a la enfermera.

___2___ b. Llegó a la guardia del hospital.

___5___ c. Fue atendida por el doctor.

___1___ d. Tuvo un accidente con una bicicleta.

___4___ e. Entrevistó a pacientes.

6 **El sistema de salud en Argentina** Identify the main characteristics of the health system in Argentina. Use these guiding questions. Answers will vary.

1. ¿Cómo es el sistema de salud: público, privado o mixto?

2. ¿Hay que pagar en los hospitales públicos?

3. ¿Qué son las guardias?

4. ¿Hay que esperar mucho para ser atendido/a?

5. ¿Cómo es la carrera de medicina?

6. ¿Qué similitudes y diferencias existen entre el sistema de salud en Argentina y el de tu país?

7 **¿Un pequeño accidente?** You were exploring the city of Buenos Aires when an aggressive pedestrian knocked you to the ground. You arrived in great pain at the **guardia** only to find the wait very long. Write your conversation with a nurse in which you explain your symptoms to convince him/her that this is not a minor accident and you should receive immediate care. Answers will vary.

_____

_____

_____

_____

_____

_____

_____

_____

_____

contextos

1 **Identificar** You will hear a series of words. Write each one in the appropriate category.

modelo

You hear: el hospital

You write: **el hospital** under **Lugares**.

Lugares	Medicinas	Condiciones y síntomas médicos
el hospital	la aspirina	la tos
la sala de emergencia	la pastilla	el resfriado
la farmacia	el antibiótico	la gripe
el consultorio		la fiebre

2 **Describir** For each drawing, you will hear two statements. Choose the one that corresponds to the drawing.

1. a.   b.

2. a.   b.

3. a. b.

4. a.   b.

c (before a consonant) and q

In Lesson 2, you learned that, in Spanish, the letter **c** before the vowels **a**, **o**, and **u** is pronounced like the *c* in the English word *car*. When the letter **c** appears before any consonant except **h**, it is also pronounced like the *c* in *car*.

clínica	bici**cl**eta	**cr**ema	do**ct**ora	o**ct**ubre

In Spanish, the letter **q** is always followed by an **u**, which is silent. The combination **qu** is pronounced like the *k* sound in the English word *kitten*. Remember that the sounds **kwa**, **kwe**, **kwi**, **kwo**, and **koo** are always spelled with the combination **cu** in Spanish, never with **qu**.

querer	par**que**	**qu**eso	**qu**ímica	mante**qu**illa

1 **Práctica** Repeat each word after the speaker, focusing on the **c** and **q** sounds.

1. quince
2. querer
3. pequeño
4. equipo

5. conductor
6. escribir
7. contacto
8. increíble

9. aquí
10. ciclismo
11. electrónico
12. quitarse

2 **Oraciones** When you hear the number, read the corresponding sentence aloud. Then listen to the speaker and repeat the sentence.

1. El doctor Cruz quiso sacarle un diente.
2. Clara siempre se maquilla antes de salir de casa.
3. ¿Quién perdió su equipaje?
4. Pienso comprar aquella camisa porque me queda bien.
5. La chaqueta cuesta quinientos cuarenta dólares, ¿no?
6. Esa cliente quiere pagar con tarjeta de crédito.

3 **Refranes** Repeat each saying after the speaker to practice the **c** and the **q** sounds.

1. Ver es creer.[1]
2. Quien mal anda, mal acaba.[2]

4 **Dictado** You will hear five sentences. Each will be said twice. Listen carefully and write what you hear.

1. Esta mañana Cristina se despertó enferma.

2. Le duele todo el cuerpo y no puede levantarse de la cama.

3. Cree que es la gripe y va a tener que llamar a la clínica de la universidad.

4. Cristina no quiere perder otro día de clase, pero no puede ir porque está muy mareada.

5. Su compañera de cuarto va a escribirle un mensaje electrónico a la profesora Crespo porque hoy tienen un examen en su clase.

[1] *Seeing is believing.*
[2] *He who lives badly, ends badly.*

estructura

4.1 The imperfect tense

1 **Identificar** Listen to each sentence and circle the verb tense you hear.

1. a. present   b. preterite   (c.) imperfect
2. a. present   (b.) preterite   c. imperfect
3. a. present   b. preterite   (c.) imperfect
4. (a.) present   b. preterite   c. imperfect
5. a. present   (b.) preterite   c. imperfect

6. a. present   b. preterite   (c.) imperfect
7. a. present   (b.) preterite   c. imperfect
8. a. present   b. preterite   (c.) imperfect
9. (a.) present   b. preterite   c. imperfect
10. a. present   (b.) preterite   c. imperfect

2 **Cambiar** Form a new sentence using the cue you hear. Repeat the correct answer after the speaker. (*6 items*)

> **modelo**
>
> Iban a casa. (Eva)
> *Eva iba a casa.*

3 **Preguntas** A reporter is writing an article about funny things people used to do when they were children. Answer her questions, using the cues in your lab manual. Then repeat the correct response after the speaker.

> **modelo**
>
> *You hear:* ¿Qué hacía Miguel de niño?
> *You see:* ponerse pajitas (*straws*) en la nariz
> *You say:* Miguel se ponía pajitas en la nariz.

1. quitarse los zapatos en el restaurante
2. vestirnos con la ropa de mamá
3. sólo querer comer dulces

4. jugar con un amigo invisible
5. usar las botas de su papá
6. comer con las manos

4 **Completar** Listen to this description of Ángela's medical problem and write the missing words in your lab manual.

(1) _____Sufría_____ Ángela porque (2) _____estornudaba_____ día y noche.

(3) _____Pensaba_____ que (4) _____tenía_____ un resfriado, pero se

(5) _____sentía_____ bastante saludable. Se (6) _____iba_____ de la biblioteca después

de poco tiempo porque les (7) _____molestaba_____ a los otros estudiantes. Sus amigas, Laura y

Petra, siempre le (8) _____decían_____ que (9) _____tenía_____ alguna alergia. Por fin,

decidió hacerse un examen médico. La doctora le dijo que ella (10) _____era_____

alérgica y que (11) _____había_____ muchas medicinas para las alergias. Finalmente, le

recetó unas pastillas. Al día siguiente (*following*), Ángela se (12) _____sentía_____ mejor

porque (13) _____sabía_____ cuál era el problema y ella dejó de estornudar después de

tomar las pastillas.

4.2 The preterite and the imperfect

1 **Identificar** Listen to each statement and identify the verbs in the preterite and the imperfect. Write them in the appropriate column.

> **modelo**
>
> *You hear:* Cuando llegó la ambulancia, el esposo estaba mareado.
> *You write:* **llegó** under *preterite*, and **estaba** under *imperfect.*

	preterite	*imperfect*
Modelo	llegó	estaba
1.	tomó	estaba
2.	lastimé	jugaba
3.		tenía, estudiaba
4.	llegó	estábamos
5.	dolió, sacó	
6.	fui, recetó	
7.		dolían, era
8.	llevó	dolía

2 **Responder** Answer the questions using the cues in your lab manual. Substitute direct object pronouns for the direct object nouns when appropriate. Repeat the correct response after the speaker.

> **modelo**
>
> *You hear:* ¿Por qué no llamaste al médico la semana pasada?
> *You see:* perder su número de teléfono
> *You say:* **Porque perdí su número de teléfono.**

1. en la mesa de la cocina
2. tener ocho años
3. lastimarse el tobillo
4. no, ponerla en la mochila

5. tomarse las pastillas
6. no, pero tener una grave infección de garganta
7. toda la mañana
8. necesitar una radiografía de la boca

3 **¡Qué nervios!** Listen as Sandra tells a friend about her day. Then read the statements in your lab manual and decide whether they are **cierto** or **falso**.

	Cierto	Falso
1. Sandra tenía mucha experiencia poniendo inyecciones.	○	⊘
2. La enfermera tenía un terrible dolor de cabeza.	○	⊘
3. La enfermera le dio una pastilla a Sandra.	⊘	○
4. El paciente trabajaba en el hospital con Sandra.	○	⊘
5. El paciente estaba muy nervioso.	○	⊘
6. Sandra le puso la inyección mientras él hablaba.	⊘	○

4.3 Constructions with **se**

1 **Escoger** Listen to each question and choose the most logical response.

1. a. Ay, se te quedó en casa.
   b. Ay, se me quedó en casa.
2. a. No, se le olvidó llamarlo.
   b. No, se me olvidó llamarlo.
3. a. Se le rompieron jugando al fútbol.
   b. Se les rompieron jugando al fútbol.

4. a. Ay, se les olvidaron.
   b. Ay, se nos olvidó.
5. a. No, se me perdió.
   b. No, se le perdió.
6. a. Se nos rompió.
   b. Se le rompieron.

2 **Preguntas** Answer each question you hear using the cue in your lab manual and the impersonal **se**. Repeat the correct response after the speaker.

> **modelo**
> *You hear:* ¿Qué lengua se habla en Costa Rica?
> *You see:* español
> *You say:* Se habla español.

1. a las seis
2. gripe
3. en la farmacia

4. en la caja
5. en la Oficina de Turismo
6. tomar el autobús #3

3 **Letreros (*Signs*)** Some or all of the type is missing on the signs in your lab manual. Listen to the speaker and write the appropriate text below each sign. The text for each sign will be repeated.

(3.) Se sale por la derecha.

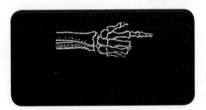

(4.) ¡No se puede hacer radiografías a mujeres embarazadas! Favor de informar a la enfermera si piensa que está embarazada.

AGENCIA REAL

(1.) Se venden casas y apartamentos. Precios razonables.

(2.) ¡Nos preocupamos por su salud! Se prohíbe fumar en el hospital.

4.4 Adverbs

1 **Completar** Listen to each statement and circle the word or phrase that best completes it.

1. a. casi   b. mal   c. ayer
2. a. con frecuencia b. además   c. ayer
3. a. poco   b. tarde   c. bien
4. a. a menudo   b. muy   c. menos
5. a. así   b. apenas   c. tranquilamente
6. a. bastante   b. a tiempo   c. normalmente

2 **Cambiar** Form a new sentence by changing the adjective in your lab manual to an adverb. Repeat the correct answer after the speaker.

> **modelo**
> You hear: Juan dibuja.
> You see: fabuloso
> You say: Juan dibuja fabulosamente.

1. regular   4. constante
2. rápido   5. general
3. feliz   6. fácil

3 **Preguntas** Answer each question you hear in the negative, using the cue in your lab manual. Repeat the correct response after the speaker.

> **modelo**
> You hear: ¿Salió bien la operación?
> You see: mal
> You say: No, la operación salió mal.

1. lentamente   4. nunca
2. tarde   5. tristemente
3. muy   6. poco

4 **Situaciones** You will hear four brief conversations. Choose the phrase that best completes each sentence in your lab manual.

1. Mónica…
   a. llegó tarde al aeropuerto.
   b. casi perdió el avión a San José.
   c. decidió no ir a San José.
2. Pilar…
   a. se preocupa por la salud de Tomás.
   b. habla con su médico.
   c. habla con Tomás sobre un problema médico.
3. La señora Blanco…
   a. se rompió la pierna hoy.
   b. quiere saber si puede correr mañana.
   c. se lastimó el tobillo hoy.
4. María está enojada porque Vicente…
   a. no va a recoger (to pick up) su medicina.
   b. no recogió su medicina ayer.
   c. no debe tomar antibióticos.

vocabulario

You will now hear the vocabulary found in your textbook on the last page of this lesson. Listen and repeat each Spanish word or phrase after the speaker.

Additional Vocabulary

Additional Vocabulary

Notes

Notes

Notes

La tecnología

5

Communicative Goals

You will learn how to:

- Talk about using technology and electronics
- Use common expressions on the telephone
- Talk about car trouble

A PRIMERA VISTA

- ¿Qué hace la chica?
- ¿Crees que usa su computadora con frecuencia?
- ¿Es una chica saludable?
- ¿Qué partes del cuerpo se ven en la foto?

Más práctica

Workbook pages 293–304
Video Manual pages 305–310
Lab Manual pages 311–316

La tecnología

Más vocabulario

la cámara digital/de video	digital/video camera
el canal	(TV) channel
el correo de voz	voice mail
el estéreo	stereo
el *fax*	fax (machine)
la pantalla táctil	touch screen
el reproductor de CD	CD player
la televisión por cable	cable television
el video	video
el archivo	file
la arroba	@ symbol
el blog	blog
la conexión inalámbrica	wireless connection
la dirección electrónica	e-mail address
Internet	Internet
el mensaje de texto	text message
la página principal	home page
el programa de computación	software
la red	network; Web
el sitio web	website
apagar	to turn off
borrar	to erase
descargar	to download
escanear	to scan
funcionar	to work
grabar	to record
guardar	to save
imprimir	to print
llamar	to call
navegar (en Internet)	to surf (the Internet)
poner, prender	to turn on
sonar (o:ue)	to ring
descompuesto/a	not working; out of order
lento/a	slow
lleno/a	full

Variación léxica

computadora ⟷ ordenador (*Esp.*),
computador (*Col.*)

descargar ⟷ bajar (*Arg., Col., Esp., Ven.*)

Supersite: MP3 Audio Files and Scripts, Digital Image Bank,
Activity Pack, Testing Program (Quizzes), **Vocabulario adicional**

el televisor

la pantalla

el reproductor de DVD

la impresora

la computadora (portátil)

el monitor

el (teléfono) celular

el ratón

el teclado

el cederrón

recursos

WB
pp. 293–294

LM
p. 311

vhlcentral.com
Lección 5

Heritage Speakers Ask heritage speakers to describe their experiences with Spanish-language Web applications, such as e-mail or websites. Do they or their families regularly visit Spanish-language websites? Which ones?

Cibercafé CORRIENTES

el control remoto

el reproductor de MP3

el disco compacto

Práctica 1 2 Supersite: MP3 Audio Files, Scripts

1

Escuchar 🎧 Escucha la conversación entre dos amigas. Después completa las oraciones.

1. María y Ana están en ___b___.
   a. una tienda   b. un cibercafé   c. un restaurante
2. A María le encantan ___b___.
   a. los celulares   b. las cámaras digitales   c. los cibercafés
3. Ana prefiere guardar las fotos en ___c___.
   a. la pantalla   b. un archivo   c. un cederrón
4. María quiere tomar un café y ___c___.
   a. poner la computadora   b. sacar fotos digitales
   c. navegar en Internet
5. Ana paga por el café y ___a___.
   a. el uso de Internet   b. la impresora   c. el cederrón

2

¿Cierto o falso? 🎧 Escucha las oraciones e indica si lo que dice cada una es **cierto** o **falso**, según el dibujo.

1. ___cierto___   5. ___cierto___
2. ___falso___   6. ___falso___
3. ___falso___   7. ___cierto___
4. ___cierto___   8. ___falso___

2 To challenge students, have them provide the correct information.

3

Oraciones Escribe oraciones usando estos elementos. Usa el pretérito y añade las palabras necesarias.

1. yo / descargar / fotos / Internet
   Yo descargué las fotos digitales por Internet.
2. tú / apagar / televisor / diez / noche
   Tú apagaste el televisor a las diez de la noche.
3. Daniel y su esposa / comprar / computadora portátil / ayer
   Daniel y su esposa compraron una computadora portátil ayer.
4. Sara y yo / ir / cibercafé / para / navegar en Internet
   Sara y yo fuimos al cibercafé para navegar en Internet.
5. Jaime / decidir / comprar / reproductor de MP3
   Jaime decidió comprar un reproductor de MP3.
6. teléfono celular / sonar / pero / yo / no contestar
   El teléfono celular sonó, pero yo no contesté.

4

Preguntas Mira el dibujo y contesta las preguntas. Answers will vary.

1. ¿Qué tipo de café es?
2. ¿Cuántas impresoras hay? ¿Cuántos ratones?
3. ¿Por qué vinieron estas personas al café?
4. ¿Qué hace el camarero?
5. ¿Qué hace la mujer en la computadora? ¿Y el hombre?
6. ¿Qué máquinas están cerca del televisor?
7. ¿Dónde hay un cibercafé en tu comunidad?
8. ¿Por qué puedes tú necesitar un cibercafé?

Más vocabulario

la autopista, la carretera	*highway*
la calle	*street*
la circulación, el tráfico	*traffic*
el garaje, el taller (mecánico)	*(mechanic's) garage; repair shop*
la licencia de conducir	*driver's license*
el/la mecánico/a	*mechanic*
la policía	*police (force)*
la velocidad máxima	*speed limit*
arrancar	*to start*
arreglar	*to fix; to arrange*
bajar(se) de	*to get off of/out of (a vehicle)*
conducir, manejar	*to drive*
estacionar	*to park*
parar	*to stop*
subir(se) a	*to get on/into (a vehicle)*

En la gasolinera

Labels in image: el capó, el cofre · Revisa el aceite. (revisar) · el carro, el coche · el parabrisas · Llena el tanque. (llenar) · el radio · la gasolina · el navegador GPS · el baúl · el volante · la llanta

---

5   Completar Completa estas oraciones con las palabras correctas.

1. Para poder conducir legalmente, necesitas... *una licencia de conducir.*
2. Puedes poner las maletas en... *el baúl.*
3. Si tu carro no funciona, debes llevarlo a... *un mecánico/taller.*
4. Para llenar el tanque de tu coche, necesitas ir a... *la gasolinera.*
5. Antes de un viaje largo, es importante revisar... *el aceite.*
6. Otra palabra para autopista es... *carretera.*
7. Mientras hablas por teléfono celular, no es buena idea... *manejar/conducir.*
8. Otra palabra para coche es... *carro.*

6   Conversación Completa la conversación con las palabras de la lista.

el aceite	la gasolina	llenar	el parabrisas	el taller
el baúl	las llantas	manejar	revisar	el volante

EMPLEADO Bienvenido al (1) ___taller___ mecánico Óscar. ¿En qué le puedo servir?

JUAN Buenos días. Quiero (2) ___llenar___ el tanque y revisar (3) ___el aceite___, por favor.

EMPLEADO Con mucho gusto. Si quiere, también le limpio (4) ___el parabrisas___.

JUAN Sí, gracias. Está un poquito sucio. La próxima semana tengo que (5) ___manejar___ hasta Buenos Aires. ¿Puede cambiar (6) ___las llantas___? Están gastadas (*worn*).

EMPLEADO Claro que sí, pero voy a tardar (*it will take me*) un par de horas.

JUAN Mejor regreso mañana. Ahora no tengo tiempo. ¿Cuánto le debo por (7) ___la gasolina___?

EMPLEADO Sesenta pesos. Y veinticinco por (8) ___revisar___ y cambiar el aceite.

Practice more at **vhlcentral.com**.

---

5 Have students create three similar sentence starters for a partner to complete. Write some on the board and have the class complete them.

¡LENGUA VIVA!

Aunque **carro** es el término que se usa en la mayoría de países hispanos, no es el único. En España, por ejemplo, se dice **coche**, y en Argentina, Chile y Uruguay se dice **auto**.

6 Ask groups to discuss car troubles they have had. Possible subjects: a visit to the mechanic, a car accident, getting a speeding ticket, etc. Write helpful vocabulary on the board. Ex: **ponerle una multa, exceder la velocidad máxima.** Have each group pick the strangest or funniest story to share with the class.

CONSULTA

For more information about **Buenos Aires**, see **Panorama**, p. 290.

CONSULTA

To review expressions like **hace… que,** see **Lección 4, Expresiones útiles,** p. 201.

Lección 5

Comunicación

7

Preguntas Trabajen en grupos y túrnense para contestar estas preguntas. Después compartan sus respuestas con la clase. Answers will vary.

1. a. ¿Tienes un teléfono celular? ¿Para qué lo usas?
   b. ¿Qué utilizas más: el teléfono o el correo electrónico? ¿Por qué?
   c. En tu opinión, ¿cuáles son las ventajas (*advantages*) y desventajas de los diferentes modos de comunicación?

2. a. ¿Con qué frecuencia usas la computadora?
   b. ¿Para qué usas Internet?
   c. ¿Tienes tu propio blog? ¿Cómo es?

3. a. ¿Miras la televisión con frecuencia? ¿Qué programas ves?
   b. ¿Dónde miras tus programas favoritos, en la tele o en la computadora?
   c. ¿Ves películas en la computadora? ¿Cuál es tu película favorita de todos los tiempos (*of all time*)?
   d. ¿A través de (*By*) qué medio escuchas música? ¿Radio, estéreo, reproductor de MP3 o computadora?

4. a. ¿Tienes licencia de conducir?
   b. ¿Cuánto tiempo hace que la conseguiste?
   c. ¿Tienes carro? Descríbelo.
   d. ¿Llevas tu carro al taller? ¿Para qué?

NOTA CULTURAL

Algunos sitios web utilizan códigos para identificar su país de origen. Éstos son los códigos para algunos países hispanohablantes:

Argentina	.ar
Colombia	.co
España	.es
México	.mx
Venezuela	.ve

8 For expansion, ask groups to write a postcard in which the problems are a direct result of the existence of technology, not its absence.

8 Possible answers: 1. Gabriela no encuentra a los amigos de Paco porque nunca están en casa, tuvo que esperar mucho por el carro y su hotel estaba muy lejos de todo. 2. No existen los mismos problemas porque existen el correo de voz y los teléfonos celulares, se puede reservar un carro en Internet y se puede buscar información sobre un hotel en la red antes del viaje.

Large Groups Stage a debate about the role of technology in today's world. Divide the class into two groups and assign each side a position. Propose this debate topic: **La tecnología: ¿beneficio o no?** Allow groups time to plan their arguments before staging the debate.

Supersite: At this point you may want to present *Vocabulario adicional: Más vocabulario para el carro y la tecnología.*

8

Postal En parejas, lean la tarjeta postal. Después contesten las preguntas. Answers will vary.

19 julio de 1979

Hola, Paco:

¡Saludos! Estamos de viaje por unas semanas. La Costa del Sol es muy bonita. No hemos encontrado (we haven't found) a tus amigos porque nunca están en casa cuando llamamos. El teléfono suena y suena y nadie contesta. Vamos a seguir llamando.

Sacamos muchas fotos muy divertidas. Cuando regresemos y las revelemos (get them developed), te las voy a enseñar. Las playas son preciosas. Hasta ahora el único problema fue que la oficina en la cual reservamos un carro perdió nuestros papeles y tuvimos que esperar mucho tiempo.

También tuvimos un pequeño problema con el hotel. La agencia de viajes nos reservó una habitación en un hotel que está muy lejos de todo. No podemos cambiarla, pero no me importa mucho. A pesar de eso, estamos contentos.

Tu hermana, Gabriela

EUROPA 12⁰⁰ ESPAÑA

Francisco Jiménez
San Lorenzo 3250
Rosario, Argentina 2000

1. ¿Cuáles son los problemas que ocurren en el viaje de Gabriela?
2. Con la tecnología de hoy, ¿existen los mismos problemas cuando se viaja? ¿Por qué?
3. Hagan una comparación entre la tecnología de los años 70 y 80 y la de hoy.
4. Imaginen que la hija de Gabriela escribe un mensaje electrónico sobre el mismo tema con fecha de hoy. Escriban ese mensaje, incorporando la tecnología actual (teléfonos celulares, Internet, cámaras digitales, etc.). Inventen nuevos problemas.

Video Synopsis **Miguel's** car has broken down again, and he has to take it to his friend **Jorge's** repair shop. In the meantime, **Maru** has bad luck with her computer. Their friends do their best to help them with their technological problems. **Miguel's** car is saved one last time, but **Maru** may not be so lucky with her computer.

En el taller

El coche de Miguel está descompuesto y Maru tiene problemas con su computadora

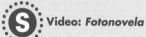 **Video:** *Fotonovela*

PERSONAJES   **MIGUEL**   **JORGE**

MIGUEL ¿Cómo lo ves?

JORGE Creo que puedo arreglarlo. ¿Me pasas la llave?

Preview Show the **En el taller** episode once without sound and have the class create a plot summary based on the visual cues. Then show the episode with sound and have the class make corrections and fill in any gaps in the plot summary.

JORGE ¿Y dónde está Maru?

MIGUEL Acaba de enviarme un mensaje de texto: "Última noticia sobre la computadora portátil: todavía está descompuesta. Moni intenta arreglarla. Voy para allá".

MARU Buenos días, Jorge.

JORGE ¡Qué gusto verte, Maru! ¿Cómo está la computadora?

MARU Mi amiga Mónica recuperó muchos archivos, pero muchos otros se borraron.

JORGE ¿Está descompuesta tu computadora?

MIGUEL No, la mía no, la suya. Una amiga la está ayudando.

JORGE Un mal día para la tecnología, ¿no?

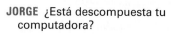

MIGUEL Ella está preparando un proyecto para ver si puede hacer sus prácticas profesionales en el Museo de Antropología.

JORGE ¿Y todo está en la computadora?

MIGUEL Y claro.

MARU Estamos en una triste situación. Yo necesito una computadora nueva, y Miguel necesita otro coche.

JORGE Y un televisor nuevo para mí, por favor.

MARU

Lección 5

Video Recap: Lección 4 Before doing this **Fotonovela** section, review the previous episode with these questions: **1.** ¿Qué estaba haciendo Jimena cuando empezó a sentirse mal? (Estaba estudiando con Elena.) **2.** ¿Quién llevó a Jimena al médico? (Elena la llevó.) **3.** ¿Cuáles eran los síntomas de Jimena? (Tosía, le dolía la garganta y estaba congestionada.)

MARU ¿Qué vamos a hacer, Miguel?

MIGUEL Tranquila, cariño. Por eso tenemos amigos como Jorge y Mónica. Nos ayudamos los unos a los otros.

JORGE ¿No te sientes afortunada, Maru? No te preocupes. Sube.

MIGUEL ¡Por fin!

MARU Gracias, Jorge. Eres el mejor mecánico de la ciudad.

MIGUEL ¿Cuánto te debo por el trabajo?

JORGE Hombre, no es nada. Guárdalo para el coche nuevo. Eso sí, recomiéndame con tus amigos.

MIGUEL Gracias, Jorge.

JORGE No manejes en carretera. Revisa el aceite cada 1.500 kilómetros y asegúrate de llenarle el tanque... No manejes con el cofre abierto. Nos vemos.

Expresiones útiles Point out the phrases **No manejes, Revisa, asegúrate, Guárdalo, recomiéndame,** and **No te preocupes**. Explain that these are **tú** commands, a direct way of telling someone to do or not to do something. Then draw attention to the words **Nos ayudamos** and tell students that this is a reciprocal reflexive construction that expresses a shared action. Point out the words **la mía** and **la suya** in the caption of video still 3 and tell the class that these are examples of stressed possessive pronouns. Tell students they will learn more about these concepts in **Estructura**.

recursos

VM
pp. 305–306

vhlcentral.com
Lección 5

Expresiones útiles

Giving instructions to a friend

¿Me pasas la llave?
Can you pass me the wrench?

No lo manejes en carretera.
Don't drive it on the highway.

Revisa el aceite cada 1.500 kilómetros.
Check the oil every 1,500 kilometers.

Asegúrate de llenar el tanque.
Make sure to fill up the tank.

No manejes con el cofre abierto.
Don't drive with the hood open.

Recomiéndame con tus amigos.
Recommend me to your friends.

Taking a phone call

Aló./Bueno./Diga.
Hello.

¿Quién habla?/¿De parte de quién?
Who is speaking/calling?

Con él/ella habla.
Speaking.

¿Puedo dejar un recado?
May I leave a message?

Reassuring someone

Tranquilo/a, cariño.
Relax, sweetie.

Nos ayudamos los unos a los otros.
We help each other out.

No te preocupes.
Don't worry.

Additional vocabulary

entregar *to hand in*
el intento *attempt*
la noticia *news*
el proyecto *project*
recuperar *to recover*

¿Qué pasó?

1 **Seleccionar** Selecciona las respuestas que completan correctamente estas oraciones.

1. Jorge intenta arreglar __b__.
   a. la computadora de Maru   b. el coche de Miguel   c. el teléfono celular de Felipe
2. Maru dice que se borraron muchos __a__ de su computadora.
   a. archivos   b. sitios web   c. mensajes de texto
3. Jorge dice que necesita un __c__.
   a. navegador GPS   b. reproductor de DVD   c. televisor
4. Maru dice que Jorge es el mejor __a__.
   a. mecánico de la ciudad   b. amigo del mundo   c. compañero de la clase
5. Jorge le dice a Miguel que no maneje su coche en __c__.
   a. el tráfico   b. el centro de la ciudad   c. la carretera

2 **Identificar** Identifica quién puede decir estas oraciones.

1. Cómprate un coche nuevo y recomiéndame con tus amigos.   Jorge
2. El mensaje de texto de Maru dice que su computadora todavía está descompuesta.   Miguel
3. Mi amiga Mónica me ayudó a recuperar muchos archivos, pero necesito una computadora nueva.   Maru
4. No conduzcas con el cofre abierto y recuerda que el tanque debe estar lleno.   Jorge
5. Muchos de los archivos de mi computadora se borraron.   Maru

MARU

MIGUEL

JORGE

3 **Problema mecánico** Trabajen en parejas para representar los papeles de un(a) mecánico/a y un(a) cliente/a que está llamando al taller porque su carro está descompuesto. Usen las instrucciones como guía.   Answers will vary.

Mecánico/a	Cliente/a
Contesta el teléfono con un saludo y el nombre del taller.	→ Saluda y explica que tu carro está descompuesto.
Pregunta qué tipo de problema tiene exactamente.	→ Explica que tu carro no arranca cuando hace frío.
Di que debe traer el carro al taller.	→ Pregunta cuándo puedes llevarlo.
Ofrece una hora para revisar el carro.	→ Acepta la hora que ofrece el/la mecánico/a.
Da las gracias y despídete.	→ Despídete y cuelga (*hang up*) el teléfono.

Ahora cambien los papeles y representen otra conversación. Ustedes son un(a) técnico/a y un(a) cliente/a. Usen estas ideas:

> el celular no guarda mensajes   la impresora imprime muy lentamente
> la computadora no descarga fotos   el reproductor de DVD está descompuesto

🎯 Practice more at **vhlcentral.com**.

3 Possible conversation:
E1: ¿Bueno?
Taller Mendoza.
E2: Buenos días. Tengo un problema con mi carro.
E1: ¿Qué pasó? ¿Cuál es el problema exactamente?
E2: El carro no arranca cuando hace frío.
E1: Tengo que revisarlo. ¿Puede venir al taller?
E2: Creo que sí. ¿A qué hora debo pasar?
E1: Tengo tiempo esta tarde a las tres.
E2: Muy bien. Es buena hora para mí también.
E1: Nos vemos a las tres. Gracias, y hasta esta tarde.
E2: Hasta luego.

Small Groups Have the class work in small groups to write questions about the **Fotonovela**. Have each group hand its questions to another group, which will write the answers. Ex: **G1:** ¿A quién le mandó un mensaje de texto Maru? **G2:** Maru le mandó un mensaje de texto a Miguel.

Extra Practice Have each student choose one of the **Fotonovela** characters and prepare a five-sentence summary of the day's events from that person's point of view. Have a few volunteers read their summaries to the class; the class will guess which character would have given each summary.

NATIONAL communication STANDARDS

3 Have students sit back-to-back to simulate a real phone conversation. Remind students that speaking on the phone requires practice because one cannot see the speaker's facial expressions. Encourage students to listen for the gist and for key information, rather than trying to understand every word.

Heritage Speakers
Ask heritage speakers to come up with additional sentences to exemplify each point in the chart. Have them write their sentences on the board without accent marks. Call on volunteers to determine which words, if any, require written accents.

Teaching Tips
• If necessary, briefly review the information about written accents in **Lección 4**, p. 187.
• Emphasize the difference in stress between **por qué** and **porque**.
• Have students work in pairs to explain which words in the **Práctica** activity need written accents and why.

Extra Practice Add an auditory aspect to this **Ortografía** section. Prepare a series of mini-dialogues. Slowly read each one aloud, pausing to allow students to write. Then, in pairs, have students check their work. Ex:
1. —¿Ésta es tu cámara? —Sí, papá la trajo de Japón para mí.
2. —¿Dónde encontraste mi mochila? —¡Pues, donde la dejaste!
3. —¿Cuándo visitó Buenos Aires Mario? —Yo sé que Laura fue allí el año pasado, ¿pero cuándo fue él? ¡Ni idea!
4. —¿Me quieres explicar por qué llegas tarde? —Porque mi carro está descompuesto.

Lección 5

Ortografía

La acentuación de palabras similares

Audio

Supersite: MP3 Audio Files, Listening Scripts

Although accent marks usually indicate which syllable in a word is stressed, they are also used to distinguish between words that have the same or similar spellings.

Él maneja **el** coche.   **Sí**, voy **si** quieres.

Although one-syllable words do not usually carry written accents, some *do* have accent marks to distinguish them from words that have the same spelling but different meanings.

Sé cocinar.   **Se** baña.   ¿Tomas **té**?   **Te** duermes.

Sé (*I know*) and **té** (*tea*) have accent marks to distinguish them from the pronouns **se** and **te**.

para **mí**   **mi** cámara   **Tú** lees.   **tu** estéreo

Mí (*Me*) and **tú** (*you*) have accent marks to distinguish them from the possessive adjectives **mi** and **tu**.

¿**Por qué** vas?   Voy **porque** quiero.

Several words of more than one syllable also have accent marks to distinguish them from words that have the same or similar spellings.

Éste es rápido.   **Este** tren es rápido.

Demonstrative pronouns have accent marks to distinguish them from demonstrative adjectives.

¿**Cuándo** fuiste?   Fui **cuando** me llamó.
¿**Dónde** trabajas?   Voy al taller **donde** trabajo.

Adverbs have accent marks when they are used to convey a question.

 Práctica Marca los acentos en las palabras que los necesitan.

ANA Alo, soy Ana. ¿Que tal? Aló/¿Qué?
JUAN Hola, pero… ¿por que me llamas tan tarde? ¿por qué?
ANA Porque mañana tienes que llevarme a la universidad. Mi auto esta dañado. está
JUAN ¿Como se daño? ¿Cómo?/dañó
ANA Se daño el sabado. Un vecino (*neighbor*) choco con (*crashed into*) el. dañó/sábado/chocó/él

 Crucigrama Utiliza las siguientes pistas (*clues*) para completar el crucigrama. ¡Ojo con los acentos!

Horizontales
1. Él _____ levanta.
4. No voy _____ no puedo.
7. Tú _____ acuestas.
9. ¿ _____ es el examen?
10. Quiero este video y _____.

Verticales
2. ¿Cómo _____ usted?
3. Eres _____ mi hermano.
5. ¿ _____ tal?
6. Me gusta _____ suéter.
8. Navego _____ la red.

Crossword grid:
- Row 1: ¹S ²E ³C
- Row 2: S ⁴P O R ⁵Q U ⁶E
- Row 3: ⁷T ⁸E M U S
- Row 4: ⁹C U Á N D O ¹⁰É S E

Game Divide the class into two teams. Assign a member of each team one of two similar words (Ex: **se/sé**). Provide one minute for students to write a sentence using the word. Award one point for each correct usage. Continue until all students have had a turn.

recursos
LM p. 312
vhlcentral.com Lección 5

 Additional Reading

El teléfono celular

connections cultures
NATIONAL STANDARDS

¿Cómo te comunicas con tus amigos y familia? En algunos países hispanos, el servicio de teléfono común° es bastante caro, por lo que el teléfono celular, más accesible y barato, es el favorito de mucha gente.

El servicio más popular entre los jóvenes es el sistema de tarjetas prepagadas°, porque no requiere de un contrato ni de cuotas° extras. En muchos países, puedes encontrar estas tarjetas en cualquier° tienda o recargar el saldo° de tu celular por Internet.

Los celulares de los años 80, grandes e incómodos, eran un símbolo de estatus y estaban limitados al uso de la voz°. Las funciones que entonces sólo existían en la ciencia ficción, ahora son una realidad. Los celulares de hoy tienen muchas funciones: cámara de fotos o de video,

agenda electrónica°, navegador GPS, juegos, conexión a Internet, reproductor de MP3... Con los teléfonos actuales se puede interactuar en las redes sociales° de Internet y, gracias a la tecnología táctil, acceder a sus aplicaciones de forma diferente y rápida.

Con la evolución de los celulares, muchas personas han dejado de usar ciertos aparatos°: ¿para qué una cámara, un reproductor de música y un celular separados si puedes tener todo en uno°?

El uso de los celulares

• En el mundo se intercambian cerca de 6 billones de mensajes de texto al año.

• En los EE.UU., el 76% de los hispanos con celular lo usan para conectarse a Internet y el 96% de los hispanos entre 18 y 29 años tiene un celular.

• América Latina tiene más de 396 millones de usuarios de teléfonos celulares. Utilizan programas de mensajería instantánea, navegan por Internet y transfieren datos como videos y fotos.

común *ordinary* prepagadas *prepaid* cuotas *fees* cualquier *any*
recargar el saldo *to buy more minutes* voz *voice*
agenda electrónica *PDA* redes sociales *social networks*
aparatos *devices* todo en uno *all in one*

ACTIVIDADES

1 **¿Cierto o falso?** Indica si lo que dicen estas oraciones es **cierto** o **falso**. Corrige la información falsa.

1. El teléfono común es un servicio caro en algunos países. Cierto.

2. Muchas personas usan más el teléfono celular que el teléfono común. Cierto.

3. Es difícil encontrar tarjetas prepagadas en los países hispanos. Falso. Puedes encontrar tarjetas prepagadas en cualquier tienda o recargar tu saldo por Internet.

4. En los años 80 los celulares eran un símbolo de estatus. Cierto.

5. Los primeros teléfonos celulares eran muy cómodos y pequeños. Falso. Los primeros teléfonos celulares eran grandes e incómodos.

6. Hoy en día muy pocas personas usan el celular para sacar fotos y oír música. Falso. Hoy en día muchas personas usan el celular para sacar fotos y oír música.

7. En los EE.UU., el 12% de los hispanos usa el celular para conectarse a Internet. Falso. En los EE.UU., el 76% de los hispanos usa el celular para conectarse a Internet.

ASÍ SE DICE

La tecnología

los audífonos (Méx., Col.), los auriculares (Arg.), los cascos (Esp.)	*headset; earphones*
el móvil (Esp.)	**el celular**
el manos libres (Amér. S.)	*hands-free system*
la memoria	*memory*
mensajear (Méx.)	**enviar y recibir mensajes de texto**

EL MUNDO HISPANO

Las bicimotos

- **Argentina** El *ciclomotor* se usa mayormente° para repartir a domicilio° comidas y medicinas.

- **Perú** La *motito* se usa mucho para el reparto a domicilio de pan fresco todos los días.

- **México** La *Vespa* se usa para evitar° el tráfico en grandes ciudades.

- **España** La población usa el *Vespino* para ir y volver al trabajo cada día.

- **Puerto Rico** Una *scooter* es el medio de transporte favorito en las zonas rurales.

- **República Dominicana** Las *moto-taxis* son el medio de transporte más económico, ¡pero no olvides el casco°!

mayormente mainly **repartir a domicilio** home delivery of **evitar** to avoid **casco** helmet

PERFIL

Los mensajes de texto

¿Qué tienen en común un **mensaje de texto** y un telegrama?: la necesidad de decir lo máximo en el menor espacio posible —y rápidamente—. Así como los abuelos se las arreglaron° para hacer más baratos sus telegramas, que se cobraban° por número de palabras, ahora los jóvenes buscan ahorrar° espacio, tiempo y dinero, en sus mensajes de texto. Esta economía del lenguaje dio origen al **lenguaje chat**, una forma de escritura muy creativa y compacta. Olvídate de la gramática, la puntuación y la ortografía: es tan flexible que evoluciona° todos los días con el uso que cada quien° le da, aunque° hay muchas palabras y expresiones ya establecidas°. Fácilmente encontrarás° abreviaturas (**xq?**, "¿Por qué?"; **tkm**, "Te quiero mucho."), sustitución de sonidos por números (**a2**, "Adiós."; **5mntrios**, "Sin comentarios."), símbolos (**ad+**, "además") y omisión de vocales y acentos (**tb**, "también"; **k tl?**, "¿Qué tal?"). Ahora que lo sabes, si un amigo te envía: **cont xfa, m dbs $!°**, puedes responderle: **ntp, ns vms + trd°**.

se las arreglaron they managed to **se cobraban** were charged **ahorrar** to save **evoluciona** evolves **cada quien** each person **aunque** although **establecidas** fixed **encontrarás** you will find **cont xfa, m dbs $!** Contesta, por favor, ¡me debes dinero! **ntp, ns vms +trd** No te preocupes, nos vemos más tarde.

🕘 Conexión Internet

¿Qué sitios web son populares entre los jóvenes hispanos?	Go to **vhlcentral.com** to find more cultural information related to this **Cultura** section.

ACTIVIDADES

2 **Comprensión** Responde a las preguntas.

1. ¿Cuáles son tres formas de decir *headset*? los audífonos, los auriculares, los cascos
2. ¿Para qué se usan las bicimotos en Argentina? para repartir a domicilio comidas y medicinas
3. ¿Qué dio origen al "lenguaje chat"? la necesidad de ahorrar espacio, tiempo y dinero
4. ¿Es importante escribir los acentos en los mensajes de texto? No. La gramática, la ortografía y la puntuación no importan en un mensaje de texto.

3 **¿Cómo te comunicas?** Escribe un párrafo breve en donde expliques qué utilizas para comunicarte con tus amigos/as (correo electrónico, redes sociales, teléfono, etc.) y de qué hablan cuando se llaman por teléfono.
Answers will vary.

3 Have students exchange their paragraphs with a classmate for peer editing.

🔊 Practice more at **vhlcentral.com**.

5.1 Familiar commands  Tutorial

NATIONAL comparisons STANDARDS

ANTE TODO In Spanish, the command forms are used to give orders or advice. You use **tú** commands (**mandatos familiares**) when you want to give an order or advice to someone you normally address with the familiar **tú**.

Affirmative tú commands

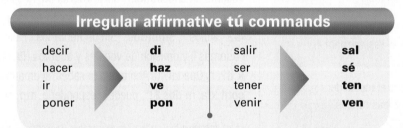

Infinitive	Present tense él/ella form	Affirmative tú command
hablar	habla	**habla** (tú)
guardar	guarda	**guarda** (tú)
prender	prende	**prende** (tú)
volver	vuelve	**vuelve** (tú)
pedir	pide	**pide** (tú)
imprimir	imprime	**imprime** (tú)

▶ Affirmative **tú** commands usually have the same form as the **él/ella** form of the present indicative.

> **Guarda** el documento antes de cerrarlo.
> *Save the document before closing it.*

> **Imprime** tu tarea para la clase de inglés.
> *Print your homework for English class.*

▶ The following verbs have irregular affirmative **tú** commands.

Irregular affirmative tú commands

decir	**di**	salir	**sal**
hacer	**haz**	ser	**sé**
ir	**ve**	tener	**ten**
poner	**pon**	venir	**ven**

> ¡**Sal** ahora mismo!
> *Leave at once!*

> **Haz** los ejercicios.
> *Do the exercises.*

▶ Since **ir** and **ver** have the same **tú** command (**ve**), context will determine the meaning.

> **Ve** al cibercafé con Yolanda.
> *Go to the cybercafé with Yolanda.*

> **Ve** ese programa… es muy interesante.
> *See that program… it's very interesting.*

Súbete al coche y préndelo.

No lo manejes en la carretera.

Teaching Tip Model the use of informal commands with simple examples using TPR and gestures. Ex: Point to a student and say: _____ , **levántate. Gracias, ahora siéntate.** Give other commands using **camina, vuelve, toca,** and **corre.**

TPR Ask individual students to comply with a series of commands requiring them to perform actions or move around the room. While the student follows the command, the class writes it down as a volunteer writes it on the board. Be sure to use both affirmative and negative commands. Ex: **Recoge ese papel. Ponlo en la basura. Regresa a tu escritorio. No te sientes. Siéntate ahora.**

Heritage Speakers Ask heritage speakers to look for an advertisement in a Spanish-language magazine or newspaper in which informal commands are used. Have students bring a copy of the ad to class. Ask them to share it with the class and explain why they think informal commands were used instead of formal ones.

Teaching Tip Contrast the negative forms of **tú** commands by giving an affirmative command followed by a negative command. Ex: _____, **camina a la puerta. No camines rápidamente.** Write the examples on the board as you go along.

Extra Practice Ask volunteers to convert affirmative **tú** commands with reflexive and object pronouns into negative commands, and vice versa. Ex: **Imprímelo. (No lo imprimas.)**

¡ATENCIÓN!

In affirmative commands, reflexive, indirect, and direct object pronouns are always attached to the end of the verb. In negative commands, these pronouns always precede the verb.

Bórralos./No los borres.

Escríbeles un mensaje electrónico./**No les escribas** un mensaje electrónico.

• • •

When a pronoun is attached to an affirmative command that has two or more syllables, an accent mark is added to maintain the original stress:

borra → **bórralos**

prende → **préndela**

imprime → **imprímelo**

▶ The negative **tú** commands are formed by dropping the final -**o** of the **yo** form of the present tense. For -**ar** verbs, add -**es**. For -**er** and -**ir** verbs, add -**as**.

Negative tú commands

Infinitive	Present tense yo form	Negative tú command
hablar	hablo	**no hables** (tú)
guardar	guardo	**no guardes** (tú)
prender	prendo	**no prendas** (tú)
volver	vuelvo	**no vuelvas** (tú)
pedir	pido	**no pidas** (tú)

Héctor, **no pares** el carro aquí.
Héctor, don't stop the car here.

No prendas la computadora todavía.
Don't turn on the computer yet.

▶ Verbs with irregular **yo** forms maintain the same irregularity in their negative **tú** commands. These verbs include **conducir, conocer, decir, hacer, ofrecer, oír, poner, salir, tener, traducir, traer, venir,** and **ver.**

No pongas el cederrón en la computadora.
Don't put the CD-ROM in the computer.

No conduzcas tan rápido.
Don't drive so fast.

▶ Note also that stem-changing verbs keep their stem changes in negative **tú** commands.

No p**ie**rdas tu celular.
Don't lose your cell phone.

No v**ue**lvas a esa gasolinera.
Don't go back to that gas station.

No rep**i**tas las instrucciones.
Don't repeat the instructions.

▶ Verbs ending in -**car**, -**gar**, and -**zar** have a spelling change in the negative **tú** commands.

sa**car**	c → **qu**	no sa**qu**es
apa**gar**	g → **gu**	no apa**gu**es
almor**zar**	z → **c**	no almuer**c**es

▶ The following verbs have irregular negative **tú** commands.

Irregular negative tú commands

dar	**no des**
estar	**no estés**
ir	**no vayas**
saber	**no sepas**
ser	**no seas**

recursos

WB
pp. 295–296

LM
p. 313

S

vhlcentral.com
Lección 5

¡INTÉNTALO! Indica los mandatos familiares afirmativos y negativos de estos verbos.

1. correr — _Corre_ más rápido. — No _corras_ más rápido.
2. llenar — _Llena_ el tanque. — No _llenes_ el tanque.
3. salir — _Sal_ ahora. — No _salgas_ ahora.
4. descargar — _Descarga_ ese documento. — No _descargues_ ese documento.
5. levantarse — _Levántate_ temprano. — No _te levantes_ temprano.
6. hacerlo — _Hazlo_ ya. — No _lo hagas_ ahora.

Lección 5

Práctica

1 **Completar** Tu mejor amigo no entiende nada de tecnología y te pide ayuda. Completa los comentarios de tu amigo con el mandato de cada verbo.

1. No ____vengas____ en una hora. ____Ven____ ahora mismo. (venir)
2. ____Haz____ tu tarea después. No la ____hagas____ ahora. (hacer)
3. No ____vayas____ a la tienda a comprar papel para la impresora. ____Ve____ a la cafetería a comprarme algo de comer. (ir)
4. No ____me digas____ que no puedes abrir un archivo. ____Dime____ que el programa de computación funciona sin problemas. (decirme)
5. ____Sé____ generoso con tu tiempo y no ____seas____ antipático si no entiendo fácilmente. (ser)
6. ____Ten____ mucha paciencia y no ____tengas____ prisa. (tener)
7. ____Apaga____ tu teléfono celular, pero no ____apagues____ la computadora. (apagar)

2 **Cambiar** Pedro y Marina no pueden ponerse de acuerdo (*agree*) cuando viajan en su carro. Cuando Pedro dice que algo es necesario, Marina expresa una opinión diferente. Usa la información entre paréntesis para formar las órdenes que Marina le da a Pedro.

> **modelo**
>
> **Pedro:** Necesito revisar el aceite del carro. (seguir hasta el próximo pueblo)
> **Marina:** No revises el aceite del carro. Sigue hasta el próximo pueblo.

1. Necesito conducir más rápido. (parar el carro) No conduzcas más rápido. Para el carro.
2. Necesito poner el radio. (hablarme) No pongas el radio. Háblame.
3. Necesito almorzar ahora. (comer más tarde) No almuerces ahora. Come más tarde.
4. Necesito sacar los discos compactos. (manejar con cuidado) No saques… Maneja…
5. Necesito estacionar el carro en esta calle. (pensar en otra opción) No estaciones… Piensa…
6. Necesito volver a esa gasolinera. (arreglar el carro en un taller) No vuelvas… Arregla…
7. Necesito leer el mapa. (pedirle ayuda a aquella señora) No leas… Pídele…
8. Necesito dormir en el carro. (acostarse en una cama) No duermas… Acuéstate…

3 **Problemas** Tú y tu compañero/a trabajan en el centro de computadoras de la universidad. Muchos estudiantes están llamando con problemas. Denles órdenes para ayudarlos a resolverlos.

Answers will vary. Suggested answers:

> **modelo**
>
> **Problema:** No veo nada en la pantalla.
> **Tu respuesta:** Prende la pantalla de tu computadora.

apagar…	descargar…	grabar…	imprimir…	prender…
borrar…	funcionar…	guardar…	navegar…	volver…

1. No me gusta este programa de computación. Descarga otro.
2. Tengo miedo de perder mi documento. Guárdalo.
3. Prefiero leer este sitio web en papel. Imprímelo.
4. Mi correo electrónico funciona muy lentamente. Borra los mensajes más viejos.
5. Busco información sobre los gauchos de Argentina. Navega en Internet.
6. Tengo demasiados archivos en mi computadora. Borra algunos archivos.
7. Mi computadora se congeló (*froze*). Apaga la computadora y luego préndela.
8. Quiero ver las fotos del cumpleaños de mi hermana. Descárgalas.

 Practice more at **vhlcentral.com**.

1 Continue this activity orally with the class, using regular verbs. Call out a negative command and designate individuals to make corresponding affirmative commands. Ex: **No sirvas la comida ahora. (Sirve la comida ahora./Sírvela ahora.)**

TPR Have the class stand in a circle. Name an infinitive and toss a foam or paper ball to a student. He or she will give the affirmative **tú** command and throw the ball to another student, who will provide the negative form.

Pairs Have pairs imagine that they are in charge of a computer lab at a university in a Spanish-speaking country. Have them make a handout of four things students must do and four things they must not do while in the lab. Instruct them to use **tú** commands throughout. Then, write **Mandatos afirmativos** and **Mandatos negativos** on the board and ask individuals to write one of their commands in the appropriate column.

3 To simplify, review the vocabulary in the word bank by asking students to make associations with each word. Ex: **imprimir (documento), descargar (programa)**

NOTA CULTURAL

Los gauchos (*nomadic cowboys*), conocidos por su habilidad (*skill*) para montar a caballo y utilizar el lazo, viven en la Región Pampeana, una llanura muy extensa ubicada en el centro de Argentina y dedicada a la agricultura (*agriculture*).

Comunicación

4 To simplify, ask students to brainstorm a list of what they might ask their classmates to do.

4 Have volunteers report to the class what they were asked to do, what they did, and what they did not do.

5 Ask comprehension questions about the ad. ¿Qué se anuncia? (cursos de informática) ¿Cómo puedes informarte? (llamar por teléfono) ¿Dónde se encuentra este tipo de anuncio? (en periódicos y revistas)

Pairs Have pairs prepare a conversation between two roommates who are getting ready for a party. Students should use affirmative and negative **tú** commands. Ex: E1: ¡Sal del baño ya! E2: ¡No me grites!

4 **Órdenes** Circula por la clase e intercambia mandatos negativos y afirmativos con tus compañeros/as. Debes seguir las órdenes que ellos te dan o reaccionar apropiadamente. Answers will vary.

modelo

Estudiante 1: Dame todo tu dinero.
Estudiante 2: No, no quiero dártelo. Muéstrame tu cuaderno.
Estudiante 1: Aquí está.
Estudiante 3: Ve a la pizarra y escribe tu nombre.
Estudiante 4: No quiero. Hazlo tú.

5 **Anuncios** Miren este anuncio. Luego, en grupos pequeños, preparen tres anuncios adicionales para tres escuelas que compiten (*compete*) con ésta. Answers will vary.

Síntesis

Supersite: Activity Pack

Extra Practice Add an auditory aspect to this grammar practice. Prepare series of commands that would be said to certain individuals. Write the names on the board and read each series aloud. Have students match the commands to each name. Ex: **No comas eso. No te subas al sofá. Tráeme las pantuflas.** (un perro)

6 **¡Tanto que hacer!** Tu profesor(a) te va a dar una lista de diligencias (*errands*). Algunas las hiciste tú y algunas las hizo tu compañero/a. Las diligencias que ya hicieron tienen esta marca ✔. Pero quedan cuatro diligencias por hacer. Dale órdenes a tu compañero/a y él/ella responde para confirmar si hay que hacerla o si ya la hizo. Answers will vary.

modelo

Estudiante 1: Llena el tanque.
Estudiante 2: Ya llené el tanque. / ¡Ay, no! Tenemos que llenar el tanque.

Lección 5

5.2   Por and para   (S) Tutorial

ANTE TODO   Unlike English, Spanish has two words that mean *for*: **por** and **para**. These two prepositions are not interchangeable. Study the following charts to see how they are used.

▶ **Por** and **para** are most commonly used to describe aspects of movement, time, and action, but in different circumstances.

Por	Para
Movement	
Through or by a place	Toward a destination
La excursión nos llevó **por** el centro.	Mis amigos van **para** el estadio.
The tour took us through downtown.	*My friends are going to the stadium.*
Time	
Duration of an event	Action deadline
Ana navegó la red **por** dos horas.	Tengo que escribir un ensayo **para** mañana.
Ana surfed the net for two hours.	*I have to write an essay by tomorrow.*
Action	
Reason or motive for an action or circumstance	Indication of for whom something is intended or done
Llegué a casa tarde **por** el tráfico.	Estoy preparando una sorpresa **para** Eduardo.
I got home late because of the traffic.	*I'm preparing a surprise for Eduardo.*

▶ Here is a list of the uses of **por** and **para**.

Por is used to indicate...

1. **Movement: Motion or a general location** . . (around, through, along, by)
   Pasamos **por** el parque y **por** el río.
   We passed by the park and along the river.

2. **Time: Duration of an action** . . . . (for, during, in)
   Estuve en la Patagonia **por** un mes.
   I was in Patagonia for a month.

3. **Action: Reason or motive for an action** . . (because of, on account of, on behalf of)
   Lo hizo **por** su familia.
   She did it on behalf of her family.

4. **Object of a search** . . . . (for, in search of)
   Vengo **por** ti a las ocho.
   I'm coming for you at eight.
   Manuel fue **por** su cámara digital.
   Manuel went in search of his digital camera.

5. **Means by which something is done** . . . (by, by way of, by means of)
   Ellos viajan **por** la autopista.
   They travel by (by way of) the highway.

6. **Exchange or substitution** . . . . (for, in exchange for)
   Le di dinero **por** el reproductor de MP3.
   I gave him money for the MP3 player.

7. **Unit of measure** . . . . (per, by)
   José manejaba a 120 kilómetros **por** hora.
   José was driving 120 kilometers per hour.

TPR Call out a sentence, omitting **por** or **para**. If students think **por** should be used in the sentence, they raise one hand. If they think **para** should be used, they raise two hands. Ex: **Tengo que leer la lección 5 _____ mañana.** (two hands); **Jimena trabaja _____ la noche.** (one hand) Avoid cases where either **por** or **para** could be used.

Video Replay the **Fotonovela** episode and pause to discuss each example of **por** and **para**. Ask students to determine the corresponding use in the charts on pp. 272–273.

¡ATENCIÓN!

Por is also used in several idiomatic expressions, including:
por aquí *around here*
por ejemplo *for example*
por eso *that's why; therefore*
por fin *finally*

AYUDA

Remember that when giving an exact time, **de** is used instead of **por** before **la mañana, la tarde,** or **la noche.**
La clase empieza a las nueve **de** la mañana.

• • •

In addition to **por**, **durante** is also commonly used to mean *for* when referring to time.
Esperé al mecánico **durante** cincuenta minutos.

Teaching Tip Create a matching activity for the uses of **para**. Write sentences exemplifying each use of **para** listed, but not in the order they are given in the text. Ex: **1. Maru escribió un mensaje para Miguel. 2. Este autobús va para Mérida. 3. Para Jimena, los estudios son importantes. 4. Jorge trabaja para un taller. 5. Jimena estudia para llegar a ser doctora. 6. El baúl es para las maletas. 7. Tengo que entregar el proyecto para la semana que viene.** Call on individual students to match each sentence with its usage.

Game Play **Concentración**. Create one card for each use of **por** and **para**, and one card with a sentence illustrating each use, for a total of 28 cards. Shuffle the cards and lay them face down. Then, taking turns, students uncover two cards at a time, trying to match a use to a sentence. The student with the most matches wins.

Extra Practice For visual learners, bring in magazine pictures and have students write sentences about them using **por** and **para**. Ex: **Este señor hace la cena para su esposa.**

Para is used to indicate...

1. Movement: Destination . . . .
(*toward, in the direction of*)

Salimos **para** Córdoba el sábado.
We are leaving for Córdoba on Saturday.

2. Time: Deadline or a specific time in the future . . . .
(*by, for*)

Él va a arreglar el carro **para** el viernes.
He will fix the car by Friday.

3. Action: Purpose or goal + [*infinitive*] . . . .
(*in order to*)

Juan estudia **para** (ser) mecánico.
Juan is studying to be a mechanic.

4. Purpose + [*noun*] . . . .
(*for, used for*)

Es una llanta **para** el carro.
It's a tire for the car.

5. The recipient of something . . . .
(*for*)

Compré una impresora **para** mi hijo.
I bought a printer for my son.

6. Comparison with others or an opinion . .
(*for, considering*)

Para un joven, es demasiado serio.
For a young person, he is too serious.

Para mí, esta lección no es difícil.
For me, this lesson isn't difficult.

7. In the employment of . . . .
(*for*)

Sara trabaja **para** Telecom Argentina.
Sara works for Telecom Argentina.

▶ In many cases it is grammatically correct to use either **por** or **para** in a sentence. The meaning of the sentence is different, however, depending on which preposition is used.

Caminé **por** el parque.
I walked through the park.

Caminé **para** el parque.
I walked to (toward) the park.

Trabajó **por** su padre.
He worked for (in place of) his father.

Trabajó **para** su padre.
He worked for his father('s company).

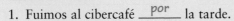

¡INTÉNTALO!   Completa estas oraciones con las preposiciones **por** o **para**.

1. Fuimos al cibercafé __por__ la tarde.
2. Necesitas un navegador GPS __para__ encontrar la casa de Luis.
3. Entraron __por__ la puerta.
4. Quiero un pasaje __para__ Buenos Aires.
5. __Para__ arrancar el carro, necesito la llave.
6. Arreglé el televisor __para__ mi amigo.
7. Estuvieron nerviosos __por__ el examen.
8. ¿No hay una gasolinera __por__ aquí?
9. El reproductor de MP3 es __para__ usted.
10. Juan está enfermo. Tengo que trabajar __por__ él.
11. Estuvimos en Canadá __por__ dos meses.
12. __Para__ mí, el español es fácil.
13. Tengo que estudiar la lección __para__ el lunes.
14. Voy a ir __por__ la carretera.
15. Compré dulces __para__ mi novia.
16. Compramos el auto __por__ un buen precio.

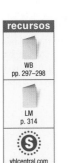

recursos

WB
pp. 297–298

LM
p. 314

S
vhlcentral.com
Lección 5

Práctica

1

Completar Completa este párrafo con las preposiciones **por** o **para**.

El mes pasado mi esposo y yo hicimos un viaje a Buenos Aires y sólo pagamos dos mil dólares (1)_por_ los pasajes. Estuvimos en Buenos Aires (2)_por_ una semana y paseamos por toda la ciudad. Durante el día caminamos (3)_por_ la plaza San Martín, el microcentro y el barrio de La Boca, donde viven muchos artistas. (4)_Por_ la noche fuimos a una tanguería, que es una especie de teatro, (5)_para_ mirar a la gente bailar tango. Dos días después decidimos hacer una excursión (6)_por_ las pampas (7)_para_ ver el paisaje y un rodeo con gauchos. Alquilamos (*We rented*) un carro y manejamos (8)_por_ todas partes y pasamos unos días muy agradables. El último día que estuvimos en Buenos Aires fuimos a Galerías Pacífico (9)_para_ comprar recuerdos (*souvenirs*) (10)_para_ nuestros hijos y nietos. Compramos tantos regalos que tuvimos que pagar impuestos (*duties*) en la aduana al regresar.

2

Oraciones Crea oraciones originales con los elementos de las columnas. Une los elementos usando **por** o **para**. Answers will vary.

> **modelo**
>
> Fuimos a Mar del Plata por razones de salud para visitar a un especialista. ◀

(no) fue al mercado	por/para	comprar frutas	por/para	¿?
(no) fuimos a las montañas	por/para	tres días	por/para	¿?
(no) fuiste a Mar del Plata	por/para	razones de salud	por/para	¿?
(no) fueron a Buenos Aires	por/para	tomar el sol	por/para	¿?

3

Describir Usa **por** o **para** y el tiempo presente para describir estos dibujos. Answers will vary.

1. _____   2. _____   3. _____

4. _____   5. _____   6. _____

 Practice more at **vhlcentral.com**.

1 Have students refer to the charts on pp. 272–273 to identify each use of **por** and **para** in the paragraph. In pairs, have them write additional sentences for the remaining uses (**por**: reason or motive, object of search, means, unit of measure / **para**: destination, deadline, purpose + [*noun*], comparison, employment).

NOTA CULTURAL

Mar del Plata es un centro turístico en la costa de Argentina. La ciudad es conocida como "la perla del Atlántico" y todos los años muchos turistas visitan sus playas y casinos.

2 Model the activity by creating a sentence with an element from each column. Emphasize that the columns can be combined in several ways. Ex: **Fueron a Buenos Aires por tres días para divertirse.**

3 Have students take turns with a partner to expand their descriptions to a short oral narrative. After each drawing has been described, ask students to pick two or three of their narratives and link them into a story.

Large Group Have students use **por** and **para** to create ten questions for a survey about technology. Ex: **¿Por cuántos minutos al día hablas por teléfono celular?** Have students administer their survey to five different people in the room. Follow up with class discussion.

Comunicación

4 Have students create new sentences, employing additional uses of **por** and **para**.

4 **Descripciones** Usa **por** o **para** y completa estas frases de manera lógica. Luego, compara tus respuestas con las de un(a) compañero/a.   Answers will vary.

1. En casa, hablo con mis amigos…
2. Mi padre/madre trabaja…
3. Ayer fui al taller…
4. Los miércoles tengo clases…
5. A veces voy a la biblioteca…

6. Esta noche tengo que estudiar…
7. Necesito… dólares…
8. Compré un regalo…
9. Mi mejor amigo/a estudia…
10. Necesito hacer la tarea…

5 Ask students about the car in the picture. Ex: ¿**Te gusta este carro? ¿Cuánto se paga por un carro así? ¿A cuántas millas por hora corre este carro?**

5 Show a picture of an old used car and ask students to create a new conversation. The parents are offering to buy their son/ daughter this car instead of the one shown in the activity.

5 **Situación** En parejas, dramaticen esta situación. Utilicen muchos ejemplos de **por** y **para**.
Answers will vary.

Hijo/a	**Padre/Madre**
Pídele dinero a tu padre/madre.	⟶ Pregúntale a tu hijo/a para qué lo necesita.
Dile que quieres comprar un carro.	⟶ Pregúntale por qué necesita un carro.
Explica tres razones por las que necesitas un carro.	⟶ Explica por qué sus razones son buenas o malas.
Dile que por no tener un carro tu vida es muy difícil.	⟶ Decide si vas a darle el dinero y explica por qué.

Síntesis

Extra Practice For students still having trouble distinguishing between **por** and **para**, have them create a mnemonic device, like a story or chant, for remembering the different uses. Ex: **Vine por la tarde y busqué por el parque, por el río y por el centro. Busqué por horas. Viajé por carro, por tren y por avión.** Do the same for **para.**

6 **Una subasta** (*auction*) Cada estudiante debe traer a la clase un objeto o una foto del objeto para vender. En grupos, túrnense para ser el/la vendedor(a) y los postores (*bidders*). Para empezar, el/la vendedor(a) describe el objeto y explica para qué se usa y por qué alguien debe comprarlo.
Answers will vary.

modelo

Vendedora: Aquí tengo un reproductor de CD. Pueden usarlo para disfrutar su música favorita o para escuchar canciones en español. Sólo hace un año que lo compré y todavía funciona perfectamente. ¿Quién ofrece $1.500 para empezar?

Postor(a) 1: Pero los reproductores de CD son anticuados. Te doy $20.

Vendedora: Ah, pero éste es muy especial porque viene con el CD que grabé cuando quería ser cantante de ópera.

Postor(a) 2: Ah, ¡entonces te doy $100!

Lección 5

5.3 Reciprocal reflexives Tutorial

ANTE TODO In **Lección 1**, you learned that reflexive verbs indicate that the subject of a sentence does the action to itself. Reciprocal reflexives, on the other hand, express a shared or reciprocal action between two or more people or things. In this context, the pronoun means *(to) each other* or *(to) one another.*

Teaching Tips
• Briefly review reflexive verbs (**Lección 1**, pp. 30–31) before beginning this grammar presentation.
• To add a visual aspect, hold up photos of celebrities and have students use reciprocal reflexives to make statements about them. Remind them they can use present, preterite, or imperfect tense. Ex: **Antes Jennifer Aniston y Brad Pitt se querían mucho, pero ahora no se hablan.**

Luis y Marta **se** miran en el espejo.
Luis and Marta look at themselves in the mirror.

Luis y Marta **se** miran.
Luis and Marta look at each other.

▶ Only the plural forms of the reflexive pronouns (**nos, os, se**) are used to express reciprocal actions because the action must involve more than one person or thing.

Cuando **nos vimos** en la calle, **nos abrazamos**.
When we saw each other on the street, we hugged (one another).

Nos ayudamos cuando usamos la computadora.
We help each other when we use the computer.

Ustedes **se** van a **encontrar** en el cibercafé, ¿no?
You are meeting (each other) at the cybercafé, right?

Las amigas **se saludaron** y **se besaron**.
The friends greeted each other and kissed (one another).

¡ATENCIÓN!

Here is a list of common verbs that can express reciprocal actions:
abrazar(se) *to hug; to embrace (each other)*
ayudar(se) *to help (each other)*
besar(se) *to kiss (each other)*
encontrar(se) *to meet (each other); to run into (each other)*
saludar(se) *to greet (each other)*

TPR Call on a pair of volunteers to act out a reciprocal action. The class will guess the action, using the verb in a sentence.

Extra Practice Write several verbs on the board and have students describe what they and their friends do together. Ex: **verse, decirse, ayudarse, reunirse**

 **¡INTÉNTALO!** Indica el reflexivo recíproco adecuado de estos verbos en el presente o el pretérito.

presente

1. (escribir) Los novios __se escriben__.
   Nosotros __nos escribimos__.
   Ana y Ernesto __se escriben__.
2. (escuchar) Mis tíos __se escuchan__.
   Nosotros __nos escuchamos__.
   Ellos __se escuchan__.
3. (ver) Nosotros __nos vemos__.
   Fernando y Tomás __se ven__.
   Ustedes __se ven__.
4. (llamar) Ellas __se llaman__.
   Mis hermanos __se llaman__.
   Pepa y yo __nos llamamos__.

pretérito

1. (saludar) Nicolás y tú __se saludaron__.
   Nuestros vecinos __se saludaron__.
   Nosotros __nos saludamos__.
2. (hablar) Los amigos __se hablaron__.
   Elena y yo __nos hablamos__.
   Ustedes __se hablan__.
3. (conocer) Alberto y yo __nos conocimos__.
   Ustedes __se conocieron__.
   Ellos __se conocieron__.
4. (encontrar) Ana y Javier __se encontraron__.
   Los primos __se encontraron__.
   Mi hermana y yo __nos encontramos__.

recursos

WB
pp. 299–300

LM
p. 315

vhlcentral.com
Lección 5

Práctica y Comunicación

1 Have students expand upon the sentences to create a story about **Laura** and **Elián** falling in love.

1 Have students rewrite the sentences, imagining that they are talking about themselves and their significant other, a close friend, or a relative.

1

Un amor recíproco Describe a Laura y a Elián usando los verbos recíprocos.

> **modelo**
>
> Laura veía a Elián todos los días. Elián veía a Laura todos los días.
> Laura y Elián *se veían todos los días.*

1. Laura conocía bien a Elián. Elián conocía bien a Laura.
   Laura y Elián se conocían bien.
2. Laura miraba a Elián con amor. Elián la miraba con amor también.
   Laura y Elián se miraban con amor.
3. Laura entendía bien a Elián. Elián entendía bien a Laura.
   Laura y Elián se entendían bien.
4. Laura hablaba con Elián todas las noches por teléfono. Elián hablaba
   con Laura todas las noches por teléfono.
   Laura y Elián se hablaban todas las noches por teléfono.
5. Laura ayudaba a Elián con sus problemas. Elián la ayudaba también
   con sus problemas.
   Laura y Elián se ayudaban con sus problemas.

2 Have pairs choose a drawing and create the story of what the characters did leading up to the moment pictured and what they did after that. Ask pairs to share their stories, and have the class vote for the most original or funniest one.

2

Describir Mira los dibujos y describe lo que estas personas hicieron. Answers will vary.
Suggested answers:

1. Las hermanas ___se abrazaron___.

2. Ellos ___se besaron___.

3. Gilberto y Mercedes ___no se miraron___ /
   ___no se hablaron___ / ___se enojaron___.

4. Tú y yo ___nos saludamos___ /
   ___nos encontramos en la calle___.

3 Have students ask follow-up questions. Ex: **¿A qué hora se vieron ayer? ¿Dónde se vieron? ¿Por qué se vieron ayer? ¿Para qué se ven ustedes normalmente?**

3

Preguntas En parejas, túrnense para hacerse estas preguntas. Answers will vary.

1. ¿Se vieron tú y tu mejor amigo/a ayer? ¿Cuándo se ven ustedes normalmente?
2. ¿Dónde se encuentran tú y tus amigos?
3. ¿Se ayudan tú y tu mejor amigo/a con sus problemas?
4. ¿Se entienden bien tus compañeros de clase?
5. ¿Dónde se conocieron tú y tu mejor amigo/a? ¿Cuánto tiempo hace que se
   conocen ustedes?
6. ¿Cuándo se dan regalos tú y tu novio/a?
7. ¿Se escriben tú y tus amigos mensajes de texto o prefieren llamarse por teléfono?
8. ¿Siempre se llevan bien tú y tu compañero/a de cuarto? Explica.

Practice more at **vhlcentral.com**.

Lección 5

5.4 Stressed possessive adjectives and pronouns **Tutorial**

ANTE TODO Spanish has two types of possessive adjectives: the unstressed (or short) forms you learned in *¡ADELANTE! UNO* **Lección 3** and the stressed (or long) forms. The stressed forms are used for emphasis or to express *of mine, of yours,* and so on.

Stressed possessive adjectives

Masculine singular	Feminine singular	Masculine plural	Feminine plural	
mío	**mía**	**míos**	**mías**	*my; (of) mine*
tuyo	**tuya**	**tuyos**	**tuyas**	*your; (of) yours* (fam.)
suyo	**suya**	**suyos**	**suyas**	*your; (of) yours* (form.); *his; (of) his; her; (of) hers; its*
nuestro	**nuestra**	**nuestros**	**nuestras**	*our; (of) ours*
vuestro	**vuestra**	**vuestros**	**vuestras**	*your; (of) yours* (fam.)
suyo	**suya**	**suyos**	**suyas**	*your; (of) yours* (form.); *their; (of) theirs*

▶ **¡Atención!** Used with **un/una**, these possessives are similar in meaning to the English expression *of mine/yours*/etc.

Juancho es **un** amigo **mío**.
Juancho is a friend of mine.

Ella es **una** compañera **nuestra**.
She is a classmate of ours.

▶ Stressed possessive adjectives agree in gender and number with the nouns they modify. While unstressed possessive adjectives are placed before the noun, stressed possessive adjectives are placed after the noun they modify.

su impresora
her printer

la impresora **suya**
her printer

nuestros televisores
our television sets

los televisores **nuestros**
our television sets

▶ A definite article, an indefinite article, or a demonstrative adjective usually precedes a noun modified by a stressed possessive adjective.

Me encantan
{
unos discos compactos **tuyos**. *I love some of your CDs.*
los discos compactos **tuyos**. *I love your CDs.*
estos discos compactos **tuyos**. *I love these CDs of yours.*

▶ Since **suyo, suya, suyos,** and **suyas** have more than one meaning, you can avoid confusion by using the construction: [*article*] + [*noun*] + **de** + [*subject pronoun*].

el teclado **suyo**

el teclado **de él/ella/usted**
el teclado **de ustedes/ellos/ellas**

Teaching Tip Write the masculine forms of the stressed possessive adjectives/pronouns on the board, and ask volunteers to give the feminine and plural forms. Emphasize that when a stressed possessive adjective is used, the word it modifies is preceded by an article.

Pairs Tell students that their laundry has gotten mixed up with their roommate's and since they are the same size and have the same tastes in clothing, they cannot tell what belongs to whom. Have them ask each other questions about different articles of clothing. Ex: —¿Son tuyos estos pantalones de rayas? —Sí, son míos. —Y, ¿estos calcetines rojos son tuyos? —Sí, son míos, pero esta camisa grandísima no es mía.

Video Replay the **Fotonovela** episode. Have students listen for each use of an unstressed possessive adjective and write down the sentence in which it occurs. Next, have students rewrite those sentences using a stressed possessive adjective. Discuss how the use of stressed possessive adjectives affected the meaning or fluidity of the sentences.

CONSULTA

This is the same construction you learned in *¡ADELANTE! UNO* **Lección 3** for clarifying **su** and **sus**. To review unstressed possessive adjectives, see *¡ADELANTE! UNO* **Estructura 3.2**, p. 139.

Lección 5

Teaching Tips
- Ask students questions using unstressed possessive adjectives or the [*article*] + [*noun*] + **de** construction before a name, having them answer with a possessive pronoun. Ex: **¿Tienes tu cuaderno? (Sí, tengo el mío.)**
- Point out that the function of the stressed possessives is to give emphasis. They are often used to point out contrasts. Ex: **¿Tu carro es azul? Pues, el carro mío es rojo. ¿Tu cámara digital no es buena? La mía es excelente.**

Possessive pronouns

▶ Possessive pronouns are used to replace a noun + [*possessive adjective*]. In Spanish, the possessive pronouns have the same forms as the stressed possessive adjectives, but they are preceded by a definite article.

la cámara **nuestra**	**la nuestra**
el navegador GPS **tuyo**	**el tuyo**
los archivos **suyos**	**los suyos**

▶ A possessive pronoun agrees in number and gender with the noun it replaces.

—Aquí está **mi coche**. ¿Dónde está **el tuyo**?
Here's my car. Where is yours?

—**El mío** está en el taller de mi hermano.
Mine is at my brother's garage.

—¿Tienes **las revistas** de Carlos?
Do you have Carlos' magazines?

—No, pero tengo **las nuestras**.
No, but I have ours.

¿También está descompuesta tu computadora?

No, la mía no, la suya.

recursos

WB
pp. 301–302

LM
p. 316

S
vhlcentral.com
Lección 5

¡INTÉNTALO! Indica las formas tónicas (*stressed*) de estos adjetivos posesivos y los pronombres posesivos correspondientes.

	adjetivos	pronombres
1. su cámara digital	la *cámara digital* suya	la suya
2. mi televisor	el televisor mío	el mío
3. nuestros discos compactos	los discos compactos nuestros	los nuestros
4. tus calculadoras	las calculadoras tuyas	las tuyas
5. su monitor	el monitor suyo	el suyo
6. mis videos	los videos míos	los míos
7. nuestra impresora	la impresora nuestra	la nuestra
8. tu estéreo	el estéreo tuyo	el tuyo
9. nuestro cederrón	el cederrón nuestro	el nuestro
10. mi computadora	la computadora mía	la mía

Extra Practice Call out a noun and subject, then ask students to say which stressed possessive adjective they would use. Ex: **discos compactos, ustedes (suyos)**

Práctica

1

Oraciones Forma oraciones con estas palabras. Usa el presente y haz los cambios necesarios.

1. un / amiga / suyo / vivir / Mendoza   Una amiga suya vive en Mendoza.
2. ¿me / prestar / calculadora / tuyo?   ¿Me prestas la calculadora tuya?
3. el / coche / suyo / nunca / funcionar / bien   El coche suyo nunca funciona bien.
4. no / nos / interesar / problemas / suyo   No nos interesan los problemas suyos.
5. yo / querer / cámara digital / mío / ahora mismo   Yo quiero la cámara digital mía ahora mismo.
6. un / amigos / nuestro / manejar / como / loco   Unos amigos nuestros manejan como locos.

2

¿Es suyo? Un policía ha capturado (*has captured*) al hombre que robó (*robbed*) en tu casa. Ahora quiere saber qué cosas son tuyas. Túrnate con un(a) compañero/a para hacer el papel del policía y usa las pistas (*clues*) para contestar las preguntas.

> **modelo**
> no/viejo
> **Policía:** Esta impresora, ¿es suya?
> **Estudiante:** No, no es mía. La mía era más vieja.

1. sí   E1: Este estéreo, ¿es suyo? E2: Sí, es mío.

2. no/pequeño   E1: Este televisor, ¿es suyo? E2: No, no es mío. El mío era más pequeño.

3. sí   E1: Estos teléfonos celulares, ¿son suyos? E2: Sí, son míos.

4. sí   E1: Esta computadora portátil, ¿es suya? E2: Sí, es mía.

5. no/grande   E1: Esta cámara de video, ¿es suya? E2: No, no es mía. La mía era más grande.

6. no/caro   E1: Estos reproductores de MP3, ¿son suyos? E2: No, no son míos. Los míos eran más caros.

3

Conversaciones Completa estas conversaciones con las formas adecuadas de los pronombres posesivos.

1. —La casa de ellos estaba en la Avenida Alvear. ¿Dónde estaba la casa de ustedes?
   —__La nuestra__ estaba en la calle Bolívar.
2. —A Carmen le encanta su monitor nuevo.
   —¿Sí? A José no le gusta __el suyo__.
3. —Puse mis discos aquí. ¿Dónde pusiste __los tuyos__, Alfonso?
   —Puse __los míos__ en el escritorio.
4. —Se me olvidó traer mis llaves. ¿Trajeron ustedes __las suyas__?
   —No, dejamos __las nuestras__ en casa.
5. —Yo compré mi computadora en una tienda y Marta compró __la suya__ en Internet. Y __la tuya__, ¿dónde la compraste?
   —__La mía__ es de Cíbermax.

Practice more at **vhlcentral.com.**

1 Have students write four additional dehydrated sentences that use stressed possessive adjectives or pronouns. Have them exchange papers with a classmate, who will "rehydrate" them.

2 Have students continue the activity, using these items: **el navegador GPS, las calculadoras, el reproductor de DVD, los ratones.**

3 To simplify, have students begin by scanning the conversations and writing the English translation of the word for each blank. Ex: 1. *Ours.* Then have them underline the noun that the pronoun refers to and state its gender and number. Ex: 1. **casa**; feminine singular.

3 Have students create conversations modeled after the ones in the activity and perform them for the class. Each one should consist of at least six lines and use as many stressed possessive adjectives and pronouns as possible.

Lección 5

Comunicación

4 Encourage students to bring in personal items to use as props, or have them print out photos of the items.

4

Vendedores competitivos Trabajen en grupos de tres. Uno/a de ustedes va a una tienda a comprar un aparato tecnológico (reproductor de MP3, computadora portátil, monitor, etc.). Los/Las otros/as dos son empleados/as de dos marcas rivales y compiten para convencer al/a la cliente/a de que compre su producto. Usen los adjetivos posesivos y túrnense para comprar y vender. ¿Quién es el/la mejor vendedor/a? Answers will vary.

> **modelo**
>
> **Estudiante 1:** Buenos días, quiero comprar un reproductor de MP3.
> **Estudiante 2:** Tengo lo que necesita. El mío, tiene capacidad para 500 canciones.
> **Estudiante 3:** El tuyo es muy viejo, con el mío también puedes ver videos…

5 Before beginning the activity, have students make a list of objects to compare. Then have them brainstorm as many different qualities or features of those objects as they can. Finally, have them list adjectives that they might use to compare the objects they have chosen.

5

Comparar Trabajen en parejas. Intenta (*Try to*) convencer a tu compañero/a de que algo que tú tienes es mejor que lo que él/ella tiene. Pueden hablar de sus carros, reproductores de MP3, teléfonos celulares, clases, horarios o trabajos. Answers will vary.

> **modelo**
>
> **Estudiante 1:** Mi computadora tiene una pantalla de quince pulgadas (*inches*). ¿Y la tuya?
> **Estudiante 2:** La mía es mejor porque tiene una pantalla de diecisiete pulgadas.
> **Estudiante 1:** Pues la mía…

Síntesis

6

Inventos locos En grupos pequeños, imaginen que construyeron un aparato tecnológico revolucionario. Dibujen su invento y descríbanlo contestando estas preguntas. Incluyan todos los detalles que crean (*that you believe*) necesarios. Luego, compártanlo con la clase. Utilicen los posesivos, **por** y **para** y el vocabulario de **Contextos**. Answers will vary.

> **modelo**
>
> Nuestro aparato se usa para cocinar huevos y funciona de una manera muy fácil...

Supersite: See the Activity Pack for an additional information gap activity to practice the material presented in this section.

Extra Practice Have students imagine that they are salespersons at a car dealership and they are writing a letter to a customer explaining why their cars are better than those of the other two dealerships in town. Students should compare several attributes of the cars and use stressed possessive adjectives and pronouns when appropriate.

- ¿Para qué se usa?
- ¿Cómo es?
- ¿Cuánto cuesta?
- ¿Qué personas van a comprar este aparato?

Recapitulación

Diagnostics

Completa estas actividades para repasar los conceptos de gramática que aprendiste en esta lección.

1 **Completar** Completa la tabla con las formas de los mandatos familiares. **8 pts.**

Infinitivo	Mandato	
	Afirmativo	**Negativo**
comer	come	no comas
hacer	haz	no hagas
sacar	saca	no saques
venir	ven	no vengas
ir	ve	no vayas

2 **Por y para** Completa el diálogo con **por** o **para**. **10 pts.**

MARIO Hola, yo trabajo (1) ___para___ el periódico de la universidad. ¿Puedo hacerte unas preguntas?

INÉS Sí, claro.

MARIO ¿Navegas mucho (2) ___por___ la red?

INÉS Sí, todos los días me conecto a Internet (3) ___para___ leer mi correo y navego (4) ___por___ una hora. También me gusta hablar (5) ___por___ *Skype* con mis amigos. Es muy bueno y, (6) ___para___ mí, es divertido.

MARIO ¿Y qué piensas sobre hacer la tarea en la computadora?

INÉS En general, me parece bien, pero (7) ___por___ ejemplo, anoche hice unos ejercicios (8) ___para___ la clase de álgebra y al final me dolieron los ojos. (9) ___Por___ eso a veces prefiero hacer la tarea a mano.

MARIO Muy bien. Muchas gracias (10) ___por___ tu tiempo.

3 **Posesivos** Completa las oraciones y confirma de quién son las cosas. **6 pts.**

1. —¿Éste es mi video? —Sí, es el ___tuyo___ (*fam.*).
2. —¿Ésta es la cámara de tu papá? —Sí, es la ___suya___.
3. — ¿Ese teléfono es de Pilar? —Sí, es el ___suyo___.
4. —¿Éstos son los cederrones de ustedes? —No, no son ___nuestros___.
5. —¿Ésta es tu computadora portátil? —No, no es ___mía___.
6. —¿Ésas son mis fotos? —Sí, son las ___suyas___ (*form.*).

RESUMEN GRAMATICAL

5.1 **Familiar commands** *pp. 268–269*

tú commands		
Infinitive	**Affirmative**	**Negative**
guardar	**guard**a	no **guard**es
volver	**vuelv**e	no **vuelv**as
imprimir	**imprim**e	no **imprim**as

▶ Irregular **tú** command forms

dar → **no des**	saber → **no sepas**
decir → **di**	salir → **sal**
estar → **no estés**	ser → **sé, no seas**
hacer → **haz**	tener → **ten**
ir → **ve, no vayas**	venir → **ven**
poner → **pon**	

▶ Verbs ending in **-car, -gar, -zar** have a spelling change in the negative **tú** commands:

sacar → no sa**qu**es
apagar → no apa**gu**es
almorzar → no almuer**c**es

5.2 **Por and para** *pp. 272–273*

▶ Uses of **por**:

motion or general location; duration; reason or motive; object of a search; means by which something is done; exchange or substitution; unit of measure

▶ Uses of **para**:

destination; deadline; purpose or goal; recipient of something; comparison or opinion; in the employment of

5.3 **Reciprocal reflexives** *p. 276*

▶ Reciprocal reflexives express a shared or reciprocal action between two or more people or things. Only the plural forms (**nos, os, se**) are used.

Cuando **nos vimos** en la calle, **nos abrazamos**.

▶ Common verbs that can express reciprocal actions:

abrazar(se), ayudar(se), besar(se), conocer(se), encontrar(se), escribir(se), escuchar(se), hablar(se), llamar(se), mirar(se), saludar(se), ver(se)

Small Groups As a class, brainstorm a list of infinitives that can be made reciprocal (**llamar, abrazar, conocer**, etc.) and write them on the board. In small groups, have students create a dialogue using at least six of these infinitives. Then have students act out their dialogues for the class. Encourage students to use lesson vocabulary.

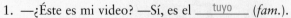

Lección 5

4 Give students these situations as items 5–8: **5. Mi amigo tiene las respuestas del examen final de historia. ¿Se las pido?** (No, no se las pidas.; Sí, pídeselas.) **6. Es el cumpleaños de mi compañero de cuarto. ¿Le compro algo?** (Sí, cómprale algo.; No, no le compres nada.) **7. Rompí la computadora portátil de mi padre. ¿Se lo digo?** (Sí, díselo; No, no se lo digas.) **8. No tengo nada de dinero. ¿Busco trabajo?** (Sí, búscalo.; No, no lo busques.)

4

Ángel y diablito A Juan le gusta pedir consejos a su ángel y a su diablito imaginarios. Completa las respuestas con mandatos familiares desde las dos perspectivas. **8 pts.**

1. Estoy manejando. ¿Voy más rápido?
   Á No, no ___vayas___ más rápido.
   D Sí, ___ve___ más rápido.

2. Es el reproductor de música de mi hermana.
   ¿Lo pongo en mi mochila?
   Á No, no ___lo pongas___ en tu mochila.
   D Sí, ___ponlo___ en tu mochila.

3. Necesito estirar (*to stretch*) las piernas.
   ¿Doy un paseo?
   Á Sí, ___da___ un paseo.
   D No, no ___des___ un paseo.

4. Mi amigo necesita imprimir algo. ¿Apago la impresora?
   Á No, no ___apagues___ la impresora.
   D Sí, ___apaga___ la impresora.

5.4 | **Stressed possessive adjectives and pronouns** *pp. 278–279*

Stressed possessive adjectives

Masculine	Feminine
mío(s)	mía(s)
tuyo(s)	tuya(s)
suyo(s)	suya(s)
nuestro(s)	nuestra(s)
vuestro(s)	vuestra(s)
suyo(s)	suya(s)

la impresora **suya** → la **suya**

las llaves **mías** → las **mías**

5 Have students create two additional dehydrated sentences. Then have them exchange papers with a classmate and complete the exercise.

5

Oraciones Forma oraciones para expresar acciones recíprocas con el tiempo indicado. **6 pts.**

> **modelo**
>
> tú y yo / conocer / bien (presente) *Tú y yo nos conocemos bien.*

1. José y Paco / llamar / una vez por semana (imperfecto)
   José y Paco se llamaban una vez por semana.
2. mi novia y yo / ver / todos los días (presente)
   Mi novia y yo nos vemos todos los días.
3. los compañeros de clase / ayudar / con la tarea (pretérito)
   Los compañeros de clase se ayudaron con la tarea.
4. tú y tu mamá / escribir / por correo electrónico / cada semana (imperfecto)
   Tú y tu mamá se escribían por correo electrónico cada semana.
5. mis hermanas y yo / entender / perfectamente (presente)
   Mis hermanas y yo nos entendemos perfectamente.
6. los profesores / saludar / con mucho respeto (pretérito)
   Los profesores se saludaron con mucho respeto.

6 To challenge students, have them first write a letter from the point of view of the friend who needs help with technology. Then have students write their suggestions according to the problems outlined in the letter.

6

La tecnología Escribe al menos seis oraciones diciéndole a un(a) amigo/a qué hacer para tener "una buena relación" con la tecnología. Usa mandatos familiares afirmativos y negativos. **12 pts.**

Answers will vary.

7

7 Explain that this expression takes the masculine possessive form because it does not refer to anything specific, as denoted by **lo que**.

Saber compartir Completa la expresión con los dos pronombres posesivos que faltan. **¡2 puntos EXTRA!**

Heritage Speakers Ask heritage speakers to come up with additional popular expressions using grammar from this lesson (**tú** commands, **por** and **para**, reciprocal reflexives, stressed possessives). Have them write the expressions on the board, leaving key words blank for classmates to guess.

" Lo que° es ___mío___
es ___tuyo/suyo___ . **"**

Lo que *What*

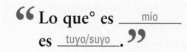

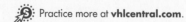

Practice more at **vhlcentral.com**.

Lectura

Antes de leer

communication
cultures
NATIONAL STANDARDS

Estrategia

Recognizing borrowed words

One way languages grow is by borrowing words from each other. English words that relate to technology often are borrowed by Spanish and other languages throughout the world. Sometimes the words are modified slightly to fit the sounds of the languages that borrow them. When reading in Spanish, you can often increase your understanding by looking for words borrowed from English or other languages you know.

Examinar el texto

Observa la tira cómica°. ¿De qué trata°?
¿Cómo lo sabes? Answers will vary.

Buscar

Esta lectura contiene una palabra tomada° del inglés. Trabaja con un(a) compañero/a para encontrarla.

el celular
_____

Repasa° las palabras nuevas relacionadas con la tecnología que aprendiste en **Contextos** y expande la lista de palabras tomadas del inglés. Answers will vary.

_____ _____

_____ _____

_____

Sobre el autor

Juan Matías Loiseau (1974–). Más conocido como Tute, este artista nació en Buenos Aires, Argentina. Estudió diseño gráfico, humorismo y cine. Sus tiras cómicas se publican en Estados Unidos, Francia y toda Latinoamérica.

tira cómica *comic strip* ¿De qué trata? *What is it about?*
tomada *taken* Repasa *Review*

 Practice more at **vhlcentral.com**.

Después de leer

Comprensión 🔊⚡

Indica si las oraciones son **ciertas** o **falsas**. Corrige las falsas.

Cierto   Falso

✓ _____ 1. Hay tres personajes en la tira cómica: un usuario de teléfono, un amigo y un empleado de la empresa (*company*) telefónica.

_____ ✓ 2. El nuevo servicio de teléfono incluye las llamadas telefónicas únicamente.
También viene con un tipo que te sigue a todos lados.

_____ ✓ 3. El empleado duerme en su casa.
Duerme al lado de la cama del usuario.

✓ _____ 4. El contrato de teléfono dura (*lasts*) un año.

_____ ✓ 5. El usuario y el amigo están trabajando (*working*). Están de vacaciones.

Preguntas 🔊⚡

Responde a estas preguntas con oraciones completas. Usa el pretérito y el imperfecto.

1. ¿Al usuario le gustaba usar el teléfono celular todo el tiempo?
No, al usuario le molestaba usar el celular todo el tiempo.

2. ¿Por qué el usuario decidió tirar el teléfono al mar?
Porque el celular y el tipo lo tenían harto.

3. Según el amigo, ¿para qué tenía el usuario que tirar el teléfono celular al mar?
El usuario tenía que tirar el teléfono al mar para recuperar su libertad.

4. ¿Qué ocurrió cuando el usuario tiró el teléfono?
El empleado fue a buscar el teléfono.

5. ¿Qué le dijo el empleado al usuario cuando salió del mar?
El empleado le dijo que tenía una llamada perdida.

Conversar

En grupos pequeños, hablen de estos temas. Answers will vary.

1. ¿Se sienten identificados/as con el usuario de teléfono de la tira cómica? ¿Por qué?

2. ¿Cuáles son los aspectos positivos y los negativos de tener teléfono celular?

3. ¿Cuál es para ustedes el límite que debe tener la tecnología en nuestras vidas?

Teaching Tip Survey the class for item 2 in **Conversar** and write their answers on the board in a two-column chart with the headings **Lo positivo** y **Lo negativo**. Then ask the class to determine which column wins out overall.

te viene *comes with* tipo *guy, dude* te avisa *alerts you* escuchás *listen (Arg.)* distraídos *careless* piso *floor* bolsa de dormir *sleeping bag* darle de baja *to suspend* harto *fed up* revolear *throw it away with energy (S. America)* bien hecho *well done* llamada perdida *missed call*

Pairs Have pairs of students work together to create an alternate ending to this comic. Then have students get together in groups and share their new endings. Have the group select one to present to the class.

Escritura

Estrategia
Listing key words

Once you have determined the purpose for a piece of writing and identified your audience, it is helpful to make a list of key words you can use while writing. If you were to write a description of your campus, for example, you would probably need a list of prepositions that describe location, such as **delante de, al lado de,** and **detrás de**. Likewise, a list of descriptive adjectives would be useful to you if you were writing about the people and places of your childhood.

By preparing a list of potential words ahead of time, you will find it easier to avoid using the dictionary while writing your first draft. You will probably also learn a few new words in Spanish while preparing your list of key words.

Listing useful vocabulary is also a valuable organizational strategy, since the act of brainstorming key words will help you to form ideas about your topic. In addition, a list of key words can help you avoid redundancy when you write.

If you were going to help someone write a personal ad, what words would be most helpful to you? Jot a few of them down and compare your list with a partner's. Did you choose the same words? Would you choose any different or additional words, based on what your partner wrote?

1. _____
2. _____
3. _____
4. _____
5. _____
6. _____

Tema
Escribir instrucciones

Un(a) amigo/a tuyo/a quiere escribir un anuncio personal en un sitio web para citas románticas. Tú tienes experiencia con esto y vas a decirle qué debe y no debe decir en su perfil°.

Escríbele un correo en el que le explicas claramente° cómo hacerlo.

Cuando escribas tu correo, considera esta información:

▶ el nombre del sitio web

▶ mandatos afirmativos que describen en detalle lo que tu amigo/a debe escribir

▶ una descripción física, sus pasatiempos, sus actividades favoritas y otras cosas originales como el tipo de carro que tiene o su signo del zodiaco

▶ su dirección electrónica, su número de teléfono celular, etc.

▶ mandatos negativos sobre cosas que tu amigo/a no debe escribir en el anuncio

Teaching Tip Have students brainstorm and categorize a list of verbs and instructions that they may use in their writing. Ask a volunteer to record students' suggestions on the board. Tell students they will be composing their e-mails using affirmative and negative **tú** commands.

perfil *profile* **claramente** *clearly*

Escuchar Audio

Lección 5

Estrategia

Recognizing the genre of spoken discourse

You will encounter many different genres of spoken discourse in Spanish. For example, you may hear a political speech, a radio interview, a commercial, a voicemail message, or a news broadcast. Try to identify the genre of what you hear so that you can activate your background knowledge about that type of discourse and identify the speakers' motives and intentions.

 To practice this strategy, you will now listen to two short selections. Identify the genre of each one.

Preparación

Mira la foto de Ricardo Moreno. ¿Puedes imaginarte qué tipo de discurso vas a oír?

Ahora escucha 🎧 ●ᔆ

Mientras escuchas a Ricardo Moreno, responde a las preguntas.

1. ¿Qué tipo de discurso es?
   a. las noticias° por radio o televisión
   b. una conversación entre amigos
   c. un anuncio comercial
   d. una reseña° de una película

2. ¿De qué habla?
   a. del tiempo   c. de un producto o servicio
   b. de su vida   d. de algo que oyó o vio

3. ¿Cuál es el propósito°?
   a. informar   c. relacionarse con alguien
   b. vender   d. dar opiniones

noticias *news* reseña *review* propósito *purpose*

Comprensión

Identificar ●ᔆ

Indica si esta información está incluida en el discurso; si está incluida, escribe los detalles que escuchaste.

	Sí	No
1. El anuncio describe un servicio.	◉	○
Venden computadoras y productos para computadoras.		
2. Explica cómo está de salud.	○	◉
3. Informa sobre la variedad de productos.	◉	○
programas de computación, impresoras, computadoras portátiles		
4. Pide tu opinión.	○	◉
5. Explica por qué es la mejor tienda.	◉	○
Tiene buenos precios y los dependientes conocen los últimos avances.		
6. Informa sobre el tiempo para mañana.	○	◉
7. Informa dónde se puede conseguir el servicio.	◉	○
en Mundo de Computación o en el sitio web		
8. Informa sobre las noticias del mundo.	○	◉

Haz un anuncio ᔆ

Con tres o cuatro compañeros, hagan un anuncio comercial de algún producto. No se olviden de dar toda la información necesaria. Después presenten su anuncio a la clase. Entre todos, decidan cuál es el mejor anuncio.

Teaching Tip Make sure students correctly identified the two genres in the **Estrategia** recording as **entrevista** and **mensaje de correo de voz**. Then have them look at the photo and describe what they see. Guide them to see that **Ricardo Moreno** is broadcasting from a radio station.

En pantalla

NATIONAL STANDARDS — communication cultures

No sólo del fútbol y el béisbol viven los aficionados hispanos; también del automovilismo°. En Argentina es el segundo deporte más popular después del fútbol. En la Fórmula 1, la leyenda del argentino Juan Manuel Fangio aún sigue viva. España tiene circuitos importantes, como Jerez y Montmeló, y pilotos reconocidos como Fernando Alonso y Pedro de la Rosa. En México encontramos la tradicional Copa Turmex y las *NASCAR Corona Series*, y pilotos como Adrián Fernández y Esteban Gutiérrez. En NASCAR, el colombiano Juan Pablo Montoya y el cubanoamericano Aric Almirola han hecho un buen papel°.

Vocabulario útil	
¿Cómo quedó?	*How does it look?*
cuénteme	*tell me*
la llama	*flame; llama (the animal)*
malinterpretar	*misunderstand*
veamos	*let's see*

Preparación

¿Alguna vez le pediste a alguien que hiciera algo y te malinterpretó o se lo pediste a la persona equivocada?
Answers will vary.

Ordenar

Ordena cronológicamente estas oraciones.

a. El dueño del taller malinterpretó el pedido. 2

b. El cliente se sorprendió cuando lo vio y se le cayó el casco (*helmet*). 5

c. Pensó que el cliente no se refería a (*didn't refer to*) las llamas de fuego sino a los animales. 3

d. El cliente pidió que pintaran (*painted*) su carro con llamas. 1

e. El dueño estaba muy orgulloso (*proud*) cuando le mostró al cliente cómo quedó el carro. 4

¿Cómo terminó?

En parejas, imaginen el final de la historia. ¿Cómo se sentían el cliente y el dueño del taller? ¿Qué ocurrió después? ¿Encontraron una solución? Usen el pretérito y el imperfecto. Answers will vary.

automovilismo *car racing* han hecho un buen papel *have done a good job*

Anuncio de Davivienda

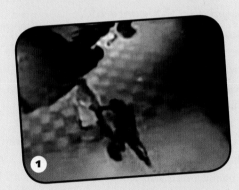

Don Álex, lo estábamos esperando.

Cuénteme. ¿Cómo quedó mi carro?

Quedó espectacular [...] Llamas por arriba, por los lados...

Teaching Tip Encourage students to come up with two endings for the video. One should be outlandishly comical, and the other should be serious.

Video: TV Clip

Practice more at **vhlcentral.com**.

Hoy día, en cualquier ciudad grande latinoamericana puedes encontrar **un cibercafé**. Allí uno puede disfrutar de° un refresco o un café mientras navega en Internet, escribe correo electrónico o chatea°. De hecho°, el negocio° del cibercafé está mucho más desarrollado° en Latinoamérica que en los Estados Unidos. En una ciudad hispana, es común ver varios en una misma cuadra°. Los cibercafés ofrecen servicios especializados que permiten su coexistencia. Por ejemplo, mientras que el cibercafé Videomax atrae° a los niños con videojuegos, el Conécta-T ofrece servicio de chat con cámara para jóvenes, y el Mundo° Ejecutivo atrae a profesionales, todos en la misma calle.

Maravillas de la tecnología

… los cibercafés se conocen comúnmente como "cabinas de Internet" y están localizados por todo el país.

Vocabulario útil	
chateando	*chatting*
comunidad indígena	*indigenous community*
localizados	*located*
usuarios	*users*

Preparación

¿Con qué frecuencia navegas en Internet? ¿Dónde lo haces, en tu casa o en un lugar público? Answers will vary.

… el primer *hotspot* de Cuzco [...] permite a los usuarios navegar de manera inalámbrica…

Elegir

Indica cuál de las dos opciones resume mejor este episodio.

a. En Cuzco, Internet es un elemento importante para las comunidades indígenas que quieren vender sus productos en otros países. Con Internet inalámbrica, estas comunidades chatean con clientes en otros países.

(b.) En Cuzco, la comunidad y los turistas usan la tecnología de los celulares e Internet para comunicarse con sus familias o vender productos. Para navegar en Internet, se pueden visitar las cabinas de Internet o ir a la Plaza de Armas con una computadora portátil.

Puedo usar Internet en medio de la plaza y nadie me molesta.

Teaching Tip To challenge students, have them write a summary in their own words.

disfrutar de *enjoy* chatea *chat (from the English verb* to chat*)* De hecho *In fact* negocio *business* desarrollado *developed* cuadra *(city) block* atrae *attracts* Mundo *World*

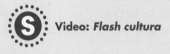 **Video: *Flash cultura***

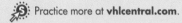 Practice more at **vhlcentral.com**.

recursos

| VM pp. 309–310 | vhlcentral.com Lección 5 |

S Video: *Panorama cultural*
Interactive map

Argentina

connections cultures NATIONAL STANDARDS

El país en cifras

▶ **Área:** 2.780.400 km² (1.074.000 millas²)
Argentina es el país de habla española más grande del mundo. Su territorio es dos veces el tamaño° de Alaska.

▶ **Población:** 42.548.000

▶ **Capital:** Buenos Aires (y su área metropolitana) —13.401.000
En el gran Buenos Aires vive más del treinta por ciento de la población total del país. La ciudad es conocida° como el "París de Suramérica" por su estilo parisino°.

Buenos Aires

▶ **Ciudades principales:**
Córdoba —1.552.000, Rosario —1.280.000, Mendoza —956.000

SOURCE: Population Division, UN Secretariat

▶ **Moneda:** peso argentino

▶ **Idiomas:** español (oficial), lenguas indígenas

Bandera de Argentina

Argentinos célebres

▶ **Jorge Luis Borges,** escritor (1899–1986)
▶ **María Eva Duarte de Perón ("Evita"),** primera dama° (1919–1952)
▶ **Mercedes Sosa,** cantante (1935–2009)
▶ **Leandro "Gato" Barbieri,** saxofonista (1932–)

tamaño *size* conocida *known* parisino *Parisian* primera dama *First Lady*
ancha *wide* mide *it measures* campo *field*

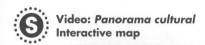

Gaucho de las pampas

ESTADOS UNIDOS

OCÉANO ATLÁNTICO

OCÉANO PACÍFICO

AMÉRICA DEL SUR

ARGENTINA

BOLIVIA

PARAGUAY

Las cataratas del Iguazú

San Miguel de Tucumán

La Cordillera de los Andes

Córdoba

CHILE

Aconcagua

Rosario

Río Paraná

URUGUAY

Buenos Aires

La Pampa

Mar del Plata

Océano Atlántico

San Carlos de Bariloche

Monte Fitz Roy (Chaltén)

Patagonia

Vista de San Carlos de Bariloche

Tierra del Fuego

recursos

| WB pp. 303–304 | VM pp. 307–308 | **S** vhlcentral.com Lección 5 |

¡Increíble pero cierto!

La Avenida 9 de Julio en Buenos Aires es la calle más ancha° del mundo. De lado a lado mide° cerca de 140 metros, lo que es equivalente a un campo° y medio de fútbol. Su nombre conmemora el Día de la Independencia de Argentina.

Historia • Inmigración europea

Se dice que Argentina es el país más "europeo" de toda Latinoamérica. Después del año 1880, inmigrantes italianos, alemanes, españoles e ingleses llegaron para establecerse en esta nación. Esta diversidad cultural ha dejado° una profunda huella° en la música, el cine y la arquitectura argentinos.

BRASIL

Artes • El tango

El tango es uno de los símbolos culturales más importantes de Argentina. Este género° musical es una mezcla de ritmos de origen africano, italiano y español, y se originó a finales del siglo XIX entre los porteños°. Poco después se hizo popular entre el resto de los argentinos y su fama llegó hasta París. Como baile, el tango en un principio° era provocativo y violento, pero se hizo más romántico durante los años 30. Hoy día, este estilo musical tiene adeptos° en muchas partes del mundo°.

Lugares • Las cataratas del Iguazú

Las famosas cataratas° del Iguazú se encuentran entre las fronteras de Argentina, Paraguay y Brasil, al norte de Buenos Aires. Cerca de ellas confluyen° los ríos Iguazú y Paraná. Estas extensas caídas de agua tienen hasta 80 metros (262 pies) de altura° y en época° de lluvias llegan a medir 4 kilómetros (2,5 millas) de ancho. Situadas en el Parque Nacional Iguazú, las cataratas son un destino° turístico muy visitado.

Artesano en Buenos Aires

¿Qué aprendiste? Responde a cada pregunta con una oración completa.

1. ¿Qué porcentaje de la población de Argentina vive en el gran Buenos Aires?
   Más del treinta por ciento de la población de Argentina vive en el gran Buenos Aires.

2. ¿Quién era Mercedes Sosa?
   Mercedes Sosa era una cantante argentina.

3. Se dice que Argentina es el país más europeo de Latinoamérica.
   ¿Por qué? Se dice que Argentina es el país más europeo de Latinoamérica porque muchos inmigrantes europeos se establecieron allí.

4. ¿Qué tipo de baile es uno de los símbolos culturales más importantes de Argentina?
   El tango es uno de los símbolos culturales más importantes de Argentina.

5. ¿Dónde y cuándo se originó el tango?
   El tango se originó entre los porteños a finales del siglo XIX.

6. ¿Cómo era el baile del tango originalmente?
   El tango era un baile provocativo y violento.

7. ¿En qué parque nacional están las cataratas del Iguazú?
   Las cataratas del Iguazú están en el Parque Nacional Iguazú.

Conexión Internet Investiga estos temas en **vhlcentral.com**.

1. Busca información sobre el tango. ¿Te gustan los ritmos y sonidos del tango? ¿Por qué? ¿Se baila el tango en tu comunidad?

2. ¿Quiénes fueron Juan y Eva Perón y qué importancia tienen en la historia de Argentina?

 Practice more at **vhlcentral.com**.

ha dejado *has left* huella *mark* género *genre* porteños *people of Buenos Aires* en un principio *at first* adeptos *followers* mundo *world* cataratas *waterfalls* confluyen *converge* altura *height* época *season* destino *destination*

Supersite/DVD: You may want to wrap up this section by playing the **Panorama cultural** video footage for this lesson.
Heritage Speakers If applicable, ask heritage speakers who use **vos** instead of **tú** to provide examples for the class.

La tecnología

la cámara digital/ de video	digital/video camera
el canal	(TV) channel
el cibercafé	cybercafé
el control remoto	remote control
el correo de voz	voice mail
el disco compacto	CD
el estéreo	stereo
el fax	fax (machine)
la pantalla táctil	touch screen
el radio	radio (set)
el reproductor de CD	CD player
el reproductor de MP3	MP3 player
el (teléfono) celular	(cell) phone
la televisión por cable	cable television
el televisor	televison set
el video	video
apagar	to turn off
funcionar	to work
llamar	to call
poner, prender	to turn on
sonar (o:ue)	to ring
descompuesto/a	not working; out of order
lento/a	slow
lleno/a	full

La computadora

el archivo	file
la arroba	@ symbol
el blog	blog
el cederrón	CD-ROM
la computadora (portátil)	(portable) computer; (laptop)
la conexión inalámbrica	wireless (connection)
la dirección electrónica	e-mail address
el disco compacto	CD
la impresora	printer
Internet	Internet
el mensaje de texto	text message
el monitor	(computer) monitor
la página principal	home page
la pantalla	screen
el programa de computación	software
el ratón	mouse
la red	network; Web
el reproductor de DVD	DVD player
el sitio web	website
el teclado	keyboard
borrar	to erase
descargar	to download
escanear	to scan
grabar	to record
guardar	to save
imprimir	to print
navegar (en Internet)	to surf (the Internet)

El carro

la autopista, la carretera	highway
el baúl	trunk
la calle	street
el capó, el cofre	hood
el carro, el coche	car
la circulación, el tráfico	traffic
el garaje, el taller (mecánico)	garage; (mechanic's) repair shop
la gasolina	gasoline
la gasolinera	gas station
la licencia de conducir	driver's license
la llanta	tire
el/la mecánico/a	mechanic
el navegador GPS	GPS
el parabrisas	windshield
la policía	police (force)
la velocidad máxima	speed limit
el volante	steering wheel
arrancar	to start
arreglar	to fix; to arrange
bajar(se) de	to get off of/out of (a vehicle)
conducir, manejar	to drive
estacionar	to park
llenar (el tanque)	to fill (the tank)
parar	to stop
revisar (el aceite)	to check (the oil)
subir(se) a	to get on/into (a vehicle)

Verbos

abrazar(se)	to hug; to embrace (each other)
ayudar(se)	to help (each other)
besar(se)	to kiss (each other)
encontrar(se) (o:ue)	to meet (each other); to run into (each other)
saludar(se)	to greet (each other)

Supersite: MP3 Audio Files, Testing Program

Otras palabras y expresiones

por aquí	around here
por ejemplo	for example
por eso	that's why; therefore
por fin	finally

Por and **para**	See pages 272–273.
Stressed possessive adjectives and pronouns	See pages 278–279.
Expresiones útiles	See page 263.

recursos

| LM p. 316 | vhlcentral.com Lección 5 |

Audio: Vocabulary Flashcards

contextos

1   **La tecnología** Fill in the blanks with the correct terms.

1. Para navegar en la red sin cables (*wires*) necesitas <u>una conexión inalámbrica</u>.

2. Para hacer videos de tu familia puedes usar <u>una cámara de video</u>.

3. Cuando vas a un sitio web, lo primero (*the first thing*) que ves es <u>la página principal</u>.

4. Si alguien te llama a tu celular y no respondes, te puede dejar un mensaje en <u>el correo de voz</u>.

5. La red de computadoras y servidores más importante del mundo es <u>Internet</u>.

6. Para poder ver muchos canales, tienes que tener <u>(la) televisión por cable</u>.

2   **Eso hacían** Match a subject from the word bank to each verb phrase. Then write complete sentences for the pairs using the imperfect.

| muchos jóvenes estadounidenses | el conductor del autobús | el mecánico de Jorge |
| el carro viejo | la impresora nueva | el teléfono celular |

1. manejar lentamente por la nieve

   <u>El conductor del autobús manejaba lentamente por la nieve.</u>

2. imprimir los documentos muy rápido

   <u>La impresora nueva imprimía los documentos muy rápido.</u>

3. revisarle el aceite al auto todos los meses

   <u>El mecánico de Jorge le revisaba el aceite al auto todos los meses.</u>

4. sonar insistentemente, pero nadie responder

   <u>El teléfono celular sonaba insistentemente, pero nadie respondía.</u>

5. no arrancar cuando llover

   <u>El carro viejo no arrancaba cuando llovía.</u>

6. navegar en Internet cuando eran niños

   <u>Muchos jóvenes estadounidenses navegaban en Internet cuando eran niños.</u>

3   **La computadora** Label the drawing with the correct terms.

1. <u>el monitor</u>

2. <u>la pantalla</u>

5. <u>la impresora</u>

3. <u>el teclado</u>

4. <u>el ratón</u>

6. <u>el reproductor de MP3</u>

7. <u>el disco compacto/el cederrón</u>

4 **Preguntas** Answer the questions with complete sentences.

1. ¿Para qué se usa la impresora?
   La impresora se usa para imprimir.

2. ¿Para qué se usan los frenos (*brakes*) del coche?
   Los frenos del coche se usan para parar.

3. ¿Qué se usa para conducir por carreteras que no conoces?
   El navegador GPS se usa para conducir por carreteras que no conoces.

4. ¿Qué se usa para llevar el carro a la derecha o a la izquierda?
   El volante se usa para llevar el carro a la derecha o a la izquierda.

5. ¿Qué se usa para cambiar los canales del televisor?
   El control remoto se usa para cambiar los canales del televisor.

6. ¿Para qué se usa la llave del carro?
   La llave del carro se usa para arrancar.

5 **Mi primer día en la carretera** Complete the paragraph with terms from the word bank.

accidente	estacionar	policía
aceite	lento	revisar
arrancar	licencia de conducir	subir
autopista	llanta	taller mecánico
calle	lleno	tráfico
descargar	parar	velocidad máxima

Después de dos exámenes, conseguí mi (1) licencia de conducir para poder manejar legalmente por primera vez. Estaba muy emocionado cuando (2) subí al carro de mi papá. El tanque estaba (3) lleno y el (4) aceite lo revisaron el día anterior (*previous*) en el (5) taller mecánico. El carro y yo estábamos listos para (6) arrancar. Primero salí por la (7) calle en donde está mi casa. Luego llegué a un área de la ciudad donde había mucha gente y también mucho (8) tráfico. Se me olvidó (9) parar en el semáforo (*light*), que estaba amarillo, y estuve cerca de tener un (10) accidente. Sin saberlo, entré en la (11) autopista interestatal (*interstate*). La (12) velocidad máxima era de 70 millas (*miles*) por hora, pero yo estaba tan nervioso que iba mucho más (13) lento, a 10 millas por hora. Vi un carro de la (14) policía y tuve miedo. Por eso volví a casa y (15) estacioné el carro en la calle. ¡Qué aventura!

estructura

5.1 Familiar commands

1 **Cosas por hacer** Read the list of things to do. Then use familiar commands to finish the e-mail from Ana to her husband, Eduardo, about the things that he has to do before their vacation.

> comprar un paquete de papel para la impresora
> ir al sitio web de la agencia de viajes y pedir la información sobre nuestro hotel
> imprimir la información
> terminar de hacer las maletas
>
> revisar el aceite del carro
> comprobar que tenemos una llanta extra
> limpiar el parabrisas
> llenar el tanque de gasolina
> venir a buscarme a la oficina

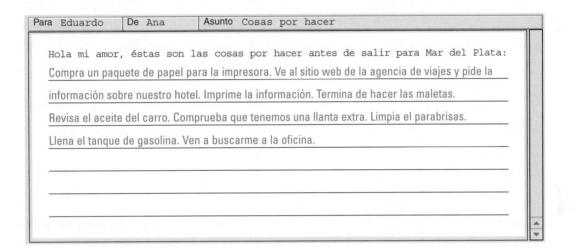

Para Eduardo	De Ana	Asunto Cosas por hacer

Hola mi amor, éstas son las cosas por hacer antes de salir para Mar del Plata:

Compra un paquete de papel para la impresora. Ve al sitio web de la agencia de viajes y pide la

información sobre nuestro hotel. Imprime la información. Termina de hacer las maletas.

Revisa el aceite del carro. Comprueba que tenemos una llanta extra. Limpia el parabrisas.

Llena el tanque de gasolina. Ven a buscarme a la oficina.

2 **Díselo** You are feeling bossy today. Give your friends instructions based on the cues provided using familiar commands.

modelo

Ramón / comprarte un disco compacto en Mendoza
Ramón, cómprame un disco compacto en Mendoza.

1. Mario / traerte la cámara digital que le regaló Gema
   Mario, tráeme la cámara digital que te regaló Gema.

2. Natalia / escribirle un mensaje de texto a su hermana
   Natalia, escríbele un mensaje de texto a tu hermana.

3. Martín / llamarlos por teléfono celular
   Martín, llámalos por teléfono celular.

4. Gloria / hacer la cama antes de salir
   Gloria, haz la cama antes de salir.

5. Carmen / no revisar el aceite hasta la semana que viene
   Carmen, no revises el aceite hasta la semana que viene.

6. Lilia / enseñarte a manejar
   Lilia, enséñame a manejar.

3 **Planes para el invierno** Rewrite this paragraph from a travel website. Use familiar commands instead of the infinitives you see.

Este invierno, (decir) adiós al frío y a la nieve. (Descubrir) una de las más grandes maravillas (*marvels*) naturales del mundo (*world*). (Ir) al Parque Nacional Iguazú en Argentina y (visitar) las hermosas cascadas. (Explorar) el parque y (mirar) las más de 400 especies de pájaros y animales que viven ahí. (Visitar) este santuario de la naturaleza en los meses de enero a marzo y (disfrutar) de una temperatura promedio de 77° F. Para unas vacaciones de aventura, (hacer) un safari por la selva (*jungle*) o (reservar) una excursión por el río Iguazú. De noche, (dormir) en uno de nuestros exclusivos hoteles en medio de la selva. (Respirar) el aire puro y (probar) la deliciosa comida de la región.

Invierno en Argentina

Este invierno, dile adiós al frío y a la nieve. Descubre una de las más grandes maravillas naturales del mundo. Ve al

Parque Nacional Iguazú en Argentina y visita las hermosas cascadas. Explora el parque y mira las más de 400 especies de

pájaros y animales que viven ahí. Visita este santuario de la naturaleza en los meses de enero a marzo y disfruta de una

temperatura promedio de 77° F. Para unas vacaciones de aventura, haz un safari por la selva o reserva una excursión por

el río Iguazú. De noche, duerme en uno de nuestros exclusivos hoteles en medio de la selva. Respira el aire puro y prueba

la deliciosa comida de la región.

4 **¿Qué hago?** Clara's brother Manuel is giving her a driving lesson, and Clara has a lot of questions. Write Manuel's answers to her questions in the form of affirmative or negative familiar commands.

> **modelo**
>
> ¿Tengo que comprar gasolina?
> *Sí, compra gasolina./No, no compres gasolina.*

1. ¿Puedo hablar por teléfono celular con mis amigos?

   Sí, habla por teléfono celular con tus amigos./No, no hables por teléfono celular con tus amigos.

2. ¿Puedo manejar en la autopista?

   Sí, maneja en la autopista./No, no manejes en la autopista.

3. ¿Debo estacionar por aquí?

   Sí, estaciona por aquí./No, no estaciones por aquí.

4. ¿Debo sacar mi licencia de conducir?

   Sí, saca tu licencia de conducir./No, no saques tu licencia de conducir.

5. ¿Puedo bajar por esta calle?

   Sí, baja por esta calle./No, no bajes por esta calle.

6. ¿Tengo que seguir el tráfico?

   Sí, sigue el tráfico./No, no sigas el tráfico.

5.2 Por and para

1 **Para éste o por aquello** Complete the sentences with **por** or **para** as appropriate.

1. Pudieron terminar el trabajo _____por_____ haber empezado (*having begun*) a tiempo.

2. Ese *fax* es _____para_____ enviar y recibir documentos de la compañía.

3. Elsa vivió en esa ciudad _____por_____ algunos meses hace diez años.

4. Mi mamá compró esta computadora portátil _____para_____ mi papá.

5. Sales _____para_____ Argentina mañana a las ocho y media.

6. Rosaura cambió el estéreo _____por_____ el reproductor de MP3.

7. El señor López necesita el informe _____para_____ el 2 de agosto.

8. Estuve estudiando toda la noche _____para_____ el examen.

9. Los turistas fueron de excursión _____por_____ las montañas.

10. Mis amigos siempre me escriben _____por_____ correo electrónico.

2 **Por muchas razones** Complete the sentences with the expressions in the word bank. Note that you will use two of them twice.

por aquí	por eso
por ejemplo	por fin

1. Ramón y Sara no pudieron ir a la fiesta anoche; _____por eso_____ no los viste.

2. Buscaron el vestido perfecto por mucho tiempo, y _____por fin_____ lo encontraron en esa tienda.

3. Creo que va a ser difícil encontrar un teclado y un monitor _____por aquí_____.

4. Pídele ayuda a uno de tus amigos, _____por ejemplo_____, Miguel, Carlos o Francisco.

5. Miguel y David no saben si podemos pasar _____por aquí_____ en bicicleta.

6. El monitor no está conectado, _____por eso_____ no funciona.

3 **Por y para** Complete the sentences with **por** or **para**.

1. Fui a comprar frutas _____por_____ (*instead of*) mi madre.

2. Fui a comprar frutas _____para_____ (*to give to*) mi madre.

3. Rita le dio dinero _____para_____ (*in order to buy*) la computadora portátil.

4. Rita le dio dinero _____por_____ (*in exchange for*) la computadora portátil.

5. La familia los llevó _____por_____ (*through*) los Andes.

6. La familia los llevó _____para_____ (*to*) los Andes.

4 **Escribir oraciones** Write sentences in the preterite, using the elements provided and **por** or **para**.

> **modelo**
>
> (tú) / salir en el auto / ¿? / Córdoba
> *Saliste en el auto para Córdoba.*

1. Ricardo y Emilia / traer un pastel / ¿? / su prima

   Ricardo y Emilia trajeron un pastel para su prima.

2. los turistas / llegar a las ruinas / ¿? / barco

   Los turistas llegaron a las ruinas por barco.

3. (yo) / tener un resfriado / ¿? / el frío

   Tuve un resfriado por el frío.

4. mis amigas / ganar dinero / ¿? / viajar a Suramérica

   Mis amigas ganaron dinero para viajar a Suramérica.

5. ustedes / buscar a Teresa / ¿? / toda la playa

   Ustedes buscaron a Teresa por toda la playa.

6. el avión / salir a las doce / ¿? / Buenos Aires

   El avión salió a las doce para Buenos Aires.

5 **Para Silvia** Complete the paragraph with **por** and **para**.

Fui a la agencia de viajes porque quería ir (1) _____para_____ Mendoza

(2) _____para_____ visitar a mi novia, Silvia. Entré (3) _____por_____ la

puerta y Marta, la agente de viajes, me dijo: "¡Tengo una oferta excelente (4) _____para_____

ti!". Me explicó que podía viajar en avión (5) _____para_____ Buenos Aires

(6) _____por_____ seiscientos dólares. Podía salir un día de semana,

(7) _____por_____ ejemplo lunes o martes. Me podía quedar en un hotel en Buenos Aires

(8) _____por_____ quince dólares (9) _____por_____ noche. Luego viajaría

(10) _____por_____ tren a Mendoza (11) _____para_____ encontrarme con

Silvia. "Debes comprar el pasaje (12) _____para_____ el fin de mes", me recomendó

Marta. Fue la oferta perfecta (13) _____para_____ mí. Llegué a Mendoza y Silvia fue a la

estación (14) _____por_____ mí. Llevé unas flores (15) _____para_____ ella.

Estuve en Mendoza (16) _____por_____ un mes y (17) _____por_____ fin

Silvia y yo nos comprometimos. Estoy loco (18) _____por_____ ella.

5.3 Reciprocal reflexives

1 **Se conocen** Complete the sentences with the reciprocal reflexives of the verbs in parentheses. Use the present tense.

1. Andrea y Daniel _____ se ven _____ (ver) todos los días.

2. Los amigos _____ se encuentran _____ (encontrar) en el centro de la ciudad.

3. El padre y la madre de Lisa _____ se quieren _____ (querer) mucho.

4. Javier y yo _____ nos saludamos _____ (saludar) por las mañanas.

5. Los compañeros de clase _____ se ayudan _____ (ayudar) con las tareas.

6. Paula y su mamá _____ se llaman _____ (llamar) por teléfono todos los días.

2 **Nos vemos** Complete the sentences with the reciprocal reflexives of the verbs in the word bank.

| abrazar | besar | encontrar | mirar | saludar |
| ayudar | despedir | llamar | querer | ver |

1. Cuando los estudiantes llegan a clase, todos _____ se saludan _____.

2. Hace seis meses que Ricardo no ve a su padre. Cuando se ven, _____ se abrazan _____.

3. Los buenos amigos _____ se ayudan _____ cuando tienen problemas.

4. Es el final de la boda. El novio y la novia _____ se besan _____.

5. Mi novia y yo nos vamos a casar porque _____ nos queremos _____ mucho.

6. Antes de irse a sus casas, todos los amigos de Irene y Vicente _____ se despiden _____.

7. Hablo todos los días con mi hermana. Nosotras _____ nos llamamos _____ todos los días.

8. Cuando Sandra sale a comer con sus amigas, ellas _____ se encuentran _____ en el restaurante.

3 **Así fue** Write sentences from the elements provided. Use reciprocal reflexives and the preterite of the verbs.

1. ayer / Felipe y Lola / enviar / mensajes por correo electrónico

   Ayer Felipe y Lola se enviaron mensajes por correo electrónico.

2. Raúl y yo / encontrar / en el centro de computación

   Raúl y yo nos encontramos en el centro de computación.

3. mis abuelos / querer / mucho toda la vida

   Mis abuelos se quisieron mucho toda la vida.

4. los protagonistas de la película / abrazar y besar / al final

   Los protagonistas de la película se abrazaron y se besaron al final.

5. esos hermanos / ayudar / a conseguir trabajo

   Esos hermanos se ayudaron a conseguir trabajo.

Workbook

4 **Noticias (News) de Alma** Read the letter from Alma, then complete the sentences about the letter with reciprocal reflexive forms of the correct verbs.

> Querida Claudia:
>
> Conocí a Manolo el mes pasado en Buenos Aires. Desde el día en que lo conocí, lo veo todos los días. Cuando salgo de la universidad me encuentro con él en algún lugar de la ciudad. Nuestro primer beso fue en el parque. Anoche Manolo me dijo que me quiere a mí y yo le dije que lo quiero mucho a él. Siempre nos ayudamos mucho con las tareas de la universidad. Llamo mucho a mi hermana y ella me llama a mí para hablar de nuestras cosas. Mi hermana me entiende muy bien y viceversa.
>
> Hasta luego,
> Alma

1. Manolo y Alma _____ se conocieron _____ el mes pasado en Buenos Aires.

2. Ellos _____ se ven _____ todos los días desde que se conocieron.

3. Manolo y Alma _____ se encuentran _____ después de clase en algún lugar de la ciudad.

4. La primera vez que _____ se besaron _____, Manolo y Alma estaban en el parque.

5. Anoche Manolo y Alma _____ se dijeron _____ que se quieren mucho.

6. Manolo y Alma siempre _____ se ayudan _____ mucho con las tareas de la universidad.

7. Alma y su hermana _____ se llaman _____ mucho para hablar de sus cosas.

8. Alma y su hermana _____ se entienden _____ muy bien.

5 **Completar** Complete each pair of sentences with the preterite of the verbs in parentheses. Use the reciprocal reflexive verb in only one sentence in each pair.

(conocer)

1. Ricardo y Juan _____ conocieron _____ a Cristina el año pasado.

2. Los González _____ se conocieron _____ en un viaje por Europa.

(saludar)

3. Los chicos _____ se saludaron _____ cuando llegaron al restaurante.

4. La camarera _____ saludó _____ a los chicos cuando les trajo el menú.

(ayudar)

5. Las enfermeras _____ ayudaron _____ al paciente a levantarse.

6. Los niños _____ se ayudaron _____ para terminar la tarea más temprano.

(ver)

7. Los mecánicos _____ vieron _____ los coches descompuestos.

8. El profesor y los estudiantes _____ se vieron _____ por primera vez en clase.

5.4 Stressed possesive adjectives and pronouns

1 **Esas cosas tuyas** Fill in the blanks with the possessive adjectives as indicated.

1. Ana nos quiere mostrar unas fotos _____ suyas _____ (*of hers*).

2. A Lorena le encanta la ropa _____ nuestra _____ (*of ours*).

3. Los turistas traen las toallas _____ suyas _____ (*of theirs*).

4. El mecánico te muestra unos autos _____ suyos _____ (*of his*).

5. El sitio web _____ suyo _____ (*of his*) es espectacular.

6. ¿Quieres probar el programa de computación _____ nuestro _____ (*of ours*)?

7. Roberto prefiere usar la computadora _____ mía _____ (*of mine*).

8. Ese ratón _____ tuyo _____ (*of yours*) es el más moderno que existe.

2 **¿De quién es?** Complete the sentences with possessive adjectives.

1. Ésa es mi computadora. Es la computadora mía _____.

2. Vamos a ver su sitio web. Vamos a ver el sitio web suyo _____.

3. Aquéllos son mis archivos. Son los archivos míos _____.

4. Quiero usar el programa de él. Quiero usar el programa suyo _____.

5. Buscamos la impresora de nosotros. Buscamos la impresora nuestra _____.

6. Ésos son los discos compactos de ella. Son los discos compactos suyos _____.

7. Tienen que arreglar tu teclado. Tienen que arreglar el teclado tuyo _____.

8. Voy a usar el teléfono celular de ustedes. Voy a usar el teléfono celular suyo _____.

3 **Los suyos** Answer the questions. Follow the model.

> **modelo**
> ¿Vas a llevar tu cámara de video?
> Sí, voy a llevar la mía.

1. ¿Prefieres usar tu cámara digital? Sí, prefiero usar la mía.

2. ¿Quieres usar nuestra conexión inalámbrica? Sí, quiero usar la suya./Sí, quiero usar la nuestra.

3. ¿Guardaste mis archivos? Sí, guardé los tuyos.

4. ¿Llenaste el tanque de su carro? Sí, llené el suyo.

5. ¿Manejó Sonia nuestro carro? Sí, manejó el nuestro./ Sí, manejó el suyo.

6. ¿Vas a comprar mi televisor? Sí, voy a comprar el tuyo.

7. ¿Tomaste los teclados de ellos? Sí, tomé los suyos.

8. ¿Tienes un blog de viajes? Sí, tengo el mío.

4

¿De quién son? Replace the question with one using **de** to clarify the possession. Then answer the question affirmatively, using a possessive pronoun.

> **modelo**
>
> ¿Es suyo el teléfono celular? (de ella)
> *¿Es de ella el teléfono celular? Sí, es suyo.*

1. ¿Son suyas las gafas? (de usted)

   ¿Son de usted las gafas? Sí, son mías.

2. ¿Es suyo el estéreo? (de Joaquín)

   ¿Es de Joaquín el estéreo? Sí, es suyo.

3. ¿Es suya la impresora? (de ellos)

   ¿Es de ellos la impresora? Sí, es suya.

4. ¿Son suyos esos reproductores de DVD? (de Susana)

   ¿Son de Susana esos reproductores de DVD? Sí, son suyos.

5. ¿Es suyo el coche? (de tu mamá)

   ¿Es de tu mamá el coche? Sí, es suyo.

6. Son suyas estas cámaras de video? (de ustedes)

   ¿Son de ustedes estas cámaras de video? Sí, son nuestras.

Síntesis

Tell the story of a romantic couple you know. Use reciprocal reflexive forms of verbs to tell what happened between them and when. Use stressed possessive adjectives and pronouns as needed to talk about their families and their difficulties. Use familiar commands to give examples of advice you give to each member of the couple on important issues. Answers will vary.

_____

_____

_____

_____

_____

_____

_____

_____

_____

_____

_____

panorama

Argentina

1 **Argentina** Fill in the blanks with the correct terms.

1. La ciudad de Buenos Aires se conoce como el _____"París de Suramérica"_____.

2. Se dice que Argentina es el país más _____europeo_____ de toda Latinoamérica.

3. Después de 1880, muchos _____inmigrantes_____ se establecieron en Argentina.

4. Los sonidos y ritmos del tango tienen raíces _____africanas_____,

_____italianas_____ y _____españolas_____.

5. A los habitantes de Buenos Aires se les llama _____porteños_____.

6. El nombre de la Avenida 9 de Julio conmemora la _____independencia_____ de Argentina.

2 **Palabras desordenadas** Unscramble the words about Argentina, using the clues.

1. DMAEZON _____Mendoza_____
(una de las ciudades principales argentinas)

2. ESEDREMC _____Mercedes_____
(nombre de una cantante argentina)

3. GAIOATNAP _____Patagonia_____
(región fría que está en la parte sur (*south*) de Argentina)

4. REGTARLNIA _____Inglaterra_____
(uno de los países de origen de muchos inmigrantes en Argentina)

5. OTÑSOERP _____porteños_____
(personas de Buenos Aires)

6. TOORVPOAVCI _____provocativo_____
(una característica del baile del tango en un principio)

3 **Datos argentinos** Fill in the blanks with the aspects of Argentina described.

1. saxofonista argentino _Leandro "Gato" Barbieri_

2. las tres mayores ciudades de Argentina _Buenos Aires, Córdoba y Rosario_

3. países de origen de muchos inmigrantes argentinos _Italia, Alemania, España e Inglaterra_

4. escritor argentino célebre _Jorge Luis Borges_

5. países que comparten las cataratas del Iguazú _Argentina, Paraguay y Brasil_

6. primera dama argentina; nació en 1919 _Evita Perón/María Eva Duarte de Perón/Evita_

4 **Fotos de Argentina** Label the photographs from Argentina.

1. _____ el tango _____

2. _____ las cataratas de Iguazú _____

5 **¿Cierto o falso?** Indicate whether the statements are **cierto** or **falso**. Correct the false statements.

1. Argentina es el país más grande del mundo.

Falso. Argentina es el país de habla hispana más grande del mundo.

2. La Avenida 9 de Julio en Buenos Aires es la calle más ancha del mundo.

Cierto.

3. Los idiomas que se hablan en Argentina son el español y el inglés.

Falso. Los idiomas que se hablan en Argentina son el español y lenguas indígenas.

4. Los inmigrantes que llegaron a Argentina eran principalmente de Europa.

Cierto.

5. El tango es un género musical con raíces indígenas y africanas.

Falso. El tango es un género musical con raíces africanas, italianas y españolas.

6. Las cataratas del Iguazú están cerca de la confluencia de los ríos Iguazú y Paraná.

Cierto.

6 **Preguntas argentinas** Answer the questions with complete sentences. Answers will vary. Suggested answers:

1. ¿Por qué se conoce a Buenos Aires como el "París de Suramérica"?

Buenos Aires se conoce como el "París de Suramérica" por su estilo parisino.

2. ¿Quién fue la primera dama de Argentina hasta 1952?

La primera dama de Argentina hasta 1952 fue María Eva Duarte de Perón/Evita Perón/Evita.

3. ¿Qué dejaron las diferentes culturas de los inmigrantes en Argentina?

Las diferentes culturas de los inmigrantes dejaron una huella profunda en la música, el cine y la arquitectura de Argentina.

4. ¿Cómo cambió el baile del tango desde su origen hasta los años 30?

En un principio, el tango era un baile provocativo y violento, pero se hizo más romántico durante los años 30.

En el taller

Lección 5
Fotonovela

Antes de ver el video

1 **¿Qué pasa?** In this image, where do you think Miguel is? What do you think he is doing, and why?

Answers will vary.

_____

_____

_____

_____

_____

_____

_____

_____

Mientras ves el video

2 **¿Qué oíste?** Watch **En el taller** and place a check mark beside what you hear.

____ 1. ¿Cuál es tu dirección electrónica?

____ 2. ¿Está descompuesta tu computadora?

✔ 3. ¿Y revisaste el aceite?

____ 4. El navegador GPS también está descompuesto.

✔ 5. Mal día para la tecnología, ¿no?

✔ 6. ¡Te están llamando!

✔ 7. Se me acabó la pila.

____ 8. Me gusta mucho la televisión por cable.

✔ 9. ¿Me pasas la llave?

✔ 10. No manejes con el cofre abierto.

3 **¿Qué viste?** Place a check mark beside what you see.

✔ 1. un teléfono celular

✔ 2. una llave

✔ 3. el cofre de un coche

____ 4. un reproductor de CD

✔ 5. un mecánico

____ 6. la pantalla de un televisor

____ 7. una arroba

____ 8. una cámara de video

✔ 9. un taller mecánico

____ 10. un archivo

4 **¿Quién dice?** Write the name of the person who said each sentence.

__Jorge__ 1. ¿Quién es el mecánico?

__Maru__ 2. Está descargando el programa antivirus ahora.

__Miguel__ 3. Acaba de enviarme un mensaje de texto.

__Jorge__ 4. Este coche tiene más de 150.000 kilómetros.

__Maru__ 5. Por favor, ¡arréglalo!

Después de ver el video

5   **Corregir** Rewrite these statements so they are true.

1. Miguel le llevó su coche a Felipe, el mecánico.

   Miguel le llevó su coche a Jorge, el mecánico.

2. La computadora de Maru funciona muy bien.

   La computadora de Maru está descompuesta.

3. Jorge no tiene problemas para arreglar el coche de Miguel.

   Jorge tiene problemas para arreglar el coche de Miguel.

4. Se le acabó la pila al teléfono celular de Miguel.

   Se le acabó la pila al teléfono celular de Maru.

5. Maru necesita una cámara digital nueva y Miguel necesita un reproductor de MP3 nuevo.

   Maru necesita una computadora nueva y Miguel necesita un coche nuevo.

6. Jorge le dice a Miguel que revise el aceite cada mil kilómetros.

   Jorge le dice a Miguel que revise el aceita cada mil quinientos kilómetros.

6   **Un mensaje** Imagine that Maru is writing a short message to a friend about today's events. Write in Spanish what you think she would say.   Answers will vary.

_____

_____

_____

_____

_____

_____

_____

_____

7   **Preguntas personales** Answer these questions in Spanish.   Answers will vary.

1. Cuando tu carro está descompuesto, ¿lo llevas a un(a) mecánico/a o lo arreglas tú mismo/a? ¿Por qué? _____

_____

_____

2. ¿Conoces a un(a) buen(a) mecánico/a? ¿Cómo se llama? _____

_____

_____

3. ¿Tienes un teléfono celular? ¿Para qué lo usas? _____

_____

_____

Panorama: Argentina	**Lección 5**
	Panorama cultural

Antes de ver el video

1 **Más vocabulario** Look over these useful words and expressions before you watch the video.

Vocabulario útil

actualmente *nowadays*	**gaucho** *cowboy*	**pintura** *paint*
barrios *neighborhood*	**género** *genre*	**salón de baile** *ballroom*
cantante *singer*	**homenaje** *tribute*	**suelo** *floor*
exponer *to exhibit*	**pareja** *partner*	**surgir** *to emerge*
extrañar *to miss*	**paso** *step*	**tocar** *to play*

2 **Completar** The previous vocabulary will be used in this video. In preparation for watching the video, complete the sentences using words from the vocabulary list. Conjugate the verbs as necessary. Some words will not be used.

1. Los artistas _____exponen_____ sus pinturas en las calles.

2. Beyoncé es una _____cantante_____ famosa.

3. El tango tiene _____pasos_____ muy complicados.

4. El jazz es un _____género_____ musical que se originó en los Estados Unidos.

5. El tango _____surgió_____ en Buenos Aires, Argentina.

6. La gente va a los _____salones de baile_____ a bailar y divertirse.

7. Las personas _____extrañan_____ mucho su país cuando tienen que vivir en el extranjero.

Mientras ves el video

3 **Marcar** Check off the cognates you hear while watching the video.

✔ 1. adultos   ✔ 7. dramático

✔ 2. aniversario   ✔ 8. exclusivamente

___ 3. arquitectura   ✔ 9. famosos

✔ 4. artistas   ✔ 10. gráfica

___ 5. demostración   ___ 11. impacto

✔ 6. conferencia   ✔ 12. musical

Después de ver el video

4 **¿Cierto o falso?** Indicate whether each statement is **cierto** or **falso**. Correct the false statements.

1. Guillermo Alio dibuja en el suelo una gráfica para enseñar a cantar.

   Falso. Alio dibuja en el suelo una gráfica para enseñar a bailar.

2. El tango es música, danza, poesía y pintura.

   Cierto.

3. Alio es un artista que baila y canta al mismo tiempo.

   Falso. Alio es un artista que baila y pinta al mismo tiempo.

4. Alio y su pareja se ponen pintura verde en los zapatos.

   Falso. Alio pone pintura negra y su pareja pone pintura roja en sus zapatos.

5. Ahora los tangos son historias de hombres que sufren por amor.

   Cierto.

6. El tango tiene un tono dramático y nostálgico.

   Cierto.

5 **Completar** Complete the sentences with words from the word bank.

actualmente	compositor	fiesta	género	homenaje	pintor	surgió	toca

1. El tango es un _____ género _____ musical que se originó en Argentina en 1880.

2. El tango _____ surgió _____ en el barrio La Boca.

3. _____ Actualmente _____ este barrio se considera un museo al aire libre.

4. En la calle Caminito se _____ toca _____ y se baila el tango.

5. Carlos Gardel fue el _____ compositor _____ de varios de los tangos más famosos.

6. En el aniversario de su muerte, sus aficionados le hacen un _____ homenaje _____.

6 **Responder** Answer the questions in Spanish. Use complete sentences.   Answers will vary.

1. ¿Por qué crees que el tango es tan famoso en todo el mundo? _____

   _____

2. ¿Te gustaría (*Would you like*) aprender a bailar tango? ¿Por qué?_____

   _____

3. ¿Qué tipo de música te gusta? Explica tu respuesta. _____

   _____

Maravillas de la tecnología

Lección 5
Flash cultura

Antes de ver el video

1 **Más vocabulario** Look over these useful words before you watch the video.

Vocabulario útil		
la afirmación cultural *cultural affirmation*	chatear *to chat*	la masificación *spread*
	el desarrollo *development*	mejorar *to improve*
alejado/a *remote*	el esfuerzo *effort*	el/la proveedor(a) *supplier*
beneficiarse *to benefit*	al extranjero *abroad*	servirse de *to make use of*
el/la cuzqueño/a *person from Cuzco*	mandar *to send*	el/la usuario/a *user*

2 **La tecnología** Complete this paragraph about technology in Peru.

En Perú, la (1) ___masificación___ de Internet benefició el (2) ___desarrollo___ de la agricultura en las comunidades indígenas. Para estas comunidades es una herramienta (*tool*) importante para obtener e intercambiar información. También, en ciudades como Cuzco, los artistas y comerciantes que son (3) ___usuarios___ de Internet pueden (4) ___mejorar___ el nivel (*level*) de ventas porque se conectan (5) ___al extranjero___ y así pueden vender sus productos en otros países.

3 **¡En español!** Look at the video still. Imagine what Omar will say about technology in Peru and write a two- or three-sentence introduction to this episode. Answers will vary.

Omar Fuentes, Perú

¡Hola a todos! ¿Saben de qué vamos a hablar hoy? _____

_____

_____

_____

_____

Mientras ves el video

4 **Completar** Watch Omar interview a young man and complete their conversation.

OMAR ¿Qué haces en medio de la Plaza de Armas usando una (1) ___computadora___?

JOVEN Estoy mandándole un (2) ___(e-)mail___ a mi novia en Quito.

OMAR ... en Quito... ¿Así que tú eres (3) ___ecuatoriano___?

JOVEN Sí, soy ecuatoriano.

OMAR Y... ¿qué tal? ¿Qué te (4) ___parece___ el Cuzco? ¿Qué te parece el Perú?

JOVEN Me encanta Cuzco porque se parece mucho a mi ciudad, pero me gusta un poco más porque puedo usar (5) ___Internet___ en medio de la plaza y (6) ___nadie___ me molesta.

5

Emparejar Identify what these people use cell phones and Internet for.

1. __b/c__

2. __d__

3. __c__

a. para escribir mensajes
   a su novia

b. para comunicarse con su
   proveedora

c. para vender sus productos
   en el extranjero

d. para hacer una videoconferencia
   y hablar con su familia

e. para chatear con amigos

Después de ver el video

6

¿Cierto o falso? Indicate whether each statement is **cierto** or **falso**.

1. En Perú, los cibercafés son lugares exclusivos para los turistas. ___falso___

2. Los cibercafés son conocidos como "cabinas de Internet" en Perú y están por todo el país. ___cierto___

3. A diferencia de los cibercafés, los teléfonos celulares ayudan a la comunicación rápida
   y económica. ___falso___

4. La comunidad indígena de Perú se beneficia de las ventajas que ofrecen los cibercafés. ___cierto___

5. En la Plaza de Armas de Cuzco es posible navegar en la red de manera inalámbrica. ___cierto___

6. Las tecnologías de la comunicación no permiten a las comunidades indígenas reafirmarse
   culturalmente. ___falso___

7

Preguntas Answer these questions. Answers will vary.

1. ¿Para qué usas Internet?

   _____

2. ¿Cómo te comunicas con tu familia y tus amigos cuando viajas?

   _____

3. ¿Piensas que la masificación de la tecnología es buena? ¿Por qué?

   _____

4. ¿Piensas que el servicio de Internet debe ser gratuito para todas las personas? ¿Por qué?

   _____

8

Un mensaje Remember the young man who was writing an e-mail to his girlfriend at the Plaza de
Armas in Cuzco? Imagine you are him and write an e-mail to his girlfriend telling her about living in
Cuzco and how technology is used there. Answers will vary.

¡Hola, mi amor! En este momento estoy en la Plaza de Armas de Cuzco. _____

_____

_____

_____

_____

contexts

Lección 5

1 **Asociaciones** Circle the word or words that are not logically associated with each word you hear.

1. la impresora   (la velocidad)   el *fax*
2. guardar   imprimir   (funcionar)
3. la carretera   el motor   (el sitio web)
4. el tanque   (el ratón)   el aceite
5. conducir   (el cibercafé)   (el reproductor de MP3)
6. (el archivo)   la televisión   (la llanta)

2 **¿Lógico o ilógico?** You will hear some statements. Decide if they are **lógico** or **ilógico**.

	Lógico	Ilógico		Lógico	Ilógico
1.	○	⊘	4.	⊘	○
2.	⊘	○	5.	⊘	○
3.	○	⊘	6.	○	⊘

3 **Identificar** For each drawing in your lab manual, you will hear two statements. Choose the statement that best corresponds to the drawing.

1. (a.)   b.   2. a.   (b.)

3. (a.)   b.   4. (a.)   b.

pronunciación

c (before e or i), s, and z

In Latin America, **c** before **e** or **i** sounds much like the *s* in *sit*.

| medi**c**ina | **c**elular | cono**c**er | pa**c**iente |

In parts of Spain, **c** before **e** or **i** is pronounced like the *th* in *think*.

| condu**c**ir | poli**c**ía | **c**ederrón | velo**c**idad |

The letter **s** is pronounced like the *s* in *sit*.

| **s**ubir | be**s**ar | **s**onar | impre**s**ora |

In Latin America, the Spanish **z** is pronounced like the *s* in *sit*.

| cabe**z**a | nari**z** | abra**z**ar | embara**z**ada |

The **z** is pronounced like the *th* in *think* in parts of Spain.

| **z**apatos | **z**ona | pla**z**a | bra**z**o |

1 **Práctica** Repeat each word after the speaker to practice pronouncing **s**, **z**, and **c** before **i** and **e**.

1. funcionar
2. policía
3. receta
4. sitio
5. disco
6. zapatos
7. zanahoria
8. marzo
9. comenzar
10. perezoso
11. quizás
12. operación

2 **Oraciones** When you hear each number, read the corresponding sentence aloud. Then listen to the speaker and repeat the sentence.

1. Vivió en Buenos Aires en su niñez, pero siempre quería pasar su vejez en Santiago.
2. Cecilia y Zulaima fueron al centro a cenar al restaurante Las Delicias.
3. Sonó el despertador a las seis y diez, pero estaba cansado y no quiso oírlo.
4. Zacarías jugaba al baloncesto todas las tardes después de cenar.

3 **Refranes** Repeat each saying after the speaker to practice pronouncing **s**, **z**, and **c** before **i** and **e**.

1. Zapatero, a tus zapatos.[1]
2. Primero es la obligación que la devoción.[2]

4 **Dictado** You will hear a friend describing Azucena's weekend experiences. Listen carefully and write what you hear during the pauses. The entire passage will be repeated so that you can check your work.

El sábado pasado Azucena iba a salir con Francisco. Se subió al carro e intentó arrancarlo, pero no funcionaba. El carro tenía gasolina y, como revisaba el aceite con frecuencia, sabía que tampoco era eso. Decidió tomar un autobús cerca de su casa. Se subió al autobús y comenzó a relajarse. Debido a la circulación llegó tarde, pero se alegró de ver que Francisco estaba esperándola.

_____

_____

_____

[1] *Mind your P's and Q's. (lit. Shoemaker, to your shoes.)*
[2] *Business before pleasure.*

estructura

5.1 Familiar commands

1 **Identificar** You will hear some sentences. If the verb is a **tú** command, circle **Sí** in your lab manual. If the verb is not a **tú** command, circle **No**.

> **modelo**
> *You hear:* Ayúdanos a encontrar el control remoto.
> *You circle:* **Sí** because **Ayúdanos** is a *tú* command.

1. Sí (No)   6. Sí (No)
2. Sí (No)   7. Sí (No)
3. (Sí) No   8. (Sí) No
4. (Sí) No   9. Sí (No)
5. (Sí) No   10. (Sí) No

2 **Cambiar** Change each command you hear to the negative. Repeat the correct answer after the speaker. (*8 items*)

> **modelo**
> Cómprame un reproductor de DVD.
> *No me compres un reproductor de DVD.*

3 **Preguntas** Answer each question you hear using an affirmative **tú** command. Repeat the correct response after the speaker. (*7 items*)

> **modelo**
> ¿Estaciono aquí?
> *Sí, estaciona aquí.*

4 **Consejos prácticos** You will hear a conversation among three friends. Using **tú** commands and the ideas presented, write six pieces of advice that Mario can follow to save some money.

1. Usa el transporte público. _____
2. Compra un carro más pequeño. _____
3. Habla menos por teléfono. _____
4. Cancela la televisión por cable. _____
5. Vende tu teléfono celular. _____
6. Apaga las luces, la televisión y la computadora. _____

5.2 Por and para

1 **Escoger** You will hear some sentences with a beep in place of a preposition. Decide if **por** or **para** should complete each sentence

> **modelo**
>
> *You hear:* El teclado es (*beep*) la computadora de Nuria.
> *You mark:* an **X** under **para**

	por	para
Modelo		X
1.		X
2.		X
3.	X	
4.	X	
5.	X	
6.	X	
7.		X
8.	X	

2 **La aventura** Complete each phrase about Jaime with **por** or **para** and the cue in your lab manual. Repeat each correct response after the speaker.

> **modelo**
>
> *You hear:* Jaime estudió
> *You see:* médico
> *You say:* Jaime estudió para médico.

1. unos meses
2. hacer sus planes
3. mil dólares
4. ver a sus padres
5. la ciudad
6. su mamá
7. pesos
8. las montañas

3 **Los planes** Listen to the telephone conversation between Antonio and Sonia and then select the best response for the questions in your lab manual.

1. ¿Por dónde quiere ir Sonia para ir a Bariloche?
   a. Quiere ir por Santiago de Chile.
   b. Va a ir por avión.

2. ¿Para qué va Sonia a Bariloche?
   a. Va para esquiar.
   b. Va para comprar esquíes.

3. ¿Por qué tiene que ir de compras Sonia?
   a. Para comprar una bolsa.
   b. Necesita un abrigo para el frío.

4. ¿Por qué quiere ir Antonio con ella hoy?
   a. Quiere ir para estar con ella.
   b. Quiere ir para comprar un regalo.

5.3 Reciprocal reflexives

1 **Escoger** Listen to each question and, in your lab manual, choose the most logical response.

1. (a.) Hace cuatro años que nos conocimos.
   b. Se vieron todos los fines de semana.
2. a. Nos besamos antes de salir a trabajar.
   (b.) No, creo que se besaron en la segunda.
3. (a.) Nos llevamos mal sólo el último año.
   b. Se llevaron mal siempre.
4. (a.) Sí, se saludan con un abrazo y también con un beso.
   b. Nos saludamos desde lejos.
5. a. Casi nunca me miraban.
   (b.) Creo que se miraban con mucho amor.
6. (a.) Sólo nos ayudamos para el examen.
   b. Se ayudan a menudo.
7. (a.) Creo que se hablan todas las noches.
   b. Le hablan mucho porque tienen celulares.
8. a. Cuando se casaron se querían mucho.
   (b.) Cada día nos queremos más.

2 **Responder** Answer each question in the affirmative. Repeat the correct answer after the speaker. (6 *items*)

> **modelo**
>
> ¿Se abrazaron tú y Carolina en la primera cita?
> Sí, *nos abrazamos en la primera cita.*

3 **Los amigos** Listen to a description of a friendship and then, in your lab manual, choose the phrase that best completes each sentence.

1. Desde los once años, los chicos _____ con frecuencia.
   (a.) se veían   b. se ayudaban   c. se besaban
2. Samuel y Andrea _____ por la amistad (*friendship*) de sus madres.
   a. se escribían   b. se entendían   (c.) se conocieron
3. Las madres de Andrea y Samuel...
   a. se ayudaban.   (b.) se conocían bien.   c. se odiaban.
4. Andrea y Samuel no _____ por un tiempo debido a (*due to*) un problema.
   a. se conocieron   (b.) se hablaron   c. se ayudaron
5. Después de un tiempo...
   a. se besaron.   (b.) se pidieron perdón.   c. se odiaron.
6. La separación sirvió para enseñarles que...
   (a.) se querían.   b. se hablaban mucho.   c. se conocían bien.
7. No es cierto. Andrea y Samuel no...
   (a.) se casaron.   b. se entendían bien.   c. se querían.
8. Los dos amigos _____ por un tiempo.
   a. se besaban   b. se comprometieron   (c.) se llevaron mal

Lab Manual

5.4 Stressed possessive adjectives and pronouns

1 **Identificar** Listen to each statement and mark an **X** in the column identifying the possessive pronoun you hear.

> **modelo**
>
> *You hear:* Ya arreglaron todos los coches, pero el tuyo no.
> *You write:* an **X** under *yours*.

	mine	*yours*	*his/hers*	*ours*	*theirs*
Modelo		**X**			
1.	X				
2.		X			
3.			X		
4.					X
5.				X	
6.	X				
7.		X			
8.			X		

2 **Transformar** Restate each sentence you hear, using the cues in your lab manual. Repeat the correct answer after the speaker.

> **modelo**
>
> *You hear:* ¿De qué año es el carro suyo?
> *You see:* mine
> *You say:* ¿De qué año es el carro mío?

1. *his*
2. *ours*
3. *yours (fam.)*
4. *theirs*
5. *mine*
6. *hers*

3 **¿Cierto o falso?** You will hear two brief conversations. Listen carefully and then indicate whether the statements in your lab manual are **cierto** or **falso**.

	Cierto	Falso
Conversación 1		
1. Pablo dice que el carro es de Ana.	○	⊘
2. Ana necesita la computadora para su trabajo.	○	⊘
3. Las películas de Ana son mejores que las de Pablo.	⊘	○
Conversación 2		
4. La computadora de Adela es muy rápida.	○	⊘
5. El navegador GPS de la prima de Adela es muy bueno.	○	⊘
6. El navegador es más de Adela que de ellos dos.	⊘	○

vocabulario

You will now hear the vocabulary found in your textbook on the last page of this lesson. Listen and repeat each Spanish word or phrase after the speaker.

Additional Vocabulary

Additional Vocabulary

Notes

Notes

Notes

La vivienda

6

Communicative Goals

You will learn how to:

- Welcome people to your home
- Describe your house or apartment
- Talk about household chores
- Give instructions

A PRIMERA VISTA

- ¿Están los chicos en casa?
- ¿Viven en una casa o en un apartamento?
- ¿Ya comieron o van a comer?
- ¿Están de buen humor o de mal humor?

Más práctica

La vivienda

Más vocabulario

las afueras	suburbs; outskirts
el alquiler	rent (payment)
el ama (*m., f.*) de casa	housekeeper; caretaker
el barrio	neighborhood
el edificio de apartamentos	apartment building
el/la vecino/a	neighbor
la vivienda	housing
el balcón	balcony
la entrada	entrance
la escalera	stairs; stairway
el garaje	garage
el jardín	garden; yard
el patio	patio; yard
el sótano	basement; cellar
la cafetera	coffee maker
el electrodoméstico	electrical appliance
el horno (de microondas)	(microwave) oven
la lavadora	washing machine
la luz	light; electricity
la secadora	clothes dryer
la tostadora	toaster
el cartel	poster
la mesita de noche	night stand
los muebles	furniture
alquilar	to rent
mudarse	to move (from one house to another)

Variación léxica

dormitorio ⟷ aposento (*Rep. Dom.*); recámara (*Méx.*)

apartamento ⟷ departamento (*Arg., Chile, Méx.*); piso (*Esp.*)

lavar los platos ⟷ lavar/fregar los trastes (*Amér. C., Rep. Dom.*)

recursos

WB pp. 355–356

LM p. 373

vhlcentral.com Lección 6

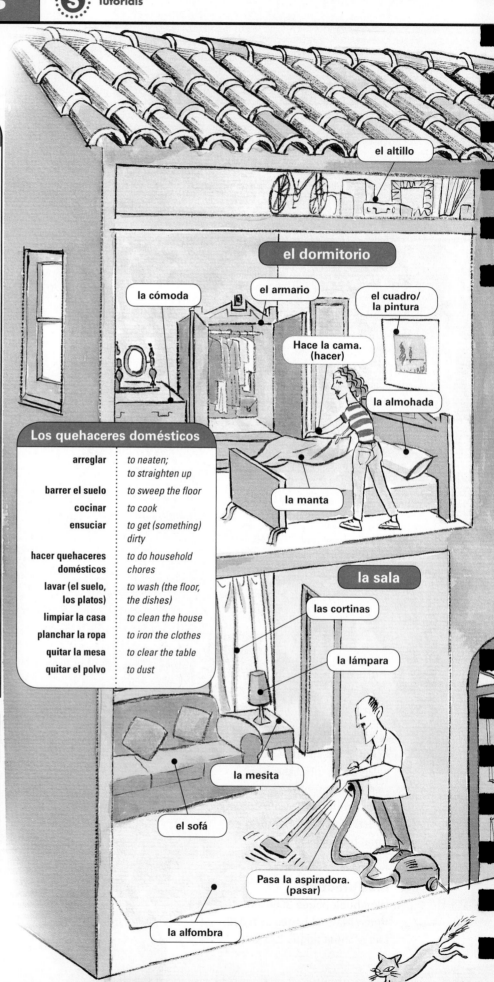

el altillo

el dormitorio

la cómoda

el armario

el cuadro/ la pintura

Hace la cama. (hacer)

la almohada

la manta

Los quehaceres domésticos

arreglar	to neaten; to straighten up
barrer el suelo	to sweep the floor
cocinar	to cook
ensuciar	to get (something) dirty
hacer quehaceres domésticos	to do household chores
lavar (el suelo, los platos)	to wash (the floor, the dishes)
limpiar la casa	to clean the house
planchar la ropa	to iron the clothes
quitar la mesa	to clear the table
quitar el polvo	to dust

la sala

las cortinas

la lámpara

la mesita

el sofá

Pasa la aspiradora. (pasar)

la alfombra

Supersite: MP3 Audio Files and Scripts, Digital Image Bank, Activity Pack, Testing Program (Quizzes), **Vocabulario adicional**

la oficina

el sillón

la pared

el estante

Sacude los muebles.
(sacudir)

la cocina

el refrigerador

el congelador

la cocina, la estufa

el horno

el lavaplatos

Saca la basura.
(sacar)

Práctica 1 2 Supersite: MP3 Audio Files, Scripts

Lección 6

1 **Escuchar** 🎧 Escucha la conversación y completa las oraciones.

1. Pedro va a limpiar primero ___la sala___.
2. Paula va a comenzar en ___la cocina___.
3. Pedro va a ___planchar la ropa___ en el sótano.
4. Pedro también va a limpiar ___la oficina___.
5. Ellos están limpiando la casa porque
   ___la madre de Pedro viene a visitarlos___.

2 **Respuestas** 🎧 Escucha las preguntas y selecciona la respuesta más adecuada. Una respuesta no se va a usar.

__3__ a. Sí, la alfombra estaba muy sucia.
__5__ b. No, porque todavía se están mudando.
__1__ c. Sí, sacudí la mesa y el estante.
____ d. Sí, puse el pollo en el horno.
__2__ e. Hice la cama, pero no limpié los muebles.
__4__ f. Sí, después de sacarla de la secadora.

2 Before listening, have students read through the items and brainstorm possible questions.

3 **Escoger** Escoge la letra de la respuesta correcta.

1. Cuando quieres tener una lámpara y un despertador cerca de tu cama, puedes ponerlos en __c__.
   a. el barrio   b. el cuadro   c. la mesita de noche
2. Si no quieres vivir en el centro de la ciudad, puedes mudarte __b__.
   a. al alquiler   b. a las afueras   c. a la vivienda
3. Guardamos (*We keep*) los pantalones, las camisas y los zapatos en __b__.
   a. la secadora   b. el armario   c. el patio
4. Para subir de la planta baja al primer piso, usas __c__.
   a. la entrada   b. el cartel   c. la escalera
5. Ponemos cuadros y pinturas en __a__.
   a. las paredes   b. los quehaceres   c. los jardines

4 **Definiciones** En parejas, identifiquen cada cosa que se describe. Luego inventen sus propias descripciones de algunas palabras y expresiones de **Contextos**.

modelo
Estudiante 1: *Es donde pones los libros.*
Estudiante 2: *el estante*

1. Es donde pones la cabeza cuando duermes. la/una almohada
2. Es el quehacer doméstico que haces después de comer. lavar los platos/ quitar la mesa
3. Algunos de ellos son las cómodas y los sillones. los muebles
4. Son las personas que viven en tu barrio. los vecinos
5. _____
6. _____

Heritage Speakers Ask heritage speakers to share additional lexical variations. Ex: **el lavaplatos/el lavavajillas; el altillo/el ático/el desván**

la taza

el vaso

la copa

Pone la mesa. (poner)

la cuchara

la servilleta

el plato

el tenedor

el cuchillo

el comedor

Supersite: At this point you may want to present *Vocabulario adicional: Más vocabulario para el hogar.*

Teaching Tip Add a visual aspect to this vocabulary presentation. Bring in silverware, plates, and glasses. As you hold up each item, have students name it and guide you in setting the table. Ex: **¿Dónde pongo el tenedor, a la derecha o a la izquierda del plato?**

5 **Completar** Completa estas frases con las palabras más adecuadas.

1. Para tomar vino necesitas... una copa
2. Para comer una ensalada necesitas... un tenedor/un plato
3. Para tomar café necesitas... una taza
4. Para poner la comida en la mesa necesitas... un plato/poner la mesa
5. Para limpiarte la boca después de comer necesitas... una servilleta
6. Para cortar (*to cut*) un bistec necesitas... un cuchillo (y un tenedor)
7. Para tomar agua necesitas... un vaso/una copa
8. Para tomar sopa necesitas... una cuchara/un plato

5 Ask volunteers to answer questions modeled on the sentence starters. Ex: **¿Qué se necesita para comer la carne?**

6 Before dividing the class into groups, model the activity using your own situation. Ex: **En casa, mi esposa siempre pasa la aspiradora, pero yo sacudo los muebles. Mi hijo...**

6 **Los quehaceres** Trabajen en grupos para indicar quién hace estos quehaceres domésticos en sus casas. Luego contesten las preguntas. Answers will vary.

barrer el suelo	lavar los platos	planchar la ropa
cocinar	lavar la ropa	sacar la basura
hacer las camas	pasar la aspiradora	sacudir los muebles

modelo

Estudiante 1: ¿Quién pasa la aspiradora en tu casa?
Estudiante 2: Mi hermano y yo pasamos la aspiradora.

1. ¿Quién hace más quehaceres, tú o tus compañeros/as?
2. ¿Quiénes hacen la mayoría de los quehaceres, los hombres o las mujeres?
3. ¿Piensas que debes hacer más quehaceres? ¿Por qué?

Practice more at **vhlcentral.com**.

Game Have students bring in real estate ads. Ask teams of three to write a description of a property. Teams then take turns reading their descriptions aloud. Other teams guess the price. The team that guesses the amount closest to the real price without going over scores one point.

Extra Practice Ask students to complete these analogies.
1. aspiradora : _____ :: lavadora : ropa (alfombra) (*Aspiradora* es a *alfombra* como *lavadora* es a *ropa*.)
2. frío : calor :: congelador: _____ (horno)
3. cama : dormitorio :: _____ : oficina (escritorio)
4. platos : cocina :: carro : _____ (garaje)

Comunicación

7 Model the activity using a magazine picture. Ex: **¡Qué comedor más desordenado! ¡Es un desastre! Alguien debe quitar los platos sucios de la mesa. También es necesario sacudir los muebles y pasar la aspiradora. La mesa y las sillas son muy bonitas, pero el comedor está muy sucio.**

Extra Practice Have students complete this cloze activity. **La vida doméstica de un estudiante universitario puede ser un desastre, ¿no? Nunca hay tiempo para hacer los ____ (quehaceres) domésticos. Sólo ____ (pasa) la aspiradora una vez al semestre y nunca ____ (sacude) los muebles. Los ____ (platos) sucios se acumulan en la ____ (cocina). Saca la ropa de la ____ (secadora) y se la pone sin ____ (planchar). Y, ¿por qué hacer la ____ (cama)? Se va a acostar en ella de nuevo este mismo día, ¿no?**

8 Draw a floor plan of a four-room apartment on the board. Ask volunteers to describe it.

CONSULTA
To review bathroom-related vocabulary, see **Lección 1, Contextos, p. 20.**

Supersite:
Activity Pack

9 Have pairs tell each other about an occasion when they have had to clean up their home for a particular reason. Ask them to share their stories with the class.

7 **La vida doméstica** En parejas, describan las habitaciones que ven en estas fotos. Identifiquen y describan cinco muebles o adornos (*accessories*) de cada foto y digan dos quehaceres que se pueden hacer en cada habitación. Answers will vary.

8 **Mi apartamento** Dibuja el plano (*floor plan*) de un apartamento amueblado (*furnished*) imaginario y escribe los nombres de las habitaciones y de los muebles. En parejas, siéntense espalda contra espalda (*sit back to back*). Uno/a de ustedes describe su apartamento mientras su compañero/a lo dibuja según la descripción. Cuando terminen, miren el segundo dibujo. ¿Es similar al dibujo original? Hablen de los cambios que se necesitan hacer para mejorar el dibujo. Repitan la actividad intercambiando papeles.
Answers will vary.

9 **¡Corre, corre!** Tu profesor(a) va a darte una serie incompleta de dibujos que forman una historia. Tú y tu compañero/a tienen dos series diferentes. Descríbanse los dibujos para completar la historia.
Answers will vary.

> **modelo**
> **Estudiante 1:** Marta quita la mesa.
> **Estudiante 2:** Francisco...

Lección 6

Video Synopsis **Felipe** and **Jimena** have promised to clean the apartment in exchange for permission to take a trip to the **Yucatán** Peninsula. **Marissa, Juan Carlos,** and **don Diego** help them finish on time.

Los quehaceres

Jimena y Felipe deben limpiar el apartamento para poder ir de viaje con Marissa.

PERSONAJES

JIMENA   FELIPE

Video: *Fotonovela*

SR. DÍAZ Quieren ir a Yucatán con Marissa, ¿verdad?

SRA. DÍAZ Entonces, les sugiero que arreglen este apartamento. Regresamos más tarde.

SR. DÍAZ Les aconsejo que preparen la cena para las 8:30.

MARISSA ¿Qué pasa?

JIMENA Nuestros papás quieren que Felipe y yo arreglemos toda la casa.

FELIPE Y que, además, preparemos la cena.

MARISSA ¡Pues, yo les ayudo!

(*Don Diego llega a ayudar a los chicos.*)

FELIPE Tenemos que limpiar la casa hoy.

JIMENA ¿Nos ayuda, don Diego?

DON DIEGO Claro. Recomiendo que se organicen en equipos para limpiar.

MARISSA Mis padres siempre quieren que mis hermanos y yo ayudemos con los quehaceres. No me molesta ayudar. Pero odio limpiar el baño.

JIMENA Lo que más odio yo es sacar la basura.

JUAN CARLOS Hola, Jimena. ¿Está Felipe? (*a Felipe*) Te olvidaste del partido de fútbol.

FELIPE Juan Carlos, ¿verdad que mi papá te considera como de la familia?

JUAN CARLOS Sí.

MARISSA Yo lleno el lavaplatos... después de vaciarlo.

DON DIEGO Juan Carlos, ¿por qué no terminas de pasar la aspiradora? Y Felipe, tú limpia el polvo. ¡Ya casi acaban!

Video Recap: Lección 5 Before doing this **Fotonovela** section, review the previous episode with these questions:
1. ¿Quién intenta arreglar la computadora de Maru? (Mónica intenta arreglarla.) 2. ¿Dónde está Miguel?
(Está en el taller de Jorge.) 3. ¿Cuánto le pagó Miguel a Jorge para arreglar su coche? (No le pagó nada.)

trescientos veintitrés | **323**

SRA. DÍAZ

SR. DÍAZ

MARISSA

JUAN CARLOS

DON DIEGO

Expresiones útiles Point out the sentences that begin with **Les sugiero que...**, **Les aconsejo que...**, and **Recomiendo que...** Explain that these are examples of the present subjunctive with verbs of will or influence. Point out that the verbs **Vengan, quédese, Venga,** and **Pase** are formal commands. Have students guess which go with **usted/ustedes.** Tell students that they will learn more about these concepts in **Estructura.**

Lección 6

(*Los chicos preparan la cena y ponen la mesa.*)

JUAN CARLOS ¿Dónde están los tenedores?

JIMENA Allá.

JUAN CARLOS ¿Y las servilletas?

MARISSA Aquí están.

FELIPE La sala está tan limpia. Le pasamos la aspiradora al sillón y a las cortinas. ¡Y también a las almohadas!

JIMENA Yucatán, ¡ya casi llegamos!

(*Papá y mamá regresan a casa.*)

SRA. DÍAZ ¡Qué bonita está la casa!

SR. DÍAZ Buen trabajo, muchachos. ¿Qué hay para cenar?

JIMENA Quesadillas. Vengan.

Teaching Tip Photocopy the **Fotonovela** Videoscript (Supersite) and white out words related to houses and household chores. Have students fill in the missing words as they watch the episode.

Pairs Have students imagine that the **Díaz** family has decided to sell the apartment. Ask pairs to write a real estate ad for the apartment. Encourage creativity. Have volunteers read their ads for the class.

SRA. DÍAZ Don Diego, quédese a cenar con nosotros. Venga.

SR. DÍAZ Sí, don Diego. Pase.

DON DIEGO Gracias.

recursos

VM
pp. 367–368

vhlcentral.com
Lección 6

Expresiones útiles

Making recommendations

Le(s) sugiero que arregle(n) este apartamento.
I suggest you tidy up this apartment.
Le(s) aconsejo que prepare(n) la cena para las ocho y media.
I recommend that you have dinner ready for eight thirty.

Organizing work

Recomiendo que se organicen en equipos para limpiar.
I recommend that you divide yourselves into teams to clean.
Yo lleno el lavaplatos... después de vaciarlo.
I'll fill the dishwasher... after I empty it.
¿Por qué no terminas de pasar la aspiradora?
Why don't you finish vacuuming?
¡Ya casi acaban!
You're almost finished!
Felipe, tú quita el polvo.
Felipe, you dust.

Making polite requests

Don Diego, quédese a cenar con nosotros.
Don Diego, stay and have dinner with us.
Venga.
Come on.
Don Diego, pase.
Don Diego, come in.

Additional vocabulary

el plumero *duster*

¿Qué pasó?

1

¿Cierto o falso? Indica si lo que dicen estas oraciones es **cierto** o **falso**. Corrige las oraciones falsas.

	Cierto	Falso
1. Felipe y Jimena tienen que preparar el desayuno. Felipe y Jimena tienen que preparar la cena.	○	⦿
2. Don Diego ayuda a los chicos organizando los quehaceres domésticos.	⦿	○
3. Jimena le dice a Juan Carlos dónde están los tenedores.	⦿	○
4. A Marissa no le molesta limpiar el baño. Marissa odia limpiar el baño.	○	⦿
5. Juan Carlos termina de lavar los platos. Juan Carlos termina de pasar la aspiradora.	○	⦿

1 Give students these additional items: 6. Marissa lleva seis platos a la mesa. (Falso. Marissa lleva seis vasos a la mesa.) 7. Después de terminar con la limpieza, don Diego se va a su casa. (Falso. Don Diego se queda a cenar.)

2

Identificar Identifica quién puede decir estas oraciones.

1. Yo les ayudo, no me molesta hacer quehaceres domésticos.   Marissa
2. No me gusta sacar la basura, pero es necesario hacerlo.   Jimena
3. Es importante que termines de pasar la aspiradora, Juan Carlos.   Don Diego
4. ¡La casa está muy limpia! ¡Qué bueno que pasamos la aspiradora!   Felipe
5. ¡Buen trabajo, chicos! ¿Qué vamos a cenar?   Sr. Díaz

JIMENA   DON DIEGO

FELIPE

SR. DÍAZ   MARISSA

2 Give students these additional items: 6. No puedo ver el partido de fútbol hoy. (Felipe) 7. ¡Vengan a comer las quesadillas! (Jimena)

3

Completar Los chicos y don Diego están haciendo los quehaceres. Adivina en qué cuarto está cada uno de ellos.

1. Jimena limpia el congelador. Jimena está en ____la cocina____.
2. Don Diego limpia el escritorio. Don Diego está en ____la oficina____.
3. Felipe pasa la aspiradora debajo de la mesa y las sillas. Felipe está en ____el comedor____.
4. Juan Carlos sacude el sillón. Juan Carlos está en ____la sala____.
5. Marissa hace la cama. Marissa está en ____el dormitorio____.

3 Ask pairs to come up with lists of other household chores that can be done in each of the rooms. Have them share their answers with the class. Keep count of the items on their lists to find out which pair came up with the most correct possibilities.

4

Mi casa Dibuja el plano de una casa o de un apartamento. Puede ser el plano de la casa o del apartamento donde vives o de donde te gustaría (*you would like*) vivir. Después, trabajen en parejas y describan lo que se hace en cuatro de las habitaciones. Para terminar, pídanse (*ask for*) ayuda para hacer dos quehaceres domésticos. Pueden usar estas frases en su conversación.   Answers will vary.

Quiero mostrarte…	Al fondo hay…
Ésta es (la cocina).	Quiero que me ayudes a (sacar la basura).
Allí yo (preparo la comida).	Por favor, ayúdame con…

4 To simplify, draw your own floor plan on the board and model the activity. Ex: **Quiero mostrarte mi casa. Ésta es la sala. Me gusta mirar la televisión allí. Aquí está la oficina. Allí hablo por teléfono y trabajo en la computadora. Ésta es la cocina, donde preparo las comidas… Quiero que me ayudes a sacudir los muebles y a pasar la aspiradora.**

NATIONAL comparisons STANDARDS

Teaching Tips
- Explain that in a few Spanish city and country names the definite article is considered part of the name, and is thus capitalized. Ex: **La Habana, La Coruña, La Haya, El Salvador.**
- Spanish treatment of titles of books, films, and works of art differs from English. In Spanish, only the first word and any proper noun gets an initial capital. Spanish treatment of the names of newspapers and magazines is the same as in English. Tell students that **El País** is a newspaper and **Muy Interesante** is a magazine. All the items mentioned are italicized in print.

Ortografía
Mayúsculas y minúsculas

 Audio

Supersite: MP3 Audio Files, Listening Scripts

Here are some of the rules that govern the use of capital letters (**mayúsculas**) and lowercase letters (**minúsculas**) in Spanish.

Los estudiantes llegaron al aeropuerto a las dos. Luego fueron al hotel.

In both Spanish and English, the first letter of every sentence is capitalized.

Rubén Blades   Panamá   Colón   los Andes

The first letter of all proper nouns (names of people, countries, cities, geographical features, etc.) is capitalized.

Cien años de soledad   Don Quijote de la Mancha
El País   Muy Interesante

The first letter of the first word in titles of books, films, and works of art is generally capitalized, as well as the first letter of any proper names. In newspaper and magazine titles, as well as other short titles, the initial letter of each word is often capitalized.

la señora Ramos   don Francisco
el presidente   Sra. Vives

Titles associated with people are *not* capitalized unless they appear as the first word in a sentence. Note, however, that the first letter of an abbreviated title is capitalized.

Último   Álex   MENÚ   PERDÓN

Accent marks should be retained on capital letters. In practice, however, this rule is often ignored.

lunes   viernes   marzo   primavera

The first letter of days, months, and seasons is <u>not</u> capitalized.

español   estadounidense   japonés   panameños

The first letter of nationalities and languages is <u>not</u> capitalized.

Profesor Herrera, ¿es cierto que somos venenosas°?

Sí, Pepito. ¿Por qué lloras?

Extra Practice Write additional titles, names, sentences, etc., all in lowercase on the board. Ask volunteers to decide which letters should be capitalized.

Extra Practice Have students scan the reading on the next page, circle all the capital letters, and explain why each is capitalized. Point out the words **árabe, españoles,** and **islámica** and have volunteers explain why they are not capitalized.

Práctica Corrige las mayúsculas y minúsculas incorrectas.

1. soy lourdes romero. Soy Colombiana.
   Soy Lourdes Romero. Soy colombiana.
2. éste Es mi Hermano álex.
   Éste es mi hermano Álex.
3. somos De panamá. Somos de Panamá.

4. ¿es ud. La sra. benavides?
   ¿Es Ud. la Sra. Benavides?
5. ud. Llegó el Lunes, ¿no?
   Ud. llegó el lunes, ¿no?

Palabras desordenadas Lee el diálogo de las serpientes. Ordena las letras para saber de qué palabras se trata. Después escribe las letras indicadas para descubrir por qué llora Pepito.

m n a a P á ⬭ ▢ ▢ ▢ ▢ ▢

s t e m r a ⬭ ▢ ▢ ▢ ▢ ▢

i g s l é n ▢ ▢ ⬭ ▢ ▢ ▢

y a U r u g u ▢ ▢ ▢ ⬭ ▢ ▢ ▢

r o ñ e s a ▢ ▢ ▢ ▢ ⬭ ▢

¡_orque _e acabo de morder° la _en_u_!

Respuestas: Panamá, martes, inglés, Uruguay, señora.
¡Porque me acabo de morder la lengua!

recursos

LM p. 374

vhlcentral.com Lección 6

venenosas *venomous* **morder** *to bite*

EN DETALLE

S Additional Reading

El patio central

En las tardes cálidas° de Oaxaca, México; Córdoba, España, o Popayán, Colombia, es un placer sentarse en **el patio central** de una casa y tomar un refresco disfrutando de° una buena conversación. De influencia árabe, esta característica arquitectónica° fue traída° a las Américas por los españoles. En la época° colonial, se construyeron casas, palacios, monasterios, hospitales y escuelas con patio central. Éste es un espacio privado e íntimo en donde se puede disfrutar del sol y de la brisa° estando aislado° de la calle.

El centro del patio es un espacio abierto. Alrededor de° él, separado por columnas, hay un pasillo cubierto°. Así, en el patio hay zonas de sol y de sombra°. El patio es una parte importante de la vivienda familiar y su decoración se cuida° mucho. En el centro del patio muchas veces hay una fuente°, plantas e incluso árboles°. El agua es un elemento muy importante en la cultura islámica porque

simboliza la purificación del cuerpo y del alma°. Por esta razón y para disminuir° la temperatura, el agua en estas construcciones es muy importante. El agua y la vegetación ayudan a mantener la temperatura fresca y el patio proporciona° luz y ventilación a todas las habitaciones.

La distribución

Las casas con patio central eran usualmente las viviendas de familias adineradas°. Son casas de dos o tres pisos. Los cuartos de la planta baja son las áreas comunes: cocina, comedor, sala, etc., y tienen puertas al patio. En los pisos superiores están las habitaciones privadas de la familia.

cálidas *hot* disfrutando de *enjoying* arquitectónica *architectural* traída *brought* época *era* brisa *breeze* aislado *isolated* Alrededor de *Surrounding* cubierto *covered* sombra *shade* se cuida *is looked after* fuente *fountain* árboles *trees* alma *soul* disminuir *lower* proporciona *provides* adineradas *wealthy*

ACTIVIDADES

1 **¿Cierto o falso?** Indica si lo que dicen las oraciones es cierto o falso. Corrige las falsas.

1. Los patios centrales de Latinoamérica tienen su origen en la tradición indígena. **Falso.** Los patios centrales tienen su origen en la arquitectura árabe.
2. Los españoles llevaron a América el concepto del patio. **Cierto.**
3. En la época colonial las casas eran las únicas construcciones con patio central. **Falso.** Se construyeron casas, palacios, monasterios, hospitales y escuelas.
4. El patio es una parte importante en estas construcciones, y es por eso que se le presta atención a su decoración. **Cierto.**

5. El patio central es un lugar de descanso que da luz y ventilación a las habitaciones. **Cierto.**
6. Las fuentes en los patios tienen importancia por razones culturales y porque bajan la temperatura. **Cierto.**
7. En la cultura española el agua simboliza salud y bienestar del cuerpo y del alma. **Falso.** En la cultura islámica el agua simboliza salud y bienestar del cuerpo y del alma.
8. Las casas con patio central eran para personas adineradas. **Cierto.**
9. Los cuartos de la planta baja son privados. **Falso.** Los cuartos de la planta baja son las áreas comunes.
10. Los dormitorios están en los pisos superiores. **Cierto.**

ASÍ SE DICE

La vivienda

el ático, el desván	el altillo
la cobija (Col., Méx.), la frazada (Arg., Cuba, Ven.)	la manta
el escaparate (Cuba, Ven.), el ropero (Méx.)	el armario
el fregadero	*kitchen sink*
el frigidaire (Perú); el frigorífico (Esp.), la nevera	el refrigerador
el lavavajillas (Arg., Esp., Méx.)	el lavaplatos

EL MUNDO HISPANO

Los muebles

- **Mecedora°** La mecedora es un mueble típico de Latinoamérica, especialmente de la zona del Caribe. A las personas les gusta relajarse mientras se mecen° en el patio.

- **Mesa camilla** Era un mueble popular en España hasta hace algunos años. Es una mesa con un bastidor° en la parte inferior° para poner un brasero°. En invierno, las personas se sentaban alrededor de la mesa camilla para conversar, jugar a las cartas o tomar café.

- **Hamaca** Se cree que los taínos hicieron las primeras hamacas con fibras vegetales. Su uso es muy popular en toda Latinoamérica para dormir y descansar.

Mecedora *Rocking chair* se mecen *they rock themselves* bastidor *frame* inferior *bottom* brasero *container for hot coals*

PERFIL

Las islas flotantes del lago Titicaca

Bolivia y Perú comparten el **lago Titicaca**, donde viven **los uros**, uno de los pueblos indígenas más antiguos de América. Hace muchos años, los uros fueron a vivir al lago escapando de **los incas.** Hoy en día, siguen viviendo allí en cuarenta **islas flotantes** que ellos mismos hacen con unos juncos° llamados **totora**. Primero tejen° grandes plataformas. Luego, con el mismo material, construyen sus casas sobre las plataformas. La totora es resistente, pero con el tiempo el agua la pudre°. Los habitantes de las islas necesitan renovar continuamente las plataformas y las casas. Sus muebles y sus barcos también están hechos° de juncos. Los uros viven de la pesca y del turismo; en las islas hay unas tiendas donde venden artesanías° hechas con totora.

PERÚ

Lago Titicaca

BOLIVIA

juncos *reeds* tejen *they weave* la pudre *rots it* hechos *made* artesanías *handcrafts*

Conexión Internet

¿Cómo son las casas modernas en los países hispanos?

Go to **vhlcentral.com** to find more cultural information related to this **Cultura** section.

ACTIVIDADES

2 **Comprensión** Responde a las preguntas.

1. Tu amigo mexicano te dice: "La **cobija** azul está en el **ropero**". ¿Qué quiere decir? La manta azul está en en el armario.

2. ¿Quiénes hicieron las primeras hamacas? ¿Qué material usaron? los taínos; fibras vegetales

3. ¿Qué grupo indígena vive en el lago Titicaca? Los uros viven en el lago Titicaca.

4. ¿Qué pueden comprar los turistas en las islas flotantes del lago Titicaca? Pueden comprar artesanías hechas con totora.

3 **Viviendas tradicionales** Escribe cuatro oraciones sobre una vivienda tradicional que conoces. Explica en qué lugar se encuentra, de qué materiales está hecha y cómo es. Answers will vary.

3 To add a visual aspect, have students find a photo of a traditional dwelling to use as the basis for the written description.

 Practice more at **vhlcentral.com**.

6.1 | # Relative pronouns **Tutorial**

ANTE TODO In both English and Spanish, relative pronouns are used to combine two sentences or clauses that share a common element, such as a noun or pronoun. Study this diagram.

> Mis padres me regalaron **la aspiradora**.
> *My parents gave me the vacuum cleaner.*

> **La aspiradora** funciona muy bien.
> *The vacuum cleaner works really well.*

> La aspiradora **que** me regalaron mis padres funciona muy bien.
> *The vacuum cleaner that my parents gave me works really well.*

> **Lourdes** es muy inteligente.
> *Lourdes is very intelligent.*

> **Lourdes** estudia español.
> *Lourdes is studying Spanish.*

> Lourdes, **quien** estudia español, es muy inteligente.
> *Lourdes, who studies Spanish, is very intelligent.*

> Eso fue todo lo que dijimos.

> Mi papá se lleva bien con Juan Carlos, quien es como mi hermano.

▶ Spanish has three frequently used relative pronouns. **¡Atención!** Even though interrogative words (**qué**, **quién**, etc.) always carry an accent, relative pronouns never carry a written accent.

que	*that; which; who*
quien(es)	*who; whom; that*
lo que	*that which; what*

▶ **Que** is the most frequently used relative pronoun. It can refer to things or to people. Unlike its English counterpart, *that*, **que** is never omitted.

> ¿Dónde está la cafetera **que** compré?
> *Where is the coffee maker (that) I bought?*

> El hombre **que** limpia es Pedro.
> *The man who is cleaning is Pedro.*

▶ The relative pronoun **quien** refers only to people, and is often used after a preposition or the personal **a**. **Quien** has only two forms: **quien** (singular) and **quienes** (plural).

> ¿Son las chicas **de quienes** me hablaste la semana pasada?
> *Are they the girls (that) you told me about last week?*

> Eva, **a quien** conocí anoche, es mi nueva vecina.
> *Eva, whom I met last night, is my new neighbor.*

Teaching Tip Compare and contrast the use of **que** and **quien** by writing some examples on the board. Ex: **Es la chica que vino con Carlos a mi fiesta. Es la chica a quien conocí en mi fiesta.** Have students deduce the rule.

Extra Practice Write these sentences on the board, and have students supply the correct relative pronoun.
1. Hay una escalera _____ sube al primer piso. (que)
2. Elena es la muchacha a _____ le presté la aspiradora. (quien)
3. ¿Dónde pusiste la ropa _____ acabas de quitarte? (que) 4. ¿Cuáles son los estudiantes a _____ les alquilas tu casa? (quienes)
5. La cómoda _____ compramos la semana pasada está en el dormitorio de mi hermana. (que)

Game Ask students to bring in some interesting pictures from magazines or the Internet, but tell them not to show these photos to one another. Divide the class into teams of three. Each team should pick a picture. One student will write an accurate description of it, and the others will write imaginary descriptions. Tell them to use relative pronouns in the descriptions. Each team will read its three descriptions aloud without showing the picture. Give the rest of the class two minutes to ask questions about the descriptions before guessing which is the accurate one. Award one point for a correct guess and two points to the team able to fool the class.

Lección 6

¡LENGUA VIVA!

In English, it is generally recommended that *who(m)* be used to refer to people, and that *that* and *which* be used to refer to things. In Spanish, however, it is perfectly acceptable to use **que** when referring to people.

Teaching Tips

• Test comprehension as you proceed by asking volunteers to answer questions about students and objects in the classroom. Ex: **¿Cómo se llama la estudiante que se sienta detrás de _____? ¿Cómo se llaman los estudiantes a quienes acabo de hacer esta pregunta? ¿Dónde está la tarea que ustedes hicieron para hoy?**

• Add a visual aspect to this grammar presentation. Line up four to five pictures. Ask questions that use relative pronouns or elicit them in student answers. Ex: **¿Quién está comiendo una hamburguesa? (El muchacho que está en la playa está comiendo una hamburguesa.) ¿Quién sabe lo que está haciendo esta muchacha? (Está quitando la mesa.)**

▶ **Quien(es)** is occasionally used instead of **que** in clauses set off by commas.

Lola, **quien** es cubana, es médica.
Lola, who is Cuban, is a doctor.

Su tía, **que** es alemana, ya llegó.
His aunt, who is German, already arrived.

▶ Unlike **que** and **quien(es), lo que** doesn't refer to a specific noun. It refers to an idea, a situation, or a past event and means *what, that which,* or *the thing that.*

Lo que me molesta es el calor.
What bothers me is the heat.

Lo que quiero es una casa.
What I want is a house.

Este supermercado tiene todo **lo que** necesito.

A Samuel no le gustó **lo que** le dijo Violeta.

¡INTÉNTALO! Completa estas oraciones con pronombres relativos.

1. Voy a utilizar los platos ___que___ me regaló mi abuela.
2. Ana comparte un apartamento con la chica a ___quien___ conocimos en la fiesta de Jorge.
3. Esta oficina tiene todo ___lo que___ necesitamos.
4. Puedes estudiar en el dormitorio ___que___ está a la derecha de la cocina.
5. Los señores ___que___ viven en esa casa acaban de llegar de Centroamérica.
6. Los niños a ___quienes___ viste en nuestro jardín son mis sobrinos.
7. La piscina ___que___ ves desde la ventana es la piscina de mis vecinos.
8. Úrsula, ___que/quien___ ayudó a mamá a limpiar el refrigerador, es muy simpática.
9. El hombre de ___quien___ hablo es mi padre.
10. ___Lo que___ te dijo Pablo no es cierto.
11. Tengo que sacudir los muebles ___que___ están en el altillo una vez al mes.
12. No entiendo por qué no lavaste los vasos ___que___ te dije.
13. La mujer a ___quien___ saludaste vive en las afueras.
14. ¿Sabes ___lo que___ necesita este dormitorio? ¡Unas cortinas!
15. No quiero volver a hacer ___lo que___ hice ayer.
16. No me gusta vivir con personas a ___quienes___ no conozco.

recursos

WB
pp. 357–358

LM
p. 375

S
vhlcentral.com
Lección 6

Extra Practice Ask students to make two short lists: **Lo que tengo en mi dormitorio** and **Lo que quiero tener en mi dormitorio**. Ask volunteers to read part of their lists to the class. Encourage a conversation by asking questions such as: **¿Es esto lo que tienes en tu dormitorio? ¿Es un _____ lo que quieres tú?**

Práctica

1

Combinar Combina elementos de la columna A y la columna B para formar oraciones lógicas.

A

1. Ése es el hombre __d__.
2. Rubén Blades, __c__.
3. No traje __e__.
4. ¿Te gusta la manta __b__?
5. ¿Cómo se llama el programa __g__?
6. La mujer __a__.

B

a. con quien bailaba es mi vecina
b. que te compró Cecilia
c. quien es de Panamá, es un cantante muy bueno
d. que arregló mi lavadora
e. lo que necesito para la clase de matemáticas
f. que comiste en el restaurante
g. que escuchaste en la radio anoche

NOTA CULTURAL

Rubén Blades es un cantante, compositor y actor panameño muy famoso. Este versátil abogado fue también Ministro de Turismo en su país (2004–2009) y fue nombrado Embajador contra el racismo por las Naciones Unidas en el 2000.

2

Completar Completa la historia sobre la casa que Jaime y Tina quieren comprar, usando los pronombres relativos **que, quien, quienes** o **lo que**.

1. Jaime y Tina son los chicos a __quienes__ conocí la semana pasada.
2. Quieren comprar una casa __que__ está en las afueras de la ciudad.
3. Es una casa __que__ era de una artista famosa.
4. La artista, a __quien__ yo conocía, murió el año pasado y no tenía hijos.
5. Ahora se vende la casa con todos los muebles __que__ ella tenía.
6. La sala tiene una alfombra __que__ ella trajo de Kuwait.
7. La casa tiene muchos estantes, __lo que__ a Tina le encanta.

3

Oraciones Javier y Ana acaban de casarse y han comprado (*they have bought*) una casa y muchas otras cosas. Combina sus declaraciones para formar una sola oración con los pronombres relativos **que, quien(es)** y **lo que**.

> **modelo**
>
> Vamos a usar los vasos nuevos mañana. Los pusimos en el comedor.
> *Mañana vamos a usar los vasos nuevos que pusimos en el comedor.*

3 Ask a volunteer to read the **modelo** aloud. Ask another volunteer to explain what word is replaced by the relative pronoun **que**.

3 Have pairs write two more sentences that contain relative pronouns and refer to **Javier** and **Ana's** new home.

1. Tenemos una cafetera nueva. Mi prima nos la regaló.
   Tenemos una cafetera nueva que mi prima nos regaló.
2. Tenemos una cómoda nueva. Es bueno porque no hay espacio en el armario.
   Tenemos una cómoda nueva, lo que es bueno porque no hay espacio en el armario.
3. Esos platos no nos costaron mucho. Están encima del horno.
   Esos platos que están encima del horno no nos costaron mucho.
4. Esas copas me las regaló mi amiga Amalia. Ella viene a visitarme mañana.
   Esas copas me las regaló mi amiga Amalia, quien/que viene a visitarme mañana.
5. La lavadora está casi nueva. Nos la regalaron mis suegros.
   La lavadora que nos regalaron mis suegros está casi nueva.
6. La vecina nos dio una manta de lana. Ella la compró en México.
   La vecina nos dio una manta de lana que compró en México.

2 Ask questions about the content of the activity. Ex: **1.** ¿Quiénes quieren comprar una casa? (Jaime y Tina) **2.** ¿Qué casa quieren comprar? (una casa que está en las afueras de la ciudad) **3.** ¿De quién era la casa? (de una artista famosa) **4.** ¿Cómo venden la casa? (con todos los muebles que tenía) **5.** ¿Qué tipo de alfombra tiene la sala? (una alfombra que la artista trajo de Kuwait)

Extra Practice Have students use relative pronouns to complete this series. **1.** ____ tenemos que hacer es buscar otro apartamento. (Lo que) **2.** El apartamento ____ tenemos sólo tiene dos dormitorios. (que) **3.** Ayer hablamos con un compañero ____ alquila una casa cerca de aquí. (que) **4.** Buscamos algo similar a ____ él tiene: tres dormitorios, dos cuartos de baño, una cocina, una sala, un comedor... ¡y un alquiler bajo! (lo que) **5.** Nos dio el nombre de unos agentes a ____ podemos contactar. (quienes)

Pairs Ask pairs of students to write a description of a new household gadget, using relative pronouns. Their descriptions should include the purpose of the gadget and how it is used.

Lección 6

Comunicación

NATIONAL communication STANDARDS

4

4 Have pairs team up to form groups of four. Each student will report on his or her partner, using the information obtained in the interview.

4 Have pairs of students write four additional questions. Ask pairs to exchange their questions with another pair.

Entrevista En parejas, túrnense para hacerse estas preguntas. Answers will vary.

1. ¿Qué es lo que más te gusta de vivir en las afueras o en la ciudad?
2. ¿Cómo son las personas que viven en tu barrio?
3. ¿Cuál es el quehacer doméstico que pagarías (*you would pay*) por no hacer?
4. ¿Quién es la persona que hace los quehaceres domésticos en tu casa?
5. ¿Hay vecinos que te caen bien? ¿Quiénes?
6. ¿De qué vecino es el coche que más te gusta?
7. ¿Cuál es el barrio de tu ciudad que más te gusta y por qué?
8. ¿Quién es la persona a quien le pedirías (*you would ask*) que te ayude con los quehaceres?
9. ¿Cuál es el lugar de la casa donde te sientes más cómodo/a? ¿Por qué?
10. ¿Qué es lo que más te gusta de tu barrio?
11. ¿Qué hace el vecino que más llama la atención?
12. ¿Qué es lo que menos te gusta de tu barrio?

5 Have groups choose their three best **adivinanzas** and present them to the class.

5

Adivinanza En grupos, túrnense para describir distintas partes de una vivienda usando pronombres relativos. Los demás compañeros tienen que hacer preguntas hasta que adivinen (*they guess*) la palabra. Answers will vary.

modelo

Estudiante 1: Es lo que tenemos en el dormitorio.
Estudiante 2: ¿Es el mueble que usamos para dormir?
Estudiante 1: No. Es lo que usamos para guardar la ropa.
Estudiante 3: Lo sé. Es la cómoda.

NATIONAL communication STANDARDS

Síntesis

6 Have pairs choose one of the items listed in the activity and develop a magazine ad. Their ad should include three sentences with relative pronouns.

6

Definir En parejas, definan las palabras. Usen los pronombres relativos **que**, **quien(es)** y **lo que**. Luego compartan sus definiciones con la clase. Answers will vary.

alquiler	flan	patio	tenedor
amigos	guantes	postre	termómetro
aspiradora	jabón	sillón	vaso
enfermera	manta	sótano	vecino

modelo

lavadora   Es lo que se usa para lavar la ropa.
pastel   Es un postre que comes en tu cumpleaños.

AYUDA

Remember that **de**, followed by the name of a material, means *made of*.

Es de algodón.
It's made of cotton.

• • •

Es un tipo de *means*
It's a kind/sort of…

Es un tipo de flor.
It's a kind of flower.

Game Divide the class into teams of four and assign one relative pronoun (**que, quien, quienes,** or **lo que**) to each team member. Call out a word or phrase from the lesson vocabulary. Allow one minute for students to write a sentence containing the vocabulary item and their assigned relative pronoun. Award teams one point for each correct sentence, plus a bonus point to the team with the most original sentence. Rotate the pronouns until every student has written four sentences.

6.2 Formal (usted/ustedes) commands 🅢 Tutorial

ANTE TODO   As you learned in **Lección 5**, the command forms are used to give orders or advice. Formal commands are used with people you address as **usted** or **ustedes**. Observe these examples, then study the chart.

Hable con ellos, don Francisco.
Talk with them, Don Francisco.

Coma frutas y verduras.
Eat fruits and vegetables.

Laven los platos ahora mismo.
Wash the dishes right now.

Beban menos té y café.
Drink less tea and coffee.

Formal commands (Ud. and Uds.)

Infinitive	Present tense yo form	Ud. command	Uds. command
limpiar	limpi**o**	limpi**e**	limpi**en**
barrer	barr**o**	barr**a**	barr**an**
sacudir	sacud**o**	sacud**a**	sacud**an**
decir (e:i)	dig**o**	dig**a**	dig**an**
pensar (e:ie)	piens**o**	piens**e**	piens**en**
volver (o:ue)	vuelv**o**	vuelv**a**	vuelv**an**
servir (e:i)	sirv**o**	sirv**a**	sirv**an**

▶ The **usted** and **ustedes** commands, like the negative **tú** commands, are formed by dropping the final **-o** of the yo form of the present tense. For **-ar** verbs, add **-e** or **-en**. For **-er** and **-ir** verbs, add **-a** or **-an**.

Don Diego, quédese a cenar con nosotros.

No se preocupen, yo los ayudo.

▶ Verbs with irregular **yo** forms maintain the same irregularity in their formal commands. These verbs include **conducir, conocer, decir, hacer, ofrecer, oír, poner, salir, tener, traducir, traer, venir,** and **ver.**

Oiga, don Manolo...
Listen, Don Manolo...

¡Salga inmediatamente!
Leave immediately!

Ponga la mesa, por favor.
Set the table, please.

Hagan la cama antes de salir.
Make the bed before leaving.

▶ Note also that verbs maintain their stem changes in **usted** and **ustedes** commands.

e:ie	o:ue	e:i
No **pierda** la llave.	**Vuelva** temprano, joven.	**Sirva** la sopa, por favor.
Cierren la puerta.	**Duerman** bien, chicos.	**Repitan** las frases.

NATIONAL
comparisons
STANDARDS

AYUDA

By learning formal commands, it will be easier for you to learn the subjunctive forms that are presented in **Estructura 6.3**, p. 336.

Teaching Tips
• Model the use of formal commands with simple examples using TPR and gestures. Ex: **Levántense. Siéntense.** Then point to individual students and give commands in an exaggerated formal tone. Ex: **Señor(ita) ____, levántese.** Give other commands using **salga/ salgan, vuelva/vuelvan,** and **venga/vengan.**
• Write a list of verbs on the board and have volunteers give commands, first to you, then to the class. Respond with humor to any impossible or inappropriate requests. Ex: **¡Ni loco/a!**

Video Replay the **Fotonovela** episode and have students write down each formal command that they hear. Have students compare their lists with a partner.

Extra Practice Describe situations and have students call out **ustedes** commands that would be used. Ex: A mother sending her kids off to overnight camp. (**Cepíllense los dientes antes de dormir.**) An aerobics class. (**Levanten los brazos.**)

AYUDA

These spelling changes are necessary to ensure that the words are pronounced correctly. See **Lección 2, Pronunciación,** p. 89, and **Lección 3, Pronunciación,** p. 149.

• • •

It may help you to study the following five series of syllables. Note that, within each series, the consonant sound doesn't change.

ca que qui co cu

za ce ci zo zu

ga gue gui go gu

ja ge gi jo ju

Teaching Tips
- Ask volunteers to write formal command forms of other verbs with spelling changes on the board. Ex: **empezar (empiece); comenzar (comience); buscar (busque); pagar (pague); llegar (llegue).**
- Test comprehension as you proceed by asking volunteers to supply the correct form of other infinitives you name.
- Point out that the written accent mark on **dé** serves to distinguish the verb form from the preposition **de.**

Extra Practice Write a list of situations on the board using singular and plural forms. Ex: **La cocina está sucia. Mis amigos y yo tenemos hambre. Tenemos miedo.** Then have students write responses in the form of commands. Ex: **Límpiela. Hagan la cena. No tengan miedo.**

▶ Verbs ending in **-car**, **-gar**, and **-zar** have a spelling change in the command forms.

sa**car**	c → qu	sa**qu**e, sa**qu**en
ju**gar**	g → gu	jue**gu**e, jue**gu**en
almor**zar**	z → c	almuer**c**e, almuer**c**en

▶ These verbs have irregular formal commands.

Infinitive	Ud. command	Uds. command
dar	**dé**	**den**
estar	**esté**	**estén**
ir	**vaya**	**vayan**
saber	**sepa**	**sepan**
ser	**sea**	**sean**

▶ To make a formal command negative, simply place **no** before the verb.

No ponga las maletas en la cama.   **No ensucien** los sillones.
Don't put the suitcases on the bed.   *Don't dirty the armchairs.*

▶ In affirmative commands, reflexive, indirect, and direct object pronouns are always attached to the end of the verb.

Siénten**se**, por favor.   Acuésten**se** ahora.
Síga**me**, Laura.   Póngan**las** en el suelo, por favor.

▶ **¡Atención!** When a pronoun is attached to an affirmative command that has two or more syllables, an accent mark is added to maintain the original stress.

limpie ⟶ límpielo   lean ⟶ léanlo
diga ⟶ dígamelo   sacudan ⟶ sacúdanlos

▶ In negative commands, these pronouns always precede the verb.

No **se** preocupe.   No **los** ensucien.
No **me lo** dé.   No **nos las** traigan.

▶ **Usted** and **ustedes** can be used with the command forms to strike a more formal tone. In such instances, they follow the command form.

Muéstrele usted la foto a su amigo.   **Tomen ustedes** esta mesa.
Show the photo to your friend.   *Take this table.*

recursos

WB
pp. 359–360

LM
p. 376

Ⓢ
vhlcentral.com
Lección 6

Teaching Tip Point out the double **n** in item 4: **Sírvannoslo.**

¡INTÉNTALO!   Indica los mandatos (*commands*) afirmativos y negativos correspondientes.

1. escucharlo (Ud.) ___Escúchelo___. ___No lo escuche___.
2. decírmelo (Uds.) ___Díganmelo___. ___No me lo digan___.
3. salir (Ud.) ___Salga___. ___No salga___.
4. servírnoslo (Uds.) ___Sírvannoslo___. ___No nos lo sirvan___.
5. barrerla (Ud.) ___Bárrala___. ___No la barra___.
6. hacerlo (Ud.) ___Hágalo___. ___No lo haga___.

Práctica

1

Completar La señora González quiere mudarse de casa. Ayúdala a organizarse. Indica el mandato formal de cada verbo.

1. ____Lea____ los anuncios del periódico y ___guárdelos___. (Leer, guardarlos)
2. ____Vaya____ personalmente y ____vea____ las casas usted misma. (Ir, ver)
3. Decida qué casa quiere y ___llame___ al agente. ___Pídale___ un contrato de alquiler. (llamar, Pedirle)
4. ___Contrate___ un camión (*truck*) para ese día y ___pregúnteles___ la hora exacta de llegada. (Contratar, preguntarles)
5. El día de la mudanza (*On moving day*) ____esté____ tranquila. ___Vuelva___ a revisar su lista para completar todo lo que tiene que hacer. (estar, Volver)
6. Primero, ___dígales___ a todos en casa que usted va a estar ocupada. No ___les diga___ que usted va a hacerlo todo. (decirles, decirles)
7. ___Saque___ tiempo para hacer las maletas tranquilamente. No ___les haga___ las maletas a los niños más grandes. (Sacar, hacerles)
8. No ___se preocupe___. ___Sepa___ que todo va a salir bien. (preocuparse, Saber)

2

¿Qué dicen? Mira los dibujos y escribe un mandato lógico para cada uno. Usa palabras que aprendiste en **Contextos**. Answers will vary. Suggested answers:

1. ___Abran sus libros, por favor.___

2. ___Cierre la puerta. ¡Hace frío!___

3. ___Traiga usted la cuenta, por favor.___

4. ___La cocina está sucia. Bárranla, por favor.___

5. ___Duerma bien, niña.___

6. ___Arreglen el cuarto, por favor. Está desordenado.___

Practice more at **vhlcentral.com**.

1 To challenge students, have them work in pairs to formulate a list of instructions for the movers. Ex: **Tengan cuidado con los platos. No pongan los cuadros en una caja**. Then, with the class, compare and contrast the commands the pairs have formulated.

2 To simplify, before starting the activity, have volunteers describe the situation in each of the drawings. Have them identify who is speaking to whom.

2 Continue the exercise by using magazine pictures. Ex: **Tengan paciencia con los niños.**

Extra Practice Add an auditory aspect to this grammar practice. Prepare a series of sentences that contain formal commands. Read each twice, pausing after the second time for students to write. Ex: **1. Saquen la basura a la calle. 2. Almuerce usted conmigo hoy. 3. Niños, jueguen en el patio. 4. Váyase inmediatamente. 5. Esté usted aquí a las diez.**

Pairs Have pairs of students write a list of commands for the president of your school. Ex: **Por favor, no suba el costo de la matrícula. Permita más fiestas en las residencias.** Then have them write a list of commands for their fellow students. Ex: **No hablen en la biblioteca.**

communication

3 Ask volunteers to offer other suggestions for the problem in the **modelo**. Ex: **Tenga usted más cuidado. Compre nuevos zapatos de tenis.**

3 Ask pairs to pick their most humorous or unusual response to present to the class.

Comunicación

3 **Solucionar** Trabajen en parejas. Un(a) estudiante presenta los problemas de la columna A y el/la otro/a los de la columna B. Usen mandatos formales y túrnense para ofrecer soluciones. Answers will vary.

> **modelo**
>
> **Estudiante 1:** Vilma se torció un tobillo jugando al tenis. Es la tercera vez.
> **Estudiante 2:** *No juegue más al tenis. / Vaya a ver a un especialista.*

A

1. Se me perdió el libro de español con todas mis notas.
2. A Vicente se le cayó la botella de vino para la cena.
3. ¿Cómo? ¿Se le olvidó traer el traje de baño a la playa?
4. Se nos quedaron los boletos en la casa. El avión sale en una hora.

B

1. Mis hijas no se levantan temprano. Siempre llegan tarde a la escuela.
2. A mi abuela le robaron (*stole*) las maletas. Era su primer día de vacaciones.
3. Nuestra casa es demasiado pequeña para nuestra familia.
4. Me preocupo constantemente por Roberto. Trabaja demasiado.

4 Have pairs write another scenario on a sheet of paper. Then ask them to exchange papers with another pair, and give them two minutes to prepare another dialogue. Have them act out their dialogues for the authors.

4 **Conversaciones** En parejas, escojan dos situaciones y preparen conversaciones para presentar a la clase. Usen mandatos formales. Answers will vary.

> **modelo**
>
> **Lupita:** Señor Ramírez, siento mucho llegar tan tarde. Mi niño se enfermó. ¿Qué debo hacer?
> **Sr. Ramírez:** *No se preocupe. Siéntese y descanse un poco.*

SITUACIÓN 1 Profesor Rosado, no vine la semana pasada porque el equipo jugaba en Boquete. ¿Qué debo hacer para ponerme al día (*catch up*)?

SITUACIÓN 2 Los invitados de la boda llegan a las cuatro de la tarde, las mesas están sin poner y el champán sin servir. Son las tres de la tarde y los camareros apenas están llegando. ¿Qué deben hacer los camareros?

SITUACIÓN 3 Mi novio es un poco aburrido. No le gustan ni el cine, ni los deportes, ni salir a comer. Tampoco habla mucho. ¿Qué puedo hacer?

▶**SITUACIÓN 4** Tengo que preparar una presentación para mañana sobre el Canal de Panamá. ¿Por dónde comienzo?

NOTA CULTURAL

El 31 de diciembre de 1999, los Estados Unidos cedió el control del **Canal de Panamá** al gobierno de Panamá, terminando así con casi cien años de administración estadounidense.

Síntesis

communication

5 **Presentar** En grupos, preparen un anuncio de televisión para presentar a la clase. El anuncio debe tratar de un detergente, un electrodoméstico o una agencia inmobiliaria (*real estate agency*). Usen mandatos, los pronombres relativos (**que, quien(es)** o **lo que**) y el **se** impersonal. Answers will vary.

> **modelo**
>
> Compre el lavaplatos Destellos. Tiene todo lo que usted desea. Es el lavaplatos que mejor funciona. Venga a verlo ahora mismo… No pierda ni un minuto más. Se aceptan tarjetas de crédito.

Supersite: See the Activity Pack for an additional information gap activity to practice the material presented in this section.

Lección 6

6.3 The present subjunctive  Tutorial

ANTE TODO With the exception of commands, all the verb forms you have been using have been in the indicative mood. The indicative is used to state facts and to express actions or states that the speaker considers to be real and definite. In contrast, the subjunctive mood expresses the speaker's attitudes toward events, as well as actions or states the speaker views as uncertain or hypothetical.

Por favor, quiten los platos de la mesa.

Les aconsejo que preparen la cena.

▶ The present subjunctive is formed very much like **usted**, **ustedes**, and *negative* **tú** commands. From the **yo** form of the present indicative, drop the **-o** ending, and replace it with the subjunctive endings.

INFINITIVE	PRESENT INDICATIVE	VERB STEM	PRESENT SUBJUNCTIVE
hablar comer escribir	**hablo como escribo**	**habl- com- escrib-**	**hable coma escriba**

▶ The present subjunctive endings are:

-ar verbs

-e	-emos
-es	-éis
-e	-en

-er and -ir verbs

-a	-amos
-as	-áis
-a	-an

Present subjunctive of regular verbs

		hablar	comer	escribir
SINGULAR FORMS	yo	habl**e**	com**a**	escrib**a**
	tú	habl**es**	com**as**	escrib**as**
	Ud./él/ella	habl**e**	com**a**	escrib**a**
PLURAL FORMS	nosotros/as	habl**emos**	com**amos**	escrib**amos**
	vosotros/as	habl**éis**	com**áis**	escrib**áis**
	Uds./ellos/ellas	habl**en**	com**an**	escrib**an**

Teaching Tip Write sentences like these on the board in two columns labeled *Indicative* and *Subjunctive*. Column 1: **Mi esposo lava los platos. Mi esposo barre el suelo. Mi esposo cocina.** Column 2: **Es importante que mi esposo lave los platos. Es urgente que mi esposo barra el suelo. Es bueno que mi esposo cocine.** Guide students to notice the difference between the indicative and subjunctive forms.

AYUDA

Note that, in the present subjunctive, **-ar** verbs use endings normally associated with present tense **-er** and **-ir** verbs. Likewise, **-er** and **-ir** verbs in the present subjunctive use endings normally associated with **-ar** verbs in the present tense. Note also that, in the present subjunctive, the **yo** form is the same as the **Ud./él/ella** form.

¡LENGUA VIVA!

You may think that English has no subjunctive, but it does! While once common, it now survives mostly in set expressions such as *If I were you…* and *Be that as it may…*

Lección 6

Teaching Tips
- Provide additional examples of the subjunctive mood in English. Ex: *I wish she were here. I insist that he take notes. I suggest you be there tomorrow.*
- Emphasize the stem changes that occur in the **nosotros/as** and **vosotros/as** forms of **-ir** stem-changing verbs.

Extra Practice Read aloud sentences that use the subjunctive, and have students repeat. Then call out a different subject for the subordinate clause. Have students say the sentence with the new subject, making all other necessary changes. Ex: **Es malo que ustedes trabajen mucho. Javier. (Es malo que Javier trabaje mucho.) Es necesario que lleguen temprano. Nosotras. (Es necesario que lleguemos temprano.)**

Extra Practice Ask students to compare family members' attitudes toward domestic life using the subjunctive. Ex: **Según los padres, es necesario que los hijos...**

AYUDA

Note that stem-changing verbs and verbs that have a spelling change have the same ending as regular verbs in the present subjunctive.

TPR Call out an infinitive and a subject pronoun (Ex: **alquilar/yo**). Toss a foam or paper ball to a student. He or she must provide the correct subjunctive form (**alquile**) and toss the ball back. Avoid verbs with irregular subjunctive forms.

▶ Verbs with irregular **yo** forms show the same irregularity in all forms of the present subjunctive.

Infinitive	Present indicative	Verb stem	Present subjunctive
conducir	conduzco	**conduzc-**	**conduzca**
conocer	conozco	**conozc-**	**conozca**
decir	digo	**dig-**	**diga**
hacer	hago	**hag-**	**haga**
ofrecer	ofrezco	**ofrezc-**	**ofrezca**
oír	oigo	**oig-**	**oiga**
parecer	parezco	**parezc-**	**parezca**
poner	pongo	**pong-**	**ponga**
tener	tengo	**teng-**	**tenga**
traducir	traduzco	**traduzc-**	**traduzca**
traer	traigo	**traig-**	**traiga**
venir	vengo	**veng-**	**venga**
ver	veo	**ve-**	**vea**

▶ To maintain the **-c, -g,** and **-z** sounds, verbs ending in **-car, -gar,** and **-zar** have a spelling change in all forms of the present subjunctive.

sacar:	sa**qu**e, sa**qu**es, sa**qu**e, sa**qu**emos, sa**qu**éis, sa**qu**en
jugar:	jue**gu**e, jue**gu**es, jue**gu**e, ju**gu**emos, ju**gu**éis, jue**gu**en
almorzar:	almuer**c**e, almuer**c**es, almuer**c**e, almor**c**emos, almor**c**éis, almuer**c**en

Present subjunctive of stem-changing verbs

▶ **-Ar** and **-er** stem-changing verbs have the same stem changes in the subjunctive as they do in the present indicative.

pensar (e:ie):	p**ie**nse, p**ie**nses, p**ie**nse, pensemos, penséis, p**ie**nsen
mostrar (o:ue):	m**ue**stre, m**ue**stres, m**ue**stre, mostremos, mostréis, m**ue**stren
entender (e:ie):	ent**ie**nda, ent**ie**ndas, ent**ie**nda, entendamos, entendáis, ent**ie**ndan
volver (o:ue):	v**ue**lva, v**ue**lvas, v**ue**lva, volvamos, volváis, v**ue**lvan

▶ **-Ir** stem-changing verbs have the same stem changes in the subjunctive as they do in the present indicative, but in addition, the **nosotros/as** and **vosotros/as** forms undergo a stem change. The unstressed **e** changes to **i**, while the unstressed **o** changes to **u**.

pedir (e:i):	p**i**da, p**i**das, p**i**da, p**i**damos, p**i**dáis, p**i**dan
sentir (e:ie):	s**ie**nta, s**ie**ntas, s**ie**nta, s**i**ntamos, s**i**ntáis, s**ie**ntan
dormir (o:ue):	d**ue**rma, d**ue**rmas, d**ue**rma, d**u**rmamos, d**u**rmáis, d**ue**rman

Irregular verbs in the present subjunctive

▶ These five verbs are irregular in the present subjunctive.

		dar	estar	ir	saber	ser
SINGULAR FORMS	yo	dé	esté	vaya	sepa	sea
	tú	des	estés	vayas	sepas	seas
	Ud./él/ella	dé	esté	vaya	sepa	sea
PLURAL FORMS	nosotros/as	demos	estemos	vayamos	sepamos	seamos
	vosotros/as	deis	estéis	vayáis	sepáis	seáis
	Uds./ellos/ellas	den	estén	vayan	sepan	sean

Irregular verbs in the present subjunctive

▶ **¡Atención!** The subjunctive form of **hay** (*there is, there are*) is also irregular: **haya.**

General uses of the subjunctive

▶ The subjunctive is mainly used to express: 1) will and influence, 2) emotion, 3) doubt, disbelief, and denial, and 4) indefiniteness and nonexistence.

▶ The subjunctive is most often used in sentences that consist of a main clause and a subordinate clause. The main clause contains a verb or expression that triggers the use of the subjunctive. The conjunction **que** connects the subordinate clause to the main clause.

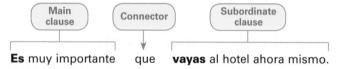

Main clause	Connector	Subordinate clause

Es muy importante   que   **vayas** al hotel ahora mismo.

▶ These impersonal expressions are always followed by clauses in the subjunctive:

Es bueno que...	**Es mejor que...**	**Es malo que...**
It's good that...	*It's better that...*	*It's bad that...*
Es importante que...	**Es necesario que...**	**Es urgente que...**
It's important that...	*It's necessary that...*	*It's urgent that...*

 **¡INTÉNTALO!**   Indica el presente de subjuntivo de estos verbos.

1. (alquilar, beber, vivir)   que yo <u>alquile, beba, viva</u>
2. (estudiar, aprender, asistir)   que tú <u>estudies, aprendas, asistas</u>
3. (encontrar, poder, tener)   que él <u>encuentre, pueda, tenga</u>
4. (hacer, pedir, dormir)   que nosotras <u>hagamos, pidamos, durmamos</u>
5. (dar, hablar, escribir)   que ellos <u>den, hablen, escriban</u>
6. (pagar, empezar, buscar)   que ustedes <u>paguen, empiecen, busquen</u>
7. (ser, ir, saber)   que yo <u>sea, vaya, sepa</u>
8. (estar, dar, oír)   que tú <u>estés, des, oigas</u>

Teaching Tips
• Point out that, in order to use the subjunctive in the subordinate clause, the conjunction **que** must be present and there must be a change of subject. Write these sentences on the board: **Es importante que limpies la cocina. Es importante limpiar la cocina.** Have a volunteer explain why the subjunctive is used only in the first sentence. Emphasize that, while the first example states one person's responsibility, the second is a broad statement about the importance of cleaning kitchens.
• Reiterate that, whereas the word *that* is usually optional in English, **que** is required in Spanish.

Extra Practice Call on two volunteers at a time. The first student writes a main clause on the board that requires the subjunctive (Ex: **Es importante que**). The second student writes an ending for the sentence (Ex: **aprendamos español.**).

Video Replay the **Fotonovela** episode and pause where appropriate to discuss each use of the subjunctive.

recursos

WB pp. 361–362

LM p. 377

vhlcentral.com
Lección 6

Lección 6

Práctica y Comunicación

1 Completar
Completa las oraciones con el presente de subjuntivo de los verbos entre paréntesis. Luego empareja las oraciones del primer grupo con las del segundo grupo.

A

1. Es mejor que ___cenemos___ en casa. (nosotros, cenar) __b__
2. Es importante que ___visites___ las casas colgadas de Cuenca. (tú, visitar) __c__
3. Señora, es urgente que le ___saque___ el diente. Tiene una infección. (yo, sacar) __e__
4. Es malo que Ana les ___dé___ tantos dulces a los niños. (dar) __a__
5. Es necesario que ___lleguen___ a la una de la tarde. (ustedes, llegar) __f__
6. Es importante que ___nos acostemos___ temprano. (nosotros, acostarse) __d__

B

a. Es importante que ___coman___ más verduras. (ellos, comer)
b. No, es mejor que ___salgamos___ a comer. (nosotros, salir)
c. Y yo creo que es bueno que ___vaya___ a Madrid después. (yo, ir)
d. En mi opinión, no es necesario que ___durmamos___ tanto. (nosotros, dormir)
e. ¿Ah, sí? ¿Es necesario que me ___tome___ un antibiótico también? (yo, tomar)
f. Para llegar a tiempo, es necesario que ___almorcemos___ temprano. (nosotros, almorzar)

NOTA CULTURAL

Las casas colgadas (*hanging*) de Cuenca, España, son muy famosas. Situadas en un acantilado (*cliff*), forman parte del paisaje de la ciudad.

2 Minidiálogos
En parejas, completen los minidiálogos con expresiones impersonales de una manera lógica. Answers will vary.

modelo

Miguelito: Mamá, no quiero arreglar mi cuarto.
Sra. Casas: *Es necesario que lo arregles. Y es importante que sacudas los muebles también.*

1. **MIGUELITO** Mamá, no quiero estudiar. Quiero salir a jugar con mis amigos.
   SRA. CASAS _____
2. **MIGUELITO** Mamá, es que no me gustan las verduras. Prefiero comer pasteles.
   SRA. CASAS _____
3. **MIGUELITO** ¿Tengo que poner la mesa, mamá?
   SRA. CASAS _____
4. **MIGUELITO** No me siento bien, mamá. Me duele todo el cuerpo y tengo fiebre.
   SRA. CASAS _____

3 Entrevista
Trabajen en parejas. Entrevístense usando estas preguntas. Expliquen sus respuestas.
Answers will vary.

1. ¿Es importante que las personas sepan una segunda lengua? ¿Por qué?
2. ¿Es urgente que los norteamericanos aprendan otras lenguas?
3. Si un(a) norteamericano/a quiere aprender francés, ¿es mejor que lo aprenda en Francia?
4. ¿Es necesario que una persona sepa decir "te amo" en la lengua nativa de su pareja?
5. ¿Es importante que un cantante de ópera entienda italiano?

2 Ask questions about **Miguelito** and his mother. Ex: **Para la Sra. Casas, ¿es necesario que Miguelito coma pasteles?** (No. Es necesario que Miguelito coma verduras.) **¿Qué quiere Miguelito?** (Quiere salir a jugar con sus amigos.) Have a volunteer explain why the second response does not take the subjunctive. (There isn't a change of subject and **que** is absent.)

3 Ask students to report on their partner's answers using complete sentences and explanations. Ex: **¿Qué opina ____ sobre los cantantes de ópera? ¿Cree que es importante que entiendan italiano?**

Subjunctive with verbs of will and influence Tutorial

ANTE TODO You will now learn how to use the subjunctive with verbs and expressions of will and influence.

Quiero que tengas dientes más blancos.

▶ Verbs of will and influence are often used when someone wants to affect the actions or behavior of other people.

Enrique **quiere** que salgamos a cenar.
Enrique wants us to go out to dinner.

Paola **prefiere** que cenemos en casa.
Paola prefers that we have dinner at home.

▶ Here is a list of widely used verbs of will and influence.

Verbs of will and influence

aconsejar	*to advise*	**pedir** (e:i)	*to ask (for)*
desear	*to wish; to desire*	**preferir** (e:ie)	*to prefer*
importar	*to be important; to matter*	**prohibir**	*to prohibit*
		querer (e:ie)	*to want*
insistir (en)	*to insist (on)*	**recomendar** (e:ie)	*to recommend*
mandar	*to order*	**rogar** (o:ue)	*to beg; to plead*
necesitar	*to need*	**sugerir** (e:ie)	*to suggest*

▶ Some impersonal expressions, such as **es necesario que, es importante que, es mejor que,** and **es urgente que,** are considered expressions of will or influence.

▶ When the main clause contains an expression of will or influence, the subjunctive is required in the subordinate clause, provided that the two clauses have different subjects.

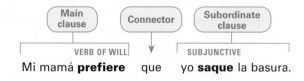

Main clause	Connector	Subordinate clause
VERB OF WILL		SUBJUNCTIVE
Mi mamá **prefiere**	que	yo **saque** la basura.

Teaching Tip Ask ten volunteers for household tips and list them in the infinitive with the student's name in parentheses. Ex: **hacer los quehaceres los sábados** (Paul); **lavar los platos en el lavaplatos** (Sara). Rephrase the first two items using verbs of will and influence. Ex: **Paul aconseja que hagamos los quehaceres los sábados. Sara recomienda que lavemos los platos en el lavaplatos.** Provide cues and have volunteers continue. Ex: **¿Qué sugiere _____?**

¡ATENCIÓN!

In English, verbs or expressions of will and influence often use a construction with an infinitive, such as *I want you to go.* This is not the case in Spanish, where the subjunctive would be used in a subordinate clause.

TPR Have students stand. At random, call out implied commands using statements with verbs of will or influence and actions that can be mimed. Ex: **Quiero que laves los platos. Insisto en que hagas la cama.** When you make a statement, point to a student to mime the action. Also use plural statements and point to more than one student. When you use negative statements, indicated students should do nothing. Keep a brisk pace.

Lección 6

Teaching Tips
- Have a volunteer read aloud the captions to the video stills. Point out that in each example the subject of the verb in the main clause is different from the subject of the verb in the subordinate clause.
- Elicit indirect object pronouns with verbs of influence by making statements that give advice and asking students for advice. Ex: **Yo siempre les aconsejo a mis estudiantes que estudien mucho. ¿Qué me recomiendan ustedes a mí?**
- Write these sentences on the board: **Quiero que almuerces en la cafetería. Quiero almorzar en la cafetería.** Ask a volunteer to explain why an infinitive is used in the second sentence instead of the subjunctive.

Extra Practice Create sentences that follow the pattern of the sentences in **¡Inténtalo!** Say the sentence, have students repeat it, then give a different subject pronoun for the subordinate clause, varying the person and number. Have students then say the sentence with the new subject, changing pronouns and verbs as necessary.

Les sugiero que arreglen este apartamento.

Recomiendo que se organicen en equipos.

▶ Indirect object pronouns are often used with the verbs **aconsejar, importar, mandar, pedir, prohibir, recomendar, rogar,** and **sugerir.**

Te aconsejo que estudies.
I advise you to study.

Le sugiero que vaya a casa.
I suggest that he go home.

Les recomiendo que barran el suelo.
I recommend that you sweep the floor.

Le ruego que no venga.
I'm begging you not to come.

▶ Note that all the forms of **prohibir** in the present tense carry a written accent, except for the **nosotros/as** form: **prohíbo, prohíbes, prohíbe, prohibimos, prohibís, prohíben.**

Ella les **prohíbe** que miren la televisión.
She prohibits them from watching TV.

Nos **prohíben** que nademos en la piscina.
They prohibit us from swimming in the swimming pool.

▶ The infinitive is used with words or expressions of will and influence if there is no change of subject in the sentence.

No quiero **sacudir** los muebles.
I don't want to dust the furniture.

Paco prefiere **descansar.**
Paco prefers to rest.

Es importante **sacar** la basura.
It's important to take out the trash.

No es necesario **quitar** la mesa.
It's not necessary to clear the table.

¡INTÉNTALO! Completa cada oración con la forma correcta del verbo entre paréntesis.

1. Te sugiero que ___vayas___ (ir) con ella al supermercado.
2. Él necesita que yo le ___preste___ (prestar) dinero.
3. No queremos que tú ___hagas___ (hacer) nada especial para nosotros.
4. Mis papás quieren que yo ___limpie___ (limpiar) mi cuarto.
5. Nos piden que la ___ayudemos___ (ayudar) a preparar la comida.
6. Quieren que tú ___saques___ (sacar) la basura todos los días.
7. Quiero ___descansar___ (descansar) esta noche.
8. Es importante que ustedes ___limpien___ (limpiar) los estantes.
9. Su tía les manda que ___pongan___ (poner) la mesa.
10. Te aconsejo que no ___salgas___ (salir) con él.
11. Mi tío insiste en que mi prima ___haga___ (hacer) la cama.
12. Prefiero ___ir___ (ir) al cine.
13. Es necesario ___estudiar___ (estudiar).
14. Recomiendo que ustedes ___pasen___ (pasar) la aspiradora.

recursos

WB
pp. 363–364

LM
p. 378

(S)
vhlcentral.com
Lección 6

Práctica

1

Completar Completa el diálogo con verbos de la lista.

cocina	haga	quiere	sea
comas	ponga	saber	ser
diga	prohíbe	sé	vaya

IRENE Tengo problemas con Vilma. Sé que debo hablar con ella. ¿Qué me recomiendas que le (1)___diga___?

JULIA Pues, necesito (2)___saber___ más antes de darte consejos.

IRENE Bueno, para empezar me (3)___prohíbe___ que traiga dulces a la casa.

JULIA Pero chica, tiene razón. Es mejor que tú no (4)___comas___ cosas dulces.

IRENE Sí, ya lo sé. Pero quiero que (5)___sea___ más flexible. Además, insiste en que yo (6)___haga___ todo en la casa.

JULIA Yo (7)___sé___ que Vilma (8)___cocina___ y hace los quehaceres todos los días.

IRENE Sí, pero siempre que hay fiesta me pide que (9)___ponga___ los cubiertos y las copas en la mesa y que (10)___vaya___ al sótano por las servilletas y los platos. ¡Es lo que más odio: ir al sótano!

JULIA Mujer, ¡Vilma sólo (11)___quiere___ que ayudes en la casa!

2

Aconsejar En parejas, lean lo que dice cada persona. Luego den consejos lógicos usando verbos como **aconsejar, recomendar** y **prohibir**. Sus consejos deben ser diferentes de lo que la persona quiere hacer. Answers will vary.

> **modelo**
>
> **Isabel:** Quiero conseguir un comedor con los muebles más caros del mundo.
>
> **Consejo:** *Te aconsejamos que consigas unos muebles menos caros.*

1. **DAVID**   Pienso poner el cuadro del lago de Maracaibo en la cocina.
2. **SARA**   Voy en bicicleta a comprar unas copas de cristal.
3. **SR. ALARCÓN**   Insisto en comenzar a arreglar el jardín en marzo.
4. **SRA. VILLA**   Quiero ver las tazas y los platos de la tienda El Ama de Casa Feliz.
5. **DOLORES**   Voy a poner servilletas de tela (*cloth*) para los cuarenta invitados.
6. **SR. PARDO**   Pienso poner todos mis muebles nuevos en el altillo.
7. **SRA. GONZÁLEZ**   Hay una fiesta en casa esta noche, pero no quiero limpiarla.
8. **CARLITOS**   Hoy no tengo ganas de hacer las camas ni de quitar la mesa.

3

Preguntas En parejas, túrnense para contestar las preguntas. Usen el subjuntivo. Answers will vary.

1. ¿Te dan consejos tus amigos/as? ¿Qué te aconsejan? ¿Aceptas sus consejos? ¿Por qué?
2. ¿Qué te sugieren tus profesores que hagas antes de terminar los cursos que tomas?
3. ¿Insisten tus amigos/as en que salgas mucho con ellos?
4. ¿Qué quieres que te regalen tu familia y tus amigos/as en tu cumpleaños?
5. ¿Qué le recomiendas tú a un(a) amigo/a que no quiere salir los sábados con su novio/a?
6. ¿Qué les aconsejas a los nuevos estudiantes de tu universidad?

---

1 Before beginning the activity, ask a volunteer to read the first line of dialogue aloud. Guide students to see that the subject of the verb in the blank is **yo**, which is implied by **me** in the main clause.

1 Have pairs write a summary of the dialogue in the third person. Ask one or two volunteers to read their summaries to the class.

2 Have students create two suggestions for each person. In the second they should use one of the impersonal expressions listed on page 338.

NOTA CULTURAL

En el **lago de Maracaibo,** en Venezuela, hay casas suspendidas sobre el agua que se llaman **palafitos**. Este tipo de construcciones les recordó a los conquistadores la ciudad de Venecia, Italia, de donde viene el nombre "Venezuela", que significa "pequeña Venecia".

3 Follow up the activity with class discussion. Ex: **¿A quiénes siempre les dan consejos sus amigos? ¿Que tipo de cosas aconsejan?**

Large Group Write the names of famous historical figures on individual sticky notes and place them on the students' backs. Have students circulate around the room, giving each other advice that will help them guess their "identity."

Comunicación

4 Ask each pair to pick their favorite response and share it with the class, who will vote for the most clever, shocking, or humorous suggestion.

4 **Inventar** En parejas, preparen una lista de seis personas famosas. Un(a) estudiante da el nombre de una persona famosa y el/la otro/a le da un consejo. Answers will vary.

> **modelo**
>
> **Estudiante 1:** Judge Judy.
> **Estudiante 2:** Le recomiendo que sea más simpática con la gente.
> **Estudiante 2:** Orlando Bloom.
> **Estudiante 1:** Le aconsejo que haga más películas.

5 Before beginning the activity, ask volunteers to describe the drawing, naming everything they see and all the chores that need to be done.

5 **Hablar** En parejas, miren la ilustración. Imaginen que Gerardo es su hermano y necesita ayuda para arreglar su casa y resolver sus problemas románticos y económicos. Usen expresiones impersonales y verbos como **aconsejar**, **sugerir** y **recomendar**. Answers will vary.

> **modelo**
>
> Es mejor que arregles el apartamento más a menudo.
> Te aconsejo que no dejes para mañana lo que puedes hacer hoy.

Síntesis

6 Have pairs compare their responses in groups of four. Ask groups to choose which among all of the suggestions are the most likely to work for **Hernán** and have them share these with the class.

6 Have pairs choose a famous couple in history or fiction. Ex: Romeo and Juliet or Napoleon and Josephine. Then have them write a letter from one of the couples to **doctora Salvamórez**. Finally, have them exchange their letters with another pair and write the corresponding responses from the doctor.

6 **La doctora Salvamórez** Hernán tiene problemas con su novia y le escribe a la doctora Salvamórez, columnista del periódico *Panamá y su gente*. Ella responde a las cartas de personas con problemas románticos. En parejas, lean el mensaje de Hernán y después usen el subjuntivo para escribir los consejos de la doctora. Answers will vary.

Estimada doctora Salvamórez:

Mi novia nunca quiere que yo salga de casa. No le molesta que vengan mis amigos a visitarme. Pero insiste en que nosotros sólo miremos los programas de televisión que ella quiere. Necesita saber dónde estoy en cada momento, y yo necesito que ella me dé un poco de independencia. ¿Qué hago?

Hernán

Lección 6

Recapitulación

 Diagnostics

Completa estas actividades para repasar los conceptos de gramática que aprendiste en esta lección.

1

Completar Completa el cuadro con la forma correspondiente del presente de subjuntivo. **12 pts.**

yo/él/ella	tú	nosotros/as	Uds./ellos/ellas
limpie	limpies	limpiemos	limpien
venga	**vengas**	vengamos	vengan
quiera	quieras	**queramos**	quieran
ofrezca	ofrezcas	ofrezcamos	**ofrezcan**

2

El apartamento ideal Completa este folleto (*brochure*) informativo con la forma correcta del presente de subjuntivo. **8 pts.**

¿Eres joven y buscas tu primera vivienda? Te ofrezco estos consejos:

■ Te sugiero que primero (tú) (1) ___escribas___ (escribir) una lista de las cosas que quieres en un apartamento.

■ Quiero que después (2) ___pienses___ (pensar) muy bien cuáles son tus prioridades. Es necesario que cada persona (3) ___tenga___ (tener) sus prioridades claras, porque el hogar (*home*) perfecto no existe.

■ Antes de decidir en qué área quieren vivir, les aconsejo a ti y a tu futuro/a compañero/a de apartamento que (4) ___salgan___ (salir) a ver la ciudad y que (5) ___conozcan___ (conocer) los distintos barrios y las afueras.

■ Pidan que el agente les (6) ___muestre___ (mostrar) todas las partes de cada casa.

■ Finalmente, como consumidores, es importante que nosotros (7) ___sepamos___ (saber) bien nuestros derechos (*rights*); por eso, deben insistir en que todos los puntos del contrato (8) ___estén___ (estar) muy claros antes de firmarlo (*signing it*).

¡Buena suerte!

Teaching Tip Review verbs with stem changes and spelling changes in the subjunctive.

RESUMEN GRAMATICAL

6.1 **Relative pronouns**   *pp. 328–329*

Relative pronouns	
que	*that; which; who*
quien(es)	*who; whom; that*
lo que	*that which; what*

6.2 **Formal commands**   *pp. 332–333*

Formal commands (**Ud.** and **Uds.**)		
Infinitive	Present tense yo form	Ud(s) command
limpiar	limpio	limpie(n)
barrer	barro	barra(n)
sacudir	sacudo	sacuda(n)

▶ Verbs with stem changes or irregular **yo** forms maintain the same irregularity in the formal commands:

hacer: yo **hago** → **Ha**ga**n** la cama.

Irregular formal commands	
dar	**dé (Ud.); den (Uds.)**
estar	**esté(n)**
ir	**vaya(n)**
saber	**sepa(n)**
ser	**sea(n)**

6.3 **The present subjunctive**   *pp. 336–338*

Present subjunctive of regular verbs		
hablar	comer	escribir
hable	coma	escriba
hables	comas	escribas
hable	coma	escriba
hablemos	comamos	escribamos
habléis	comáis	escribáis
hablen	coman	escriban

Extra Practice Call out verbs and have volunteers give the singular and plural command forms Ex: **barrer (barra, barran)** Repeat the drill with the subjunctive, varying the subject pronouns. Ex: **dormir/nosotros (que nosotros durmamos).**

Lección 6

3 Have students circle the noun or idea to which each relative pronoun refers.

3 Have students work in pairs to create four additional sentences using relative pronouns.

3 **Relativos** Completa las oraciones con **lo que**, **que** o **quien**. 〔8 pts.〕

1. Me encanta la alfombra ___que___ está en el comedor.
2. Mi amiga Tere, con ___quien___ trabajo, me regaló ese cuadro.
3. Todas las cosas ___que___ tenemos vienen de la casa de mis abuelos.
4. Hija, no compres más cosas. ___Lo que___ debes hacer ahora es organizarlo todo.
5. La agencia de decoración de ___que___ le hablé se llama Casabella.
6. Esas flores las dejaron en la puerta mis nuevos vecinos, a ___quienes___ aún (*yet*) no conozco.
7. Leonor no compró nada, porque ___lo que___ le gustaba era muy caro.
8. Mi amigo Aldo, a ___quien___ visité ayer, es un cocinero excelente.

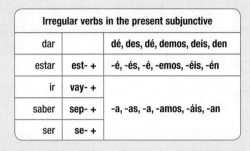

Irregular verbs in the present subjunctive		
dar		dé, des, dé, demos, deis, den
estar	est- +	-é, -és, -é, -emos, -éis, -én
ir	vay- +	
saber	sep- +	-a, -as, -a, -amos, -áis, -an
ser	se- +	

6.4 **Subjunctive with verbs of will and influence** *pp. 340–341*

▶ Verbs of will and influence: **aconsejar, desear, importar, insistir (en), mandar, necesitar, pedir (e:i), preferir (e:ie), prohibir, querer (e:ie), recomendar (e:ie), rogar (o:ue), sugerir (e:ie)**

4 To simplify, have students begin by scanning the paragraph and identifying which blanks call for **usted** commands and which call for **ustedes** commands.

4 Tell students that some answers will contain object pronouns (items 2 and 10).

4 **Preparando la casa** Martín y Ángela van a hacer un curso de verano en Costa Rica y una vecina va a cuidarles (*take care of*) la casa mientras ellos no están. Completa las instrucciones de la vecina con mandatos formales. Usa cada verbo una sola vez y agrega pronombres de objeto directo o indirecto si es necesario. 〔10 pts.〕

arreglar	dejar	hacer	pedir	sacudir
barrer	ensuciar	limpiar	poner	tener

Primero, (1) ___hagan___ ustedes las maletas. Las cosas que no se llevan a Costa Rica, (2) ___pónganlas___ en el altillo. Ángela, (3) ___arregle/limpie___ las habitaciones y Martín, (4) ___limpie/arregle___ usted la cocina y el baño. Después, los dos (5) ___barran___ el suelo y (6) ___sacudan___ los muebles de toda la casa. Ángela, no (7) ___deje___ sus joyas (*jewelry*) en el apartamento. (8) ___Tengan___ cuidado ¡y no (9) ___ensucien___ nada antes de irse! Por último, (10) ___pídanle___ a alguien que recoja (*pick up*) su correo.

5 Before beginning this activity, have pairs discuss their own habits regarding chores.

5 Have students imagine they have two roommates, and ask them to rewrite their sentences using **ustedes** commands.

Heritage Speakers Ask heritage speakers to think of other popular phrases or quotes that use formal command forms. Have them write the phrases on the board, leaving blanks for classmates to guess the commands.

5 **Los quehaceres** A tu compañero/a de cuarto no le gusta ayudar con los quehaceres. Escribe al menos seis oraciones dándole consejos para hacer más divertidos los quehaceres. 〔12 pts.〕

Answers will vary.

modelo
Te sugiero que pongas música mientras lavas los platos…

6 **El circo** Completa esta famosa frase que tiene su origen en el circo (*circus*). 〔2 puntos EXTRA!〕

" ¡___Pasen___ (Pasar) ustedes y ___vean___ (ver)! El espectáculo va a comenzar. "

Practice more at **vhlcentral.com**.

Lectura

NATIONAL STANDARDS — communication cultures

Antes de leer

Estrategia
Locating the main parts of a sentence

Did you know that a text written in Spanish is an average of 15% longer than the same text written in English? Since the Spanish language tends to use more words to express ideas, you will often encounter long sentences when reading in Spanish. Of course, the length of sentences varies with genre and with authors' individual styles. To help you understand long sentences, identify the main parts of the sentence before trying to read it in its entirety. First locate the main verb of the sentence, along with its subject, ignoring any words or phrases set off by commas. Then reread the sentence, adding details like direct and indirect objects, transitional words, and prepositional phrases.

Examinar el texto

Mira el formato de la lectura. ¿Qué tipo de documento es? ¿Qué cognados encuentras en la lectura? ¿Qué te dicen sobre el tema de la selección?

¿Probable o improbable?

Mira brevemente el texto e indica si estas oraciones son probables o improbables.

1. Este folleto° es de interés turístico. probable
2. Describe un edificio moderno cubano. improbable
3. Incluye algunas explicaciones de arquitectura. probable
4. Espera atraer° a visitantes al lugar. probable

Oraciones largas

Mira el texto y busca algunas oraciones largas. Con un(a) compañero/a, identifiquen las partes principales de la oración y después examinen las descripciones adicionales. ¿Qué significan las oraciones?

Teaching Tips
• Students should see from the layout (cover page with title, photo, and phone numbers; interior pages with an introduction and several headings followed by short paragraphs) that this is a brochure. Revealing cognates are **información** (cover) and **residencia oficial del Presidente de Panamá** (introduction).

folleto *brochure* atraer *to attract* épocas *time periods*

Bienvenidos al
Palacio de las Garzas

El palacio está abierto de martes a domingo.
Para más información,
llame al teléfono 507-226-7000.
También puede solicitar° un folleto
a la casilla° 3467,
Ciudad de Panamá, Panamá.

Después de leer

Ordenar 🖉 S

Pon estos eventos en el orden cronológico adecuado.

__3__ El palacio se convirtió en residencia presidencial.

__2__ Durante diferentes épocas°, maestros, médicos y banqueros ejercieron su profesión en el palacio.

__4__ El Dr. Belisario Porras ocupó el palacio por primera vez.

__1__ Los españoles construyeron el palacio.

__5__ Se renovó el palacio.

__6__ Los turistas pueden visitar el palacio de martes a domingo.

• Ask pairs to create a couple of long sentences. Have them point out the main verb and subject.

 Practice more at **vhlcentral.com**.

Variación léxica Point out that in Spanish, **planta baja** means *ground floor*. The second story is called **el primer piso**, the third story is **el segundo piso**, and so forth. In the **Palacio de las Garzas**, **el segundo piso** is also **la planta alta** (*top floor*). trescientos cuarenta y siete

347

El Palacio de las Garzas° es la residencia oficial del Presidente de Panamá desde 1903. Fue construido en 1673 para ser la casa de un gobernador español. Con el paso de los años fue almacén, escuela, hospital, aduana, banco y por último, palacio presidencial.

En la actualidad el edificio tiene tres pisos, pero los planos originales muestran una construcción de un piso con un gran patio en el centro. La restauración del palacio comenzó en el año 1922 y los trabajos fueron realizados por el arquitecto Villanueva-Myers y el pintor Roberto Lewis. El palacio, un monumento al estilo colonial, todavía conserva su elegancia y buen gusto, y es una de las principales atracciones turísticas del barrio Casco Viejo°.

Planta baja

El Patio de las Garzas

Una antigua puerta de hierro° recibe a los visitantes. El patio interior todavía conserva los elementos originales de la construcción: piso de mármol°, columnas cubiertas° de nácar° y una magnífica fuente° de agua en el centro. Aquí están las nueve garzas que le dan el nombre al palacio y que representan las nueve provincias de Panamá.

Primer piso

El Salón Amarillo

Aquí el turista puede visitar una galería de cuarenta y un retratos° de gobernadores y personajes ilustres de Panamá. La principal atracción de este salón es el sillón presidencial, que se usa especialmente cuando hay cambio de presidente. Otros atractivos de esta área son el comedor Los Tamarindos, que se destaca° por la elegancia de sus muebles y sus lámparas de cristal, y el Patio Andaluz, con sus coloridos mosaicos que representan la unión de la cultura indígena y la española.

El Salón Dr. Belisario Porras

Este elegante y majestuoso salón es uno de los lugares más importantes del Palacio de las Garzas. Lleva su nombre en honor al Dr. Belisario Porras, quien fue tres veces presidente de Panamá (1912–1916, 1918–1920 y 1920–1924).

Segundo piso

Es el área residencial del palacio y el visitante no tiene acceso a ella. Los armarios, las cómodas y los espejos de la alcoba fueron comprados en Italia y Francia por el presidente Porras, mientras que las alfombras, cortinas y frazadas° son originarias de España.

solicitar *request* casilla *post office box* Garzas *Herons* Casco Viejo *Old Quarter*
hierro *iron* mármol *marble* cubiertas *covered* nácar *mother-of-pearl*
fuente *fountain* retratos *portraits* se destaca *stands out* frazadas *blankets*

Preguntas

Contesta las preguntas.

1. ¿Qué sala es notable por sus muebles elegantes y sus lámparas de cristal? el comedor Los Tamarindos

2. ¿En qué parte del palacio se encuentra la residencia del presidente? en el segundo piso

3. ¿Dónde empiezan los turistas su visita al palacio? en el Patio de las Garzas

4. ¿En qué lugar se representa artísticamente la rica herencia cultural de Panamá? en el Patio Andaluz

5. ¿Qué salón honra la memoria de un gran panameño? el Salón Dr. Belisario Porras

6. ¿Qué partes del palacio te gustaría (*would you like*) visitar? ¿Por qué? Explica tu respuesta.
Answers will vary.

Conversación

En grupos de tres o cuatro estudiantes, hablen sobre lo siguiente: Answers will vary.

1. ¿Qué tiene en común el Palacio de las Garzas con otras residencias presidenciales u otras casas muy grandes?

2. ¿Te gustaría vivir en el Palacio de las Garzas? ¿Por qué?

3. Imagina que puedes diseñar tu palacio ideal. Describe los planos para cada piso del palacio.

Small Groups In small groups, ask students to compare the **Palacio de las Garzas** to other official residences, historic homes, or government buildings they have visited.

Heritage Speakers Ask heritage speakers to give a brief presentation about a famous government building in their family's home country. Tell them to include recommendations to visitors about what rooms and objects are particularly noteworthy and should not be missed. If possible, they should illustrate their presentation with photographs or brochures.

Escritura

Estrategia
Using linking words

You can make your writing sound more sophisticated by using linking words to connect simple sentences or ideas and create more complex sentences. Consider these passages, which illustrate this effect:

Without linking words

En la actualidad el edificio tiene tres pisos. Los planos originales muestran una construcción de un piso con un gran patio en el centro. La restauración del palacio comenzó en el año 1922. Los trabajos fueron realizados por el arquitecto Villanueva-Myers y el pintor Roberto Lewis.

With linking words

En la actualidad el edificio tiene tres pisos, pero los planos originales muestran una construcción de un piso con un gran patio en el centro. La restauración del palacio comenzó en el año 1922 y los trabajos fueron realizados por el arquitecto Villanueva-Myers y el pintor Roberto Lewis.

Linking words	
cuando	when
mientras	while
o	or
pero	but
porque	because
pues	since
que	that; who; which
quien(es)	who
sino	but (rather)
y	and

Estrategia Review the linking words. Point out that they are all words with which students are familiar. Have pairs use a few of them in sentences, and ask volunteers to share their sentences with the class.

Tema

Escribir un contrato de arrendamiento°

Eres el/la administrador(a)° de un edificio de apartamentos. Prepara un contrato de arrendamiento para los nuevos inquilinos°. El contrato debe incluir estos detalles:

▶ la dirección° del apartamento y del/de la administrador(a)

▶ las fechas del contrato

▶ el precio del alquiler y el día que se debe pagar

▶ el precio del depósito

▶ información y reglas° acerca de:
   la basura
   el correo
   los animales domésticos
   el ruido°
   los servicios de electricidad y agua
   el uso de electrodomésticos

▶ otros aspectos importantes de la vida comunitaria

Teaching Tip Review with students the details suggested for inclusion in the lease agreement. You may wish to present the following terms students can use in their agreements: **arrendador** (*landlord*), **propietario** (*owner*), **estipulaciones** (*stipulations*), **parte** (*party*), **de anticipación/de antelación** (*in advance*). Give students samples of legal documents in Spanish (downloadable from the Internet).

contrato de arrendamiento *lease* **administrador(a)** *manager* **inquilinos** *tenants* **dirección** *address* **reglas** *rules* **ruido** *noise*

Escuchar Audio

Lección 6

Estrategia
Using visual cues

Visual cues like illustrations and headings provide useful clues about what you will hear.

 To practice this strategy, you will listen to a passage related to the following photo. Jot down the clues the photo gives you as you listen.

Preparación

Mira el dibujo. ¿Qué pistas te da para comprender la conversación que vas a escuchar? ¿Qué significa *bienes raíces*?

Ahora escucha

Mira los anuncios de esta página y escucha la conversación entre el señor Núñez, Adriana y Felipe. Luego indica si cada descripción se refiere a la casa ideal de Adriana y Felipe, a la casa del anuncio o al apartamento del anuncio.

Oraciones	La casa ideal	La casa del anuncio	El apartamento del anuncio
Es barato.	___	___	✓
Tiene cuatro alcobas.	___	✓	___
Tiene una oficina.	✓	___	___
Tiene un balcón.	___	___	✓
Tiene una cocina moderna.	___	✓	___
Tiene un jardín muy grande.	___	✓	___
Tiene un patio.	✓	___	___

18G

Bienes raíces

Se vende.
4 alcobas, 3 baños, cocina moderna, jardín con árboles frutales.
B/. 225.000

Se alquila.
2 alcobas, 1 baño.
Balcón.
Urbanización Las Brisas. B/. 525

Comprensión

Preguntas

1. ¿Cuál es la relación entre el señor Núñez, Adriana y Felipe? ¿Cómo lo sabes? El Sr. Núñez es el padre de Adriana y Felipe es su esposo.
2. ¿Qué diferencia de opinión hay entre Adriana y Felipe sobre dónde quieren vivir? Felipe prefiere vivir en la ciudad, pero Adriana quiere vivir en las afueras.
3. Usa la información de los dibujos y la conversación para entender lo que dice Adriana al final. ¿Qué significa "todo a su debido tiempo"? Answers will vary.

Conversación

En parejas, túrnense para hacer y responder a las preguntas.
Answers will vary.

1. ¿Qué tienen en común el apartamento y la casa del anuncio con el lugar donde tú vives?
2. ¿Qué piensas de la recomendación del señor Núñez?
3. ¿Qué tipo de sugerencias te da tu familia sobre dónde vivir?
4. ¿Dónde prefieres vivir tú, en un apartamento o en una casa? Explica por qué.

Teaching Tip Explain to students that **alcoba** is another word for *bedroom*.

 Practice more at **vhlcentral.com**.

En pantalla

NATIONAL STANDARDS — communication cultures

En los países hispanos el costo del servicio de electricidad y de los electrodomésticos es muy caro. Es por eso que no es muy común tener muchos electrodomésticos. Por ejemplo, en los lugares donde hace mucho calor, mucha gente no tiene aire acondicionado°; utiliza los ventiladores°, que usan menos electricidad. Muchas personas lavan los platos a mano o barren el suelo en vez de usar un lavaplatos o una aspiradora.

Vocabulario útil

fabrica	*manufactures*
lavavajillas	**lavaplatos**
aislante	*insulation*
campanas	*hoods*

Preparación

¿Lavas tu ropa, cocinas, barres? ¿Te piden que hagas algunos quehaceres domésticos en casa?

Identificar

Indica lo que veas en el anuncio.

✔ 1. llaves

___ 2. sofá

✔ 3. puerta

✔ 4. oficina

✔ 5. bebé (*baby*)

✔ 6. calle

✔ 7. despertador

___ 8. altillo

El apartamento

Trabajen en grupos pequeños. Imaginen que terminaron la universidad, consiguieron el trabajo (*job*) de sus sueños (*dreams*) y comparten un apartamento en el centro de una gran ciudad. Describan el apartamento, los muebles y los electrodomésticos y digan qué quehaceres haca cada quien.

Teaching Tip Before you show the video, have students look at the video stills, read the captions, and predict what is being sold in this commercial.

aire acondicionado *air conditioning* ventiladores *fans* se agradece *is appreciated*

Anuncio de Balay

Sabemos lo mucho que se agradece°...

... en algunos momentos...

... un poco de silencio.

 Video: TV Clip

 Practice more at **vhlcentral.com**.

NATIONAL
cultures
STANDARDS

Lección 6

En el sur de la Ciudad de México hay una construcción que fusiona° el funcionalismo con elementos de la cultura mexicana. Es la casa y estudio° en que el muralista Diego Rivera y su esposa, Frida Kahlo, vivieron hasta 1934. El creador fue el destacado° arquitecto y pintor mexicano Juan O'Gorman, amigo de la pareja. Como Frida y Diego necesitaban cada uno un lugar tranquilo para trabajar, O'Gorman hizo dos casas, cada una con un taller°, conectadas por un puente° en la parte superior°. En 1981, años después de la muerte de los artistas, se creó ahí el Museo Casa Estudio Diego Rivera y Frida Kahlo. Este museo busca conservar, investigar y difundir° la obra° de estos dos mexicanos, como lo hace el Museo Casa de Frida Kahlo, que vas a ver a continuación.

Vocabulario útil

jardinero	*gardener*
muros	*walls*
la silla de ruedas	*wheelchair*
las valiosas obras	*valuable works*

Preparación

Imagina que eres un(a) artista, ¿cómo sería (*would be*) tu casa? ¿Sería muy diferente de la casa en donde vives ahora? Answers will vary.

¿Cierto o falso?

Indica si lo que dicen estas oraciones es **cierto** o **falso**.

1. La casa de Frida Kahlo está en el centro de México, D.F. Falso.
2. La casa de Frida se transformó en un museo en los años 50. Cierto.
3. Frida Kahlo vivió sola en su casa. Falso.
4. Entre las obras que se exhiben está el cuadro (*painting*) *Las dos Fridas*. Cierto.
5. El jardinero actual (*current*) jamás conoció ni a Frida ni a Diego. Falso.
6. En el museo se exhiben la silla de ruedas y los aparatos ortopédicos de Frida. Cierto.

fusiona *fuses* estudio *studio* destacado *prominent* taller *art studio* puente *bridge* parte superior *top* difundir *to spread* obra *work*

La casa de Frida

El hogar en que nació la pintora Frida Kahlo en 1907 se caracteriza por su arquitectura típicamente mexicana...

Esta casa tiene varios detalles que revelan el amor de esta mexicana por la cultura de su país, por ejemplo, la cocina.

Uno de los espacios más atractivos de esta casa es este estudio que Diego instaló...

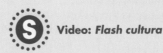 **Video:** *Flash cultura*

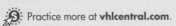 Practice more at **vhlcentral.com**.

recursos

VM
pp. 371–372

vhlcentral.com
Lección 6

Panamá

NATIONAL STANDARDS
connections
cultures

El país en cifras

▸ **Área:** 78.200 km² (30.193 millas²), *aproximadamente el área de Carolina del Sur*

▸ **Población:** 3.773.000

▸ **Capital:** La Ciudad de Panamá —1.527.000

▸ **Ciudades principales:** Colón, David

SOURCE: Population Division, UN Secretariat

▸ **Moneda:** balboa; es equivalente al dólar estadounidense.

En Panamá circulan los billetes de dólar estadounidense. El país centroamericano, sin embargo, acuña° su propia moneda. "El peso" es una moneda grande equivalente a cincuenta centavos°. La moneda de cinco centavos es llamada frecuentemente "real".

▸ **Idiomas:** español (oficial), lenguas indígenas, inglés *Muchos panameños son bilingües. La lengua materna del 14% de los panameños es el inglés.*

Bandera de Panamá

Panameños célebres

▸ **Mariano Rivera,** beisbolista (1969–)

▸ **Mireya Moscoso,** política (1946–)

▸ **Rubén Blades,** músico y político (1948–)

acuña *mints* centavos *cents*
peaje *toll* promedio *average*

recursos

| WB pp. 365–366 | VM pp. 369–370 | vhlcentral.com Lección 6 |

Un turista disfruta del bosque tropical colgado de un cable.

Mujer kuna lavando una mola

ESTADOS UNIDOS
OCÉANO ATLÁNTICO
PANAMÁ
AMÉRICA DEL SUR

COSTA RICA

Lago Gatún
Canal de Panamá
Islas San Blas
Bocas del Toro
Cordillera de San Blas
Mar Caribe
Colón
Río Chepo
Serranía de Tabasará
Ciudad de Panamá
David
Río Cobre
Isla del Rey
Océano Pacífico
Golfo de Panamá
Isla de Coiba

Ruinas de un fuerte panameño

¡Increíble pero cierto!

¿Conocías estos datos sobre el Canal de Panamá?

• Gracias al Canal de Panamá, el viaje en barco de Nueva York a Tokio es 3.000 millas más corto.

• Su construcción costó 639 millones de dólares.

• Hoy lo usan en promedio 39 barcos al día.

• El peaje° promedio° cuesta 54.000 dólares.

Tokio
Nueva York
PANAMÁ

Lugares • El Canal de Panamá

El Canal de Panamá conecta el océano Pacífico con el océano Atlántico. La construcción de este cauce° artificial empezó en 1903 y concluyó diez años después. Es una de las principales fuentes° de ingresos° del país, gracias al dinero que aportan los más de 14.000 buques° que transitan anualmente por esta ruta y a las actividades comerciales que se han desarrollado° en torno a° ella.

Artes • La mola

La mola es una forma de arte textil de los kunas, una tribu indígena que vive principalmente en las islas San Blas. Esta pieza artesanal se confecciona con fragmentos de tela° de colores vivos. Algunos de sus diseños son abstractos, inspirados en las formas del coral, y otros son geométricos, como en las molas más tradicionales. Antiguamente, estos tejidos se usaban sólo como ropa, pero hoy día también sirven para decorar las casas.

Naturaleza • El mar

Panamá, cuyo° nombre significa "lugar de muchos peces°", es un país muy frecuentado por los aficionados del buceo y la pesca. El territorio panameño cuenta con una gran variedad de playas en los dos lados del istmo°, con el mar Caribe a un lado y el océano Pacífico al otro. Algunas zonas costeras están destinadas al turismo. Otras están protegidas por la diversidad de su fauna marina, en la que abundan los arrecifes° de coral, como el Parque Nacional Marino Isla Bastimentos.

COLOMBIA

Vista de la Ciudad de Panamá

¿Qué aprendiste? Responde a cada pregunta con una oración completa.

1. ¿Cuál es la lengua materna del catorce por ciento de los panameños?
   El inglés es la lengua materna del catorce por ciento de los panameños.
2. ¿A qué unidad monetaria (*monetary unit*) es equivalente el balboa?
   El balboa es equivalente al dólar estadounidense.
3. ¿Qué océanos une el Canal de Panamá?
   El Canal de Panamá une los océanos Atlántico y Pacífico.
4. ¿Quién es Mariano Rivera?
   Mariano Rivera es un beisbolista panameño.
5. ¿Qué son las molas?
   Las molas son una forma de arte textil de los kunas.
6. ¿Cómo son los diseños de las molas?
   Algunos diseños son abstractos y otros son geométricos.
7. ¿Para qué se usan las molas?
   Las molas se usan como ropa y para decorar las casas.
8. ¿Cómo son las playas de Panamá?
   Son muy variadas; unas están destinadas al turismo, otras tienen valor ecológico.
9. ¿Qué significa "Panamá"?
   "Panamá" significa "lugar de muchos peces".

Conexión Internet Investiga estos temas en **vhlcentral.com**.

Practice more at **vhlcentral.com**.

1. Investiga la historia de las relaciones entre Panamá y los Estados Unidos y la decisión de devolver (*give back*) el Canal de Panamá. ¿Estás de acuerdo con la decisión? Explica tu opinión.
2. Investiga sobre los kunas u otro grupo indígena de Panamá. ¿En qué partes del país viven? ¿Qué lenguas hablan? ¿Cómo es su cultura?

cauce *channel* fuentes *sources* ingresos *income* buques *ships* han desarrollado *have developed* en torno a *around* tela *fabric*
cuyo *whose* peces *fish* istmo *isthmus* arrecifes *reefs*
Supersite/DVD: You may want to wrap up this section by playing the **Panorama cultural** video footage for this lesson.

Las viviendas

las afueras	suburbs; outskirts
el alquiler	rent (payment)
el ama (*m., f.*) de casa	housekeeper; caretaker
el barrio	neighborhood
el edificio de apartamentos	apartment building
el/la vecino/a	neighbor
la vivienda	housing
alquilar	to rent
mudarse	to move (from one house to another)

Los cuartos y otros lugaress

el altillo	attic
el balcón	balcony
la cocina	kitchen
el comedor	dining room
el dormitorio	bedroom
la entrada	entrance
la escalera	stairs; stairway
el garaje	garage
el jardín	garden; yard
la oficina	office
el pasillo	hallway
el patio	patio; yard
la sala	living room
el sótano	basement; cellar

Supersite: MP3 Audio Files, Testing Program

Los muebles y otras cosas

la alfombra	carpet; rug
la almohada	pillow
el armario	closet
el cartel	poster
la cómoda	chest of drawers
las cortinas	curtains
el cuadro	picture
el estante	bookcase; bookshelves
la lámpara	lamp
la luz	light; electricity
la manta	blanket
la mesita	end table
la mesita de noche	night stand
los muebles	furniture
la pared	wall
la pintura	painting; picture
el sillón	armchair
el sofá	couch; sofa

Los electrodomésticos

la cafetera	coffee maker
la cocina, la estufa	stove
el congelador	freezer
el electrodoméstico	electric appliance
el horno (de microondas)	(microwave) oven
la lavadora	washing machine
el lavaplatos	dishwasher
el refrigerador	refrigerator
la secadora	clothes dryer
la tostadora	toaster

La mesa

la copa	wineglass; goblet
la cuchara	(table or large) spoon
el cuchillo	knife
el plato	plate
la servilleta	napkin
la taza	cup
el tenedor	fork
el vaso	glass

Los quehaceres domésticos

arreglar	to neaten; to straighten up
barrer el suelo	to sweep the floor
cocinar	to cook
ensuciar	to get (something) dirty
hacer la cama	to make the bed
hacer quehaceres domésticos	to do household chores
lavar (el suelo, los platos)	to wash (the floor, the dishes)
limpiar la casa	to clean the house
pasar la aspiradora	to vacuum
planchar la ropa	to iron the clothes
poner la mesa	to set the table
quitar la mesa	to clear the table
quitar el polvo	to dust
sacar la basura	to take out the trash
sacudir los muebles	to dust the furniture

Verbos y expresiones verbales

aconsejar	to advise
insistir (en)	to insist (on)
mandar	to order
recomendar (e:ie)	to recommend
rogar (o:ue)	to beg; to plead
sugerir (e:ie)	to suggest
Es bueno que…	It's good that…
Es importante que…	It's important that…
Es malo que…	It's bad that…
Es mejor que…	It's better that…
Es necesario que…	It's necessary that…
Es urgente que…	It's urgent that…

Relative pronouns	See page 328.
Expresiones útiles	See page 323.

Audio: Vocabulary Flashcards

contextos

1 **Los aparatos domésticos** Answer the questions with complete sentences.

> **modelo**
>
> Julieta quiere comer pan tostado. ¿Qué tiene que usar Julieta?
> **Julieta tiene que usar una tostadora.**

1. La ropa de Joaquín está sucia. ¿Qué necesita Joaquín?
   Joaquín necesita una lavadora.

2. Clara lavó la ropa. ¿Qué necesita Clara ahora?
   Clara necesita una secadora ahora.

3. Los platos de la cena están sucios. ¿Qué se necesita?
   Se necesita un lavaplatos.

4. Rita quiere hacer hielo (ice). ¿Dónde debe poner el agua?
   Rita debe poner el agua en el congelador.

2 **¿En qué habitación?** Label these items as belonging to **la cocina**, **la sala**, or **el dormitorio**.

1. el lavaplatos la cocina
2. el sillón la sala/el dormitorio
3. la cama el dormitorio
4. el horno la cocina

5. la almohada el dormitorio
6. la cafetera la cocina
7. la mesita de noche el dormitorio
8. la cómoda el dormitorio

3 **¿Qué hacían?** Complete the sentences, describing the domestic activity in each drawing. Use the imperfect tense.

1. Ramón sacaba la basura.

2. Rebeca hacía la cama.

3. Mi tío Juan pasaba la aspiradora.

4. Isabel sacudía los muebles.

4 **Una es diferente** Fill in the blank with the word that doesn't belong in each group.

1. sala, plato, copa, vaso, taza __sala__

2. cuchillo, altillo, plato, copa, tenedor __altillo__

3. cocina, balcón, patio, jardín, garaje __cocina__

4. cartel, estante, pintura, lavadora, cuadro __lavadora__

5. dormitorio, sala, comedor, cafetera, oficina __cafetera__

6. lavadora, escalera, secadora, lavaplatos, tostadora __escalera__

5 **Crucigrama** Complete the crossword puzzle.

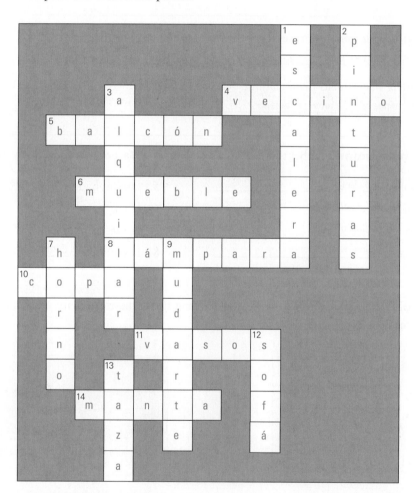

Horizontales

4. El hombre que vive al lado de tu casa.
5. Julieta habló con Romeo desde su _____.
6. sillón, mesa, cama o silla
8. Lo que prendes cuando necesitas luz.
10. Lo que se usa para tomar vino.
11. Usas estas cosas para tomar agua o soda.
14. Lo que usas cuando hace frío de noche.

Verticales

1. Lo que usas para ir de un piso a otro.
2. obras (*works*) de Picasso, de Goya, etc.
3. pagar dinero cada mes por vivir en un lugar
7. _____ de microondas
9. Si vas a vivir en otro lugar, vas a _____.
12. Donde se pueden sentar tres o cuatro personas.
13. Lo que usas para tomar el café.

estructura

6.1 Relative pronouns

1 **Relativamente** Complete the sentences with **que**, **quien**, or **quienes**.

1. La persona a _____quien_____ debes conocer es Marta.
2. El restaurante _____que_____ más me gusta es Il Forno.
3. Los amigos a _____quienes_____ fue a visitar son Ana y Antonio.
4. Doña María, _____quien/que_____ me cuidaba cuando yo era niña, vino a verme.
5. El estudiante _____que_____ mejor conozco de la clase es Gustavo.
6. La habitación _____que_____ tiene las paredes azules es la tuya.
7. Los primos con _____quienes_____ mejor me llevo son Pedro y Natalia.
8. El profesor _____que_____ sabe la respuesta está en la biblioteca ahora.

2 **Conversación telefónica** You're talking on the phone with your mother, who wants to catch up on everything in your life. Answer her questions using the words in parentheses.

> **modelo**
>
> ¿Qué es lo que tienes en el altillo? (un álbum de fotos)
> *Lo que tengo en el altillo es un álbum de fotos.*

1. ¿Qué es lo que preparas en la cocina? (el almuerzo)
   Lo que preparo en la cocina es el almuerzo.

2. ¿Qué es lo que buscas en el estante? (mi libro favorito)
   Lo que busco en el estante es mi libro favorito.

3. ¿Qué es lo que te gusta hacer en verano? (ir al campo)
   Lo que me gusta hacer en verano es ir al campo.

4. ¿Qué es lo que vas a poner en el balcón? (un sofá)
   Lo que voy a poner en el balcón es un sofá.

5. ¿Qué es lo que tienes en el armario? (mucha ropa)
   Lo que tengo en el armario es mucha ropa.

6. ¿Qué es lo que le vas a regalar a tu hermana? (una cafetera)
   Lo que le voy a regalar a mi hermana es una cafetera.

3 **¿Que o lo que?** Complete the sentences with **que** or **lo que**.

1. El pastel de cumpleaños _____que_____ me trajo mi abuela estuvo delicioso.
2. _____Lo que_____ más les gusta a Pedro y Andrés es jugar al baloncesto.
3. Miguel perdió las llaves, _____lo que_____ le hizo llegar tarde al dentista.
4. Ricardo y Ester querían los muebles _____que_____ vieron en la tienda.

4 **Pronombres relativos** Complete the sentences with **que**, **quien**, **quienes**, or **lo que**.

1. Los vecinos _____que_____ viven frente a mi casa son muy simpáticos.

2. Rosa y Pepe viajan mucho, _____lo que_____ los expone a muchas culturas.

3. Las amigas con _____quienes_____ estudias en la universidad son de varias ciudades.

4. El apartamento _____que_____ Rebeca y Jorge alquilaron está cerca del centro.

5. Adrián y Daniel, _____que/quienes_____ estudian física, son expertos en computación.

6. Rubén debe pedirle la aspiradora a Marcos, a _____quien_____ le regalaron una.

5 **Mi prima Natalia** Complete the paragraph with **que**, **quien**, **quienes**, or **lo que**.

Natalia, (1) _____que/quien_____ es mi prima, tiene un problema. Natalia es la prima

(2) _____que_____ más quiero de todas las que tengo. (3) _____Lo que_____ le pasa a Natalia

es que siempre está muy ocupada. Su novio, a (4) _____quien_____ conoció hace dos años, quiere pasar

más tiempo con ella. La clase (5) _____que_____ más le gusta a Natalia es la clase de francés.

Natalia, (6) _____que/quien_____ ya habla inglés y español, quiere aprender el francés muy bien. Tiene

dos amigos franceses con (7) _____quienes_____ practica el idioma. Natalia también está en el equipo

de natación, (8) _____lo que_____ le toma dos horas todas las mañanas. Las otras nadadoras

(9) _____que_____ están en el equipo la necesitan siempre en las prácticas. Además, a Natalia le

gusta visitar a sus padres, a (10) _____quienes_____ ve casi todos los fines de semana. También ve

con frecuencia a los parientes y amigos (11) _____que_____ viven en su ciudad. ¡Este verano

(12) _____lo que_____ Natalia necesita son unas vacaciones!

6 **Lo que me parece** Rewrite each sentence using **lo que**.

> **modelo**
> A mí me gusta comer en restaurantes.
> *Lo que a mí me gusta es comer en restaurantes.*

1. Raúl dijo una mentira.
   Lo que Raúl dijo fue una mentira.

2. Conseguiste enojar a Victoria.
   Lo que conseguiste fue enojar a Victoria.

3. Lilia va a comprar una falda.
   Lo que Lilia va a comprar es una falda.

4. Ellos preparan una sorpresa.
   Lo que ellos preparan es una sorpresa.

5. A Teo y a mí nos gusta la nieve.
   Lo que a Teo y a mí nos gusta es la nieve.

6.2 Formal (usted/ustedes) commands

1 **Háganlo así** Complete the commands, using the verbs in parentheses.

Usted

1. (lavar) ____Lave____ la ropa con el nuevo detergente.

2. (salir) ____Salga____ de su casa y disfrute del aire libre.

3. (decir) ____Diga____ todo lo que piensa hacer hoy.

4. (beber) No ____beba____ demasiado en la fiesta.

5. (venir) ____Venga____ preparado para pasarlo bien.

6. (irse) No ____se vaya____ sin probar la langosta de Maine.

Ustedes

7. (comer) No ____coman____ con la boca abierta.

8. (oír) ____Oigan____ música clásica en casa.

9. (poner) No ____pongan____ los codos (*elbows*) en la mesa.

10. (traer) ____Traigan____ un regalo a la fiesta de cumpleaños.

11. (ver) ____Vean____ programas de televisión educativos.

12. (conducir) ____Conduzcan____ con recaución (*caution*) por la ciudad.

2 **Por favor** Give instructions to people cleaning a house by changing the verb phrases into formal commands.

> **modelo**
> sacudir la alfombra
> *Sacuda la alfombra, por favor.*

1. traer la aspiradora
   Traiga la aspiradora, por favor.

2. arreglar el coche
   Arregle el coche, por favor.

3. bajar al sótano
   Baje al sótano, por favor.

4. apagar la cafetera
   Apague la cafetera, por favor.

5. venir a la casa
   Venga a la casa, por favor.

3 **Para emergencias** Rewrite this hotel's emergency instructions, replacing each **debe** + (*infinitive*) with formal commands.

Querido huésped:

Debe leer estas instrucciones para casos de emergencia. Si ocurre (*occurs*) una emergencia, debe tocar la puerta antes de abrirla. Si la puerta no está caliente, debe salir de la habitación con cuidado (*carefully*). Al salir, debe doblar a la derecha por el pasillo y debe bajar por la escalera de emergencia. Debe mantener la calma y debe caminar lentamente. No debe usar el ascensor durante una emergencia. Debe dejar su equipaje en la habitación en caso de emergencia. Al llegar a la planta baja, debe salir al patio o a la calle. Luego debe pedir ayuda a un empleado del hotel.

Querido huésped:

Lea estas instrucciones para casos de emergencia. Si ocurre una emergencia, toque la puerta antes de abrirla. Si la puerta

no está caliente, salga de la habitación con cuidado. Al salir, doble a la derecha por el pasillo y baje por la escalera de

emergencia. Mantenga la calma y camine lentamente. No use el ascensor durante una emergencia. Deje su equipaje en la

habitación en caso de emergencia. Al llegar a la planta baja, salga al patio o a la calle. Luego pida ayuda a un empleado

del hotel.

_____

_____

_____

_____

4 **Lo opuesto** Change each command to express the opposite sentiment.

> **modelo**
> Recéteselo a mi hija.
> **No se lo recete a mi hija.**

1. Siéntense en la cama. No se sienten en la cama.

2. No lo limpie ahora. Límpielo ahora.

3. Lávenmelas mañana. No me las laven mañana.

4. No nos los sirvan. Sírvannoslos.

5. Sacúdalas antes de ponerlas. No las sacuda antes de ponerlas.

6. No se las busquen. Búsquenselas.

7. Despiértenlo a las ocho. No lo despierten a las ocho.

8. Cámbiesela por otra. No se la cambie por otra.

9. Pídanselos a Martín. No se los pidan a Martín.

10. No se lo digan hoy. Díganselo hoy.

6.3 The present subjunctive

1 **Oraciones** Complete the sentences with the present subjunctive of the verb in parentheses.

1. Es bueno que ustedes _____coman_____ (comer) frutas, verduras y yogures.

2. Es importante que Laura y yo _____estudiemos_____ (estudiar) para el examen de física.

3. Es urgente que el doctor te _____mire_____ (mirar) la rodilla y la pierna.

4. Es malo que los niños no _____lean_____ (leer) mucho de pequeños (*when they are little*).

5. Es mejor que (tú) les _____escribas_____ (escribir) un mensaje antes de llamarlos.

6. Es necesario que (yo) _____pase_____ (pasar) por la casa de Mario por la mañana.

2 **El verbo correcto** Complete the sentences with the present subjunctive of the verbs from the word bank.

almorzar	hacer	oír	poner	traducir	venir
conducir	ofrecer	parecer	sacar	traer	ver

1. Es necesario que (yo) _____venga_____ a casa temprano para ayudar a mi mamá.

2. Es bueno que (la universidad) _____ofrezca_____ muchos cursos por semestre.

3. Es malo que (ellos) _____almuercen_____ justo antes de ir a nadar a la piscina.

4. Es urgente que (Lara) _____traduzca_____ estos documentos legales.

5. Es mejor que (tú) _____conduzcas_____ más lento para evitar (*avoid*) accidentes.

6. Es importante que (ella) no _____ponga_____ la cafetera en la mesa.

7. Es bueno que (tú) _____traigas_____ las fotos para verlas en la fiesta.

8. Es necesario que (él) _____vea_____ la casa antes de comprarla.

9. Es malo que (nosotros) no _____saquemos_____ la basura todas las noches.

10. Es importante que (ustedes) _____hagan_____ los quehaceres domésticos.

3 **Opiniones** Rewrite these sentences using the present subjunctive of the verbs in parentheses.

1. Mi padre dice que es importante que yo (estar) contenta con mi trabajo.
   Mi padre dice que es importante que yo esté contenta con mi trabajo.

2. Rosario cree que es bueno que la gente (irse) de vacaciones más a menudo.
   Rosario cree que es bueno que la gente se vaya de vacaciones más a menudo.

3. Creo que es mejor que Elsa (ser) la encargada del proyecto.
   Creo que es mejor que Elsa sea la encargada del proyecto.

4. Es importante que les (dar) las gracias por el favor que te hicieron.
   Es importante que les des las gracias por el favor que te hicieron.

5. Él piensa que es malo que muchos estudiantes no (saber) otras lenguas.
   Él piensa que es malo que muchos estudiantes no sepan otras lenguas.

6. El director dice que es necesario que (haber) una reunión de la facultad.
   El director dice que es necesario que haya una reunión de la facultad.

4

Es necesario Write sentences using the elements provided and the present subjunctive of the verbs.

> **modelo**
>
> malo / Roberto / no poder / irse de vacaciones
> **Es malo que Roberto no pueda irse de vacaciones.**

1. importante / Nora / pensar / las cosas antes de tomar una decisión

   Es importante que Nora piense en las cosas antes de tomar una decisión.

2. necesario / (tú) / entender / la situación de esas personas

   Es necesario que entiendas la situación de esas personas.

3. bueno / Clara / sentirse / cómoda en el apartamento nuevo

   Es bueno que Clara se sienta cómoda en el apartamento nuevo.

4. urgente / mi madre / mostrarme / los papeles que llegaron

   Es urgente que mi madre me muestre los papeles que llegaron.

5. mejor / David / dormir / antes de conducir la motocicleta

   Es mejor que David duerma antes de conducir la motocicleta.

6. malo / los niños / pedirles / tantos regalos a sus abuelos

   Es malo que los niños les pidan tantos regalos a sus abuelos.

5

Sí, es bueno Answer the questions using the words in parentheses and the present subjunctive.

> **modelo**
>
> ¿Tiene Álex que terminar ese trabajo hoy? (urgente)
> **Sí, es urgente que Álex termine ese trabajo hoy.**

1. ¿Debemos traer el pasaporte al aeropuerto? (necesario)

   Sí, es necesario que traigan el pasaporte al aeropuerto./Sí, es necesario que traigamos el pasaporte al aeropuerto.

2. ¿Tienes que hablar con don Mario? (urgente)

   Sí, es urgente que hable con don Mario.

3. ¿Debe David ir a visitar a su abuela todas las semanas? (bueno)

   Sí, es bueno que David vaya a visitar a su abuela todas las semanas.

4. ¿Puede Mariana llamar a Isabel para darle las gracias? (importante)

   Sí, es importante que Mariana llame a Isabel para darle las gracias.

5. ¿Va Andrés a saber lo que le van a preguntar en el examen? (mejor)

   Sí, es mejor que Andrés sepa lo que le van a preguntar en el examen.

6.4 Subjunctive with verbs of will and influence

1 **Preferencias** Complete the sentences with the present subjuntive of the verbs in parentheses.

1. Rosa quiere que tú _____escojas_____ (escoger) el sofá para la sala.

2. La mamá de Susana prefiere que ella _____estudie_____ (estudiar) medicina.

3. Miranda insiste en que Luisa _____sea_____ (ser) la candidata a vicepresidenta.

4. Rita y yo deseamos que nuestros padres _____viajen_____ (viajar) a Panamá.

5. A Eduardo no le importa que nosotros _____salgamos_____ (salir) esta noche.

6. La agente de viajes nos recomienda que _____nos quedemos_____ (quedarnos) en ese hotel.

2 **Compra una casa** Read the following suggestions for buying a house. Then write a note to a friend, repeating the advice and using the present subjunctive of the verbs.

Antes de comprar una casa:
- Se aconseja tener un agente inmobiliario (*real estate*).
- Se sugiere buscar una casa en un barrio seguro (*safe*).
- Se insiste en mirar los baños, la cocina y el sótano.
- Se recomienda comparar precios de varias casas antes de decidir.
- Se aconseja hablar con los vecinos del barrio.

Te aconsejo que tengas un agente inmobiliario. Te sugiero que busques una casa en un barrio seguro. Insisto en que mires los baños, la cocina y el sótano. Te recomiendo que compares los precios de varias casas antes de decidir. Te aconsejo que hables con los vecinos del barrio.

3 **Instrucciones** Write sentences using the elements provided and the present subjunctive. Replace the indirect objects with indirect object pronouns.

modelo

(a ti) / Simón / sugerir / terminar la tarea luego
Simón te sugiere que termines la tarea luego.

1. (a Daniela) / José / rogar / escribir esa carta de recomendación

   José le ruega que escriba esa carta de recomendación.

2. (a ustedes) / (yo) / aconsejar / vivir en las afueras de la ciudad

   Les aconsejo que vivan en las afueras de la ciudad.

3. (a ellos) / la directora / prohibir / estacionar frente a la escuela

   La directora les prohíbe que estacionen frente a la escuela.

4. (a mí) / (tú) / sugerir / alquilar un apartamento en el barrio

   Me sugieres que alquile un apartamento en el barrio.

Workbook

4 **¿Subjuntivo o infinitivo?** Write sentences using the elements provided. Use the subjunctive of the verbs when required.

1. Marina / querer / yo / traer / la compra a casa

   Marina quiere que yo traiga la compra a casa.

2. Sonia y yo / preferir / buscar / la información en Internet

   Sonia y yo preferimos buscar la información en Internet.

3. el profesor / desear / nosotros / usar / el diccionario

   El profesor desea que nosotros usemos el diccionario.

4. ustedes / necesitar / escribir / una carta al consulado

   Ustedes necesitan escribir una carta al consulado.

5. (yo) / preferir / Manuel / ir / al apartamento por mí

   Prefiero que Manuel vaya al apartamento por mí.

6. Ramón / insistir en / buscar / las alfombras de la casa

   Ramón insiste en buscar las alfombras de la casa.

Síntesis

Imagine that you are going away for the weekend and you are letting some of your friends stay in your house. Write instructions for your houseguests asking them how to take care of the house. Use formal commands, the phrases **Es bueno**, **Es mejor**, **Es importante**, **Es necesario**, and **Es malo**, and the verbs **aconsejar**, **pedir**, **necesitar**, **prohibir**, **recomendar**, **rogar**, and **sugerir** to describe how to make sure that your house is in perfect shape when you get home.   Answers will vary.

_____

_____

_____

_____

_____

_____

_____

_____

_____

_____

panorama

Panamá

1 **Datos panameños** Complete the sentences with the correct information.

1. _____ Rubén Blades _____ es un músico y político célebre de Panamá.

2. Una de las principales fuentes de ingresos de Panamá es _____ el Canal de Panamá _____.

3. Las _____ molas _____ son una forma de arte textil de la tribu indígena kuna.

4. Algunos diseños de las molas se inspiran en las formas del _____ coral _____.

2 **Relativamente** Rewrite each pair of sentences as one sentence. Use relative pronouns to combine the sentences.

> **modelo**
> La Ciudad de Panamá es la capital de Panamá. Tiene más de un millón de habitantes.
> La Ciudad de Panamá, que tiene más de un millón de habitantes, es la capital de Panamá.

1. La moneda de Panamá es equivalente al dólar estadounidense. Se llama el balboa.

   La moneda de Panamá, que se llama el balboa, es equivalente al dólar estadounidense.

2. El Canal de Panamá se empezó a construir en 1903. Éste une los océanos Atlántico y Pacífico.

   El Canal de Panamá, que une los océanos Atlántico y Pacífico, se empezó a construir en 1903.

3. La tribu indígena de los kuna vive principalmente en las islas San Blas. Ellos hacen molas.

   La tribu indígena de los kuna, que hace molas, es de las islas San Blas.

4. Panamá es un sitio excelente para el buceo. Panamá significa "lugar de muchos peces".

   Panamá, que significa "lugar de muchos peces", es un sitio excelente para el buceo.

3 **Geografía panameña** Fill in the blanks with the correct geographical name.

1. la capital de Panamá la Ciudad de Panamá

2. ciudades principales de Panamá la Ciudad de Panamá, Colón y David

3. países que limitan (*border*) con Panamá Costa Rica y Colombia

4. mar al norte (*north*) de Panamá el mar Caribe

5. océano al sur (*south*) de Panamá el océano Pacífico

6. por donde pasan más de 14.000 buques por año el Canal de Panamá

7. en donde vive la tribu indígena de los kuna las islas San Blas

8. parque donde se protege la fauna marina el Parque Nacional Marino Isla Bastimentos

4 **Viaje a Panamá** Complete the phrases with the correct information. Then write a paragraph of a tourist brochure about Panama. Use formal commands in the paragraph. The first sentence is done for you.

1. viajar en avión a la _____Ciudad de Panamá_____, capital de Panamá

2. visitar el país centroamericano, donde circulan los billetes de _____dólar estadounidense_____

3. conocer a los panameños; la lengua natal del 14% de ellos es _____el inglés_____

4. ir al Canal de Panamá, que une los océanos _____Atlántico_____ y _____Pacífico_____

5. ver las _____molas_____ que hace la tribu indígena kuna y decorar la casa con ellas

6. bucear en las playas de gran valor _____ecológico_____ por la riqueza y diversidad de su vida marina

Viaje en avión a la Ciudad de Panamá, capital de Panamá. Visite el país centroamericano, donde circulan los billetes de dólar estadounidense. Conozca a los panameños; la lengua natal del 14% de ellos es el inglés. Vaya al Canal de Panamá, que une los océanos Atlántico y Pacífico. Vea las molas que hace la tribu indígena kuna y decore la casa con ellas. Bucee en las playas de gran valor ecológico por la riqueza y diversidad de su vida marina.

_____

_____

_____

_____

_____

5 **¿Cierto o falso?** Indicate whether the statements are **cierto** or **falso**. Correct the false statements.

1. Panamá tiene aproximadamente el tamaño de California.

   Falso. El área de Panamá tiene aproximadamente al tamaño de Carolina del Sur.

2. La moneda panameña, que se llama el balboa, es equivalente al dólar estadounidense.

   Cierto.

3. La lengua natal de todos los panameños es el inglés.

   Falso. La lengua natal del 14% de los panameños es el inglés.

4. El Canal de Panamá une los océanos Pacífico y Atlántico.

   Cierto.

5. Las molas tradicionales siempre se usaron para decorar las casas.

   Falso. Las molas tradicionales antes sólo se usaban como ropa pero hoy día también se usan para decorar las casas.

Los quehaceres

Lección 6
Fotonovela

Antes de ver el video

1 **En la casa** In this episode, Jimena and Felipe need to clean the house if they want to travel with Marissa to the Yucatan Peninsula. Look at the image and describe what you think is going on. Answers will vary.

_____

_____

_____

_____

_____

_____

_____

Mientras ves el video

2 **¿Cierto o falso?** Watch **Los quehaceres** and indicate whether each statement is **cierto** or **falso**.

	Cierto	Falso
1. A Jimena le gusta sacar la basura.	○	⦾
2. Felipe y Jimena deben limpiar la casa porque sus papás les pagaron el viaje.	⦾	○
3. Marissa sabe cómo cambiar la bolsa de la aspiradora.	○	⦾
4. Las servilletas estaban sobre la lavadora.	○	⦾
5. Don Diego y los chicos prepararon quesadillas para cenar.	⦾	○

3 **¿Qué cosas ves?** Place a check mark beside what you see.

✔ 1. un lavaplatos   ✔ 4. vasos   ✔ 7. platos

____ 2. un garaje   ✔ 5. un sofá   ____ 8. un sótano

____ 3. un jardín   ____ 6. un balcón   ✔ 9. tenedores

4 **Ordenar** Number the events from one to five, in the order they occur.

4 a. Don Diego les sugiere a las chicas que se organicen en equipos para limpiar.

5 b. Juan Carlos pone la mesa.

3 c. Marissa quiere quitar la bolsa de la aspiradora.

1 d. La señora Díaz entra a la cocina y saluda a sus hijos.

2 e. Jimena le dice a Felipe que limpie el baño.

Después de ver el video

5 **Seleccionar** Write the letter of the word or words that match each sentence.

1. La señora Díaz les pide a sus hijos que quiten ____ de la mesa.

   a. los vasos   b. las tazas   (c.) los platos

2. La señora Díaz les ____ a sus hijos que limpien ____ si quieren viajar.

   a. ruega; el patio   (b.) sugiere; el apartamento   c. recomienda; el altillo

3. Jimena va a limpiar ____ y ____.

   (a.) el refrigerador; la estufa   b. el armario; la pared   c. el sillón; la lámpara

4. Don Diego le aconseja a Felipe que quite el polvo del ____.

   a. sótano   b. garaje   (c.) estante

5. Juan Carlos no sabe dónde están ____.

   a. las copas   b. los vasos   (c.) los tenedores

6 **Preguntas** Answer the following questions in Spanish.

1. Según el señor Díaz, ¿para qué hora deben preparar la cena Jimena y Felipe?

   Según el Sr. Díaz, Jimena y Felipe deben preparar la cena para las ocho y media.

2. ¿Qué les piden sus padres a Marissa y a sus hermanos?

   Sus padres les piden a Marissa y a sus hermanos que ayuden con los quehaceres.

3. ¿Quiénes se sientan en el sofá para ver el partido de fútbol?

   Juan Carlos y Felipe se sientan en el sofá para ver el partido de fútbol.

4. ¿Quién cambia la bolsa de la aspiradora?

   Felipe cambia la bolsa de la aspiradora.

5. ¿Qué dice la señora Díaz cuando ve el apartamento limpio?

   La señora Díaz dice "¡Qué bonita está la casa!" cuando ve el apartamento limpio.

7 **Escribir** Imagine that you are one of the characters. Write a paragraph from that person's point of view, summarizing what happened in the episode. Answers will vary.

Panorama: Panamá

Antes de ver el video

1 **Más vocabulario** Look over these useful words before you watch the video.

Vocabulario útil		
anualmente *annually*	impresionante *incredible*	según *according to*
arrecife *reef*	lado *side*	sitio *site*
disfrutar *to enjoy*	peces *fish*	torneo *tournament*
especies *species*	precioso *beautiful*	

2 **Responder** This video talks about the best places to dive and surf in Panama. In preparation for watching this video, answer these questions about surfing. Answers will vary.

1. ¿Te gusta el *surf*? ¿Por qué?

_____

_____

_____

2. ¿Practicas este deporte? ¿Conoces a alguien que lo practique? ¿Dónde lo practica(s)?

_____

_____

_____

Mientras ves el video

3 **Ordenar** Number the items in the order in which they appear in the video.

a. __1__

b. __3__

c. __2__

Mientras ves el video

4   **Emparejar** Find the items in the second column that correspond to the ones in the first.

1. La isla Contadora es la más grande __b__
2. Allí siempre hace calor, __d__
3. En Panamá, los visitantes pueden bucear en el océano Pacífico por la mañana __f__
4. Las islas de San Blas son 365, __e__
5. En Santa Catarina los deportistas disfrutan de __c__

a. por la noche.
b. del archipiélago.
c. la playa blanca y el agua color turquesa.
d. por eso se puede bucear en todas las estaciones.
e. una para cada día del año.
f. y en el mar Caribe por la tarde.

5   **Responder** Answer the questions in Spanish. Use complete sentences.

1. ¿Qué país centroamericano tiene archipiélagos en el océano Pacífico y en el mar Caribe?

   Panamá tiene archipiélagos en el océano Pacífico y en el mar Caribe.

2. ¿Por qué Las Perlas es un buen lugar para bucear?

   Las Perlas es un buen lugar para bucear porque allí hay miles de especies tropicales de peces y muchos arrecifes de

   corales y siempre hace mucho calor.

3. ¿Cómo llegan los turistas a la isla Contadora?

   Los turistas llegan a la isla Contadora por barco o por avión.

4. ¿Cómo se llaman los indígenas que viven en las islas San Blas?

   Los indígenas kuna viven en las islas San Blas.

5. ¿Adónde van los mejores deportistas de *surfing* del mundo?

   Los mejores deportistas de surfing del mundo van a Santa Catarina.

6   **Pasatiempos** Complete this chart in Spanish. Answers will vary.

Mis deportes/ pasatiempos favoritos	Por qué me gustan	Dónde/cuándo los practico

La casa de Frida

Antes de ver el video

1   **Más vocabulario** Look over these useful words before you watch the video.

Vocabulario útil		
el alma *soul*	contar con *to have; to feature*	el relicario *locket*
la artesanía *crafts*	convertirse en *to become*	el retrato *portrait*
el barro *clay*	la muleta *crutch*	la urna *urn*
la ceniza *ash*	el recorrido *tour*	el vidrio soplado *blown glass*

2   **Emparejar** Match each definition to the appropriate word.

1. Es un aparato que ayuda a caminar a las personas que no pueden hacerlo por sí solas (*by themselves*). las muletas/la muleta

2. Es el recipiente (*container*) donde se ponen las cenizas de la persona muerta. la urna

3. Es una pintura de una persona. el retrato

4. tener, poseer contar con

5. camino o itinerario en un museo, en parques, etc. el recorrido

6. Transformarse en algo distinto de lo que era antes. convertirse en

3   **¡En español!** Look at the video still. Imagine what Carlos will say about **La casa de Frida** and write a two- or three-sentence introduction to this episode.   Answers will vary.

Carlos López, México

¡Bienvenidos a otro episodio de *Flash cultura*! Soy Carlos López desde... _____

_____

_____

_____

Mientras ves el video

4   **¿Dónde están?** Identify where these items are located in Frida's museum.

¿Dónde están?	La cocina	La habitación
1. barro verde de Oaxaca	✔	
2. la urna con sus cenizas		✔
3. los aparatos ortopédicos		✔
4. vidrio soplado	✔	
5. la cama original		✔
6. artesanía de Metepec	✔	

5 **Impresiones** Listen to what these people say, and match the captions to the appropriate person.

1. __c__

2. __b__

3. __e__

4. __d__

a. Me encanta que todavía (*still*) tienen todas las cosas de Frida en su lugar…

b. … tenemos la gran bendición (*blessing*) de que contamos con un jardinero que… trabajó (*worked*) para ellos.

c. A mí lo que más me gusta es la cocina y los jardines.

d. El espacio más impresionante de esta casa es la habitación de Frida.

e. … para mí fueron unas buenas personas…

Después de ver el video

6 **Ordenar** Put Carlos' actions in the correct order.

__5__ a. Habló con distintas personas sobre el museo y sus impresiones.

__1__ b. Caminó por las calles de Coyoacán.

__6__ c. Pasó por el estudio y terminó el recorrido en la habitación de Frida.

__3__ d. Mostró el cuadro *Viva la vida* y otras pinturas de Frida.

__4__ e. Recorrió la cocina.

__2__ f. Llegó al Museo Casa de Frida Kahlo.

7 **¿Qué te gustó más?** Choose an aspect of Frida's house and describe it. Is it similar to or different from your own house? What do you find interesting about it? Answers will vary.

_____

_____

_____

_____

_____

_____

_____

contextos

Lección 6

1   **Describir**   Listen to each sentence and write the number of the sentence below the drawing of the household item mentioned.

a. _____3_____

b. _____7_____

c. _____2_____

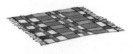

d. _____8_____

e. _____6_____

f. _____1_____

g. _____4_____

h. _____5_____

2   **Identificar**   You will hear a series of words. Write the word that does not belong in each series.

1. _____el armario_____   4. _____la pared_____   7. _____la servilleta_____

2. _____el tenedor_____   5. _____el alquiler_____   8. _____la vivienda_____

3. _____el cartel_____   6. _____el cuchillo_____

3   **Quehaceres domésticos**   Your children are complaining about the state of things in your house. Respond to their complaints by telling them what household chores they should do to correct the situation. Repeat the correct response after the speaker. (*6 items*)

> **modelo**
> La ropa está arrugada (*wrinkled*).
> Debes planchar la ropa.

4   **En la oficina de la agente inmobiliaria**   Listen to this conversation between Mr. Fuentes and a real estate agent. Then read the statements in your lab manual and decide whether they are **cierto** or **falso**.

	Cierto	Falso
1. El señor Fuentes quiere alquilar una casa.	○	☑
2. El señor Fuentes quiere vivir en las afueras.	☑	○
3. Él no quiere pagar más de 900 balboas al mes.	○	☑
3. Él vive solo (*alone*).	○	☑
5. El edificio de apartamentos tiene ascensor.	☑	○
6. El apartamento tiene lavadora.	○	☑

pronunciación

The letter **x**

In Spanish, the letter **x** has several sounds. When the letter **x** appears between two vowels, it is usually pronounced like the *ks* sound in *eccentric* or the *gs* sound in *egg salad*.

con**exi**ón   **exa**men   **saxo**fón

If the letter **x** is followed by a consonant, it is pronounced like *s* or *ks*.

ex**pl**icar   se**xt**o   e**xc**ursión

In Old Spanish, the letter **x** had the same sound as the Spanish **j**. Some proper names and some words from native languages like Náhuatl and Maya have retained this pronunciation.

Don Qui**x**ote   Oa**x**aca   Te**x**as

1   **Práctica** Repeat each word after the speaker, focusing on the **x** sound.

1. éxito
2. reflexivo
3. exterior
4. excelente
5. expedición
6. mexicano
7. expresión
8. examinar
9. excepto
10. exagerar
11. contexto
12. Maximiliano

2   **Oraciones** When you hear the number, read the corresponding sentence aloud. Then listen to the speaker and repeat the sentence.

1. Xavier Ximénez va de excursión a Ixtapa.
2. Xavier es una persona excéntrica y se viste de trajes extravagantes.
3. Él es un experto en lenguas extranjeras.
4. Hoy va a una exposición de comidas exóticas.
5. Prueba algunos platos exquisitos y extraordinarios.

3   **Refranes** Repeat each saying after the speaker to practice the **x** sound.

1. Ir por extremos no es de discretos.[1]
2. El que de la ira se deja vencer, se expone a perder.[2]

4   **Dictado** You will hear five sentences. Each will be said twice. Listen carefully and write what you hear.

1. Doña Ximena vive en un edificio de apartamentos en el extremo de la Ciudad de México.
2. Su apartamento está en el sexto piso.
3. Ella es extranjera.
4. Viene de Extremadura, España.
5. A doña Ximena le gusta ir de excursión y le fascina explorar lugares nuevos.

[1] *Prudent people don't go to extremes.*
[2] *He who allows anger to overcome him, risks losing.*

estructura

6.1 Relative pronouns

1   **Escoger** You will hear some sentences with a beep in place of the relative pronoun. Decide whether **que**, **quien**, or **lo que** should complete each sentence and circle it.

> **modelo**
>
> *You hear:* (*Beep*) me gusta de la casa es el jardín.
> *You circle:* **Lo que** *because the sentence is* **Lo que me gusta de la casa es el jardín.**

1. (que)   quien   lo que
2. que   (quien)   lo que
3. (que)   quien   lo que
4. que   quien   (lo que)
5. que   (quien)   lo que

6. (que)   quien   lo que
7. Que   Quien   (Lo que)
8. (que)   quien   lo que
9. que   (quien)   lo que
10. que   quien   (lo que)

2   **Completar** You will hear some incomplete sentences. Choose the correct ending for each sentence.

1. a. con que trabaja tu amiga.
   (b.) que se mudó a Portobelo.
2. (a.) que vende muebles baratos.
   b. que trabajábamos.
3. (a.) a quienes escribí son mis primas.
   b. de quien te escribí.

4. a. con que barres el suelo.
   (b.) que queremos vender.
5. (a.) lo que deben.
   b. que deben.
6. a. que te hablo es ama de casa.
   (b.) en quien pienso es ama de casa.

3   **Preguntas** Answer each question you hear using a relative pronoun and the cues in your lab manual. Repeat the correct response after the speaker.

> **modelo**
>
> *You hear:* ¿Quiénes son los chicos rubios?
> *You see:* mis primos / viven en Colón
> *You say:* Son mis primos que viven en Colón.

1. chica / conocí en el café
2. el cliente / llamó ayer
3. chico / se casa Patricia

4. agente / nos ayudó
5. vecinos / viven en la casa azul
6. chica / trabajo

4   **Un robo (*break-in*)** There has been a theft at the Riveras' house. The detective they have hired has gathered all the family members in the living room to reveal the culprit. Listen to his conclusions. Then complete the list of clues (**pistas**) in your lab manual and answer the question.

Pistas

1. El reloj que estaba roto
2. La taza que estaba sucia (en el lavaplatos)
3. La almohada que tenía dos pelos (pelirrojos)

Pregunta

¿Quién se llevó las cucharas de la abuela y por qué se las llevó? La tía Matilde se llevó las cucharas de la abuela porque necesitaba dinero.

6.2 Formal (usted/ustedes) commands

1 Identificar You will hear some sentences. If the verb is a formal command, circle **Sí**. If the verb is not a command, circle **No**.

> **modelo**
>
> *You hear:* Saque la basura.
> *You circle:* **Sí** because **Saque** is a formal command.

1.	Sí	(No)	6.	(Sí)	No
2.	(Sí)	No	7.	Sí	(No)
3.	(Sí)	No	8.	Sí	(No)
4.	Sí	(No)	9.	Sí	(No)
5.	(Sí)	No	10.	(Sí)	No

2 Cambiar A physician is giving a patient advice. Change each sentence you hear from an indirect command to a formal command. Repeat the correct answer after the speaker. (*6 items*)

> **modelo**
>
> Usted tiene que dormir ocho horas cada noche.
> **Duerma** *ocho horas cada noche.*

3 Preguntas Answer each question you hear in the affirmative using a formal command and a direct object pronoun. Repeat the correct response after the speaker. (*8 items*)

> **modelo**
>
> ¿Cerramos las ventanas?
> Sí, *ciérrenlas.*

4 Más preguntas Answer each question you hear using a formal command and the cue in your lab manual. Repeat the correct response after the speaker.

> **modelo**
>
> *You hear:* ¿Debo llamar al señor Rodríguez?
> *You see:* no / ahora
> *You say:* No, no lo llame ahora.

1. no
2. a las cinco
3. sí / aquí
4. no
5. el primer día del mes
6. que estamos ocupados

5 ¿Cómo llegar? Julia is going to explain how to get to her home. Listen to her instructions, then number the instructions in your lab manual in the correct order. Two items will not be used.

_____2_____ a. entrar al edificio que está al lado del Banco Popular

_____ b. tomar el ascensor al cuarto piso

_____5_____ c. buscar las llaves debajo de la alfombra

_____ d. ir detrás del edificio

_____1_____ e. bajarse del metro en la estación Santa Rosa

_____3_____ f. subir las escaleras al tercer piso

_____4_____ g. caminar hasta el final del pasillo

6.3 The present subjunctive

1 **Escoger** You will hear some sentences with a beep in place of a verb. Decide which verb should complete each sentence and circle it.

> **modelo**
>
> *You hear:* Es urgente que (*beep*) al médico.
> *You see:* vas vayas
> *You say:* **vayas** because the sentence is **Es urgente que vayas al médico**.

1. tomamos   (tomemos)
2. (conduzcan)   conducen
3. (aprenda)   aprendee
4. arreglas   (arregles)

5. se acuestan   (se acuesten)
6. sabes   (sepas)
7. (almorcemos)   almorzamos
8. (se mude)   se muda

2 **Cambiar** You are a Spanish instructor, and it's the first day of class. Tell your students what it is important for them to do using the cues you hear. (*8 items*)

> **modelo**
>
> hablar español en la clase
> **Es importante que ustedes hablen español en la clase.**

3 **Transformar** Change each sentence you hear to the subjunctive mood using the expression in your lab manual. Repeat the correct answer after the speaker.

> **modelo**
>
> *You hear:* Pones tu ropa en el armario.
> *You see:* Es necesario
> *You say:* **Es necesario que pongas tu ropa en el armario.**

1. Es mejor   4. Es importante
2. Es urgente   5. Es bueno
3. Es malo   6. Es necesario

4 **¿Qué pasa aquí?** Listen to this conversation. Then choose the phrase that best completes each sentence in your lab manual.

1. Esta conversación es entre...
   a. un empleado y una clienta.
   b. un hijo y su madre.
   c. un camarero y la dueña de un restaurante.
2. Es necesario que Mario...
   a. llegue temprano.
   b. se lave las manos.
   c. use la lavadora.
3. Es urgente que Mario...
   a. ponga las mesas.
   b. quite las mesas.
   c. sea listo.

6.4 Subjunctive with verbs of will and influence

1 **Identificar** Listen to each sentence. If you hear a verb in the subjunctive, mark **Sí**. If you don't hear the subjunctive, mark **No**.

1. (Sí)   No   4. Sí   (No)
2. Sí   (No)   5. Sí   (No)
3. (Sí)   No   6. (Sí)   No

2 **Transformar** Some people are discussing what they or their friends want to do. Say that you don't want them to do those things. Repeat the correct response after the speaker. (*6 items*)

> **modelo**
>
> Esteban quiere invitar a tu hermana a una fiesta.
> **No quiero que Esteban invite a mi hermana a una fiesta.**

3 **Situaciones** Listen to each situation and make a recommendation using the cues in your lab manual. Repeat the correct response after the speaker.

> **modelo**
>
> *You hear:* Sacamos una "F" en el examen de química.
> *You see:* estudiar más
> *You say:* **Les recomiendo que estudien más.**

1. ponerte un suéter
2. quedarse en la cama
3. regalarles una tostadora
4. no hacerlo
5. comprarlas en la Casa Bonita
6. ir a La Cascada

4 **¿Qué hacemos?** Listen to this conversation and answer the questions in your lab manual.

1. ¿Qué quiere el señor Barriga que hagan los chicos?
   El señor Barriga quiere que los chicos le paguen el alquiler (hoy mismo).

2. ¿Qué le pide el chico?
   (El chico) Le pide que les dé más tiempo.

3. ¿Qué les sugiere el señor a los chicos?
   Les sugiere que les pidan dinero a sus padres y que Juan Carlos encuentre otro trabajo pronto.

4. ¿Qué tienen que hacer los chicos si no consiguen el dinero?
   Los chicos tienen/van a tener que mudarse.

5. Al final, ¿en qué insiste el señor Barriga?
   Al final, el señor Barriga insiste en que le paguen el alquiler mañana por la mañana.

vocabulario

You will now hear the vocabulary found in your textbook on the last page of this lesson. Listen and repeat each Spanish word or phrase after the speaker.

Additional Vocabulary

Additional Vocabulary

Notes

Notes

Plan de escritura

(1) Ideas y organización

Begin by organizing your writing materials. If you prefer to write by hand, you may want to have a few spare pens and pencils on hand, as well as an eraser or correction fluid. If you prefer to use a word-processing program, make sure you know how to type Spanish accent marks, the **tilde,** and Spanish punctuation marks. Then make a list of the resources you can consult while writing. Finally, make a list of the basic ideas you want to cover. Beside each idea, jot down a few Spanish words and phrases you may want to use while writing.

(2) Primer borrador

Write your first draft, using the resources and ideas you gathered in **Ideas y organización.**

(3) Comentario

Exchange papers with a classmate and comment on each other's work, using these questions as a guide. Begin by mentioning what you like about your classmate's writing.

a. How can your classmate make his or her writing clearer, more logical, or more organized?

b. What suggestions do you have for making the writing more interesting or complete?

c. Do you see any spelling or grammatical errors?

(4) Redacción

Revise your first draft, keeping in mind your classmate's comments. Also, incorporate any new information you may have. Before handing in the final version, review your work using these guidelines:

a. Make sure each verb agrees with its subject. Then check the gender and number of each article, noun, and adjective.

b. Check your spelling and punctuation.

c. Consult your **Anotaciones para mejorar la escritura** (see description below) to avoid repetition of previous errors.

(5) Evaluación y progreso

You may want to share what you've written with a classmate, a small group, or the entire class. After your instructor has returned your paper, review the comments and corrections. On a separate sheet of paper, write the heading **Anotaciones para mejorar** (*Notes for improving*) **la escritura** and list your most common errors. Place this list and your corrected document in your writing portfolio (**Carpeta de trabajos**) and consult it from time to time to gauge your progress.

Spanish Terms for Direction Lines and Classroom Use

Below is a list of useful terms that you might hear your instructor say in class. It also includes Spanish terms that appear in the direction lines of your textbook.

En las instrucciones — *In direction lines*

Cambia/Cambien...	*Change...*
Camina/Caminen por la clase.	*Walk around the classroom.*
Ciertas o falsas	*True or false*
Cierto o falso	*True or false*
Circula/Circulen por la clase.	*Walk around the classroom.*
Completa las oraciones de una manera lógica.	*Complete the sentences logically.*
Con un(a) compañero/a...	*With a classmate...*
Contesta las preguntas.	*Answer the questions.*
Corrige las oraciones falsas.	*Correct the false statements.*
Cuenta/Cuenten...	*Tell...*
Di/Digan...	*Say...*
Discute/Discutan...	*Discuss...*
En grupos...	*In groups...*
En parejas...	*In pairs...*
Entrevista...	*Interview...*
Escúchala	*Listen to it*
Forma oraciones completas.	*Create/Make complete sentences.*
Háganse preguntas.	*Ask each other questions.*
Haz el papel de...	*Play the role of...*
Haz los cambios necesarios.	*Make the necessary changes.*
Indica/Indiquen si las oraciones...	*Indicate if the sentences...*
Intercambia/Intercambien...	*Exchange...*
Lee/Lean en voz alta.	*Read aloud.*
Pon/Pongan...	*Put...*
...que mejor completa...	*...that best completes...*
Reúnete...	*Get together...*
...se da/dan como ejemplo.	*...is/are given as a model.*
Toma nota...	*Take note...*
Tomen apuntes.	*Take notes.*
Túrnense...	*Take turns...*

Palabras útiles — *Useful words*

la adivinanza	*riddle*
el anuncio	*advertisement/ad*
los apuntes	*notes*
el borrador	*draft*
la canción	*song*
la concordancia	*agreement*
el contenido	*contents*
el cortometraje	*short film*
eficaz	*efficient*
la encuesta	*survey*
el equipo	*team*
el esquema	*outline*
el folleto	*brochure*
las frases	*phrases*
la hoja de actividades	*activity sheet/handout*
la hoja de papel	*piece of paper*
la información errónea	*incorrect information*
el/la lector(a)	*reader*
la lectura	*reading*
las oraciones	*sentences*
la ortografía	*spelling*
el papel	*role*
el párrafo	*paragraph*
el paso	*step*
la(s) persona(s) descrita(s)	*the person (people) described*
la pista	*clue*
por ejemplo	*for example*
el propósito	*purpose*
los recursos	*resources*
el reportaje	*report*
los resultados	*results*
según	*according to*
siguiente	*following*
la sugerencia	*suggestion*
el sustantivo	*noun*
el tema	*topic*
último	*last*
el último recurso	*last resort*

Verbos útiles *Useful verbs*

adivinar	*to guess*
anotar	*to jot down*
añadir	*to add*
apoyar	*to support*
averiguar	*to find out*
cambiar	*to change*
combinar	*to combine*
compartir	*to share*
comprobar (o:ue)	*to check*
corregir (e:i)	*to correct*
crear	*to create*
devolver (o:ue)	*to return*
doblar	*to fold*
dramatizar	*to act out*
elegir (e:i)	*to choose/select*
emparejar	*to match*
entrevistar	*to interview*
escoger	*to choose*
identificar	*to identify*
incluir	*to include*
informar	*to report*
intentar	*to try*
intercambiar	*to exchange*
investigar	*to research*
marcar	*to mark*
preguntar	*to ask*
recordar (o:ue)	*to remember*
responder	*to answer*
revisar	*to revise*
seguir (e:i)	*to follow*
seleccionar	*to select*
subrayar	*to underline*
traducir	*to translate*
tratar de	*to be about*

Expresiones útiles *Useful expressions*

Ahora mismo.	*Right away.*
¿Cómo no?	*But of course.*
¿Cómo se dice _____ en español?	*How do you say _____ in Spanish?*
¿Cómo se escribe _____?	*How do you spell _____?*
¿Comprende(n)?	*Do you understand?*
Con gusto.	*With pleasure.*
Con permiso.	*Excuse me.*
De acuerdo.	*Okay.*
De nada.	*You're welcome.*
¿De veras?	*Really?*
¿En qué página estamos?	*What page are we on?*
¿En serio?	*Seriously?*
Enseguida.	*Right away.*
hoy día	*nowadays*
Más despacio, por favor.	*Slower, please.*
Muchas gracias.	*Thanks a lot.*
No entiendo.	*I don't understand.*
No hay de qué.	*Don't mention it.*
No importa.	*No problem./It doesn't matter.*
¡No me digas!	*You don't say!*
No sé.	*I don't know.*
¡Ojalá!	*Hopefully!*
Perdone.	*Pardon me.*
Por favor.	*Please.*
Por supuesto.	*Of course.*
¡Qué bien!	*Great!*
¡Qué gracioso!	*How funny!*
¡Qué pena!	*What a shame/pity!*
¿Qué significa _____?	*What does _____ mean?*
Repite, por favor.	*Please repeat.*
Tengo una pregunta.	*I have a question.*
¿Tiene(n) alguna pregunta?	*Do you have any questions?*
Vaya(n) a la página dos.	*Go to page 2.*

Glossary of Grammatical Terms

ADJECTIVE A word that modifies, or describes, a noun or pronoun.

muchos libros
many books

un hombre **rico**
a rich man

las mujeres **altas**
the tall women

Demonstrative adjective An adjective that specifies which noun a speaker is referring to.

esta fiesta
this party

ese chico
that boy

aquellas flores
those flowers

Possessive adjective An adjective that indicates ownership or possession.

mi mejor vestido
my best dress

Éste es **mi** hermano.
This is my brother.

Stressed possessive adjective A possessive adjective that emphasizes the owner or possessor.

Es un libro **mío**.
It's my book./It's a book of mine.

Es amiga **tuya**; yo no la conozco.
She's a friend of yours; I don't know her.

ADVERB A word that modifies, or describes, a verb, adjective, or other adverb.

Pancho escribe **rápidamente**.
Pancho writes quickly.

Este cuadro es **muy** bonito.
This picture is very pretty.

ARTICLE A word that points out a noun in either a specific or a non-specific way.

Definite article An article that points out a noun in a specific way.

el libro
the book

la maleta
the suitcase

los diccionarios
the dictionaries

las palabras
the words

Indefinite article An article that points out a noun in a general, non-specific way.

un lápiz
a pencil

una computadora
a computer

unos pájaros
some birds

unas escuelas
some schools

CLAUSE A group of words that contains both a conjugated verb and a subject, either expressed or implied.

Main (or Independent) clause A clause that can stand alone as a complete sentence.

Pienso ir a cenar pronto.
I plan to go to dinner soon.

Subordinate (or Dependent) clause A clause that does not express a complete thought and therefore cannot stand alone as a sentence.

Trabajo en la cafetería **porque necesito dinero para la escuela**.
I work in the cafeteria because I need money for school.

COMPARATIVE A construction used with an adjective or adverb to express a comparison between two people, places, or things.

Este programa es **más interesante que** el otro.
This program is more interesting than the other one.

Tomás no es **tan alto como** Alberto.
Tomás is not as tall as Alberto.

CONJUGATION A set of the forms of a verb for a specific tense or mood or the process by which these verb forms are presented.

Preterite conjugation of **cantar**:
cant**é**   cant**amos**
cant**aste**   cant**asteis**
cant**ó**   cant**aron**

CONJUNCTION A word used to connect words, clauses, or phrases.

Susana es de Cuba **y** Pedro es de España.
Susana is from Cuba and Pedro is from Spain.

No quiero estudiar **pero** tengo que hacerlo.
I don't want to study, but I have to.

CONTRACTION The joining of two words into one. The only contractions in Spanish are **al** and **del**.

Mi hermano fue **al** concierto ayer.
*My brother went **to the** concert yesterday.*

Saqué dinero **del** banco.
*I took money **from the** bank.*

DIRECT OBJECT A noun or pronoun that directly receives the action of the verb.

Tomás lee **el libro.** **La** pagó ayer.
*Tomás reads **the book.*** *She paid **it** yesterday.*

GENDER The grammatical categorizing of certain kinds of words, such as nouns and pronouns, as masculine, feminine, or neuter.

Masculine
articles el, un
pronouns él, lo, mío, éste, ése, aquél
adjective simpático

Feminine
articles la, una
pronouns ella, la, mía, ésta, ésa, aquélla
adjective simpática

IMPERSONAL EXPRESSION A third-person expression with no expressed or specific subject.

Es muy importante. Llueve mucho.
It's very important. *It's raining hard.*

Aquí **se habla** español.
*Spanish **is spoken** here.*

INDIRECT OBJECT A noun or pronoun that receives the action of the verb indirectly; the object, often a living being, to or for whom an action is performed.

Eduardo **le** dio un libro **a Linda.**
*Eduardo gave a book **to Linda.***

La profesora **me** dio una C en el examen.
*The professor gave **me** a C on the test.*

INFINITIVE The basic form of a verb. Infinitives in Spanish end in -ar, -er, or -ir.

hablar correr abrir
to speak *to run* *to open*

INTERROGATIVE An adjective or pronoun used to ask a question.

¿**Quién** habla? ¿**Cuántos** compraste?
***Who** is speaking?* ***How many** did you buy?*

¿**Qué** piensas hacer hoy?
***What** do you plan to do today?*

INVERSION Changing the word order of a sentence, often to form a question.

Statement: Elena pagó la cuenta del restaurante.

Inversion: ¿Pagó Elena la cuenta del restaurante?

MOOD A grammatical distinction of verbs that indicates whether the verb is intended to make a statement or command or to express a doubt, emotion, or condition contrary to fact.

Imperative mood Verb forms used to make commands.

Di la verdad. Caminen ustedes conmigo.
Tell the truth. *Walk with me.*

¡Comamos ahora!
Let's eat now!

Indicative mood Verb forms used to state facts, actions, and states considered to be real.

Sé que **tienes** el dinero.
*I know that **you have** the money.*

Subjunctive mood Verb forms used principally in subordinate (dependent) clauses to express wishes, desires, emotions, doubts, and certain conditions, such as contrary-to-fact situations.

Prefieren que **hables** en español.
*They prefer that **you speak** in Spanish.*

Dudo que Luis **tenga** el dinero necesario.
*I doubt that Luis **has** the necessary money.*

NOUN A word that identifies people, animals, places, things, and ideas.

hombre gato
man *cat*

México casa
Mexico *house*

libertad libro
freedom *book*

NUMBER A grammatical term that refers to singular or plural. Nouns in Spanish and English have number. Other parts of a sentence, such as adjectives, articles, and verbs, can also have number.

Singular	Plural
una cosa	unas cosas
a thing	*some things*
el profesor	los profesores
the professor	*the professors*

NUMBERS Words that represent amounts.

Cardinal numbers Words that show specific amounts.

cinco minutos
five minutes

el año dos mil veintitrés
the year 2023

Ordinal numbers Words that indicate the order of a noun in a series.

el **cuarto** jugador	la **décima** hora
*the **fourth** player*	*the **tenth** hour*

PAST PARTICIPLE A past form of the verb used in compound tenses. The past participle may also be used as an adjective, but it must then agree in number and gender with the word it modifies.

Han **buscado** por todas partes.
*They have **searched** everywhere.*

Yo no había **estudiado** para el examen.
*I hadn't **studied** for the exam.*

Hay una **ventana abierta** en la sala.
*There is an **open window** in the living room.*

PERSON The form of the verb or pronoun that indicates the speaker, the one spoken to, or the one spoken about. In Spanish, as in English, there are three persons: first, second, and third.

Person	Singular	Plural
1st	yo *I*	nosotros/as *we*
2nd	tú, Ud. *you*	vosotros/as, Uds. *you*
3rd	él, ella *he, she*	ellos, ellas *they*

PREPOSITION A word or words that describe(s) the relationship, most often in time or space, between two other words.

Anita es **de** California.
*Anita is **from** California.*

La chaqueta está **en** el carro.
*The jacket is **in** the car.*

Marta se peinó **antes de** salir.
*Marta combed her hair **before** going out.*

PRESENT PARTICIPLE In English, a verb form that ends in -*ing*. In Spanish, the present participle ends in -**ndo**, and is often used with **estar** to form a progressive tense.

Mi hermana está **hablando** por teléfono ahora mismo.
*My sister is **talking** on the phone right now.*

PRONOUN A word that takes the place of a noun or nouns.

Demonstrative pronoun A pronoun that takes the place of a specific noun.

Quiero **ésta**.
*I want **this one**.*

¿Vas a comprar **ése**?
*Are you going to buy **that one**?*

Juan prefirió **aquéllos**.
*Juan preferred **those** (over there).*

Object pronoun A pronoun that functions as a direct or indirect object of the verb.

Te digo la verdad.
*I'm telling **you** the truth.*

Me lo trajo Juan.
*Juan brought **it** to **me**.*

Reflexive pronoun A pronoun that indicates that the action of a verb is performed by the subject on itself. These pronouns are often expressed in English with -*self: myself, yourself*, etc.

Yo **me** bañé antes de salir.
*I bathed **(myself)** before going out.*

Elena **se** acostó a las once y media.
*Elena **went to bed** at eleven-thirty.*

Relative pronoun A pronoun that connects a subordinate clause to a main clause.

El chico **que** nos escribió viene de visita mañana.
*The boy **who** wrote us is coming to visit tomorrow.*

Ya sé **lo que** tenemos que hacer.
*I already know **what** we have to do.*

Subject pronoun A pronoun that replaces the name or title of a person or thing, and acts as the subject of a verb.

Tú debes estudiar más.
***You** should study more.*

Él llegó primero.
***He** arrived first.*

SUBJECT A noun or pronoun that performs the action of a verb and is often implied by the verb.

María va al supermercado.
***María** goes to the supermarket.*

(Ellos) Trabajan mucho.
***They** work hard.*

Esos **libros** son muy caros.
*Those **books** are very expensive.*

SUPERLATIVE A word or construction used with an adjective or adverb to express the highest or lowest degree of a specific quality among three or more people, places, or things.

De todas mis clases, ésta es la **más interesante**.
*Of all my classes, this is the **most interesting**.*

Raúl es el **menos simpático** de los chicos.
*Raúl is the **least pleasant** of the boys.*

TENSE A set of verb forms that indicates the time of an action or state: past, present, or future.

Compound tense A two-word tense made up of an auxiliary verb and a present or past participle. In Spanish, **estar** and **haber** are auxiliary verbs.

En este momento, **estoy estudiando**.
*At this time, **I am studying**.*

El paquete no **ha llegado** todavía.
*The package **has not arrived** yet.*

Simple tense A tense expressed by a single verb form.

María **estaba** enferma anoche.
*María **was** sick last night.*

Juana **hablará** con su mamá mañana.
*Juana **will speak** with her mom tomorrow.*

VERB A word that expresses actions or states of being.

Auxiliary verb A verb used with a present or past participle to form a compound tense. **Haber** is the most commonly used auxiliary verb in Spanish.

Los chicos **han** visto los elefantes.
*The children **have** seen the elephants.*

Espero que **hayas** comido.
*I hope you **have** eaten.*

Reflexive verb A verb that describes an action performed by the subject on itself and is always used with a reflexive pronoun.

Me compré un carro nuevo.
*I **bought myself** a new car.*

Pedro y Adela **se levantan** muy temprano.
*Pedro and Adela **get (themselves) up** very early.*

Spelling change verb A verb that undergoes a predictable change in spelling, in order to reflect its actual pronunciation in the various conjugations.

practicar	c→qu	practico	practiqué
dirigir	g→j	dirigí	dirijo
almorzar	z→c	almorzó	almorcé

Stem-changing verb A verb whose stem vowel undergoes one or more predictable changes in the various conjugations.

entender (e:ie)	entiendo
pedir (e:i)	piden
dormir (o:ue, u)	duermo, durmieron

Verb Conjugation Tables

The verb lists

The list of verbs below, and the model-verb tables that start on page A-11 show you how to conjugate every verb taught in ¡**ADELANTE!** Each verb in the list is followed by a model verb conjugated according to the same pattern. The number in parentheses indicates where in the verb tables you can find the conjugated forms of the model verb. If you want to find out how to conjugate **divertirse**, for example, look up number 33, **sentir**, the model for verbs that follow the **e:ie** stem-change pattern.

How to use the verb tables

In the tables you will find the infinitive, present and past participles, and all the simple forms of each model verb. The formation of the compound tenses of any verb can be inferred from the table of compound tenses, pages A-11 and A-12, either by combining the past participle of the verb with a conjugated form of **haber** or by combining the present participle with a conjugated form of **estar**.

abrazar (z:c) like cruzar (37)
abrir like vivir (3) *except* past participle is **abierto**
aburrir(se) like vivir (3)
acabar de like hablar (1)
acampar like hablar (1)
acompañar like hablar (1)
aconsejar like hablar (1)
acordarse (o:ue) like contar (24)
acostarse (o:ue) like contar (24)
adelgazar (z:c) like cruzar (37)
afeitarse like hablar (1)
ahorrar like hablar (1)
alegrarse like hablar (1)
aliviar like hablar (1)
almorzar (o:ue) like contar (24) *except* (z:c)
alquilar like hablar (1)
andar like hablar (1) *except* preterite stem is **anduv-**
anunciar like hablar (1)
apagar (g:gu) like llegar (41)
aplaudir like vivir (3)
apreciar like hablar (1)
aprender like comer (2)
apurarse like hablar (1)
arrancar (c:qu) like tocar (43)
arreglar like hablar (1)
asistir like vivir (3)
aumentar like hablar (1)

ayudar(se) like hablar (1)
bailar like hablar (1)
bajar(se) like hablar (1)
bañarse like hablar (1)
barrer like comer (2)
beber like comer (2)
besar(se) like hablar (1)
borrar like hablar (1)
brindar like hablar (1)
bucear like hablar (1)
buscar (c:qu) like tocar (43)
caber (4)
caer(se) (5)
calentarse (e:ie) like pensar (30)
calzar (z:c) like cruzar (37)
cambiar like hablar (1)
caminar like hablar (1)
cantar like hablar (1)
casarse like hablar (1)
cazar (z:c) like cruzar (37)
celebrar like hablar (1)
cenar like hablar (1)
cepillarse like hablar (1)
cerrar (e:ie) like pensar (30)
cobrar like hablar (1)
cocinar like hablar (1)
comenzar (e:ie) (z:c) like empezar (26)
comer (2)
compartir like vivir (3)
comprar like hablar (1)
comprender like comer (2)

comprometerse like comer (2)
comunicarse (c:qu) like tocar (43)
conducir (c:zc) (6)
confirmar like hablar (1)
conocer (c:zc) (35)
conseguir (e:i) (g:gu) like seguir (32)
conservar like hablar (1)
consumir like vivir (3)
contaminar like hablar (1)
contar (o:ue) (24)
contestar like hablar (1)
contratar like hablar (1)
controlar like hablar (1)
conversar like hablar (1)
correr like comer (2)
costar (o:ue) like contar (24)
creer (y) (36)
cruzar (z:c) (37)
cuidar like hablar (1)
cumplir like vivir (3)
dañar like hablar (1)
dar (7)
deber like comer (2)
decidir like vivir (3)
decir (e:i) (8)
declarar like hablar (1)
dejar like hablar (1)
depositar like hablar (1)
desarrollar like hablar (1)
desayunar like hablar (1)

descansar like hablar (1)
descargar like llegar (41)
describir like vivir (3) *except* past participle is descrito
descubrir like vivir (3) *except* past participle is descubierto
desear like hablar (1)
despedirse (e:i) like pedir (29)
despertarse (e:ie) like pensar (30)
destruir (y) (38)
dibujar like hablar (1)
dirigir (g:j) like vivir (3) *except* (g:j)
disfrutar like hablar (1)
divertirse (e:ie) like sentir (33)
divorciarse like hablar (1)
doblar like hablar (1)
doler (o:ue) like volver (34) *except* past participle is regular
dormir(se) (o:ue, u) (25)
ducharse like hablar (1)
dudar like hablar (1)
durar like hablar (1)
echar like hablar (1)
elegir (e:i) like pedir (29) *except* (g:j)
emitir like vivir (3)
empezar (e:ie) (z:c) (26)
enamorarse like hablar (1)

encantar like hablar (1)
encontrar(se) (o:ue) like contar (24)
enfermarse like hablar (1)
engordar like hablar (1)
enojarse like hablar (1)
enseñar like hablar (1)
ensuciar like hablar (1)
entender (e:ie) (27)
entrenarse like hablar (1)
entrevistar like hablar (1)
enviar (envío) (39)
escalar like hablar (1)
escanear like hablar (1)
escoger (g:j) like proteger (42)
escribir like vivir (3) *except* past participle is **escrito**
escuchar like hablar (1)
esculpir like vivir (3)
esperar like hablar (1)
esquiar (esquío) like enviar (39)
establecer (c:zc) like conocer (35)
estacionar like hablar (1)
estar (9)
estornudar like hablar (1)
estudiar like hablar (1)
evitar like hablar (1)
explicar (c:qu) like tocar (43)
faltar like hablar (1)
fascinar like hablar (1)
firmar like hablar (1)
fumar like hablar (1)
funcionar like hablar (1)
ganar like hablar (1)
gastar like hablar (1)
grabar like hablar (1)
graduarse (gradúo) (40)
guardar like hablar (1)
gustar like hablar (1)
haber (hay) (10)
hablar (1)
hacer (11)
importar like hablar (1)
imprimir like vivir (3)
indicar (c:qu) like tocar (43)
informar like hablar (1)
insistir like vivir (3)
interesar like hablar (1)
invertir (e:ie) like sentir (33)

invitar like hablar (1)
ir(se) (12)
jubilarse like hablar (1)
jugar (u:ue) (g:gu) (28)
lastimarse like hablar (1)
lavar(se) like hablar (1)
leer (y) like creer (36)
levantar(se) like hablar (1)
limpiar like hablar (1)
llamar(se) like hablar (1)
llegar (g:gu) (41)
llenar like hablar (1)
llevar(se) like hablar (1)
llover (o:ue) like volver (34) *except* past participle is regular
luchar like hablar (1)
mandar like hablar (1)
manejar like hablar (1)
mantener(se) (e:ie) like tener (20)
maquillarse like hablar (1)
mejorar like hablar (1)
merendar (e:ie) like pensar (30)
mirar like hablar (1)
molestar like hablar (1)
montar like hablar (1)
morir (o:ue, u) like dormir (25) *except* past participle is **muerto**
mostrar (o:ue) like contar (24)
mudarse like hablar (1)
nacer (c:zc) like conocer (35)
nadar like hablar (1)
navegar (g:gu) like llegar (41)
necesitar like hablar (1)
negar (e:ie) like pensar (30) *except* (g:gu)
nevar (e:ie) like pensar (30)
obedecer (c:zc) like conocer (35)
obtener (e:ie) like tener (20)
ocurrir like vivir (3)
odiar like hablar (1)
ofrecer (c:zc) like conocer (35)
oír (13)
olvidar like hablar (1)
pagar (g:gu) like llegar (41)
parar like hablar (1)
parecer (c:zc) like conocer (35)

pasar like hablar (1)
pasear like hablar (1)
patinar like hablar (1)
pedir (e:i) (29)
peinarse like hablar (1)
pensar (e:ie) (30)
perder (e:ie) like entender (27)
pescar (c:qu) like tocar (43)
pintar like hablar (1)
planchar like hablar (1)
poder (o:ue) (14)
poner(se) (15)
practicar (c:qu) like tocar (43)
preferir (e:ie) like sentir (33)
preguntar like hablar (1)
prender like comer (2)
preocuparse like hablar (1)
preparar like hablar (1)
presentar like hablar (1)
prestar like hablar (1)
probar(se) (o:ue) like contar (24)
prohibir (prohíbo) like vivir (3)
proteger (g:j) (42)
publicar (c:qu) like tocar (43)
quedar(se) like hablar (1)
querer (e:ie) (16)
quitar(se) like hablar (1)
recetar like hablar (1)
recibir like vivir (3)
reciclar like hablar (1)
recoger (g:j) like proteger (42)
recomendar (e:ie) like pensar (30)
recordar (o:ue) like contar (24)
reducir (c:zc) like conducir (6)
regalar like hablar (1)
regatear like hablar (1)
regresar like hablar (1)
reír(se) (e:i) (31)
relajarse like hablar (1)
renunciar like hablar (1)
repetir (e:i) like pedir (29)
resolver (o:ue) like volver (34)
respirar like hablar (1)
revisar like hablar (1)

rogar (o:ue) like contar (24) *except* (g:gu)
romper(se) like comer (2) *except* past participle is **roto**
saber (17)
sacar (c:qu) like tocar (43)
sacudir like vivir (3)
salir (18)
saludar(se) like hablar (1)
secar(se) (c:qu) like tocar (43)
seguir (e:i) (32)
sentarse (e:ie) like pensar (30)
sentir(se) (e:ie) (33)
separarse like hablar (1)
ser (19)
servir (e:i) like pedir (29)
solicitar like hablar (1)
sonar (o:ue) like contar (24)
sonreír (e:i) like reír(se) (31)
sorprender like comer (2)
subir like vivir (3)
sudar like hablar (1)
sufrir like vivir (3)
sugerir (e:ie) like sentir (33)
suponer like poner (15)
temer like comer (2)
tener (e:ie) (20)
terminar like hablar (1)
tocar (c:qu) (43)
tomar like hablar (1)
torcerse (o:ue) like volver (34) *except* (c:z) and past participle is regular; e.g., yo tuerzo
toser like comer (2)
trabajar like hablar (1)
traducir (c:zc) like conducir (6)
traer (21)
transmitir like vivir (3)
tratar like hablar (1)
usar like hablar (1)
vender like comer (2)
venir (e:ie) (22)
ver (23)
vestirse (e:i) like pedir (29)
viajar like hablar (1)
visitar like hablar (1)
vivir (3)
volver (o:ue) (34)
votar like hablar (1)

Regular verbs: simple tenses

1. hablar
Participles: hablando, hablado

	INDICATIVE					SUBJUNCTIVE		IMPERATIVE
Infinitive	Present	Imperfect	Preterite	Future	Conditional	Present	Past	
hablar	hablo	hablaba	hablé	hablaré	hablaría	hable	hablara	
	hablas	hablabas	hablaste	hablarás	hablarías	hables	hablaras	habla tú (no hables)
	habla	hablaba	habló	hablará	hablaría	hable	hablara	hable Ud.
	hablamos	hablábamos	hablamos	hablaremos	hablaríamos	hablemos	habláramos	hablemos
	habláis	hablabais	hablasteis	hablaréis	hablaríais	habléis	hablarais	hablad (no habléis)
	hablan	hablaban	hablaron	hablarán	hablarían	hablen	hablaran	hablen Uds.

2. comer
Participles: comiendo, comido

	INDICATIVE					SUBJUNCTIVE		IMPERATIVE
Infinitive	Present	Imperfect	Preterite	Future	Conditional	Present	Past	
comer	como	comía	comí	comeré	comería	coma	comiera	
	comes	comías	comiste	comerás	comerías	comas	comieras	come tú (no comas)
	come	comía	comió	comerá	comería	coma	comiera	coma Ud.
	comemos	comíamos	comimos	comeremos	comeríamos	comamos	comiéramos	comamos
	coméis	comíais	comisteis	comeréis	comeríais	comáis	comierais	comed (no comáis)
	comen	comían	comieron	comerán	comerían	coman	comieran	coman Uds.

3. vivir
Participles: viviendo, vivido

	INDICATIVE					SUBJUNCTIVE		IMPERATIVE
Infinitive	Present	Imperfect	Preterite	Future	Conditional	Present	Past	
vivir	vivo	vivía	viví	viviré	viviría	viva	viviera	
	vives	vivías	viviste	vivirás	vivirías	vivas	vivieras	vive tú (no vivas)
	vive	vivía	vivió	vivirá	viviría	viva	viviera	viva Ud.
	vivimos	vivíamos	vivimos	viviremos	viviríamos	vivamos	viviéramos	vivamos
	vivís	vivíais	vivisteis	viviréis	viviríais	viváis	vivierais	vivid (no viváis)
	viven	vivían	vivieron	vivirán	vivirían	vivan	vivieran	vivan Uds.

All verbs: compound tenses

PERFECT TENSES

INDICATIVE

Present Perfect		Past Perfect		Future Perfect		Conditional Perfect	
he		había		habré		habría	
has	hablado	habías	hablado	habrás	hablado	habrías	hablado
ha	comido	había	comido	habrá	comido	habría	comido
hemos	vivido	habíamos	vivido	habremos	vivido	habríamos	vivido
habéis		habíais		habréis		habríais	
han		habían		habrán		habrían	

SUBJUNCTIVE

Present Perfect		Past Perfect	
haya		hubiera	
hayas	hablado	hubieras	hablado
haya	comido	hubiera	comido
hayamos	vivido	hubiéramos	vivido
hayáis		hubierais	
hayan		hubieran	

PROGRESSIVE TENSES

	INDICATIVE				SUBJUNCTIVE	
Present Progressive	**Past Progressive**	**Future Progressive**	**Conditional Progressive**		**Present Progressive**	**Past Progressive**
estoy	estaba	estaré	estaría		esté	estuviera
estás	estabas	estarás	estarías		estés	estuvieras
está hablando	estaba hablando	estará hablando	estaría hablando		esté hablando	estuviera hablando
estamos comiendo	estábamos comiendo	estaremos comiendo	estaríamos comiendo		estemos comiendo	estuviéramos comiendo
estáis viviendo	estabais viviendo	estaréis viviendo	estaríais viviendo		estéis viviendo	estuvierais viviendo
están	estaban	estarán	estarían		estén	estuvieran

Irregular verbs

Infinitive	INDICATIVE					SUBJUNCTIVE		IMPERATIVE
	Present	**Imperfect**	**Preterite**	**Future**	**Conditional**	**Present**	**Past**	
4 caber	**quepo**	cabía	**cupe**	**cabré**	**cabría**	**quepa**	**cupiera**	
	cabes	cabías	**cupiste**	**cabrás**	**cabrías**	**quepas**	**cupieras**	cabe tú (no **quepas**)
Participles:	cabe	cabía	**cupo**	**cabrá**	**cabría**	**quepa**	**cupiera**	**quepa** Ud.
cabiendo	cabemos	cabíamos	**cupimos**	**cabremos**	**cabríamos**	**quepamos**	**cupiéramos**	**quepamos**
cabido	cabéis	cabíais	**cupisteis**	**cabréis**	**cabríais**	**quepáis**	**cupierais**	cabed (no **quepáis**)
	caben	cabían	**cupieron**	**cabrán**	**cabrían**	**quepan**	**cupieran**	**quepan** Uds.
5 caer(se)	**caigo**	caía	caí	caeré	caería	**caiga**	**cayera**	
	caes	caías	**caíste**	caerás	caerías	**caigas**	**cayeras**	cae tú (no **caigas**)
Participles:	cae	caía	**cayó**	caerá	caería	**caiga**	**cayera**	**caiga** Ud.
cayendo	caemos	caíamos	**caímos**	caeremos	caeríamos	**caigamos**	**cayéramos**	**caigamos**
caído	caéis	caíais	**caísteis**	caeréis	caeríais	**caigáis**	**cayerais**	caed (no **caigáis**)
	caen	caían	**cayeron**	caerán	caerían	**caigan**	**cayeran**	**caigan** Uds.
6 conducir	**conduzco**	conducía	**conduje**	conduciré	conduciría	**conduzca**	**condujera**	
(c:zc)	conduces	conducías	**condujiste**	conducirás	conducirías	**conduzcas**	**condujeras**	conduce tú (no **conduzcas**)
	conduce	conducía	**condujo**	conducirá	conduciría	**conduzca**	**condujera**	**conduzca** Ud.
Participles:	conducimos	conducíamos	**condujimos**	conduciremos	conduciríamos	**conduzcamos**	**condujéramos**	**conduzcamos**
conduciendo	conducís	conducíais	**condujisteis**	conduciréis	conduciríais	**conduzcáis**	**condujerais**	conducid (no **conduzcáis**)
conducido	conducen	conducían	**condujeron**	conducirán	conducirían	**conduzcan**	**condujeran**	**conduzcan** Uds.

7. dar
Participles: dando, dado

Mood	Forms
Present	doy, das, da, damos, dais, dan
Imperfect	daba, dabas, daba, dábamos, dabais, daban
Preterite	di, diste, dio, dimos, disteis, dieron
Future	daré, darás, dará, daremos, daréis, darán
Conditional	daría, darías, daría, daríamos, daríais, darían
Present Subjunctive	dé, des, dé, demos, deis, den
Past Subjunctive	diera, dieras, diera, diéramos, dierais, dieran
Imperative	da tú (no des), dé Ud., demos, dad (no deis), den Uds.

8. decir (e:i)
Participles: diciendo, dicho

Mood	Forms
Present	digo, dices, dice, decimos, decís, dicen
Imperfect	decía, decías, decía, decíamos, decíais, decían
Preterite	dije, dijiste, dijo, dijimos, dijisteis, dijeron
Future	diré, dirás, dirá, diremos, diréis, dirán
Conditional	diría, dirías, diría, diríamos, diríais, dirían
Present Subjunctive	diga, digas, diga, digamos, digáis, digan
Past Subjunctive	dijera, dijeras, dijera, dijéramos, dijerais, dijeran
Imperative	di tú (no digas), diga Ud., digamos, decid (no digáis), digan Uds.

9. estar
Participles: estando, estado

Mood	Forms
Present	estoy, estás, está, estamos, estáis, están
Imperfect	estaba, estabas, estaba, estábamos, estabais, estaban
Preterite	estuve, estuviste, estuvo, estuvimos, estuvisteis, estuvieron
Future	estaré, estarás, estará, estaremos, estaréis, estarán
Conditional	estaría, estarías, estaría, estaríamos, estaríais, estarían
Present Subjunctive	esté, estés, esté, estemos, estéis, estén
Past Subjunctive	estuviera, estuvieras, estuviera, estuviéramos, estuvierais, estuvieran
Imperative	está tú (no estés), esté Ud., estemos, estad (no estéis), estén Uds.

10. haber
Participles: habiendo, habido

Mood	Forms
Present	he, has, ha, hemos, habéis, han
Imperfect	había, habías, había, habíamos, habíais, habían
Preterite	hube, hubiste, hubo, hubimos, hubisteis, hubieron
Future	habré, habrás, habrá, habremos, habréis, habrán
Conditional	habría, habrías, habría, habríamos, habríais, habrían
Present Subjunctive	haya, hayas, haya, hayamos, hayáis, hayan
Past Subjunctive	hubiera, hubieras, hubiera, hubiéramos, hubierais, hubieran
Imperative	

11. hacer
Participles: haciendo, hecho

Mood	Forms
Present	hago, haces, hace, hacemos, hacéis, hacen
Imperfect	hacía, hacías, hacía, hacíamos, hacíais, hacían
Preterite	hice, hiciste, hizo, hicimos, hicisteis, hicieron
Future	haré, harás, hará, haremos, haréis, harán
Conditional	haría, harías, haría, haríamos, haríais, harían
Present Subjunctive	haga, hagas, haga, hagamos, hagáis, hagan
Past Subjunctive	hiciera, hicieras, hiciera, hiciéramos, hicierais, hicieran
Imperative	haz tú (no hagas), haga Ud., hagamos, haced (no hagáis), hagan Uds.

12. ir
Participles: yendo, ido

Mood	Forms
Present	voy, vas, va, vamos, vais, van
Imperfect	iba, ibas, iba, íbamos, ibais, iban
Preterite	fui, fuiste, fue, fuimos, fuisteis, fueron
Future	iré, irás, irá, iremos, iréis, irán
Conditional	iría, irías, iría, iríamos, iríais, irían
Present Subjunctive	vaya, vayas, vaya, vayamos, vayáis, vayan
Past Subjunctive	fuera, fueras, fuera, fuéramos, fuerais, fueran
Imperative	ve tú (no vayas), vaya Ud., vamos, id (no vayáis), vayan Uds.

13. oír (y)
Participles: oyendo, oído

Mood	Forms
Present	oigo, oyes, oye, oímos, oís, oyen
Imperfect	oía, oías, oía, oíamos, oíais, oían
Preterite	oí, oíste, oyó, oímos, oísteis, oyeron
Future	oiré, oirás, oirá, oiremos, oiréis, oirán
Conditional	oiría, oirías, oiría, oiríamos, oiríais, oirían
Present Subjunctive	oiga, oigas, oiga, oigamos, oigáis, oigan
Past Subjunctive	oyera, oyeras, oyera, oyéramos, oyerais, oyeran
Imperative	oye tú (no oigas), oiga Ud., oigamos, oíd (no oigáis), oigan Uds.

14 poder (o:ue)
Participles: **pudiendo**, podido

	INDICATIVE					SUBJUNCTIVE		IMPERATIVE
	Present	Imperfect	Preterite	Future	Conditional	Present	Past	
	puedo	podía	**pude**	**podré**	**podría**	**pueda**	**pudiera**	
	puedes	podías	**pudiste**	**podrás**	**podrías**	**puedas**	**pudieras**	**puede** tú (no **puedas**)
	puede	podía	**pudo**	**podrá**	**podría**	**pueda**	**pudiera**	**pueda** Ud.
	podemos	podíamos	**pudimos**	**podremos**	**podríamos**	podamos	**pudiéramos**	podamos
	podéis	podíais	**pudisteis**	**podréis**	**podríais**	podáis	**pudierais**	poded (no podáis)
	pueden	podían	**pudieron**	**podrán**	**podrían**	**puedan**	**pudieran**	**puedan** Uds.

15 poner
Participles: poniendo, **puesto**

	INDICATIVE					SUBJUNCTIVE		IMPERATIVE
	Present	Imperfect	Preterite	Future	Conditional	Present	Past	
	pongo	ponía	**puse**	**pondré**	**pondría**	**ponga**	**pusiera**	
	pones	ponías	**pusiste**	**pondrás**	**pondrías**	**pongas**	**pusieras**	**pon** tú (no **pongas**)
	pone	ponía	**puso**	**pondrá**	**pondría**	**ponga**	**pusiera**	**ponga** Ud.
	ponemos	poníamos	**pusimos**	**pondremos**	**pondríamos**	**pongamos**	**pusiéramos**	**pongamos**
	ponéis	poníais	**pusisteis**	**pondréis**	**pondríais**	**pongáis**	**pusierais**	poned (no **pongáis**)
	ponen	ponían	**pusieron**	**pondrán**	**pondrían**	**pongan**	**pusieran**	**pongan** Uds.

16 querer (e:ie)
Participles: queriendo, querido

	INDICATIVE					SUBJUNCTIVE		IMPERATIVE
	Present	Imperfect	Preterite	Future	Conditional	Present	Past	
	quiero	quería	**quise**	**querré**	**querría**	**quiera**	**quisiera**	
	quieres	querías	**quisiste**	**querrás**	**querrías**	**quieras**	**quisieras**	**quiere** tú (no **quieras**)
	quiere	quería	**quiso**	**querrá**	**querría**	**quiera**	**quisiera**	**quiera** Ud.
	queremos	queríamos	**quisimos**	**querremos**	**querríamos**	queramos	**quisiéramos**	**queramos**
	queréis	queríais	**quisisteis**	**querréis**	**querríais**	queráis	**quisierais**	quered (no queráis)
	quieren	querían	**quisieron**	**querrán**	**querrían**	**quieran**	**quisieran**	**quieran** Uds.

17 saber
Participles: sabiendo, sabido

	INDICATIVE					SUBJUNCTIVE		IMPERATIVE
	Present	Imperfect	Preterite	Future	Conditional	Present	Past	
	sé	sabía	**supe**	**sabré**	**sabría**	**sepa**	**supiera**	
	sabes	sabías	**supiste**	**sabrás**	**sabrías**	**sepas**	**supieras**	sabe tú (no **sepas**)
	sabe	sabía	**supo**	**sabrá**	**sabría**	**sepa**	**supiera**	**sepa** Ud.
	sabemos	sabíamos	**supimos**	**sabremos**	**sabríamos**	**sepamos**	**supiéramos**	**sepamos**
	sabéis	sabíais	**supisteis**	**sabréis**	**sabríais**	**sepáis**	**supierais**	sabed (no **sepáis**)
	saben	sabían	**supieron**	**sabrán**	**sabrían**	**sepan**	**supieran**	**sepan** Uds.

18 salir
Participles: saliendo, salido

	INDICATIVE					SUBJUNCTIVE		IMPERATIVE
	Present	Imperfect	Preterite	Future	Conditional	Present	Past	
	salgo	salía	salí	**saldré**	**saldría**	**salga**	saliera	
	sales	salías	saliste	**saldrás**	**saldrías**	**salgas**	salieras	**sal** tú (no **salgas**)
	sale	salía	salió	**saldrá**	**saldría**	**salga**	saliera	**salga** Ud.
	salimos	salíamos	salimos	**saldremos**	**saldríamos**	**salgamos**	saliéramos	**salgamos**
	salís	salíais	salisteis	**saldréis**	**saldríais**	**salgáis**	salierais	salid (no **salgáis**)
	salen	salían	salieron	**saldrán**	**saldrían**	**salgan**	salieran	**salgan** Uds.

19 ser
Participles: siendo, sido

	INDICATIVE					SUBJUNCTIVE		IMPERATIVE
	Present	Imperfect	Preterite	Future	Conditional	Present	Past	
	soy	era	**fui**	seré	sería	sea	fuera	
	eres	eras	**fuiste**	serás	serías	seas	fueras	**sé** tú (no seas)
	es	era	**fue**	será	sería	sea	fuera	sea Ud.
	somos	**éramos**	**fuimos**	seremos	seríamos	seamos	**fuéramos**	seamos
	sois	erais	**fuisteis**	seréis	seríais	seáis	fuerais	sed (no seáis)
	son	eran	**fueron**	serán	serían	sean	fueran	sean Uds.

20 tener (e:ie)
Participles: teniendo, tenido

	INDICATIVE					SUBJUNCTIVE		IMPERATIVE
	Present	Imperfect	Preterite	Future	Conditional	Present	Past	
	tengo	tenía	**tuve**	**tendré**	**tendría**	**tenga**	**tuviera**	
	tienes	tenías	**tuviste**	**tendrás**	**tendrías**	**tengas**	**tuvieras**	**ten** tú (no **tengas**)
	tiene	tenía	**tuvo**	**tendrá**	**tendría**	**tenga**	**tuviera**	**tenga** Ud.
	tenemos	teníamos	**tuvimos**	**tendremos**	**tendríamos**	**tengamos**	**tuviéramos**	**tengamos**
	tenéis	teníais	**tuvisteis**	**tendréis**	**tendríais**	**tengáis**	**tuvierais**	tened (no **tengáis**)
	tienen	tenían	**tuvieron**	**tendrán**	**tendrían**	**tengan**	**tuvieran**	**tengan** Uds.

Verb tables

21 traer

Participles: **trayendo**, **traído**

	INDICATIVE					SUBJUNCTIVE		IMPERATIVE
Infinitive	Present	Imperfect	Preterite	Future	Conditional	Present	Past	
traer	**traigo**	traía	**traje**	traeré	traería	**traiga**	**trajera**	
	traes	traías	**trajiste**	traerás	traerías	**traigas**	**trajeras**	trae tú (no **traigas**)
	trae	traía	**trajo**	traerá	traería	**traiga**	**trajera**	**traiga** Ud.
	traemos	traíamos	**trajimos**	traeremos	traeríamos	**traigamos**	**trajéramos**	**traigamos**
	traéis	traíais	**trajisteis**	traeréis	traeríais	**traigáis**	**trajerais**	traed (no **traigáis**)
	traen	traían	**trajeron**	traerán	traerían	**traigan**	**trajeran**	**traigan** Uds.

22 venir (e:ie)

Participles: **viniendo**, venido

	INDICATIVE					SUBJUNCTIVE		IMPERATIVE
Infinitive	Present	Imperfect	Preterite	Future	Conditional	Present	Past	
venir	**vengo**	venía	**vine**	**vendré**	**vendría**	**venga**	**viniera**	
	vienes	venías	**viniste**	**vendrás**	**vendrías**	**vengas**	**vinieras**	**ven** tú (no **vengas**)
	viene	venía	**vino**	**vendrá**	**vendría**	**venga**	**viniera**	**venga** Ud.
	venimos	veníamos	**vinimos**	**vendremos**	**vendríamos**	**vengamos**	**viniéramos**	**vengamos**
	venís	veníais	**vinisteis**	**vendréis**	**vendríais**	**vengáis**	**vinierais**	venid (no **vengáis**)
	vienen	venían	**vinieron**	**vendrán**	**vendrían**	**vengan**	**vinieran**	**vengan** Uds.

23 ver

Participles: **viendo**, **visto**

	INDICATIVE					SUBJUNCTIVE		IMPERATIVE
Infinitive	Present	Imperfect	Preterite	Future	Conditional	Present	Past	
ver	**veo**	**veía**	**vi**	veré	vería	**vea**	**viera**	
	ves	**veías**	**viste**	verás	verías	**veas**	**vieras**	**ve** tú (no **veas**)
	ve	**veía**	**vio**	verá	vería	**vea**	**viera**	**vea** Ud.
	vemos	**veíamos**	**vimos**	veremos	veríamos	**veamos**	**viéramos**	**veamos**
	veis	**veíais**	**visteis**	veréis	veríais	**veáis**	**vierais**	ved (no **veáis**)
	ven	**veían**	**vieron**	verán	verían	**vean**	**vieran**	**vean** Uds.

Stem-changing verbs

24 contar (o:ue)

Participles: contando, contado

	INDICATIVE					SUBJUNCTIVE		IMPERATIVE
Infinitive	Present	Imperfect	Preterite	Future	Conditional	Present	Past	
contar	**cuento**	contaba	conté	contaré	contaría	**cuente**	contara	
	cuentas	contabas	contaste	contarás	contarías	**cuentes**	contaras	**cuenta** tú (no **cuentes**)
	cuenta	contaba	contó	contará	contaría	**cuente**	contara	**cuente** Ud.
	contamos	contábamos	contamos	contaremos	contaríamos	contemos	contáramos	contemos
	contáis	contabais	contasteis	contaréis	contaríais	contéis	contarais	contad (no contéis)
	cuentan	contaban	contaron	contarán	contarían	**cuenten**	contaran	**cuenten** Uds.

25 dormir (o:ue)

Participles: **durmiendo**, dormido

	INDICATIVE					SUBJUNCTIVE		IMPERATIVE
Infinitive	Present	Imperfect	Preterite	Future	Conditional	Present	Past	
dormir	**duermo**	dormía	dormí	dormiré	dormiría	**duerma**	**durmiera**	
	duermes	dormías	dormiste	dormirás	dormirías	**duermas**	**durmieras**	**duerme** tú (no **duermas**)
	duerme	dormía	**durmió**	dormirá	dormiría	**duerma**	**durmiera**	**duerma** Ud.
	dormimos	dormíamos	dormimos	dormiremos	dormiríamos	**durmamos**	**durmiéramos**	**durmamos**
	dormís	dormíais	dormisteis	dormiréis	dormiríais	**durmáis**	**durmierais**	dormid (no **durmáis**)
	duermen	dormían	**durmieron**	dormirán	dormirían	**duerman**	**durmieran**	**duerman** Uds.

26 empezar (e:ie) (z:c)

Participles: empezando, empezado

	INDICATIVE					SUBJUNCTIVE		IMPERATIVE
Infinitive	Present	Imperfect	Preterite	Future	Conditional	Present	Past	
empezar	**empiezo**	empezaba	**empecé**	empezaré	empezaría	**empiece**	empezara	
	empiezas	empezabas	empezaste	empezarás	empezarías	**empieces**	empezaras	**empieza** tú (no **empieces**)
	empieza	empezaba	empezó	empezará	empezaría	**empiece**	empezara	**empiece** Ud.
	empezamos	empezábamos	empezamos	empezaremos	empezaríamos	**empecemos**	empezáramos	**empecemos**
	empezáis	empezabais	empezasteis	empezaréis	empezaríais	**empecéis**	empezarais	empezad (no **empecéis**)
	empiezan	empezaban	empezaron	empezarán	empezarían	**empiecen**	empezaran	**empiecen** Uds.

27 entender (e:ie) — Participles: entendiendo, entendido

	Present	Imperfect	Preterite	Future	Conditional	Subj. Present	Subj. Past	Imperative
	entiendo	entendía	entendí	entenderé	entendería	entienda	entendiera	
	entiendes	entendías	entendiste	entenderás	entenderías	entiendas	entendieras	entiende tú (no entiendas)
	entiende	entendía	entendió	entenderá	entendería	entienda	entendiera	entienda Ud.
	entendemos	entendíamos	entendimos	entenderemos	entenderíamos	entendamos	entendiéramos	entendamos
	entendéis	entendíais	entendisteis	entenderéis	entenderíais	entendáis	entendierais	entended (no entendáis)
	entienden	entendían	entendieron	entenderán	entenderían	entiendan	entendieran	entiendan Uds.

28 jugar (u:ue) (g:gu) — Participles: jugando, jugado

	Present	Imperfect	Preterite	Future	Conditional	Subj. Present	Subj. Past	Imperative
	juego	jugaba	jugué	jugaré	jugaría	juegue	jugara	
	juegas	jugabas	jugaste	jugarás	jugarías	juegues	jugaras	juega tú (no juegues)
	juega	jugaba	jugó	jugará	jugaría	juegue	jugara	juegue Ud.
	jugamos	jugábamos	jugamos	jugaremos	jugaríamos	juguemos	jugáramos	juguemos
	jugáis	jugabais	jugasteis	jugaréis	jugaríais	juguéis	jugarais	jugad (no juguéis)
	juegan	jugaban	jugaron	jugarán	jugarían	jueguen	jugaran	jueguen Uds.

29 pedir (e:i) — Participles: pidiendo, pedido

	Present	Imperfect	Preterite	Future	Conditional	Subj. Present	Subj. Past	Imperative
	pido	pedía	pedí	pediré	pediría	pida	pidiera	
	pides	pedías	pediste	pedirás	pedirías	pidas	pidieras	pide tú (no pidas)
	pide	pedía	pidió	pedirá	pediría	pida	pidiera	pida Ud.
	pedimos	pedíamos	pedimos	pediremos	pediríamos	pidamos	pidiéramos	pidamos
	pedís	pedíais	pedisteis	pediréis	pediríais	pidáis	pidierais	pedid (no pidáis)
	piden	pedían	pidieron	pedirán	pedirían	pidan	pidieran	pidan Uds.

30 pensar (e:ie) — Participles: pensando, pensado

	Present	Imperfect	Preterite	Future	Conditional	Subj. Present	Subj. Past	Imperative
	pienso	pensaba	pensé	pensaré	pensaría	piense	pensara	
	piensas	pensabas	pensaste	pensarás	pensarías	pienses	pensaras	piensa tú (no pienses)
	piensa	pensaba	pensó	pensará	pensaría	piense	pensara	piense Ud.
	pensamos	pensábamos	pensamos	pensaremos	pensaríamos	pensemos	pensáramos	pensemos
	pensáis	pensabais	pensasteis	pensaréis	pensaríais	penséis	pensarais	pensad (no penséis)
	piensan	pensaban	pensaron	pensarán	pensarían	piensen	pensaran	piensen Uds.

31 reír(se) (e:i) — Participles: riendo, reído

	Present	Imperfect	Preterite	Future	Conditional	Subj. Present	Subj. Past	Imperative
	río	reía	reí	reiré	reiría	ría	riera	
	ríes	reías	reíste	reirás	reirías	rías	rieras	ríe tú (no rías)
	ríe	reía	rió	reirá	reiría	ría	riera	ría Ud.
	reímos	reíamos	reímos	reiremos	reiríamos	riamos	riéramos	riamos
	reís	reíais	reísteis	reiréis	reiríais	riáis	rierais	reíd (no riáis)
	ríen	reían	rieron	reirán	reirían	rían	rieran	rían Uds.

32 seguir (e:i) (gu:g) — Participles: siguiendo, seguido

	Present	Imperfect	Preterite	Future	Conditional	Subj. Present	Subj. Past	Imperative
	sigo	seguía	seguí	seguiré	seguiría	siga	siguiera	
	sigues	seguías	seguiste	seguirás	seguirías	sigas	siguieras	sigue tú (no sigas)
	sigue	seguía	siguió	seguirá	seguiría	siga	siguiera	siga Ud.
	seguimos	seguíamos	seguimos	seguiremos	seguiríamos	sigamos	siguiéramos	sigamos
	seguís	seguíais	seguisteis	seguiréis	seguiríais	sigáis	siguierais	seguid (no sigáis)
	siguen	seguían	siguieron	seguirán	seguirían	sigan	siguieran	sigan Uds.

33 sentir (e:ie) — Participles: sintiendo, sentido

	Present	Imperfect	Preterite	Future	Conditional	Subj. Present	Subj. Past	Imperative
	siento	sentía	sentí	sentiré	sentiría	sienta	sintiera	
	sientes	sentías	sentiste	sentirás	sentirías	sientas	sintieras	siente tú (no sientas)
	siente	sentía	sintió	sentirá	sentiría	sienta	sintiera	sienta Ud.
	sentimos	sentíamos	sentimos	sentiremos	sentiríamos	sintamos	sintiéramos	sintamos
	sentís	sentíais	sentisteis	sentiréis	sentiríais	sintáis	sintierais	sentid (no sintáis)
	sienten	sentían	sintieron	sentirán	sentirían	sientan	sintieran	sientan Uds.

| | INDICATIVE | | | | | SUBJUNCTIVE | | IMPERATIVE |
Infinitive	Present	Imperfect	Preterite	Future	Conditional	Present	Past	
34 volver (o:ue)	**vuelvo**	volvía	volví	volveré	volvería	**vuelva**	volviera	
	vuelves	volvías	volviste	volverás	volverías	**vuelvas**	volvieras	**vuelve** tú (no **vuelvas**)
	vuelve	volvía	volvió	volverá	volvería	**vuelva**	volviera	**vuelva** Ud.
Participles:	volvemos	volvíamos	volvimos	volveremos	volveríamos	volvamos	volviéramos	volvamos
volviendo	volvéis	volvíais	volvisteis	volveréis	volveríais	volváis	volvierais	volved (no volváis)
vuelto	**vuelven**	volvían	volvieron	volverán	volverían	**vuelvan**	volvieran	**vuelvan** Uds.

Verbs with spelling changes only

| | INDICATIVE | | | | | SUBJUNCTIVE | | IMPERATIVE |
Infinitive	Present	Imperfect	Preterite	Future	Conditional	Present	Past	
35 conocer (c:zc)	**conozco**	conocía	conocí	conoceré	conocería	**conozca**	conociera	
	conoces	conocías	conociste	conocerás	conocerías	**conozcas**	conocieras	conoce tú (no **conozcas**)
	conoce	conocía	conoció	conocerá	conocería	**conozca**	conociera	**conozca** Ud.
Participles:	conocemos	conocíamos	conocimos	conoceremos	conoceríamos	**conozcamos**	conociéramos	**conozcamos**
conociendo	conocéis	conocíais	conocisteis	conoceréis	conoceríais	**conozcáis**	conocierais	conoced (no **conozcáis**)
conocido	conocen	conocían	conocieron	conocerán	conocerían	**conozcan**	conocieran	**conozcan** Uds.
36 creer (y)	creo	creía	**creí**	creeré	creería	crea	**creyera**	
	crees	creías	**creíste**	creerás	creerías	creas	**creyeras**	cree tú (no creas)
	cree	creía	**creyó**	creerá	creería	crea	**creyera**	crea Ud.
Participles:	creemos	creíamos	**creímos**	creeremos	creeríamos	creamos	**creyéramos**	creamos
creyendo	creéis	creíais	**creísteis**	creeréis	creeríais	creáis	**creyerais**	creed (no creáis)
creído	creen	creían	**creyeron**	creerán	creerían	crean	**creyeran**	crean Uds.
37 cruzar (z:c)	cruzo	cruzaba	**crucé**	cruzaré	cruzaría	**cruce**	cruzara	
	cruzas	cruzabas	cruzaste	cruzarás	cruzarías	**cruces**	cruzaras	cruza tú (no **cruces**)
	cruza	cruzaba	cruzó	cruzará	cruzaría	**cruce**	cruzara	**cruce** Ud.
Participles:	cruzamos	cruzábamos	cruzamos	cruzaremos	cruzaríamos	**crucemos**	cruzáramos	**crucemos**
cruzando	cruzáis	cruzabais	cruzasteis	cruzaréis	cruzaríais	**crucéis**	cruzarais	cruzad (no **crucéis**)
cruzado	cruzan	cruzaban	cruzaron	cruzarán	cruzarían	**crucen**	cruzaran	**crucen** Uds.
38 destruir (y)	**destruyo**	destruía	destruí	destruiré	destruiría	**destruya**	**destruyera**	
	destruyes	destruías	destruiste	destruirás	destruirías	**destruyas**	**destruyeras**	**destruye** tú (no **destruyas**)
	destruye	destruía	**destruyó**	destruirá	destruiría	**destruya**	**destruyera**	**destruya** Ud.
Participles:	destruimos	destruíamos	destruimos	destruiremos	destruiríamos	**destruyamos**	**destruyéramos**	**destruyamos**
destruyendo	destruís	destruíais	destruisteis	destruiréis	destruiríais	**destruyáis**	**destruyerais**	destruid (no **destruyáis**)
destruido	**destruyen**	destruían	**destruyeron**	destruirán	destruirían	**destruyan**	**destruyeran**	**destruyan** Uds.
39 enviar (envío)	**envío**	enviaba	envié	enviaré	enviaría	**envíe**	enviara	
	envías	enviabas	enviaste	enviarás	enviarías	**envíes**	enviaras	**envía** tú (no **envíes**)
	envía	enviaba	envió	enviará	enviaría	**envíe**	enviara	**envíe** Ud.
Participles:	enviamos	enviábamos	enviamos	enviaremos	enviaríamos	**enviemos**	enviáramos	enviemos
enviando	enviáis	enviabais	enviasteis	enviaréis	enviaríais	**enviéis**	enviarais	enviad (no **enviéis**)
enviado	**envían**	enviaban	enviaron	enviarán	enviarían	**envíen**	enviaran	**envíen** Uds.

Infinitive	INDICATIVE					SUBJUNCTIVE		IMPERATIVE
	Present	Imperfect	Preterite	Future	Conditional	Present	Past	
40 graduarse (gradúo)	gradúo	graduaba	gradué	graduaré	graduaría	gradúe	graduara	
	gradúas	graduabas	graduaste	graduarás	graduarías	gradúes	graduaras	gradúa tú (no gradúes)
	gradúa	graduaba	graduó	graduará	graduaría	gradúe	graduara	gradúe Ud.
Participles:	graduamos	graduábamos	graduamos	graduaremos	graduaríamos	graduemos	graduáramos	graduemos
graduando	graduáis	graduabais	graduasteis	graduaréis	graduaríais	graduéis	graduarais	graduad (no graduéis)
graduado	gradúan	graduaban	graduaron	graduarán	graduarían	gradúen	graduaran	gradúen Uds.
41 llegar (g:gu)	llego	llegaba	llegué	llegaré	llegaría	llegue	llegara	
	llegas	llegabas	llegaste	llegarás	llegarías	llegues	llegaras	llega tú (no llegues)
	llega	llegaba	llegó	llegará	llegaría	llegue	llegara	llegue Ud.
Participles:	llegamos	llegábamos	llegamos	llegaremos	llegaríamos	lleguemos	llegáramos	lleguemos
llegando	llegáis	llegabais	llegasteis	llegaréis	llegaríais	lleguéis	llegarais	llegad (no lleguéis)
llegado	llegan	llegaban	llegaron	llegarán	llegarían	lleguen	llegaran	lleguen Uds.
42 proteger (g:j)	protejo	protegía	protegí	protegeré	protegería	proteja	protegiera	
	proteges	protegías	protegiste	protegerás	protegerías	protejas	protegieras	protege tú (no protejas)
	protege	protegía	protegió	protegerá	protegería	proteja	protegiera	proteja Ud.
Participles:	protegemos	protegíamos	protegimos	protegeremos	protegeríamos	protejamos	protegiéramos	protejamos
protegiendo	protegéis	protegíais	protegisteis	protegeréis	protegeríais	protejáis	protegierais	proteged (no protejáis)
protegido	protegen	protegían	protegieron	protegerán	protegerían	protejan	protegieran	protejan Uds.
43 tocar (c:qu)	toco	tocaba	toqué	tocaré	tocaría	toque	tocara	
	tocas	tocabas	tocaste	tocarás	tocarías	toques	tocaras	toca tú (no toques)
	toca	tocaba	tocó	tocará	tocaría	toque	tocara	toque Ud.
Participles:	tocamos	tocábamos	tocamos	tocaremos	tocaríamos	toquemos	tocáramos	toquemos
tocando	tocáis	tocabais	tocasteis	tocaréis	tocaríais	toquéis	tocarais	tocad (no toquéis)
tocado	tocan	tocaban	tocaron	tocarán	tocarían	toquen	tocaran	toquen Uds.

Guide to Vocabulary

All active vocabulary in ¡ADELANTE! is presented in this glossary. The first number after an entry refers to the volume of ¡ADELANTE! where the word is activated; the second refers to the lesson number.

aceite 2.2 (Activated in *¡ADELANTE!* **DOS** , Lección 2)

posible 3.1 (Activated in *¡ADELANTE!* **TRES** , Lección 1)

Note on alphabetization

For purposes of alphabetization, **ch** and **ll** are not treated as separate letters, but **ñ** follows **n**. Therefore, in this glossary you will find that **año**, for example, appears after **anuncio**.

Abbreviations used in this glossary

adj.	adjective	*form.*	formal	*pl.*	plural
adv.	adverb	*indef.*	indefinite	*poss.*	possessive
art.	article	*interj.*	interjection	*prep.*	preposition
conj.	conjunction	*i.o.*	indirect object	*pron.*	pronoun
def.	definite	*m.*	masculine	*ref.*	reflexive
d.o.	direct object	*n.*	noun	*sing.*	singular
f.	feminine	*obj.*	object	*sub.*	subject
fam.	familiar	*p.p.*	past participle	*v.*	verb

Spanish-English

A

a *prep.* at; to **1.1**
  ¿A qué hora...? At what time...? **1.1**
  a dieta on a diet **3.3**
  a la derecha to the right **1.2**
  a la izquierda to the left **1.2**
  a la plancha grilled **2.2**
  a la(s) + *time* at + *time* **1.1**
  a menos que unless **3.1**
  a menudo *adv.* often **2.4**
  a nombre de in the name of **1.5**
  a plazos in installments **3.4**
  A sus órdenes. At your service.
  a tiempo *adv.* on time **2.4**
  a veces *adv.* sometimes **2.4**
  a ver let's see **1.2**
¡Abajo! *adv.* Down! **3.3**
abeja *f.* bee
abierto/a *adj.* open **1.5, 3.2**
abogado/a *m., f.* lawyer **3.4**
abrazar(se) *v.* to hug; to embrace (each other) **2.5**
abrazo *m.* hug
abrigo *m.* coat **1.6**
abril *m.* April **1.5**
abrir *v.* to open **1.3**
abuelo/a *m., f.* grandfather; grandmother **1.3**
abuelos *pl.* grandparents **1.3**
aburrido/a *adj.* bored; boring **1.5**

aburrir *v.* to bore **2.1**
aburrirse *v.* to get bored **3.5**
acabar de (+ *inf.*) *v.* to have just done something **1.6**
acampar *v.* to camp **1.5**
accidente *m.* accident **2.4**
acción *f.* action **3.5**
  de acción action (genre) **3.5**
aceite *m.* oil **2.2**
aceptar: ¡Acepto casarme contigo! I'll marry you! **3.5**
ácido/a *adj.* acid **3.1**
acompañar *v.* to accompany **3.2**
aconsejar *v.* to advise **2.6**
acontecimiento *m.* event **3.6**
acordarse (de) (o:ue) *v.* to remember **2.1**
acostarse (o:ue) *v.* to go to bed **2.1**
activo/a *adj.* active **3.3**
actor *m.* actor **3.4**
actriz *f.* actor **3.4**
actualidades *f., pl.* news; current events **3.6**
acuático/a *adj.* aquatic **1.4**
adelgazar *v.* to lose weight; to slim down **3.3**
además (de) *adv.* furthermore; besides **2.4**
adicional *adj.* additional
adiós *m.* good-bye **1.1**
adjetivo *m.* adjective
administración de empresas *f.* business administration **1.2**
adolescencia *f.* adolescence **2.3**
¿adónde? *adv.* where (to)? (destination) **1.2**
aduana *f.* customs **1.5**

aeróbico/a *adj.* aerobic **3.3**
aeropuerto *m.* airport **1.5**
afectado/a *adj.* affected **3.1**
afeitarse *v.* to shave **2.1**
aficionado/a *adj.* fan **1.4**
afirmativo/a *adj.* affirmative
afuera *adv.* outside **1.5**
afueras *f., pl.* suburbs; outskirts **2.6**
agencia de viajes *f.* travel agency **1.5**
agente de viajes *m., f.* travel agent **1.5**
agosto *m.* August **1.5**
agradable *adj.* pleasant **1.5**
agua *f.* water **2.2**
  agua mineral mineral water **2.2**
aguantar *v.* to endure, to hold up **3.2**
ahora *adv.* now **1.2**
  ahora mismo right now **1.5**
ahorrar *v.* to save (money) **3.2**
ahorros *m.* savings **3.2**
aire *m.* air **1.5**
ajo *m.* garlic **2.2**
al (*contraction of* **a + el**) **1.2**
  al aire libre open-air **1.6**
  al contado in cash **3.2**
  (al) este (to the) east **3.2**
  al fondo (de) at the end (of) **2.6**
  al lado de beside **1.2**
  (al) norte (to the) north **3.2**
  (al) oeste (to the) west **3.2**
  (al) sur (to the) south **3.2**
alcoba *f.* bedroom **2.6**
alcohol *m.* alcohol **3.3**
alcohólico/a *adj.* alcoholic **3.3**

alegrarse (de) *v.* to be happy 3.1
alegre *adj.* happy; joyful 1.5
alegría *f.* happiness 2.3
alemán, alemana *adj.* German 1.3
alérgico/a *adj.* allergic 2.4
alfombra *f.* carpet; rug 2.6
algo *pron.* something; anything 2.1
algodón *m.* cotton 1.6
alguien *pron.* someone; somebody; anyone 2.1
algún, alguno/a(s) *adj.* any; some 2.1
alimento *m.* food
  alimentación *f.* diet
aliviar *v.* to reduce 3.3
  aliviar el estrés/la tensión to reduce stress/tension 3.3
allá *adv.* over there 1.2
allí *adv.* there 1.2
  allí mismo right there 3.2
alma *f.* soul 2.3
almacén *m.* department store 1.6
almohada *f.* pillow 2.6
almorzar (o:ue) *v.* to have lunch 1.4
almuerzo *m.* lunch 2.2
aló *interj.* hello (*on the telephone*) 2.5
alquilar *v.* to rent 2.6
alquiler *m.* rent (payment) 2.6
altar *m.* altar 2.3
altillo *m.* attic 2.6
alto/a *adj.* tall 1.3
aluminio *m.* aluminum 3.1
ama de casa *m., f.* housekeeper; caretaker 2.6
amable *adj.* nice; friendly
amarillo/a *adj.* yellow 1.6
amigo/a *m., f.* friend 1.3
amistad *f.* friendship 2.3
amor *m.* love 2.3
  amor a primera vista love at first sight 2.3
anaranjado/a *adj.* orange 1.6
ándale *interj.* come on 3.2
andar *v.* **en patineta** to skateboard 1.4
ángel *m.* angel 2.3
anillo *m.* ring 3.5
animal *m.* animal 3.1
aniversario (de bodas) *m.* (wedding) anniversary 2.3
anoche *adv.* last night 1.6
anteayer *adv.* the day before yesterday 1.6
antes *adv.* before 2.1
  antes (de) que *conj.* before 3.1
  antes de *prep.* before 2.1
antibiótico *m.* antibiotic 2.4
antipático/a *adj.* unpleasant 1.3
anunciar *v.* to announce; to advertise 3.6
anuncio *m.* advertisement 3.4
año *m.* year 1.5
  año pasado last year 1.6
apagar *v.* to turn off 2.5

aparato *m.* appliance
apartamento *m.* apartment 2.6
apellido *m.* last name 1.3
apenas *adv.* hardly; scarcely 2.4
aplaudir *v.* to applaud 3.5
apreciar *v.* to appreciate 3.5
aprender (a + *inf.*) *v.* to learn 1.3
apurarse *v.* to hurry; to rush 3.3
aquel, aquella *adj.* that (over there) 1.6
aquél, aquélla *pron.* that (over there) 1.6
aquello *neuter, pron.* that; that thing; that fact 1.6
aquellos/as *pl. adj.* those (over there) 1.6
aquéllos/as *pl. pron.* those (ones) (over there) 1.6
aquí *adv.* here 1.1
  Aquí está(n)... Here is/ are... 1.5
árbol *m.* tree 3.1
archivo *m.* file 2.5
arete *m.* earring 1.6
Argentina *f.* Argentina 1.1
argentino/a *adj.* Argentine 1.3
armario *m.* closet 2.6
arqueología *f.* archaeology 1.2
arqueólogo/a *m., f.* archaeologist 3.4
arquitecto/a *m., f.* architect 3.4
arrancar *v.* to start (*a car*) 2.5
arreglar *v.* to fix; to arrange 2.5; to neaten; to straighten up 2.6
arreglarse *v.* to get ready 2.1; to fix oneself (*clothes, hair, etc., to go out*) 2.1
arriba: hasta arriba to the top 3.3
arroba *f.* @ symbol 2.5
arroz *m.* rice 2.2
arte *m.* art 1.2
artes *f., pl.* arts 3.5
artesanía *f.* craftsmanship; crafts 3.5
artículo *m.* article 3.6
artista *m., f.* artist 1.3
artístico/a *adj.* artistic 3.5
arveja *f.* pea 2.2
asado/a *adj.* roast 2.2
ascenso *m.* promotion 3.4
ascensor *m.* elevator 1.5
así *adv.* like this; so (*in such a way*) 2.4
asistir (a) *v.* to attend 1.3
aspiradora *f.* vacuum cleaner 2.6
aspirante *m., f.* candidate; applicant 3.4
aspirina *f.* aspirin 2.4
atún *m.* tuna 2.2
aumentar *v.* to grow; to get bigger 3.1
aumentar *v.* **de peso** to gain weight 3.3
aumento *m.* increase 3.4
  aumento de sueldo pay raise 3.4

aunque although
autobús *m.* bus 1.1
automático/a *adj.* automatic
auto(móvil) *m.* auto(mobile) 1.5
autopista *f.* highway 2.5
ave *f.* bird 3.1
avenida *f.* avenue
aventura *f.* adventure 3.5
  de aventura adventure (genre) 3.5
avergonzado/a *adj.* embarrassed 1.5
avión *m.* airplane 1.5
¡Ay! *interj.* Oh!
  ¡Ay, qué dolor! Oh, what pain!
ayer *adv.* yesterday 1.6
ayudar(se) *v.* to help (each other) 2.5, 2.6
azúcar *m.* sugar 2.2
azul *adj. m., f.* blue 1.6

B

bailar *v.* to dance 1.2
bailarín/bailarina *m., f.* dancer 3.5
baile *m.* dance 3.5
bajar(se) de *v.* to get off of/out of (a vehicle) 2.5
bajo/a *adj.* short (*in height*) 1.3
bajo control under control 2.1
balcón *m.* balcony 2.6
balde *m.* bucket 1.5
ballena *f.* whale 3.1
baloncesto *m.* basketball 1.4
banana *f.* banana 2.2
banco *m.* bank 3.2
banda *f.* band 3.5
bandera *f.* flag
bañarse *v.* to bathe; to take a bath 2.1
baño *m.* bathroom 2.1
barato/a *adj.* cheap 1.6
barco *m.* boat 1.5
barrer *v.* to sweep 2.6
  barrer el suelo to sweep the floor 2.6
barrio *m.* neighborhood 2.6
bastante *adv.* enough; rather 2.4
basura *f.* trash 2.6
baúl *m.* trunk 2.5
beber *v.* to drink 1.3
bebida *f.* drink 2.2
  bebida alcohólica *f.* alcoholic beverage 3.3
béisbol *m.* baseball 1.4
bellas artes *f., pl.* fine arts 3.5
belleza *f.* beauty 3.2
beneficio *m.* benefit 3.4
besar(se) *v.* to kiss (each other) 2.5
beso *m.* kiss 2.3
biblioteca *f.* library 1.2
bicicleta *f.* bicycle 1.4
bien *adj.* well 1.1
bienestar *m.* well-being 3.3
bienvenido(s)/a(s) *adj.* welcome 1.1

billete *m.* paper money; ticket
billón *m.* trillion
biología *f.* biology 1.2
bisabuelo/a *m., f.* great-grand-father/great-grandmother 1.3
bistec *m.* steak 2.2
bizcocho *m.* biscuit
blanco/a *adj.* white 1.6
blog *m.* blog 2.5
(blue)jeans *m., pl.* jeans 1.6
blusa *f.* blouse 1.6
boca *f.* mouth 2.4
boda *f.* wedding 2.3
boleto *m.* ticket 1.2, 3.5
bolsa *f.* purse, bag 1.6
bombero/a *m., f.* firefighter 3.4
bonito/a *adj.* pretty 1.3
borrador *m.* eraser 1.2
borrar *v.* to erase 2.5
bosque *m.* forest 3.1
   bosque tropical tropical forest; rain forest 3.1
bota *f.* boot 1.6
botella *f.* bottle 2.3
   botella de vino bottle of wine 2.3
botones *m., f. sing.* bellhop 1.5
brazo *m.* arm 2.4
brindar *v.* to toast (*drink*) 2.3
bucear *v.* to scuba dive 1.4
bueno *adv.* well
buen, bueno/a *adj.* good 1.3, 1.6
   buena forma good shape (*physical*) 3.3
   Buenas noches. Good evening; Good night. 1.1
   Buenas tardes. Good afternoon. 1.1
   buenísimo/a extremely good
   Bueno. Hello. (on telephone) 2.5
   Buenos días. Good morning. 1.1
bulevar *m.* boulevard
buscar *v.* to look for 1.2
buzón *m.* mailbox 3.2

C

caballero *m.* gentleman, sir 2.2
caballo *m.* horse 1.5
cabe: no cabe duda de there's no doubt 3.1
cabeza *f.* head 2.4
cada *adj. m., f.* each 1.6
caerse *v.* to fall (down) 2.4
café *m.* café 1.4; *adj. m., f.* brown 1.6; *m.* coffee 2.2
cafeína *f.* caffeine 3.2
cafetera *f.* coffee maker 2.6
cafetería *f.* cafeteria 1.2
caído/a *p.p.* fallen 3.2
caja *f.* cash register 1.6
cajero/a *m., f.* cashier 3.2
   cajero automático *m.* ATM 3.2
calavera de azúcar *f.* skull made out of sugar 2.3

calcetín (calcetines) *m.* sock(s) 1.6
calculadora *f.* calculator 1.2
calentamiento global *m.* global warming 3.1
calentarse (e:ie) *v.* to warm up 3.3
calidad *f.* quality 1.6
calle *f.* street 2.5
caloría *f.* calorie 3.3
calzar *v.* to take size... shoes 1.6
cama *f.* bed 1.5
cámara digital *f.* digital camera 2.5
cámara de video *f.* video camera 2.5
camarero/a *m., f.* waiter/waitress 2.2
camarón *m.* shrimp 2.2
cambiar (de) *v.* to change 2.3
cambio: de cambio in change 2.3
cambio *m.* **climático** climate change 3.1
cambio *m.* **de moneda** currency exchange
caminar *v.* to walk 1.2
camino *m.* road
camión *m.* truck; bus
camisa *f.* shirt 1.6
camiseta *f.* t-shirt 1.6
campo *m.* countryside 1.5
canadiense *adj.* Canadian 1.3
canal *m.* (TV) channel 2.5, 3.5
canción *f.* song 3.5
candidato/a *m., f.* candidate 3.6
canela *f.* cinnamon 2.4
cansado/a *adj.* tired 1.5
cantante *m., f.* singer 3.5
cantar *v.* to sing 1.2
capital *f.* capital city 1.1
capó *m.* hood 2.5
cara *f.* face 2.1
caramelo *m.* caramel 2.3
carne *f.* meat 2.2
   carne de res *f.* beef 2.2
carnicería *f.* butcher shop 3.2
caro/a *adj.* expensive 1.6
carpintero/a *m., f.* carpenter 3.4
carrera *f.* career 3.4
carretera *f.* highway 2.5
carro *m.* car; automobile 2.5
carta *f.* letter 1.4; (playing) card 1.5
cartel *m.* poster 2.6
cartera *f.* wallet 1.4, 1.6
cartero *m.* mail carrier 3.2
casa *f.* house; home 1.2
casado/a *adj.* married 2.3
casarse (con) *v.* to get married (to) 2.3
casi *adv.* almost 2.4
catorce fourteen 1.1
cazar *v.* to hunt 3.1
cebolla *f.* onion 2.2
cederrón *m.* CD-ROM 2.5
celebrar *v.* to celebrate 2.3
cementerio *m.* cemetery 2.3
cena *f.* dinner 2.2
cenar *v.* to have dinner 1.2

centro *m.* downtown 1.4
   centro comercial shopping mall 1.6
cepillarse los dientes/el pelo *v.* to brush one's teeth/one's hair 2.1
cerámica *f.* pottery 3.5
cerca de *prep.* near 1.2
cerdo *m.* pork 2.2
cereales *m., pl.* cereal; grains 2.2
cero *m.* zero 1.1
cerrado/a *adj.* closed 1.5, 3.2
cerrar (e:ie) *v.* to close 1.4
cerveza *f.* beer 2.2
césped *m.* grass
ceviche *m.* marinated fish dish 2.2
   ceviche de camarón *m.* lemon-marinated shrimp 2.2
chaleco *m.* vest
champán *m.* champagne 2.3
champiñón *m.* mushroom 2.2
champú *m.* shampoo 2.1
chaqueta *f.* jacket 1.6
chau *fam. interj.* bye 1.1
cheque *m.* (bank) check 3.2
   cheque (de viajero) *m.* (traveler's) check 3.2
chévere *adj., fam.* terrific
chico/a *m., f.* boy/girl 1.1
chino/a *adj.* Chinese 1.3
chocar (con) *v.* to run into
chocolate *m.* chocolate 2.3
choque *m.* collision 3.6
chuleta *f.* chop (*food*) 2.2
   chuleta de cerdo *f.* pork chop 2.2
cibercafé *m.* cybercafé
ciclismo *m.* cycling 1.4
cielo *m.* sky 3.1
cien(to) one hundred 1.2
ciencia *f.* science 1.2
   ciencias ambientales environmental sciences 1.2
   de ciencia ficción *f.* science fiction (genre) 3.5
científico/a *m., f.* scientist 3.4
cierto/a *adj.* certain 3.1
   es cierto it's certain 3.1
   no es cierto it's not certain 3.1
cima *f.* top, peak 3.3
cinco five 1.1
cincuenta fifty 1.2
cine *m.* movie theater 1.4
cinta *f.* (audio)tape
cinta caminadora *f.* treadmill 3.3
cinturón *m.* belt 1.6
circulación *f.* traffic 2.5
cita *f.* date; appointment 2.3
ciudad *f.* city 1.4
ciudadano/a *m., f.* citizen 3.6
Claro (que sí). *fam.* Of course.
clase *f.* class 1.2
   clase de ejercicios aeróbicos *f.* aerobics class 3.3
clásico/a *adj.* classical 3.5
cliente/a *m., f.* customer 1.6
clínica *f.* clinic 2.4

Span-Eng

cobrar *v.* to cash (a check) 3.2
coche *m.* car; automobile 2.5
cocina *f.* kitchen; stove 2.3, 2.6
cocinar *v.* to cook 2.6
cocinero/a *m., f.* cook, chef 3.4
cofre *m.* hood 3.2
cola *f.* line 3.2
colesterol *m.* cholesterol 3.3
color *m.* color 1.6
comedia *f.* comedy; play 3.5
comedor *m.* dining room 2.6
comenzar (e:ie) *v.* to begin 1.4
comer *v.* to eat 1.3
comercial *adj.* commercial;
  business-related 3.4
comida *f.* food; meal 1.4, 2.2
como like; as 2.2
¿cómo? what?; how? 1.1
  ¿Cómo es...? What's... like? 1.3
  ¿Cómo está usted? *form.*
    How are you? 1.1
  ¿Cómo estás? *fam.* How are
    you? 1.1
  ¿Cómo les fue...? *pl.* How
    did... go for you? 3.3
  ¿Cómo se llama usted?
    (form.) What's your name? 1.1
  ¿Cómo te llamas? *(fam.)*
    What's your name? 1.1
cómoda *f.* chest of drawers 2.6
cómodo/a *adj.* comfortable 1.5
compañero/a de clase *m., f.*
  classmate 1.2
compañero/a de cuarto *m., f.*
  roommate 1.2
compañía *f.* company; firm 3.4
compartir *v.* to share 1.3
completamente *adv.* completely
  1.5, 3.4
compositor(a) *m., f.* composer 3.5
comprar *v.* to buy 1.2
compras *f., pl.* purchases 1.5
  ir de compras to go shopping 1.5
comprender *v.* to understand 1.3
comprobar *v.* to check
comprometerse (con) *v.* to get
  engaged (to) 2.3
computación *f.* computer
  science 1.2
computadora *f.* computer 1.1
computadora portátil *f.* portable
  computer; laptop 2.5
comunicación *f.* communication 3.6
comunicarse (con) *v.* to
  communicate (with) 3.6
comunidad *f.* community 1.1
con *prep.* with 1.2
  Con él/ella habla. Speaking.
    (on phone) 2.5
  con frecuencia *adv.*
    frequently 2.4
  Con permiso. Pardon me;
    Excuse me. 1.1
  con tal (de) que provided
    (that) 3.1
concierto *m.* concert 3.5
concordar *v.* to agree

concurso *m.* game show;
  contest 3.5
conducir *v.* to drive 1.6, 2.5
conductor(a) *m., f.* driver 1.1
conexión *f.* **inalámbrica** wireless
  (connection) 2.5
confirmar *v.* to confirm 1.5
confirmar *v.* **una reservación** *f.*
  to confirm a reservation 1.5
confundido/a *adj.* confused 1.5
congelador *m.* freezer 2.6
congestionado/a *adj.* congested;
  stuffed-up 2.4
conmigo *pron.* with me 1.4, 2.3
conocer *v.* to know; to be
  acquainted with 1.6
conocido *adj.; p.p.* known
conseguir (e:i) *v.* to get; to
  obtain 1.4
consejero/a *m., f.* counselor;
  advisor 3.4
consejo *m.* advice
conservación *f.* conservation 3.1
conservar *v.* to conserve 3.1
construir *v.* to build
consultorio *m.* doctor's office 2.4
consumir *v.* to consume 3.3
contabilidad *f.* accounting 1.2
contador(a) *m., f.* accountant 3.4
contaminación *f.* pollution 3.1
  **contaminación del aire/del
    agua** air/water pollution 3.1
contaminado/a *adj.* polluted 3.1
contaminar *v.* to pollute 3.1
contar (o:ue) *v.* to count; to tell 1.4
contento/a *adj.* happy; content 1.5
contestar *v.* to answer 1.2
contigo *fam. pron.* with
  you 1.5, 2.3
contratar *v.* to hire 3.4
control *m.* control 2.1
  control remoto remote
    control 2.5
controlar *v.* to control 3.1
conversación *f.* conversation 1.1
conversar *v.* to converse, to chat 1.2
copa *f.* wineglass; goblet 2.6
corazón *m.* heart 2.4
corbata *f.* tie 1.6
corredor(a) *m., f.* **de bolsa**
  stockbroker 3.4
correo *m.* mail; post office 3.2
  correo de voz *m.*
    voice mail 2.5
  correo electrónico *m.*
    e-mail 1.4
correr *v.* to run 1.3
cortesía *f.* courtesy
cortinas *f., pl.* curtains 2.6
corto/a *adj.* short (*in length*) 1.6
cosa *f.* thing 1.1
Costa Rica *f.* Costa Rica 1.1
costar (o:ue) *v.* to cost 1.6
costarricense *adj.* Costa
  Rican 1.3
cráter *m.* crater 3.1

creer *v.* to believe 3.1
  creer (en) *v.* to believe (in) 1.3
  no creer (en) *v.* not to
    believe (in) 3.1
creído/a *adj., p.p.* believed 3.2
crema de afeitar *f.* shaving
  cream 1.5, 2.1
crimen *m.* crime; murder 3.6
cruzar *v.* to cross 3.2
cuaderno *m.* notebook 1.1
cuadra *f.* (city) block 3.2
¿cuál(es)? which?; which
  one(s)? 1.2
  ¿Cuál es la fecha de hoy?
    What is today's date? 1.5
cuadro *m.* picture 2.6
cuadros *m., pl.* plaid 1.6
cuando when 2.1; 3.1
¿cuándo? when? 1.2
¿cuánto(s)/a(s)? how much/how
  many? 1.1
  ¿Cuánto cuesta...? How
    much does... cost? 1.6
  ¿Cuántos años tienes? How
    old are you? 1.3
cuarenta forty 1.2
cuarto de baño *m.* bathroom 2.1
cuarto *m.* room 1.2, 2.1
cuarto/a *adj.* fourth 1.5
  menos cuarto quarter to
    (time) 1.1
  y cuarto quarter after (time) 1.1
cuatro four 1.1
cuatrocientos/as four
  hundred 1.2
Cuba *f.* Cuba 1.1
cubano/a *adj.* Cuban 1.3
cubiertos *m., pl.* silverware
cubierto/a *p.p.* covered
cubrir *v.* to cover
cuchara *f.* (table or large) spoon 2.6
cuchillo *m.* knife 2.6
cuello *m.* neck 2.4
cuenta *f.* bill 2.3; account 3.2
  cuenta corriente *f.* checking
    account 3.2
  cuenta de ahorros *f.* savings
    account 3.2
cuento *m.* short story 3.5
cuerpo *m.* body 2.4
cuidar *v.* to take care of 3.1
cultura *f.* culture 1.2, 3.5
cumpleaños *m., ing.*
  birthday 2.3
cumplir años *v.* to have a
  birthday 2.3
cuñado/a *m., f.* brother-in-law;
  sister-in-law 1.3
currículum *m.* résumé 3.4
curso *m.* course 1.2

D

danza *f.* dance 3.5
dañar *v.* to damage; to break
  down 2.4

dar *v.* to give **1.6, 2.3**
  dar un consejo *v.* to give advice **1.6**
  darse con *v.* to bump into; to run into (something) **2.4**
  darse prisa *v.* to hurry; to rush **3.3**
de *prep.* of; from **1.1**
  ¿De dónde eres? *fam.* Where are you from? **1.1**
  ¿De dónde es usted? *form.* Where are you from? **1.1**
  ¿De parte de quién? Who is speaking/calling? (*on phone*) **2.5**
  ¿de quién...? whose...? (*sing.*) **1.1**
  ¿de quiénes...? whose...? (*pl.*) **1.1**
  de algodón (made) of cotton **1.6**
  de aluminio (made) of aluminum **3.1**
  de buen humor in a good mood **1.5**
  de compras shopping **1.5**
  de cuadros plaid **1.6**
  de excursión hiking **1.4**
  de hecho in fact
  de ida y vuelta roundtrip **1.5**
  de la mañana in the morning; A.M. **1.1**
  de la noche in the evening; at night; P.M. **1.1**
  de la tarde in the afternoon; in the early evening; P.M. **1.1**
  de lana (made) of wool **1.6**
  de lunares polka-dotted **1.6**
  de mal humor in a bad mood **1.5**
  de mi vida of my life **3.3**
  de moda in fashion **1.6**
  De nada. You're welcome. **1.1**
  de niño/a as a child **2.4**
  de parte de on behalf of **2.5**
  de plástico (made) of plastic **3.1**
  de rayas striped **1.6**
  de repente suddenly **1.6**
  de seda (made) of silk **1.6**
  de vaqueros western (genre) **3.5**
  de vez en cuando from time to time **2.4**
  de vidrio (made) of glass **3.1**
debajo de *prep.* below; under **1.2**
deber (+ *inf.*) *v.* should; must; ought to **1.3**
  Debe ser... It must be... **1.6**
deber *m.* responsibility; obligation **3.6**
debido a due to (the fact that)
débil *adj.* weak **3.3**
decidido/a *adj.* decided **3.2**
decidir (+ *inf.*) *v.* to decide **1.3**
décimo/a *adj.* tenth **1.5**

decir (e:i) *v.* **(que)** to say (that); to tell (that) **1.4, 2.3**
  decir la respuesta to say the answer **1.4**
  decir la verdad to tell the truth **1.4**
  decir mentiras to tell lies **1.4**
declarar *v.* to declare; to say **3.6**
dedo *m.* finger **2.4**
dedo del pie *m.* toe **2.4**
deforestación *f.* deforestation **3.1**
dejar *v.* to let **2.6**; to quit; to leave behind **3.4**
  dejar de (+ *inf.*) *v.* to stop (*doing something*) **3.1**
  dejar una propina *v.* to leave a tip **2.3**
del (*contraction of* **de + el**) of the; from the
delante de *prep.* in front of **1.2**
delgado/a *adj.* thin; slender **1.3**
delicioso/a *adj.* delicious **2.2**
demás *adj.* the rest
demasiado *adj., adv.* too much **1.6**
dentista *m., f.* dentist **2.4**
dentro de (diez años) within (ten years) **3.4**; inside
dependiente/a *m., f.* clerk **1.6**
deporte *m.* sport **1.4**
deportista *m.* sports person
deportivo/a *adj.* sports-related **1.4**
depositar *v.* to deposit **3.2**
derecha *f.* right **1.2**
  a la derecha de to the right of **1.2**
derecho *adv.* straight (ahead) **3.2**
derechos *m., pl.* rights **3.6**
desarrollar *v.* to develop **3.1**
desastre (natural) *m.* (natural) disaster **3.6**
desayunar *v.* to have breakfast **1.2**
desayuno *m.* breakfast **2.2**
descafeinado/a *adj.* decaffeinated **3.3**
descansar *v.* to rest **1.2**
descargar *v.* to download **2.5**
descompuesto/a *adj.* not working; out of order **2.5**
describir *v.* to describe **1.3**
descrito/a *p.p.* described **3.2**
descubierto/a *p.p.* discovered **3.2**
descubrir *v.* to discover **3.1**
desde *prep.* from **1.6**
desear *v.* to wish; to desire **1.2**
desempleo *m.* unemployment **3.6**
desierto *m.* desert **3.1**
desigualdad *f.* inequality **3.6**
desordenado/a *adj.* disorderly **1.5**
despacio *adv.* slowly **2.4**
despedida *f.* farewell; good-bye
despedir (e:i) *v.* to fire **3.4**
despedirse (de) (e:i) *v.* to say good-bye (to) **2.1**
despejado/a *adj.* clear (*weather*)
despertador *m.* alarm clock **2.1**
despertarse (e:ie) *v.* to wake up **2.1**

después *adv.* afterwards; then **2.1**
  después de after **2.1**
  después de que *conj.* after **3.1**
destruir *v.* to destroy **3.1**
detrás de *prep.* behind **1.2**
día *m.* day **1.1**
  día de fiesta holiday **2.3**
diario *m.* diary **1.1**; newspaper **3.6**
diario/a *adj.* daily **2.1**
dibujar *v.* to draw **1.2**
dibujo *m.* drawing **3.5**
  dibujos animados *m., pl.* cartoons **3.5**
diccionario *m.* dictionary **1.1**
dicho/a *p.p.* said **3.2**
diciembre *m.* December **1.5**
dictadura *f.* dictatorship **3.6**
diecinueve nineteen **1.1**
dieciocho eighteen **1.1**
dieciséis sixteen **1.1**
diecisiete seventeen **1.1**
diente *m.* tooth **2.1**
dieta *f.* diet **3.3**
  comer una dieta equilibrada to eat a balanced diet **3.3**
diez ten **1.1**
difícil *adj.* difficult; hard **1.3**
Diga. Hello. (*on phone*) **2.5**
diligencia *f.* errand **3.2**
dinero *m.* money **1.6**
dirección *f.* address **3.2**
  dirección electrónica *f.* e-mail address **2.5**
director(a) *m., f.* director; (*musical*) conductor **3.5**
dirigir *v.* to direct **3.5**
disco compacto compact disc (CD) **2.5**
discriminación *f.* discrimination **3.6**
discurso *m.* speech **3.6**
diseñador(a) *m., f.* designer **3.4**
diseño *m.* design
disfraz *m.* costume
disfrutar (de) *v.* to enjoy; to reap the benefits (of) **3.3**
disminuir *v.* to reduce **3.6**
diversión *f.* fun activity; entertainment; recreation **1.4**
divertido/a *adj.* fun **2.1**
divertirse (e:ie) *v.* to have fun **2.3**
divorciado/a *adj.* divorced **2.3**
divorciarse (de) *v.* to get divorced (from) **2.3**
divorcio *m.* divorce **2.3**
doblar *v.* to turn **3.2**
doble *adj.* double
doce twelve **1.1**
doctor(a) *m., f.* doctor **1.3, 2.4**
documental *m.* documentary **3.5**
documentos de viaje *m., pl.* travel documents
doler (o:ue) *v.* to hurt **2.4**
dolor *m.* ache; pain **2.4**
  dolor de cabeza *m.* head ache **2.4**
doméstico/a *adj.* domestic **2.6**

domingo *m.* Sunday **1.2**
don *m.* Mr.; sir **1.1**
doña *f.* Mrs.; ma'am **1.1**
donde *adv.* where
  ¿Dónde está...? *Where is...?* **1.2**
  ¿dónde? where? **1.1**
dormir (o:ue) *v.* to sleep **1.4**
dormirse (o:ue) *v.* to go to sleep;
  to fall asleep **2.1**
dormitorio *m.* bedroom **2.6**
dos two **1.1**
  dos veces *f.* twice; two times **1.6**
doscientos/as two hundred **1.2**
drama *m.* drama; play **3.5**
dramático/a *adj.* dramatic **3.5**
dramaturgo/a *m., f.* playwright **3.5**
droga *f.* drug **3.3**
drogadicto/a *adj.* drug addict **3.3**
ducha *f.* shower **2.1**
ducharse *v.* to shower; to take a
  shower **2.1**
duda *f.* doubt **3.1**
dudar *v.* to doubt **3.1**
  no dudar *v.* not to doubt **3.1**
dueño/a *m., f.* owner; landlord **2.2**
dulces *m., pl.* sweets; candy **2.3**
durante *prep.* during **2.1**
durar *v.* to last **3.6**

E

e *conj. (used instead of **y** before
  words beginning with **i** and **hi**)*
  and **1.4**
echar *v.* to throw
  echar (una carta) al buzón *v.*
  to put (a letter) in the
  mailbox; to mail **3.2**
ecología *f.* ecology **3.1**
ecológico/a *adj.* ecological **3.1**
ecologista *m., f.* ecologist **3.1**
economía *f.* economics **1.2**
ecoturismo *m.* ecotourism **3.1**
Ecuador *m.* Ecuador **1.1**
ecuatoriano/a *adj.* Ecuadorian **1.3**
edad *f.* age **2.3**
edificio *m.* building **2.6**
  edificio de apartamentos
  apartment building **2.6**
(en) efectivo *m.* cash **1.6**
ejercer *v.* to practice/exercise (a
  degree/profession) **3.4**
ejercicio *m.* exercise **3.3**
  ejercicios aeróbicos
  aerobic exercises **3.3**
  ejercicios de estiramiento
  stretching exercises **3.3**
ejército *m.* army **3.6**
el *m., sing., def. art.* the **1.1**
él *sub. pron.* he **1.1;**
  obj. pron. him
elecciones *f., pl.* election **3.6**
electricista *m., f.* electrician **3.4**
electrodoméstico *m.* electric
  appliance **2.6**
elegante *adj. m., f.* elegant **1.6**

elegir (e:i) *v.* to elect **3.6**
ella *sub. pron.* she **1.1;** *obj. pron.* her
ellos/as *sub. pron.* they **1.1;** them
embarazada *adj.* pregnant **2.4**
emergencia *f.* emergency **2.4**
emitir *v.* to broadcast **3.6**
emocionante *adj. m., f.* exciting
empezar (e:ie) *v.* to begin **1.4**
empleado/a *m., f.* employee **1.5**
empleo *m.* job; employment **3.4**
empresa *f.* company; firm **3.4**
en *prep.* in; on; at **1.2**
  en casa at home **2.1**
  en caso (de) que in case
  (that) **3.1**
  en cuanto as soon as **3.1**
  en efectivo in cash **3.2**
  en exceso in excess; too
  much **3.3**
  en línea in-line **1.4**
  en mi nombre in my name
  en punto on the dot; exactly;
  sharp *(time)* **1.1**
  en qué in what; how **1.2**
  ¿En qué puedo servirles?
  How can I help you? **1.5**
  en vivo live **2.1**
enamorado/a (de) *adj.* in
  love (with) **1.5**
enamorarse (de) *v.* to fall in love
  (with) **2.3**
encantado/a *adj.* delighted;
  pleased to meet you **1.1**
encantar *v.* to like very much;
  to love *(inanimate objects)* **2.1**
  ¡Me encantó! *I* loved it! **3.3**
encima de *prep.* on top of **1.2**
encontrar (o:ue) *v.* to find **1.4**
encontrar(se) (o:ue) *v.* to meet
  (each other); to run into (each
  other) **2.5**
  encontrarse con to meet up
  with **2.1**
encuesta *f.* poll; survey **3.6**
energía *f.* energy **3.1**
  energía nuclear nuclear
  energy **3.1**
  energía solar solar energy **3.1**
enero *m.* January **1.5**
enfermarse *v.* to get sick **2.4**
enfermedad *f.* illness **2.4**
enfermero/a *m., f.* nurse **2.4**
enfermo/a *adj.* sick **2.4**
enfrente de *adv.* opposite; facing **3.2**
engordar *v.* to gain weight **3.3**
enojado/a *adj.* mad; angry **1.5**
enojarse (con) *v.* to get angry
  (with) **2.1**
ensalada *f.* salad **2.2**
ensayo *m.* essay **1.3**
enseguida *adv.* right away
enseñar *v.* to teach **1.2**
ensuciar *v.* to get (something)
  dirty **2.6**
entender (e:ie) *v.* to understand **1.4**
enterarse *v.* to find out **3.4**
entonces *adv.* so, then **1.5, 2.1**

entrada *f.* entrance **2.6;** ticket **3.5**
entre *prep.* between; among **1.2**
entregar *v.* to hand in **2.5**
entremeses *m., pl.* hors
  d'oeuvres; appetizers **2.2**
entrenador(a) *m., f.* trainer **3.3**
entrenarse *v.* to practice; to
  train **3.3**
entrevista *f.* interview **3.4**
entrevistador(a) *m., f.*
  interviewer **3.4**
entrevistar *v.* to interview **3.4**
envase *m.* container **3.1**
enviar *v.* to send; to mail **3.2**
equilibrado/a *adj.* balanced **3.3**
equipado/a *adj.* equipped **3.3**
equipaje *m.* luggage **1.5**
equipo *m.* team **1.4**
equivocado/a *adj.* wrong **1.5**
eres *fam.* you are **1.1**
es he/she/it is **1.1**
  Es bueno que... It's good
  that... **2.6**
  Es de... He/She is from... **1.1**
  es extraño it's strange **3.1**
  es igual it's the same **1.5**
  Es importante que... It's
  important that... **2.6**
  es imposible it's impossible **3.1**
  es improbable it's
  improbable **3.1**
  Es malo que... It's bad
  that... **2.6**
  Es mejor que... It's better
  that... **2.6**
  Es necesario que... It's
  necessary that... **2.6**
  es obvio it's obvious **3.1**
  es ridículo it's ridiculous **3.1**
  es seguro it's sure **3.1**
  es terrible it's terrible **3.1**
  es triste it's sad **3.1**
  Es urgente que... It's urgent
  that... **2.6**
  Es la una. It's one o'clock. **1.1**
  es una lástima it's a shame **3.1**
  es verdad it's true **3.1**
esa(s) *f., adj.* that; those **1.6**
ésa(s) *f., pron.* that (one);
  those (ones) **1.6**
escalar *v.* to climb **1.4**
  escalar montañas *v.* to climb
  mountains **1.4**
escalera *f.* stairs; stairway **2.6**
escalón *m.* step **3.3**
escanear *v.* to scan **2.5**
escoger *v.* to choose **2.2**
escribir *v.* to write **1.3**
  **escribir un mensaje
  electrónico** to write an
  e-mail message **1.4**
  escribir una postal
  to write a postcard **1.4**
  escribir una carta to write a
  letter **1.4**
escrito/a *p.p.* written **3.2**
escritor(a) *m., f.* writer **3.5**

escritorio *m.* desk **1.2**
escuchar *v.* to listen to **1.2**
  escuchar la radio to listen (to) the radio **1.2**
  escuchar música to listen (to) music **1.2**
escuela *f.* school **1.1**
esculpir *v.* to sculpt **3.5**
escultor(a) *m., f.* sculptor **3.5**
escultura *f.* sculpture **3.5**
ese *m., sing., adj.* that **1.6**
ése *m., sing., pron.* that one **1.6**
eso *neuter, pron.* that; that thing **1.6**
esos *m., pl., adj.* those **1.6**
ésos *m., pl., pron.* those (ones) **1.6**
España *f.* Spain **1.1**
español *m.* Spanish (language) **1.2**
español(a) *adj. m., f.* Spanish **1.3**
espárragos *m., pl.* asparagus **2.2**
especialidad: las especialidades del día today's specials **1.2**
especialización *f.* major **1.2**
espectacular *adj.* spectacular **3.3**
espectáculo *m.* show **3.5**
espejo *m.* mirror **2.1**
esperar *v.* to hope; to wish **3.1**
  esperar (+ *inf.*) *v.* to wait (for); to hope **1.2**
esposo/a *m., f.* husband/wife; spouse **1.3**
esquí (acuático) *m.* (water) skiing **1.4**
esquiar *v.* to ski **1.4**
esquina *m.* corner **3.2**
está he/she/it is, you are
  Está (muy) despejado. It's (very) clear. (*weather*)
  Está lloviendo. It's raining. **1.5**
  Está nevando. It's snowing. **1.5**
  Está (muy) nublado. It's (very) cloudy. (*weather*) **1.5**
  Está bien. That's fine. **2.5**
esta(s) *f., adj.* this; these **1.6**
  esta noche tonight **1.4**
ésta(s) *f., pron.* this (one); these (ones) **1.6**
  Ésta es... *f.* This is... (*introducing someone*) **1.1**
establecer *v.* to establish **3.4**
estación *f.* station; season **1.5**
  estación de autobuses bus station **1.5**
  estación del metro subway station **1.5**
  estación de tren train station **1.5**
estacionamiento *m.* parking lot **3.2**
estacionar *v.* to park **2.5**
estadio *m.* stadium **1.2**
estado civil *m.* marital status **2.3**
Estados Unidos *m., pl.* (EE.UU.; E.U.) United States **1.1**
estadounidense *adj. m., f.* from the United States **1.3**

estampado/a *adj.* print
estampilla *f.* stamp **3.2**
estante *m.* bookcase; bookshelves **2.6**
estar *v.* to be **1.2**
  estar a dieta to be on a diet **3.3**
  estar aburrido/a to be bored **1.5**
  estar afectado/a (por) to be affected (by) **3.1**
  estar bajo control to be under control **2.1**
  estar cansado/a to be tired **1.5**
  estar contaminado/a to be polluted **3.1**
  estar de acuerdo to agree **3.4**
  Estoy de acuerdo. I agree. **3.4**
  No estoy de acuerdo. I don't agree. **3.4**
  estar de moda to be in fashion **1.6**
  estar de vacaciones *f., pl.* to be on vacation **1.5**
  estar en buena forma to be in good shape **3.3**
  estar enfermo/a to be sick **2.4**
  estar harto/a de... to be sick of **3.6**
  estar listo/a to be ready **3.3**
  estar perdido/a to be lost **3.2**
  estar roto/a to be broken **2.4**
  estar seguro/a to be sure **1.5**
  estar torcido/a to be twisted; to be sprained **2.4**
  No está nada mal. It's not bad at all. **1.5**
estatua *f.* statue **3.5**
este *m.* east **3.2**
este *m., sing., adj.* this **1.6**
éste *m., sing., pron.* this (one) **1.6**
  Éste es... *m.* This is... (*introducing someone*) **1.1**
estéreo *m.* stereo **2.5**
estilo *m.* style
estiramiento *m.* stretching **3.3**
esto *neuter pron.* this; this thing **1.6**
estómago *m.* stomach **2.4**
estornudar *v.* to sneeze **2.4**
estos *m., pl., adj.* these **1.6**
éstos *m., pl., pron.* these (ones) **1.6**
estrella *f.* star **3.1**
  estrella de cine *m., f.* movie star **3.5**
estrés *m.* stress **3.3**
estudiante *m., f.* student **1.1, 1.2**
estudiantil *adj. m., f.* student **1.2**
estudiar *v.* to study **1.2**
estufa *f.* stove **2.6**
estupendo/a *adj.* stupendous **1.5**
etapa *f.* stage **2.3**
evitar *v.* to avoid **3.1**
examen *m.* test; exam **1.2**
  examen médico physical exam **2.4**
excelente *adj. m., f.* excellent **1.5**

exceso *m.* excess; too much **3.3**
excursión *f.* hike; tour; excursion **1.4**
excursionista *m., f.* hiker
experiencia *f.* experience **3.6**
explicar *v.* to explain **1.2**
explorar *v.* to explore
expresión *f.* expression
extinción *f.* extinction **3.1**
extranjero/a *adj.* foreign **3.5**
extrañar *v.* to miss **3.4**
extraño/a *adj.* strange **3.1**

F

fábrica *f.* factory **3.1**
fabuloso/a *adj.* fabulous **1.5**
fácil *adj.* easy **1.3**
falda *f.* skirt **1.6**
faltar *v.* to lack; to need **2.1**
familia *f.* family **1.3**
famoso/a *adj.* famous **3.4**
farmacia *f.* pharmacy **2.4**
fascinar *v.* to fascinate **2.1**
favorito/a *adj.* favorite **1.4**
fax *m.* fax (machine) **2.5**
febrero *m.* February **1.5**
fecha *f.* date **1.5**
¡Felicidades! Congratulations! **2.3**
¡Felicitaciones! Congratulations! **2.3**
feliz *adj.* happy **1.5**
  ¡Feliz cumpleaños! Happy birthday! **2.3**
fenomenal *adj.* great, phenomenal **1.5**
feo/a *adj.* ugly **1.3**
festival *m.* festival **3.5**
fiebre *f.* fever **2.4**
fiesta *f.* party **2.3**
fijo/a *adj.* fixed, set **1.6**
fin *m.* end **1.4**
  fin de semana weekend **1.4**
finalmente *adv.* finally **3.3**
firmar *v.* to sign (*a document*) **3.2**
física *f.* physics **1.2**
flan (de caramelo) *m.* baked (caramel) custard **2.3**
flexible *adj.* flexible **3.3**
flor *f.* flower **3.1**
folclórico/a *adj.* folk; folkloric **3.5**
folleto *m.* brochure
fondo *m.* end **2.6**
forma *f.* shape **3.3**
formulario *m.* form **3.2**
foto(grafía) *f.* photograph **1.1**
francés, francesa *adj. m., f.* French **1.3**
frecuentemente *adv.* frequently **2.4**
frenos *m., pl.* brakes
frente (frío) *m.* (cold) front **1.5**
fresco/a *adj.* cool **1.5**
frijoles *m., pl.* beans **2.2**
frío/a *adj.* cold **1.5**
frito/a *adj.* fried **2.2**

fruta *f.* fruit 2.2
frutería *f.* fruit store 3.2
fuera *adv.* outside
fuerte *adj. m., f.* strong 3.3
fumar *v.* to smoke 3.3
  (no) fumar *v.* (not) to
  smoke 3.3
funcionar *v.* to work 2.5; to
  function
fútbol *m.* soccer 1.4
fútbol americano *m.* football 1.4
futuro/a *adj.* future 3.4
  en el futuro in the future 3.4

G

gafas (de sol) *f., pl.* (sun)
  glasses 1.6
gafas (oscuras) *f., pl.* (sun)glasses
galleta *f.* cookie 2.3
ganar *v.* to win 1.4;
  to earn (money) 3.4
ganga *f.* bargain 1.6
garaje *m.* garage; (mechanic's)
  repair shop 2.5;
  garage (*in a house*) 2.6
garganta *f.* throat 2.4
gasolina *f.* gasoline 2.5
gasolinera *f.* gas station 2.5
gastar *v.* to spend (*money*) 1.6
gato *m.* cat 3.1
gemelo/a *m., f.* twin 1.3
genial *adj.* great 3.4
gente *f.* people 1.3
geografía *f.* geography 1.2
gerente *m., f.* manager 2.2, 3.4
gimnasio *m.* gymnasium 1.4
gobierno *m.* government 3.1
golf *m.* golf 1.4
gordo/a *adj.* fat 1.3
grabar *v.* to record 2.5
gracias *f., pl.* thank you; thanks 1.1
  Gracias por invitarme.
  Thanks for inviting me. 2.3
graduarse (de/en) *v.* to graduate
  (from/in) 2.3
gran, grande *adj.* big; large 1.3
grasa *f.* fat 3.3
gratis *adj. m., f.* free of charge 3.2
grave *adj.* grave; serious 2.4
grillo *m.* cricket
gripe *f.* flu 2.4
gris *adj. m., f.* gray 1.6
gritar *v.* to scream, to shout 2.1
grito *m.* scream 1.5
guantes *m., pl.* gloves 1.6
guapo/a *adj.* handsome; good-
  looking 1.3
guardar *v.* to save (on a
  computer) 2.5
guerra *f.* war 3.6
guía *m., f.* guide
gustar *v.* to be pleasing to; to
  like 1.2
  Me gustaría... I would like...

gusto *m.* pleasure 1.1
  El gusto es mío. The pleasure
  is mine. 1.1
  Mucho gusto. Pleased to meet
  you. 1.1
  ¡Qué gusto verlo/la! *(form.)*
  How nice to see you! 3.6
  ¡Qué gusto verte! *(fam.)*
  How nice to see you! 3.6

H

haber *(auxiliar) v.* to have (done
  something) 3.3
habitación *f.* room 1.5
  habitación doble double
  room 1.5
  habitación individual single
  room 1.5
hablar *v.* to talk; to speak 1.2
hacer *v.* to do; to make 1.4
  Hace buen tiempo. The
  weather is good. 1.5
  Hace (mucho) calor. It's (very)
  hot. (*weather*) 1.5
  Hace fresco. It's cool.
  (*weather*) 1.5
  Hace (mucho) frío. It's (very)
  cold. (*weather*) 1.5
  Hace mal tiempo. The weather
  is bad. 1.5
  Hace (mucho) sol. It's (very)
  sunny. (*weather*) 1.5
  Hace (mucho) viento. It's
  (very) windy. (*weather*) 1.5
  hacer cola to stand in line 3.2
  hacer diligencias to run
  errands 3.2
  hacer ejercicio to exercise 3.3
  hacer ejercicios aeróbicos to
  do aerobics 3.3
  **hacer ejercicios de
  estiramiento** to do stretching
  exercises 3.3
  hacer el papel (de) to play the
  role (of) 3.5
  hacer gimnasia to work out 3.3
  hacer juego (con) to match
  (with) 1.6
  hacer la cama to make the
  bed 2.6
  hacer las maletas to pack
  (one's) suitcases 1.5
  **hacer quehaceres
  domésticos** to do household
  chores 2.6
  hacer (wind)surf to (wind)
  surf 1.5
  hacer turismo to go sightseeing
  hacer un viaje
  to take a trip 1.5
  **¿Me harías el honor de
  casarte conmigo?** Would
  you do me the honor of
  marrying me? 3.5

hacia *prep.* toward 3.2
hamburguesa *f.* hamburger 2.2
hasta *prep.* until 1.6; toward
  Hasta la vista. See you later. 1.1
  Hasta luego. See you later. 1.1
  Hasta mañana. See you
  tomorrow. 1.1
  Hasta pronto. See you soon. 1.1
  hasta que until 3.1
hay there is; there are 1.1
  Hay (mucha) contaminación.
  It's (very) smoggy.
  Hay (mucha) niebla. It's (very)
  foggy.
  Hay que It is necessary that 3.2
  No hay de qué. You're
  welcome. 1.1
  No hay duda de There's no
  doubt 3.1
hecho/a *p.p.* done 3.2
heladería *f.* ice cream shop 3.2
helado/a *adj.* iced 2.2
helado *m.* ice cream 2.3
hermanastro/a *m., f.*
  stepbrother/stepsister 1.3
hermano/a *m., f.* brother/sister 1.3
hermano/a mayor/menor *m., f.*
  older/younger brother/sister 1.3
hermanos *m., pl.* siblings
  (brothers and sisters) 1.3
hermoso/a *adj.* beautiful 1.6
hierba *f.* grass 3.1
hijastro/a *m., f.* stepson/
  stepdaughter 1.3
hijo/a *m., f.* son/daughter 1.3
  hijo/a único/a *m., f.* only
  child 1.3
  hijos *m., pl.* children 1.3
híjole *interj.* wow 1.6
historia *f.* history 1.2; story 3.5
hockey *m.* hockey 1.4
hola *interj.* hello; hi 1.1
hombre *m.* man 1.1
  hombre de negocios *m.*
  businessman 3.4
hora *f.* hour 1.1; the time
horario *m.* schedule 1.2
horno *m.* oven 2.6
  horno de microondas *m.*
  microwave oven 2.6
horror *m.* horror 3.5
  de horror horror (genre) 3.5
hospital *m.* hospital 2.4
hotel *m.* hotel 1.5
hoy *adv.* today 1.2
  hoy día *adv.* nowadays
  Hoy es... Today is... 1.2
hueco *m.* hole 1.4
huelga *f.* strike (*labor*) 3.6
hueso *m.* bone 2.4
huésped *m., f.* guest 1.5
huevo *m.* egg 2.2
humanidades *f.,
  pl.* humanities 1.2
huracán *m.* hurricane 3.6

I

ida *f.* one way (*travel*)
idea *f.* idea **1.4**
iglesia *f.* church **1.4**
igualdad *f.* equality **3.6**
igualmente *adv.* likewise **1.1**
impermeable *m.* raincoat **1.6**
importante *adj. m., f.*
　important **1.3**
importar *v.* to be important to;
　to matter **2.1**
imposible *adj. m., f.* impossible **3.1**
impresora *f.* printer **2.5**
imprimir *v.* to print **2.5**
improbable *adj. m., f.*
　improbable **3.1**
impuesto *m.* tax **3.6**
incendio *m.* fire **3.6**
increíble *adj. m., f.* incredible **1.5**
indicar cómo llegar *v.* to give
　directions **3.2**
individual *adj.* private (*room*) **1.5**
infección *f.* infection **2.4**
informar *v.* to inform **3.6**
informe *m.* report; paper
　(*written work*) **3.6**
ingeniero/a *m., f.* engineer **1.3**
inglés *m.* English (*language*) **1.2**
inglés, inglesa *adj.* English **1.3**
inodoro *m.* toilet **2.1**
insistir (en) *v.* to insist (on) **2.6**
inspector(a) de aduanas *m., f.*
　customs inspector **1.5**
inteligente *adj. m., f.*
　intelligent **1.3**
intento *m.* intent **2.5**
intercambiar *v.* to exchange
interesante *adj. m., f.*
　interesting **1.3**
interesar *v.* to be interesting to;
　to interest **2.1**
internacional *adj. m., f.*
　international **3.6**
Internet Internet **2.5**
inundación *f.* flood **3.6**
invertir (e:ie) *v.* to invest **3.4**
invierno *m.* winter **1.5**
invitado/a *m., f.* guest **2.3**
invitar *v.* to invite **2.3**
inyección *f.* injection **2.4**
ir *v.* to go **1.4**
　ir a (+ *inf.*) *to* be going to do
　　something **1.4**
　ir de compras to go
　　shopping **1.5**
　**ir de excursión (a las
　　montañas)** to go for a hike
　　(in the mountains) **1.4**
　ir de pesca to go fishing
　ir de vacaciones to go on
　　vacation **1.5**
　ir en autobús to go by bus **1.5**
　ir en auto(móvil) to go by
　　auto(mobile); to go by car **1.5**
　ir en avión to go by plane **1.5**
　ir en barco to go by boat **1.5**
　ir en metro to go by subway
　ir en motocicleta to go by
　　motorcycle **1.5**
　ir en taxi to go by taxi **1.5**
　ir en tren to go by train
irse *v.* to go away; to leave **2.1**
italiano/a *adj.* Italian **1.3**
izquierda *f.* left **1.2**
　a la izquierda de to the left
　　of **1.2**

J

jabón *m.* soap **2.1**
jamás *adv.* never; not ever **2.1**
jamón *m.* ham **2.2**
japonés, japonesa *adj.*
　Japanese **1.3**
jardín *m.* garden; yard **2.6**
jefe, jefa *m., f.* boss **3.4**
jengibre *m.* ginger **2.4**
joven *adj. m., f., sing.* (**jóvenes**
　pl.) young **1.3**
　joven *m., f., sing.* (**jóvenes** *pl.*)
　　youth; young person **1.1**
joyería *f.* jewelry store **3.2**
jubilarse *v.* to retire (from
　work) **2.3**
juego *m.* game
jueves *m., sing.* Thursday **1.2**
jugador(a) *m., f.* player **1.4**
jugar (u:ue) *v.* to play **1.4**
　jugar a las cartas *f., pl.* to
　　play cards **1.5**
jugo *m.* juice **2.2**
　jugo de fruta *m.* fruit juice **2.2**
julio *m.* July **1.5**
jungla *f.* jungle **3.1**
junio *m.* June **1.5**
juntos/as *adj.* together **2.3**
juventud *f.* youth **2.3**

K

kilómetro *m.* kilometer **1.1**

L

la *f., sing., def. art.* the **1.1**
la *f., sing., d.o. pron.* her, it,
　form. you **1.5**
laboratorio *m.* laboratory **1.2**
lago *m.* lake **3.1**
lámpara *f.* lamp **2.6**
lana *f.* wool **1.6**
langosta *f.* lobster **2.2**
lápiz *m.* pencil **1.1**
largo/a *adj.* long **1.6**
las *f., pl., def. art.* the **1.1**
las *f., pl., d.o. pron.* them; *form.*
　you **1.5**
lástima *f.* shame **3.1**
lastimarse *v.* to injure oneself **2.4**
　lastimarse el pie to injure
　　one's foot **2.4**

lata *f.* (*tin*) can **3.1**
lavabo *m.* sink **2.1**
lavadora *f.* washing machine **2.6**
lavandería *f.* laundromat **3.2**
lavaplatos *m., sing.* dishwasher **2.6**
lavar *v.* to wash **2.6**
　lavar (el suelo, los platos) to
　　wash (the floor, the dishes) **2.6**
lavarse *v.* to wash oneself **2.1**
　lavarse la cara to wash one's
　　face **2.1**
　lavarse las manos to wash
　　one's hands **2.1**
le *sing., i.o. pron.* to/for him, her,
　form. you **1.6**
　Le presento a... *form.* I would
　　like to introduce you to
　　(name). **1.1**
lección *f.* lesson **1.1**
leche *f.* milk **2.2**
lechuga *f.* lettuce **2.2**
leer *v.* to read **1.3**
　leer correo electrónico
　　to read e-mail **1.4**
　leer un periódico to read a
　　newspaper **1.4**
　leer una revista to read a
　　magazine **1.4**
leído/a *p.p.* read **3.2**
lejos de *prep.* far from **1.2**
lengua *f.* language **1.2**
　lenguas extranjeras *f., pl.*
　　foreign languages **1.2**
lentes de contacto *m., pl.*
　contact lenses
　lentes (de sol) (sun)glasses
lento/a *adj.* slow **2.5**
les *pl., i.o. pron.* to/
　for them, *form.* you **1.6**
letrero *m.* sign **3.2**
levantar *v.* to lift **3.3**
　levantar pesas to lift
　　weights **3.3**
levantarse *v.* to get up **2.1**
ley *f.* law **3.1**
libertad *f.* liberty; freedom **3.6**
libre *adj. m., f.* free **1.4**
librería *f.* bookstore **1.2**
libro *m.* book **1.2**
licencia de conducir *f.* driver's
　license **2.5**
limón *m.* lemon **2.2**
limpiar *v.* to clean **2.6**
　limpiar la casa *v.* to clean the
　　house **2.6**
limpio/a *adj.* clean **1.5**
línea *f.* line **1.4**
listo/a *adj.* ready; smart **1.5**
literatura *f.* literature **1.2**
llamar *v.* to call **2.5**
　llamar por teléfono to call on
　　the phone
llamarse *v.* to be called;
　to be named **2.1**
llanta *f.* tire **2.5**
llave *f.* key **1.5**; wrench **2.5**
llegada *f.* arrival **1.5**

llegar *v.* to arrive 1.2
llenar *v.* to fill 2.5, 3.2
  llenar el tanque to fill the tank 2.5
  llenar (un formulario) to fill out (a form) 3.2
lleno/a *adj.* full 2.5
llevar *v.* to carry 1.2; to wear; to take 1.6
  llevar una vida sana to lead a healthy lifestyle 3.3
  llevarse bien/mal (con) to get along well/badly (with) 2.3
llorar *v.* to cry 3.3
llover (o:ue) *v.* to rain 1.5
  Llueve. It's raining. 1.5
lluvia *f.* rain
lo *m., sing. d.o. pron.* him, it, *form.* you 1.5
  ¡Lo he pasado de película! I've had a fantastic time! 3.6
  lo que that which; what 2.6
  Lo siento. I'm sorry. 1.1
loco/a *adj.* crazy 1.6
locutor(a) *m., f.* (TV or radio) announcer 3.6
lodo *m.* mud
los *m., pl., def. art.* the 1.1
los *m. pl., d.o. pron.* them, *form.* you 1.5
luchar (contra/por) *v.* to fight; to struggle (against/for) 3.6
luego *adv.* later 1.1; then 2.1
lugar *m.* place 1.2, 1.4
luna *f.* moon 3.1
lunares *m.* polka dots 1.6
lunes *m., sing.* Monday 1.2
luz *f.* light; electricity 2.6

M

madrastra *f.* stepmother 1.3
madre *f.* mother 1.3
madurez *f.* maturity; middle age 2.3
maestro/a *m., f.* teacher 3.4
magnífico/a *adj.* magnificent 1.5
maíz *m.* corn 2.2
mal, malo/a *adj.* bad 1.3
maleta *f.* suitcase 1.1
mamá *f.* mom 1.3
mandar *v.* to order 2.6; to send; to mail 3.2
manejar *v.* to drive 2.5
manera *f.* way 3.4
mano *f.* hand 1.1
manta *f.* blanket 2.6
mantener *v.* to maintain 3.3
  mantenerse en forma to stay in shape 3.3
mantequilla *f.* butter 2.2
manzana *f.* apple 2.2
mañana *f.* morning, a.m. 1.1; tomorrow 1.1
mapa *m.* map 1.2
maquillaje *m.* makeup 2.1
maquillarse *v.* to put on makeup 2.1

mar *m.* sea 1.5
maravilloso/a *adj.* marvelous 1.5
mareado/a *adj.* dizzy; nauseated 2.4
margarina *f.* margarine 2.2
mariscos *m., pl.* shellfish 2.2
marrón *adj. m., f.* brown 1.6
martes *m., sing.* Tuesday 1.2
marzo *m.* March 1.5
más *pron.* more 1.2
  más de (+ número) more than 2.2
  más tarde later (on) 2.1
  más... que more... than 2.2
masaje *m.* massage 3.3
matemáticas *f., pl.* mathematics 1.2
materia *f.* course 1.2
matrimonio *m.* marriage 2.3
máximo/a *adj.* maximum 2.5
mayo *m.* May 1.5
mayonesa *f.* mayonnaise 2.2
mayor *adj.* older 1.3
  el/la mayor *adj.* eldest 2.2; oldest
me *sing., d.o. pron.* me 1.5; *sing. i.o. pron.* to/for me 1.6
  Me duele mucho. It hurts me a lot. 2.4
  Me gusta... I like... 1.2
  No me gustan nada. I don't like them at all. 1.2
  Me gustaría(n)... I would like... 3.5
  Me llamo... My name is... 1.1
  Me muero por... I'm dying to (for)...
mecánico/a *m., f.* mechanic 2.5
mediano/a *adj.* medium
medianoche *f.* midnight 1.1
medias *f., pl.* pantyhose, stockings 1.6
medicamento *m.* medication 2.4
medicina *f.* medicine 2.4
médico/a *m., f.* doctor 1.3; *adj.* medical 2.4
medio/a *adj.* half 1.3
  medio ambiente *m.* environment 3.1
  medio/a hermano/a *m., f.* half-brother/half-sister 1.3
  mediodía *m.* noon 1.1
  medios de comunicación *m., pl.* means of communication; media 3.6
y media thirty minutes past the hour (time) 1.1
mejor *adj.* better 2.2
  el/la mejor *m., f.* the best 2.2
mejorar *v.* to improve 3.1
melocotón *m.* peach 2.2
menor *adj.* younger 1.3
  el/la menor *m., f.* youngest 2.2
menos *adv.* less 2.4
  menos cuarto..., menos quince... *quarter* to... (time) 1.1
  menos de (+ número) fewer than 2.2
  menos... que less... than 2.2

mensaje *m.* **de texto** text message 2.5
mensaje electrónico *m.* e-mail message 1.4
mentira *f.* lie 1.4
menú *m.* menu 2.2
mercado *m.* market 1.6
  mercado al aire libre open-air market 1.6
merendar (e:ie) *v.* to snack 2.2; to have an afternoon snack
merienda *f.* afternoon snack 3.3
mes *m.* month 1.5
mesa *f.* table 1.2
mesita *f.* end table 2.6
  mesita de noche night stand 2.6
meterse en problemas *v.* to get into trouble 3.1
metro *m.* subway 1.5
mexicano/a *adj.* Mexican 1.3
México *m.* Mexico 1.1
mí *pron., obj. of prep.* me 2.2
mi(s) *poss. adj.* my 1.3
microonda *f.* microwave 2.6
  horno de microondas *m.* microwave oven 2.6
miel *f.* honey 2.4
mientras *conj.* while 2.4
miércoles *m., sing.* Wednesday 1.2
mil *m.* one thousand 1.2
  mil millones billion
milla *f.* mile 2.5
millón *m.* million 1.2
millones (de) *m.* millions (of)
mineral *m.* mineral 3.3
minuto *m.* minute 1.1
mío(s)/a(s) *poss.* my; (of) mine 2.5
mirar *v.* to look (at); to watch 1.2
  mirar (la) televisión to watch television 1.2
mismo/a *adj.* same 1.3
mochila *f.* backpack 1.2
moda *f.* fashion 1.6
módem *m.* modem
moderno/a *adj.* modern 3.5
molestar *v.* to bother; to annoy 2.1
monitor *m.* (computer) monitor 2.5
  monitor(a) *m., f.* trainer
mono *m.* monkey 3.1
montaña *f.* mountain 1.4
montar *v.* **a caballo** to ride a horse 1.5
montón: un montón de a lot of 1.4
monumento *m.* monument 1.4
morado/a *adj.* purple 1.6
moreno/a *adj.* brunet(te) 1.3
morir (o:ue) *v.* to die 2.2
mostrar (o:ue) *v.* to show 1.4
motocicleta *f.* motorcycle 1.5
motor *m.* motor
muchacho/a *m., f.* boy; girl 1.3
mucho/a *adj., adv.* a lot of; much 1.2; many 1.3

(Muchas) gracias. Thank you (very much); Thanks (a lot). **1.1**

muchas veces *adv.* a lot; many times **2.4**

Mucho gusto. Pleased to meet you. **1.1**

muchísimo very much **1.2**

mudarse *v.* to move (from one house to another) **2.6**

muebles *m., pl.* furniture **2.6**

muela *f.* tooth

muerte *f.* death **2.3**

muerto/a *p.p.* died **3.2**

mujer *f.* woman **1.1**

mujer de negocios *f.* business woman **3.4**

mujer policía *f.* female police officer

multa *f.* fine

mundial *adj. m., f.* worldwide

mundo *m.* world **2.1, 3.1**

muro *m.* wall **3.3**

músculo *m.* muscle **3.3**

museo *m.* museum **1.4**

música *f.* music **1.2, 3.5**

musical *adj. m., f.* musical **3.5**

músico/a *m., f.* musician **3.5**

muy adv. very **1.1**

(Muy) bien, gracias. (Very) well, thanks. **1.1**

N

nacer *v.* to be born **2.3**

nacimiento *m.* birth **2.3**

nacional *adj. m., f.* national **3.6**

nacionalidad *f.* nationality **1.1**

nada nothing **1.1**; not anything **2.1**

nada mal not bad at all **1.5**

nadar *v.* to swim **1.4**

nadie *pron.* no one, nobody, not anyone **2.1**

naranja *f.* orange **2.2**

nariz *f.* nose **2.4**

natación *f.* swimming **1.4**

natural *adj. m., f.* natural **3.1**

naturaleza *f.* nature **3.1**

navegador *m.* **GPS** GPS **2.5**

navegar (en Internet) *v.* to surf (the Internet) **2.5**

Navidad *f.* Christmas **2.3**

necesario/a *adj.* necessary **2.6**

necesitar (+ *inf.*) *v.* to need **1.2**

negar (e:ie) *v.* to deny **3.1**

no negar (e:ie) *v.* not to deny **3.1**

negocios *m., pl.* business; commerce **3.4**

negro/a *adj.* black **1.6**

nervioso/a *adj.* nervous **1.5**

nevar (e:ie) *v.* to snow **1.5**

Nieva. It's snowing. **1.5**

ni... ni neither... nor **2.1**

niebla *f.* fog

nieto/a *m., f.* grandson/ granddaughter **1.3**

nieve *f.* snow

ningún, ninguno/a(s) *adj.* no; none; not any **2.1**

niñez *f.* childhood **2.3**

niño/a *m., f.* child **1.3**

no no; not **1.1**

¿no? right? **1.1**

No cabe duda de... There is no doubt... **3.1**

no es seguro it's not sure **3.1**

no es verdad it's not true **3.1**

No está nada mal. It's not bad at all. **1.5**

no estar de acuerdo to disagree

No estoy seguro. I'm not sure.

no hay there is not; there are not **1.1**

No hay de qué. You're welcome. **1.1**

No hay duda de... There is no doubt... **3.1**

¡No me diga(s)! You don't say!

No me gustan nada. I don't like them at all. **1.2**

no muy bien not very well **1.1**

No quiero. I don't want to. **1.4**

No sé. I don't know.

No se preocupe. (*form.*) Don't worry. **2.1**

No te preocupes. (*fam.*) Don't worry. **2.1**

no tener razón to be wrong **1.3**

noche *f.* night **1.1**

nombre *m.* name **1.1**

norte *m.* north **3.2**

norteamericano/a *adj.* (North) American **1.3**

nos *pl., d.o. pron.* us **1.5**; *pl., i.o. pron.* to/for us **1.6**

Nos vemos. See you. **1.1**

nosotros/as *sub. pron.* we **1.1**; *obj. pron.* us

noticia *f.* news **2.5**

noticias *f., pl.* news **3.6**

noticiero *m.* newscast **3.6**

novecientos/as nine hundred **1.2**

noveno/a *adj.* ninth **1.5**

noventa ninety **1.2**

noviembre *m.* November **1.5**

novio/a *m., f.* boyfriend/ girlfriend **1.3**

nube *f.* cloud **3.1**

nublado/a *adj.* cloudy **1.5**

Está (muy) nublado. It's very cloudy. **1.5**

nuclear *adj. m., f.* nuclear **3.1**

nuera *f.* daughter-in-law **1.3**

nuestro(s)/a(s) *poss. adj.* our **1.3**; (of ours) **2.5**

nueve nine **1.1**

nuevo/a *adj.* new **1.6**

número *m.* number **1.1**; (shoe) size **1.6**

nunca *adv.* never; not ever **2.1**

nutrición *f.* nutrition **3.3**

nutricionista *m., f.* nutritionist **3.3**

O

o or **2.1**

o... o either... or **2.1**

obedecer *v.* to obey **3.6**

obra *f.* work (*of art, literature, music, etc.*) **3.5**

obra maestra *f.* masterpiece **3.5**

obtener *v.* to obtain; to get **3.4**

obvio/a *adj.* obvious **3.1**

océano *m.* ocean

ochenta eighty **1.2**

ocho eight **1.1**

ochocientos/as eight hundred **1.2**

octavo/a *adj.* eighth **1.5**

octubre *m.* October **1.5**

ocupación *f.* occupation **3.4**

ocupado/a *adj.* busy **1.5**

ocurrir *v.* to occur; to happen **3.6**

odiar *v.* to hate **2.3**

oeste *m.* west **3.2**

oferta *f.* offer

oficina *f.* office **2.6**

oficio *m.* trade **3.4**

ofrecer *v.* to offer **1.6**

oído *m.* (sense of) hearing; inner ear **2.4**

oído/a *p.p.* heard **3.2**

oír *v.* to hear **1.4**

Oiga/Oigan. *form., sing./pl.* Listen. (*in conversation*) **1.1**

Oye. *fam., sing.* Listen. (*in conversation*) **1.1**

ojalá (que) *interj.* I hope (that); I wish (that) **3.1**

ojo *m.* eye **2.4**

olvidar *v.* to forget **2.4**

once eleven **1.1**

ópera *f.* opera **3.5**

operación *f.* operation **2.4**

ordenado/a *adj.* orderly **1.5**

ordinal *adj.* ordinal (*number*)

oreja *f.* (outer) ear **2.4**

organizarse *v.* to organize oneself **2.6**

orquesta *f.* orchestra **3.5**

ortografía *f.* spelling

ortográfico/a *adj.* spelling

os *fam., pl. d.o. pron.* you **1.5**; *fam., pl. i.o. pron.* to/for you **1.6**

otoño *m.* autumn **1.5**

otro/a *adj.* other; another **1.6**

otra vez again

P

paciente *m., f.* patient **2.4**

padrastro *m.* stepfather **1.3**

padre *m.* father **1.3**

padres *m., pl.* parents **1.3**

pagar *v.* to pay **1.6, 2.3**

pagar a plazos to pay in installments **3.2**

pagar al contado to pay in cash **3.2**

pagar en efectivo to pay in cash **3.2**
pagar la cuenta to pay the bill **2.3**
página *f.* page **2.5**
  página principal *f.* home page **2.5**
país *m.* country **1.1**
paisaje *m.* landscape **1.5**
pájaro *m.* bird **3.1**
palabra *f.* word **1.1**
paleta helada *f.* popsicle **1.4**
pálido/a *adj.* pale **3.2**
pan *m.* bread **2.2**
  pan tostado *m.* toasted bread **2.2**
panadería *f.* bakery **3.2**
pantalla *f.* screen **2.5**
  pantalla táctil *f.* touch screen **2.5**
pantalones *m., pl.* pants **1.6**
  pantalones cortos *m., pl.* shorts **1.6**
pantuflas *f.* slippers **2.1**
papa *f.* potato **2.2**
  papas fritas *f., pl.* fried potatoes; French fries **2.2**
papá *m.* dad **1.3**
  papás *m., pl.* parents **1.3**
papel *m.* paper **1.2**; role **3.5**
papelera *f.* wastebasket **1.2**
paquete *m.* package **3.2**
par *m.* pair **1.6**
  par de zapatos pair of shoes **1.6**
para *prep.* for; in order to; by; used for; considering **2.5**
  para que so that **3.1**
parabrisas *m., sing.* windshield **2.5**
parar *v.* to stop **2.5**
parecer *v.* to seem **1.6**
pared *f.* wall **2.6**
pareja *f.* (married) couple; partner **2.3**
parientes *m., pl.* relatives **1.3**
parque *m.* park **1.4**
párrafo *m.* paragraph
parte: de parte de on behalf of **2.5**
partido *m.* game; match (*sports*) **1.4**
pasado/a *adj.* last; past **1.6**
  pasado *p.p.* passed
pasaje *m.* ticket **1.5**
  pasaje de ida y vuelta *m.* roundtrip ticket **1.5**
pasajero/a *m., f.* passenger **1.1**
pasaporte *m.* passport **1.5**
pasar *v.* to go through **1.5**
  pasar la aspiradora to vacuum **2.6**
  pasar por el banco to go by the bank **3.2**
  pasar por la aduana to go through customs
  pasar tiempo to spend time
  pasarlo bien/mal to have a good/bad time **2.3**

pasatiempo *m.* pastime; hobby **1.4**
pasear *v.* to take a walk; to stroll **1.4**
  pasear en bicicleta to ride a bicycle **1.4**
  pasear por to walk around **1.4**
pasillo *m.* hallway **2.6**
pasta *f.* **de dientes** toothpaste **2.1**
pastel *m.* cake; pie **2.3**
  pastel de chocolate *m.* chocolate cake **2.3**
  pastel de cumpleaños *m.* birthday cake
pastelería *f.* pastry shop **3.2**
pastilla *f.* pill; tablet **2.4**
patata *f.* potato **2.2**
  patatas fritas *f., pl.* fried potatoes; French fries **2.2**
patinar (en línea) *v.* to (in-line) skate **1.4**
patineta *f.* skateboard **1.4**
patio *m.* patio; yard **2.6**
pavo *m.* turkey **2.2**
paz *f.* peace **3.6**
pedir (e:i) *v.* to ask for; to request **1.4**; to order (*food*) **2.2**
  pedir prestado *v.* to borrow **3.2**
  pedir un préstamo *v.* to apply for a loan **3.2**
  Todos me dijeron que te pidiera disculpas de su parte. They all told me to ask you to excuse them/ forgive them. **3.6**
peinarse *v.* to comb one's hair **2.1**
película *f.* movie **1.4**
peligro *m.* danger **3.1**
peligroso/a *adj.* dangerous **3.6**
pelirrojo/a *adj.* red-haired **1.3**
pelo *m.* hair **2.1**
pelota *f.* ball **1.4**
peluquería *f.* beauty salon **3.2**
peluquero/a *m., f.* hairdresser **3.4**
pensar (e:ie) *v.* to think **1.4**
  pensar (+ inf.) *v.* to intend to; to plan to (do *something*) **1.4**
  pensar en *v.* to think about **1.4**
pensión *f.* boardinghouse
peor *adj.* worse **2.2**
  el/la peor *adj.* the worst **2.2**
pequeño/a *adj.* small **1.3**
pera *f.* pear **2.2**
perder (e:ie) *v.* to lose; to miss **1.4**
perdido/a *adj.* lost **3.1, 3.2**
Perdón Pardon me.; Excuse me. **1.1**
perezoso/a *adj.* lazy
perfecto/a *adj.* perfect **1.5**
periódico *m.* newspaper **1.4**
periodismo *m.* journalism **1.2**
periodista *m., f.* journalist **1.3**
permiso *m.* permission
pero *conj.* but **1.2**
perro *m.* dog **3.1**

persona *f.* person **1.3**
personaje *m.* character **3.5**
  personaje principal *m.* main character **3.5**
pesas *f. pl.* weights **3.3**
pesca *f.* fishing
pescadería *f.* fish market **3.2**
pescado *m.* fish (cooked) **2.2**
pescar *v.* to fish **1.5**
peso *m.* weight **3.3**
pez *m., sing.* (**peces** *pl.*) fish (live) **3.1**
pie *m.* foot **2.4**
piedra *f.* stone **3.1**
pierna *f.* leg **2.4**
pimienta *f.* black pepper **2.2**
pintar *v.* to paint **3.5**
pintor(a) *m., f.* painter **3.4**
pintura *f.* painting; picture **2.6, 3.5**
piña *f.* pineapple
piscina *f.* swimming pool **1.4**
piso *m.* floor (of a building) **1.5**
pizarra *f.* blackboard **1.2**
planchar la ropa *v.* to iron the clothes **2.6**
planes *m., pl.* plans **1.4**
planta *f.* plant **3.1**
  planta baja *f.* ground floor **1.5**
plástico *m.* plastic **3.1**
plato *m.* dish (in a meal) **2.2**; *m.* plate **2.6**
  plato principal *m.* main dish **2.2**
playa *f.* beach **1.5**
plaza *f.* city or town square **1.4**
plazos *m., pl.* periods; time **3.2**
pluma *f.* pen **1.2**
plumero *m.* duster **2.6**
población *f.* population **3.1**
pobre *adj. m., f.* poor **1.6**
pobrecito/a *adj.* poor thing **1.3**
pobreza *f.* poverty
poco/a *adj.* little; few **1.5; 2.4**
poder (o:ue) *v.* to be able to; can **1.4**
  ¿Podría pedirte algo? Could I ask you something? **3.5**
  ¿Puedo dejar un recado? May I leave a message? **2.5**
poema *m.* poem **3.5**
poesía *f.* poetry **3.5**
poeta *m., f.* poet **3.5**
policía *f.* police (force) **2.5**
política *f.* politics **3.6**
político/a *m., f.* politician **3.4**; *adj.* political **3.6**
pollo *m.* chicken **2.2**
  pollo asado *m.* roast chicken **2.2**
ponchar *v.* to go flat
poner *v.* to put; to place **1.4**; to turn on (*electrical appliances*) **2.5**
  poner la mesa to set the table **2.6**
  poner una inyección to give an injection **2.4**
  ponerle el nombre to name someone/something **2.3**

ponerse (+ *adj.*) *v.* to become
(+ *adj.*) 2.1; to put on 2.1
por *prep.* in exchange for; for;
by; in; through; around; along;
during; because of; on account
of; on behalf of; in search of;
by way of; by means of 2.5
  por aquí around here 2.5
  por ejemplo for example 2.5
  por eso that's why;
therefore 2.5
  por favor please 1.1
  por fin finally 2.5
  por la mañana in the
morning 2.1
  por la noche at night 2.1
  por la tarde in the
afternoon 2.1
  por lo menos *adv.* at least 2.4
  ¿por qué? why? 1.2
  Por supuesto. Of course.
  por teléfono by phone; on the
phone
  por último finally 2.1
porque *conj.* because 1.2
portátil *adj. m., f.* portable 2.5
portero/a *m., f.* doorman/
doorwoman 1.1
porvenir *m.* future 3.4
  por el porvenir for/to the
future 3.4
posesivo/a *adj.* possessive 1.3
posible *adj.* possible 3.1
  es posible it's possible 3.1
  no es posible it's not
possible 3.1
postal *f.* postcard
postre *m.* dessert 2.3
practicar *v.* to practice 1.2
  practicar deportes *m., pl.* to
play sports 1.4
precio (fijo) *m.* (fixed; set)
price 1.6
preferir (e:ie) *v.* to prefer 1.4
pregunta *f.* question
preguntar *v.* to ask (*a question*) 1.2
premio *m.* prize; award 3.5
prender *v.* to turn on 2.5
prensa *f.* press 3.6
preocupado/a (por) *adj.* worried
(about) 1.5
preocuparse (por) *v.* to worry
(about) 2.1
preparar *v.* to prepare 1.2
preposición *f.* preposition
presentación *f.* introduction
presentar *v.* to introduce; to
present 3.5; to put on (*a
performance*) 3.5
  Le presento a... I would like
to introduce you to (name).
(*form.*) 1.1
  Te presento a... I would like
to introduce you to (name).
(*fam.*) 1.1
presiones *f., pl.* pressures 3.3
prestado/a *adj.* borrowed

préstamo *m.* loan 3.2
prestar *v.* to lend; to loan 1.6
primavera *f.* spring 1.5
primer, primero/a *adj.* first 1.2,
1.5
primo/a *m., f.* cousin 1.3
principal *adj. m., f.* main 2.2
prisa *f.* haste
  darse prisa *v.* to hurry;
to rush 3.3
probable *adj. m., f.* probable 3.1
  es probable it's probable 3.1
  no es probable it's not
probable 3.1
probar (o:ue) *v.* to taste; to
try 2.2
probarse (o:ue) *v.* to try on 2.1
problema *m.* problem 1.1
profesión *f.* profession 1.3, 3.4
profesor(a) *m., f.* teacher 1.1, 1.2
programa *m.* 1.1
  programa de computación
m. software 2.5
  programa de entrevistas *m.*
talk show 3.5
  programa de realidad *m.*
reality show 3.5
programador(a) *m., f.* computer
programmer 1.3
prohibir *v.* to prohibit 2.4;
to forbid
pronombre *m.* pronoun
pronto *adv.* soon 2.4
propina *f.* tip 2.3
propio/a *adj.* own 3.4
proteger *v.* to protect 3.1
proteína *f.* protein 3.3
próximo/a *adj.* next 1.3, 3.4
proyecto *m.* project 2.5
prueba *f.* test; quiz 1.2
psicología *f.* psychology 1.2
psicólogo/a *m., f.* psychologist 3.4
publicar *v.* to publish 3.5
público *m.* audience 3.5
pueblo *m.* town 1.4
puerta *f.* door 1.2
Puerto Rico *m.* Puerto Rico 1.1
puertorriqueño/a *adj.* Puerto
Rican 1.3
pues *conj.* well
puesto *m.* position; job 3.4
puesto/a *p.p.* put 3.2
puro/a *adj.* pure 3.1

Q

que *pron.* that; which; who 2.6
  ¿En qué...? In which...? 1.2
  ¡Qué...! How...!
  ¡Qué dolor! What pain!
  ¡Qué ropa más bonita!
What pretty clothes! 1.6
  ¡Qué sorpresa! What a surprise!
  ¿qué? what? 1.1
  ¿Qué día es hoy? What day is
it? 1.2

¿Qué hay de nuevo? What's
new? 1.1
¿Qué hora es? What time
is it? 1.1
¿Qué les parece? What do
you (*pl.*) think?
¿Qué onda? What's up? 3.2
¿Qué pasa? What's happening?
What's going on? 1.1
¿Qué pasó? What happened? 2.5
¿Qué precio tiene? What is
the price?
¿Qué tal...? How are you?;
How is it going? 1.1
¿Qué talla lleva/usa? What
size do you wear? 1.6
¿Qué tiempo hace? How's
the weather? 1.5
quedar *v.* to be left over;
to fit (*clothing*) 2.1; to
be left behind; to be located 3.2
quedarse *v.* to stay; to remain 2.1
quehaceres domésticos *m.,
pl.* household chores 2.6
quemar (un CD/DVD)
v. to burn (a CD/DVD)
querer (e:ie) *v.* to want; to love 1.4
queso *m.* cheese 2.2
quien(es) *pron.* who; whom;
that 2.6
  ¿quién(es)? who?; whom? 1.1
  ¿Quién es...? Who is...? 1.1
  ¿Quién habla? Who is
speaking/calling? (*phone*) 2.5
química *f.* chemistry 1.2
quince fifteen 1.1
  menos quince quarter to
(time) 1.1
  y quince quarter after (time) 1.1
quinceañera *f.* young
woman celebrating her
fifteenth birthday 2.3
quinientos/as *adj.* five hundred 1.2
quinto/a *adj.* fifth 1.5
quisiera *v.* I would like 3.5
quitar el polvo *v.* to dust 2.6
quitar la mesa *v.* to
clear the table 2.6
quitarse *v.* to take off 2.1
quizás *adv.* maybe 1.5

R

racismo *m.* racism 3.6
radio *f.* radio (*medium*) 1.2;
m. radio (set) 1.2
radiografía *f.* X-ray 2.4
rápido *adv.* quickly 2.4
ratón *m.* mouse 2.5
ratos libres *m., pl.* spare (free)
time 1.4
raya *f.* stripe 1.6
razón *f.* reason
rebaja *f.* sale 1.6
receta *f.* prescription 2.4
recetar *v.* to prescribe 2.4

Span-Eng

recibir *v.* to receive 1.3
reciclaje *m.* recycling 3.1
reciclar *v.* to recycle 3.1
recién casado/a *m.,*
  f. newlywed 2.3
recoger *v.* to pick up 3.1
recomendar (e:ie) *v.* to
  recommend 2.2, 2.6
recordar (o:ue) *v.* to remember 1.4
recorrer *v.* to tour an area
recuperar *v.* to recover 2.5
recurso *m.* resource 3.1
  recurso natural *m.* natural
    resource 3.1
red *f.* network; Web 2.5
reducir *v.* to reduce 3.1
refresco *m.* soft drink 2.2
refrigerador *m.* refrigerator 2.6
regalar *v.* to give (a gift) 2.3
regalo *m.* gift 1.6
regatear *v.* to bargain 1.6
región *f.* region; area 3.1
regresar *v.* to return 1.2
regular *adv.* so-so; OK 1.1
reído *p.p.* laughed 3.2
reírse (e:i) *v.* to laugh 2.3
relaciones *f., pl.* relationships
relajarse *v.* to relax 2.3
reloj *m.* clock; watch 1.2
renovable *adj.* renewable 3.1
renunciar (a) *v.* to resign
  (from) 3.4
repetir (e:i) *v.* to repeat 1.4
reportaje *m.* report 3.6
reportero/a *m., f.* reporter;
  journalist 3.4
representante *m., f.*
  representative 3.6
reproductor de CD *m.* CD
  player 2.5
reproductor de DVD *m.* DVD
  player 2.5
reproductor de MP3 *m.* MP3
  player 2.5
resfriado *m.* cold (*illness*) 2.4
residencia estudiantil *f.*
  dormitory 1.2
resolver (o:ue) *v.* to resolve;
  to solve 3.1
respirar *v.* to breathe 3.1
responsable *adj.* responsible 2.2
respuesta *f.* answer
restaurante *m.* restaurant 1.4
resuelto/a *p.p.* resolved 3.2
reunión *f.* meeting 3.4
revisar *v.* to check 2.5
  revisar el aceite *v.* to check
    the oil 2.5
revista *f.* magazine 1.4
rico/a *adj.* rich 1.6; *adj.* tasty;
  delicious 2.2
ridículo/a *adj.* ridiculous 3.1
río *m.* river 3.1
rodilla *f.* knee 2.4
rogar (o:ue) *v.* to beg; to
  plead 2.6
rojo/a *adj.* red 1.6

romántico/a *adj.* romantic 3.5
romper *v.* to break 2.4
  romperse la pierna *v.* to break
    one's leg 2.4
romper (con) *v.* to break up
  (with) 2.3
ropa *f.* clothing; clothes 1.6
  ropa interior *f.* underwear 1.6
rosado/a *adj.* pink 1.6
roto/a *adj.* broken 2.4, 3.2
rubio/a *adj.* blond(e) 1.3
ruso/a *adj.* Russian 1.3
rutina *f.* routine 2.1
  rutina diaria *f.* daily routine 2.1

S

sábado *m.* Saturday 1.2
saber *v.* to know; to know how 1.6;
  to taste 2.2
  saber a to taste like 2.2
sabrosísimo/a *adj.* extremely
  delicious 2.2
sabroso/a *adj.* tasty; delicious 2.2
sacar *v.* to take out
  sacar buena notas to get
    good grades 1.2
  sacar fotos to take photos 1.5
  sacar la basura to take out
    the trash 2.6
  sacar(se) un diente to have a
    tooth removed 2.4
sacudir *v.* to dust 2.6
  sacudir los muebles to dust
    the furniture 2.6
sal *f.* salt 2.2
sala *f.* living room 2.6; room
  sala de emergencia(s)
    emergency room 2.4
salario *m.* salary 3.4
salchicha *f.* sausage 2.2
salida *f.* departure; exit 1.5
salir *v.* to leave 1.4; to go out 2.9
  salir (con) to go out (with);
    to date 2.3
  salir de to leave from
  salir para to leave for (*a place*)
salmón *m.* salmon 2.2
salón de belleza *m.* beauty
  salon 3.2
salud *f.* health 2.4
saludable *adj.* healthy 2.4
saludar(se) *v.* to greet (each
  other) 2.5
saludo *m.* greeting 1.1
  saludos a... greetings to... 1.1
sandalia *f.* sandal 1.6
sandía *f.* watermelon
sándwich *m.* sandwich 2.2
sano/a *adj.* healthy 2.4
se *ref. pron.* himself, herself,
  itself, *form.* yourself,
  themselves, yourselves 2.1
se *impersonal* one 2.4
  Se hizo... He/she/it became...
secadora *f.* clothes dryer 2.6

secarse *v.* to dry oneself 2.1
sección de (no) fumar *f.* (non)
  smoking section 2.2
secretario/a *m., f.* secretary 3.4
secuencia *f.* sequence
seda *f.* silk 1.6
sedentario/a *adj.* sedentary;
  related to sitting 3.3
seguir (e:i) *v.* to follow; to
  continue 1.4
según according to
segundo/a *adj.* second 1.5
seguro/a *adj.* sure; safe 1.5
seis six 1.1
seiscientos/as six hundred 1.2
sello *m.* stamp 3.2
selva *f.* jungle 3.1
semáforo *m.* traffic light 3.2
semana *f.* week 1.2
  fin *m.* **de semana** weekend 1.4
  semana *f.* **pasada** last week 1.6
semestre *m.* semester 1.2
sendero *m.* trail; trailhead 3.1
sentarse (e:ie) *v.* to sit down 2.1
sentir(se) (e:ie) *v.* to feel 2.1;
  to be sorry; to regret 3.1
señor (Sr.); don *m.* Mr.; sir 1.1
señora (Sra.); doña *f.* Mrs.;
  ma'am 1.1
señorita (Srta.) *f.* Miss 1.1
separado/a *adj.* separated 2.3
separarse (de) *v.* to separate
  (from) 2.3
septiembre *m.* September 1.5
séptimo/a *adj.* seventh 1.5
ser *v.* to be 1.1
  ser aficionado/a (a) to be a
    fan (of) 1.4
  ser alérgico/a (a) to be allergic
    (to) 2.4
  ser gratis to be free of
    charge 3.2
serio/a *adj.* serious
servicio *m.* service 3.3
servilleta *f.* napkin 2.6
servir (e:i) *v.* to help 1.5; to
  serve 2.2
sesenta sixty 1.2
setecientos/as seven hundred 1.2
setenta seventy 1.2
sexismo *m.* sexism 3.6
sexto/a *adj.* sixth 1.5
sí *adv.* yes 1.1
si *conj.* if 1.4
SIDA *m.* AIDS 3.6
sido *p.p.* been 3.3
siempre *adv.* always 2.1
siete seven 1.1
silla *f.* seat 1.2
sillón *m.* armchair 2.6
similar *adj. m., f.* similar
simpático/a *adj.* nice; likeable 1.3
sin *prep.* without 1.2, 3.1
  sin duda without a doubt
  sin embargo however
  sin que *conj.* without 3.1
sino but (rather)

síntoma *m.* symptom 2.4
sitio *m.* place 1.3
sitio *m.* **web** website 2.5
situado/a *p.p.* located
sobre *m.* envelope 3.2; *prep.* on; over 1.2
  sobre todo above all 3.1
(sobre)población *f.* (over)population 3.1
sobrino/a *m., f.* nephew; niece 1.3
sociología *f.* sociology 1.2
sofá *m.* couch; sofa 2.6
sol *m.* sun 1.4; 1.5; 3.1
solar *adj. m., f.* solar 3.1
soldado *m., f.* soldier 3.6
soleado/a *adj.* sunny
solicitar *v.* to apply (*for a job*) 3.4
solicitud (de trabajo) *f.* (job) application 3.4
sólo *adv.* only 1.3
solo/a *adj.* alone
soltero/a *adj.* single 2.3
solución *f.* solution 3.1
sombrero *m.* hat 1.6
Son las dos. It's two o'clock. 1.1
sonar (o:ue) *v.* to ring 2.5
sonreído *p.p.* smiled 3.2
sonreír (e:i) *v.* to smile 2.3
sopa *f.* soup 2.2
sorprender *v.* to surprise 2.3
sorpresa *f.* surprise 2.3
sótano *m.* basement; cellar 2.6
soy I am 1.1
  Soy de... I'm from... 1.1
su(s) *poss. adj.* his; her; its; *form.* your; their 1.3
subir(se) a *v.* to get on/into (*a vehicle*) 2.5
sucio/a *adj.* dirty 1.5
sudar *v.* to sweat 3.3
suegro/a *m., f.* father-in-law; mother-in-law 1.3
sueldo *m.* salary 3.4
suelo *m.* floor 2.6
suéter *m.* sweater 1.6
sufrir *v.* to suffer 2.4
  sufrir muchas presiones to be under a lot of pressure 3.3
  sufrir una enfermedad to suffer an illness 2.4
sugerir (e:ie) *v.* to suggest 2.6
supermercado *m.* supermarket 3.2
suponer *v.* to suppose 1.4
sur *m.* south 3.2
sustantivo *m.* noun
suyo(s)/a(s) *poss.* (of) his/her; (of) hers; (of) its; (of) *form.* your, (of) yours, (of) their 2.5

T

tabla de (wind)surf *f.* sufboard/sailboard 1.3
tal vez *adv.* maybe 1.5
talentoso/a *adj.* talented 3.5
talla *f.* size 1.6
  talla grande *f.* large

taller *m.* **mecánico** garage; mechanic's repairshop 2.5
también *adv.* also; too 1.2; 2.1
tampoco *adv.* neither; not either 2.1
tan *adv.* so 1.5
  tan... como as... as 2.2
  tan pronto como *conj.* as soon as 3.1
tanque *m.* tank 2.5
tanto *adv.* so much
  tanto... como as much... as 2.2
tantos/as como as many... as 2.2
tarde *f.* afternoon; evening; P.M. 1.1; *adv.* late 2.1
tarea *f.* homework 1.2
tarjeta *f.* (post) card
tarjeta de crédito *f.* credit card 1.6
tarjeta postal *f.* postcard
taxi *m.* taxi 1.5
taza *f.* cup 2.6
te *sing., fam., d.o. pron.* you 1.5; *sing., fam., i.o. pron.* to/for you 1.6
  Te presento a... *fam.* I would like to introduce you to (name). 1.1
  ¿Te gustaría? Would you like to? 3.5
  ¿Te gusta(n)... ? Do you like... ? 1.2
té *m.* tea 2.2
  té helado *m.* iced tea 2.2
teatro *m.* theater 3.5
teclado *m.* keyboard 2.5
técnico/a *m., f.* technician 3.4
tejido *m.* weaving 3.5
teleadicto/a *m., f.* couch potato 3.3
teléfono (celular) *m.* (cell) phone 2.5
telenovela *f.* soap opera 3.5
teletrabajo *m.* telecommuting 3.4
televisión *f.* television 1.2; 2.5
televisión por cable *f.* cable television 2.5
televisor *m.* television set 2.5
temer *v.* to fear 3.1
temperatura *f.* temperature 2.4
temporada *f.* period of time 1.5
temprano *adv.* early 2.1
tenedor *m.* fork 2.6
tener *v.* to have 1.3
  tener... años to be... years old 1.3
  Tengo... años. I'm... years old. 1.3
  tener (mucho) calor to be (very) hot 1.3
  tener (mucho) cuidado to be (very) careful 1.3
  tener dolor to have pain 2.4
  tener éxito to be successful 3.4
  tener fiebre to have a fever 2.4
  tener (mucho) frío to be (very) cold 1.3

tener ganas de (+ *inf.*) to feel like (*doing something*) 1.3
tener (mucha) hambre *f.* to be (very) hungry 1.3
tener (mucho) miedo (de) to be (very) afraid (of); to be (very) scared (of) 1.3
tener miedo (de) que to be afraid that
tener planes *m., pl.* to have plans 1.4
tener (mucha) prisa to be in a (big) hurry 1.3
tener que (+ *inf.*) *v.* to have to (*do something*) 1.3
tener razón *f.* to be right 1.3
tener (mucha) sed *f.* to be (very) thirsty 1.3
tener (mucho) sueño to be (very) sleepy 1.3
tener (mucha) suerte to be (very) lucky 1.3
tener tiempo to have time 1.4
tener una cita to have a date; to have an appointment 2.3
tenis *m.* tennis 1.4
tensión *f.* tension 3.3
tercer, tercero/a *adj.* third 1.5
terco/a *adj.* stubborn 2.4
terminar *v.* to end; to finish 1.2
  terminar de (+ *inf.*) *v.* to finish (*doing something*) 1.4
terremoto *m.* earthquake 3.6
terrible *adj. m., f.* terrible 3.1
ti *obj. of prep., fam.* you
tiempo *m.* time 1.4; weather 1.5
  tiempo libre free time
tienda *f.* shop; store 1.6
tierra *f.* land; soil 3.1
tinto/a *adj.* red (wine) 2.2
tío/a *m., f.* uncle; aunt 1.3
tíos *m., pl.* aunts and uncles 1.3
título *m.* title 3.4
tiza *f.* chalk 1.2
toalla *f.* towel 2.1
tobillo *m.* ankle 2.4
tocar *v.* to play (*a musical instrument*) 3.5; to touch
todavía *adv.* yet; still 1.3, 1.5
todo *m.* everything 1.5
  Todo está bajo control. Everything is under control. 2.1
todo(s)/a(s) *adj.* all 1.4; whole
todos *m., pl.* all of us; *m., pl.* everybody; everyone
todos los días *adv.* every day 2.4
tomar *v.* to take; to drink 1.2
  tomar clases *f., pl.* to take classes 1.2
  tomar el sol to sunbathe 1.4
  tomar en cuenta to take into account
  tomar fotos *f., pl.* to take photos 1.5
  tomar la temperatura to take someone's temperature 2.4

Span–Eng

tomar una decisión to make a decision **3.3**
tomate *m.* tomato **2.2**
tonto/a *adj.* silly; foolish **1.3**
torcerse (o:ue) (el tobillo) *v.* to sprain (one's ankle) **2.4**
torcido/a *adj.* twisted; sprained **2.4**
tormenta *f.* storm **3.6**
tornado *m.* tornado **3.6**
tortuga (marina) *f.* (sea) turtle **3.1**
tos *f., sing.* cough **2.4**
toser *v.* to cough **2.4**
tostado/a *adj.* toasted **2.2**
tostadora *f.* toaster **2.6**
trabajador(a) *adj.* hard-working **1.3**
trabajar *v.* to work **1.2**
trabajo *m.* job; work **3.4**
traducir *v.* to translate **1.6**
traer *v.* to bring **1.4**
tráfico *m.* traffic **2.5**
tragedia *f.* tragedy **3.5**
traído/a *p.p.* brought **3.2**
traje *m.* suit **1.6**
  traje (de baño) *m.* (bathing) suit **1.6**
trajinera *f.* type of barge **1.3**
tranquilo/a *adj.* calm; quiet **3.3**
  Tranquilo. Don't worry.; Be cool. **2.1**
  Tranquilo, cariño. Relax, sweetie. **2.5**
transmitir *v.* to broadcast **3.6**
tratar de (+ *inf.*) *v.* to try (*to do something*) **3.3**
trece thirteen **1.1**
treinta thirty **1.1, 1.2**
  y treinta thirty minutes past the hour (time) **1.1**
tren *m.* train **1.5**
tres three **1.1**
trescientos/as three hundred **1.2**
trimestre *m.* trimester; quarter **1.2**
triste *adj.* sad **1.5**
tú *fam. sub. pron.* you **1.1**
  Tú eres... You are... **1.1**
tu(s) *fam. poss. adj.* your **1.3**
turismo *m.* tourism **1.5**
turista *m., f.* tourist **1.1**
turístico/a *adj.* touristic
tuyo(s)/a(s) *fam. poss. pron.* your; (of) yours **2.5**

U

Ud. *form. sing.* you **1.1**
Uds. *form., pl.* you **1.1**
último/a *adj.* last **2.1**
  la última vez the last time **2.1**
un, uno/a *indef. art.* a; one **1.1**
  uno/a *m., f., sing. pron.* one **1.1**
   a la una at one o'clock **1.1**
  una vez once; one time **1.6**
  una vez más one more time **2.3**

único/a *adj.* only **1.3**; unique **2.3**
universidad *f.* university; college **1.2**
unos/as *m., f., pl. indef. art.* some **1.1**
  los unos a los otros each other **2.5**
  unos/as *pron.* some **1.1**
urgente *adj.* urgent **2.6**
usar *v.* to wear; to use **1.6**
usted (Ud.) *form. sing.* you **1.1**
  ustedes (Uds.) *form., pl.* you **1.1**
útil *adj.* useful
uva *f.* grape **2.2**

V

vaca *f.* cow **3.1**
vacaciones *f. pl.* vacation **1.5**
valle *m.* valley **3.1**
vamos *let's* go **1.4**
vaquero *m.* cowboy **3.5**
  de vaqueros *m., pl.* western (genre) **3.5**
varios/as *adj. m. f., pl.* various; several **2.2**
vaso *m.* glass **2.6**
veces *f., pl.* times **1.6**
vecino/a *m., f.* neighbor **2.6**
veinte twenty **1.1**
veinticinco twenty-five **1.1**
veinticuatro twenty-four **1.1**
veintidós twenty-two **1.1**
veintinueve twenty-nine **1.1**
veintiocho twenty-eight **1.1**
veintiséis twenty-six **1.1**
veintisiete twenty-seven **1.1**
veintitrés twenty-three **1.1**
veintiún, veintiuno/a twenty-one **1.1**
vejez *f.* old age **2.3**
velocidad *f.* speed **2.5**
  velocidad máxima *f.* speed limit **2.5**
vencer *v.* to expire **2.2**
vendedor(a) *m., f.* salesperson **1.6**
vender *v.* to sell **1.6**
venir *v.* to come **1.3**
ventana *f.* window **1.2**
ver *v.* to see **1.4**
  a ver *v.* let's see **1.2**
  ver películas *f., pl.* to see movies **1.4**
verano *m.* summer **1.5**
verbo *m.* verb
verdad *f.* truth
  ¿verdad? right? **1.1**
verde *adj., m. f.* green **1.6**
verduras *pl., f.* vegetables **2.2**
vestido *m.* dress **1.6**
vestirse (e:i) *v.* to get dressed **2.1**
vez *f.* time **1.6**
viajar *v.* to travel **1.2**
viaje *m.* trip **1.5**
viajero/a *m., f.* traveler **1.5**
vida *f.* life **2.3**

video *m.* video **1.1, 2.5**
videoconferencia *f.* videoconference **3.4**
videojuego *m.* video game **1.4**
vidrio *m.* glass **3.1**
viejo/a *adj.* old **1.3**
viento *m.* wind **1.5**
viernes *m., sing.* Friday **1.2**
vinagre *m.* vinegar **2.2**
vino *m.* wine **2.2**
  vino blanco *m.* white wine **2.2**
  vino tinto *m.* red wine **2.2**
violencia *f.* violence **3.6**
visitar *v.* to visit **1.4**
  visitar monumentos *m., pl.* to visit monuments **1.4**
visto/a *p.p.* seen **3.2**
vitamina *f.* vitamin **3.3**
viudo/a *adj.* widower/widow **2.3**
vivienda *f.* housing **2.6**
vivir *v.* to live **1.3**
vivo/a *adj.* bright; lively; living
volante *m.* steering wheel **2.5**
volcán *m.* volcano **3.1**
vóleibol *m.* volleyball **1.4**
volver (o:ue) *v.* to return **1.4**
volver a ver(te, lo, la) *v.* to see (you, him, her) again **3.6**
vos *pron.* you
vosotros/as *fam., pl.* you **1.1**
votar *v.* to vote **3.6**
vuelta *f.* return trip
vuelto/a *p.p.* returned **3.2**
vuestro(s)/a(s) *poss. adj.* your **1.3**; (of) yours *fam.* **2.5**

W

walkman *m.* walkman

Y

y *conj.* and **1.1**
  y cuarto quarter after (time) **1.1**
  y media half-past (time) **1.1**
  y quince quarter after (time) **1.1**
  y treinta thirty (minutes past the hour) **1.1**
  ¿Y tú? *fam.* And you? **1.1**
  ¿Y usted? *form.* And you? **1.1**
ya *adv.* already **1.6**
yerno *m.* son-in-law **1.3**
yo *sub. pron.* I **1.1**
  Yo soy... I'm... **1.1**
yogur *m.* yogurt **2.2**

Z

zanahoria *f.* carrot **2.2**
zapatería *f.* shoe store **3.2**
zapatos de tenis *m., pl.* tennis shoes, sneakers **1.6**

English-Spanish

A

a **un/a** *m., f., sing.; indef. art.* 1.1
@ (*symbol*) **arroba** *f.* 2.5
A.M. **mañana** *f.* 1.1
able: be able to **poder (o:ue)** *v.* 1.4
above all **sobre todo** 3.1
accident **accidente** *m.* 2.4
accompany **acompañar** *v.* 3.2
account **cuenta** *f.* 3.2
  on account of **por** *prep.* 2.5
accountant **contador(a)** *m., f.* 3.4
accounting **contabilidad** *f.* 1.2
ache **dolor** *m.* 2.4
acquainted: be acquainted
  with **conocer** *v.* 1.6
action (genre) **de acción** *f.* 3.5
active **activo/a** *adj.* 3.3
actor **actor** *m.*, **actriz** *f.* 3.4
addict (*drug*) **drogadicto/a** *adj.* 3.3
additional **adicional** *adj.*
address **dirección** *f.* 3.2
adjective **adjetivo** *m.*
adolescence **adolescencia** *f.* 2.3
adventure (genre) **de aventura** *f.* 3.5
advertise **anunciar** *v.* 3.6
advertisement **anuncio** *m.* 3.4
advice **consejo** *m.* 1.6
  give advice **dar consejos** 1.6
advise **aconsejar** *v.* 2.6
advisor **consejero/a** *m., f.* 3.4
aerobic **aeróbico/a** *adj.* 3.3
  aerobics class **clase de
    ejercicios aeróbicos** 3.3
  to do aerobics **hacer ejercicios
    aeróbicos** 3.3
affected **afectado/a** *adj.* 3.1
  be affected (by) **estar** *v.*
    afectado/a (por) 3.1
affirmative **afirmativo/a** *adj.*
afraid: be (very) afraid (of) **tener
  (mucho) miedo (de)** 1.3
  be afraid that **tener miedo
    (de) que**
after **después de** *prep.* 2.1;
  después de que *conj.* 3.1
afternoon **tarde** *f.* 1.1
afterward **después** *adv.* 2.1
again **otra vez**
age **edad** *f.* 2.3
agree **concordar** *v.*
agree **estar** *v.* **de acuerdo** 3.4
  I agree. **Estoy de acuerdo.** 3.4
  I don't agree. **No estoy de
    acuerdo.** 3.4
agreement **acuerdo** *m.* 3.4
AIDS **SIDA** *m.* 3.6
air **aire** *m.* 3.1
  air pollution **contaminación
    del aire** 3.1
airplane **avión** *m.* 1.5
airport **aeropuerto** *m.* 1.5
alarm clock **despertador** *m.* 2.1
alcohol **alcohol** *m.* 3.3

to consume alcohol **consumir
  alcohol** 3.3
alcoholic **alcohólico/a** *adj.* 3.3
all **todo(s)/a(s)** *adj.* 1.4
  all of us **todos** 1.1
  all over the world **en todo el
    mundo**
allergic **alérgico/a** *adj.* 2.4
  be allergic (to) **ser alérgico/a
    (a)** 2.4
alleviate **aliviar** *v.*
almost **casi** *adv.* 2.4
alone **solo/a** *adj.*
along **por** *prep.* 2.5
already **ya** *adv.* 1.6
also **también** *adv.* 1.2; 2.1
altar **altar** *m.* 2.3
aluminum **aluminio** *m.* 3.1
  (made) of aluminum **de
    aluminio** 3.1
always **siempre** *adv.* 2.1
American (*North*)
  norteamericano/a *adj.* 1.3
among **entre** *prep.* 1.2
amusement **diversión** *f.*
and **y** 1.1, **e** (*before words
  beginning with i or hi*) 1.4
  And you? **¿Y tú?** *fam.* 1.1;
    ¿Y usted? *form.* 1.1
angel **ángel** *m.* 2.3
angry **enojado/a** *adj.* 1.5
  get angry (with) **enojarse** *v.*
    (con) 2.1
animal **animal** *m.* 3.1
ankle **tobillo** *m.* 2.4
anniversary **aniversario** *m.* 2.3
  (wedding) anniversary
    aniversario *m.*
    (de bodas) 2.3
announce **anunciar** *v.* 3.6
announcer (*TV/radio*) **locutor(a)**
  m., f. 3.6
annoy **molestar** *v.* 2.1
another **otro/a** *adj.* 1.6
answer **contestar** *v.* 1.2;
  respuesta *f.*
antibiotic **antibiótico** *m.* 2.4
any **algún, alguno/a(s)** *adj.* 2.1
anyone **alguien** *pron.* 2.1
anything **algo** *pron.* 2.1
apartment **apartamento** *m.* 2.6
apartment building **edificio de
  apartamentos** 2.6
appear **parecer** *v.*
appetizers **entremeses** *m., pl.* 2.2
applaud **aplaudir** *v.* 3.5
apple **manzana** *f.* 2.2
appliance (electric)
  electrodoméstico *m.* 2.6
applicant **aspirante** *m., f.* 3.4
application **solicitud** *f.* 3.4
  job application **solicitud de
    trabajo** 3.4
apply (*for a job*) **solicitar** *v.* 3.4
  apply for a loan **pedir (e:i)** *v.*
    un préstamo 3.2
appointment **cita** *f.* 2.3

have an appointment **tener** *v.*
  una cita 2.3
appreciate **apreciar** *v.* 3.5
April **abril** *m.* 1.5
aquatic **acuático/a** *adj.*
archaeologist **arqueólogo/a**
  m., f. 3.4
archaeology **arqueología** *f.* 1.2
architect **arquitecto/a** *m., f.* 3.4
area **región** *f.* 3.1
Argentina **Argentina** *f.* 1.1
Argentine **argentino/a** *adj.* 1.3
arm **brazo** *m.* 2.4
armchair **sillón** *m.* 2.6
army **ejército** *m.* 3.6
around **por** *prep.* 2.5
  around here **por aquí** 2.5
arrange **arreglar** *v.* 2.5
arrival **llegada** *f.* 1.5
arrive **llegar** *v.* 1.2
art **arte** *m.* 1.2
  (fine) arts **bellas artes** *f., pl.* 3.5
article **artículo** *m.* 3.6
artist **artista** *m., f.* 1.3
artistic **artístico/a** *adj.* 3.5
arts **artes** *f., pl.* 3.5
as **como** 2.2
  as a child **de niño/a** 2.4
  as... as **tan... como** 2.2
  as many... as **tantos/as...
    como** 2.2
  as much... as **tanto...
    como** 2.2
  as soon as **en cuanto** *conj.* 3.1;
    tan pronto como *conj.* 3.1
ask (*a question*) **preguntar** *v.* 1.2
  ask for **pedir (e:i)** *v.* 1.4
asparagus **espárragos** *m., pl.* 2.2
aspirin **aspirina** *f.* 2.4
at **a** *prep.* 1.1; **en** *prep.* 1.2
  at + *time* **a la(s)** + *time* 1.1
  at home **en casa** 2.1
  at least **por lo menos** 2.4
  at night **por la noche** 2.1
  at the end (of) **al fondo (de)** 2.6
  At what time...? **¿A qué
    hora...?** 1.1
  At your service. **A sus
    órdenes.**
ATM **cajero automático** *m.* 3.2
attempt **intento** *m.* 2.5
attend **asistir (a)** *v.* 1.3
attic **altillo** *m.* 2.6
attract **atraer** *v.* 1.4
audience **público** *m.* 3.5
August **agosto** *m.* 1.5
aunt **tía** *f.* 1.3
  aunts and uncles **tíos** *m., pl.* 1.3
automobile **automóvil** *m.* 1.5;
  carro *m.*; **coche** *m.* 2.5
autumn **otoño** *m.* 1.5
avenue **avenida** *f.*
avoid **evitar** *v.* 3.1
award **premio** *m.* 3.5

B

backpack **mochila** *f.* 1.2
bad **mal, malo/a** *adj.* 1.3
  It's bad that... **Es malo
    que...** 2.6
  It's not at all bad. **No está
    nada mal.** 1.5
bag **bolsa** *f.* 1.6
bakery **panadería** *f.* 3.2
balanced **equilibrado/a** *adj.* 3.3
  to eat a balanced diet **comer
    una dieta equilibrada** 3.3
balcony **balcón** *m.* 2.6
ball **pelota** *f.* 1.4
banana **banana** *f.* 2.2
band **banda** *f.* 3.5
bank **banco** *m.* 3.2
bargain **ganga** *f.* 1.6;
  regatear *v.* 1.6
baseball (*game*) **béisbol** *m.* 1.4
basement **sótano** *m.* 2.6
basketball (*game*) **baloncesto**
  m. 1.4
bathe **bañarse** *v.* 2.1
bathing suit **traje** *m.* **de baño** 1.6
bathroom **baño** *m.* 2.1;
  cuarto de baño *m.* 2.1
be **ser** *v.* 1.1; **estar** *v.* 1.2
  be... years old **tener... años** 1.3
  be sick of... **estar harto/a
    de...** 3.6
beach **playa** *f.* 1.5
beans **frijoles** *m., pl.* 2.2
beautiful **hermoso/a** *adj.* 1.6
beauty **belleza** *f.* 3.2
  beauty salon **peluquería** *f.* 3.2;
    salón *m.* **de belleza** 3.2
because **porque** *conj.* 1.2
  because of **por** *prep.* 2.5
become (+ *adj.*) **ponerse**
  (+ *adj.*) 2.1; **convertirse** *v.*
bed **cama** *f.* 1.5
  go to bed **acostarse (o:ue)** *v.* 2.1
bedroom **alcoba** *f.*; **dormitorio** *m.*
  2.6; **recámara** *f.*
beef **carne de res** *f.* 2.2
been **sido** *p.p.* 3.3
beer **cerveza** *f.* 2.2
before **antes** *adv.* 2.1; **antes de**
  prep. 2.1; **antes (de) que**
  conj. 3.1
beg **rogar (o:ue)** *v.* 2.6
begin **comenzar (e:ie)** *v.* 1.4;
  empezar (e:ie) *v.* 1.4
behalf: on behalf of **de parte de** 2.5
behind **detrás de** *prep.* 1.2
believe (in) **creer** *v.* **(en)** 1.3;
  creer *v.* 3.1
  not to believe **no creer** 3.1
believed **creído/a** *p.p.* 3.2
bellhop **botones** *m., f. sing.* 1.5
below **debajo de** *prep.* 1.2
belt **cinturón** *m.* 1.6
benefit **beneficio** *m.* 3.4
beside **al lado de** *prep.* 1.2
besides **además (de)** *adv.* 2.4

best **mejor** *adj.*
  the best **el/la mejor** *m., f.* 2.2;
better **mejor** *adj.* 2.2
  It's better that... **Es mejor
    que...** 2.6
between **entre** *prep.* 1.2
beverage **bebida** *f.*
  alcoholic beverage **bebida
    alcohólica** *f.* 3.3
bicycle **bicicleta** *f.* 1.4
big **gran, grande** *adj.* 1.3
bill **cuenta** *f.* 2.3
billion **mil millones**
biology **biología** *f.* 1.2
bird **ave** *f.* 3.1; **pájaro** *m.* 3.1
birth **nacimiento** *m.* 2.3
birthday **cumpleaños** *m., sing.* 2.3
  have a birthday **cumplir** *v.*
    años 2.3
black **negro/a** *adj.* 1.6
blackboard **pizarra** *f.* 1.2
blanket **manta** *f.* 2.6
block (city) **cuadra** *f.* 3.2
blog **blog** *m.* 2.5
blond(e) **rubio/a** *adj.* 1.3
blouse **blusa** *f.* 1.6
blue **azul** *adj. m., f.* 1.6
boarding house **pensión** *f.*
boat **barco** *m.* 1.5
body **cuerpo** *m.* 2.4
bone **hueso** *m.* 2.4
book **libro** *m.* 1.2
bookcase **estante** *m.* 2.6
bookshelves **estante** *m.* 2.6
bookstore **librería** *f.* 1.2
boot **bota** *f.* 1.6
bore **aburrir** *v.* 2.1
bored **aburrido/a** *adj.* 1.5
  be bored **estar** *v.* **aburrido/a** 1.5
  get bored **aburrirse** *v.* 3.5
boring **aburrido/a** *adj.* 1.5
born: be born **nacer** *v.* 2.3
borrow **pedir (e:i)** *v.*
  prestado 3.2
borrowed **prestado/a** *adj.*
boss **jefe** *m.*, **jefa** *f.* 3.4
bother **molestar** *v.* 2.1
bottle **botella** *f.* 2.3
  bottle of wine **botella de
    vino** 2.3
bottom **fondo** *m.*
boulevard **bulevar** *m.*
boy **chico** *m.* 1.1;
  muchacho *m.* 1.3
boyfriend **novio** *m.* 1.3
brakes **frenos** *m., pl.*
bread **pan** *m.* 2.2
break **romper** *v.* 2.4
  break (one's leg) **romperse
    (la pierna)** 2.4
  break down **dañar** *v.* 2.4
  break up (with) **romper** *v.*
    (con) 2.3
breakfast **desayuno** *m.* 1.2, 2.2
  have breakfast **desayunar** *v.* 1.2
breathe **respirar** *v.* 3.1
bring **traer** *v.* 1.4

broadcast **transmitir** *v.* 3.6;
  emitir *v.* 3.6
brochure **folleto** *m.*
broken **roto/a** *adj.* 2.4, 3.2
  be broken **estar roto/a** 2.4
brother **hermano** *m.* 1.3
  brother-in-law **cuñado** *m., f.* 1.3
  brothers and sisters **hermanos**
    m., pl. 1.3
brought **traído/a** *p.p.* 3.2
brown **café** *adj.* 1.6;
  marrón *adj.* 1.6
brunet(te) **moreno/a** *adj.* 1.3
brush **cepillar** *v.* 2.1
  brush one's hair **cepillarse el
    pelo** 2.1
  brush one's teeth **cepillarse los
    dientes** 2.1
bucket **balde** *m.* 1.5
build **construir** *v.* 1.4
building **edificio** *m.* 2.6
bump into (*something
  accidentally*) **darse con** 2.4;
  (*someone*) **encontrarse** *v.* 2.5
burn (a CD/DVD) **quemar** *v.*
  (un CD/DVD)
bus **autobús** *m.* 1.1
  bus station **estación** *f.* **de
    autobuses** 1.5
business **negocios** *m. pl.* 3.4
  business administration
    administración *f.* **de
    empresas** 1.2
  business-related **comercial**
    adj. 3.4
businessperson **hombre** *m.* **/
  mujer** *f.* **de negocios** 3.4
busy **ocupado/a** *adj.* 1.5
but **pero** *conj.* 1.2; (*rather*) **sino**
  conj. (*in negative sentences*)
butcher shop **carnicería** *f.* 3.2
butter **mantequilla** *f.* 2.2
buy **comprar** *v.* 1.2
by **por** *prep.* 2.5; **para** *prep.* 2.5
  by means of **por** *prep.* 2.5
  by phone **por teléfono** 2.5
  by way of **por** *prep.* 2.5
bye **chau** *interj. fam.* 1.1

C

cable television **televisión** *f.*
  por cable *m.* 2.5
café **café** *m.* 1.4
cafeteria **cafetería** *f.* 1.2
caffeine **cafeína** *f.* 3.3
cake **pastel** *m.* 2.3
  chocolate cake **pastel de
    chocolate** *m.* 2.3
calculator **calculadora** *f.* 1.2
call **llamar** *v.* 2.5
  be called **llamarse** *v.* 2.1
  call on the phone **llamar
    por teléfono**
calm **tranquilo/a** *adj.* 3.3
calorie **caloría** *f.* 3.3

camera **cámara** *f.* 2.5
camp **acampar** *v.* 1.5
can (*tin*) **lata** *f.* 3.1
can **poder (o:ue)** *v.* 1.4
   Could I ask you something?
    ¿Podría pedirte algo? 3.5
Canadian **canadiense** *adj.* 1.3
candidate **aspirante** *m., f.* 3.4;
   candidato/a *m., f.* 3.6
candy **dulces** *m., pl.* 2.3
capital city **capital** *f.* 1.1
car **coche** *m.* 2.5; **carro** *m.* 2.5;
   auto(móvil) *m.* 1.5
caramel **caramelo** *m.* 2.3
card **tarjeta** *f.*; (*playing*)
   carta *f.* 1.5
care: take care of **cuidar** *v.* 3.2
career **carrera** *f.* 3.4
careful: be (very) careful **tener** *v.*
   (mucho) cuidado 1.3
caretaker **ama** *m., f.* **de casa** 2.6
carpenter **carpintero/a** *m., f.* 3.4
carpet **alfombra** *f.* 2.6
carrot **zanahoria** *f.* 2.2
carry **llevar** *v.* 1.2
cartoons **dibujos** *m, pl.*
   animados 3.5
case: in case (that) **en caso (de)**
   que 3.1
cash (a check) **cobrar** *v.* 3.2;
   cash **(en) efectivo** 1.6
   cash register **caja** *f.* 1.6
   pay in cash **pagar** *v.* **al contado**
   3.2; **pagar en efectivo** 3.2
cashier **cajero/a** *m., f.*
cat **gato** *m.* 3.1
CD **disco compacto** *m.* 2.5
CD player **reproductor de**
   CD *m.* 2.5
CD-ROM **cederrón** *m.* 2.5
celebrate **celebrar** *v.* 2.3
celebration **celebración** *f.*
cellar **sótano** *m.* 2.6
(cell) phone **(teléfono)**
   celular *m.* 2.5
cemetery **cementerio** *m.* 2.3
cereal **cereales** *m., pl.* 2.2
certain **cierto/a** *adj.*;
   seguro/a *adj.* 3.1
   it's (not) certain **(no) es**
   cierto/seguro 3.1
chalk **tiza** *f.* 1.2
champagne **champán** *m.* 2.3
change **cambiar** *v.* **(de)** 2.3
change: in change **de cambio** 1.2
channel (*TV*) **canal** *m.* 2.5; 3.5
character (*fictional*) **personaje**
   m. 2.5, 3.5
   (main) character **personaje**
   (principal) *m.* 3.5
chat **conversar** *v.* 1.2
cheap **barato/a** *adj.* 1.6
check **comprobar (o:ue)** *v.*;
   revisar *v.* 2.5; (*bank*) **cheque**
   m. 3.2
   check the oil **revisar el**
   aceite 2.5

checking account **cuenta** *f.*
   corriente 3.2
cheese **queso** *m.* 2.2
chef **cocinero/a** *m., f.* 3.4
chemistry **química** *f.* 1.2
chest of drawers **cómoda** *f.* 2.6
chicken **pollo** *m.* 2.2
child **niño/a** *m., f.* 1.3
childhood **niñez** *f.* 2.3
children **hijos** *m., pl.* 1.3
Chinese **chino/a** *adj.* 1.3
chocolate **chocolate** *m.* 2.3
   chocolate cake **pastel** *m.* **de**
   chocolate 2.3
cholesterol **colesterol** *m.* 3.3
choose **escoger** *v.* 2.2
chop (*food*) **chuleta** *f.* 2.2
Christmas **Navidad** *f.* 2.3
church **iglesia** *f.* 1.4
cinnamon **canela** *f.* 2.4
citizen **ciudadano/a** *m., f.* 3.6
city **ciudad** *f.* 1.4
class **clase** *f.* 1.2
   take classes **tomar clases** 1.2
classical **clásico/a** *adj.* 3.5
classmate **compañero/a** *m., f.* **de**
   clase 1.2
clean **limpio/a** *adj.* 1.5;
   limpiar *v.* 2.6
   clean the house *v.* **limpiar la**
   casa 2.6
clear (*weather*) **despejado/a** *adj.*
   clear the table **quitar la**
   mesa 2.6
   It's (very) clear. (*weather*)
   Está (muy) despejado.
clerk **dependiente/a** *m., f.* 1.6
climate change **cambio**
   climático *m.* 3.1
climb **escalar** *v.* 1.4
   climb mountains **escalar**
   montañas 1.4
clinic **clínica** *f.* 2.4
clock **reloj** *m.* 1.2
close **cerrar (e:ie)** *v.* 1.4
closed **cerrado/a** *adj.* 1.5
closet **armario** *m.* 2.6
clothes **ropa** *f.* 1.6
   clothes dryer **secadora** *f.* 2.6
clothing **ropa** *f.* 1.6
cloud **nube** *f.* 3.1
cloudy **nublado/a** *adj.* 1.5
   It's (very) cloudy. **Está (muy)**
   nublado. 1.5
coat **abrigo** *m.* 1.6
coffee **café** *m.* 2.2
   coffee maker **cafetera** *f.* 2.6
cold **frío** *m.* 1.5;
   (*illness*) **resfriado** *m.* 2.4
   be (*feel*) (very) cold **tener**
   (mucho) frío 1.3
   It's (very) cold. (*weather*) **Hace**
   (mucho) frío. 1.5
college **universidad** *f.* 1.2
collision **choque** *m.* 3.6
color **color** *m.* 1.6
comb one's hair **peinarse** *v.* 2.1

come **venir** *v.* 1.3
come on **ándale** *interj.* 3.2
comedy **comedia** *f.* 3.5
comfortable **cómodo/a** *adj.* 1.5
commerce **negocios** *m., pl.* 3.4
commercial **comercial** *adj.* 3.4
communicate (with) **comunicarse**
   v. **(con)** 3.6
communication **comunicación**
   f. 3.6
   means of communication
   medios *m. pl.* **de**
   comunicación 3.6
community **comunidad** *f.* 1.1
company **compañía** *f.* 3.4;
   empresa *f.* 3.4
comparison **comparación** *f.*
completely **completamente**
   adv. 3.4
composer **compositor(a)** *m., f.* 3.5
computer **computadora** *f.* 1.1
   computer monitor **monitor**
   m. 2.5
   computer programmer
   programador(a) *m., f.* 1.3
   computer science **computación**
   f. 1.2
concert **concierto** *m.* 3.5
conductor (*musical*) **director(a)**
   m., f. 3.5
confirm **confirmar** *v.* 1.5
   confirm a reservation **confirmar**
   una reservación 1.5
confused **confundido/a** *adj.* 1.5
congested **congestionado/a**
   adj. 2.4
Congratulations! **¡Felicidades!**;
   ¡Felicitaciones! *f. pl.* 2.3
conservation **conservación** *f.* 3.1
conserve **conservar** *v.* 3.1
considering **para** *prep.* 2.3
consume **consumir** *v.* 3.3
container **envase** *m.* 3.1
contamination **contaminación** *f.*
content **contento/a** *adj.* 1.5
contest **concurso** *m.* 3.5
continue **seguir (e:i)** *v.* 1.4
control **control** *m.*; **controlar** *v.* 3.1
   be under control **estar bajo**
   control 2.1
conversation **conversación** *f.* 1.1
converse **conversar** *v.* 1.2
cook **cocinar** *v.* 2.6;
   cocinero/a *m., f.* 3.4
cookie **galleta** *f.* 2.3
cool **fresco/a** *adj.* 1.5
   Be cool. **Tranquilo.** 2.1
   It's cool. (weather) **Hace**
   fresco. 1.5
corn **maíz** *m.* 2.2
corner **esquina** *f.* 3.2
cost **costar (o:ue)** *v.* 1.6
Costa Rica **Costa Rica** *f.* 1.1
Costa Rican **costarricense** *adj.* 1.3
costume **disfraz** *m.*
cotton **algodón** *f.* 1.6
   (made of) cotton **de algodón** 1.6

couch **sofá** *m.* 2.6
couch potato **teleadicto/a**
   m., f. 3.3
cough **tos** *f.* 2.4; **toser** *v.* 2.4
counselor **consejero/a** *m., f.* 3.4
count **contar (o:ue)** *v.* 1.4
country (*nation*) **país** *m.* 1.1
countryside **campo** *m.* 1.5
(married) couple **pareja** *f.* 2.3
course **curso** *m.* 1.2; **materia** *f.* 1.2
courtesy **cortesía** *f.*
cousin **primo/a** *m., f.* 1.3
cover **cubrir** *v.*
covered **cubierto/a** *p.p.*
cow **vaca** *f.* 3.1
crafts **artesanía** *f.* 3.5
craftsmanship **artesanía** *f.* 3.5
crater **cráter** *m.* 3.1
crazy **loco/a** *adj.* 1.6
create **crear** *v.*
credit **crédito** *m.* 1.6
   credit card **tarjeta** *f.* **de**
     crédito 1.6
crime **crimen** *m.* 3.6
cross **cruzar** *v.* 3.2
cry **llorar** *v.* 3.3
Cuba **Cuba** *f.* 1.1
Cuban **cubano/a** *adj.* 1.3
culture **cultura** *f.* 1.2, 3.5
cup **taza** *f.* 2.6
currency exchange **cambio** *m.*
  de moneda
current events **actualidades** *f.,*
   pl. 3.6
curtains **cortinas** *f., pl.* 2.6
custard (*baked*) **flan** *m.* 2.3
custom **costumbre** *f.* 1.1
customer **cliente/a** *m., f.* 1.6
customs **aduana** *f.* 1.5
   customs inspector **inspector(a)**
     m., f. **de aduanas** 1.5
cybercafé **cibercafé** *m.*
cycling **ciclismo** *m.* 1.4

D

dad **papá** *m.* 1.3
daily **diario/a** *adj.* 2.1
   daily routine **rutina** *f.* **diaria** 2.1
damage **dañar** *v.* 2.4
dance **bailar** *v.* 1.2; **danza** *f.* 3.5;
   baile *m.* 3.5
dancer **bailarín/bailarina** *m.,*
   f. 3.5
danger **peligro** *m.* 3.1
dangerous **peligroso/a** *adj.* 3.6
date (*appointment*) **cita** *f.* 2.3;
   (*calendar*) **fecha** *f.* 1.5;
   (*someone*) **salir** *v.* **con**
   (alguien) 2.3
   have a date **tener una cita** 2.3
daughter **hija** *f.* 1.3
daughter-in-law **nuera** *f.* 1.3
day **día** *m.* 1.1
   day before yesterday
     anteayer *adv.* 1.6

deal: It's not a big deal.
   No es para tanto. 2.6
death **muerte** *f.* 2.3
decaffeinated **descafeinado/a**
   adj. 3.3
December **diciembre** *m.* 1.5
decide **decidir** *v.* (+ *inf.*) 1.3
decided **decidido/a** *adj. p.p.* 3.2
declare **declarar** *v.* 3.6
deforestation **deforestación** *f.* 3.1
delicious **delicioso/a** *adj.* 2.2;
   rico/a *adj.* 2.2; **sabroso/a**
   adj. 2.2
delighted **encantado/a** *adj.* 1.1
dentist **dentista** *m., f.* 2.4
deny **negar (e:ie)** *v.* 3.1
   not to deny **no dudar** 3.1
department store **almacén** *m.* 1.6
departure **salida** *f.* 1.5
deposit **depositar** *v.* 3.2
describe **describir** *v.* 1.3
described **descrito/a** *p.p.* 3.2
desert **desierto** *m.* 3.1
design **diseño** *m.*
designer **diseñador(a)** *m., f.* 3.4
desire **desear** *v.* 1.2
desk **escritorio** *m.* 1.2
dessert **postre** *m.* 2.3
destroy **destruir** *v.* 3.1
develop **desarrollar** *v.* 3.1
diary **diario** *m.* 1.1
dictatorship **dictadura** *f.* 3.6
dictionary **diccionario** *m.* 1.1
die **morir (o:ue)** *v.* 2.2
died **muerto/a** *p.p.* 3.2
diet **dieta** *f.* 3.3; **alimentación**
   balanced diet **dieta**
     equilibrada 3.3
   be on a diet **estar a dieta** 3.3
difficult **difícil** *adj. m., f.* 1.3
digital camera **cámara** *f.*
   digital 2.5
dining room **comedor** *m.* 2.6
dinner **cena** *f.* 1.2, 2.2
   have dinner **cenar** *v.* 1.2
direct **dirigir** *v.* 3.5
director **director(a)** *m., f.* 3.5
dirty **ensuciar** *v.*; **sucio/a** *adj.* 1.5
   get (something) dirty **ensuciar**
     v. 2.6
disagree **no estar de acuerdo**
disaster **desastre** *m.* 3.6
discover **descubrir** *v.* 3.1
discovered **descubierto/a** *p.p.* 3.2
discrimination **discriminación**
   f. 3.6
dish **plato** *m.* 2.2, 2.6
   main dish **plato principal** *m.* 2.2
dishwasher **lavaplatos** *m.,*
   sing. 2.6
disorderly **desordenado/a** *adj.* 1.5
dive **bucear** *v.* 1.4
divorce **divorcio** *m.* 2.3
divorced **divorciado/a** *adj.* 2.3
   get divorced (from) **divorciarse**
     v. **(de)** 2.3
dizzy **mareado/a** *adj.* 2.4

do **hacer** *v.* 1.4
   do aerobics **hacer ejercicios**
     aeróbicos 3.3
   do household chores **hacer**
     quehaceres domésticos 2.6
   do stretching exercises **hacer**
     ejercicios de estiramiento 3.3
   (I) don't want to. **No quiero.** 1.4
doctor **doctor(a)** *m., f.* 1.3; 2.4;
   médico/a *m., f.* 1.3
documentary (*film*) **documental**
   m. 3.5
dog **perro** *m.* 3.1
domestic **doméstico/a** *adj.*
   domestic appliance
     electrodoméstico *m.*
done **hecho/a** *p.p.* 3.2
door **puerta** *f.* 1.2
doorman/doorwoman
   portero/a *m., f.* 1.1
dormitory **residencia** *f.*
   estudiantil 1.2
double **doble** *adj.* 1.5
   double room **habitación** *f.*
     doble 1.5
doubt **duda** *f.* 3.1; **dudar** *v.* 3.1
   not to doubt **no dudar** 3.1
   There is no doubt that...
     No cabe duda de 3.1;
     No hay duda de 3.1
Down with... ! **¡Abajo el/la...!**
download **descargar** *v.* 2.5
downtown **centro** *m.* 1.4
drama **drama** *m.* 3.5
dramatic **dramático/a** *adj.* 3.5
draw **dibujar** *v.* 1.2
drawing **dibujo** *m.* 3.5
dress **vestido** *m.* 1.6
   get dressed **vestirse (e:i)** *v.* 2.1
drink **beber** *v.* 1.3; **bebida**
   f. 2.2; **tomar** *v.* 1.2
drive **conducir** *v.* 1.6; **manejar**
   v. 2.5
driver **conductor(a)** *m., f.* 1.1
drug **droga** *f.* 3.3
   drug addict **drogadicto/a**
     adj. 3.3
dry oneself **secarse** *v.* 2.1
during **durante** *prep.* 2.1; **por**
   prep. 2.5
dust **sacudir** *v.* 2.6;
   quitar *v.* **el polvo** 2.6
   dust the furniture **sacudir los**
     muebles 2.6
duster **plumero** *m.* 2.6
DVD player **reproductor** *m.* **de**
   DVD 2.5

E

each **cada** *adj.* 1.6
each other **los unos a los**
   otros 2.5
eagle **águila** *f.*
ear (outer) **oreja** *f.* 2.4
early **temprano** *adv.* 2.1

earn **ganar** *v.* 3.4
earring **arete** *m.* 1.6
earthquake **terremoto** *m.* 3.6
ease **aliviar** *v.*
east **este** *m.* 3.2
  to the east **al este** 3.2
easy **fácil** *adj. m., f.* 1.3
eat **comer** *v.* 1.3
ecological **ecológico/a** *adj.* 3.1
ecologist **ecologista** *m., f.* 3.1
ecology **ecología** *f.* 3.1
economics **economía** *f.* 1.2
ecotourism **ecoturismo** *m.* 3.1
Ecuador **Ecuador** *m.* 1.1
Ecuadorian **ecuatoriano/a** *adj.* 1.3
effective **eficaz** *adj. m., f.*
egg **huevo** *m.* 2.2
eight **ocho** 1.1
eight hundred **ochocientos/as** 1.2
eighteen **dieciocho** 1.1
eighth **octavo/a** 1.5
eighty **ochenta** 1.2
either... or **o... o** *conj.* 2.1
eldest **el/la mayor** 2.2
elect **elegir** *v.* 3.6
election **elecciones** *f. pl.* 3.6
electric appliance
  electrodoméstico *m.* 2.6
electrician **electricista** *m., f.* 3.4
electricity **luz** *f.* 2.6
elegant **elegante** *adj. m., f.* 1.6
elevator **ascensor** *m.* 1.5
eleven **once** 1.1
e-mail **correo** *m.* **electrónico** 1.4
  e-mail message **mensaje** *m.*
    electrónico 1.4
  read e-mail **leer** *v.* **el correo**
    electrónico 1.4
e-mail address **dirrección** *f.*
  electrónica 2.5
embarrassed **avergonzado/a**
  adj. 1.5
embrace (each other) **abrazar(se)**
  v. 2.5
emergency **emergencia** *f.* 2.4
  emergency room **sala** *f.* **de**
    emergencia 2.4
employee **empleado/a** *m., f.* 1.5
employment **empleo** *m.* 3.4
end **fin** *m.* 1.4; **terminar** *v.* 1.2
  end table **mesita** *f.* 2.6
endure **aguantar** *v.* 3.2
energy **energía** *f.* 3.1
engaged: get engaged (to)
  comprometerse *v.* **(con)** 2.3
engineer **ingeniero/a** *m., f.* 1.3
English (*language*) **inglés** *m.* 1.2;
  inglés, inglesa *adj.* 1.3
enjoy **disfrutar** *v.* **(de)** 3.3
enough **bastante** *adv.* 2.4
entertainment **diversión** *f.* 1.4
entrance **entrada** *f.* 2.6
envelope **sobre** *m.* 3.2
environment **medio ambiente**
  m. 3.1
environmental sciences **ciencias**
  ambientales 1.2

equality **igualdad** *f.* 3.6
equipped **equipado/a** *adj.* 3.3
erase **borrar** *v.* 2.5
eraser **borrador** *m.* 1.2
errand **diligencia** *f.* 3.2
essay **ensayo** *m.* 1.3
evening **tarde** *f.* 1.1
event **acontecimiento** *m.* 3.6
every day **todos los días** 2.4
everything **todo** *m.* 1.5
  Everything is under control.
    Todo está bajo control. 2.1
exactly **en punto** 1.1
exam **examen** *m.* 1.2
excellent **excelente** *adj.* 1.5
excess **exceso** *m.* 3.3
  in excess **en exceso** 3.3
exchange **intercambiar** *v.*
  in exchange for **por** 2.5
exciting **emocionante** *adj. m., f.*
excursion **excursión** *f.*
excuse **disculpar** *v.*
Excuse me. (*May I?*) **Con**
  permiso. 1.1; (*I beg your*
  pardon.) **Perdón.** 1.1
exercise **ejercicio** *m.* 3.3;
  hacer *v.* **ejercicio** 3.3; (a
  degree/profession) **ejercer** *v.* 3.4
exit **salida** *f.* 1.5
expensive **caro/a** *adj.* 1.6
experience **experiencia** *f.* 3.6
expire **vencer** *v.* 3.2
explain **explicar** *v.* 1.2
explore **explorar** *v.*
expression **expresión** *f.*
extinction **extinción** *f.* 3.1
eye **ojo** *m.* 2.4

F

fabulous **fabuloso/a** *adj.* 1.5
face **cara** *f.* 2.1
facing **enfrente de** *prep.* 3.2
fact: in fact **de hecho**
factory **fábrica** *f.* 3.1
fall (down) **caerse** *v.* 2.4
  fall asleep **dormirse (o:ue)**
    v. 2.1
  fall in love (with) **enamorarse**
    v. **(de)** 2.3
fall (season) **otoño** *m.* 1.5
fallen **caído/a** *p.p.* 3.2
family **familia** *f.* 1.3
famous **famoso/a** *adj.* 3.4
fan **aficionado/a** *adj.* 1.4
  be a fan (of) **ser aficionado/a**
    (a) 1.4
far from **lejos de** *prep.* 1.2
farewell **despedida** *f.*
fascinate **fascinar** *v.* 2.1
fashion **moda** *f.* 1.6
  be in fashion **estar de moda** 1.6
fast **rápido/a** *adj.*
fat **gordo/a** *adj.* 1.3; **grasa** *f.* 3.3
father **padre** *m.* 1.3
father-in-law **suegro** *m.* 1.3

favorite **favorito/a** *adj.* 1.4
fax (machine) **fax** *m.* 2.5
fear **temer** *v.* 3.1
February **febrero** *m.* 1.5
feel **sentir(se) (e:ie)** *v.* 2.1
  feel like (*doing something*) **tener**
    ganas de (+ inf.) 1.3
festival **festival** *m.* 3.5
fever **fiebre** *f.* 2.4
  have a fever **tener** *v.* **fiebre** 2.4
few **pocos/as** *adj. pl.*
  fewer than **menos de**
    (*+ number*) 2.2
field: major field of study
  especialización *f.*
fifteen **quince** 1.1
  fifteen-year-old girl celebrating her
    birthday **quinceañera** *f.* 2.3
fifth **quinto/a** 1.5
fifty **cincuenta** 1.2
fight (for/against) **luchar** *v.* **(por/**
  contra) 3.6
figure (*number*) **cifra** *f.*
file **archivo** *m.* 2.5
fill **llenar** *v.* 2.5
  fill out (a form) **llenar (un**
    formulario) 3.2
  fill the tank **llenar el tanque** 2.5
finally **finalmente** *adv.* 3.3; **por**
  último 2.1; **por fin** 2.5
find **encontrar (o:ue)** *v.* 1.4
  find (each other) **encontrar(se)**
  find out **enterarse** *v.* 3.4
fine **multa** *f.*
(fine) arts **bellas artes** *f., pl.* 3.5
finger **dedo** *m.* 2.4
finish **terminar** *v.* 1.2
  finish (*doing something*)
    terminar *v.* **de (+ inf.)** 1.4
fire **incendio** *m.* 3.6; **despedir**
  (e:i) *v.* 3.4
firefighter **bombero/a** *m., f.* 3.4
firm **compañía** *f.* 3.4; **empresa**
  f. 3.4
first **primer, primero/a** 1.2, 1.5
fish (*food*) **pescado** *m.* 2.2;
  pescar *v.* 1.5; (*live*) **pez** *m.,*
  sing. (**peces** *pl.*) 3.1
  fish market **pescadería** *f.* 3.2
fishing **pesca** *f.*
fit (*clothing*) **quedar** *v.* 2.1
five **cinco** 1.1
five hundred **quinientos/as** 1.2
fix (*put in working order*) **arreglar**
  v. 2.5; (*clothes, hair, etc. to go*
  out) **arreglarse** *v.* 2.1
fixed **fijo/a** *adj.* 1.6
flag **bandera** *f.*
flexible **flexible** *adj.* 3.3
flood **inundación** *f.* 3.6
floor (*of a building*) **piso** *m.* 1.5;
  suelo *m.* 2.6
  ground floor **planta baja** *f.* 1.5
  top floor **planta** *f.* **alta**
flower **flor** *f.* 3.1
flu **gripe** *f.* 2.4
fog **niebla** *f.*

folk **folclórico/a** *adj.* 3.5
follow **seguir (e:i)** *v.* 1.4
food **comida** *f.* 1.4, 2.2
foolish **tonto/a** *adj.* 1.3
foot **pie** *m.* 2.4
football **fútbol** *m.* **americano** 1.4
for **para** *prep.* 2.5; **por** *prep.* 2.5
    for example **por ejemplo** 2.5
    for me **para mí** 2.2
forbid **prohibir** *v.*
foreign **extranjero/a** *adj.* 3.5
    foreign languages **lenguas**
        f., pl. **extranjeras** 1.2
forest **bosque** *m.* 3.1
forget **olvidar** *v.* 2.4
fork **tenedor** *m.* 2.6
form **formulario** *m.* 3.2
forty **cuarenta** *m.* 1.2
four **cuatro** 1.1
four hundred **cuatrocientos/**
    as 1.2
fourteen **catorce** 1.1
fourth **cuarto/a** *m., f.* 1.5
free **libre** *adj. m., f.* 1.4
    be free (of charge) **ser**
        gratis 3.2
    free time **tiempo libre**; spare
        (free) time **ratos libres** 1.4
freedom **libertad** *f.* 3.6
freezer **congelador** *m.* 2.6
French **francés, francesa** *adj.* 1.3
    French fries **papas** *f., pl.*
        fritas 2.2; **patatas** *f., pl.*
        fritas 2.2
frequently **frecuentemente**
    adv. 2.4; **con frecuencia**
    adv. 2.4
Friday **viernes** *m., sing.* 1.2
fried **frito/a** *adj.* 2.2
    fried potatoes **papas** *f., pl.*
        fritas 2.2; **patatas** *f., pl.*
        fritas 2.2
friend **amigo/a** *m., f.* 1.3
friendly **amable** *adj. m., f.*
friendship **amistad** *f.* 2.3
from **de** *prep.* 1.1; **desde** *prep.* 1.6
    from the United States
        estadounidense *m., f.*
        adj. 1.3
    from time to time **de vez en**
        cuando 2.4
    He/She/It is from... **Es de...**;
        I'm from... **Soy de...** 1.1
front: (cold) front **frente**
    (frío) *m.* 1.5
fruit **fruta** *f.* 2.2
    fruit juice **jugo** *m.* **de fruta** 2.2
    fruit store **frutería** *f.* 3.2
full **lleno/a** *adj.* 2.5
fun **divertido/a** *adj.* 2.1
    fun activity **diversión** *f.* 1.4
    have fun **divertirse (e:ie)** *v.* 2.3
function **funcionar** *v.*
furniture **muebles** *m., pl.* 2.6
furthermore **además (de)** *adv.* 2.4
future **futuro** *adj.* 3.4; **porvenir**
    m. 3.4

for/to the future **por el**
    porvenir 3.4
in the future **en el futuro** 3.4

G

gain weight **aumentar** *v.* **de**
    peso 3.3; **engordar** *v.* 3.3
game **juego** *m.*; *(match)*
    partido *m.* 1.4
    game show **concurso** *m.* 3.5
garage *(in a house)* **garaje** *m.* 2.6;
    garaje *m.* 2.5; **taller**
    (mecánico) 2.5
garden **jardín** *m.* 2.6
garlic **ajo** *m.* 2.2
gas station **gasolinera** *f.* 2.5
gasoline **gasolina** *f.* 2.5
gentleman **caballero** *m.* 2.2
geography **geografía** *f.* 1.2
German **alemán, alemana** *adj.* 1.3
get **conseguir (e:i)** *v.* 1.4;
    obtener *v.* 3.4
    get along well/badly (with)
        llevarse bien/mal (con) 2.3
    get bigger **aumentar** *v.* 3.1
    get bored **aburrirse** *v.* 3.5
    get good grades **sacar buenas**
        notas 1.2
    get into trouble **meterse en**
        problemas 3.1
    get off of (a vehicle) **bajar(se)** *v.*
        de 2.5
    get on/into (a vehicle) **subir(se)**
        v. **a** 2.5
    get out of (a vehicle) **bajar(se)**
        v. **de** 2.5
    get ready **arreglarse** *v.* 2.1
    get up **levantarse** *v.* 2.1
gift **regalo** *m.* 1.6
ginger **jengibre** *m.* 2.4
girl **chica** *f.* 1.1; **muchacha** *f.* 1.3
girlfriend **novia** *f.* 1.3
give **dar** *v.* 1.6, 2.3;
    (as a gift) **regalar** 2.3
    give directions **indicar cómo**
        llegar 3.2
glass *(drinking)* **vaso** *m.* 2.6;
    vidrio *m.* 3.1
    (made) of glass **de vidrio** 3.1
glasses **gafas** *f., pl.* 1.6
    sunglasses **gafas** *f., pl.* **de sol** 1.6
global warming **calentamiento**
    global 3.1
gloves **guantes** *m., pl.* 1.6
go **ir** *v.* 1.4
    go away **irse** 2.1
    go by boat **ir en barco** 1.5
    go by bus **ir en autobús** 1.5
    go by car **ir en auto(móvil)** 1.5
    go by motorcycle **ir en**
        motocicleta 1.5
    go by plane **ir en avión** 1.5
    go by taxi **ir en taxi** 1.5
    go by the bank **pasar por el**
        banco 3.2

go down; **bajar(se)** *v.*
go on a hike (in the mountains)
    ir de excursión (a las
    montañas) 1.4
go out **salir** *v.* 2.3
go out (with) **salir** *v.* **(con)** 2.3
go up **subir** *v.*
Let's go. **Vamos.** 1.4
goblet **copa** *f.* 2.6
going to: be going to *(do something)*
    ir a (+ inf.) 1.4
golf **golf** *m.* 1.4
good **buen, bueno/a** *adj.* 1.3, 1.6
    Good afternoon. **Buenas**
        tardes. 1.1
    Good evening. **Buenas**
        noches. 1.1
    Good morning. **Buenos días.** 1.1
    Good night. **Buenas noches.** 1.1
    It's good that... **Es bueno**
        que... 2.6
goodbye **adiós** *m.* 1.1
    say goodbye (to) **despedirse** *v.*
        (de) (e:i) 2.1
good-looking **guapo/a** *adj.* 1.3
government **gobierno** *m.* 3.1
GPS **navegador GPS** *m.* 2.5
graduate (from/in) **graduarse** *v.*
    (de/en) 2.3
grains **cereales** *m., pl.* 2.2
granddaughter **nieta** *f.* 1.3
grandfather **abuelo** *m.* 1.3
grandmother **abuela** *f.* 1.3
grandparents **abuelos** *m., pl.* 1.3
grandson **nieto** *m.* 1.3
grape **uva** *f.* 2.2
grass **hierba** *f.* 3.1
grave **grave** *adj.* 2.4
gray **gris** *adj. m., f.* 1.6
great **fenomenal** *adj. m., f.* 1.5;
    genial *adj.* 3.4
great-grandfather **bisabuelo** *m.* 1.3
great-grandmother **bisabuela** *f.* 1.3
green **verde** *adj. m., f.* 1.6
greet (each other) **saludar(se)** *v.* 2.5
greeting **saludo** *m.* 1.1
    Greetings to... **Saludos a...** 1.1
grilled **a la plancha** 2.2
ground floor **planta baja** *f.* 1.5
grow **aumentar** *v.* 3.1
guest *(at a house/hotel)* **huésped**
    m., f. 1.5; *(invited to a function)*
    invitado/a *m., f.* 2.3
guide **guía** *m., f.* 3.1
gymnasium **gimnasio** *m.* 1.4

H

hair **pelo** *m.* 2.1
hairdresser **peluquero/a** *m., f.* 3.4
half **medio/a** *adj.* 1.3
    half-brother **medio**
        hermano 1.3
    half-sister **media hermana** 1.3
    half-past... *(time)* **...y media** 1.1
hallway **pasillo** *m.* 2.6

ham **jamón** m. 2.2
hamburger **hamburguesa** f. 2.2
hand **mano** f. 1.1
hand in **entregar** v. 2.5
handsome **guapo/a** adj. 1.3
happen **ocurrir** v. 3.6
happiness **alegría** v. 2.3
Happy birthday! **¡Feliz
    cumpleaños!** 2.3
happy **alegre** adj. 1.5; **contento/a**
    adj. 1.5; **feliz** adj. m., f. 1.5
    be happy **alegrarse** v. **(de)** 3.1
hard **difícil** adj. m., f. 1.3
hard-working **trabajador(a)**
    adj. 1.3
hardly **apenas** adv. 2.4
hat **sombrero** m. 1.6
hate **odiar** v. 2.3
have **tener** v. 1.3
    have time **tener tiempo** 1.4
    have to (do something) **tener que**
        (+ inf.) 1.3; **deber (+ inf.)**
    have a tooth removed **sacar(se)**
        un diente 2.4
he **él** 1.1
head **cabeza** f. 2.4
headache **dolor** m. **de cabeza** 2.4
health **salud** f. 2.4
healthy **saludable** adj. m., f. 2.4;
    sano/a adj. 2.4
    lead a healthy lifestyle **llevar** v.
        una vida sana 3.3
hear **oír** v. 1.4
heard **oído/a** p.p. 3.2
hearing: sense of hearing **oído** m. 2.4
heart **corazón** m. 2.4
Hello. **Hola.** 1.1; (on the
    telephone) **Aló.** 2.5;
    Bueno. 2.5; **Diga.** 2.5
help **ayudar** v. 2.6; **servir**
    (e:i) v. 1.5
    help each other **ayudarse** v. 2.5
her **su(s)** poss. adj. 1.3; (of) hers
    suyo(s)/a(s) poss. 2.5
    her **la** f., sing., d.o. pron. 1.5
    to/for her **le** f., sing., i.o. pron. 1.6
here **aquí** adv. 1.1
    Here is/are... **Aquí está(n)...** 1.5
Hi. **Hola.** 1.1
highway **autopista** f. 2.5;
    carretera f. 2.5
hike **excursión** f. 1.4
    go on a hike **hacer una excursión**
        1.5; **ir de excursión** 1.4
hiker **excursionista** m., f.
hiking **de excursión** 1.4
him: to/for him **le** m., sing., i.o.
    pron. 1.6
hire **contratar** v. 3.4
his **su(s)** poss. adj. 1.3; (of) his
    suyo(s)/a(s) poss. pron. 2.5
    his **lo** m., sing., d.o. pron. 1.5
history **historia** f. 1.2; 3.5
hobby **pasatiempo** m. 1.4
hockey **hockey** m. 1.4
hold up **aguantar** v. 3.2
hole **hueco** m. 1.4

holiday **día** m. **de fiesta** 2.3
home **casa** f. 1.2
    home page **página** f.
        principal 2.5
homework **tarea** f. 1.2
honey **miel** f. 2.4
hood **capó** m. 2.5; **cofre** m. 2.5
hope **esperar** v. **(+ inf.)** 1.2;
    esperar v. 3.1
    I hope (that) **ojalá (que)** 3.1
horror (genre) **de horror** m. 3.5
hors d'oeuvres **entremeses** m.,
    pl. 2.2
horse **caballo** m. 1.5
hospital **hospital** m. 2.4
hot: be (feel) (very) hot **tener**
    (mucho) calor 1.3
    It's (very) hot. **Hace (mucho)**
        calor. 1.5
hotel **hotel** m. 1.5
hour **hora** f. 1.1
house **casa** f. 1.2
household chores **quehaceres** m.
    pl. **domésticos** 2.6
housekeeper **ama** m., f. **de casa** 2.6
housing **vivienda** f. 2.6
How... ! **¡Qué...!**
    how **¿cómo?** adv. 1.1
    How are you? **¿Qué tal?** 1.1
    How are you? **¿Cómo estás?**
        fam. 1.1
    How are you? **¿Cómo está**
        usted? form. 1.1
    How can I help you? **¿En qué**
        puedo servirles? 1.5
    How did it go for you...?
        ¿Cómo le/les fue...? 3.3
    How is it going? **¿Qué tal?** 1.1
    How is the weather? **¿Qué**
        tiempo hace? 3.3
    How much/many?
        ¿Cuánto(s)/a(s)? 1.1
    How much does... cost?
        ¿Cuánto cuesta...? 1.6
    How old are you? **¿Cuántos**
        años tienes? fam. 1.3
however **sin embargo**
hug (each other) **abrazar(se)** v. 2.5
humanities **humanidades** f., pl. 1.2
hundred **cien, ciento** 1.2
hungry: be (very) hungry **tener** v.
    (mucha) hambre 1.3
hunt **cazar** v. 3.1
hurricane **huracán** m. 3.6
hurry **apurarse** v. 3.3; **darse**
    prisa v. 3.3
    be in a (big) hurry **tener** v.
        (mucha) prisa 1.3
hurt **doler (o:ue)** v. 2.4
    It hurts me a lot... **Me duele**
        mucho... 2.4
husband **esposo** m. 1.3

I

I **yo** 1.1

I am... **Yo soy...** 1.1
I hope (that) **Ojalá (que)**
    interj. 3.1
I wish (that) **Ojalá (que)**
    interj. 3.1
ice cream **helado** m. 2.3
    ice cream shop **heladería** f. 3.2
iced **helado/a** adj. 2.2
    iced tea **té** m. **helado** 2.2
idea **idea** f. 1.4
if **si** conj. 1.4
illness **enfermedad** f. 2.4
important **importante** adj. 1.3
    be important to **importar** v. 2.1
    It's important that... **Es**
        importante que... 2.6
impossible **imposible** adj. 3.1
    it's impossible **es imposible** 3.1
improbable **improbable** adj. 3.1
    it's improbable **es**
        improbable 3.1
improve **mejorar** v. 3.1
in **en** prep. 1.2; **por** prep. 2.5
    in the afternoon **de la tarde** 1.1;
        por la tarde 2.1
    in a bad mood **de mal**
        humor 1.5
    in the direction of **para** prep. 1.1
    in the early evening **de la**
        tarde 1.1
    in the evening **de la noche** 1.1;
        por la tarde 2.1
    in a good mood **de buen**
        humor 1.5
    in the morning **de la**
        mañana 1.1; **por la**
        mañana 2.1
    in love (with)
        enamorado/a (de) 1.5
    in search of **por** prep. 2.5
in front of **delante de** prep. 1.2
increase **aumento** m. 3.4
incredible **increíble** adj. 1.5
inequality **desigualdad** f. 3.6
infection **infección** f. 2.4
inform **informar** v. 3.6
injection **inyección** f. 2.4
    give an injection **poner una**
        inyección v. 2.4
injure (oneself) **lastimarse** 2.4
    injure (one's foot) **lastimarse** v.
        (el pie) 2.4
inner ear **oído** m. 2.4
inside **dentro** adv.
insist (on) **insistir** v. **(en)** 2.6
installments: pay in installments
    pagar v. **a plazos** 3.2
intelligent **inteligente** adj. 1.3
intend to **pensar** v. **(+ inf.)** 1.4
interest **interesar** v. 2.1
interesting **interesante** adj. 1.3
    be interesting to **interesar** v. 2.1
international **internacional**
    adj. m., f. 3.6
Internet **Internet** 2.5
interview **entrevista** f. 3.4;
    interview **entrevistar** v. 3.4

interviewer **entrevistador(a)** *m.,*
f. 3.4
introduction **presentación** *f.*
I would like to introduce you to
(name)... **Le presento a...**
form. 1.1; **Te presento a...**
fam. 1.1
invest **invertir (e:ie)** *v.* 3.4
invite **invitar** *v.* 2.3
iron (clothes) **planchar** *v.* **la**
ropa 2.6
it **lo/la** *sing., d.o., pron.* 1.5
Italian **italiano/a** *adj.* 1.3
its **su(s)** *poss. adj.* 1.3,
suyo(s)/a(s) *poss. pron.* 2.5
it's the same **es igual** 1.5

J

jacket **chaqueta** *f.* 1.6
January **enero** *m.* 1.5
Japanese **japonés, japonesa**
adj. 1.3
jeans **(blue)jeans** *m., pl.* 1.6
jewelry store **joyería** *f.* 3.2
job **empleo** *m.* 3.4; **puesto**
m. 3.4; **trabajo** *m.* 3.4
job application **solicitud** *f.* **de**
trabajo 3.4
jog **correr** *v.*
journalism **periodismo** *m.* 1.2
journalist **periodista** *m., f.* 1.3;
reportero/a *m., f.* 3.4
joy **alegría** *f.* 2.3
give joy **dar** *v.* **alegría** 2.3
joyful **alegre** *adj.* 1.5
juice **jugo** *m.* 2.2
July **julio** *m.* 1.5
June **junio** *m.* 1.5
jungle **selva, jungla** *f.* 3.1
just **apenas** *adv.*
have just done something
acabar de (+ *inf.***)** 1.6

K

key **llave** *f.* 1.5
keyboard **teclado** *m.* 2.5
kilometer **kilómetro** *m.* 2.5
kiss **beso** *m.* 2.3
kiss each other **besarse** *v.* 2.5
kitchen **cocina** *f.* 2.3, 2.6
knee **rodilla** *f.* 2.4
knife **cuchillo** *m.* 2.6
know **saber** *v.* 1.6; **conocer** *v.* 1.6
know how **saber** *v.* 1.6

L

laboratory **laboratorio** *m.* 1.2
lack **faltar** *v.* 2.1
lake **lago** *m.* 3.1
lamp **lámpara** *f.* 2.6
land **tierra** *f.* 3.1
landlord **dueño/a** *m., f.* 2.2

landscape **paisaje** *m.* 1.5
language **lengua** *f.* 1.2
laptop (computer) **computadora**
f. **portátil** 2.5
large **grande** *adj.* 1.3
large (*clothing size*) **talla**
grande
last **durar** *v.* 3.6; **pasado/a**
adj. 1.6; **último/a** *adj.* 2.1
last name **apellido** *m.* 1.3
last night **anoche** *adv.* 1.6
last week **semana** *f.* **pasada** 1.6
last year **año** *m.* **pasado** 1.6
the last time **la última vez** 2.1
late **tarde** *adv.* 2.1
later (on) **más tarde** 2.1
See you later. **Hasta la vista.** 1.1;
Hasta luego. 1.1
laugh **reírse (e:i)** *v.* 2.3
laughed **reído** *p.p.* 3.2
laundromat **lavandería** *f.* 3.2
law **ley** *f.* 3.1
lawyer **abogado/a** *m., f.* 3.4
lazy **perezoso/a** *adj.*
learn **aprender** *v.* **(a +** *inf.***)** 1.3
least, at **por lo menos** *adv.* 2.4
leave **salir** *v.* 1.4; **irse** *v.* 2.1
leave a tip **dejar una**
propina 2.3
leave behind **dejar** *v.* 3.4
leave for (*a place*) **salir para**
leave from **salir de**
left **izquierda** *f.* 1.2
be left over **quedar** *v.* 2.1
to the left of **a la izquierda**
de 1.2
leg **pierna** *f.* 2.4
lemon **limón** *m.* 2.2
lend **prestar** *v.* 1.6
less **menos** *adv.* 2.4
less... than **menos... que** 2.2
less than **menos de (+** *number***)**
lesson **lección** *f.* 1.1
let **dejar** *v.* 2.6
let's see **a ver**
letter **carta** *f.* 1.4, 3.2
lettuce **lechuga** *f.* 2.2
liberty **libertad** *f.* 3.6
library **biblioteca** *f.* 1.2
license (*driver's*) **licencia** *f.* **de**
conducir 2.5
lie **mentira** *f.* 1.4
life **vida** *f.* 2.3
of my life **de mi vida** 3.3
lifestyle: lead a healthy lifestyle
llevar una vida sana 3.3
lift **levantar** *v.* 3.3
lift weights **levantar pesas** 3.3
light **luz** *f.* 2.6
like **gustar** *v.* 1.2; **como**
prep. 2.2
I don't like them at all. **No me**
gustan nada. 1.2
I like... **Me gusta(n)...** 1.2
like this **así** *adv.* 2.4
like very much **encantar** *v.*;
fascinar *v.* 2.1

Do you like...? **¿Te**
gusta(n)...? 1.2
likeable **simpático/a** *adj.* 1.3
likewise **igualmente** *adv.* 1.1
line **línea** *f.* 1.4; **cola** (*queue*) *f.* 3.2
listen (to) **escuchar** *v.* 1.2
Listen! (*command*) **¡Oye!** *fam.,*
sing. 1.1; **¡Oiga/Oigan!**
form., sing./pl. 1.1
listen to music **escuchar**
música 1.2
listen (to) the radio **escuchar la**
radio 1.2
literature **literatura** *f.* 1.2
little (*quantity*) **poco/a** *adj.* 1.5;
poco *adv.* 2.4
live **vivir** *v.* 1.3; **en vivo** *adj.* 2.1
living room **sala** *f.* 2.6
loan **préstamo** *m.* 3.2; **prestar**
v. 1.6, 3.2
lobster **langosta** *f.* 2.2
located **situado/a** *adj.*
be located **quedar** *v.* 3.2
long **largo/a** *adj.* 1.6
look (at) **mirar** *v.* 1.2
look for **buscar** *v.* 1.2
lose **perder (e:ie)** *v.* 1.4
lose weight **adelgazar** *v.* 3.3
lost **perdido/a** *adj.* 3.1, 3.2
be lost **estar perdido/a** 3.2
lot, a **muchas veces** *adv.* 2.4
lot of, a **mucho/a** *adj.* 1.2, 1.3;
un montón de 1.4
love (*another person*) **querer**
(e:ie) *v.* 1.4; (*inanimate objects*)
encantar *v.* 2.1; **amor** *m.* 2.3
in love **enamorado/a** *adj.* 1.5
I loved it! **¡Me encantó!** 3.3
love at first sight **amor a**
primera vista 2.3
lucky: be (very) lucky **tener**
(mucha) suerte 1.3
luggage **equipaje** *m.* 1.5
lunch **almuerzo** *m.* 1.4, 2.2
have lunch **almorzar (o:ue)**
v. 1.4

M

ma'am **señora (Sra.); doña** *f.* 1.1
mad **enojado/a** *adj.* 1.5
magazine **revista** *f.* 1.4
magnificent **magnífico/a** *adj.* 1.5
mail **correo** *m.* 3.2; **enviar** *v.,*
mandar *v.* 3.2; **echar**
(una carta) al buzón 3.2
mail carrier **cartero** *m.* 3.2
mailbox **buzón** *m.* 3.2
main **principal** *adj. m., f.* 2.2
maintain **mantener** *v.* 3.3
major **especialización** *f.* 1.2
make **hacer** *v.* 1.4
make a decision **tomar una**
decisión 3.3
make the bed **hacer la**
cama 2.6

makeup **maquillaje** *m.* 2.1
  put on makeup **maquillarse** *v.* 2.1
man **hombre** *m.* 1.1
manager **gerente** *m., f.* 2.2, 3.4
many **mucho/a** *adj.* 1.3
  many times **muchas veces** 2.4
map **mapa** *m.* 1.2
March **marzo** *m.* 1.5
margarine **margarina** *f.* 2.2
marinated fish **ceviche** *m.* 2.2
  lemon-marinated shrimp **ceviche** *m.* **de camarón** 2.2
marital status **estado** *m.* **civil** 2.3
market **mercado** *m.* 1.6
  open-air market **mercado al aire libre** 1.6
marriage **matrimonio** *m.* 2.3
married **casado/a** *adj.* 2.3
  get married (to) **casarse** *v.* **(con)** 2.3
  I'll marry you! **¡Acepto casarme contigo!** 3.5
marvelous **maravilloso/a** *adj.* 1.5
massage **masaje** *m.* 3.3
masterpiece **obra maestra** *f.* 3.5
match (*sports*) **partido** *m.* 1.4
match (with) **hacer** *v.* **juego (con)** 1.6
mathematics **matemáticas** *f., pl.* 1.2
matter **importar** *v.* 2.1
maturity **madurez** *f.* 2.3
maximum **máximo/a** *adj.* 2.5
May **mayo** *m.* 1.5
May I leave a message? **¿Puedo dejar un recado?** 2.5
maybe **tal vez** 1.5; **quizás** 1.5
mayonnaise **mayonesa** *f.* 2.2
me **me** *sing., d.o. pron.* 1.5
  to/for me **me** *sing., i.o. pron.* 1.6
meal **comida** *f.* 1.4, 2.2
means of communication **medios** *m., pl.* **de comunicación** 3.6
meat **carne** *f.* 2.2
mechanic **mecánico/a** *m., f.* 2.5
  mechanic's repair shop **taller mecánico** 2.5
media **medios** *m., pl.* **de comunicación** 3.6
medical **médico/a** *adj.* 2.4
medication **medicamento** *m.* 2.4
medicine **medicina** *f.* 2.4
medium **mediano/a** *adj.*
meet (each other) **encontrar(se)** *v.* 2.5; **conocer(se)** *v.* 2.2
  meet up with **encontrarse con** 2.1
meeting **reunión** *f.* 3.4
menu **menú** *m.* 2.2
message **mensaje** *m.*
Mexican **mexicano/a** *adj.* 1.3
Mexico **México** *m.* 1.1
microwave **microonda** *f.* 2.6
  microwave oven **horno** *m.* **de microondas** 2.6
middle age **madurez** *f.* 2.3

midnight **medianoche** *f.* 1.1
mile **milla** *f.* 2.5
milk **leche** *f.* 2.2
million **millón** *m.* 1.2
  million of **millón de** 1.2
mine **mío(s)/a(s)** *poss.* 2.5
mineral **mineral** *m.* 3.3
  mineral water **agua** *f.* **mineral** 2.2
minute **minuto** *m.* 1.1
mirror **espejo** *m.* 2.1
Miss **señorita (Srta.)** *f.* 1.1
miss **perder (e:ie)** *v.* 1.4; **extrañar** *v.* 3.4
mistaken **equivocado/a** *adj.*
modern **moderno/a** *adj.* 3.5
mom **mamá** *f.* 1.3
Monday **lunes** *m., sing.* 1.2
money **dinero** *m.* 1.6
monitor **monitor** *m.* 2.5
monkey **mono** *m.* 3.1
month **mes** *m.* 1.5
monument **monumento** *m.* 1.4
moon **luna** *f.* 3.1
more **más** 1.2
  more... than **más... que** 2.2
  more than **más de (+ *number*)** 2.2
morning **mañana** *f.* 1.1
mother **madre** *f.* 1.3
mother-in-law **suegra** *f.* 1.3
motor **motor** *m.*
motorcycle **motocicleta** *f.* 1.5
mountain **montaña** *f.* 1.4
mouse **ratón** *m.* 2.5
mouth **boca** *f.* 2.4
move (*from one house to another*) **mudarse** *v.* 2.6
movie **película** *f.* 1.4
  movie star **estrella** *f.* **de cine** 3.5
  movie theater **cine** *m.* 1.4
MP3 player **reproductor** *m.* **de MP3** 2.5
Mr. **señor (Sr.); don** *m.* 1.1
Mrs. **señora (Sra.); doña** *f.* 1.1
much **mucho/a** *adj.* 1.2, 1.3
  very much **muchísimo/a** *adj.* 1.2
mud **lodo** *m.*
murder **crimen** *m.* 3.6
muscle **músculo** *m.* 3.3
museum **museo** *m.* 1.4
mushroom **champiñón** *m.* 2.2
music **música** *f.* 1.2, 3.5
musical **musical** *adj., m., f.* 3.5
musician **músico/a** *m., f.* 3.5
must **deber** *v.* **(+ *inf.*)** 3
  It must be... **Debe ser...** 1.6
my **mi(s)** *poss. adj.* 1.3; **mío(s)/a(s)** *poss. pron.* 2.5

N

name **nombre** *m.* 1.1
  be named **llamarse** *v.* 2.1
  in the name of **a nombre de** 1.5

last name **apellido** *m.* 1.3
My name is... **Me llamo...** 1.1
name someone/ something **ponerle el nombre** 2.3
napkin **servilleta** *f.* 2.6
national **nacional** *adj. m., f.* 3.6
nationality **nacionalidad** *f.* 1.1
natural **natural** *adj. m., f.* 3.1
  natural disaster **desastre** *m.* **natural** 3.6
  natural resource **recurso** *m.* **natural** 3.1
nature **naturaleza** *f.* 3.1
nauseated **mareado/a** *adj.* 2.4
near **cerca de** *prep.* 1.2
neaten **arreglar** *v.* 2.6
necessary **necesario/a** *adj.* 2.6
  It is necessary that... **Hay que...** 2.6, 3.2
neck **cuello** *m.* 2.4
need **faltar** *v.* 2.1; **necesitar** *v.* **(+ *inf.*)** 1.2
neighbor **vecino/a** *m., f.* 2.6
neighborhood **barrio** *m.* 2.6
neither **tampoco** *adv.* 2.1
neither... nor **ni... ni** *conj.* 2.1
nephew **sobrino** *m.* 1.3
nervous **nervioso/a** *adj.* 1.5
network **red** *f.* 2.5
never **nunca** *adj.* 2.1; **jamás** 2.1
new **nuevo/a** *adj.* 1.6
newlywed **recién casado/a** *m., f.* 2.3
news **noticias** *f., pl.* 3.6; **actualidades** *f., pl.* 3.6; **noticia** *f.* 2.5
newscast **noticiero** *m.* 3.6
newspaper **periódico** 1.4; **diario** *m.* 3.6
next **próximo/a** *adj.* 1.3, 3.4
  next to **al lado de** *prep.* 1.2
nice **simpático/a** *adj.* 1.3; **amable** *adj. m., f.*
niece **sobrina** *f.* 1.3
night **noche** *f.* 1.1
  night stand **mesita** *f.* **de noche** 2.6
nine **nueve** 1.1
nine hundred **novecientos/as** 1.2
nineteen **diecinueve** 1.1
ninety **noventa** 1.2
ninth **noveno/a** 1.5
no **no** 1.1; **ningún, ninguno/a(s)** *adj.* 2.1
  no one **nadie** *pron.* 2.1
nobody **nadie** 2.1
none **ningún, ninguno/a(s)** *adj.* 2.1
noon **mediodía** *m.* 1.1
nor **ni** *conj.* 2.1
north **norte** *m.* 3.2
  to the north **al norte** 3.2
nose **nariz** *f.* 2.4
not **no** 1.1
  not any **ningún, ninguno/a(s)** *adj.* 2.1

not anyone **nadie** *pron.* 2.1
not anything **nada** *pron.* 2.1
not bad at all **nada mal** 1.5
not either **tampoco** *adv.* 2.1
not ever **nunca** *adv.* 2.1;
  jamás *adv.* 2.1
not very well **no muy bien** 1.1
not working **descompuesto/a**
  adj. 2.5
notebook **cuaderno** *m.* 1.1
nothing **nada** 1.1; 2.1
noun **sustantivo** *m.*
November **noviembre** *m.* 1.5
now **ahora** *adv.* 1.2
nowadays **hoy día** *adv.*
nuclear **nuclear** *adj. m., f.* 3.1
  nuclear energy **energía**
    nuclear 3.1
number **número** *m.* 1.1
nurse **enfermero/a** *m., f.* 2.4
nutrition **nutrición** *f.* 3.3
nutritionist **nutricionista**
  m., f. 3.3

O

o'clock: It's... o'clock **Son**
  las... 1.1
  It's one o'clock. **Es la una.** 1.1
obey **obedecer** *v.* 3.6
obligation **deber** *m.* 3.6
obtain **conseguir (e:i)** *v.* 1.4;
  obtener *v.* 3.4
obvious **obvio/a** *adj.* 3.1
  it's obvious **es obvio** 3.1
occupation **ocupación** *f.* 3.4
occur **ocurrir** *v.* 3.6
October **octubre** *m.* 1.5
of **de** *prep.* 1.1
  Of course. **Claro que sí.;**
    Por supuesto.
offer **oferta** *f.;* **ofrecer**
  (c:zc) *v.* 1.6
office **oficina** *f.* 2.6
  doctor's office **consultorio** *m.* 2.4
often **a menudo** *adv.* 2.4
Oh! **¡Ay!**
oil **aceite** *m.* 2.2
OK **regular** *adj.* 1.1
  It's okay. **Está bien.**
old **viejo/a** *adj.* 1.3
old age **vejez** *f.* 2.3
older **mayor** *adj. m., f.* 1.3
  older brother, sister **hermano/a**
    mayor *m., f.* 1.3
oldest **el/la mayor** 2.2
on **en** *prep.* 1.2; **sobre** *prep.* 1.2
  on behalf of **por** *prep.* 2.5
  on the dot **en punto** 1.1
  on time **a tiempo** 2.4
  on top of **encima de** 1.2
once **una vez** 1.6
one **un, uno/a** *m., f., sing. pron.* 1.1
  one hundred **cien(to)** 1.2
  one million **un millón** *m.* 1.2
  one more time **una vez más** 2.3

one thousand **mil** 1.2
one time **una vez** 1.6
onion **cebolla** *f.* 2.2
only **sólo** *adv.* 1.3; **único/a**
  adj. 1.3
  only child **hijo/a único/a**
    m., f. 1.3
open **abierto/a** *adj.* 1.5, 3.2;
  abrir *v.* 1.3
open-air **al aire libre** 1.6
opera **ópera** *f.* 3.5
operation **operación** *f.* 2.4
opposite **enfrente de** *prep.* 3.2
or **o** *conj.* 2.1
orange **anaranjado/a** *adj.* 1.6;
  naranja *f.* 2.2
orchestra **orquesta** *f.* 3.5
order **mandar** 2.6; *(food)* **pedir**
  (e:i) *v.* 2.2
  in order to **para** *prep.* 2.5
orderly **ordenado/a** *adj.* 1.5
ordinal *(numbers)* **ordinal** *adj.*
organize oneself
  organizarse *v.* 2.6
other **otro/a** *adj.* 1.6
ought to **deber** *v.* **(+ inf.)** *adj.* 1.3
our **nuestro(s)/a(s)** *poss.*
  adj. 1.3; *poss. pron.* 2.5
out of order **descompuesto/a**
  adj. 2.5
outside **afuera** *adv.* 1.5
outskirts **afueras** *f., pl.* 2.6
oven **horno** *m.* 2.6
over **sobre** *prep.* 1.2
(over)population **(sobre)**
  población *f.* 3.1
over there **allá** *adv.* 1.2
own **propio/a** *adj.* 3.4
owner **dueño/a** *m., f.* 2.2

P

p.m. **tarde** *f.* 1.1
pack (one's suitcases) **hacer** *v.* **las**
  maletas 1.5
package **paquete** *m.* 3.2
page **página** *f.* 2.5
pain **dolor** *m.* 2.4
  have pain **tener** *v.* **dolor** 2.4
paint **pintar** *v.* 3.5
painter **pintor(a)** *m., f.* 3.4
painting **pintura** *f.* 2.6, 3.5
pair **par** *m.* 1.6
  pair of shoes **par** *m.* **de**
    zapatos 1.6
pale **pálido/a** *adj.* 3.2
pants **pantalones** *m., pl.* 1.6
pantyhose **medias** *f., pl.* 1.6
paper **papel** *m.* 1.2; *(report)*
  informe *m.* 3.6
Pardon me. *(May I?)* **Con**
  permiso. 1.1; *(Excuse me.)*
  Pardon me. **Perdón.** 1.1
parents **padres** *m., pl.* 1.3;
  papás *m., pl.* 1.3

park **estacionar** *v.* 2.5; **parque**
  m. 1.4
parking lot **estacionamiento**
  m. 3.2
partner *(one of a married couple)*
  pareja *f.* 2.3
party **fiesta** *f.* 2.3
passed **pasado/a** *p.p.*
passenger **pasajero/a** *m., f.* 1.1
passport **pasaporte** *m.* 1.5
past **pasado/a** *adj.* 1.6
pastime **pasatiempo** *m.* 1.4
pastry shop **pastelería** *f.* 3.2
patient **paciente** *m., f.* 2.4
patio **patio** *m.* 2.6
pay **pagar** *v.* 1.6
  pay in cash **pagar** *v.* **al**
    contado; pagar en
    efectivo 3.2
  pay in installments **pagar** *v.* **a**
    plazos 3.2
  pay the bill **pagar la**
    cuenta 2.3
pea **arveja** *m.* 2.2
peace **paz** *f.* 3.6
peach **melocotón** *m.* 2.2
peak **cima** *f.* 3.3
pear **pera** *f.* 2.2
pen **pluma** *f.* 1.2
pencil **lápiz** *m.* 1.1
people **gente** *f.* 1.3
pepper *(black)* **pimienta** *f.* 2.2
per **por** *prep.* 2.5
perfect **perfecto/a** *adj.* 1.5
period of time **temporada** *f.* 1.5
person **persona** *f.* 1.3
pharmacy **farmacia** *f.* 2.4
phenomenal **fenomenal** *adj.* 1.5
photograph **foto(grafía)** *f.* 1.1
physical *(exam)* **examen** *m.*
  médico 2.4
physician **doctor(a), médico/a**
  m., f. 1.3
physics **física** *f. sing.* 1.2
pick up **recoger** *v.* 3.1
picture **cuadro** *m.* 2.6;
  pintura *f.* 2.6
pie **pastel** *m.* 2.3
pill (tablet) **pastilla** *f.* 2.4
pillow **almohada** *f.* 2.6
pineapple **piña** *f.*
pink **rosado/a** *adj.* 1.6
place **lugar** *m.* 1.2, 1.4; **sitio** *m.*
  1.3; **poner** *v.* 1.4
plaid **de cuadros** 1.6
plans **planes** *m., pl.* 1.4
  have plans **tener planes** 1.4
plant **planta** *f.* 3.1
plastic **plástico** *m.* 3.1
  (made) of plastic **de**
    plástico 3.1
plate **plato** *m.* 2.6
play **drama** *m.* 3.5; **comedia**
  f. 3.5; **jugar (u:ue)** *v.* 1.4; *(a*
  musical instrument) **tocar** *v.*
  3.5; *(a role)* **hacer el papel**
  de 3.5; *(cards)* **jugar a (las**

cartas) 1.5; (sports)
practicar deportes 1.4
player **jugador(a)** m., f. 1.4
playwright **dramaturgo/a**
m., f. 3.5
plead **rogar (o:ue)** v. 2.6
pleasant **agradable** adj. 1.5
please **por favor** 1.1
Pleased to meet you. **Mucho
gusto.** 1.1; **Encantado/a.**
adj. 1.1
pleasing: be pleasing to **gustar** v. 2.1
pleasure **gusto** m. 1.1
The pleasure is mine. **El gusto
es mío.** 1.1
poem **poema** m. 3.5
poet **poeta** m., f. 3.5
poetry **poesía** f. 3.5
police (force) **policía** f. 2.5
political **político/a** adj. 3.6
politician **político/a** m., f. 3.4
politics **política** f. 3.6
polka-dotted **de lunares** 1.6
poll **encuesta** f. 3.6
pollute **contaminar** v. 3.1
polluted **contaminado/a** m., f. 3.1
be polluted **estar
contaminado/a** 3.1
pollution **contaminación** f. 3.1
pool **piscina** f. 1.4
poor **pobre** adj., m., f. 1.6
poor thing **pobrecito/a** adj. 1.3
popsicle **paleta helada** f. 1.4
population **población** f. 3.1
pork **cerdo** m. 2.2
pork chop **chuleta** f. **de
cerdo** 2.2
portable **portátil** adj. 2.5
portable computer
computadora f.
portátil 2.5
position **puesto** m. 3.4
possessive **posesivo/a** adj. 1.3
possible **posible** adj. 3.1
it's (not) possible **(no) es
posible** 3.1
post office **correo** m. 3.2
postcard **postal** f.
poster **cartel** m. 2.6
potato **papa** f. 2.2; **patata** f. 2.2
pottery **cerámica** f. 3.5
practice **entrenarse** v. 3.3;
practicar v. 1.2; (a degree/
profession) **ejercer** v. 3.4
prefer **preferir (e:ie)** v. 1.4
pregnant **embarazada** adj. f. 2.4
prepare **preparar** v. 1.2
preposition **preposición** f.
prescribe (medicine) **recetar**
v. 2.4
prescription **receta** f. 2.4
present **regalo** m. 1.6;
presentar v. 3.5
press **prensa** f. 3.6
pressure **presión** f.
be under a lot of pressure **sufrir
muchas presiones** 3.3

pretty **bonito/a** adj. 1.3
price **precio** m. 1.6
(fixed, set) price **precio** m.
fijo 1.6
print **estampado/a** adj.;
imprimir v. 2.5
printer **impresora** f. 2.5
private (room) **individual** adj.
prize **premio** m. 3.5
probable **probable** adj. 3.1
it's (not) probable **(no) es
probable** 3.1
problem **problema** m. 1.1
profession **profesión** f. 1.3; 3.4
professor **profesor(a)** m., f.
program **programa** m. 1.1
programmer **programador(a)**
m., f. 1.3
prohibit **prohibir** v. 2.4
project **proyecto** m. 2.5
promotion (career)
ascenso m. 3.4
pronoun **pronombre** m.
protect **proteger** v. 3.1
protein **proteína** f. 3.3
provided (that) **con tal (de)
que** conj. 3.1
psychologist **psicólogo/a**
m., f. 3.4
psychology **psicología** f. 1.2
publish **publicar** v. 3.5
Puerto Rican **puertorriqueño/a**
adj. 1.3
Puerto Rico **Puerto Rico** m. 1.1
pull a tooth **sacar una muela**
purchases **compras** f., pl. 1.5
pure **puro/a** adj. 3.1
purple **morado/a** adj. 1.6
purse **bolsa** f. 1.6
put **poner** v. 1.4; **puesto/a**
p.p. 3.2
put (a letter) in the mailbox
**echar (una carta) al
buzón** 3.2
put on (a performance)
presentar v. 3.5
put on (clothing) **ponerse**
v. 2.1
put on makeup **maquillarse**
v. 2.1

Q

quality **calidad** f. 1.6
quarter (academic) **trimestre**
m. 1.2
quarter after (time) **y cuarto** 1.1;
y quince 1.1
quarter to (time) **menos
cuarto** 1.1; **menos
quince** 1.1
question **pregunta** f. 1.2
quickly **rápido** adv. 2.4
quiet **tranquilo/a** adj. 3.3
quit **dejar** v. 3.4
quiz **prueba** f. 1.2

R

racism **racismo** m. 3.6
radio (medium) **radio** f. 1.2
radio (set) **radio** m. 2.5
rain **llover (o:ue)** v. 1.5;
lluvia f.
It's raining. **Llueve.** 1.5; **Está
lloviendo.** 1.5
raincoat **impermeable** m. 1.6
rain forest **bosque** m. **tropical** 3.1
raise (salary) **aumento de
sueldo** 3.4
rather **bastante** adv. 2.4
read **leer** v. 1.3; **leído/a** p.p. 3.2
read e-mail **leer correo
electrónico** 1.4
read a magazine **leer una
revista** 1.4
read a newspaper **leer un
periódico** 1.4
ready **listo/a** adj. 1.5
(Are you) ready? **¿(Están)
listos?** 3.3
reality show **progama de
realidad** m. 3.5
reap the benefits (of) **disfrutar** v.
(de) 3.3
receive **recibir** v. 1.3
recommend **recomendar (e:ie)**
v. 2.2; 2.6
record **grabar** v. 2.5
recover **recuperar** v. 2.5
recreation **diversión** f. 1.4
recycle **reciclar** v. 3.1
recycling **reciclaje** m. 3.1
red **rojo/a** adj. 1.6
red-haired **pelirrojo/a** adj. 1.3
reduce **reducir** v. 3.1; disminuir v. 3.4
reduce stress/tension **aliviar el
estrés/la tensión** 3.3
refrigerator **refrigerador** m. 2.6
region **región** f. 3.1
regret **sentir (e:ie)** v. 3.1
related to sitting **sedentario/a**
adj. 3.3
relatives **parientes** m., pl. 1.3
relax **relajarse** v. 2.3
Relax, sweetie. **Tranquilo/a,
cariño.** 2.5
remain **quedarse** v. 2.1
remember **recordar (o:ue)** v. 1.4;
acordarse (o:ue) v. **(de)** 2.1
remote control **control remoto**
m. 2.5
renewable **renovable** adj. 3.1
rent **alquilar** v. 2.6; (payment)
alquiler m. 2.6
repeat **repetir (e:i)** v. 1.4
report **informe** m. 3.6; **reportaje**
m. 3.4
reporter **reportero/a** m., f. 3.4
representative **representante**
m., f. 3.6
request **pedir (e:i)** v. 1.4
reservation **reservación** f. 1.5
resign (from) **renunciar (a)** v. 3.4

resolve **resolver (o:ue)** *v.* 3.1
resolved **resuelto/a** *p.p.* 3.2
resource **recurso** *m.* 3.1
responsibility **deber** *m.* 3.6;
 responsabilidad *f.*
responsible **responsable** *adj.* 2.2
rest **descansar** *v.* 1.2
restaurant **restaurante** *m.* 1.4
résumé **currículum** *m.* 3.4
retire (from work) **jubilarse** *v.* 2.3
return **regresar** *v.* 1.2; **volver
 (o:ue)** *v.* 1.4
returned **vuelto/a** *p.p.* 3.2
rice **arroz** *m.* 2.2
rich **rico/a** *adj.* 1.6
ride a bicycle **pasear** *v.* **en
 bicicleta** 1.4
ride a horse **montar** *v.* **a
 caballo** 1.5
ridiculous **ridículo/a** *adj.* 3.1
 it's ridiculous **es ridículo** 3.1
right **derecha** *f.* 1.2
 be right **tener razón** 1.3
 right? (*question tag*) **¿no?** 1.1;
  ¿verdad? 1.1
 right away **enseguida** *adv.*
 right now **ahora mismo** 1.5
 right there **allí mismo** 3.2
 to the right of **a la
  derecha de** 1.2
rights **derechos** *m.* 3.6
ring **anillo** *m.* 3.5
ring (a doorbell) **sonar (o:ue)** *v.* 2.5
river **río** *m.* 3.1
road **camino** *m.*
roast **asado/a** *adj.* 2.2
roast chicken **pollo** *m.* **asado** 2.2
rollerblade **patinar en línea** *v.*
romantic **romántico/a** *adj.* 3.5
room **habitación** *f.* 1.5; **cuarto**
 m. 1.2; 2.1
 living room **sala** *f.* 2.6
roommate **compañero/a**
 m., f. **de cuarto** 1.2
roundtrip **de ida y vuelta** 1.5
 roundtrip ticket **pasaje** *m.* **de
  ida y vuelta** 1.5
routine **rutina** *f.* 2.1
rug **alfombra** *f.* 2.6
run **correr** *v.* 1.3
 run errands **hacer
  diligencias** 3.2
 run into (*have an accident*)
  chocar (con) *v.*; (*meet
  accidentally*) **encontrar(se)
  (o:ue)** *v.* 2.5; (*run into
  something*) **darse (con)** 2.4
 run into (each other)
  encontrar(se) (o:ue) *v.* 2.5
rush **apurarse, darse prisa** *v.* 3.3
Russian **ruso/a** *adj.* 1.3

S

sad **triste** *adj.* 1.5; 3.1
 it's sad **es triste** 3.1

safe **seguro/a** *adj.* 1.5
said **dicho/a** *p.p.* 3.2
sailboard **tabla de
 windsurf** *f.* 1.5
salad **ensalada** *f.* 2.2
salary **salario** *m.* 3.4; **sueldo**
 m. 3.4
sale **rebaja** *f.* 1.6
salesperson **vendedor(a)** *m., f.* 1.6
salmon **salmón** *m.* 2.2
salt **sal** *f.* 2.2
same **mismo/a** *adj.* 1.3
sandal **sandalia** *f.* 1.6
sandwich **sándwich** *m.* 2.2
Saturday **sábado** *m.* 1.2
sausage **salchicha** *f.* 2.2
save (*on a computer*) **guardar**
 v. 2.5; save (money) **ahorrar**
 v. 3.2
savings **ahorros** *m.* 3.2
 savings account **cuenta** *f.* **de
  ahorros** 3.2
say **decir** *v.* 1.4; **declarar** *v.* 3.6
say (that) **decir (que)** *v.* 1.4, 2.3
 say the answer **decir la
  respuesta** 1.4
scan **escanear** *v.* 2.5
scarcely **apenas** *adv.* 2.4
scared: be (very) scared (of) **tener
 (mucho) miedo (de)** 1.3
schedule **horario** *m.* 1.2
school **escuela** *f.* 1.1
science **ciencia** *f.* 1.2
 science fiction **ciencia ficción**
  f. 3.5
scientist **científico/a** *m., f.* 3.4
scream **grito** *m.* 1.5; **gritar**
 v. 2.1
screen **pantalla** *f.* 2.5
scuba dive **bucear** *v.* 1.4
sculpt **esculpir** *v.* 3.5
sculptor **escultor(a)** *m., f.* 3.5
sculpture **escultura** *f.* 3.5
sea **mar** *m.* 1.5
 (sea) turtle **tortuga
  (marina)** *f.* 3.1
season **estación** *f.* 1.5
seat **silla** *f.* 1.2
second **segundo/a** 1.5
secretary **secretario/a** *m., f.* 3.4
sedentary **sedentario/a** *adj.* 3.3
see **ver** *v.* 1.4
 see (you, him, her) again **volver
  a ver(te, lo, la)** 3.6
 see movies **ver películas** 1.4
 See you. **Nos vemos.** 1.1
 See you later. **Hasta la vista.** 1.1;
  Hasta luego. 1.1
 See you soon. **Hasta
  pronto.** 1.1
 See you tomorrow. **Hasta
  mañana.** 1.1
seem **parecer** *v.* 1.6
seen **visto/a** *p.p.* 3.2
sell **vender** *v.* 1.6
semester **semestre** *m.* 1.2
send **enviar; mandar** *v.* 3.2

separate (from) **separarse** *v.*
 (de) 2.3
separated **separado/a** *adj.* 2.3
September **septiembre** *m.* 1.5
sequence **secuencia** *f.*
serious **grave** *adj.* 2.4
serve **servir (e:i)** *v.* 2.2
service **servicio** *m.* 3.3
set (*fixed*) **fijo/a** *adj.* 1.6
 set the table **poner la mesa** 2.6
seven **siete** 1.1
seven hundred **setecientos/as** 1.2
seventeen **diecisiete** 1.1
seventh **séptimo/a** 1.5
seventy **setenta** 1.2
several **varios/as** *adj. pl.* 2.2
sexism **sexismo** *m.* 3.6
shame **lástima** *f.* 3.1
 it's a shame **es una lástima** 3.1
shampoo **champú** *m.* 2.1
shape **forma** *f.* 3.3
 be in good shape **estar en
  buena forma** 3.3
 stay in shape **mantenerse en
  forma** 3.3
share **compartir** *v.* 1.3
sharp (*time*) **en punto** 1.1
shave **afeitarse** *v.* 2.1
shaving cream **crema** *f.* **de
 afeitar** 1.5, 2.1
she **ella** 1.1
shellfish **mariscos** *m., pl.* 2.2
ship **barco** *m.*
shirt **camisa** *f.* 1.6
shoe **zapato** *m.* 1.6
 shoe size **número** *m.* 1.6
 shoe store **zapatería** *f.* 3.2
 tennis shoes **zapatos** *m., pl.* **de
  tenis** 1.6
shop **tienda** *f.* 1.6
shopping, to go **ir de
 compras** 1.5
 shopping mall **centro
  comercial** *m.* 1.6
short (*in height*) **bajo/a** *adj.* 1.3;
 (*in length*) **corto/a** *adj.* 1.6
short story **cuento** *m.* 3.5
shorts **pantalones cortos**
 m., pl. 1.6
should (*do something*) **deber** *v.*
 (+ inf.) 1.3
shout **gritar** *v.* 2.1
show **espectáculo** *m.* 3.5;
 mostrar (o:ue) *v.* 1.4
 game show **concurso** *m.* 3.5
shower **ducha** *f.* 2.1; **ducharse**
 v. 2.1
shrimp **camarón** *m.* 2.2
siblings **hermanos/as** *pl.* 1.3
sick **enfermo/a** *adj.* 2.4
 be sick **estar enfermo/a** 2.4
 get sick **enfermarse** *v.* 2.4
sign **firmar** *v.* 3.2; **letrero** *m.* 3.2
silk **seda** *f.* 1.6
 (made of) silk **de seda** 1.6
silly **tonto/a** *adj.* 1.3
since **desde** *prep.*

sing **cantar** *v.* 1.2
singer **cantante** *m., f.* 3.5
single **soltero/a** *adj.* 2.3
   single room **habitación** *f.*
    individual 1.5
sink **lavabo** *m.* 2.1
sir **señor (Sr.), don** m. 1.1;
   caballero *m.* **2.2**
sister **hermana** *f.* 1.3
sister-in-law **cuñada** *f.* 1.3
sit down **sentarse (e:ie)** *v.* 2.1
six **seis** 1.1
six hundred **seiscientos/as** 1.2
sixteen **dieciséis** 1.1
sixth **sexto/a** 1.5
sixty **sesenta** 1.2
size **talla** *f.* 1.6
   shoe size **número** *m.* 1.6
(in-line) skate **patinar (en línea)** 1.4
skateboard **andar en patineta**
   v. 1.4
ski **esquiar** *v.* 1.4
skiing **esquí** *m.* 1.4
   water-skiing **esquí** *m.*
    acuático 1.4
skirt **falda** *f.* 1.6
skull made out of sugar **calavera**
   de azúcar *f.* 2.3
sky **cielo** *m.* 3.1
sleep **dormir (o:ue)** *v.* 1.4
   go to sleep **dormirse**
    (o:ue) v. 2.1
sleepy: be (very) sleepy **tener**
   (mucho) sueño 1.3
slender **delgado/a** *adj.* 1.3
slim down **adelgazar** *v.* 3.3
slippers **pantuflas** *f.* 2.1
slow **lento/a** *adj.* 2.5
slowly **despacio** *adv.* 2.4
small **pequeño/a** *adj.* 1.3
smart **listo/a** *adj.* 1.5
smile **sonreír (e:i)** *v.* 2.3
smiled **sonreído** *p.p.* 3.2
smoggy: It's (very) smoggy. **Hay**
   (mucha) contaminación.
smoke **fumar** *v.* 2.2; 3.3
   (not) to smoke **(no) fumar** 3.3
smoking section **sección** *f.* **de**
   fumar 2.2
   (non) smoking section **sección**
    de (no) fumar *f.* 2.2
snack **merendar** *v.* 2.2; 3.3;
   afternoon snack **merienda** *f.* 3.3
   have a snack **merendar** *v.*
sneakers **los zapatos de tenis** 1.6
sneeze **estornudar** *v.* 2.4
snow **nevar (e:ie)** *v.* 1.5; **nieve** *f.*
snowing: It's snowing. **Nieva.** 1.5;
   Está nevando. 1.5
so (*in such a way*) **así** *adv.* 2.4;
   tan *adv.* 1.5
   so much **tanto** *adv.*
   so-so **regular** 1.1
   so that **para que** *conj.* 3.1
soap **jabón** *m.* 2.1
soap opera **telenovela** *f.* 3.5
soccer **fútbol** *m.* 1.4

sociology **sociología** *f.* 1.2
sock(s) **calcetín (calcetines)**
   m. 1.6
sofa **sofá** *m.* 2.6
soft drink **refresco** *m.* 2.2
software **programa** *m.* **de**
   computación 2.5
soil **tierra** *f.* 3.1
solar **solar** *adj., m., f.* 3.1
   solar energy **energía solar** 3.1
soldier **soldado** *m., f.* 3.6
solution **solución** *f.* 3.1
solve **resolver (o:ue)** *v.* 3.1
some **algún, alguno/a(s)** *adj.*
   2.1; **unos/as** *pron./ m., f., pl;*
   indef., art. 1.1
somebody **alguien** *pron.* 2.1
someone **alguien** *pron.* 2.1
something **algo** *pron.* 2.1
sometimes **a veces** *adv.* 2.4
son **hijo** *m.* 1.3
song **canción** *f.* 3.5
son-in-law **yerno** *m.* 1.3
soon **pronto** *adv.* 2.4
   See you soon. **Hasta pronto.** 1.1
sorry: be sorry **sentir (e:ie)** *v.* 3.1
   I'm sorry. **Lo siento.** 1.1
soul **alma** *f.* 2.3
soup **sopa** *f.* 2.2
south **sur** *m.* 3.2
   to the south **al sur** 3.2
Spain **España** *f.* 1.1
Spanish (*language*) **español**
   m. 1.2; **español(a)** *adj.* 1.3
spare (free) time **ratos libres** 1.4
speak **hablar** *v.* 1.2
   Speaking. (*on the phone*) **Con**
    él/ella habla. 2.5
special: today's specials **las**
   especialidades del día 2.2
spectacular **espectacular** *adj. m.,*
   f. 3.3
speech **discurso** *m.* 3.6
speed **velocidad** *f.* 2.5
   speed limit **velocidad** *f.*
    máxima 2.5
spelling **ortografía** *f.,*
   ortográfico/a *adj.*
spend (*money*) **gastar** *v.* 1.6
spoon (*table or large*) **cuchara**
   f. 2.6
sport **deporte** *m.* 1.4
   sports-related **deportivo/a**
    adj. 1.4
spouse **esposo/a** *m., f.* 1.3
sprain (one's ankle) **torcerse**
   (o:ue) *v.* (el tobillo) 2.4
sprained **torcido/a** *adj.* 2.4
   be sprained **estar torcido/a** 2.4
spring **primavera** *f.* 1.5
(city or town) square **plaza** *f.* 1.4
stadium **estadio** *m.* 1.2
stage **etapa** *f.* 2.3
stairs **escalera** *f.* 2.6
stairway **escalera** *f.* 2.6
stamp **estampilla** *f.* 3.2; **sello**
   m. 3.2

stand in line **hacer** *v.* **cola** 3.2
star **estrella** *f.* 3.1
start (*a vehicle*) **arrancar** *v.* 2.5
station **estación** *f.* 1.5
statue **estatua** *f.* 3.5
status: marital status **estado** *m.*
   civil 2.3
stay **quedarse** *v.* 2.1
   stay in shape **mantenerse en**
    forma 3.3
steak **bistec** *m.* 2.2
steering wheel **volante** *m.* 2.5
step **escalón** *m.* 3.3
stepbrother **hermanastro** *m.* 1.3
stepdaughter **hijastra** *f.* 1.3
stepfather **padrastro** *m.* 1.3
stepmother **madrastra** *f.* 1.3
stepsister **hermanastra** *f.* 1.3
stepson **hijastro** *m.* 1.3
stereo **estéreo** *m.* 2.5
still **todavía** *adv.* 1.5
stockbroker **corredor(a)** *m., f.* **de**
   bolsa 3.4
stockings **medias** *f., pl.* 1.6
stomach **estómago** *m.* 2.4
stone **piedra** *f.* 3.1
stop **parar** *v.* 2.5
   stop (*doing something*) **dejar de**
    (+ inf.) 3.1
store **tienda** *f.* 1.6
storm **tormenta** *f.* 3.6
story **cuento** *m.* 3.5; **historia**
   f. 3.5
stove **cocina, estufa** *f.* 2.6
straight **derecho** *adv.* 3.2
   straight (ahead) **derecho** 3.2
straighten up **arreglar** *v.* 2.6
strange **extraño/a** *adj.* 3.1
   it's strange **es extraño** 3.1
street **calle** *f.* 2.5
stress **estrés** *m.* 3.3
stretching **estiramiento** *m.* 3.3
   do stretching exercises **hacer**
    ejercicios *m. pl.* **de**
    estiramiento 3.3
strike (*labor*) **huelga** *f.* 3.6
stripe **raya** *f.* 1.6
   striped **de rayas** 1.6
stroll **pasear** *v.* 1.4
strong **fuerte** *adj. m., f.* 3.3
struggle (for/against) **luchar** *v.*
   (por/contra) 3.6
student **estudiante** *m., f.* 1.1; 1.2;
   estudiantil *adj.* 1.2
study **estudiar** *v.* 1.2
stuffed-up (*sinuses*)
   congestionado/a *adj.* 2.4
stupendous **estupendo/a** *adj.* 1.5
style **estilo** *m.*
suburbs **afueras** *f., pl.* 2.6
subway **metro** *m.* 1.5
   subway station **estación** *f.*
    del metro 1.5
successful: be successful **tener**
   éxito 3.4
such as **tales como**
suddenly **de repente** *adv.* 1.6

suffer **sufrir** *v.* 2.4
  suffer an illness **sufrir una enfermedad** 2.4
sugar **azúcar** *m.* 2.2
suggest **sugerir (e:ie)** *v.* 2.6
suit **traje** *m.* 1.6
suitcase **maleta** *f.* 1.1
summer **verano** *m.* 1.5
sun **sol** *m.* 1.5; 3.1
sunbathe **tomar** *v.* **el sol** 1.4
Sunday **domingo** *m.* 1.2
(sun)glasses **gafas** *f., pl.* **(de sol)** 1.6
sunny: It's (very) sunny. **Hace (mucho) sol.** 1.5
supermarket **supermercado** *m.* 3.2
suppose **suponer** *v.* 1.4
sure **seguro/a** *adj.* 1.5
  be sure **estar seguro/a** 1.5
surf (*the Internet*) **navegar** *v.* **(en Internet)** 2.5
surfboard **tabla de surf** *f.* 1.5
surprise **sorprender** *v.* 2.3; **sorpresa** *f.* 2.3
survey **encuesta** *f.* 3.6
sweat **sudar** *v.* 3.3
sweater **suéter** *m.* 1.6
sweep the floor **barrer el suelo** 2.6
sweets **dulces** *m., pl.* 2.3
swim **nadar** *v.* 1.4
swimming **natación** *f.* 1.4
  swimming pool **piscina** *f.* 1.4
symptom **síntoma** *m.* 2.4

T

table **mesa** *f.* 1.2
tablespoon **cuchara** *f.* 2.6
tablet (*pill*) **pastilla** *f.* 2.4
take **tomar** *v.* 1.2; **llevar** *v.* 1.6
  take care of **cuidar** *v.* 3.1
  take someone's temperature **tomar** *v.* **la temperatura** 2.4
  take (wear) a shoe size **calzar** *v.* 1.6
  take a bath **bañarse** *v.* 2.1
  take a shower **ducharse** *v.* 2.1
  take off **quitarse** *v.* 2.1
  take out the trash **sacar la basura** *v.* 2.6
  take photos **tomar** *v.* **fotos** 1.5; **sacar** *v.* **fotos** 1.5
talented **talentoso/a** *adj.* 3.5
talk **hablar** *v.* 1.2
  talk show **programa** *m.* **de entrevistas** 3.5
tall **alto/a** *adj.* 1.3
tank **tanque** *m.* 2.5
taste **probar (o:ue)** *v.* 2.2; **saber** *v.* 2.2
  taste like **saber a** 2.2
tasty **rico/a** *adj.* 2.2; **sabroso/a** *adj.* 2.2
tax **impuesto** *m.* 3.6
taxi **taxi** *m.* 1.5
tea **té** *m.* 2.2

teach **enseñar** *v.* 1.2
teacher **profesor(a)** *m., f.* 1.1, 1.2; **maestro/a** *m., f.* 3.4
team **equipo** *m.* 1.4
technician **técnico/a** *m., f.* 3.4
telecommuting **teletrabajo** *m.* 3.4
telephone **teléfono** 2.5
television **televisión** *f.* 1.2; 2.5
  television set **televisor** *m.* 2.5
tell **contar** *v.* 1.4; **decir** *v.* 1.4
tell (that) **decir** *v.* **(que)** 1.4, 2.3
  tell lies **decir mentiras** 1.4
  tell the truth **decir la verdad** 1.4
temperature **temperatura** *f.* 2.4
ten **diez** 1.1
tennis **tenis** *m.* 1.4
  tennis shoes **zapatos** *m., pl.* **de tenis** 1.6
tension **tensión** *f.* 3.3
tenth **décimo/a** 1.5
terrible **terrible** *adj. m., f.* 3.1
  it's terrible **es terrible** 3.1
terrific **chévere** *adj.*
test **prueba** *f.* 1.2; **examen** *m.* 1.2
text message **mensaje** *m.* **de texto** 2.5
Thank you. **Gracias.** *f., pl.* 1.1
  Thank you (very much). **(Muchas) gracias.** 1.1
  Thanks (a lot). **(Muchas) gracias.** 1.1
  Thanks for inviting me. **Gracias por invitarme.** 2.3
that **que, quien(es), lo que** *pron.* 2.6
  that (one) **ése, ésa, eso** *pron.* 1.6; **ese, esa,** *adj.* 1.6
  that (*over there*) **aquél, aquélla, aquello** *pron.* 1.6; **aquel, aquella** *adj.* 1.6
  that which **lo que** *conj.* 2.6
  that's why **por eso** 2.5
the **el** *m.,* **la** *f. sing.,* **los** *m.,* **las** *f., pl.* 1.1
theater **teatro** *m.* 3.5
their **su(s)** *poss. adj.* 1.3; **suyo(s)/a(s)** *poss. pron.* 2.5
them **los/las** *pl., d.o. pron.* 1.5
  to/for them **les** *pl., i.o. pron.* 1.6
then (*afterward*) **después** *adv.* 2.1; (*as a result*) **entonces** *adv.* 1.5, 2.1; (*next*) **luego** *adv.* 2.1; **pues** *adv.* 3.3
there **allí** *adv.* 1.2
  There is/are… **Hay…** 1.1
  There is/are not… **No hay…** 1.1
therefore **por eso** 2.5
these **éstos, éstas** *pron.* 1.6; **estos, estas** *adj.* 1.6
they **ellos** *m.,* **ellas** *f. pron.*
  They all told me to ask you to excuse them/forgive them. **Todos me dijeron que te pidiera disculpas de su parte.** 3.6
thin **delgado/a** *adj.* 1.3
thing **cosa** *f.* 1.1

think **pensar (e:ie)** *v.* 1.4; (believe) **creer** *v.*
  think about **pensar en** *v.* 1.4
third **tercero/a** 1.5
thirsty: be (very) thirsty **tener (mucha) sed** 1.3
thirteen **trece** 1.1
thirty **treinta** 1.1; 1.2; thirty (*minutes past the hour*) **y treinta; y media** 1.1
this **este, esta** *adj.;* **éste, ésta, esto** *pron.* 1.6
  This is… (*introduction*) **Éste/a es…** 1.1
those **ésos, ésas** *pron.* 1.6; **esos, esas** *adj.* 1.6
those (over there) **aquéllos, aquéllas** *pron.* 1.6; **aquellos, aquellas** *adj.* 1.6
thousand **mil** *m.* 1.6
three **tres** 1.1
three hundred **trescientos/as** 1.2
throat **garganta** *f.* 2.4
through **por** *prep.* 2.5
Thursday **jueves** *m., sing.* 1.2
thus (*in such a way*) **así** *adv.*
ticket **boleto** *m.* 1.2, 3.5; **pasaje** *m.* 1.5
tie **corbata** *f.* 1.6
time **tiempo** *m.* 1.4; **vez** *f.* 1.6
  have a good/bad time **pasarlo bien/mal** 2.3
  I've had a fantastic time. **Lo he pasado de película.** 3.6
  What time is it? **¿Qué hora es?** 1.1
  (At) What time…? **¿A qué hora…?** 1.1
times **veces** *f., pl.* 1.6
  many times **muchas veces** 2.4
  two times **dos veces** 1.6
tip **propina** *f.* 2.3
tire **llanta** *f.* 2.5
tired **cansado/a** *adj.* 1.5
  be tired **estar cansado/a** 1.5
to **a** *prep.* 1.1
toast (*drink*) **brindar** *v.* 2.3
  toast **pan** *m.* **tostado**
toasted **tostado/a** *adj.* 2.2
  toasted bread **pan tostado** *m.* 2.2
toaster **tostadora** *f.* 2.6
today **hoy** *adv.* 1.2
  Today is… **Hoy es…** 1.2
toe **dedo** *m.* **del pie** 2.4
together **juntos/as** *adj.* 2.3
toilet **inodoro** *m.* 2.1
tomato **tomate** *m.* 2.2
tomorrow **mañana** *f.* 1.1
  See you tomorrow. **Hasta mañana.** 1.1
tonight **esta noche** *adv.* 1.4
too **también** *adv.* 1.2; 2.1
  too much **demasiado** *adv.* 1.6; **en exceso** 3.3
tooth **diente** *m.* 2.1
toothpaste **pasta** *f.* **de dientes** 2.1

top **cima** *f.* 3.3
  to the top **hasta arriba** *f.* 3.3
tornado **tornado** *m.* 3.6
touch **tocar** *v.* 3.5
touch screen **pantalla táctil** *f.* 2.5
tour **excursión** *f.* 1.4;
  recorrido *m.* 3.1
tour an area **recorrer** *v.*
tourism **turismo** *m.* 1.5
tourist **turista** *m., f.* 1.1;
  turístico/a *adj.*
toward **hacia** *prep.* 3.2;
  para *prep.* 2.5
towel **toalla** *f.* 2.1
town **pueblo** *m.* 1.4
trade **oficio** *m.* 3.4
traffic **circulación** *f.* 2.5;
  tráfico *m.* 2.5
  traffic light **semáforo** *m.* 3.2
tragedy **tragedia** *f.* 3.5
trail **sendero** *m.* 3.1
  trailhead **sendero** *m.* 3.1
train **entrenarse** *v.* 3.3;
  tren *m.* 1.5
  train station **estación** *f.* **de**
    tren *m.* 1.5
trainer **entrenador(a)** *m., f.* 3.3
translate **traducir** *v.* 1.6
trash **basura** *f.* 2.6
travel **viajar** *v.* 1.2
  travel agent **agente** *m., f.*
    de viajes 1.5
traveler **viajero/a** *m., f.* 1.5
  (traveler's) check **cheque (de**
    viajero) 3.2
treadmill **cinta caminadora** *f.* 3.3
tree **árbol** *m.* 3.1
trillion **billón** *m.*
trimester **trimestre** *m.* 1.2
trip **viaje** *m.* 1.5
  take a trip **hacer un viaje** 1.5
tropical forest **bosque** *m.*
  tropical 3.1
true: it's (not)
  true **(no) es verdad** 3.1
trunk **baúl** *m.* 2.5
truth **verdad** *f.*
try **intentar** v.; **probar**
  (o:ue) *v.* 2.2
  try (*to do something*) **tratar de**
    (+ *inf.*) 3.3
  try on **probarse (o:ue)** *v.* 2.1
t-shirt **camiseta** *f.* 1.6
Tuesday **martes** *m., sing.* 1.2
tuna **atún** *m.* 2.2
turkey **pavo** *m.* 2.2
turn **doblar** *v.* 3.2
  turn off (*electricity/appliance*)
    apagar *v.* 2.5
  turn on (*electricity/appliance*)
    poner *v.* 2.5; **prender** *v.* 2.5
twelve **doce** 1.1
twenty **veinte** 1.1
twenty-eight **veintiocho** 1.1
twenty-five **veinticinco** 1.1
twenty-four **veinticuatro** 1.1
twenty-nine **veintinueve** 1.1

twenty-one **veintiún,**
  veintiuno/a 1.1
twenty-seven **veintisiete** 1.1
twenty-six **veintiséis** 1.1
twenty-three **veintitrés** 1.1
twenty-two **veintidós** 1.1
twice **dos veces** 1.6
twin **gemelo/a** *m., f.* 1.3
twisted **torcido/a** *adj.* 2.4
  be twisted **estar torcido/a** 2.4
two **dos** 1.1
  two hundred **doscientos/as** 1.2
  two times **dos veces** 1.6

U

ugly **feo/a** *adj.* 1.3
uncle **tío** *m.* 1.3
under **bajo** *adv.* 2.1;
  debajo de *prep.* 1.2
understand **comprender** *v.* 1.3;
  entender (e:ie) *v.* 1.4
underwear **ropa interior** 1.6
unemployment **desempleo** *m.* 3.6
unique **único/a** *adj.* 2.3
United States **Estados Unidos**
  (EE.UU.) *m. pl.* 1.1
university **universidad** *f.* 1.2
unless **a menos que** *conj.* 3.1
unpleasant **antipático/a** *adj.* 1.3
until **hasta** *prep.* 1.6; **hasta que**
  conj. 3.1
up **arriba** *adv.* 3.3
urgent **urgente** *adj.* 2.6
  It's urgent that... **Es urgente**
    que... 3.6
us **nos** *pl., d.o. pron.* 1.5
  to/for us **nos** *pl., i.o. pron.* 1.6
use **usar** *v.* 1.6
used for **para** *prep.* 2.5
useful **útil** *adj. m., f.*

V

vacation **vacaciones** *f., pl.* 1.5
  be on vacation **estar de**
    vacaciones 1.5
  go on vacation **ir de**
    vacaciones 1.5
vacuum **pasar** *v.* **la aspiradora** 2.6
  vacuum cleaner **aspiradora** *f.* 2.6
valley **valle** *m.* 3.1
various **varios/as** *adj. m., f. pl.* 2.2
vegetables **verduras** *pl., f.* 2.2
verb **verbo** *m.*
very **muy** *adv.* 1.1
  very much **muchísimo** *adv.* 1.2
  (Very) well, thank you. **(Muy)**
    bien, gracias. 1.1
video **video** *m.* 1.1
  video camera **cámara** *f.* **de**
    video 2.5
videoconference
  videoconferencia *f.* 3.4
video game **videojuego** *m.* 1.4
vinegar **vinagre** *m.* 2.2

violence **violencia** *f.* 3.6
visit **visitar** *v.* 1.4
  visit monuments **visitar**
    monumentos 1.4
vitamin **vitamina** *f.* 3.3
voice mail **correo de voz** *m.* 2.5
volcano **volcán** *m.* 3.1
volleyball **vóleibol** *m.* 1.4
vote **votar** *v.* 3.6

W

wait (for) **esperar** *v.* **(+** *inf.*) 1.2
waiter/waitress **camarero/a**
  m., f. 2.2
wake up **despertarse (e:ie)**
  v. 2.1
walk **caminar** *v.* 1.2
  take a walk **pasear** *v.* 1.4
  walk around **pasear por** 1.4
walkman **walkman** *m.*
wall **pared** *f.* 2.6; **muro** *m.* 3.3
wallet **cartera** *f.* 1.4, 1.6
want **querer (e:ie)** *v.* 1.4
war **guerra** *f.* 3.6
warm (oneself) up **calentarse**
  (e:ie) *v.* 3.3
wash **lavar** *v.* 2.6
  wash one's face/hands **lavarse**
    la cara/las manos 2.1
  wash (the floor, the dishes)
    lavar (el suelo, los
    platos) 2.6
  wash oneself **lavarse** *v.* 2.1
washing machine **lavadora** *f.* 2.6
wastebasket **papelera** *f.* 1.2
watch **mirar** *v.* 1.2; **reloj** *m.* 1.2
  watch television **mirar (la)**
    televisión 1.2
water **agua** *f.* 2.2
  water pollution **contaminación**
    del agua 3.1
  water-skiing **esquí** *m.*
    acuático 1.4
way **manera** *f.* 3.4
we **nosotros(as)** *m., f.* 1.1
weak **débil** *adj. m., f.* 3.3
wear **llevar** *v.* 1.6; **usar** *v.* 1.6
weather **tiempo** *m.*
  The weather is bad. **Hace mal**
    tiempo. 1.5
  The weather is good. **Hace**
    buen tiempo. 1.5
weaving **tejido** *m.* 3.5
Web **red** *f.* 2.5
website **sitio** *m.* **web** 2.5
wedding **boda** *f.* 2.3
Wednesday **miércoles** *m.,*
  sing. 1.2
week **semana** *f.* 1.2
weekend **fin** *m.* **de semana** 1.4
weight **peso** *m.* 3.3
  lift weights **levantar** *v.* **pesas**
    f., pl. 3.3
welcome **bienvenido(s)/a(s)**
  adj. 1.1

well: (Very) well, thanks. **(Muy) bien, gracias.** 1.1
well-being **bienestar** *m.* 3.3
well organized **ordenado/a** *adj.*
west **oeste** *m.* 3.2
  to the west **al oeste** 3.2
western (*genre*) **de vaqueros** 3.5
whale **ballena** *f.* 3.1
what **lo que** *pron.* 2.6
what? **¿qué?** 1.1
  At what time…? **¿A qué hora…?** 1.1
  What a pleasure to… ! **¡Qué gusto (+** *inf.***)…** 3.6
  What day is it? **¿Qué día es hoy?** 1.2
  What do you guys think? **¿Qué les parece?** 2.3
  What happened? **¿Qué pasó?** 2.5
  What is today's date? **¿Cuál es la fecha de hoy?** 1.5
  What nice clothes! **¡Qué ropa más bonita!** 1.6
  What size do you wear? **¿Qué talla lleva (usa)?** 1.6
  What time is it? **¿Qué hora es?** 1.1
  What's going on? **¿Qué pasa?** 1.1
  What's happening? **¿Qué pasa?** 1.1
  What's… like? **¿Cómo es…?** 1.3
  What's new? **¿Qué hay de nuevo?** 1.1
  What's the weather like? **¿Qué tiempo hace?** 1.5
  What's up? **¿Qué onda?** 3.2
  What's wrong? **¿Qué pasó?** 2.5
  What's your name? **¿Cómo se llama usted?** *form.* 1.1; **¿Cómo te llamas (tú)?** *fam.* 1.1
when **cuando** *conj.* 2.1; 3.1
When? **¿Cuándo?** 1.2
where **donde**
where (to)? (*destination*) **¿adónde?** 1.2; (*location*) **¿dónde?** 1.1
  Where are you from? **¿De dónde eres (tú)?** (*fam.*) 1.1; **¿De dónde es (usted)?** (*form.*) 1.1
  Where is…? **¿Dónde está…?** 1.2
  (to) where? **¿adónde?** 1.2
which **que** *pron.*, **lo que** *pron.* 2.6
which? **¿cuál?** 1.2; **¿qué?** 1.2
  In which…? **¿En qué…?** 1.2
  which one(s)? **¿cuál(es)?** 1.2
while **mientras** *conj.* 2.4
white **blanco/a** *adj.* 1.6
  white wine **vino blanco** 2.2
who **que** *pron.* 2.6; **quien(es)** *pron.* 2.6

who? **¿quién(es)?** 1.1
Who is…? **¿Quién es…?** 1.1
  Who is calling/speaking? (*on phone*) **¿De parte de quién?** 2.5
  Who is speaking? (*on phone*) **¿Quién habla?** 2.5
whole **todo/a** *adj.*
whom **quien(es)** *pron.* 2.6
whose? **¿de quién(es)?** 1.1
why? **¿por qué?** 1.2
widower/widow **viudo/a** *adj.* 2.3
wife **esposa** *f.* 1.3
win **ganar** *v.* 1.4
wind **viento** *m.* 1.5
window **ventana** *f.* 1.2
windshield **parabrisas** *m., sing.* 2.5
windy: It's (very) windy. **Hace (mucho) viento.** 1.5
wine **vino** *m.* 2.2
  red wine **vino tinto** 2.2
  white wine **vino blanco** 2.2
wineglass **copa** *f.* 2.6
winter **invierno** *m.* 1.5
wireless (connection) **conexión inalámbrica** *f.* 2.5
wish **desear** *v.* 1.2; **esperar** *v.* 3.1
  I wish (that) **ojalá (que)** 3.1
with **con** *prep.* 1.2
  with me **conmigo** 1.4; 2.3
  with you **contigo** *fam.* 1.5, 2.3
within (ten years) **dentro de (diez años)** *prep.* 3.4
without **sin** *prep.* 1.2; 3.1; 3.3; **sin que** *conj.* 3.1
woman **mujer** *f.* 1.1
wool **lana** *f.* 1.6
  (made of) wool **de lana** 1.6
word **palabra** *f.* 1.1
work **trabajar** *v.* 1.2; **funcionar** *v.* 2.5; **trabajo** *m.* 3.4
  work (*of art, literature, music, etc.*) **obra** *f.* 3.5
  work out **hacer gimnasia** 3.3
world **mundo** *m.* 2.2, 3.1
worldwide **mundial** *adj. m., f.*
worried (about) **preocupado/a (por)** *adj.* 1.5
worry (about) **preocuparse** *v.* **(por)** 2.1
  Don't worry. **No se preocupe.** *form.* 2.1; **Tranquilo.; No te preocupes.;** *fam.* 2.1
worse **peor** *adj. m., f.* 2.2
worst **el/la peor** 2.2
Would you like to…? **¿Te gustaría…?** *fam.* 1.4
Would you do me the honor of marrying me? **¿Me harías el honor de casarte conmigo?** 3.5
wow **híjole** *interj.* 1.6
wrench **llave** *f.* 2.5
write **escribir** *v.* 1.3
  write a letter/post card/e-mail

message **escribir una carta/postal/mensaje electrónico** 1.4
writer **escritor(a)** *m., f* 3.5
written **escrito/a** *p.p.* 3.2
wrong **equivocado/a** *adj.* 1.5
  be wrong **no tener razón** 1.3

X

X-ray **radiografía** *f.* 2.4

Y

yard **jardín** *m.* 2.6; **patio** *m.* 2.6
year **año** *m.* 1.5
  be… years old **tener… años** 1.3
yellow **amarillo/a** *adj.* 1.6
yes **sí** *interj.* 1.1
yesterday **ayer** *adv.* 1.6
yet **todavía** *adv.* 1.5
yogurt **yogur** *m.* 2.2
you **tú** *fam.* **usted (Ud.)** *form. sing.* **vosotros/as** *m., f. fam.* **ustedes (Uds.)** *form.* 1.1; (to, for) you *fam. sing.* **te** *pl.* **os** 1.6; *form. sing.* **le** *pl.* **les** 1.6
  you **te** *fam., sing.,* **lo/la** *form., sing.,* **os** *fam., pl.,* **los/las** *form., pl, d.o. pron.* 1.5
You don't say! **¡No me digas!** *fam.;* **¡No me diga!** *form.* 2.5
You are… **Tú eres…** 1.1
You're welcome. **De nada.** 1.1; **No hay de qué.** 1.1
young **joven** *adj. sing.* **(jóvenes** *pl.***)** 1.3
  young person **joven** *m., f. sing.* **(jóvenes** *pl.***)** 1.1
  young woman **señorita (Srta.)** *f.*
younger **menor** *adj. m., f.* 1.3
younger: younger brother, sister **hermano/a menor** *m., f.* 1.3
youngest **el/la menor** *m., f.* 2.2
your **su(s)** *poss. adj. form.* 1.3
  your **tu(s)** *poss. adj. fam. sing.* 1.3
  your **vuestro/a(s)** *poss. adj. form. pl.* 1.3
  your(s) *form.* **suyo(s)/a(s)** *poss. pron. form.* 2.5
  your(s) **tuyo(s)/a(s)** *poss. fam. sing.* 2.5
  your(s) **vuestro(s)/a(s)** *poss. fam.* 2.5
youth *f.* **juventud** 2.3

Z

zero **cero** *m.* 1.1

As in the glossary, the level and lesson of ¡**ADELANTE!** where each item is found is indicated by the two numbers separated by a decimal:

- 1.6 = ¡*ADELANTE!* **UNO** , Lección 6
- 3.4 = ¡*ADELANTE!* **TRES** , Lección 4

Text Credits

163 "Elegia nocturna" ©Carlos Pellicer.

Comic Credits

284-285 "El celular" ©TUTE.

Television Credits

50 "Champu Sedal" ©Unilever, Argentina.
112 "Jumbo Mountainbike" ©El Comercial, Perú.
168 "Totofútbol" By permission of Javier Ugarte (director).
226 "Down Taxco" By permission of Jean Marie Boursicot.
288 "¿Me lo compras?" By permission of Davivienda.
350 "Balay" By permission of Jean Marie Boursicot.

Photography and Art Credits

All images © Vista Higher Learning unless otherwise noted. Fotonovela photos provided by Carolina Zapata.

Cover: (full pg) José Blanco.

Front Matter (IAE): IAE-36 (t) Amy Baron; (b) Martín Bernetti; **IAE-37** (t) Janet Dracksdorf; (m) Carolina Zapata; (b) Martín Bernetti.

Lección de repaso: 1 (full pg) © Denis Doyle/Getty Images; **2** (t) © FogStock LLC/ Index Open; (b) © Dean Uhlinger/ Corbis; **3** (t) © Corel/Corbis; (b) Anne Loubet; **6** Martín Bernetti; **7** Janet Dracksdorf; **8** © JOEL NITO/AFP/Getty Images; **9** © Sylvain Cazenave/Corbis.

Lesson One: 19 (full pg) © Flying Colours Ltd/Getty Images; **28** © Stewart Cohen/Blend Images/Corbis; **29** (t) Ali Burafi; (b) Janet Dracksdorf; **31** (l, r) Martín Bernetti; **33** (l) Martín Bernetti; (r) © Ariel Skelley/Corbis; **36** José Blanco; **37** Martín Bernetti; **46–47** © DIDEM HIZAR/Fotolia.com; **48** © i love images/Alamy; **49** Martín Bernetti; **50** © Kevin Dodge/ Masterfile; **52** (t, mtr) Martín Bernetti; (mbl) © RICHARD SMITH/CORBIS SYGMA; (mbr) © Charles & Josette Lenars/ Corbis; (b) © Yann Arthus-Bertrand/Corbis; **53** (tl) Martín Bernetti; (tr) © Mick Roessler/Corbis; (bl) © Jeremy Horner/ Corbis; (br) © Marshall Bruce/iStockphoto.

Lesson Two: 79 (full pg) © Mark Leibowitz/Masterfile; **85** (l) Mauricio Osorio; (r) Anne Loubet; **90** (l) Rachel Distler; (r) © Greg Elms/Lonely Planet Images/Getty Images; **91** (t) © Carlos Cazalis/Corbis; (bl) © Studio Bonisolli/Stockfood; (br) © Carlos Cazalis/Corbis; **94** Paula Díez; **96** (l) © Pixtal/Age Fotostock; (r) José Blanco; **100** (l) Ventus Pictures; (r) José Blanco; **101** (l) José Blanco; (r) Ventus Pictures; **110** Vanessa Bertozzi; **111** © Jack Hollingsworth/Getty Images; **114** (t) © Henryk Sadura/Shutterstock.com; (mt) © Dave G. Houser/Corbis; **114** (mb) © Henryk Sadura/Shutterstock.com; (b) © Dave G. Houser/Corbis; **115** (tl) © Jenkedco/Shutterstock.com; (tr) © Michael & Patricia Fogden/Corbis; (bl) © Vladimir Korostyshevskiy/Shutterstock.com; (br) © Paul W. Liebhardt/Corbis; **127** (l) © Michael & Patricia Fogden/Corbis; (r) © Paul W. Liebhardt/Corbis.

Lesson Three: 141 (full pg) © Susana/Fotocolombia.com; **145** Martín Bernetti; **150** (l) © Sylwia Blaszczyszyn/Dreamstime.com; (r) © PictureNet/Corbis; **151** (t) © Simon Cruz/AP Wide World Photos; (b) © Rune Hellestad/Corbis; **164** (t) © Katrina Brown/123RF; (b) Esteban Corbo; **165** Armando Brito; **166** © Blend Images/Alamy; **170** (tl, tr, mtr) Lauren Krolick; (mtl) Kathryn Alena Korf; (mbl) © Bettmann/Corbis; (mbr) © MACARENA MINGUELL/AFP/Getty Images; (b) Bruce R. Korf; **171** (tl) Lars Rosen Gunnilstam; (tr, br) Lauren Krolick; (bl) © Nikolay Starchenko/Shutterstock.com; **182** (l) Lauren Krolick; (r) Lars Rosen Gunnilstam.

Lesson Four: 195 (full pg) © Custom Medical Stock Photo/Alamy; 204 (t) Ali Burafi; (b) © Ricardo Figueroa/AP Wide World Photos; 205 (t) Gianni Dagli Orti/The Art Archive at Art Resource, NY; (m) © Photolicensors International AG/Alamy; (b) © AFP/Getty Images; 209 © ISO K° - photography/Fotolia.com; 213 Oscar Artavia Solano; 214 (tl) © LisaInGlasses/iStockphoto; (tr) © Krek/Dreamstime.com; 219 Martín Bernetti; 222 © Corel/Corbis; 223 © Galen Rowell/Mountain Light; 224 © Anthony Redpath/Masterfile; 225 Paula Díez; 228 (tl, tr, mm, mr) Oscar Artavia Solano; (ml) © Bill Gentile/Corbis; (b) © Bob Winsett/Corbis; 229 (tl) © Frank Burek/Corbis; (mr) © Martin Rogers/Corbis; (ml) Janet Dracksdorf; (b) Oscar Artavia Solano.

Lesson Five: 257 (full pg) Paula Díez; 266 (l) © Ariel Skelley/Getty Images; (r) Paula Díez; 267 (t) © Zsolt Nyulaszi/Shutterstock.com; (b) © M. Timothy O'Keefe/Alamy; 271 © LdF/iStockphoto; 275 Katie Wade; 276 (l, r) Paula Díez; 280 (t) © gmnicholas/iStockphoto; (ml, bm) Martín Bernetti; (mml) © Auris/iStockphoto; (mmr) © NickyBlade/iStockphoto; (mr, bl) © LdF/iStockphoto; (br) Liliana Bobadilla; 286 © Chad Johnston/Masterfile; 287 © morchella/Fotolia.com; 290 (t, b) Ali Burafi; (ml) María Eugenia Corbo; (mm) © Galen Rowell/Corbis; (mr) Lauren Krolick; 291 (tl) María Eugenia Corbo; (tr, m, b) Ali Burafi; 304 (l, r) Ali Burafi.

Lesson Six: 317 (full pg) © Rolf Bruderer/Corbis; 320 (t) © TerryJ/iStockphoto; (b) © Harry Neave/Fotolia.com; 326 (l) © Dusko Despotovic/Corbis; (r) Martín Bernetti; 327 (l) Maribel Garcia; 329 (l) © Monkeybusinessimages/Dreamstime.com; (r) Anne Loubet; 330 © Blend Images/Alamy; 346 © Danny Lehman/Corbis; 348 Martín Bernetti; 352 (tl) © Kevin Schafer/Corbis; (tr) © Danny Lehman/Corbis; (b) © Hernan H. Hernandez A./Shutterstock.com; 352 (tl, mr) © Danny Lehman/Corbis; (ml) Photo courtesy of www.Tahiti-Tourisme.com; (b) © Claudio Lovo/Shutterstock.com.

About the Author

José A. Blanco founded Vista Higher Learning in 1998. A native of Barranquilla, Colombia, Mr. Blanco holds degrees in Literature and Hispanic Studies from Brown University and the University of California, Santa Cruz. He has worked as a writer, editor, and translator for Houghton Mifflin and D.C. Heath and Company and has taught Spanish at the secondary and university levels. Mr. Blanco is also the co-author of several other Vista Higher Learning programs: **Panorama, Aventuras,** and **¡Viva!** at the introductory level, **Ventanas, Facetas, Enfoques, Imagina,** and **Sueña** at the intermediate level, and **Revista** at the advanced conversation level.

About the Illustrators

Yayo, an internationally acclaimed illustrator, was born in Colombia. He has illustrated children's books, newspapers, and magazines, and has been exhibited around the world. He currently lives in Montreal, Canada.

Pere Virgili lives and works in Barcelona, Spain. His illustrations have appeared in textbooks, newspapers, and magazines throughout Spain and Europe.

Born in Caracas, Venezuela, **Hermann Mejía** studied illustration at the *Instituto de Diseño de Caracas*. Hermann currently lives and works in the United States.